The book of Job is included within the canon of Scripture, not to perplex, or provoke debate, but for proclamation. It is not merely a message about God, it is a message from God and, as with all divine revelation, it is meant to be preached. Yet relatively few preachers feel comfortable doing that! In these pages a preacher-theologian guides us through the sermons of one of the greatest preacher-theologians of church history and through them opens valuable windows on the message of this enigmatic book. He provides us with helpful hermeneutical keys to unlock the teaching it contains. He also gives us an insight into the dynamics by which it works. The end product is to pave the way for Job to be used more powerfully and practically in the pulpit. In so doing it will open this book for all who struggle with suffering and the problem of evil, but more than that, it will open this book for everyone as the revelation of God in all his sovereignty and righteousness.

**Mark G. Johnston**
**Grove Chapel, Camberwell**

This book began life as Derek Thomas' doctoral dissertation. As his PhD supervisor, I have worked through the material underlying this book a number of times and I am delighted that it is now available to a wider audience. Like Calvin himself, Derek Thomas is both an academic and a pastor. He works in the Church (First Presbyterian Church, Jackson) and also in the Academy (Reformed Theological Seminary) and therefore brings to this study a commendable combination of gifts. In addition, he is a fine preacher and is therefore well placed to lead us in a study of Calvin's own preaching. This is a solid piece of work, not for the fainthearted but, for those who persevere, there is a depth of riches to be mined.

**A.T.B. McGowan**
**Highland Theological College, Dingwall**

Calvin's Sermons on Job are a fascinating part of his voluminous heritage. Derek Thomas's able exposition guides us through some of the key issues raised by the text. His work contains valuable lessons both for the understanding of Calvin and for the task of the preacher today.

**Anthony N. S. Lane**
**London Bible College**

This is a solid and comprehensive analysis of a central theme in one of Calvin's major series of sermons, preached when he was at the summit of his influence in Geneva. It is both accessible to the serious general reader and equipped with the apparatus of learning for Calvinian experts. The author is not afraid to pursue an independent line in relation to main currents of interpretation of Calvin. All through he keeps a close eye on the pastoral bearing of this homiletic theology. He has given us a valuable addition to Calvin studies on a somewhat neglected part of his corpus.

**David F. Wright**
**New College, Edinburgh**

# Proclaiming the Incomprehensible God

## Calvin's Teaching on Job

Derek Thomas

**MENTOR**

Copyright © Derek Thomas 2004

ISBN 1 85792 922 5

Published in 2004
in the
Mentor imprint
by
Christian Focus Publications,
Geanies House, Ross-shire, IV20 1TW, Scotland

www.christianfocus.com

Cover Design by Alister MacInnes

Printed and bound by W.S. Bookwell, Finland

All rights reserved. No part of this publication may be reproduced, stored in a retrieval system, or transmitted, in any form, by any means, electronic, mechanical, photocopying, recording or otherwise without the prior permission of the publisher or a license permitting restricted copying. In the U.K. such licenses are issued by the Copyright Licensing Agency, 90 Tottenham Court Road, London W1P 9HE.

# Contents

Preface ................................................................. 7

Introduction ......................................................... 9

1. A Good Case:
Calvin's Understanding of the Book of Job .......... 29

2. The Incomprehensible Righteousness of God ... 93

3. The Incomprehensibility of God ................... 151

4. Interpreting the Hand of God:
Calvin's Pastoral Understanding of Job ............... 225

5. A Christological Focus? ................................. 305

Conclusion ....................................................... 373

Bibliography .................................................... 381

Subject Index ...................................................411

Author Index .................................................. 415

To

Bill and Marty May

# Preface

The following pages once comprised my doctoral dissertation completed in the year 2000 at the University of Wales, Lampeter through the agency of Highland Theological College at Dingwall, Scotland. It is reproduced here with only minor changes.

John Calvin preached a series of one hundred and fifty-nine sermons on the Book of Job in the years 1554-55, whilst a minister in Geneva. In the course of these sermons, Calvin reveals a particular understanding of the Book of Job in general, as well as offering insights into the nature of divine providence in particular, which adds significantly to the more systematic output of the *Institutes*.

Whilst previous studies of these sermons have focused on individual aspects or difficulties in these sermons, in this book I have attempted to engage in a comprehensive analysis of their contents, thereby providing a perspective on Calvin's pastoral theology as a whole. I have tried to focus on some of the more difficult aspects that emerge, including the concept of innocent suffering, what Calvin refers to as 'double justice', and his view of metaphysical redemption. Note has been taken of recent studies on Calvin, particularly those discussions relating to Calvin's christological focus in the Old Testament. A conclusion is offered suggesting that Calvin's output is not as rigorously christological as has been suggested.

A quick glance at the pages will reveal the large number of 'scholarly' references, many of which contain citations in French or Latin. Many readers will see this as 'surplus to requirements,' but some, serious students of the Reformer, not having access to the *Calvini Opera*, will hopefully find their inclusion valuable for further research into Calvin's method.

As always in these things, a number of people have been involved in its production to whom I owe an enormous debt of gratitude. These include: student-assistants, Peter Wang, Mark Levine, Marshall Brown and John Tweeddale who proofread some of the manuscript; Reformed Theological Seminary library staff, especially Ken Elliott; friends and colleagues, Dr. Duncan Rankin, Dr. J. Ligon Duncan III, Dr. Dennis Ireland, Dr. Ralph Davis, Dr. John Currid, Dr. Knox Chamblin and Dr. David Jussely, for their support; Dr. Sinclair Ferguson and Professor

S. Leahy, who first suggested the idea of a thesis on Calvin's sermons on Job; Dr. Andrew McGowan, my supervisor, whose insights and encouragement proved the most stimulating academic experience of my life; the Executive Committee and administration of Reformed Theological Seminary, and especially its President, Dr. Ric Cannada, for granting me a sabbatical leave of absence to see this dissertation through publication; Malcolm Maclean, and the staff of Christian Focus Publications for the enthusiasm they have shown for this book; and to my wife and family for the sacrifices they made in the production of this volume.

Finally, I owe a considerable debt of gratitude to Bill and Marty May for the help they afforded me during this project and it is to them I dedicate the work.

# Introduction

...these sermons are particularly valuable, not only because they are prime examples of Calvin's sermonic style but also because of their insights into the message of the book of Job (I. John Hesselink, review of *Calvin's Sermons on Job*, in *Sixteenth Century Journal* 26:1 (1995): 177).

The whole life of Christians ought to be a sort of practice of godliness [*pietatis*]... [*Institutes* III.xix.2].

*Tota Christianorum vita quaedam pietatis meditatio esse debet...*[*CO* 2:614].

Studies on John Calvin's understanding of divine providence have tended to overlook his homiletical work in the 159 sermons he preached on the Book of Job. Karl Barth and John Murray, for example, though writing from different perspectives, both contend vehemently that the *locus classicus* for Calvin's understanding of the doctrine of providence is *Institutes* I.xvi-xviii.[1] This part of the *Institutes* certainly occupied Calvin's attention throughout his life as successive revisions were made up to the final edition of 1559. In particular, it is clear that the relationship between providence and predestination continued to exercise Calvin's mind; for in the final edition discussion of predestination was removed from Book I to Book III. xxi-xxiv.[2]

No doubt there was a pastoral significance in transferring the doctrine of predestination from the section dealing with God the Creator to the section dealing with the role of the Holy Spirit in the application of redemption.[3] The most important reason underlying this change was the need to locate predestination within a more christological setting.[4] The consequent dislocation of providence and predestination begs the question as to the extent by which Calvin's understanding of providence was actually governed by christological considerations.

Calvin's sermonic output adds significantly to our understanding of his theology, not least in giving us a window to view the various applications each particular doctrine affords. In the sermonic material, for example, Calvin as a preacher has time to digress and develop issues in a way that the commentaries and the *Institutes* cannot.[5] An examination of Calvin's sermonic output, particularly as it focuses on the doctrine of providence, would then seem appropriate.[6]

In 1971 T. H. L. Parker observed that "The sixteenth century was, above all things, the age of the Bible. How strange, then, that this area of its history has, apart from some well-trodden paths, been neglected."[7] Since that time, major studies of Calvin's exegetical foundations have sought to fill this gap in our knowledge of the sixteenth century.[8] Some attempts have been made to examine the import of the Joban sermons in particular, including highly significant works by Thomas F. Torrance, Richard Stauffer, Erwin Mülhaupt and Josef Bohatec, and especially the works of Susan Schreiner and William J. Bouwsma.[9] Some of these deal only tangentially with the Joban sermons, or at best thematically. Thus, Torrance, for example, treats the material only insofar as it supports his understanding of Calvin's doctrine of man and natural theology. Bohatec is eager to point out the relationship of faith and providence (providence is known by faith and not by reason) and describes the content of providential faith (*Vorsehungsglaube*). This he does, citing not only the *Institutes*, but also drawing heavily on Calvin's commentary on the Book of Psalms, making only a couple of references to the *Sermons on Job*.[10] Richard Stauffer cites the Joban material by way of support for his view that Calvin's preaching centered on a doctrine of God and his attributes.[11] Stauffer's work, *Dieu, la création et la Providence dans la prédication de Calvin*, published in 1978, is an impressive work dealing with aspects of Calvin's doctrine and preaching. Avoiding some of the more controversial issues, Stauffer highlights distinctive theological accents in Calvin's preaching over a wide range of sources, including the sermons on the Book of Job. He concludes that Calvin's sermonic output represents more fully the theology found more systematically in the *Institutes*. Rather, what we have in the sermons complements and even modifies it. Stauffer, therefore, attempts a partial reformulation of Calvin's theology as has been understood from the *Institutes*. In point of fact, his reformulation is confined to the themes of Book 1 of the *Institutes*.

Important and impressive as Stauffer's work undoubtedly is, there is always the suspicion that in selecting his quotations carefully, he has managed to point up areas of tension between the sermonic and the didactic, a tension created by the genre of preaching. Calvin himself, after all, would have been aware of these tensions had they been substantive.[12] In any case, we shall argue that the emphasis given to the incomprehensibility of God in the sermonic material dealing with the book of Job is in harmony, and not tension, with the didactic accounts of the *Institutes*.

In particular, Stauffer argues that in the sermons, Calvin adds to the emphasis given in the *Institutes* on the attributes of God (*les attributes de Dieu*). These "attributes" include, simplicity, impassibility, immutability, wisdom, incomprehensibility and infinity.[13] Significantly, when Stauffer comes to illustrate Calvin's emphasis upon the incomprehensibility of God, he cites three of Calvin's sermons on Job (19, 47 and 147). Significant as this is, we shall show in this thesis that the emphasis is even greater than Stauffer records.

Bouwsma, likewise, expounds Calvin using the Joban sermons, amongst other sources, as the basis of his conclusions.[14] Bouwsma's contribution to our understanding of Calvin has already proved to be highly influential. His work is more than a biography; it is a portrait from an entirely fresh perspective. Though elements of psychological analysis intrude, Bouwsma conveys a portrait of "two Calvins": one from the old world of medieval synthesis and another from the new world of sixteenth century humanism and the Renaissance.[15] The second Calvin was "a philosopher, a rationalist and a schoolman in the high Scholastic tradition represented by Thomas Aquinas."[16] The other Calvin "was a rhetorician and humanist, a skeptical fideist in the manner of the followers of William of Ockham, flexible to the point of opportunism, and a revolutionary in spite of himself."[17]

This "two Calvins" approach inevitably focuses on the differences and tensions in Calvin's thought, rather than on any possible harmonization. Interestingly, Bouwsma argues that because Calvin's doctrine of the secret providence of God is surrounded by mystery ("God's purpose remains, for the most part, incomprehensible even to believers"[18]), the doctrine has no practical value. As we shall see, this is far from the case. Since it lies at the heart of the message of Job, it has considerable practical value, not least in underlying the need for humility, subjection and faith. However, Bouwsma engages in an extensive analysis of Calvin's understanding of those aspects of providence about which we can discern something of God's purposes and attributes.[19] This will form the theme of chapter 4.

It is clear that Bouwsma has researched the Joban sermons carefully. In some 140 footnotes, he cites from 70 of the sermons.[20]

As Hesselink notes, in an article commenting upon the many and varied reactions to Bouwsma's work, "this book is a brilliant tour de force, quite unmatched in Calvin literature."[21] However, Bouwsma's work, considered by many to be the most important on Calvin for some time, is also, by others, considered flawed.[22] In particular, the attempt to discern "two Calvins" in relation to his use of the incomprehensibility of God on the one hand, and the knowability of God on the other, borders on the schizophrenic. It is surely possible to outline that these two aspects – the hidden and the revealed – are not in tension, but actually complement each other.

In particular, Bouwsma's characterisation of Calvin's high view of God's majesty as nominalistic seems misplaced.[23] It is just as cogent to suggest that Calvin was being influenced by *biblical*, rather than *philosophical* categories. The very text of Job, as T. H. L. Parker has argued, influenced both the language and style of Calvin's preaching.[24] It was the power of exegesis that led Calvin to emphasise this feature. Similarly, Bouwsma argues that it is a philosophical consideration that leads Calvin to claim that human creatureliness and the incomprehensibility of God leads to uncertainty about the possibility of certain knowledge.[25] This raises several issues, not least the questionable statement about the certainty of knowledge: Calvin is not claiming skepticism about all knowledge, but is simply arguing that our knowledge is limited and necessarily finite. Here too, as we shall see, it is the biblical text of Job rather than philosophy which is moulding Calvin's thought.[26] Indeed, Bouwsma's work lacks sufficient interaction with the spiritual aspects behind Calvin's life. Arguably, it was this which influenced him more than anything else.[27]

All of this still posits a need to examine the Joban sermons for what they are in themselves rather than as proof texts for particular dogmas. As Schreiner remarked in 1986, "we have yet to understand how Calvin exegetically interpreted Job as a whole."[28] Eight years later, Schreiner responded with a definitive work of her own, *Where Shall Wisdom be Found? Calvin's Exegesis of Job from Medieval and Modern Perspectives*, a follow-up to her earlier work, *The Theater of His Glory*.[29] *Where Shall Wisdom be Found?* is an expansive treatment in which Calvin's particular understanding of Job is compared (and contrasted) with such diverse figures as the Spanish Jewish philosopher Maimonides, whose explanation of the book of Job is found in his *Guide of the Perplexed*, written before 1190,

*Introduction* 13

Thomas Aquinas' literal interpretation written in the 1260s, and such modern interpreters as Archibald MacLeish, Elie Weisel and Franz Kafka. Given these parameters, Schreiner is necessarily selective, choosing particular issues of study: Calvin's assessment of Elihu as "a true doctor of the church," the nominalism that lies behind Calvin's analysis of the relationship between God's power and justice, and the idea of future judgment as the resolution of the tension between sin and suffering.[30]

In keeping with Schreiner's earlier plea, *Where Shall Wisdom be Found?* does attempt to interpret Job "as a whole." And yet, gaps still remain in the understanding of what Calvin was attempting to accomplish by choosing Job as the theme for weekday sermons for a period of almost fourteen months, from February 1554 to March 1555.

**The Object of this Book in Relation to Recent Scholarship**

Our object in examining the *Sermons on Job*, preached by Calvin in 1554 and 1555, is in order to deepen our understanding of pastoral ministry.[31] In particular, we shall focus upon the way in which Calvin's doctrine of the incomprehensibility of God informs his understanding of divine providence, and see how he uses this insight as a pastoral tool in dealing with suffering. We shall then ask, in the light of recent Calvin studies, the extent to which this understanding of providence requires a christological interpretation.

Previous studies of Calvin's sermons on the book of Job have not addressed his pastoral theology in detail. Most studies have only referred tangentially to the Joban material, selecting evidence in support of particular themes and issues, but never dealing with the material as a whole. In addition to the material by Schreiner, Bouwsma, Torrance and Stauffer already mentioned, an unpublished study by Peter Miln has explored these sermons from a largely historical perspective.[32]

Though no formal statement of it exists, Miln's thesis appears to be that Calvin's *Sermons on Job* is a work "for all men in all ages."[33] Miln is concerned to show that since suffering is ever-present, Calvin's expositions on the Book of Job have a timeless quality about them.

Miln attempts to place these sermons within a definite time-period: one in which Calvin and Job have definite connections and similarities. "Job stands as the symbol, yet the person vividly presented is Calvin himself," Miln writes.[34] His first chapter attempts to set the sermons within the context of the struggles of Calvin's own personal life and those of Geneva leading up to the years 1554 and 1555.

Chapter 2 deals with the history of preaching in the broader context of the sixteenth century. Miln contends that the Reformers understood the Christian ministry to be essentially prophetic rather than sacerdotal.[35] The contributions of William Perkins (1558-1602) are considered, as well as the recent research of T. H. L. Parker and William Bouwsma. Miln then goes on to demonstrate Calvin's dependence on the rhetorical devices of Cicero. Miln corroborates the view expressed by Emil Doumergue in his seven-volume work on Calvin, that the essential Calvin is to be found in his preaching.[36]

Chapter 3 is devoted to a consideration of what Miln thinks is the general theological emphasis of the Joban sermons. He writes: "the life of the Christian is a life under God's hand."[37] For Miln, the key issues are those of justification and our relationship to Christ. "Whilst dealing with an Old Testament theme, Calvin is still able to proclaim the centrality of Jesus Christ."[38] And again, "The absolute sovereignty of God leads man to total self-abnegation, and to complete consecration and service to the Glory of God. This can only be done in Christ, who alone is the Way."[39] Thus, for Miln, there is an "intensely Christocentric nature" to these sermons.[40]

Miln also has much to say about Calvin's "Protestant ethic," in which the capitalist creation of wealth is not for personal aggrandizement, but in order that the poor might benefit from works of charity.[41] He underlines Calvin's concern with predestination, though adding that it would be "wrong to make predestination, however central a theme of the Sermons, one of the main planks of Calvin's platform from the ethical point of view."[42]

Chapter 4 raises some theological concerns, including what Miln calls "[Calvin's] utter theocentricity."[43] Here, Miln withdraws from his earlier statement regarding Christocentricity: "We note here a sharp contrast with Luther's practice where every sermon concentrated on a Christ centred approach to whatever topic was in hand. This was so even when dealing with passages from the Old Testament. Whilst Luther was concerned to point to Christ, Calvin was concerned to point to God in His triune fullness."[44]

It is in this chapter that Miln raises Calvin's use of the incomprehensibility of God: "It is God's majesty, incomprehensibility and power which confronts us."[45] Miln suggests that Calvin's intention is to emphasize our need for humility before God. The incomprehensible righteousness of God, what Calvin sometimes calls "double justice" that there exists a righteousness in God which transcends that righteousness which is revealed in the law, and before which even the pure angels of heaven are unclean this receives passing mention on pages 160 and again at 257. In the final chapter, Chapter 7, Miln will actually conclude by saying that the single *leitmotif* of these sermons is "the incomprehensibility and the majesty of God."[46] Despite this affirmation, Miln does not establish comprehensively that this is indeed so.

In chapter 5 Miln argues that Calvin has both a general and particular doctrine of providence. General providence is concerned with God's upholding of the universe and his government of it. Particular providence, for example, is concerned to outline God's action in the day to day life of Job. Miln shows how the latter is especially useful in pastoral applications to the lives of the people of God. This is followed by a chapter dealing with the doctrine of election, in which Miln contends that the sermons form one of the greatest treatises against Free Will. Miln, at times, considers issues not contained within the Joban material. For example, he maintains that Calvin espoused a view of limited rather than universal atonement.[47]

Despite this recent thesis on Calvin's Sermons on Job, a study of these Sermons remains necessary for the following reasons:

1. Almost half of the thesis sets the biographical and historical background to the Sermons on Job and this has resulted in an inadequate treatment of important theological concepts, including double justice and ontological mediation.

2. Though Miln suggests that incomprehensibility is "the single *leitmotif*," he has not sufficiently addressed Calvin's use of the term in the Sermons or Calvin's use of the idea elsewhere.

3. Miln's suggestion that these Sermons are "intensely Christocentric" does not appear to be substantiated by the evidence of the sermons themselves. We shall show that Calvin is less than Christocentric in many of the Sermons.

Furthermore, many studies in Calvin have suffered from an uncritical acceptance of a Barthian position whereby Calvin's theology is regarded as having a christological focus. As we shall see, the Joban material provides no basis for such a thesis. Moreover, Calvin's twofold knowledge of God (the *duplex cognitio Dei*) forms a theological paradigm that embraces the Reformer's understanding of the Book of Job, as well as providing a basis upon which theological and pastoral advice can be given in response to human suffering and the problem of pain.[48]

Attempts have been made to break down the barriers erected between Calvin's dogmatics on the one hand and Calvin's spirituality on the other.[49] As Brian Armstrong comments: "…it is notable that those who seek to define a primary aspect of Calvin's theological formulations by calling attention to his spirituality, to his piety, are pointing in the proper direction."[50] Accepting, by way of definition, that piety is a human response to the knowledge of God, it is impossible to study the Joban sermons in any depth without confronting the Reformer's concern for piety. We will see that the Joban material significantly adds to our understanding of that kernel of spirituality found in chapter 17 of the 1539 edition of the *Institutes*.[51] It is essential that these sermons be examined from the perspective of human pain and of how, for Calvin, such outward conformity to Christ through suffering provides a necessary mark of true spirituality.[52] This study will support the view that there is a line of continuity from the dogmatic to the homiletic in the development of the Reformer's understanding of piety.

**Overview**

We shall engage in a thorough survey of the sermons on Job, examining them within the broader context of Calvin's writing. In chapter 1, we shall attempt to identify some of the leading theological issues that Calvin discerns in this material, showing the Reformer's interest in a range of theological foci.

In chapter 2, we shall show that in Calvin's attempt to provide a comprehensive and logically consistent theodicy, addressing the tension between God's justice and power, the Reformer fails to completely absolve himself from the charge of nominalism.[53] Whilst denying the concept of absolute power (unconstrained by divine justice) Calvin's doctrine of "double justice" leads to a notion of metaphysical redemption that remained a part of his dogmatic thought to the end, as can be seen in the final edition of the *Institutes*.[54]

Chapter 3 will identify the doctrine of God's incomprehensibility as the interpretative key in the understanding of the Book of Job for the Reformer. We shall see that this incomprehensibility is quite different from the irrationality and arbitrariness of nominalism. No comprehensive study hitherto has focused as sharply on this issue. What emerges in these sermons is a twofold inability to comprehend God, arising in the first place from metaphysical reasons of finitude and creatureliness, and in the second place from ethical culpability due to the Fall rendering man intellectually and morally unable to fulfil that role for which he was created. We shall show that this is a theme that runs throughout Calvin's output, underscoring Calvin's concern at the very deepest level that the lesson of the Book of Job, as well as the key to Christian piety in general, is submission to a sovereign and incomprehensible God.[55] Although Schreiner has touched on these aspects, her work has not sufficiently addressed the all-embracing nature of the doctrine of God's incomprehensibility in Calvin's formulation of the essence of the Joban polemic.[56] This work will uncover this evidence.

In chapter 4, we shall survey the material outlining Calvin's pastoral method in the interpretation of providence in the life of Job. We shall attempt to define precisely how the Reformer viewed suffering and what its function may be in the life of the righteous. In particular we shall identify those aspects of trial that call forth particular responses in the Christian as embodying the essence of piety.

In chapter 5, we shall show that Calvin did not attempt an overtly christological interpretation of providence. In fact, no attempt was made to specify a particular Christ-focus.

## References

[1] Karl Barth, *Church Dogmatics*, trans. G. W. Bromiley and R. J. Ehrlich (Edinburgh: T. & T. Clark, 1961), III/3: 30. Also, Barth, on page 115, confines Calvin's discussion of the divine *concursus*, in relation to divine providence, to *Institutes* I.16-18. John Murray eulogizes: "No treatment of God's sovereignty has surpassed that which we find in the last three chapters of Book I of *Institutes*." See "Calvin on the Sovereignty of God," in John Murray, *Collected Writings of John Murray*, vol. 4 (Edinburgh: Banner of Truth Trust, 1982), 191. Similarly, Francois Wendel, *Calvin: The Origins and Development of His Religious Thought*, trans. Philip Mairet (Glasgow: Collins, 1976), 177-184; Timothy George, *Theology of the Reformers* (Nashville, TN: Broadman Press, 1988), 204-213; Wilhelm Niesel, *The Theology of Calvin*, trans. Harold Knight (Philadelphia: Westminster Press, 1956), 70-79; Heinrich Heppe, *Reformed Dogmatics*, trans. G. T. Thomson (Grand Rapids: Baker Book House, 1984), 251-280; A. M. Hunter, *The Teaching of Calvin* (London: James Clarke, 1950), 135-151; B. A. Gerrish, *Grace and Gratitude: The Eucharistic Theology of John Calvin* (Edinburgh: T. & T. Clark, 1993), 30.

Additionally, even where no such assertion is made as to the centrality of *Institutes* I:xvi-xviii, the fact that discussions of Calvin's doctrine of providence are limited to these passages confirms the belief that this remains the *locus classicus* for most writers. See, for example, Emil Brunner, *The Christian Doctrine of Creation and Redemption: Dogmatics, Vol. II*, trans. Olive Wyon (London: Lutterworth, 1960), 148-192; Reinhold Seeberg, *The History of Doctrines*, vol. 2, trans. Charles E. Hays (Grand Rapids: Baker Book House, 1977), 396-398; G. C. Berkouwer, *Studies in Dogmatics: The Providence of God* (Grand Rapids: Eerdmans, 1980); Otto Weber, *Foundations of Dogmatics*, vol. 1 (Grand Rapids: Eerdmans, 1981), 502-525; Edward Dowey, *The Knowledge of God in Calvin's Theology* (Grand Rapids: Eerdmans, 1994), 129-130, 145-146; Charles Partee, *Calvin and Classical Philosophy* (Leiden: E. J. Brill, 1977), 126-147.

This is not to deny that some of these writers also allude to other important sources of Calvin's doctrine of providence. Thus Wendel, for example, alludes to Calvin's *Against the Libertines* (1545) and his *Treatise on Predestination* in the appendix to the *Consensus Genevensis* (1552). John Murray makes reference to Calvin's tract *The Eternal Predestination of God* (1552), and especially his commentary on Romans, *The Epistle to the Romans* (Grand Rapids, MI: Eerdmans, 1973), 192-199. Ronald S. Wallace cites *Institutes* II.ii.7, II.iv.5, III.xx.51 and III.xxiii.9 as significant in Calvin's doctrine of providence, in *Calvin, Geneva and the Reformation* (Edinburgh: Scottish Academic Press, 1988), 261-270. Cf. Wallace's *Calvin's Doctrine of the Christian Life* (Edinburgh/London: Oliver and Boyd, 1959), 123-140. Some of these treatments make a passing reference to Calvin's commentaries and sermons, even if no further examination of them is made.

[2] The closeness of the relationship between providence and predestination can be seen in the synonymity of the use of terms in the 1536 edition of the *Institutes*. In the passage describing the church as the number of the elect, Calvin speaks of the members of the church as those who "have been chosen by God's *eternal providence*..." [italics mine] *Institutes of the Christian Religion* (1536), trans. Ford Lewis Battles (Grand Rapids, MI: Eerdmans, 1975), 58. ...*quia quotquot aeterna Dei providentia electi sunt*...[*CO* 1:73]. Similar references occur in the 1559 edition at III. xxiii. 3, 5 and 6. [*CO* 2:700-704]. For differing analyses of this issue, see D. N. Wiley, "Calvin's Doctrine of Predestination: His Principal Soteriological and Polemical Doctrine" (Ph.D. diss., Duke University, 1971), 175-222; Richard A. Muller, *Christ and the Decree: Christology and Predestination in Reformed Theology from Calvin to Perkins* (Durham, NC: The Labyrinth Press, 1986), 22-24; F. Wendel, *Calvin: Origins and Development of his Religious Thought*, trans. P. Mairet (New York: Harper and Row, 1963), 177-184, 263-284; H. Strohl, "La Pensée de Calvin sur la Providence divine," *Revue d'Histoire et de Philosophie religieuses* 22 (1942): 154-169; Etienne de Peyer, "Calvin's Doctrine of Providence," *The Evangelical Quarterly* 10 (1938): 30-44; W. Niesel, *The Theology of Calvin*, trans. H. Knight (Philadelphia: Westminster Press, 1956),

66-74; Fred Klooster, *Calvin's Doctrine of Predestination* (Grand Rapids, MI: Calvin Theological Seminary, 1961), 8-15.

[3] In the first edition (1536) predestination is found in the discussion of the article of the Church in the Apostles Creed as noted above. In the editions of 1539-1554 the doctrine is discussed in the context of soteriological issues. In the final, 1559 edition, the subject of providence is dislocated from the discussion of predestination and brought back into Book I. In the *First Genevan Catechism* (1537), predestination immediately follows Christology. The *Revised Catechism* (1542) returned to the arrangement of the *Institutes* of 1536. The *French Confession* (1559) has predestination follow the doctrine of sin, thus preceding Christology and soteriology.

[4] This, among other issues, has implications for the doctrine of assurance and the denial by Wilhem Niesel, for example, that Calvin had any place in his theology for the *syllogismus practicus*. Niesel, *The Theology of Calvin*, 168-69. For a refutation of this position, see Muller, *Christ and the Decree*, 25-27.

[5] According to Fritz Büsser, Calvin "strongly desired not to be considered as author of only *one* book, the *Institutio*....Alongside the *Institutio* and in numerous ways related to it stand Calvin's commentaries on many writings of the Old and New Testaments." Büsser, "Bullinger as Calvin's Model in Biblical Exposition: An Examination of Calvin's Preface to the Epistle to the Romans," in *In Honour of John Calvin, 1509-64: papers from the 1986 International Calvin Symposium, McGill University*, ed. E. J. Furcha. ARC Supplement 3 (Montreal: Faculty of Religious Studies, McGill University, 1987), 64-65. See also in this regard, John H. Leith, *John Calvin's Doctrine of the Christian Life* (Louisville, KY: Westminster/John Knox Press, 1989); R. S. Wallace, *Calvin's Doctrine of the Christian Life* (Edinburgh: Oliver and Boyd, 1959); Dennis Tamburello, *Union with Christ: John Calvin and the Mysticism of St. Bernard* (Louisville: Westminster/John Knox, 1994).

Richard Stauffer, for example, claims that the sermons do not only represent an unsystematised form of the theology found in the *Institutes*, but complement and even correct that theology: "*Ses sermons contiennent ainsi, épars, les éléments d'un véritable exposé de dogmatique, une dogmatique qui, sur de nombreux points, enrichit, amende ou "adoucit" l'*Institution *de la religion chrestienne.*" *Dieu, la création et la providence dans la prédication de Calvin*. Basler und Berner Studien zur historischen und systematischen Theologie, no. 33 (Bern: Peter Lang, 1978), 12. In making this claim, Stauffer assumes a certain interpretation of the *Institutes* that others have denied. Cf. T. H. L. Parker's comments in his review of this work in *Scottish Journal of Theology* 33:1 (1980): 73-75.

[6] Calvin himself, in his "Last Will and Testament," gives his sermonic output great weight. Writing in April 1564, barely a month before he died, he writes: "I protest also that I have endeavoured, according to the measure of grace he has given me, to teach his word in purity, both in my sermons and writings (*enseigner purement sa Parole, tant en sermons que par escrit*)..." *Selected Works of John Calvin: Tracts and Letters*, ed. Henry Beveridge and

Jules Bonnet, trans. Marcus Robert Gilchrist, 7 vols. (Grand Rapids: Baker Book House, 1983), 7:366. [*CO* 20:299]. Calvin himself regarded the *Institutes* as in many ways definitive of his doctrinal position. Cf. Calvin's introductory remarks to the *Institutes* about the brevity of his commentaries because of what he had written in the *Institutes*: *Itaque, hac veluti strata via, si quas posthac scripturae enarrationes edidero, quia non necesse habebo de dogmatibus longas disputationes instituere, et in locos communes evagari, eas compendio semper astringam* [*CO* 2:3-4].

[7] T. H. L. Parker, *Calvin's New Testament Commentaries* (Grand Rapids: Eerdmans, 1971), vii. David L. Puckett's impressive work examining the charge that Calvin's exegesis of the Old Testament was too "Jewish", lacking in a specific agenda to Christianize the text, deals exclusively with Calvin's Old Testament commentaries. This persuasive thesis can be supplemented by an examination of Calvin's sermonic output. Of interest to the current study, Puckett's work makes no reference to the Joban sermons, David L. Pucket, *John Calvin's Exegesis of the Old Testament* (Louisville: Westminster/John Knox, 1995).

[8] These studies include Richard C. Gamble, "*Brevitas et Facilitas*: Toward an Understanding of Calvin's Hermeneutic," *Westminster Theological Journal* 47 (1985): 1-17; "Calvin as Theologian and Exegete: Is There Anything New?" *Calvin Theological Journal* 23 (1988): 178-94; Alexandre Ganoczy and Stefan Scheld, *Die Hermeneutik Calvins: Geistesgeschichtliche Voraussetzungen und Grundzüge*, Veröffentlichungen des Instituts für Europaische Geschichte 114 (Weisbaden: Steiner Verlag, 1983); Alexandre Ganoczy, "Calvin als Paulinischer Theologe," in *Calvinus Theologus*, ed. W. H. Neuser (Neukirchen: Neukirchener Verlag, 1976), 36-99; Benoit Girardin, *Rhétorique et Théologique: Calvin, Le Commentaire de l'Epître aux Romains* (Paris: Éditions Beauchesne, 1979); Elsie Anne McKee, "Calvin's Exegesis of Romans 12:8 – Social, Accidental, or Theological," *Calvin Theological Journal* 23 (1988): 6-18; Richard A. Muller, "The Hermeneutic of Promise and Fulfillment in Calvin's Exegesis of the Old Testament Prophecies of the Kingdom," in *The Bible in the Sixteenth Century*, ed. David Steinmetz, *Duke Monographs in Medieval and Renaissance Studies*, 11 (Durham, N.C.: Duke University Press, 1990), 68-82; T. H. L. Parker, "Calvin the Exegete: Change and Development," in *Calvinus Ecclesiae Doctor*, ed. W. H. Neuser (Kampen, 1981), 33-46; *Calvin's New Testament Commentaries* (Louisville, KY: Westminster/John Knox Press, 1993); *Calvin's Old Testament Commentaries* (Edinburgh: T. & T. Clark, 1986); Barbara Pitkin, "What Pure Eyes Could See: Faith, Creation, and History in John Calvin's Theology" Ph.D. diss., Chicago, 1994); Susan Schreiner, "Through a Mirror Dimly," *Calvin Theological Journal* 21 (Nov, 1986): 175-93; David Steinmetz: "Calvin and Abraham: The Interpretations of Romans 4 in the Sixteenth Century," *Church History* 57 (1988): 443-55; "Calvin and the Patristic Exegesis of Paul," in *The Bible in the Sixteenth Century*, ed. by David C. Steinmetz, 100-118, 231-235; Thomas F. Torrance, *The Hermeneutics of John Calvin* (Edinburgh:

Scottish Academic Press, 1988); Marten Woudstra, "Calvin Interprets What 'Moses Reports': Observations on Calvin's Commentary on Exodus 1-19," *Calvin Theological Journal* 21 (1986): 151-74; David F. Wright, "Calvin's Pentateuchal Criticism: Equity, Hardness of Heart, and Divine Accommodation in the Mosaic Harmony Commentary," *Calvin Theological Journal* 21 (1986): 33-50. Several of the English language articles listed above as well as other important articles on hermeneutical aspects in Calvin have been reprinted in *Calvin and Hermeneutics*, vol. 6 of *Articles on Calvin and Calvinism*, 14 vols., ed. Richard C. Gamble (Hamden, Conn.: Garland Publishing, 1992).

On a different level, Serene Jones' work, *Calvin and the Rhetoric of Piety* (Louisville, Kentucky: Westminster/John Knox Press, 1995), attempts to examine Calvin's theology from the point of view of linguistic analysis and rhetorical style. It is doubtful, as Richard Muller notes, whether Calvin would have recognized a "rhetoric of piety," and to suggest, as this work does, that it is possible to separate personal godliness from correct expression of doctrine and denial of heresy is misguided. See Richard Muller's review of Jones' work in *Calvin Theological Journal* 31 (1996): 582-583. Like Bouwsma's work, Jones abstracts Calvin from historical context in favour of a contemporary self-understanding. Meaningful historical engagement thus becomes impossible. Such a work is almost bound to be subjective in its approach and, somewhat surprisingly, the sermons are not considered. Cf. Francis Higman, *The Style of John Calvin in His French Polemical Treatises* (Oxford: Oxford University Press, 1967).

[9] Thomas F. Torrance, *Calvin's Doctrine of Man* (London: Lutterworth Press, 1949); Richard Stauffer, *Dieu, la création et la providence dans la prédication de Calvin* (Berne, 1978); Erwin Mülhaupt, *Die Predigt Calvins: Ihre Geschichte, Ihre Form und Ihre Religiösen Grundgedanken* Arbeiten zur Kirchengeschichte, 18 (Berlin: Walter de Gruyter, 1931); Josef Bohatec, "Calvins Vorsehungslehre," in *Calvinstudien: Festschrift zum 400. Geburtstag Johann Calvins* (Leipzig: Rudolph Haupt, 1909); Susan Schreiner, in addition to the work mentioned above, see *Where Shall Wisdom Be Found? Calvin's Exegesis of Job from Medieval and Modern Perspectives* (Chicago, London: The University of Chicago Press, 1994); William J. Bouwsma, *John Calvin: A Sixteenth-Century Portrait* (New York/Oxford: Oxford University Press, 1988), esp. 162-176.

[10] Josef Bohatec, "Calvins Vorsehungslehre," in *Calvinstudien* (Leipzig), 339-441, esp. 353, 380. For his use of the Psalms commentary, see 387-93. Cf. Barbara Pitkin, "What Pure Eyes Could See: Faith, Creation, and History in John Calvin's Theology" (Ph.D. diss., University of Chicago, 1994), 237-307.

[11] Stauffer's references to the Joban sermons in *Dieu, la création et la providence dans la prédication de Calvin* are extensive and represent perhaps the most elaborate attempt yet to summarise the contents of the Joban sermons.

[12] To cite T. H. L. Parker's review of this work: "Did Calvin really change his

mind as he walked up the street from his study in 11 rue des Chanoines to mount the pulpit in St. Pierre?" *Scottish Journal of Theology* 33:1 (1980): 73-75. T. H. L. Parker would be critical of this thesis, of course, since he himself has expressed the research on the sermonic material "largely superfluous," since we already possess Calvin's own doctrinal synthesis in the *Institutes*. See, T. H. L. Parker, *The Oracles of God: An Introduction to the Preaching of John Calvin* (London: Butterworth, 1947), 81.

[13] Stauffer, *op. cit.*, 105.

[14] William J. Bouwsma, *John Calvin: A Sixteenth Century Portrait* (New York: Oxford University Press, 1988).

[15] *Op. cit.*, 230.

[16] *Idem*. Bouwsma suggests that this Calvin was "chiefly driven by a terror that took shape for him in the metaphor of the abyss."

[17] *Op. cit.*, 231. Bouwsma goes on to add: "This Calvin did seek, because he neither trusted nor needed, what passes on earth for intelligibility and order; instead, he was inclined to celebrate the paradoxes and mystery at the heart of existence."

[18] *Op. cit.*, 168. Calvin can say of election that it has no practical value! Cf., 36.

[19] *Op. cit.*, 168-172.

[20] Curiously, these are from the first half of the sermons on Job, only seven citations coming from Sermons 100-159. Some of his quotations are incorrectly cited, as we shall point out in the course of the thesis.

[21] I. John Hesselink, "Reactions to Bouwsma's Portrait of 'John Calvin'," in *Calvinus Sacrae Scripturae Professor: Calvin as Confessor of Holy Scripture*, ed. Wilhelm H. Neuser (Grand Rapids: Eerdmans, 1994), 209-213.

[22] Brian Armstrong has been especially critical. Reviewing the work for *Church History*, he contends: "If Bouwsma has discovered two Calvins, the reader also finds many Bouwsmas: The psychohistorian who believes he can get inside Calvin's mind; the iconoclast who gleefully destroys all theological images erected of Calvin; the scholar of humanism who opens new vistas for Calvin studies; the Lucien Febvre disciple writing to characterize an age as much as an individual; and, as always, the poet whose masterful pen always delights. His 'portrait' of Calvin is a pastiche of quotations and observations which create a veritable work of art; it will occasion varied response. Theologians will be distraught, perhaps not recognizing the man at all; historians will be uneasy, thinking the strokes too bold, the generalizations too sweeping; sociologists/psychologists will be ecstatic, perceiving the 'real' Calvin has been discovered; literary scholars will be delighted, finding again that all really creative hues come from humane letters; and the generalist will be fascinated by a many-faceted panorama which has something for everyone" (*Church History* 58, March 1989, 106). T.H.L. Parker is uncharacteristically scathing in his response, accusing Bouwsma of knowing Calvin better than Calvin knew himself. "This seems to me the end of meaningful commerce with the past," he concludes (*Calvin: An Introduction to His Thought*, Louisville, Kentucky: Westminster/John Knox Press, 1995, 11).

[23] *Op. cit.*, 107.
[24] T. H. L. Parker, *Calvin's Preaching*, 79-92, esp. 91, where Parker alludes to the Joban sermons and their effect on Calvin's style and emphasis
[25] *Op. cit.*, 153.
[26] Despite these criticisms, Bouwsma's contribution to Calvin studies continues to be profound.
[27] C.f. Jeannine Olson, *Theological Studies* 50.1 (1989), 190.
[28] Schreiner, "Through a Mirror Dimly," 176.
[29] Schreiner, Susan E. *The Theater of His Glory: Nature and the Natural Order in the Thought of John Calvin* (Grand Rapids, Mich.: Baker Books, 1991). Schreiner contends in *The Theater of His Glory* that providence was like a "proscenium arch" in the *Institutes*, thereby spanning the entire work. In *Where Shall Wisdom be Found?*, she takes this even further to cover the Joban sermons in particular.
[30] For reviews of Schreiner's work, *Where Shall Wisdom be Found?*, see David F. Wright, *Journal of Religion* 76 (1996): 639-640; Fred W. Graham, *Sixteenth Century Journal* 26 (1994): 430-431; Kathleen M. O'Connor, *Theological Studies* 56 (1995): 188; Craig S. Farmer, *Pro Ecclesia* 5 (1996): 504-507; Raymond C. Ortland, *Journal of the Evangelical Theological Society* 39 (1996): 292.
[31] A great deal of attention has been given to the issue of finding what is central in Calvin's theology. In the nineteenth century, scholars like A. Schweitzer suggested the doctrine of predestination, whilst H. Bauke and in this century, A. Ganoczy, suggest a *complexio oppositorum*. More recently, W. Bouwsma and B. G. Armstrong have revealed a skepticism over any attempt at formulating a systematic theology from Calvin's published writings. Joseph McLelland has whimsically commented this way: "John Calvin's method has been analyzed almost *ad nauseam*, and with conflicting conclusions: a method utterly systematic, boldly dialectical, badly confused, deliberately paradoxical" ("Renaissance in Theology: Calvin's 1536 Institutio—Fresh Start or False?" in *In Honour of John Calvin, 1509-64: Papers from the 1986 International Calvin Symposium, McGill University*, ed. E. J. Furcha. ARC Supplement 3, Montreal: Faculty of Religious Studies, McGill University, 1987, 156).

Of importance here is the helpful research of Cornelius P. Venema, "The Twofold Nature of the Gospel in Calvin's Theology: The *Duplex gratia dei* and the Interpretation of Calvin's Theology" (Ph.D. diss., Princeton Theological Seminary, 1985), 4-6. Some have criticized even this approach, the *centrally important dogma* approach, as fruitless. Among them, Bauke, Ganoczy, Battles, Bouwsma and Armstrong. For a defense of this latter position, see Richard C. Gamble, "Calvin as Theologian and Exegete: Is There Anything New?" *Calvin Theological Journal* 23 (1988): 187.

[32] Peter Miln, "Hommes D'une Bonne Cause: Calvin's Sermons on the Book of Job" (Ph.D. diss., University of Nottingham, 1989).
[33] Miln, 17.

[34] Miln, 21. Later, he writes, "Calvin was Job" (*Ibid.*, 97). Cf. the words of the final chapter, "In Job's spiritual journey, we find Calvin's also" (*Ibid.*, 251-252).

[35] *Ibid.*, 68.

[36] *Ibid.*, 140. C.f. E. Doumergue, *Jean Calvin, les hommes et les choses de son temps*. 7 vols. (Lausanne: G. Bridel & Co., 1899-1927).

[37] *Ibid.*, 97.

[38] *Ibid.*, 98.

[39] *Ibid.*, 101.

[40] *Ibid.*, 125.

[41] *Ibid.*, 121.

[42] *Ibid.*, 130.

[43] *Ibid.*, 142.

[44] *Idem*. He goes to say that, "it is clear that for Calvin Christ, for man, is indeed the cornerstone, and within the context of the Godhead it is to Christ that he principally points." Miln later argues that despite living in the Old Testament, Job is elect "in Christ" (240-242).

[45] *Ibid.*, 155.

[46] *Ibid.*, 256.

[47] *Ibid.*, 228.

[48] "First, as much in the fashioning of the universe as in the general teaching of Scripture the Lord shows himself to be simply the Creator. Then in the face of Christ he shows himself the Redeemer. Of the resulting twofold knowledge of [God] we shall now discuss the first aspect: the second will be dealt with in its proper place" (I.ii.2). *Quia ergo Dominus primum simpliciter creator tam in mundi opificio, quam in generali scripturae doctrina, deinde in Christi facie redemptor apparet, hinc duplex emergit eius cognitio: quarum nunc prior tractanda est, altera deinde suo ordine sequetur* [*CO* 2:34]. References to the 1559 edition of the *Institutes* will be cited by book, chapter and section and will be taken from the standard English translation: *Calvin: Institutes of the Christian Religion*, ed. John T. McNeill and trans. Ford Lewis Battles, 2 vols., Library of Christian Classics, vols. 20-21 (Philadelphia: Westminster Press, 1960) [*CO* 2:31-1118]. Battles notes that the explicit nomenclature of a twofold knowledge of God was added to the 1559 edition, adding by way of explanation that this distinction "is basic to the structure of the completed work" (*Institutes* 40 n3). Scholars, like Dowey, argue that the knowledge of God the Creator is dealt with in Book 1, whilst Books 2–4 cover the knowledge of God the Redeemer. Dowey's analysis is a little more intricate than this, but this summary captures his overall analysis (*Knowledge of God in Calvin's Theology*, 42). For a summary of current discussions in this area, see Richard C. Gamble, "Current Trends in Calvin Research, 1982-1990," in *Calvinus Sacrae Scripturae Professor*, ed. W. Neuser (Grand Rapids: Eerdmans, 1994), 105-8.

Dowey's criticism of Battles' contention that the *duplex cognitio Dei* fundamentally structures the whole of Calvin's thought is pertinent here but lies outside the scope of this thesis. We shall show that the *duplex* is certainly apparent as a structuring paradigm for the Joban sermons and would lend some support to Battles' position. For Battles' position, see F. L. Battles, "*Calculus Fidei*: Some Ruminations on the Structure of the Theology of John Calvin," in *Interpreting John Calvin* (Grand Rapids: Baker Book House, 1996), 139-178, esp. 155-160. Dowey's response was to an earlier printing of this article in *Calvinus Ecclesiae Doctor*, ed. W. H. Neuser (Kampen: Kok, 1978), 85-110, and appears in "The Structure of Calvin's Theological Thought as Influenced by the Two-fold Knowledge of God," in *Calvinus Ecclesiae Genevensis Custos*, ed. Wilhelm Neuser (Bern: Peter Lang, 1984), 135-148. See also Richard C. Gamble, "Exposition and Method in Calvin," *Westminster Theological Journal* 49 (1987): 153-165.

[49] Bouwsma, for example, writes: "Calvin's spirituality has received little explicit attention from scholars, partly because the concept of spirituality has had little place in Protestant scholarship, owing to the tendency among later Calvinists to view Calvin chiefly as a dogmatic theologian" (W. Bouwsma, "The Spirituality of John Calvin," in *Christian Spirituality: High Middle Ages and Reformation*, ed. Jill Raitt, New York: Crossroad, 1987, 333). See also Richard C. Gamble, "Calvin and Sixteenth-Century Spirituality: Comparison with the Anabaptists," *Calvin Theological Journal* 31 (1996): 335-58; "Calvin as Theologian and Exegete: Is There Anything New?" *Calvin Theological Journal* 23 (1988), 178-194; Lucien Richard, "The Devotio Moderna," in *Devotio Moderna: The Spirituality of John Calvin* (Atlanta: John Knox, 1974), 12-47; Howard G. Hageman, "Reformed Spirituality," in *Protestant Spiritual Traditions*, ed. Frank C. Senn (New York: Paulist, 1986); Ford Lewis Battles, *The Piety of Calvin: An Anthology Illustrative of the Spirituality of the Reformer* (Grand Rapids: Baker, 1978), 13-26; Alexandre Ganoczy, *The Young Calvin*, trans. David Foxgrover and Wade Provo (Philadelphia: Westminster, 1987), 194-208.

[50] B. Armstrong, "The Nature and Structure of Calvin's Thought according to the *Institutes*: Another Look," in *John Calvin's "Institutes"—His Opus Magnum: Proceedings of the Second South African Congress for Calvin Research*, ed. B. Van der Walt (Potchefstroom: Potchefstroom University for Christian Higher Education, 1986), 59-60.

[51] The section is entitled "On the Christian Life" [*CO* 1:1123-1152]. This section was translated into English in 1549 as *The Life and Conversation of a Christian Man* and has been reprinted several times since under the title *Golden Booklet of the True Christian Life*. See also Battles' translation in *The Piety of John Calvin*, trans. and ed. Ford Lewis Battles (Grand Rapids: Baker Book House, 1978), 51-83.

[52] Thus, in the *Institutes*, Calvin could insist that conformity to Christ's death, mortification, to give it its proper name, is what we can expect from God and is fully compliant with his will for us. *Institutes* I.xvi.3 [*CO* 2:146-147]. And in the commentary on John, Calvin can say: "The godly are pressed down by various afflictions; they are held tight in hard straits; they suffer

hunger or nakedness or disease; they are worried by reproaches; they seem every moment to be almost swallowed up by death. Let this then be their continual meditation, that it is a sowing which will yield fruit in its season" (*Commentary on the Gospel according to John* [John 12:24], vol. 2, trans. T. H. L. Parker, ed. David W. Torrance and Thomas F. Torrance, Grand Rapids: Eerdmans, 1961, 37). *Sit igitur haec continua piorum meditatio, quum premuntur variis aerumnis, quum angustiis constricti tenentur, quum fame aut nuditate aut morbis laborant quum iniuriis vexantur, quum videntur singulis momentis propemodum a morte absorbendi, hanc esse sationem, quae suo tempore fructum profert* [*CO* 47:288].

[53] Cf. the remarks of Berkouwer: "Sovereignty 'in itself' is a compassionateless concept quite as inspiring of dread as is blind fate" (G. C. Berkouwer, *The Providence of God*, Grand Rapids: Eerdmans, 1952, 254).

[54] Important and definitive work on the concept of universal mediatorship in Calvin has been done by David Willis, but he makes no mention of the Joban material. The fact that Calvin speaks directly to this issue, in relation to unfallen angels and their continual culpability in the face of a righteousness which is over and above that which is revealed in the law (Calvin's exposition of Job 4:18, and cited again in the 1559 edition of the *Institutes* at III.xii.1 [*CO* 2:554], cited as Job 4:17), adds significantly to our understanding of Calvin's exposition of Christ's role as the Mediator. See David Willis, *Calvin's Catholic Christology*, vol. 2 of *Studies in Medieval and Reformation Thought*, ed. H. A. Oberman (Leiden: E. J. Brill, 1966), 67-78.

[55] Cf. the remark made by Brian G. Armstrong: "If there is one fundamental assumption which underlies the whole of Calvin's theology it is found, I believe, in the dictum of St. Augustine that 'man is created for fellowship or communion with God and is restless until he finds his rest in that God' " ("The Nature and Structure of Calvin's Thought according to the *Institutes*: Another Look," in *John Calvin's "Institutes"—His Opus Magnum: Proceedings of the Second South African Congress for Calvin Research*, ed. B. Van der Walt, Potchefstroom: Potchefstroom University for Christian Higher Education, 1986, 61).

[56] Schreiner, in her analysis of the Joban sermons, touches on Calvin's doctrine of God's incomprehensibility at several points, suggesting that "the transcendence and sovereignty of God play a major role in both the *Institutes* and the *Sermons on Job*" (*Where Shall Wisdom be Found?*, 92). And again: "...Calvin continually directs Job not merely to God's incomprehensibility but to God's knowable revelation, which stands, he promises, in continuity with God's hiddenness" (*Ibid.*, 120). Schreiner continues at the beginning of the next chapter by saying: "...Calvin finds that the correct perspective was one that took full account of the incomprehensibility of God and the obscurity of divine providence" (*Ibid.*, 121). See also Schreiner's contrast of Calvin and Maimonides on this issue (*ibid.*, 151).

The English citations in this chapter from the Joban sermons are taken from the facsimile editon, published in 1993 by The Banner of Truth: *Sermons on Job*, trans. Arthur Golding [facsimile 1574] (Edinburgh: The Banner of Truth, 1993). After careful study and elimination, this edition derives the majority of its text from the following edition:

>Calvin, Jean, 1509-1564. Sermons of Master Iohn Calvin, vpon booke of Iob [London]: Imprinted by Lvcas Harison and George Byshop, 1574. [36], 737 [i.e. 751], [1] p. ; 36 cm. (fol.)
>NOTES: Colophon: Imprinted at London by Henrie Binneman, for Lucas Harison and George Bishop. Anno. 1574. Signatures: a4 *6**8A-Y8 Aa-Yy8 Aaa-Ccc8. Title within border (with date 1574), probably engraved by Nicholas Hilliard, McKerrow and Ferguson, Title-page borders, no. 148. Printer's device at end. Numerous errors in paging. "The Epistle Dedicatorie" to Robert Dudley, Early of Leicester, by Arthur Golding, sig. A2r-a3v.
>INDEXED: Pollard & Redgrave, STC, 4444 ; McAlpin Cat., v.1,p.70.

However, the title page, the table, and the last 3 sermons are all taken from:

>Calvin, Jean, 1509-1564. Sermons of Maister Iohn Caluin, vpon the booke of Iob, translated out of French by Arthur Golding. Londini : [Printed by Thomas Dawson] Impensis Georgij Bishop [and Thomas Woodcocke], 1584. [36], 751, [1] p. ;
>NOTES: Colophon reads: Imprinted in London at the three Cranes in the Vintree, by Thomas Dawson, for George Byshop and Thomas Woodcocke. Anno 1584.
>A variant of the edition with "impensis Thomas Woodcocke."
>INDEXED: Pollard & Redgrave, STC (2nd ed.)/ 4447.5

Complicating the identification of the edition are several changes that appear to have been made by the Banner of Truth in the production of this volume. They appear to have fixed the pagination errors which most cataloguers use as cues to the identification of exact printings and editions. They also appear to have altered the year on the title page and colophon from 1584 to 1574. The Banner of Truth edition does not contain the dedicatory epistle or translator's preface which was contained in all the 16th century editons.

In the *Calvini Opera*, the 159 Joban sermons are located in volumes 33-35 of *Ioannis Calvini opera quae supersunt omnia,* ed. Wilhelm Baum, Edward Cunitz, and Edward Reuss, 59 vols., [hereafter, *CO*].

# Chapter 1

# A Good Case: Calvin's Understanding of the Book of Job

[I]n The Book of Job is set forth a declaration of such sublimity as to humble our minds (*Institutes* I.xvii.2).

The stories of sufferers such as Job were not only historical but paradigmatic. It was precisely the paradigmatic nature of that history which gave Job's story its timeless and recurring significance for Calvin's audience (Susan Schreiner, *Where Shall Wisdom be Found?*, 8).

For some time now scholars have recognised that Calvin's sermons are an indispensable resource if we are to appreciate all the nuances of his theology. Recent works have confirmed this by highlighting the subtlety of Calvinian rhetoric on the major theological themes.[1] In an illuminating passage in sermon 78, Calvin seemed to be self-consciously aware of the importance of his task as a preacher:

> For afflictions are as diseases: and if a phisition vse one medicine for all diseases, what a thing will that bee? Some disease is whote, and some is colde: some disease requireth that a man shoulde be kept drie, and some other that hee shoulde bee refreshed with moysture: one disease will haue a man kept close, and another will haue him to go abrode. Ye see then that a Phisition shall kill his patientes, if he haue not a regarde of their diseases: yea and it behoueth him also too bee acquainted with the complexions of pacients. Euen so ought wee to consider of those whome God visiteth wyth afflictions.[2]

The sermons provide Calvin, then, with a vehicle for expressing his theological convictions in a different manner from his more celebrated theological writings. Here we will examine, as a case in point, Calvin's preaching on the Book of Job, evaluating some of these subtleties of paracletic ministry.[3]

In this chapter we shall attempt to do three things: first, we shall make reference to the historical setting in which the sermons on Job were delivered; second, we shall document and comment upon recent literature that reference the Joban sermons; and third, we shall highlight

29

the major theological and pastoral motifs that surface throughout the course of Calvin's expositions on Job.

## Historical Setting of the Joban Sermons

That Calvin should have turned to the book of Job in the years 1554 and 1555 is in one sense at least without surprise.[4] Six months before the commencement of the Joban sermons, on 13 August 1553, Michael Servetus arrived in Geneva, making his way that afternoon to hear Calvin preach in Saint Pierre.[5] Despite Calvin's protests for a more humane method than burning, the eventual decision of 25 October 1553 by the magistrates of Geneva to have Servetus executed as a heretic was to bring down upon the Reformer a torrent of criticism.[6] In the years leading up to the Servetus affair, Calvin's enemies had been looking for opportunities to criticise him. Writing to Bullinger in September 1553, some time after the commencement of the sermons on Job, Calvin recounts how the Servetus issue still troubled his relationship with the *Conseil*:

> Indeed they cause you this trouble, despite our remonstrances; but they have reached such a pitch of folly and madness, that they regard with suspicion whatever we say to them. So much so, that were I to allege that it is clear at mid-day, they would forthwith begin to doubt of it.[7]

In the previous year, 1552, the rise of the Libertines and the general opposition to Calvin had made it impossible for him to leave the city for a month.[8] Tensions in the city were at such levels that Calvin felt unable to attend the wedding of his friend Christopher Fabri.[9] Calvin eventually left Geneva, only because he heard that Farel was dying.[10]

In 1553, the issue of ecclesiastical discipline, thought to have been decided in the *Ordonnances* of 1541, was challenged by the so-called *Petit Conseil*. In the February elections of 1552, Calvin's long-standing opponent Ami Perrin was elected as first syndic. Pierre Tissot, Perrin's brother-in-law, became the city's lieutenant. The "Perrinist" party (otherwise known as the Libertines) sought to challenge the agreed policy with regard to ecclesiastical discipline insisting that, prior to the Easter communion of 1553, they be sent a list of all those currently excommunicated together with a list of reasons. The challenge to Calvin was incontrovertible. On 15 February 1553, Calvin wrote to the persecuted French believers on his need of being "tamed" by such trials:

It is very difficult for me not to boil over when someone gets impassioned. Yet so far no one has ever heard me shouting. But I lack the chief thing of all, and that is being trained by these scourges of the Lord in true humility. And therefore it is all the more necessary that I should be tamed by the free rebukes of my brethren.[11]

By Monday, 24 July, Calvin asked to be allowed to resign. The request was denied.

Matters worsened in September; the case of Philibert Berthelier's request to be absolved by the *Petit Conseil* instead of the *Consistoire* highlighted the distance between the state and church.[12] Berthelier, together with two companions, Philibert Bonna and Balthasar Sept, had been imprisoned and excommunicated for their conduct. Balthasar, upon release, applied for permission to baptise his child, which the *Consistoire* refused.[13] They also sought attendance at the celebration of the Lord's Supper. By Sunday, 3 September, following a warning for the excommunicated not to present themselves at the Lord's Supper, Calvin evidently thought this might be his last sermon in Geneva. He preached on the farewell address of Paul to the elders at Ephesus (Acts 20:13-38). During the administration of the sacrament, the armed Libertines present made a gesture as though they might seize the sacrament forcibly. Calvin spread his arms over the table and defied them and they left.[14] However, Calvin was not dismissed as he had feared. The case of Philibert Berthelier would drag on throughout the following year, eventually to be settled in the *Consistoire*'s favor in January of 1555.

In addition, Calvin's health was always a matter of great concern. In 1563-64 Calvin could write to his physicians in Montpellier in considerable detail about the "ulcer in the haemorrhoid veins," "nephritis," and the passing of stones "so big that it tore the urinary canal."[15] But, even in 1553, Calvin's delivery was said to be asthmatic and painful. Job would seem to have been an obvious choice for Calvin to turn to in his preaching.

Earlier that summer, perhaps recalling the very issues in Job, Calvin wrote (not for the first time) to five French prisoners in Lyons. After exhorting them to faith and constancy in their trials, Calvin muses on the apparent injustice of their condition:

> It is strange, indeed, to human reason, that the children of God should be so surfeited with afflictions, while the wicked disport themselves in

delights; but even more so, that the slaves of Satan should tread us under foot, as we say, and triumph over us. However, we have wherewith to comfort ourselves in all our miseries, looking for that happy issue which is promised to us, that he will not only deliver us by his angels, but will himself wipe away the tears from our eyes.[16]

Geneva, too, was in turmoil. Support for Calvin was minimal. Reforming the city was costly: Calvin was ridiculed.[17] William Naphy has outlined the possible background to some of Calvin's rare remarks about the situation in Geneva in the course of the Joban sermons.[18] Preaching in September 1554, on Job 23, Calvin refers to how honest men can barely walk the streets without being shouted out at and abused.[19] Preaching the following month on Job 29, Calvin speaks of those in authority as filled with pride.[20] The promotion of Calvin's opponents in the elections of 1553 and 1554 brought forth from Calvin a charge that they were "rascalles" and "nothing at all."[21] In an otherwise rare moment, Calvin refers in three consecutive sermons to a particular incident that he had witnessed in which a "strumpet" had been imprisoned, only to be given "great Tartes" by way of a seeming reward. "What a dealing is that?" Calvin asks?[22] In conditions of injustice and civil strife, Job seemed an appropriate book to turn to for guidance.

Calvin had several distinguished forerunners who had turned to Job for a series of sermons – notably Ambrose, Augustine, Gregory the Great, Hilary, Jerome, and Aquinas.[23] Did any of these former exegetes influence Calvin? On the contrary, it soon becomes apparent from Calvin's Sermons how dissimilar they are from the great works of his predecessors in this field. Gregory, for example, had written thirty-five books, filling six volumes on Job, outlining the traditional literal, allegorical and moral senses of each line. As a sixth-century Christian, Gregory had viewed the Old Testament allegorically and typologically, each verse of Job alluding to Christ in some way. Calvin, on the other hand, as we shall see, was careful and reticent in his use of typology and critical of the use of allegory.[24] Susan Schreiner has concluded that Calvin "knew the *general* lines of both the Gregorian and Thomistic traditions."[25] She adds:

> He explicitly rejected the allegorical meanings that stem from the *Moralia*. Like those who stood in the Thomistic tradition, Calvin expounded the literal sense of the text and believed that "literally" the Book of Job is about the doctrine of providence.[26]

For Calvin then, the Book of Job is first and foremost a book about God.[27] Its accents are essentially theological in nature. In that sense, Calvin had not turned to Job because of its obvious themes of suffering and trial: Calvin did not believe the book of Job contained solutions to these great moral dilemmas of the universe. Rather, he sought to turn the congregation in Geneva, and his own soul, to the reality of God's sovereignty and power in the contingencies of seemingly disordered life. Nowhere is this power more radically shown than in Calvin's opening remarks on the 26 February, 1554. Giving to his congregation a summary of the Book of Job, Calvin exhorts:

> The thing that we haue briefly to beare in mynde in this storie, is, that God hath suche a soueraintie ouer his creatures, as he may dispose of them at his pleasure.[28]

The sermons were recorded by the professional stenographer, Denis Raguenier, who had been employed as such since 29 September, 1549.[29] The *Sermons on Job* were first published in French in 1563, during Calvin's lifetime.[30] This was the period of the outbreak of the first of the Civil Wars of Religion in France, following the Massacre of Vassy in 1562. A second edition was published in French in 1569, following the Reformer's death, at the point when the Huguenots' cause looked bleak during the second Civil War. A third French edition appeared at the beginning of the seventeenth century (1611) following the assassination of Henri IV and the persecution that followed it. A German translation was made in 1587-88, followed by a Latin translation in 1593.[31] Before that, however, an English translation was made by Arthur Golding in 1574, barely over a decade following their initial publication in French.[32] Given their popularity (four English editions were published in the first ten years following Golding's translation, far outstripping the popularity of the English edition of the *Institutes*), it is difficult to understand Calvin's initial reluctance in seeing their publication.[33] We know of no plans by the Reformer to write a commentary on Job, for example. But part of their popularity, no doubt, lay in the fact that Calvin's preaching bore little reference to Geneva itself. Concerned as he was with the exposition of the text, the relevance of these sermons became immediately applicable wherever they were read.

### Recent Literature Referencing Calvin's Sermons on Job

Earlier works examining the theological structure of Calvin's thought have consistently ignored the contribution of the sermons, particularly the sermons on Job.[34] Several important works have appeared over the past fifty years that have attempted to redress this imbalance. In 1957, T. F. Torrance published his highly important work, *Calvin's Doctrine of Man*, which is replete with Joban references.[35] The importance of this book lies in the fact that Calvin studies began to take seriously the contribution that Calvin's sermons have in our understanding of his overall theology, which had up until this time been largely ignored in favour of the study of the *Institutes* and the commentaries. In 1978, Richard Stauffer published his equally important book, *Dieu, la création et la Providence dans la prédication de Calvin*.[36] Stauffer's work sought to analyse Calvin's preaching, highlighting theological accents, particularly the attributes of God and their relationship to the doctrine of providence.[37] This work is important in our present study.

Ten years later, Mary Potter Engel published her own analysis of Calvin research. Suggesting that, despite Torrance's contribution, a major gap existed in our understanding of Calvin's anthropology, Engel outlined her idea of dual perspectives in Calvin's eschatology, something which she claimed was entirely absent in Torrance and which thereby distorted his understanding of Calvin.[38] Engel, like Torrance, engages significantly with the Joban sermons.

In the same year, William J. Bouwsma published his distinctive and well-received biography of Calvin, *John Calvin: A Sixteenth Century Portrait*.[39] This "humanist," Renaissance portrayal of Calvin has exercised a massive influence on modern scholarship.[40] For our purpose it is notable that Bouwsma has almost 150 citations from the Joban sermons.[41] More recently, Susan Schreiner has published two books in which Calvin's sermons on Job have been the focus of her attention. In *The Theater of His Glory*, first published in 1991, Schreiner focuses largely on the doctrine of creation and the debate on natural law.[42] This was followed in 1994 by perhaps the most important work of all as far as this work is concerned, *Where Shall Wisdom be Found? Calvin's Exegesis of Job from Medieval and Modern Perspectives*.[43] Following an analysis of Calvin's understanding of Job in comparison with Gregory and Aquinas, Schreiner points out two areas of difficulty in the Joban sermons:

Calvin's distinctive understanding of God's justice and his power. Calvin has recourse to a notion of the "secret justice of God," before which even the pure angels of heaven are unclean. In addition, Calvin, according to Schreiner, comes perilously close to nominalism in his rhetoric of God's "absolute power."[44] Calvin, of course, denies this vehemently.[45] We shall consider both of these issues later. Schreiner's works make an invaluable contribution to Calvin studies, particularly to the place and importance of the Joban sermons in the overall framework of Calvin's theology.

Other more recent works have emerged, which may appear to have advanced this field of study.[46] However that may be, there is still scope to identify and describe the full range of pastoral application Calvin makes in these sermons. This work will be concerned not only with the applications Calvin makes but also with the care he took in comprehending the text of the Book of Job.[47]

Calvin's place within the development of the rhetorical tradition is an interesting issue that goes beyond the bounds of this current thesis.[48] Avoiding contrived logic and overly-refined language, Calvin (as did Zwingli, Wycliffe, Bullinger and others) turned to the running commentary approach, or "homily," of the Church Fathers.[49] In a fascinating statement in the "reply to Sadolet," written from Strassburg in 1539, Calvin complains about the esoteric nature of much of the preaching of the scholastics.

> For, as sermons were then usually divided, the first half was devoted to those misty questions of the schools which might astonish the rude populace, while the second contained sweet stories, or not unamusing speculations, by which the hearers might be kept on the alert. Only a few expressions were thrown in from the Word of God, that by their majesty they might procure credit for these frivolities. But as soon as our Reformers raised the standard, all these absurdities, in one moment, disappeared from amongst us.[50]

The Joban sermons consistently reveal Calvin's method of taking a few verses and sticking rigidly throughout to an exposition of their meaning so as to prevent himself from wandering from the text. Such "pericopic" preaching ensured variety of thematic material, but did not necessarily prevent the Reformer from personal themes of interest when the text suggested it. It is with such themes that the rest of this chapter will be devoted.

## Theological and Pastoral Motifs in the Joban Sermons

The sermons provide us with a comprehensive account of the kind of themes Calvin was prepared to consider as part of his ordinary preaching. No doctrine was sacrosanct so long as it was part of the meaning of the text in question. In these sermons, Calvin shows interest in expanding on certain themes that he believes are central to the core of the Joban material, such issues as sin and suffering, the *imago Dei* and the imitation of Christ, holiness and heaven, providence and perseverance. In this chapter, we shall provide an outline of the main theological loci of Calvin's Joban sermons. No attempt will be made in this chapter to examine these individual issues in detail; rather, our intent will be to indicate the main features of discussion that preoccupy the Reformer in the exegetical discipline of explaining the text of Job. Some of these issues will emerge as important in themselves, important because of highly controversial corollaries that emerge by way of consequence.

What was it about the message of Calvin's sermons on Job that gripped the French and English speaking world of the sixteenth century? There are several inter-related strands that coalesce to form an answer to this question.[51] All of these deserve a fuller treatment than is given here: but an overall treatment will catch something of the burden of Calvin's preaching. We will consider these under four broad categories of consideration: the doctrine of man, the doctrine of revelation, the doctrine of providence and the doctrine of faith.

### The *imago Dei*

We have already noted the contributions of Torrance and Engel in the understanding the prominence given by Calvin to anthropology in these sermons.[52] Within the somewhat inadequate anthropology of the sixteenth century, several key issues emerge here.[53] These comprise the issues of creation, the constituent elements of human nature, the *imago Dei*, and the Fall of mankind. These issues have been dealt with extensively by both Torrance and Engel, who cite numerous passages from the Joban sermons, and our purpose here will be merely to summarise and comment.

On the creation of man, Calvin is eloquent: the creation of man displays the glory of God.

> God hath so abaced vs in our begetting, as he will haue his power, ryghtuousnesse and wisdome the better knowne therby.[54]

Earlier, in the same sermon, Calvin could add:

> God doth (as a ma[n] might say) looke vpon himselfe, and behold himselfe in men as it were in a glasse: and it is not without cause that he looked vppon all that he made and found it good. But man is his principall work, and the excellentest of all his creatures.[55]

Distancing himself from Manichaeism, Calvin can insist that since the body is God's workmanship, it is not itself evil.[56]

The soul, which "is conceyued in the mothers wombe,"[57] is immortal, not by any power within itself, but because God has "breathed hys owne power into them."[58] As for the constituent parts of man, the soul is the principal part, and this displayed in turn by reason and understanding:

> Is not our soule the excellentest part of vs? And how ought that to be interteyned? Not with eating and drinking: But there is a thing agreeable too the nature of it, which is to haue reason and vnderstanding, that our life be not brutish, but that we may shewe ourselues to be creatures formed after the Image of God.[59]

As this reference illustrates, Calvin often identified the soul with reason and understanding or even truth.[60] As God's workmanship, created with faculties of reason, we are meant to use our minds, Calvin insists:

> God hath not set men in this world to bereeue them of al vnderstanding. For he will not haue them like Asses or horses: he hath indued them with reason, and would haue them to use vnderstanding.[61]

And in a touching pastoral comment, Calvin warns against the rash judgement of those whose intelligence is in question:

> When we see a starke idiot hath no wit nor reason, it behoueth vs to looke well vpon him, for he is a mirrour of our nature. Whence come the reason and vnderstanding that wee haue? Is it not the singuler gift of God? Then let all those whiche haue reason and vnderstanding, know that it is God which hath indued them with such grace, and therefore that they bee the more bounde vntoo him... whereas our Lord hath made some more sharpe witted than others, and giuen them more handesomenesse to compasse the things that they vndertake, so as they forecast, and conclude, and bring all their matters to passe wisely, and compasse many things in short time: and othersome are so slowe and dull witted, that a man must be faine, as it were to beate it into their heades with beetles, if hee will learne them anything: such diuersitie

among men sheweth euidently, that if we haue any power too iudge and discerne aright, it is the special gift of God.[62]

The Joban material gives Calvin a rich source from which to cull the nuances of sin and depravity. After all, depravity is the accusation made against Job by his three friends and about which Job constantly protests his innocence. And whilst Calvin, at least initially, is sympathetic to Job's plea, he is not cowed into any denial of the issue of human depravity itself. "When any of vs is begotten," he says, "then doeth the myre shewe it self: that is too say, wee be full of infection and filthinesse."[63] The extent of the infection of sin is total: not a part of our created beings remains unaffected.[64] From our birth the "seed" of sin is "inclosed in vs."[65] Thus, Calvin can conclude: "there is nothing in them but euill."[66] And thus the malady is both intensive and extensive.[67] Whilst Calvin avoids discussion of the origin of sin as such, he carefully distinguishes original sin and the creation of man as something holy. Sin is not of God's creating:

> Whereas sinne is in mans nature: it is not of Gods putting in by creation but by reason that Sata[n] did spread his naughtinesse further abrode at such time as man was beguyled by his wylinesse, to disappoint the benefit of God.[68]

This, then, provides Satan with his point of contact: "he discouereth the euill which is in men."[69] And further, though Calvin is careful to avoid the immediate connection of sin and suffering in the way that Job's friends see it, he does insist that sin is the cause of all our miseries.[70]

The doctrines of original sin and total depravity provide Calvin with ample scope to discourse on the issues of the bondage of the will and the inability of man to save himself. In a lengthy account of the matter in Sermon 53, Calvin attacks the "papacie" for "forging of free will." He elaborates:

> And to what end tendeth all this, but that men should like well of themselues, and thinke themselues to haue some goodnesse in them? Not that any body dareth saye that a man is able to saue himselfe. For euen in the papacie it will be confessed that we haue neede of Gods grace, not only in forgiuing oure sinnes, but also in aiding vs with his holy spirite. And yet for all this, they say not that all commeth of him. The Papists will not confess that. But they say that we haue a certaine portion

of goodnesse in ourselues, and that God had neede to help vs out with the rest. Lo howe God is made a cohelper: that is to say, he must help our infirmitie, but yet must we on our sides be companions with him. The deuill hath so bewitched men, as he maketh them beleeue they be I wote not what: and yet for all that, we see also, that too the worldward men stande greatly in their owne conceits.[71]

For Calvin, the Joban dilemma is acute because in Job's suffering, the image of God is assaulted.[72] The doctrine of the *imago Dei*, in particular, has been a focal issue for scholars. Is the image of God completely destroyed by the Fall of mankind, or do the remnants of this broken image still remain? That Calvin is ambivalent on this issue is self-evident even upon a cursory reading of the Joban sermons. On the one hand, Calvin is eager to speak of Adam's original creation as "a mirror of the excellent glorie that shyneth fully in God."[73] Man is God's "workmanship" by reason of creation itself.[74] Adam's original image-bearing character enabled him to be wise about the creation in which God had placed him.[75] However, the Joban sermons provide Calvin with extensive reasons for an explanation of man's present condition.[76] As a consequence of Adam's fall, and his representation of us, man's present condition apart from intervening grace is dire indeed. The *imago Dei* is now "marred,"[77] "disfigured,"[78] and "turned into darkness."[79] Calvin can go further in his rhetoric of the *imago Dei*:

> Wee must not looke onely too our first creation: for the hope that wee shall haue thereby, will bee verie slender, bicause Gods Image is as it were blotted oute in vs by Adams sinne.[80]

As has frequently been noted, Calvin's rhetoric becomes intense at this point, speaking of fallen man as "monsters, and worse than brute beasts."[81] Calvin is taking issue, of course, with the view held by Aquinas, for example, that the Fall simply meant the loss of something additional to man's nature, the added gift of grace (*donum superadditum*).[82]

And yet, some remnant of the image remains in the form of discernment, "some discretion imprinted in our heartes too discerne good and euill."[83] It is Calvin's view that as this image is more fully restored, so our knowledge of God and his ways increase with it.[84] But, where is this *imago* most clearly seen? The Joban sermons reveal that the image of God is most clearly seen in man's capacity to reason, in the conscience, and in fellowship.[85]

This broken image is, according to Calvin, restored in regeneration:

> When we do well, it is not of ourselues (for there can nothing be drawne from vs but al filthinesse and beggerie, as we are corrupted of nature) but our Lorde poureth his goodnesse and righteousnesse vpon vs. Then if he shew vs the favor in regenerating vs by his holy Spirit, that we liue holily, we are as glasses in the which his image is as it were represented: and this is a brightnesse which commeth fro[m] aboue, but sheweth itself here beneth.[86]

### The doctrine of revelation: The more excellent way

The Joban sermons provided Calvin with a vehicle for commenting upon the nature of Scripture as the Word of God. In some ways, the very opening sentences of Calvin's treatment on Job disclose the Reformer's persuasion that the story of Job, as Scripture, is the best source of relief for his ailing listeners. It is his conviction that this is not just a story, but that it is the Word of God. In an important and lengthy passage in sermon 144, Calvin expands on the idea that God is revealed in his Word in a more "excellent" way than in his works. Repeating his view that there is sufficient revelation of God in the world so as to render everyone without excuse, Calvin adds:

> For although he bee manifested to the whole worlde, and all creatures are inuited too prayse him, yea and that they be constreyned and inforced therevntoo: yet is there a farre other more mightie and royall power in the worde that is preached vnto us.[87]

For Calvin, all of Scripture has a practical use. "There is nothing there which is not for our profite," he proclaimed.[88] Not to heed God's Word when it is heard is, then, to "peruert the order of nature, and become as it were monsters, and worse than brute beasts."[89] Thus, Calvin commends the value of God's Word to the people of Geneva and beyond. The Word of God is a "burning fire… to clenze away all the drosse and superfluities that are in vs."[90] It is the Christian's "armour" and weapon whereby we resist the devil.[91] We are to yield obedience to the Word of God because of its authority.[92] Because "all that belongeth too our welfare is comprehended therein," we ought to receive it with "a cheerefull and louing affection."[93] Rightly applied, God's Word gives strength to "such as are weake" and relief to "such as are feeble and vtterly cast downe."[94] We should content ourselves with the Holy Scriptures.[95] Indeed, Calvin goes as far as to suggest that "God is present with vs by the means of his worde."[96] Calvin insists upon the perspicuity of Scripture:

> We shall find for a certaintie that our Lord setteth vs forth such a maiestie in his word, as is able too make all creatures to quake: and yet is there also a simplicitie, to the end to make it to bee receyued of the most ignora[n]t and unskilfull: [moreover] there is so great light in it, as wee may vnderstand it without going to schoole, at leastwise if wee bee teachable: for it is not without cause that he calleth himself purposely the schoolmauster of the lowely and little ones.[97]

Using his favourite metaphor, Calvin explains that Scripture is accommodated to our understanding.[98] "We must not," Calvin urges elsewhere, "couet too knowe ought, sauing that which God hath declared too vs with his owne mouth."[99] God's Word may appear "darke" to us, but, "that cometh not of itself, but of the blindnesse which is in our dull wits."[100]

There is, too, a relationship between Scripture as the Word of God and preaching. For Calvin, preaching is God's way of making himself and his saving purposes known. The Reformer makes the point clearly in Sermon 122:

> If a doctrine that is preached bee good and holy, and we are conuinced that it is so: then if wee yeelde not with all reuerence too frame ourselues thereafter, wee shall not be guiltie of resisting a man, but it is all one as if we spited the liuing God.[101]

For Calvin, preaching is not Scripture. As T. H. L. Parker has pointed out, Scripture is definitive and sovereign; preaching must be derivative and subordinate.[102] Preaching is the Word of God inasmuch as it conveys the biblical doctrine or message. Nowhere is this more forcefully put than in a sermon on 1 Timothy 3:2, giving an explanation of the apostle Paul's requirement of an elder that he be "apt to teach:"

> For it is not S. Pauls meaning here in this placve, that we should colour the matter and make a shewe only, & clappe our hands at him in sporting wise, and say, Oh excellently well spoken, Oh marvelous knowledge, Oh fine wit. There is no suche dealing must be vsed: be he that preacheth must begin at himselfe, & so indeuour to draw the whole flocke, to the obedience of God, to haue them walke in feare and humblenesse, and

watchfully... When a man goeth vp into the pulpit is it to be seene a farre of, and only to haue an higher place than the rest? No, no: but to the end that God may speake vnto vs by the mouth of man, and be so gratious to vs, to shewe himselfe here amongst vs, and wil haue a mortall man to be his messenger: and will hereby also proue the obedience of our faith.[103]

For Calvin, preaching is God's "familiar" word. Contrasting the revelation of God in the thunderstorm, Calvin explains Elihu's contribution in chapter 37 in the following way:

> Elihu speaketh not of the woorde, which is dayly preached vnto vs, for vs to take learning by it, and wherein God doth familiarly shewe vs his goodnesse; but by Gods roaring voyce, and by the noise that proceedeth out of his mouth...[104]

Calvin's preaching on Job also emphasises the possibility of the knowledge of God. Concluding the first sermon, Calvin expresses his conviction that we must keep our eyes "fastened vpon God." He goes on to explain what he means:

> To the ende we may know, that we be created to his glorie, to serue him and to worship him. For although he haue no neede of vs as our neybours haue, nor is either the better or the worse for our seruice: yet is it his will to haue reasonable creatures which shuld know him, and in knowing him, yeeld him that whiche belongeth vnto him.[105]

The theme of knowing God had, of course, been Calvin's key to theology since 1536 and the publication of the first edition of the *Institutes*.[106] By 1554, Calvin had already settled his view that "the sum of sacred doctrine is contained in these two parts: the knowledge of God and of ourselves."[107] This knowledge, though real, is provisional and limited to that measure of revelation that God has given of himself. Calvin explains:

> God hath giuen vs a way too know him, which is conuenient and fit for vs. He could well giue vs the full and perfect light at this day: but he seeth it is not for our profite, and therefore hee giueth vs but a certaine portion, and he applieth himselfe vnto vs. And therefore, let it not greeue vs too haue this knowledge of God as yet by measure, as it is giuen vs in the Scripture, and to wait till he haue bereft vs of this mortall body, and specially till he haue wholly refourmed our mindes that they maye bee no more so wrapped in these worldlinesse, and earthlinesse, and specially in the sinfulnesse that proceedeth of the sinne of Adam.[108]

Calvin's pastoral theology is theocentric; his elaborate unfolding of the nature of God in the *Institutes*, particularly in Book 1, finds an expansive canvas in the Joban sermons. Nor, as Harold Dekker points out, does Calvin feel the need to differentiate between the various persons of the Godhead in his Trinitarian preaching. Calvin seldom mentions one of the persons of the Trinity separately without setting him in dynamic relationship to the Godhead. To treat them independently was for him to hazard idolatry.[109]

It is into this situation that Calvin urged his hearers to heed the doctrine of providence. In the opening sentences of the first sermon on Job, Calvin sets out his reasons for doing so at the very start; the book of Job, Calvin suggests,

> "sheweth vs howe we be in Gods hande, and that it lyeth in him to determine of our lyfe, and to dispose of the same according to his good pleasure: and that it is our dutie to submit ourselues vnto him with al humblenesse and obedience..."[110]

Lest they misunderstand, Calvin repeats it in the second sermon on Job:

> He can dispose of his creatures at his owne pleasure, and that although we be at our wits ende, and see not the reason why God handleth men so roughly: yet it becommeth vs to cast downe our eyes, and to confesse that he is righteous, and to wayt his leysure, vntil he discouer vnto vs the cause why he disposeth things so.[111]

Clearly, for Calvin, a theological truth about God provided his hearers with a reason for hope and stability in their lives: God's providence embraces the totality of our existence. This provides Calvin with a means of defining true discipleship:

> We can not be truely his subiects, vntill we acknowledge the right that he hath ouer vs, and giue him all his titles and dignities. He is our Mayster and Lorde: we must then giue him all reuerence.[112]

## Not by chance: The doctrine of divine providence

The mention of perseverance brings us to a complementary, and perhaps greater, truth for Calvin: the sovereignty of God's providence in a seemingly fortuitous world.[113] We shall examine Calvin's doctrine of providence in greater detail in further chapters, but for now it is of interest to note the comprehensive nature of Calvin's thinking on this subject in 1554 and 1555, some four or five years before the final edition of the *Institutes* would appear, where providence would take a prominent part in the opening chapters.[114] In Sermon 5, discussing the vexed issue of the role of Satan in the suffering of Job, Calvin has recourse to comment on the possible dualism that may arise. Calvin is insistent: "Satan can do no more than he hath leaue to do."[115] "Nothing happened," he adds later, "without his prouidence."[116] For Calvin, the involvement of God in the tragedy of Job is such that "God findeth the meane that the euill which is in Satan, is turned to our welfare."[117] It is the doctrine of God that is uppermost in Calvin's exposition of Job. It is God's *majesty* that is invoked by the unfolding of this tale.[118] More than an explanation of theodicy, Job is an uncovering of the very character of God himself. Conscious of adversity, Calvin may well have been drawn to Job's tale as a mirror of his own life; but it is an engagement with the issues that reflect who God is and what God is like that emerged. Calvin finds parallels in the lives of other biblical characters in addition to Job. Adam, Noah, Abraham, Isaac, Jacob — all these knew suffering in the course of their discipleship. But it is David with whom Calvin more closely associates Job than any other.[119] In Sermon 5 again, as Calvin gives an explanation for the role of Satan in the plight of Job, a parallel is drawn with David and his numbering of the people of Israel. "It was the Diuell that stirred up all the mischief," Calvin adds.[120] As in the Job story, David persevered, not by any inherent power within himself, but by "a speciall working of his [God's] owne power in him."[121]

In the fourth sermon, Calvin began by reminding his hearers:

> "While we liue here belowe, we be not gouerned by fortune, but God hath an eye vpon vs, and full authoritie ouer vs... God hath the direction of the worlde, and that there is not any thing done, which is not disposed by him."[122]

Similarly, in bringing his expositions of Job to a close, Calvin has recourse to mention that in the diversity of birds (geese, swans, eagles, doves, etc.): "God doth therein shewe vs his prouidence."[123] This is, for Calvin, God's sovereignty at work in this world, something which he is always eager to defend. We are to honour this sovereignty, be humbled by it, defend it.

For wherein consisteth the soueraintie and dominion which he hath ouer vs? In our acknowledging, not only of his power: but also of his infinite goodnesse, wisedome, righteousnesse, mercie, and iustice. When wee haue that once: then do we glorify him. Well then, if men thinke Gods doings vnreasonable, if they blame him of crueltie, if they chase against him through impaciencie, or if they be offended at any thing that he doth: out of all doubt they go about to bereeue him of his diuine glory, and that cannot bee done without making war against him.[124]

The reference to "fortune" in the fourth sermon, cited above, reminds us of an emphasis that Calvin is eager to make here in the Sermons on Job as well as elsewhere in the *Institutes* and the commentaries. In Sermon 91, for example, Calvin, who believed that we are predisposed to believe in fortune, remarks:

[I]t is a verie sore temptation too the faythfull, when things are confuzed in the world, so as it may seeme that God medleth no more with them, but that fortune ruleth and gouerneth all things. And this hath beene the cause of all these diuelish Prouerbes. That all things are tossed by casuall fortune, That things are blindly guyded, That God playeth with men as with a tennisball, That there is neyther reason, nor measure in his doings, but rather that all things are gouerened by a certayne secrete necessitie, and That God vouchsafeth not too think vppon vs. Behold the blasphemies that haue raigned at all tymes. And why? For as (I haue sayde alreadie) mannes witte is dazeled when hee goeth about to iudge of things that are out of order, and which passe oure iudgement and reason.[125]

For Calvin, providence is a belief that God overrules everything that happens. What happens may be beyond our ability to grasp and understand; the suddenness and complexity—the *abyss* of providence, even the seeming harshness of it, may call into question our assurance of God's rule, but not the rule itself.[126] God's hand is firmly on the tiller.[127] Calvin distinguishes between "general" and "special" providence.[128] God's providence "intervenes" in this world. Thus, the sea is only curtailed by God's power:

Wheras wee haue drye ground to dwell vpon, let vs not think that that happeneth through anye other cause, than for that it is God's will to lodge vs here.[129]

God is, then, responsible for the unexpected in history:

Let vs knowe that in a minute of an houre he can finishe his worke, yea when there shall be no meanes, nor things any whit disposed thereto.[130]

Again and again, Calvin is eager that we learn from providence: God's interventions are purposive and educative:

> At all times since men dwelt vpon the earth, it hath bene Gods will that there should alwayes be some recordes of his iudgements, and therefore that wee must not bee so dull and blockish as not to consider the things that God hath done for our instruction.[131]

Thus, for Calvin, as we shall see in later chapters, providence consists in an all-embracing involvement of God in creation, nations, the birth, life and death of man, the successes and failures of our lives, things that seem accidental and insignificant.[132] Of special significance is Calvin's close reading of the place of prayer: that God answers prayer though not Job's for his own recovery at first. This is one of the seminal issues of the book of Job.[133] Equally, the presence and power of evil belongs under this rubric. In summary, God permits evil, punishes evil with evil, brings good out of evil, uses evil to test and educate Job; and there is the eschatological hope held out again and again that one day, God will deliver us from the power and presence of evil altogether.[134]

## The "excellent mirrour": Job as a model of perseverance

Calvin's summary of the book of Job is succinct and memorable:

> Herewithall we haue further to marke, that in al this disputation, Iob maynteineth a good case, and contrarywyse his aduersaries maynteyne an euill case. And yet it is more, that Iob maynteyning a good quarell, did handle it ill, and that the other setting foorth an vniust matter, did conuey it well. The vnderstanding of this, will be as a key to open vntoo vs all this whole booke.[135]

Calvin underscores the exemplary quality of Job's character as verified by God himself in the opening verse of the prologue (Job 1:1). Thus, in the very opening words of the first sermon on Job, he speaks of Job's "patientnesse."[136] Job is "an excellent mirrour" of one who "resisted temptations, and continued stedfastly in obedience vnto God."[137] In this way, Job encourages us to "walke in singlesse of heart," "feare God," and to "stande vpon our garde to withdraw ourselues from euill."[138]

Job's *bonne cause* is not so much Job's plea of "innocence;" Calvin does not use this language in describing Job. In fact, as we shall see, Calvin's patience with Job's plea runs into difficulty in the course of the sermons. For example, in Sermon 37, Calvin wishes to underline the point that there is no such thing as innocence before God, for that would imply sinlessness:

> There is no finding of any perfect rightuousnesse heere in men, neyther is it to be sayde, that God is beholding to them, and that they may go to law with him, or that they haue deserued well at his hand, and that he cannot find any fault in them or in their lyfe.[139]

So, what is the *bonne cause*?

> It is in that hee knoweth, that God dothe not euer punishe menne according to the measure of their sinnes, but hath his secrete iudgementes, whereof he maketh not vs priuie, and therfore that it behoueth vs to wayte till he reuele vnto vs for what cause he dothe this or that. Thus is he in this whole discourse persuaded, that God doth not always punish me[n] according to the measure of their sinnes; and therevpon assureth himselfe, that hee is not a man reiected of God, as they would make him to beleeue. Beholde heere a good and true case, notwithstanding that it be ill handled.[140]

The evil case — "God doth alwayes punishe men according to the measure of their sinnes"[141] —is one that Calvin roundly repudiates; but, its appeal, perhaps due to its very simplicity, was as great in the sixteenth century as it was in Job's and remains so in our own time. It was due to the fact that Job continued in his steadfastness that Calvin was able to urge Job upon his hearers as a model for the age in which his hearers lived.

Calvin was not shy of pointing out the grave possibility of apostasy for the wavering soul. Election guarantees perseverance, but not of the disingenuous. It is always possible to *profess* faith and fall away. Thus, even within the Joban struggles, Calvin can allude to the possibility that this may be the test: to confirm the sufferer's perseverance.

> But when God hath bene so gracious to a man as to leade him forth, not for a moneth onely but for a yeare, three, or ten, so as he hath liued a long while in the knowledge of God and of his owne saluation: if he afterwarde become a rebell and a renegate, and holde not out to the last steppe: is it

not a farre greater fault, than if a man that hath not yet taken a good and sufficient deepe roote, shoulde turne away and ouershoote himselfe through some lightnesse? For if a man haue tasted what is good, and anon after do turne away from it: verely he shall not be excused before God: but yet wil men haue pitie vpon him for that he is so turned away before he haue receyed full instruction. But when a man hath folowed the right way a long time, and hath seemed to be of the constanter sort, and yet is withdrawne fro[m] it: what excuse can there bee for him?[142]

Job's modelling of steadfastness is only to a degree. Calvin examines, in the course of the sermons, the nature and testing of faith. In Sermon 72, Calvin gives us a definition of faith. The nature of faith is "to gather itself in such wise vnto God, as it wanders not abrode, nor bee drawne away as wee commonly bee."[143] Calvin, whilst speaking in the language of assurance whenever he defines the essence of faith, nevertheless recognises a need to separate this from a discussion on how faith responds in different circumstances. This is particularly acute whenever Calvin speaks of faith in relation to trials.

Clearly, we would expect in Calvin's examination of Job's struggle that faith be tested.[144] Calvin speaks to this issue reassuringly. The definition of faith in itself is something Calvin speaks of in terms of the language of assurance.[145] Thus faith looks to God's promises in trouble:

> For herein also doeth our fayth shewe itself: namely if in the midds of our aduersities we can fasten our eyes vpon Gods graciouse promises.[146]

It is in this sense that Calvin can say: "faith is an vncorruptible seede in our soules."[147] Calvin thus appeals to the doctrine of predestination as a source of assurance of faith:

> Be glad… for your names are written in Gods registers to your euerlasting saluation. Is not this ynough to content vs? Wee be not like these fooles that haue none other immortalitie than too make themeselues too bee spoken of. For that were ouergreat fondnesse. But wee know that God hath written our names in his booke, and ingroced the recorde with his owne hande, that is too say, in his owne euerlasting determination, (for Gods hande is the vnchaungeable ordinance that hee hath appoynted) and afterwarde ratified the whole with the bloud of our Lorde Iesus Christ, and finally sealed it by the working of his holy spirite. Seing then that we

haue our memoriall there among the Angelles of heauen, and among the Patriarkes, Prophets and Apostles: haue wee not cause too bee contented? And so albeit that our remembrance bee razed out of the worlde: yet shall wee looze nothing by it.[148]

The experience of faith, however, is something different from the nature of faith in itself. Here we find Calvin applying pastoral judgements on the relationship between faith and trial. Thus, he can say:

> For if we could imbrace Gods promises with true fayth, would they not be of sufficient power to make vs to mount ouer all the temptations that do so reigne ouer vs?[149]

And again:

> If we be not patient, our faith must needes vanishe away.[150]

A man might find himself complaining in his trial, as Job did, but faith

> Ouerruleth oure affections. When we trust in God, and call vpon him, it is not as much to say as we should neuer haue any bickerings in our selues. But fayth must get the vpper hand.[151]

Calvin recognises that there may be weak faith and strong faith. There can exist a faith that is conscious of its own fragility.[152] Thus he can exhort that faith may be "well established, not in pride and ouerweening, but in true lowlinesse."[153] We should not doubt God's power to save us, he exhorts at one point.[154] Thus, too, in the midst of trial the consciousness of faith may be very small. Responding to Job's words in 9:17, "He hath smitte[n] mee downe with a whirlewynd, and he hath wounded me without cause," Calvin can say, "But God giueth vs as it were a sparke of brightnesse, and he giueth vs some feeling of faith, howbeit that we nother know it nor can discerne it."[155] Thus, there are times when "we shoulde not always feele his fatherly loue which he vseth towards vs, too asswage and to sweeten our sorrowes withall."[156]

Thus, whatever Calvin may have written about the nature of faith in itself, it does not preclude him from asserting in more pastoral contexts the need for faith to be strengthened from the assaults of various trials.[157]

The Christian life is to be viewed as one of submission to God in the face of struggle. The doctrine of God that emerges in these sermons is necessarily one closely related to the doctrine of suffering. Calvinism has often been equated with prosperity; the view of Tawney in his *Religion and the Rise of Capitalism* is a noted example.[158] To the advice of the three friends, that suffering is always punishment, Calvin responds with a corrective: sometimes this is true, but equally, sometimes this is not. In fact, suffering is a part of what we can expect as Christians. In a famous comment on 1 Peter 1:11, Calvin remarks that

> the government of the Church of Christ has been so divinely constituted from the beginning that the Cross has been the way to victory, death the way to life.[159]

It is the message reiterated in the Joban sermons:

> it is impossible that Gods children should liue in this world and not be in many perils continually.[160]

The Joban sermons, therefore, form a focused example of Calvin's doctrine of mortification, one in which the death of Christ forms a model for self-denial and cross-bearing.[161] Ronald Wallace notes that Calvin speaks of mortification in both an inward and an outward respect. Using such passages as Romans 6 and Colossians 3:5, Calvin alludes to the inward respect of self-denial and renouncing the works of the flesh; but equally, he points to passages, such as Romans 8:29, 2 Corinthians 4:10, Philippians 3:10, and 2 Timothy 2:11, in which Paul speaks of the Christian as undergoing not simply an inward conformity to Christ in His death but also a conformity in outward condition of life brought about through the concrete experience of suffering and consisting of such suffering. There are passages where "to die with Christ" means being actually brought down on the way to physical death, and "to be conformed to Christ" means actually to be made like Him in outward form before the eyes of the world in suffering and shame.[162]

Both aspects of this "*duplex mortificatio*"[163] are evidenced in Calvin's unfolding of the Joban struggle. In Sermon 66, Calvin provides what almost amounts to a definition of the life of faith:

> Lo what the lyfe of the faythfull is in effect: that is to wit, that they shall neuer bee without manye temptations: and specially that we be subject

to so many miseries during the tyme that we be in this earthly wayfaring, that such as indeuer too serue God best, ceasse not to be often ouerpressed with many inconueniences, and manye afflictions. But what for that? Whe[n] we be astonished… let vs fight against such temptations, and let vs holde on in the right way without starting out of it. And although we sine much hardnesse in ourselues, let vs pray God to giue vs such an inuincible strength, as we may continue in his seruice euen to the end, notwithstanding that Satan labour too thrust vs out of it.[164]

Yet, in maintaining the *duplex mortificatio*, Calvin insists that inward mortification remains the priority.

The cheefe battell that we haue to fyghte, is againste oureselues and against our owne vices, and that is the thing wherein we must imploy our whole force.[165]

This, over and above everything else, seems to be the main lesson that Job learned in the course of the trial. Alluding to Job's confession of sin in Job 42:6 in the penultimate sermon, Calvin discourses on the causes and nature of true repentance.

Therefore let vs marke wel, that true repentance importeth a hating of the sin, yea eue[n] to the vttermost, insomuch as a man misliketh & hateth himselfe because he is not such a one as he ought to be, and for loue of Gods rightuousnes he condemneth all that is in himself, & seeketh al means possibly to be vncased out of that old skin wherein he is wrapped. This is the true tryall of our repentance.[166]

If there is a lesson to be learned from the "tryall of our repentance," there is a similar and related one to be learned from "the tryall of our fayth:"

For fayth is not without fighting: it behoueth hir [sic] to bee throughly exercized. And howe is that done? By the diuels casting of many occasions of unbeleefe and misbeleefe in our way. Thus ye see the true tryall of our fayth.[167]

There is nothing for it, Calvin urges, but to submit to God's providence without murmuring and complaining:

Lette vs learne to submit ourselues vnto God, and let vs not bee so frowarde and madde, as to wishe to exempt ourselues from the subiection of him that created and shaped vs… When a man can so submit himselfe to God with all reuerece and lowlwinesse, and so renounce himself as to say, it is meete that thy Creator should haue the vpper hande of thee, and bee thy mayster: that is a good beginning.[168]

For Calvin's audience, this was a call to patience:

> Well Lord, we are in thy hande, it is not for vs to stinte thee, nor to taske thee to the present time, too saye thou shalt do this or that but inasmuch as thou hast told vs that thou canst ende oure miseries, yea and bring them to a happie and desirable end: Lorde we will paciently waite for that whiche thou hast promised vs.[169]

A subset to the idea of struggle is the concept of self-control. Calvin's preaching on Job expresses a plea for self-control amidst the provocations to despair. Taming what Calvin calls "the affections" is a prerequisite to living the Christian life. Amidst the torrent of issues that aggravated the times, Calvin confesses in only the seventh sermon on Job, "there is nothing more hard than to moderate a mans selfe in suche wise, as we may keepe rule and compasse."[170] "Our affections," he adds later, "are like wyld beastes: which dash vs against God."[171] A loss of control here, something of which Calvin perceived Job was to become guilty, was a sign of godlessness rather than true piety:

> Our passions must bee repressed, and we must hold them in awe, yea and wee must as it were fetter them: that is too say, wee must doo the vttermoste that wee can too abate the headye frantiknesse that is in them.[172]

The Lord's people "tempt God manifestly if we desire to passe our bounds," he suggests.[173] The sermons on Job were then meant to galvanise the faithful to emotional maturity.

Peter Leithart has written of the Stoical elements that are present in Calvin's interpretation of various responses to grief in the Bible.[174] He cites the seventh sermon on Job in which Calvin says: "for were we as a block of wood, or as a stone, it were no vertue at all in vs.... The brute beasts haue somtime no feeling, yet are they not pacient for all that."[175] This is part of the inner tension of which Calvin writes in the *Institutes*, in which the heart entertains a "contradiction" between the natural senses and the call to godliness:

> Scripture praises the saints for their forbearance when, so afflicted with harsh misfortune, they do not break or fall; so stabbed with bitterness, they are at the same time flooded with spiritual joy; so pressed by apprehension, they recover their breath, revived by God's consolation.

In the meantime, their hearts still harbor a contradiction between their natural sense, which flees and dreads what it feels adverse to itself, and their disposition to godliness, which even through these difficulties presses toward obedience to the divine will.[176]

Nowhere is this inner struggle more apparent than in the life of prayer.[177]

Calvin's preaching on Job was designed to convey the transitory nature of this life. In Sermon 28, Calvin urges his listeners to consider the nature of life itself:

> We see now howe men beeing considered in themselues, haue nothing in them but deadlinesse…. What are men then? A wind: a smoke. Howebeeit forasmuch as God hath breathed a continuing power intoo vs: therefore wee bee immortall.[178]

The fleeting nature of this life, something which suffering and trial force into sharp perspective, is an issue Calvin reflects on in these sermons. "Then must wee consider," he urges, "euen by eye sight, that our lyfe fleeteth and slydeth away from vs."[179] Death is a product of the Fall of man in the Garden.

> When we consider that our life vanisheth away in a moment, let vs consider also from whence the same swiftnesse proceedeth: that is to witte, from sinne.[180]

Indeed, Calvin says with some emphasis, "I need not to go farre too feele death."[181] Living in a sin-cursed world, where life is uncertain, ought to make us long for the heavenly life. Indeed, suffering not only anticipates its release in the world to come; it also provides foretastes of it when God is pleased to draw near and relieve the pain:

> For although the miseries be innumerable wherewith men be oppressed: yet must we wey them in the balance with the honoure that God doth vs in making vs Lords ouer his creatures to haue dominion ouer them heere bylow, as his childre[n], whome he maketh to feele him as a father towards vs, and moreouer bycause his setting of vs heere in this world is to aduance vs aloft, that is to witte to the heauenly life, wherof he giueth vs some perceyuerance and feeling aforehand.[182]

One further feature of these sermons worthy of noting is that they provide Calvin with a vehicle for consolation, which we would today call "counseling." Preaching on 2 Timothy 3:16-17, shortly after completing the Sermons on Job, Calvin comments:

> When I expound the holy Scripture I must alwayes compasse my selfe by it, that they that heare mee, may receiue profit of the doctrine which I put forth, and be edified to their salvation. If I haue not this affection, and if I do not procure their edifying that heare me, I commit sacrilege, and prophane the worde of GOD.[183]

Similarly, Calvin could say in the Joban sermons:

> When we deale with Gods word, it beoueth vs too set some certaine marke before vs, that we wander not heere and there, but deuide it aright, as they that knowe to what end they speake, that our talke be not rouing and gadding too and fro. For else we may speake many good words, but none of them shal serue to any purpose.[184]

This means that the preacher must range over the entire corpus of human ills, alluding to every facet of human experience, for "some man must bee handled after one fashion, and some man after another."[185] This, as we saw at the beginning of this chapter, required for Calvin a subtlety of exegetical and rhetorical skill such that the application of the text be made with care and sensitivity: the Joban sermons are meant to be a 'phisition' for sick souls.[186]

Nevertheless, Calvin's exegesis of Job does not resolve all the difficulties of interpretation: Calvin is often ambivalent on Job's defense of innocence; he can engage in moralistic denunciations that sound very much like the theology of Job's friends; he descends into a tortuous explanation of the existence of "double justice" in his defence of God's providence that leads him into the murky waters of absolutism, something that he also vehemently denies. But, he can also disclose a pastor's heart that is acquainted with grief and sorrow as he uncovers the hidden depths of pain in his hearers. This will form our study in chapter 2. Moreover, as we examine Calvin's doctrine of providence, we find that he focuses on the incomprehensibility of God not only as a summary of the book of Job itself but as a pastoral tool to reduce the apparent tension between God's justice and power. The doctrine of God's incomprehensibility will be our study in chapters 3 and 4. At the same time, it will become apparent that the elements of Christology in the Joban sermons, so clearly labelled by some scholars as definitive of Calvin's whole system of theology, are strangely muted.[187] We will be concentrating on this in the final chapter.

## References

[1] On Calvin's rhetoric in the *Institutes*, see Quirinus Breen, "John Calvin and the Rhetorical Tradition," in *Church History* vol. 26 (1957), 3-21; Serene Jones, *Calvin and the Rhetoric of Piety* (Louisville, Kentucky: Westminster John Knox Press, 1995). A lacuna exists in the analysis of the sermonic material, particularly in the way certain themes and emphases are given, complementing the more systematic cohesion of the *Institutes*.

On Calvin's own view of the dangers of rhetoric in the Joban sermons, see 11 (Job 3:2-10), 51.a.68, where he refers to those who "may not seeme to haue bene at schoole to learne fine Rhetorike." *...il n'y a celuy qu'il ne semble avoir esté à l'escole pour avoir belle faconde* [*CO* 33:151].

[2] 78 (Job 21:1-6), 366.a.59. *Car il y a une prudence singuliere requise en cest endroit ainsi que nous avons veu par ci devant. Car les afflictions sont comme maladies: et si un medecin use d'un mesme remede envers tous malades, et que sera-ce? Il y a quelque maladie chaude, il y en a une froide, il y en aura une qui voudra que l'homme soit desseché, et l'autre qu'il soit refreschi, l'une qu'il soit reserré, et l'autre relasché. Voila donc comme un medecin meurtrira les malades, quand il n'aura point le regard aux maladies: mesmes il faut avoir cognu les complexions des malades. Ainsi en est-il, que nous devons contempler ceux que Dieu visite par afflictions* [*CO* 34:206].

[3] In a comment on the word *paraklesis*, 'exhortation,' in Hebrews 13:22, Calvin says: "We must learn from this that Scripture is not given us to silence the voice of the pastors among us, and that we are not to be impatient when the same exhortations keep sounding in our ears" (Hebrews and I and II Peter, trans. W. B. Johnston, ed. David W. Torrance and Thomas F. Torrance, *Calvin's New Testament Commentaries*, Grand Rapids: Eerdmans, rpt. 1989, 216).

[4] The attempt to date precisely Calvin's sermons on Job is, according to T. H. L. Parker, "doomed to failure" (*Calvin's Preaching*, Louisville, Kentucky: Westminster/John Knox Press, 1992, 168). Parker reasons that if the sermons on Deuteronomy began on Wednesday, 20 March 1555, the last sermon of Job must have been on the previous Friday or Saturday, 15 or 16 March 1555. Working backwards, and assuming that Calvin preached according to his usual plan of preaching each weekday of alternative weeks with a sermon on the intervening Wednesday, this dates the beginning of the 159 Job sermons on 26 February 1554.

Calvin turned to the Old Testament a great deal during the fifteen-year span from August 1549 to February 1564. Of the 2,042 sermons that he preached, 1,437 were on the Old Testament. See A. Baumgartner *Calvin hébraisant et interprete de l'Ancien Testament* (Paris: Librarie Fischbacher, 1889), 30f. Cf. Anthony G. Baxter, "John Calvin's Use and Hermeneutics of the Old Testament," Ph.D. diss., University of Sheffield, 1987, 5.

[5] T. H. L. Parker, *John Calvin: A Biography* (Philadelphia: Westminster Press, 1975), 117.

⁶ Among Calvin's most vehement critics was Sébastien Castellion (1515-1563), to whom Calvin had refused admission to the ministry. In 1553 he was appointed professor of Greek at the University of Basel. Following Servetus' execution, Castellion was to write in March 1554, barely a few weeks after the commencement of Calvin's series of sermons on Job, *De Haereticis an sint persequendi*, an anthology of early and sixteenth-century writers denouncing executions for religious reasons. The book occasioned great irritation in Geneva, and both Calvin and Beza engaged in criticism of him. See Hans Rudolf Guggisberg, "Castellion, Sébastien," in *The Oxford Encyclopedia of the Reformation*, ed. Hans J. Hillerbrand, vol. 1 (New York, Oxford: Oxford University Press, 1996), 271-272. For an analysis of the Servetus affair, see Alister E. McGrath, *A Life of John Calvin* (Oxford, England; Cambridge, Massachusetts: Blackwell Publishers, 1990), 114-120.

Calvin makes a reference to Servetus in the sixteenth sermon, alluding to him as, "that cursed creature that was burned....That wicked creature," adding that "the deuill had caried him away" .16, (Job 4:12-19), 72.b.59. "*malheureux qui a esté bruslé...le meschant fait ce deshonneur à Dieu...le diable l'avoit transporté...* [CO 33:204].

⁷ *Select Works of John Calvin: Tracts and Letters*, ed. Henry Beveridge and Jules Bonnet, Vol. 5, 427. *Nobis quidem reclamantibus vobis facessunt hanc molestiam, sed eo venerunt amentiae et furoris, ut illis suspectum sit quidquid loquimur. Itaque si dicerem, meridiem lucere, protinus dubitare inciperent* [CO 14:611].

⁸ On the Libertines, see "Calvin's Treatise 'Against the Libertines'," trans. Robert Wilkie and Allen Verhey, *Calvin Theological Journal* 15.2 (November, 1980), 190-219.

⁹ Also known as Christopher Libertet. Writing on 13 January 1553, Calvin could say: "I should gladly have been present at your marriage, had I not been detained at home by the wickedness of those who cease not to bring destruction upon themselves and the community by their madness. I have good reason to call it madness, for they have never exhibited more unbridled licentiousness. I shall say nothing of their mischievous plots for the destruction of the faith, of their gross contempt of God, of their impious conspiracies for the scattering of the Church, of the foul Epicurism of their whole life; and this, not because these are light evils, but because they are not unknown to you. The entire Republic is at present in disorder, and they are striving to root up the established order of things. Had your marriage been a month later, I should have had more leisure. I cannot move a foot at present. I have not been through the city-gates for a month past, not even for recreation." *Select Works of John Calvin: Tracts and Letters*, ed. Henry Beveridge and Jules Bonnet, vol. 5, 387-8. *Libenter nuptiis interfuissem, nisi me domi retineret eorum improbitas, qui in suam et communem perniciem furere non desinunt. Furorem merito appello, quum nunquam magis effraeni licentia grassati sint. Scelerata consilia labefactandae fidei, crassum Dei contemptum, impias dissipandae ecclesiae conspirationes, foedum in tota*

*vita Epicurismum omitto. Non quia haec levia mala sint, sed quia non sunt vobis ignota. Nunc totum reipublicae suae ordinem et statum convellere moliuntur. Si mense uno serius duxisses uxorem poteram esse liberior. Nunc pedem movere non licet. Iam elapsus est mensis ex quo porta urbis egressus non sum, ne animi quidem levandi causa* [*CO* 14:455-456].

For a treatment of Calvin's doctrine of providence as seen in his correspondence, see Pieter C. Potgieter, "The Providence of God in Calvin's Correspondence," in *Calvin: Erbe und Auftrag*, ed. Willem van't Spijker (Kampen: Kok Pharos Publishing House, 1991), 85-96.

[10] In the event, of course, Farel did not die, but recovered sufficiently to marry a woman considerably younger than himself and, in the end, outlived Calvin himself.

[11] The translation is Parker's (T. H. L. Parker, *John Calvin A Biography*, 115). The letter is not included in the Beveridge/Bonnet edition of Calvin's letters. *Hactenus tamen me nemo vociferantem audivit. Sed quod omnium erat caput, mihi deest, ut istis Domini ferulis ad veram humilitatem erudiar. Quo magis necesse est liberis fratrum castigationibus domari* [*CO* 14:478].

[12] Philibert Berthelier was part of a group of inter-related families in Geneva who called themselves *les enfants de Genève*. Berthelier himself was a coarse man who, along with others, had tried to prevent Calvin from preaching by exaggerating fits of coughing. On the Libertines, see Jeannine E. Olson, "Libertines," in *The Oxford Encyclopedia of the Reformation*, ed. Hans J. Hillerbrand (New York, Oxford: Oxford University Press, 1996), vol. 2, 423-424.

[13] For a full account, see W. G. Naphy, *Calvin and the Consolidation of the Genevan Reformation* (Manchester/New York: Manchester University Press, 1994), 151-152.

[14] According to Beza's account, "Calvin, though he had been informed of what was done only two days before the usual period of celebrating the Lord's Supper, raised his voice and his hand in the course of his sermon. After he had spoken at some length of the despisers of sacred mysteries, he cried out, in the words of Chrysostom, 'I will die sooner than this hand shall stretch forth the sacred things of the Lord to those who have been judged despisers.' These words, strangely, had such an effect upon these men, however lawless, that Perrin secretly advised Berthelier not to come forward to the table. The sacrament was celebrated with extraordinary silence, not without some degree of trembling, as if the Deity himself were actually present" (Theodore Beza [Bèze], *The Life of John Calvin*, trans. Henry Beveridge [a translation of Beza's second *Life of Calvin* in 1844], reprinted with minor alterations in the *Banner of Truth Magazine* 227/228, August/September, 1982, 41).

[15] *CO* 20:253. On Calvin's medical history, see J. Wilkinson, "The medical history of John Calvin," in *Proceedings of the Royal College of Physicians of Edinburgh* 22 (1992), 368-383.

[16] Ibid., 413. *C'est chose estrange au sens humain que les enfans de Dieu*

*soyent saoulez dangoisse, cependant que les meschans sesgayent en leurs delices: mais encores plus que les esclaves de Satan nous mettent les pieds sur la gorge, comme on dit, et facent leur triomphe de nous. Si est-ce que nous avons a nous consoler en toutes nos miseres, attendans ceste heureuse issue laquelle nous est promise, que non seulement il nous delivrera par ses Anges, mais aussi luy-mesme torchera les larmes de nos yeux* [*CO* 14:563].

The prisoners were Mathieu Dimonet, Denis Peloquin of Blois, Louis de Marsac, gentlemen of the Bourbonnais, and one of Dimonet's cousins. The letter is addressed to Peloquin and Louis de Marsac. These five students had been declared guilty of heresy and delivered over to the Judge Ordinary of Lyons. Transferred from dungeon to dungeon, and recently transferred from Paris to Lyons to await their fate, in a trial that had lasted for over a year, the young men were sentenced, on 1 March 1553, to the stake. Calvin had written an earlier letter on March 7 of that year, and another on May 16. On the place of suffering in Calvin's letters, see, Jean-Daniel Benoit, *Calvin in his Letters*, trans. Richard Haig (Sutton Courtenay Press, 1991), 50-51 [*CO* 14:490-492], 126-127 [*CO* 14:544-547].

[17] Beza records that it was fairly common for dogs to be named "Calvin," sometimes shortened to "Cain." Calvin was also hissed and booed at in the streets. Some, including Philibert Berthelier, deliberately coughed through his sermons, passing wind or belching when Calvin complained. As Parker explains: "When Calvin remonstrated to the Council, Berthelier coarsely replied that if he stopped them coughing, 'nous peterons et roterons' " (Parker, *John Calvin: A Biography*, 99).

[18] William Naphy, *Calvin and the consolidation of the Genevan Reformation* (Manchester/New York: Manchester University Press, 1994), 157-159.

[19] *Ibid.*, 157. *CO* 34:377.

[20] *Ibid. CO* 34:563.

[21] *Ibid.*, 158. 104 (Job 34:16-20), 617.b.64, 69. *CO* 34:161.

[22] *Ibid.*, 73 (Job 20:1-7), 342.b.46. *CO* 34:143. C.f. sermons 74 and 75 for further allusions.

[23] Ambrose (c. 339-397), *De interpellatione Iob et david*, in *Sancti Ambrosii Opera* ed. Carolus Schenkl, Corpus Scriptorum ecclesiasticorum latinorum (Vienna: Hoelder-Pinchler-Tempsky, 1866-), vol. 32.2 (1897), 209-296; Augustine (354-430), *Adnotationum in Job liber unus*, Patrologiae Cursus Completus, Series Latina, ed. J. P. Migne (hereafter, PL) (Paris, 1844-80), 34:825-86; Gregory the Great (c. 540-604), *Libri XXXV, Moralium*, PL 75:515-1162; 76:9-782; *Morals on the Book of Job, Translated with Notes and Indices*, 3 vols. (Oxford: H. Parker, 1844-50); Hilary (c. 315-67), *Tractatus in Job* (fragment), PL 10:723-24; Jerome (c. 243-420), *Commentarii in lubrum Job*, PL 26:619-802; *Liber Job* (a translation), PL 28:1079-1122; Thomas Aquinas (c. 1225-74), *Expositio super Iob ad litteram*, in *Opera omnia*, iussu Leonis XIII P.M. edita, cura et studio Fratrum Praedicatorum, vol. 26 (Rome, 1965). For a fuller bibliography of pre-sixteenth century works on Job, see David J.

Clines, *Job 1-20*, Word Biblical Commentary, 17 (Dallas, Texas: Word Books, 1989), lxv-lxix.

In addition to works on the book of Job itself, Calvin would have access to the great treatises on providence, including Augustine's *De ordine*, which comprise the third and fourth dialogues he wrote while in seclusion in the villa of Cassiciacum in 386, the year of his conversion to Christianity. See "Divine Providence and the Problem of Evil," trans. Robert P. Russell, in *The Fathers of the Church*, vol. 5 (New York: CIMA Publishing Co., Inc., 1948), 239-334. Shortly before his death, Augustine was to write of this early work, saying: "In these books is treated the important question of whether the order of God's providence embraces everything good and everything evil" (*Retractationes*, I:3). See also John Chrysostom, "No One Can Harm the Man Who Does Not Injure Himself," trans. W. R. Stephens, in *Nicene and Post-Nicene Fathers*, ed. P. Schaff, et al., series 1, vol. 9 (Grand Rapids: Eerdmans, 1954), 269-284; Ambrose, "The Prayer of Job and David," in *Seven Exegetical Works*, trans. M. P. McHugh, in *The Fathers of the Church*, vol. 65 (Washington, D.C.: Catholic University of America Press, 1972), 376-85; Tertullian, *Ad Nationes*, in *Ante-Nicene Fathers*, ed. by A. Roberts and J. Donaldson (Grand Rapids, MI: Eerdmans, 1973), III:109-147.

[24] We shall return to this issue in a later chapter, but see David L. Puckett, *John Calvin's Exegesis of the Old Testament* (Louisville, Kentucky: Westminster John Knox Press, 1995), 105-138. Puckett's fine work makes no mention of the Joban sermons.

[25] Susan Schreiner, *Where Shall Wisdom be Found?: Calvin's Exegesis of Job from Medieval and Modern Perspectives* (Chicago, London: The University of Chicago Press, 1994), 9. Schreiner summarises the debate over how much influence medieval theology had on Calvin, alluding to the views of Wendel, who thought Calvin was influenced by Ockham and Scotus; Reuter, who thought Calvin had been influenced by John Mair (d.1550); Ganoczy, who has written that in the 1536 *Institutes* Calvin demonstrates a leaning towards Peter Lombard; and Alister McGrath, who argues for the influence of a "general medieval current," something which he identifies with Gregory of Rimini and the "schola augustiniana moderna." Schreiner's point is that in these discussions, it is the young Calvin that is under discussion. In the sermons on Job (1554-1555), Calvin "had greater knowledge regarding medieval theology." 7-8.

For Scotist influences in Calvin, see Williston Walker, *John Calvin the Organiser of Reformed Protestantism, 1509-1564* (New York: Schocken Books, 1969 [1906]), 149, 418; Clarke Huston Irwin, *John Calvin: the man and his work* (London: The Religious Tract Society, 1909), 179. The view was roundly attacked by B. B. Warfield, *Calvin and Augustine* (Grand Rapids: Presbyterian and Reformed Publishing Company, 1971), 154-158. Warfield is particularly critical of Ritschl's contention that a nominalist conception of God survived in Calvin's doctrine of double predestination, giving the grounds for a certain "arbitrariness" in God's actions. According to Warfield:

"A thing is not made right by the mere fact that he wills it but that the fact that he wills it (which fact Scripture may witness to us) is proof enough to us that it is right" (*Op. cit.*, 155, n.46).

[26] *Ibid.*, 9. The point is that the sermons on Job do not disclose any particular sources. It is a remarkable fact that, whilst Calvin does allude to other interpretations, he does not name any specific source. We find Calvin dismissing the allegorical interpretation towards the end of the series on Job. In Sermon 156, in discussing the exact meaning of the reference to Leviathan in Job 40:20, Calvin writes: "It is an euill thing to dally with the holie Scripture by transforming of it intoo allegories, nother ought allegories to be drawn but out of a naturall meening as we see that Saint Paule doth in the Epistle to the Galathians and in other places." 156 (Job 40:20-41:25), 733.a.34. *car de se iouër de l'Escriture saincte la transformant en allegorie, c'est une chose mauvaise: et les allegories ne doivent estre tirees sinon du sense naturel: comme nous voyons que sainct Paul en fait en l'Espistre aux Galatiens et en d'autres passages* [*CO* 35:466].

[27] It would seem fitting, following the attacks upon Calvin by Albert Pighius in 1542 and more recently by Jerome Bolsec in 1551, that Calvin should take up a systematic exposition of a work of Scripture largely dominated by the doctrine of providence. Bolsec, in particular, had attempted, in his outburst on October 16 at the weekly meeting of the Congregation, to drive home the logical inconsistencies of the doctrine of predestination, a doctrine that he believed to be inherently deterministic. He had challenged Geneva to give any evidence of it in either Augustine or the Bible. Calvin, and the other Genevan ministers, had made God into an idol. *Registres de la Compagnie des pasteurs de Genève au temps de Calvin*, publiés sous la direction des Archives d'Etat de Genève par R. M. Kingdon et J. 'F. Bergier, t. I: 1546-1553, t. II. 1553-1564 (Geneva, 1964 and 1962), 81.

On the Bolsec controversy and background, including possible connections with Pighius, see Ian McPhee, "Conserver or Transformer of Calvin's Theology? A Study of the Origins and Development of Theodore Beza's Thought, 1550-1570" (Ph.D. diss., Cambridge, 1979), 7-24; P. Holtrop, *The Bolsec Controversy on Predestination from 1551 to1555* (Lewiston, N.Y.: Edwin Mellen, 1993).

[28] I (Job 1:1), 1.a.28 . *Voila donc ce que nous avons à retenir en brief de l'histoire, c'est que Dieu a un tel empire sur ses creatures, qu'il en peut disposer à son plaisir...* [*CO* 33:21].

[29] Raguenier had begun the work of recording in shorthand some of Calvin's sermons on Acts and Jeremiah some months prior to this, but was then employed by a society formed to help the refugees who had flocked into Geneva, mainly from France, *La compagnie des étrangers*. He was paid half a minister's salary for the task. He had to record in short-hand about six thousand words per hour, using quill and ink (pencils not being invented until 1564). Numerous scribes were employed in the transcription of this shorthand into longhand, Raguenier apparently dictating from his notes.

Raguenier died in 1560 or 1561, after recording the sixty-fifth sermon on *The Harmony of the Gospels*. See T. H. L. Parker, *Calvin's Preaching*, 65-75. Bernard Gagnebin has estimated Calvin's total *recorded* homiletic output at more than 2,300 sermons. Since formal recording did not begin until 1549, ten years after Calvin began to preach, this figure probably represents little more than half of the total number of sermons Calvin preached. See Bernard Gagnebin, "L'incroyable histoire des sermons de Calvin," *Bulletin de la société d'histoire et d'archéologie de Genève* 10 (1951/55), 311-334.

[30] The only other completed series of sermons published during Calvin's lifetime were *Ephesians* (1562), *Galatians* (1563) and the *Pastoral Epistles* (1563). Selections of sermons taken from larger series were also published, including a series on Melchisedek (1560), Abraham (1561) and Jacob and Esau (1562) taken from his sermons on Genesis; Hezekiah (1562), taken from the series on Isaiah; Psalm 119 (1554), from a sporadic selection of the Psalms; and the Ten Commandments (1562), taken from the sermons on Deuteronomy. Some have hinted at the connection between the publication of these *Sermons on Job* and the Huguenot cause in France, alluding to the fact that Gaspard II de Coligny (1519-1572), admiral of France and Huguenot leader, had by this time signalled his adherence to the Reformed cause in January 1561. Irwin Hoch de Long cites as fact that Admiral Coligny valued the sermons so highly that he read one of them every morning and evening, deriving such benefit from them that he called them his "panchrestum medicamentum" —a healing and soothing balm in all the vicissitudes of life. See Irwin Hoch de Long, "Calvin as an Interpreter of the Bible," in *The Reformed Church Review* 4:13 (1909), 171; see also, Ariste Viguié, "Les Sermons de Calvin sur le livre de Job," in *Bulletin de la Societé de l'histoire du Protestantisme Francais*, vol. XXXI (1982), 466, 504, 548-555. On the style of Calvin's French syntax, see Peter Miln, "Hommes D'une Bonne Cause" (Ph.D. diss., Nottingham University 1989), 52-91; F. M. Higman, *The Style of John Calvin in his French Polemical Treatises* (Oxford: Oxford University Press, 1967); Serene Jones, *The Rhetoric of Piety* Columbia Series in Reformed Theology, (Louisville, KY: Westminster/John Knox Press, 1995); Q. Breen, "John Calvin and The Rhetorical Tradition," in *Church History* vol. 26 (1957), 3-21.

[31] A separate German translation of the concluding prayers in the Job sermons was also made and published in 1592.

[32] Arthur Golding (1536?-1605?) was responsible for a number of other English translations of Calvin's sermons, including *Galatians* (1574), *Ephesians* (1576) and *Deuteronomy* (1583). T. H. L. Parker says of him, "Golding writes a strong, energetic prose, keeping close enough to the original to do justice to Calvin's own style" (*Calvin's Preaching*, 72-73). Born in London, Golding is said to have been educated at Queens' College, Cambridge, but his name is not to be found in the college register. In 1549 he was in the service of the Protector Somerset. Among his accomplishments was the translation of Ovid's *Metamorphoses* in April 1567 (said to have

been known to Shakespeare), and Seneca's *De Beneficiis* in 1577-78. Said to have Puritan sympathies, he concentrated on the translation of works by Calvin and Beza. Among his patrons were Sir William Cecil, Sir Christopher Hatton, the Earl of Leicester, the Earl of Essex, Sir William Mildmay, Lord Cobham and the Earl of Huntingdon. He was a member of the Elizabethan Society of Antiquaries, founded by Archbishop Parker in 1572. His sole original publication was a prose "Discourse upon the Earthquake that happened throughe this realme of England and other places of Christendom, the first of April 1580...," in which he alluded to the judgement of God upon the godlessness of the age. His translation of Calvin's Joban sermons, "Sermons of M. John Caluin vpon the Booke of Iob," was first published in London in 1574 and dedicated in December 1573 to Robert, Earl of Essex (according to the *Dictionary of National Biography*, ed. Sir Leslie Stephen and Sir Sidney Lee, vol. VII, Oxford: Oxford University Press, 1967-68, 75-77. According to Stam, it is dedicated to Robert Dudley, Earl of Leicester, 113). Reprints followed in 1579, 1580 and 1584.

Two different editions of Golding's translation of Job's sermons were printed by Henry Binneman for Lucas Harrison and George Bishop in 1574, perhaps because the Company required a printer to keep a book in print and available for sale in order to maintain the copyright. No more than 1,250 copies of a work could be printed from any one type setting, a rule that ensured the continuation of labour for the Company. The two editions are in quite distinct type settings. Further impressions were made of these editions in the same year. On the edition used in this thesis, see note on page 28. See, further, David Henry Stam, "England's Calvin: A Study of the Publication of John Calvin's Works in Tudor England" (Ph.D. thesis, Northwestern University, 1978), 21, 101. See also, Ellen Borger Monsma, "The Preaching Style of Jean Calvin: An Analysis of the Psalm Sermons of the Supplementa Calviniana" (Ph.D. diss., Rutgers University, 1986), 8-19.

[33] Copies of the 1536 edition of the *Institutes* made their way to England, together with the subsequent French and Latin editions that culminated in the final 1559 edition as we now know it. The first English translation of the completed 1559 edition was made by Thomas Norton in 1561 and published by Reginald Wolfe and Richard Harrison. This edition served as the standard English translation until the nineteenth century. A section of Book III (chapters vi to x) had been translated earlier by Thomas Broke and published in London by John Day and William Seres early in 1549, under the title *Of the life or conuersation of a Christian man, a right godly treatise*. In the same year, Broke (sometimes, though wrongly, attributed to Miles Coverdale) translated Calvin's treatise on the sacraments, which first appeared in French in 1541 under the title *Petit traicté de la Saincte cene* [CO 5:429-459], and in Latin in 1545, under the title *Libellus de coena Domini*. The English translation, printed by John Day and William Seres, probably in 1548, appeared under the title *A faythful and most godly treatyse concernyng the most sacred sacrament*. In the preface, Broke speaks of having translated other sections

of the *Institutes*. Other translations were made, though not published, by John Daus (Dawes, Dauys), and Norton, in the preface to his own translation, writes of having been in possession of a copy of the translation. An entirely new edition was published in 1562, correcting some "three hundred faults." See Stam, 30, 55-67.

[34] For example, Wilhelm Niesel includes only a half dozen references to the Joban material, in *The Theology of Calvin*, trans. Harold Knight (Philadelphia: The Westminster Press, 1956). Karl Barth, similarly, in his examination of Calvin's theology, includes five references only, in *The Theology of John Calvin*, trans. Geoffrey W. Bromiley (Grand Rapids, Cambridge, U.K.: Eerdmans;, 1995 [1922]). Interestingly, four of these references occur within the first eight pages of the book indicating a potential importance for Barth of these sermons in the formulation of his understanding of Calvin's doctrine of God. Similarly, only a few references occur in the seminal works Dowey, Parker, Wallace and Wendel. See Edward A Dowey, Jr, *The Knowledge of God in Calvin's Theology* (Grand Rapids: Eerdmans, 1994 [1952]); John T. McNeill, *The History and Character of Calvinism* (New York: Oxford University Press, 1977); T. H. L. Parker, *The Oracles of God* (London: 1947); *The Doctrine of the Knowledge of God* (Edinburgh: Oliver & Boyd, 1969 [1953]); R. S. Wallace, *Calvin's Doctrine of the Word and Sacrament* (Edinburgh: Oliver & Boyd, 1953), *The Christian Life* (Edinburgh: Oliver & Boyd, 1959); François Wendel, *Calvin, sources et evolution de sa pensée religieuse* (Paris, 1950); English translation: *Origins and Development of his Religious Thought*, trans. by P. Mairet (New York: Harper and Row, 1963).

[35] T. F. Torrance, *Calvin's Doctrine of Man* (Grand Rapids: Eerdmans, 1957).

[36] Richard Stauffer, *Dieu, la création et la Providence dans la prédication de Calvin* (Bern, Frankfurt am Main, Las Vegas: Peter Lang, 1978).

[37] On Calvin's doctrine of providence, see John Calvin, *A Defense of the Secret Providence of God...* (1558), trans. Henry Cole trans. (London, 1927); see also, "John Calvin's View of Divine Providence," a translation from Calvin's French Tracts by Paul Wells, in *The Banner of Truth* 66:36-40; for the original, see *Contre la Secte phantastique et furieuse des Libertins. Qui se nomment spirituelz.* (1545) [*CO* 7:145-248]; Ronald J. VanderMolen, "Providence as Mystery, Providence as Revelation: Puritan and Anglican Modifications of John Calvin's Doctrine of Providence" *Church History* 47 (March 1978) 1:27-47.

[38] Mary Potter Engel, *John Calvin's Perspectival Anthropology* (Atlanta, Georgia: Scholars Press, 1988). Engel's attempt to set anthropology apart from his theology as a whole, particularly the knowledge of God, is almost certainly doomed to failure. See the review of her work by Charles Partee, *The Journal of Religion* 69 (1989), 553-554.

[39] William J. Bouwsma, *John Calvin: A Sixteenth Century Portrait* (New York, Oxford: Oxford University Press, 1988). Though widely acclaimed, Bouwsma's psychological schema in the understanding of Calvin has received criticism from some. T. H. L. Parker, for example, sees the point of

view that suggests we understand the sixteenth century better than Calvin did (a point of view he imputes to Bouwsma) as problematic. "On this basis," Parker adds, "an author can mean anything we want him to mean." See, T. H. L. Parker, *Calvin: An Introduction to his Thought* (Louisville, Kentucky: Westminster/John Knox Press, 1995), 11.

[40] The attempt to understand Calvin within the context of the medieval era, rather than in stark contrast to it, has been fostered by, amongst others, Heiko Oberman, *The Harvest of Medieval Theology: Gabriel Biel and Late Medieval Nominalism* (Grand Rapids: Eerdmans, 1967); also, *The Dawn of the Reformation* (Edinburgh: T. & T. Clark; Grand Rapids: Eerdmans, 1992). See also David C. Steinmetz, *Misericordia Dei: The Theology of Jannes von Staupitz in its Late Medieval Setting* (Leiden: E. J. Brill, 1968); James S. Preus, *From Shadow to Promise: Old Testament Interpretation from Augustine to Luther* (Cambridge, Mass.: Belknap Press, 1969).

[41] Our research into Bouwsma's citations from Job reveal that a number of them are incorrectly cited. Some of these will be noted in the text of this volume.

[42] Susan E. Schreiner, *The Theater of His Glory* (Grand Rapids: Baker, 1995 [1991]). *The Theater of His Glory*, a borrowed phrase from the *Institutes* (I.v.8; I.vi.2; I.xiv.20; II.vi.1), is an analysis of Calvin's understanding of the natural order and his dependence on, and agreement with, medieval and ancient traditions. Schreiner contends that twentieth-century understanding of Calvin has been unduly confused by the Barth–Brunner debate. She concludes that Calvin "stood in continuity with the past teachings of the church." *Op. cit.*, 2.

[43] Schreiner, *op. cit.* Schreiner's method is comparative: examining Calvin's understanding of Job with that of Gregory the Great (in his *Moralia*, written in the late sixth century), the Spanish Jewish philosopher Maimonides (in his *Guide of the Perplexed* written in 1190), and Thomas Aquinas' exposition of Job (written c. 1261-1264). Schreiner's conclusions are to the effect that Calvin shows some lines of continuity with his medieval predecessors, particularly Aquinas: "Calvin preaches on the Book of Job within what is basically the Thomistic framework," *Op. cit.*, 91; but Calvin is also distinctive in his contribution to the understanding of Job.

Schreiner follows this analysis with an examination of modern interpretations of Job, ranging from Norman Habel, Edwin Good and Carl Jung to literary recastings of Job by H. G. Wells, Archibald Macleish, Elie Wiesel and Franz Kafka. The absence of any transcendent God in these interpretations ends up in darkness, a world "without justice, without revelation, without hope, and without understanding" (*Op. cit.*,190).

[44]This is something, of course, that Calvin vigorously denies in the *Institutes*; see 1.17.2 [*CO* 2:155-156]; cf. "The Secret Providence of God," published as a separate treatise together with "The Eternal Predestination of God" in *Calvin's Calvinism*, trans. Henry Cole (Grand Rapids, MI: Reformed Publishing Association, nd), 248, where Calvin attacks the "Sorbonic dogma

...in the promulgation of which the Papal theologians so much pride themselves, 'that the power of God is absolute and tyrannical,' I utterly abhor. For it would be easier to force away the light of the sun from his heat, or his heat from his fire, than to separate the power of God from his justice." *Itaque Sorbonicum illud dogma, in quo sibi plaudunt papales theologastri, detestor: quod potentiam absolutam Deo affingit. Solis enim lucem a calore avellere, imo suum ab igne calorem, facilius erit, quam Dei potentiam separare a iustitia* [*CO* 8:361].

[45] In Sermon 88, Calvin understands Job himself as taking the position that God's power is absolute. It is a notion that the Reformer is quick to judge. It is "euill." Preceding the judgement, Calvin remarks that for Job to view God's power "to bee so absolute and lawlesse is as much as to make him a Tirant, which were utterly contrarie to his maiestie. For our Lord wil not vse might without right, nother is he lesse rightfull than mightful: his rightfulnesse and mightfulnesse are things inseparable." 88 (Job 23:1-7), 413.b.68. *Car combien que la puissance de Dieu soit infinie, si est-ce que de la faire ainsi absolue, c'est imaginer en luy une tyrannie, et cela est du tout contraire à sa maiesté, car nostre Seigneur ne veut point estre puissant qu'il ne soit iuste: et ce sont choses inseparables, que sa iustice et sa puissance* [*CO* 34:336]. A little later in the same sermon, Calvin is even more forthright: "Wheras the doctors of Sorbon say that God hath an absolute or lawlesse power, it is a diuelish blasphemie forged in hell, for it ought not once to enter into a faithfull mannes head." 415.a.44. *Et de fait, quand ces docteurs Sorboniques disent, que Dieu a une puissance absoluë, c'est un blaspheme diabolique qui a esté forgé aux enfers* [*CO* 34:339-340]. Calvin's point is that God does have a power that may *seem* to be lawless, but it isn't: there is a secret law concerning which we may know nothing.

[46] E.g., Serene Jones, *Calvin and the Rhetoric of Piety* (Louisville, Kentucky: Westminster John Knox Press, 1995). Jones' contribution has been criticised within its own rhetorical parameters, and its reductionistic attempt to speak of a "rhetoric of piety" (rather than, say, a "rhetoric of dogmatic exposition" or even a "rhetoric of polemic") creates an association of piety that lacks precise theological expression. See the review of this work by Richard A. Muller in *Calvin Theological Journal* 31 (1996), 582-583.

[47] For an examination of Calvin's method of comprehending the text of Scripture, see David L. Puckett, *John Calvin's Exegesis of the Old Testament* (Louisville, Kentucky: Westminster John Knox Press, 1995).

[48] See Jones, *Calvin and the Rhetoric of Piety*; Rodolphe Peter, "Rhetorique et prédication selon Calvin," *Revue d'histoire et de philosophie religieuses* 55 (1975), 249-272. Olivier Millet's *Calvin et la dynamique de la parole: Étude de la rhétorique réformée* (1992) is a major study of the language and structure of the Calvin's writings.

[49] See T. H. L. Parker, *Calvin's Preaching*, 17-32; Ellen Roger Monsma, *The Preaching Style of Jean Calvin: An Analysis of the Psalm Sermons of the Supplementa Calviniana* (Ph.D. thesis, Rutgers University 1986), 84-94.

According to Parker's analysis of 1,064 sermons, only twenty-three (about two per cent) are not part of a sequential series.

[50] *Calvin's Selected Works*, ed. Henry Beveridge and Jules Bonnet, vol. 1 (Grand Rapids, MI: Baker Books, 1983) 40. *Sic enim fere distributae erant conciones, ut dimidia pars caliginosis illis scholarum quaestionibus daretur, quae rudem plebeculam obstupefacerent: altera suaves fabellas, aut non inamoenas speculationes contineret, quibus populi alacritas excitaretur. Paucae tantum voculae ex Dei verbo aspergebantur, quae fidem talibus nugamentis sua maiestate conciliarent* [*CO* 5:396].

[51] The issue of centrality in Calvin's theology has received considerable attention. As far back as 1954, John T. McNeill could write: "Calvin formerly stirred debate because people agreed or disagreed with his teaching. Recently, men have been in disagreement over what his teaching was" (*The History and Character of Calvinism*, New York: Oxford University Press, 1967, 202). Prior to this, T. H. L. Parker could express the view that no particular doctrine in Calvin dominated his theological structure. See T. H. L. Parker, "The Approach to Calvin," *The Evangelical Quarterly* 16 (1944), 165-172. Cf. the more recent article by Tony Lane, "The Quest for the Historical Calvin," *The Evangelical Quarterly* 55 (1983), 95-113. Mary Potter Engel has outlined the main phases of the debate. See her *John Calvin's Perspectival Anthropology* (Atlanta, Georgia: Scholars Press, 1988), ix-xii. In the mid-nineteenth century, Alexander Schweizer and Ferdinand Christian Baur contended that predestination was the central dogma in Calvin. See Alexander Schweizer, *Die Glaubenslehre der evangelische-reformierten Kirche dargestellt und den Quellen belegt*, 2 vols. (Zurich: Orell, Fussli, 1944-47), 1:8; Ferdinand Christian Baur, *Lehrbuch der Christlichen Dogmengeschichte* (Tübingen:Fues, 1858), 279-84. The turning point came in 1922 when Herman Bauke questioned the centrality of any one single doctrine. See Herman Bauke, *Dei Probleme der Theologie Calvins* (Leipzig: Hinrichs'schen, 1922), 20. Since Bauke, two strands are discernible: the first nodding in his direction whilst insisting on what may be regarded as the 'heart' of Calvin's theology. Amongst these, T. F. Torrance's christological approach and Edward A. Dowey's emphasis upon the knowledge of God have been the most influential. Alister McGrath contends that Jesus Christ forms the central feature of Calvin's theology. See Alister McGrath, *A Life of John Calvin* (Oxford: Basil Blackwell, 1990), 149. It will be a part of the contention of this book that a consistent christological focus in Calvin cannot be sustained in his preaching on Job. Indeed, the lack of Christology at points where the text of Job might lead one to expect it, is one of the more telling features of these sermons. The other strand since Bauke takes his position further, insisting that Calvin's theology is essentially contradictory. Amongst these, John Leith, in his "Calvin's Theological Method and the Ambiguities in his Theology," in *Reformation Studies*, ed. F. H. Littell (Richmond: John Knox, 1962); and Richard Stauffer, "Dieu, la création et la providence dans l'oeuvre homilétique de Calvin," *La Revue Réformée 27-28* (1976-77), 196-207. Mary

Potter Engel has attempted to bridge this gap by way of resorting to the idea of different perspectives in Calvin. For a sympathetic, though ultimately critical, review of this attempt, see Tony Lane, "Recent Calvin Literature: A Review Article," *Themelios* 16 (1991), 21-22.

It is the contention of this work that the Joban sermons reflect no single doctrine as a 'controlling principle', but that a string of substantive concerns form a spectrum of exegetical and pastoral concerns for the Reformer, even when some appear more dominant than others and when taken together may appear paradoxical. Charles Partee has made a significant point in contributing to this discussion of a central dogma in Calvin's theology. "It is difficult, if not impossible," he writes, "to approach Calvin's theology without a point of view, and some points of viewing are more adequate than others" (Charles Partee, "Calvin's Central Dogma Again," *The Sixteenth Century Journal* 18.2 , 1987, 192). Partee goes on to speak of several keys that unlock Calvin's theology, whilst emphasising the theme of union with Christ.

[52] Care needs to be taken, however, since it has been questioned as to whether or not it is possible to isolate a comprehensive Calvinian anthropology from his doctrine of God. See the reviews by Muller and Partee noted above.

[53] Cf. Barth's comment that sixteenth-century Reformers lacked an adequate (biblical) understanding of human personality. *Church Dogmatics*, III:2, 384.

[54] 39 (Job 10:7-15), 181.a.35. *Voila Dieu qui nous a tellement humiliez en nostre generation, que cependant il veut que sa vertu, et iustice, et sagesse soyent tant mieux cognues* [*CO* 33:483]. Even man's fingernails are "a lookingglasse of Gods prouidence to vs." 39 (Job 10:7-15), 183.a.43. *Un miroir de la providence de Dieu* [*CO* 33:488].

[55] 39 (Job 10:7-15), 180.a.64. *Dieu par maniere de dire, se mire et se contemple aux hommes: ce n'est point sans cause qu'il a regardé tout ce qu'il avoit fait, et qu'il l'a trouvé bon. Or est-il ainsi que l'homme est le principal ouvrage et le plus excellent qui soit entre toutes les creatures* [*CO* 33:481]. Cf. Niesel, *The Theology of Calvin*, trans. Harold Knight (Philadelphia: The Westminster Press, 1956), 64.

[56] "Not that the very substance (as men terme it) of our bodies and of our soules is an euill thing: for we be God's workmanship...Our bodies in their owne being, are the good creatures of God." 58 (Job 15:11-16), 274.a.25. *Non pas que la substance (comme on appelle) de nos corps, et de nos ames soit une chose mauvaise: car nous sommes creatures de Dieu... essence sont creatures de Dieu bonnes* [*CO* 33:728].

[57] 12 (Job 3:11-19), 56.a.43. *Conceuë au ventre de la mere* [*CO* 33:162]. Cf. Institutes I.xv.6 [*CO* 2:140-141].

[58] 28 (Job 7:7-15), 128.b.52. *Dieu leur a inspiré sa vertu* [*CO* 33:348]. Cf. "Our soules are not immortall of their owne power, nother is the lyfe of them enclosed in themselues as though it had his roote there. Where is their lyfe then? In God. So farre foorthe then as God, putteth any droppe or spark of lyfe into menes soules: so farre foorth haue they liuelinesse in them, and not otherwise." 39 (Job 10:7-15), 184.a.33. *Nos ames ne sont point immortelles de*

*leur propre vertu, que leur vie n'est point là enclose, comme si elle y avoit sa racine. Où est-ce donc qu'est leur vie? En Dieu. Entant donc que Dieu met quelque goutte et quelque estincelle de vie en l'ame des hommes, voilà comme il y a vigeur, et non autrement* [*CO* 33:491]. Cf. Torrance, *Calvin's Doctrine of Man*, 27; Niesel, 66.

[59] 107 (Job 29:18-25), 504.a.32. *Or maintenant la partie la plus excellente de nous, n'est ce pas l'ame? Et l'ame comment doit-elle estre entretenue? Ce n'est point par boire ne manger, mais il y a une chose qui est convenable à sa nature, c'est que nous ayons raison et intelligence, afin que nostre vie ne soit point brutale, que nous monstrions que nous sommes creatures formees à l'image de Dieu* [*CO* 34:577]. Cf. "The cheef part of men consisteth not in the shape that is seen with our eye, but in that which dwelleth within it." 39 (Job 10:7-15), 183.a.51. *Le principal des hommes ne consiste point en ceste figure qu'on voit à l'oeil: mais en ce qu'il habite là dedans* [*CO* 33:488]. Bouwsma incorrectly references this as CO 33:480, and in addition alludes to it as an example of the body's imprisonment of the soul. *Op. cit.*, 79. This appears to go beyond the meaning of the words Calvin uses at this point. However, in an earlier sermon, he does say: "Our bodies are prisons, as darke to hinder vs from the beholding of God, as if we were alreadie vnder the earth." 17 (Job 4:20-5:2), 75.a.43. *Car nos corps sont des prisons aussi obscures pour empescher que nous ne regardions à Dieu, comme si desia nous estions sous terre* [*CO* 33:210].

[60] 39 (Job 10:7-15), 181.a.65. *Il y a intelligence et raison, il y a verité* [*CO* 33:483].

[61] 103 (Job 28:10-28), 484.a.62. *Dieu n'a point mis les hommes en ce monde pour les priver de toute intelligence: car il ne veut point qu'ils soyent semblables à des asnes ou à des chevaux, il les a douëz de raison, et a voulu qu'ils fussent entendus* [*CO* 34:523]. Cf. 94 (Job 25:1-6), 442.a.17 [*CO* 34:411]; 137 (Job 35:8-11), 645.b.45, 646.a.38 [*CO* 35:237,238]; 53 (Job 14:1-4), 248.a.22 [*CO* 33:659]. This draws from Bouwsma a flurry of comments about Calvin's "intellectualized Christianity." Far from having forgotten his medieval background, he was evidently steeped in the classical heritage still. In addition, Bouwsma adds: "The Reformation slogan *scriptura sola* was intrinsically naïve; and Calvin's claim that Scripture was his 'only guide,' and acquiescence in its 'plain doctrines,' his 'constant rule of wisdom,' could never have been more than an aspiration." *Op. cit.*, 98.

[62] 101 (Job 27:19-28:9), 476.b.57. *Voyons-nous un homme du tout idiot, qui n'ait point de sens ne de raison? Là il nous faut arrester: car c'est un miroir de nostre nature. D'où vient la raison et l'intelligence que nous avons? N'est-ce point un don singulier que Dieu nous a fait? Ainsi donc tous ceux qui ont esprit et intelligence, qu'ils cognoissent que Dieu les a douez d'une telle grace, et qu'ils en sont d'autant plus obligez à luy... nostre Seigneur en fait les uns plus aigus que les autres, qu'ils ont industrie pour venir à bout de ce qu'ils entrepennent, qu'ils concluent, qu'ils deliberent, qu'ils font prudemment toutes leurs affaires, et comprendront en peu de temps*

beaucoup de choses: les autres sont tardifs et pesans, tellement qu'il faut frapper comme à grans coups de marteau, quand on leur voudra apprendre quelque chose: une telle diversité qui est entre les hommes, monstre clairement que si nous avons quelque vertu de bien iuger et discerner, c'est un don especial de Dieu* [CO 34:503]. "Beetles" (Fr. *marteau*) refer to an implement consisting of a heavy weight, usually of wood, with a handle or stock, used for driving wedges or pegs.

⁶³ 39 (Job 10:7-15), 184.a.9. *Quand chacun de nous est engendré, voila la bouë qui se monstre, c'est à dire, que nous sommes pleins d'infection et d'ordure* [CO 33:490].

⁶⁴ "For wheras God created our soules good, they notwithstanding are infected with euill and there is not one droppe of goodnesse in the which is not stained and utterly imbaced." 58 (Job 15:11-16), 274.a.31. *Car nos ames estans créees de Dieu bonnes toutes fois elles sont infectees du mal, et n'y a point une seule goutte de bien qui ne soit infecté, qui ne soit aneanti* [CO 33:728-729].

⁶⁵ "In what state doeth God find vs when wee come out of our mothers womb? It is true that the naughtinesse which is in vs is not perceyued: but yet haue we the seede thereof inclosed in vs, so as we bee cursed already bycause wee come of acursed and crabbed stocke." 52 (Job 13:23-28) 246.a.44. *En quel estat est ce que Dieu nous trouve quand nous sortons du ventre de la mere? Il est vrai qu'on n'apperçoit pas encores la malice qui est en nous: mais si est-ce que nous en avons la semence enclose, que nous sommes desia maudits pource que nous sommes d'une race maudite et perverse* [CO 33:654].

⁶⁶ 4 (Job 1:6-8), 17.b.40. *Car il n'y a que mal* [CO 33:65]. Cf. "We see also how men be wholly giuen to euill, in so much as they peruert the things that are good and holie, and when God hath declared his will vnto them, they turne it altogither backward and to the flat contrarie." 3 (Job 1:1), 11.b.33. *Au reste nous voyons aussi comme les hommes sont adonnez du tout à mal, veu qu'ils pervertissent les choses bonnes et sainctes: et quand Dieu leur a declaré sa volonté, ils la convertissent tout au rebours, et à l'opposite* [CO 33:49]. Cf. "We haue not so much as one drop of goodnesse." 58 (Job 15:11-16), 274.b.56. *Qu'il n'y a en nous que confusion horrible, que nous n'avons point une seule goutte de bien* [CO 33:730].

⁶⁷ "They are abhominable, and filthy, and drinke iniquitie as water: that is to say, their proper nurrishment is sinne, and there is not so much as one droppe of goodnesse to be found in them: and to be short, lyke as the body draweth hi[s] sustenance of meate and drinke: so also men haue none other stuffe in them but sinne: all is corrupted.... When God hathe looked downe, and when he hathe examined men throughly, there is not one, no not euen one, but hee is infected and stinking before him, and lothely in his sight." 58 (Job 15:11-16), 274.a.19. ... *qu'ils sont abominables, qu'ils sont puants, ils hument l'iniquité comme l'eau? C'est à dire, leur propre nourriture est peché, et on ne trouvera point une seule goutte de bien en eux: bref tout*

*ainsi que le corps tirera sa substance de la viande, et du boire: anssi les hommes n'ont autre substance en eux que peché, tout y est corrompu... Que quand Dieu a regardé, qu'il a fait examen sur les hommes, qu'il n'y a point eu un seul, non iusques à un qui ne soit infecté et puant devant luy, et lequel il n'ait en abomination* [CO 33:728-729]. Cf. Torrance, *Calvin's Doctrine of Man*, 87 n10.

[68] 4 (Job 1:6-8), 16.a.19. *Comme quand le peché est en la nature des hommes, ce n'est pas que Dieu l'y ait mis de creation, mais c'est pource que Satan a espandu sa malice plus loin, quand l'homme a esté seduit par son astuce pour subvertir le bien de Dieu* [CO 33:60].

[69] 5 (Job 1:9-12), 19.a.64. *Qu'il descouvre le mal qui est vonlontiers aux hommes* [CO 33:69].

[70] "... we haue cause to sighe and sob, for asmuch as we be in a bottomlesse pit of all miseries, so long as we be here... the state of menne is miserable: but wee must consider wherefore God hath made vs subiect to so many inconueniences: namely because of Sinne." 11 (Job 3:2-10), 48.b.40. *qu'il y a dequoy gemir et pleurer, d'autant que quand nous sommes ici, nous sommes en un abysme de toutes miseres... que la condition des hommes estoit miserable: mais il nous faut regarder pourquoy Dieu nous a assubiettis à tant de maux: c'est à cause du peché* [CO 33:144].

[71] 53 (Job 14:1-4), 250.a.67. *Et à quelle fin tend tout cela, sinon à ce que les hommes se plaisent, et qu'ils cuident avoir quelque bien en eux? Non pas qu'on ose dire que l'homme est suffisant pour se sauver. Car on confessera en la Papauté que nous aurons besoin de la grace de Dieu, non seulement à ce qu'il nous pardonne nos pechez, mais qu'il nous aide de son S. Esprit. Cependant toutes fois, ce n'est pas qu'ils disent que tout procede de lui. Les Papistes ne confesseront pas cela: mais ils disent, qu'ayans quelque portion de bien, nous avons besoin que Dieu nous subviene. Voila donc Dieu qui sera coadiuteur: c'est à dire, il nous aidera en nos infirmitez, mais il faut que de nostre part nous soyons ses compagnons. Le diable a tellement ensorcelé les hommes, qu'il leur a fait à croire, qu'ils sont ici ie ne say quoy: mais cependant nous voyons aussi quant à ce monde comme les hommes se plaisent* [CO 33:665].

[72] "God hath fashioned vs after his owne image and likenesse, whereby he meaneth to haue his glorie shine in vs." 11 (Job 3:1-10), 48.b.16. *Quand il n'y auroit que cela, que Dieu nous forme à son image et semblance, qu'il veut que sa gloire reluise en nous* [CO 33:143].

[73] "Adam was created after the image of God, and indewed with excellent giftes of grace, yea and vnsubiect to death. And what importeth that image of God? A perfectnesse, a rightuousnesse, and a soundnesse wherethrough God vttered his greate riches, so that in effect man was as a mirrour of the excellent glorie that shyneth fully in God." 53 (Job 14:1-4), 248.b.22. *Adam a esté creé à l'image de Dieu, doué de graces excellentes, et mesmes il n'estoit pas subiet à la mort. Car ceste image de Dieu qu'emporte-elle? Une droiture, une iustice et integrité, que Dieu avoit là desployé ses grans thresors,*

*tellement qu'en somme l'homme estoit comme un miroir de ceste gloire excellente qui reluit pleinement en Dieu* [*CO* 33:659-660]. Cf. "For hee hath giuen men vnderstanding, and printed his Image in them... I cannot looke vppon another, but I must needes see my selfe as in a looking glasse." 113 (Job 31:9-15), 534.b.5. *Il leur a donné intelligence, imprimant son image en eux. D'autre part ie ne puis pas contempler un homme, que ie ne me voye là comme en un miroir* [*CO* 34:660]. And again: "God doth (as a ma[n] might say) looke vpon himselfe, and behold himselfe as it were in a glasse." 39 (Job 10:7-15), 180.a.64. *Dieu par maniere de dire, se mire et se contemple aux hommes* [*CO* 33:481]. Cf. *Institutes* I.xv.3 [*CO* 2:136-138].

[74] "Must wee not pretende to bee loued at Gods hande for any desertes of our owne, but bicause he sees we are his workemanship. True it is that we are his workemanship alreadie, in that wee bee men: but there is yet more, that is to wit, he hath fashioned vs new again after his own Image, through the grace of our Lorde Iesus Christ." 66 (Job 14:16-22), 261.a.23. *Il ne faut point donc que nous pretendions d'estre aimez de Dieu pour aucuns merites qui soyent en nous, mais d'autant qu'il voit que nous sommes son ouvrage. Or il est vrai, entant que nous sommes hommes, que desia nous sommes sa fracture: mais il y a plus, c'est qu'il nous a reformez à son image par la grace de nostre Seigneur Iesus Christ* [*CO* 33:693].

At one point, Calvin makes a distinction between male and female in his discussion on the *imago Dei*. Citing 1 Corinthians 11:7, the point where Paul refers to the issue of covering the head in worship, Calvin says: "True it is that the image of GOD is printed alyke in them bothe: but yet is the woman inferiour too the man, and wee must go by those degrees whiche God hathe set in the order of nature. So then, it is reason that God shoulde bee glorified bothe in males and females: howebeit that hee must cheefly bee glorified at the birthe of a manchilde." 11 (Job 3:2-10), 49.b.45. *Il est vray que l'image de Dieu est bien inprimee par tout: mais si est-ce que la femme est inferieure à l'homme; il faut que nous allions par ces degrez-là que Dieu a instituez en l'ordre de nature. Ainsi donc c'est raison que Dieu soit glorifié et aux masles, et aux femelles: toutesfois il doit estre principalement glorifié, quand un homme, c'est à dire un masle sera nay...*[*CO* 33:146-147].

[75] "Adam was formed after the image of God, to haue vnderstanding of all things that pertayned to him." 102 (Job 28:10-28), 481.b.30. *Adam qui est formé à l'image de Dieu, pour avoir intelligence de tout ce qui luy appartenoit* [*CO* 34:515].

[76] As Gerrish indicates, Calvin adopts a three-fold schema of salvation-history in the *Institutes*: creation, Fall and redemption, consummation. See Brian Gerrish, *Reformers in Profile*, 155. Actually, as some of these citations that follow indicate, Calvin distinguishes, in these sermons, the fallen condition from the renewed condition in Christ to an extent that would necessitate a four-fold schema. Engel criticises Torrance at this very point of insufficient sensitivity to these differences. *Op. cit.*, 10-24.

[77] "For God created vs after his own Image, and that Image was marred by

the sinne of Adam." 137 (Job 35:8-11), 646.a.62. *...car il nous avoit creez à son image, et ceste image là a esté corrompue par le peché d'Adam* [*CO* 35:238].

[78] "For we were created after the Image of God. And what maner of Image is it nowe? It is a disfigured one: wee be so defaced, that the marke which God had put intoo vs to bee glorified thereby, is turned into his dishonour." 122 (Job 33:1-7), 576.b.12. *Nous avons esté creez à l'image de Dieu: et ceste image-la quelle est elle? Elle est desfiguree: nous sommes tellement pervertis, que la marque que Dieu avoit mise en nous pour y estre glorifié, est tournee en son opprobre* [*CO* 35:47-48]. Cf. the language in the Deuteronomy sermons, in which Calvin speaks of the *imago* being "wholly defaced and wiped out in vs by the sinne of Adam: we are accursed, we are by nature shut out from all hope of life." 141 (Deut. 24:19-22), 869.a.2. *Nostre Seigneur nous a creez à son image et semblance. Il est vray: mais tout cela estoit effacé en nous par le peché d'Adam, nous sommes maudits, nous sommes de nature forclos de toute esperance de vie* [*CO* 28:205].

[79] "All the light which we haue of nature, is turned into darknesse." 137 (Job 35:8-11), 646.a.53. *Tout la clarté que nous avons de bature est convertie en tenebres* [*CO* 35:288].

[80] 56 (Job 14:16-22), 261.a.43. *Il ne faut pas que nous regardions seulement à nostre creation premiere (car la fiance que nous devons prendre seroit bien maigre, d'autant que l'image de Dieu est comme effacee en nous par le peché d'Adam)* [*CO* 33:694]. Calvin occasionally speaks to the issue of the relationship between Adam's sin and the rest of mankind. In Sermon 53, for example, in which the issue of sin and depravity are very much to the fore, Calvin has this to say: "Like as God created all mankynd after his owne image in the persone of Adam: euen so also through Adams sin, not only Adam himself, but consequently also all his offspring were depryued and shet out from the grace that had bene bestowed vpon him. And whereof commeth that? Bycause wee were all inclosed within his persone, according to the will of God." 53 (Job 14:1-4), 248.b.49. *Que comme Dieu en la personne d'Adam avoit creé à son image tout le genre humain: ainsi Adam par le peché n'est pas seulement privé et banni des graces qui lui estoient conferees: mais tout son lignage par consequent. Et d'où procede cela? Pource que nous estions tous enclos en sa personne, selon la volonté de Dieu* [*CO* 33:660-661]. Niesel points out on the basis of this citation that Calvin held to a creationist view of the origin of the soul. "Original sin does not devolve upon us through any physical process such as biological heredity. It is no inherited malady." Niesel, *The Theology of Calvin*, 84. Calvin goes on to say a little later in the same sermon: "For we were not created to the end that death should haue dominion ouer vs. That is come vpon vs from our father Adam, in somuch as all of vs are giltie [of his sinne]." 249.a.38. *Car nous n'avons point esté creez à telle condition, que la mort dominast sur nous: cela est survenu de nostre pere, tellement que nous en sommes tous coulpables* [*CO* 33:662].

*A Good Case: Calvin's Understanding of the Book of Job* 73

⁸¹ 128 (Job 33:29-34:3), 605.a.11. *monstres et pires que les bestes brutes* [*CO* 35:126]. Cf. the sermons on Ephesians: "If a man, then, is considered in himself and in his own nature, what shall he be able to say? See, a creature cursed of God and worthy to be refused acceptance in the common range of all other creatures, even worms, flies, lice and vermin. For there is more worth in all the world's vermin than there is in man. For man is a creature in which God's image is effaced, and the good he put into it corrupted." *Sermons on Ephesians* (Edinburgh: Banner of Truth, 1973), 133. *Quand donc l'homme sera considéré en soy et en sa nature, que pourra-on dire? Voilá une creature maudite de Dieu, laquelle est digne d'estre reiettee du rang commun de toutes autres creatures, des vers, des poux, des puces et des vermines: car il y a plus de valeur en toutes les vermines du monde, qu'il n'y a pas en; l'homme: car c'est une creature où l'image de Dieu est effacee, où le bien qu'il y avoit mis est corrompu* [*CO* 51:355]. For another reference to "defaced" in these Ephesian sermons, see earlier in the same sermon: "We are fashioned anew according to the image that was lost and utterly defaced in us by Adam's sin." *Op. cit.*, 129. *Que nous soyons reformez à ceste image qui a esté perdue, et laquelle par le peché d'Adam a esté effacee en nous* [*CO* 51:350]. Cf. David Holwerda, "The Christian Self-Image," in *Exploring the Heritage of John Calvin*, ed. David Holwerda (Grand Rapids: Baker Books, 1976), 80. Several writers have cited this reference incorrectly in their respective works, suggesting that it is taken from the Joban sermons, e.g., T. F. Torrance, *Calvin's Doctrine of Man*, 88 (as Serm. On Job 2:1f.); David Cairns, *The Image of God in Man*, 296n14 (as, Sermon on Job 2,1 seq.); B. A. Gerrish, "The Mirror of God's Goodness: A Key Metaphor in Calvin's View of Man," in *The Old Protestantism and the New* (The University of Chicago Press, 1982), 346n9 (where he admits to citing Cairns). Calvin can, too, make the point that there is in man something additional that is not found in the beasts: "the brute beasts are not parttakers of the life that is in men, but that there is in men a dignitie farre greater and of much more value." 39 (Job 10:7-12), 181.b.1. *ne leur est point commune avec les bestes brutes: mais qu'il y a une dignité beaucoup plus grande et plus à priser* [*CO* 33:483].

⁸² *Summa*, I-II.74. Torrance makes the point that Calvin agrees with the Roman Catholic view of the *imago Dei* as related in some way to the *donum superadditum*. *Calvin's Doctrine of Man*, 68-69. But note should be taken, too, of Calvin's own criticisms of Roman Catholic interpretations of this in *Institutes* II.ii.2,4,12,16. [*CO* 2:186-190, 195-196, 199].

⁸³ "True it is, that when wee come intoo this worlde, wee bring some remnant of Gods Image wherein Adam was created: howebeit the same Image is so disfigured, as wee bee full of unrightuousnesse, and there is nothing but blindnesse and ignorance in our minde." 55 (Job 14:13-15), 259.b.21. *Il est vrai que nous apportons encores quelque trace de l'image de Dieu, en laquelle avoit esté creé Adam, mais ceste image-la est tellement desfiguree que nous sommes pleins d'iniquitez, en nostre esprit il n'y a qu'aveuglement et ignorance* [*CO* 33:689-690]. Cf. "In the midst of our ignorance and of all

our errour and superstitions, our Lord doeth hold vs still convicted and bound vnto him in an inestimable bonde, for that he aduanceth vs aboue the brute beastes, by leauing vs some discretion imprinted in our heartes too discerne good and euill." 137 (Job 35:8-11), 646.a.69. *C'est qu'au milieu de toute nostre ignorance et de tous nos erreurs, et de toutes nos superstitions, encores nostre Seigneur nous tient convaineus, que nous avons une obligation inestimable envers lui de ce qu'il nous esleve par dessus les bestes brutes, quand il nous laisse quelque discretion de bien et de mal imprimee en nos coeurs* [*CO* 35:238-239]. Cf. "God to the intent to make vs excell Oxen, Asses, Dogges, and Swyne, hath printed his image in vs. And wherein in consisteth this image, but in the hauing of discretion to descerne between good and euill?" 20 (Deut. 4:3-6), 120.a.20. *Dieu pour nous rendre plus excellens que les boeufs, les asnes, les chiens, les pourceaux, a imprimé son image en nous: et ceste image ici en quoy consiste elle, sinon que nous ayons discretion du bien et du mal?* [*CO* 26:120]. Cf. Calvin's suggestion that in the diversity of fallen human nature we see "some remaining traces [*notas*] of the image of God, which distinguish the entire human race from the other creatures." *Institutes* II.ii.17. *Caeterum in hac diversitate conspicimus tamen aliquas imaginis Dei superstites notas, quae totum humanum genus ab aliis creaturis distinguant.*[*CO* 2:200]. Cf. Comm. On Genesis 1:26 [*CO* 23:25-26]; Comm. On James 3:9 where he speaks of the *lineaments* [*lineamenta*] of the image [*CO* 55:411]; and in the Comm. On Genesis 9:6, where he speaks of the *remnant* of the image: "Should any object, that this divine image has been obliterated, the solution is easy: first, there yet exists some remnant of it, so that man is possessed of no small dignity." *Si quis obiiciat imaginem illam deletam esse: solutio facilis est, manere adhuc aliquid residuum, ut praestet non parva dignitate homo* [*CO*23:147]. For other examples, see Engel,*Op. cit.*, 15-16; Torrance, *Calvin's Doctrine of Man*, 87-95.

[84] "Wee cannot atteyne to the full knowledge of Gods workes and to the causes of the same, vntill we be transformed into his image." 82 (Job 21:22-34), 384.b.30. *Que nous ne pouvons point pleinement cognoistre ce que c'est des oeuvres de Dieu, et la raison d'icelles, iusques à ce que nous soyons transfigurez en son image* [*CO* 34:256]. And again, alluding to 1 John 3:2: "It say it behoueth vs to holde ourselues within our owne slendernesse, praying God to rid vs of this mortall flesh, to the intent we may behold him as he is, when we become like vnto him... and... in wayting for that day, he reforme vs presently after his owne image, to the end we may behold him the better." 143 (Job 26:25-33), 671.a.42. *Lors, di-ie, il nous faut tenir en nostre petitesse, prians Dieu qu'il nous despouille de ceste chair mortelle, afin que nous le voyons tel qu'il est, quand nous serons semblables à luy, ... Et au reste en attendant ce iour-la, qu'il nous reforme auiourd'huy à son image, afin que nous le puissions mieux contempler* [*CO* 35:305].

[85] "The image of God is imprinted in vs, bycause we haue vnderstanding and reason, bycause wee discerne between good and euill, and bycause

men are borne too haue some order and common societie among themselues, so as euery manne hath a conscience of his owne to tell him what is euill and what is good." *Que l'image de Dieu est imprimee en nous, d'autant que nous avons intelligence et raison, que nous discernons entre le bien et le mal, que les hommes sont nais pour avoir quelque ordre, quelque police entre eux: qu'un chacun a sa conscience qui lui rend tesmoignage que cela est mauvais, que cela est bon.* 39 (Job 10:7-15), 183.b.37 [*CO* 33:489]. Cf. A. A. Hoekema, *Created in God's Image* (Grand Rapids: Eerdmans, 1986), 42-49.

[86] 83 (Job 22:1-8), 390.b.17. *Ainsi donc quand nous faisons bien, cela n'est pas de nous (car on n'en sauroit arracher que toute ordure et povreté, comme nous sommes corrompus de nature) mais nostre Seigneur espand sa bonté et sa iustice sur nous. Si donc il nous fait ceste grace en nous regenerant par son sainct Esprit, que nous vivions sainctement, nous sommes comme des miroirs ausquels son image est là comme representee: et c'est une clarté laquelle vient d'enhaut, mais elle se monstre ici bas* [*CO* 34:272]. In a sermon cited earlier, Calvin makes a similar remark regarding regeneration and its effects upon the *imago Dei* in the form of prayer: "But forasmuch as God of his owne infinite mercie hath renued vs, and adopted vs too bee his children in our Lorde Iesus Christ, and imprinted his Image againe in vs; therein wee bee hys woorkemanship, and maye come with our heades vpright too call vpon him, and assure ourselues that he will not shake vs off, but that wee shall be welcome too him." 56 (Job 14:16-22), 261.a.46. *Mais puis que Dieu par sa misericorde infinie nous a reformez, et nous a adoptez pour ses enfans en nostre Seigneur Iesus Christ, qu'il a imprimé son image en nous: voila comme nous sommes sa facture afin que nous puissions venir la teste levee pour l'invoquer, que nous puissions este asseurez qu'il ne nous reiettera point, mais que nous lui serons à gré* [*CO* 33:694].

[87] 144 (Job 37:1-6), 678.b.36. *Car combien qu'il se soit manifesté à tout le monde, et que toutes creatures soyent conviees à le louër, et mesmes qu'elles y soyent contraintes et forcees, si est-ce qu'il y a bien une autre vertu et plus magnifique en la doctrine qui nous est preschee* [*CO* 35:324].

[88] 103 (Job 28:10-24), 485.b.44. *Pource que là il n'y a rien qui ne nous soit utile* [*CO* 34:526]. Cf. Calvin's words in the *Institutes*: "For Scripture is the school of the Holy Spirit, in which, as nothing is omitted that is both necessary and useful to know, so nothing is taught but what is expedient to know." (III.xxi.3). *Est enim scriptura schola spiritus sancti, in qua ut nihil praetermissum est scitu et necessarium et utile, sic nihil docetur nisi quod scire conducat* [*CO* 2:681]. And again, in Sermon 57: "For what is the marke that God ameth at when hee setteth his woorde afore us? It is too holde vs in awe, and too make vs too walke in his feare, and obedience: and also to make vs put our whole trust in him, and too call vpon him, seeing wee bee destitute of the spirite of wisedom, rightuousnesse, power and life." 57 (Job 15:1-10), 267.b.5. *Car à quoy est-ce que Dieu tend, quand il nous propose sa parole? C'est de nous tenir en bride, et nous faire cheminer en sa crainte, et en son obeissance: et puis que ayons du tout nostre fiance en luy, que nous*

*l'invoquions, veu que nous sommes destituez d'esprit de sagesse, de iustice, de vertu, et de vie* [CO 33:711].

[89] 128 (Job 33:29-34:3), 605.a.10. *pervertissent l'ordre de nature, mesmes qu'ils sont comme monstres et pires que les bestes brutes* [CO 35:126].

[90] 77 (Job 20:26-29), 362.a.6. *feu... afin de purger toutes les ordures et superfluitez qui sont en nous* [CO 34:194].

[91] 6 (Job 1:13-19), 28.b.13. *les armures* [CO 33:92].

[92] 122 (Job 33:1-7), 574.a.4. *quand Dieu nous fait ceste grace de parler en son nom qu'il faut bien que nous donnions autorité à sa parole, et que nous la facions valoir* [CO 35:41].

[93] 14 (Job 4:1-6), 64.a.11. *Or par cela nous devons estre tant plus incitez à recevoir la parole de Dieu avec un desir, et avec une affection allaigre et amiable, quand nous voyons que tout ce qui nous est propre pour nostre salut, est là comprins* [CO 33:182].

[94] 95 (Job 26:1-7), 445.a.10. *fortifier ceux qui sont debiles, et les relever* [CO 34:419].

[95] 16 (Job 3:12-19), 73.a.8. *nous contentions de l'escriture saincte* [CO 33:204].

[96] 80 (Job 21:13-15), 376.a.8. *Puis qu'ainsi est donc que Dieu nous est present par le moyen de sa parole...* [CO 34:232].

[97] 147 (Job 38:1-4), 689.a.60. *Car quand nous aurons bien conté et rabbatu le tout, il est certain que nostre Seigneur nous propose une maiesté en sa parole, qui est pour faire trembler toutes creatures: il y a aussi une simplicité, afin de la faire recevoir aux plus ignorans et idiots: il y a une clarté si grande que nous y pouvons mordre sans avoir esté à l'escole, voire si nous sommes dociles: car ce n'est pas sans cause que notamment il s'appelle maistre des humbles et des petits* [CO 35:352]. For a discussion of Calvin's use of the metaphor of Scripture as a "schoolmauster," see, T. H. L. Parker, *Calvin's Preaching*, 25-28.

[98] 8 (Job 2:1-6), 35.a. 30. *Que l'Escriture s'accommode à nostre raison* [CO 33:109].

[99] 17 (Job 4:20-5:2), 78.b. 40. *Que nous ne devons appeter de rien savoir, sinon ce que Dieu nous a declaré de sa propre bouche* [CO 33:219].

[100] 124 (Job 33:14-17), 583.a.12. *et quand sa parole nous est obscure, ce n'est point qu'elle soit telle de soy, cela ne procede sinon de nostre aveuglement que nous avons nos esprits eslourdis* [CO 35:65].

[101] 122 (Job 33:1-7), 575.a.40. *Que si une doctrine qui est mise en avant, est saincte, et que nous en soyons convaincus: si nous ne sommes humiliez en toute crainte pour nous y renger, nous ne serons point coulpables d'avoir resisté à l'homme qui parloit à nous: mais c'est autant comme si nous despitions le Dieu vivant* [CO 35:44].

[102] T. H. L. Parker, *Calvin's Preaching*, 23.

[103] 22 (1 Tim. 3:2-4), 269.a.40. *Car sainct Paul ne veut pas qu'on face ici une parade seulement, et qu'un homme se monstre et que chacun luy applaudisse pour dire, O voilà bien parlé, ô le grand sçavoir, ô l'esprit*

*subtil! Il n'est pas question de tout cela: mais il faut que celuy qui presche, commence par soy, et puis qu'il tasche d'attirer tout le troupeau à l'obeissance de Dieu, et qu'il y aille en crainte, en humilité et en solicitude: cependant que tous cognoissent que c'est pour eux que Dieu a establi un tel ordre. Quand un homme sera monté en chaire, est-ce afin qu'il soit regardé de loin, et qu'il soit en preeminence? Nenni: mais c'est afin que Dieu parle à nous par la bouche d'un homme: et il nous fait ceste grace-là de se presenter ici, et veut qu'un homme mortel soit son messager: et par cela il veut aussi esprouver l'obeissance de nostre foy.* [CO 53:266].

[104] 144 (Job 37:1-6), 676.a.54. *Ici Eliu ne parle point de la parole qui nous est iournellement preschee afin que nous soyons enseignez par icelle, et où Dieu nous declare privement sa bonté: mais il appelle la voix de Dieu bruyante, et le son procedant de sa bouche...* [CO 35:318].

[105] 1 (Job 1:1), 4.b.25. *A fin que nous sachions que nous sommes creez à sa gloire, pour le servir et adorer: car combien qu'il n'ait pas affaire de nous, comme auront nos prochains, et que cela ne luy apporte ne chaud ne froid, si est-ce qu'il a voulu avoir des creatures raisonnables, qui le cognneussent, et l'ayans cognu, luy rendissent ce qu'il luy appartient* [CO 33:31]. The literature and research on Calvin's doctrine of the knowledge of God is extensive, and to elucidate it all here would take us beyond the scope of this thesis. We shall return to this theme in chapter 3, when we consider the doctrine of God's incomprehensibility.

[106] Ford Lewis Battles has called it , "The Kernel of Calvin's Faith." See *The Piety of John Calvin: An Anthology Illustrative of the Spirituality of the Reformer*, ed. and trans. Ford Lewis Battles (Grand Rapids: Baker Book House, 1978), 43; see also his essay, "*Calculus Fidei*: Some Ruminations on the Structure of the Theology of John Calvin," in *Interpreting John Calvin*, ed. Robert Benedetto (Grand Rapids: Baker Book House, 1966), 149.

[107] *Institutes* I.i.1. *Tota fere sapientiae nostrae summa, quae vera demum ac solida sapientia censeri debeat, duabus partibus constat, Dei cognitione et nostri* [CO 2:31]. For Calvin the knowledge of God is asserted in terms of several propositions: first, that it consists in more than the natural man's awareness of God; second, that it is more than any subjective experience we have of God; third, that it is more than knowing about God; and fourth, that is more than knowing God, in the sense that it intermingles with the knowledge we have of ourselves. Calvin, in fact, makes this point in the first sermon, cited above, by urging that we keep our eyes fastened "vpon God and our neybour."

[108] 40 (Job 10:16-17), 189.a.56. *Mais notons que Dieu nous a donné une façon de le cognoistre qui nous est propre et convenable: il nous pourroit bien bailler une clarté entiere et parfaite auiourd'hui: mais il voit que cela ne nous est point utile: et pourtant il nous en donne quelque portion certaine, il s'accommode à nous. Et ainsi qu'il ne nous face point mal d'avoir maintenant par mesure ceste cognoissance de Dieu, comme elle nous est donné en l'Escriture, attendans qu'il nous ait despouillez de ce*

*corps mortel, qu'il ait mesmes du tout reformé nos ames, qu'elles ne soyent plus ainsi enveloppes de ce qui est de l'homme, et de la terre, et mesmes de ce qu'il y a des vices procedans du peché d'Adam* [*CO* 33:504].

[109] Harold Dekker, *Sermons on Job* (Grand Rapids, Michigan: Baker Book House, 1979), xxviii.

[110] 1 (Job 1:1), 1.a.15. *Or l'histoire qui est ici escrite nous monstre, comme nous sommes en la main de Dieu, et que c'est à luy d'ordonner de nostre vie, et d'en disposer selon son bon plaisir, et que nostre office est, de nous rendre subiets à luy en toute humilité, et obeissance...* [*CO* 33:21].

[111] 2 (Job 1:2-5), 7.a.44. *...qu'il peut disposer de ses creatures à son plaisir, qu'il nous faut baisser les yeux encores que nous soyons confus, ne voyans point la raison pourquoi Dieu traitte ainsi rudement les hommes, et faut que nous confessions qu'il est iuste, attendans qu'il nous revele pourquoi c'est qu'il dispose les choses ainsi* [*CO* 33:38]. Cf. Sermon 5: "God hath the soueraine dominion ouer all his creatures, so as they must needes yeelde vnto him, and turne themselues whethersoeuer he thinketh good." 5 (Job 1:9-12), 22.a.27. *Mais d'autant que Dieu a l'empire souverain sur toutes ses creatures, et qu'il faut qu'il les plie, et les tourne là où bon luy semble* [*CO* 33:75].

[112] 80 (Job 21:13-15), 377.a.36. *Dieu declare par cela que nous ne pouvons lui estre vrayement suiets, iusques à taut que nous ayons cognu le droit qu'il a sur nous, et que nous lui ayons donné tous ses titres et qualitez. Il est nostre maistre et Seigneur: il faut donc que nous lui portions toute reverence* [*CO* 34:236].

[113] Providence is God's very active *gubernatio* of everything on earth. He is not only creator, but also provider and guide. Calvin based this dogma on the very will of God. "Since God's will is said to be the cause of all things, I have made his providence the determinative principle for all human plans and works, not only in order to display its force in the elect, who are ruled by the Holy Spirit, but also to compel the reprobate to obedience." *Institutes* I.xviii.2. *Summa haec sit: quum Dei voluntas dicitur rerum omnium esse causa, providentiam eius statui moderatricem in cunctis hominum consiliis et operibus, ut non tantum vim suam exserat in electis, qui spiritu sancto reguntur, sed etiam reprobos in obsequium cogat* [*CO* 2:170].

Calvin seemed particularly conscious of the providence of God in his personal life, as is evident from his testimony of what happened in Geneva, which he recorded in the preface to the commentary on the Psalms: "Thus it came to pass, that I was withdrawn from the study of philosophy, and was put to the study of law. To this pursuit I endeavored faithfully to apply myself, in obedience to the will of my father; but God, by the secret guidance of his providence, at length gave a different direction to my course." *Ita factum est, ut revocatus a philosophiae studio, ad leges discendas traherer, quibus tametsi ut patris voluntati obsequerer fidelem operam impendere conatus sum, Deus tamen arcano providentiae suae fraeno cursum meum alio tandem reflexit* [*CO* 31:21].

[114] *Institutes* I.xvi-xviii [*CO* 2:144-174]; "The Secret Providence of God," published as a separate treatise together with "The Eternal Predestination of God" in *Calvin's Calvinism*, trans. Henry Cole (Grand Rapids, MI: Reformed Publishing Association, nd), 223-256 [*CO* 8:347-366]; *Consensus Genevensis*, [*CO* 8:348-349]. In the opening section on providence in the *Institutes*, Calvin links the discussion with that of creation: "*Moreover*, to make God a momentary Creator, who once for all finished his work, would be cold and barren..." (I.xvi.1, emphasis added) [*CO* 8:347-366]. Calvin specifically refers to Job in this section. See I.xvii.2 [*CO* 2:155-156]. For Schreiner, for example, Calvin's understanding of the Book of Job is essentially the doctrine of providence. This is, of course, true, but the sermons reflect a variety of concerns as we intend to show in this chapter. For Calvin, as we shall argue, the Book of Job is about God Himself, God in His majesty and incomprehensibility. Providence provides for us a sub-set of the doctrine of God.

[115] 5 (Job 1:9-12), 22.b.14. *tellement que Satan ne peut sinon ce qui luy est permis.*[*CO* 33:77].

[116] *Ibid.*, 23.b.14. *Que rien n'estoit advenu sans sa providence* [*CO* 33:79].

[117] *Ibid.*, 23.a.12. *Or cependant Dieu trouvera le moyen, que le mal qui est en Satan nous sera converti à salut* [*CO* 33:78]. Calvin adds: "God turneth the euill into good, when he maketh all Satans stinges to serue vs as medicines, wherby he purgeth vs of the vyces that lye hid in vs." 23.a.47. *Nous voyons donc comme Dieu, convertit le mal en bien, quand il nous fait servir tous les aiguillons de Satan à medecine, et que par ce moyen-la il nous purge des vices qui sont cachez en nous* [*CO* 33:78-79].

[118] "We shall neuer attayne to the knowledge of Gods Maiestie, except we be caried vp aboue all our owne abilitie," Calvin adds in closing. Once again, it is God's Majesty that is singled out. *Ibid.*, 23.b.24. *Car nous ne parviendrons iamais à la cognoissance de la maiesté de Dieu, si ce n'est que nous soyons eslevez par dessus toutes nos facultez* [*CO* 33:80].

[119] For a fuller treatment, see Schreiner, *Where Shall Wisdom be Found?*, 95-105.

[120] 5 (Job 1:9-12), 22.b.47. *C'est le diable qui a suscité tout ce mal, quand David a ainsi nombré le peuple de Dieu.*[*CO* 33:77]. For a similar parallel with David, see 108 (Job 30:1-10), 508.a.10, in which Calvin comments on the cursing of David by Shimei (2 Samuel 16:5-14) and how David accepts the "heavenly providence (*providence celeste*)" of God [*CO* 34:587]. He continues: "Dauid, who was a man subiect to passions as we be, and yet notwithstanding submitteth himselfe willingly, when he perceiued it to be Gods will that hee should bee as it were torn in peeces, yea though it were wrongfully."*David, qui estoit homme suiet à passions comme nous: mais tant y a qu'il s'est assuietti volontairement, quand il a cognu que la volonté de Deiu estoit telle qu'il fust là comme desciré par pieces, voire combien que ce fust à tort* [*CO* 34:587].

[121] 108 (Job 30:1-10), 507.b.41. *Dieu avoit voulu declarer en luy une vertu especiale* [*CO* 34:586].

[122] 4 (Job 1:6-8), 14.a.58. *Que vivans ici bas, nous ne sommes point gouvernez par fortune, mais que Dieu a l'oeil sur nous, et qu'il y a toute autorité... Dieu a la conduite du monde, et que rien ne se fait, qui ne soit disposé par luy* [*CO* 33:57]. On Calvin's disavowal of chance, or fortune, see W. Niesel, *The Theology of Calvin*, trans. Harold Knight (Philadelphia: The Westminster Press, 1956), 70-79.

[123] 153 (Job 39:22-35), 720.a.49. *Dieu alors nous demonstre sa providence* [*CO* 35:433].

[124] 94 (Job 15:1-6), 441.a.32. *Car en quoy est-ce que consiste l'empire et la principauté qu'il a sur nous? C'est quand non seulement nous cognoissons sa vertu, mais sa bonté et sagesse infinie, sa iustice, sa misericorde, ses iugemens: quand nous avons cela, nous le glorifions. Or donc quand les hommes ne trouvent point de raison en ce que Dieu fait, quand ils l'accusent de cruauté, ou que par impatience ils se despittent à l'encontre de luy, ou qu'ils sont scandalisez de ce qu'il fait: il n'y a nulle doute qu'ils ne taschent de le despouiller de sa gloire divine: et cela ne se peut faire sans batailler contre luy* [*CO* 34:409]. The almost casual listing of God's attributes in the above citation is similar to the way Calvin speaks of the "virtues" or "attributes" of God in the *Institutes*. See the use of *virtutes Dei* in I.ii.1; v.7,9,10; x.2 [*CO* 2:34, 46, 47-48, 72-73]. See also the use of *attributa* in I.xiii.4, [*CO* 2:91-92], and *epitheta* in I.xiii.1 [*CO* 2:89-90]. Cf. the opening words of the 1536 edition: "Nearly the whole of sacred doctrine consists in these two parts: knowledge of God and of ourselves. Surely, we ought for the present to learn the following things about God. To hold with sure faith, first that he is infinite wisdom, righteousness, goodness, mercy, truth, power and life." *The Institutes of the Christian Religion* (1536), trans. Ford Lewis Battles (Grand Rapids: Eerdmans, 1975), 15. *Summa fere sacrae doctrinae duabus his partibus constat: Cognitione Dei ac nostri* [*CO* 1:27]. As Warfield notes, if this listing of the attributes does not survive in the final edition of the *Institutes*, something very like it appears in several passages as noted above. See Warfield, *Calvin and Augustine*, 166.

[125] 91 (Job 24:1-9), 427.a.18. *Que c'est une tentation bien mauvaise aux fideles, quand les choses sont confuses au monde, et qu'il semble que Dieu ne s'en mesle plus: mais que fortune gouverne et domine. Et voila qui a esté cause de ces proverbes diaboliques, Que tout se demene par cas fortuit, Qu'il y a une conduite aveugle des choses, et que Dieu se iouë des hommes comme de pelotes, qu'il n'y a ne raison ne mesure, ou bien que tout se gouverne par quelque necessité secrete, et que Dieu ne daigne pas penser de nous. Voila ces blasphemes qui ont regné de tout temps. Et pourquoy? Car (comme i'au desia dit) le sens humain s'esblouit, quand nous voulons iuger des choses confuses, et qui outrepassent nostre iugement et raison* [*CO* 34:371]. Calvin sometimes refers to fortune as *Epicureanism*. Cf. *Institutes* I.xvii.1 [*CO* 2:154]. Cf. "there is no erratic power or action or motion in creatures but they are governed by God's secret plan in such a way that nothing happens except what is knowingly and willingly decreed by him."

*Ab hac igitur infidelitate qui cavere volet, memoria semper teneat, non erraticam vel potentiam, vel actionem, vel motionem esse in creaturis; sed arcano Dei consilio sic regi, ut nihil contingat nisi ab ipso sciente et volente decretum.* Institutes I.xvi.3 [*CO* 2:147]. For other examples of the denial of fortune, see *Institutes* I.xvi.8-10 [*CO* 2:151-153]. For similar remarks in the commentaries, see his comment on Ezekiel 10:17: "God sustains the world by his energy, he governs everything, however remote, so that not even a sparrow falls to the ground without his decree." *Deus enim nunquam feriatur. Sustinet mundum sua virtute, minima quaeque gubernat, ut non cadat in terram passerculus sine eius decreto* [*CO* 40:220]. Cf. commentary on Isaiah 7:19 [*CO* 31:160-161].

[126] Cf. "We must concede to God that he may have reasons for his plan that are hidden from us." *Institutes* II.xi.14. *Hoc enim esset nimium nobis arrogare, non concedere Deo ut consilii sui rationes habeat quae nos lateant* [*CO* 2:339]. Calvin can make the point that the hiddenness of God's plan from us is not dissimilar to fortune. "However all things may be ordained by God's plan, according to a sure dispensation, for us they are fortuitous." *Institutes* I.xvi.9. *Dicam igitur, utcunque ordinentur omnia Dei consilio certa dispensatione, nobis tamen esse fortuita* [*CO* 2:152]. Bouwsma, italicising the word "are" in the previous citation suggests that to attribute things to an incomprehensible God and to fortune is only a semantic difference. But, this fails to recognise the force of Calvin's statement. Things may appear fortuitous; but, the belief that God's ways are ordered and ultimately for the good of his people keeps Job, as well as the faithful, going in troubled times. See, Bouwsma, *Op. cit.*, 278n60. This is Calvin's pastoral theology of providence. This implies what Calvin calls "the elevated mind:" "I readily admit that no man can form a right judgment of the providence of God, but he who elevates his mind above the earth." Commentary on Psa. 73:16. *Et sane de providentia Dei neminem fateor recte iudicare, nisi qui supra terram conscendit* [*CO* 31:682]. As we shall show in the following chapters of this thesis, this theme plays a significant part in the Joban sermons. For Calvin's use of "abyss" in dealing with providence, see *Institutes* I.xvii.2 [*CO* 2:155-156]. C.f "His judgment is a profound abyss." Commentary on Matt. 11:26. *Saepe inculcat, sua iudicia profundam esse abyssum* [*CO* 45:319].

[127] Cf. "He not only founded the heaven and earth at first, but governs all things according to his power. To own that God made the world, but maintain that he sits idle (Lt. *Otiosa*) in heaven, and takes no concern in the management of it, is to cast an impious aspersion upon his power." Commentary on Psa. 135:6. *Nam qui Deum fatentur mundi creatorem, et sedere otiosum ni coelo fingunt abiecta mundi cura, eum sua virtute impie spoliant* [*CO* 32:359].

[128] Cf. *Institutes* I.xvi.4. "Every species of things is moved by a secret instinct of nature as if it were obeying an eternal command of God and is proceeding spontaneously because God had once appointed it." [*CO* 2:147-148]. See Susan Schreiner, *Theater of His Glory*, p.31; C. Partee, *Calvin and Classical Philosophy*, 126-145; Etienne de Peyer, "Calvin's Doctrine of

Providence," *The Evangelical Quarterly* 10 (1938): 30-44; François Wendel, *Calvin, The Origins and Development of His Religious Thought*, trans. Philip Mairet (New York: Harper & Row, 1963), 173-180.

[129] 34 (Job 9:7-15), 156.b.37. *Ne pensons point que ce que nous avons quelque lieu sec pour habiter, cela soit sinon d'autant que Dieu nous veut ici loger.* [*CO* 33:420]. Cf. "He suffereth not the world to be vtterly ouerwhelmed, but holdeth it still by a secret brydle…" 79 (Job 21:7-12), 371.b.31. *Veu qu'il ne permet pas que le monde soit du tout abysmé, mais qu'il y a encores quelque bride secrette* [*CO* 34:220]. And earlier in the same sermon: "the wicked may well prosper and have all things as they would wish, and yet for all that, that wee must not bee out of quiet as though all things were gouerned by fortune and that there were nothing but disorder heere bilowe." 371.a.67. *Et a voulu monstrer que les meschans peuvent bien prosperer, que toutes choses leur viendront à souhait: mais que pour cela il ne faut point que nous soyons troublez, comme si tout se gouvernoit par fortune, qu'il n'y eust que confusion ici bas* [*CO* 34:220].

[130] 81 (Job 21:16-21), 381.b.47. *Que nous cognoissions qu'en une minute de temps il pourra achever son oeuvre, mesmes quand il n'y aura point de moyen, et que les choses n'y seront nullement disposees* [*CO* 34:248]. Bouwsma regards the view as "radical." See, Bouwsma, *John Calvin: A Sixteenth Century Portrait* (New York and Oxford: Oxford University Press, 1988), 166. Calvin continues: "For God is aboue all this comon ordre of nature, so that he can worke after a fashion that is new and strange to vs." 381.b.69. *Car Dieu est par dessus tout cest ordre commun de nature, tellement qu'i peut besongner d'une façon qui nous est estrange et nouvelle* [*CO* 34:248].

[131] 73 (Job 20:1-7), 343.a.53. *Ainsi donc notons bien ce mot, comme il emporte beaucoup à la verité, c'est assavoir, que de tout temps, et depuis que les hommes habitent en terre, Dieu a voulu qu'il y eust tousiours quelques tesmoignages de ses iugemens: et ainsi qu'il ne faut point que nous soyons si eslourdis et hebetez, que nous ne cognoissions ce que Dieu fait pour nostre instruction.* [*CO* 34:145].

[132] For God's providence in rulers, see the following example: "If some poore man be afflicted, or if there light any aduersitie vpon him, there will be regard had of it: for we be comonly inured with such matters. But when a prince that seemed to be hoyssed vp aloft, is cast downe, there we be more touched, and wee must needs espie Gods prouidence if we be not to blockish." 48 (Job 12:17-25), 223.a.32. *Si quelque povre homme estoit affligé, ou qu'il luy advint quelque calamité on n'y prendra point garde (car nous sommes tout accaustumez à ces choses) mais quand un Prince, qui semble estre eslevé en haut est abbatu, là nous sommes plus touchez, et faut que nous cognoissions la providence de Dieu, si nous ne sommes bien stupides* [*CO* 33:593]. Cf. God "sheweth vs his power by holding the Sea as it were in Cheynes, and by limiting it within bounds which it cannot ouerpasse… it pleaseth God to make the thunder to rattle, and to moue any tempest in the

ayre." 96 (Job 26:8-14), 452.a.30. *quand il tient la mer comme enchainee, qu'il y a mis des bornes qu'elle ne peut outrepasser: .. quand il lui plaist de faire esclatter les tonnerres, et qu'il esmeut quelque tempeste au ciel...* [*CO* 34:438]. Cf. *Institutes* I.v.6 [*CO* 2:45-46]. For God's sovereignty over the nations: "People inlargeth and spreadeth out their bounds very far, and then God hemmeth it in." 48 (Job 12:17-25), 226.a.19. *Un autre s'eslargit et estendra ses limites bien loin, et puis Dieu le renserre* [*CO* 33:601].

[133] "The chiefe seruice therefore that God requyreth of vs, is that we call vpon him, knowing that when we come vnto him in truth, he will make vs partakers of all his benefites, and so gouerne vs by his spirite, that we shall neuer be bereft of his graces." 80 (Job 21:13-15), 378.b.31. *Voila donc le principal service que Dieu demande de nous, c'est que nous l'invoquions, sachans que quand nous y viendrons en verité, il nous fera participans de tous ses biens, et nous gouvernera par son sainct Esprit, en telle sorte que nous ne serons iamais despouillez de ses graces* [*CO* 34:240]. Cf. "The very object of this our severe afflcition, is to awaken us amidst our slothfulness." Commentary on Daniel 9:18, Vol. XIII, 182. *Huc spectat quum nos ita severe affligit, ut expergefaciat nostram pigritiem* [*CO* 41:158].

[134] Early in the sermons on Job, Calvin has cause to reflect on the relationship of God and evil. The presence of Satan tempts him to the use of the language of permission. But Calvin is insistent: "It is commonly alleged for answere, that when wicked folke doe any euill, God woorketh not that: but only suffereth it, and simply giueth them leaue. But seeing hee hath authoritie and power to let them: is not his suffering or permission on all one as if he did it himself? Therfore that is but a verie fonde excuse, and God hath no neede of our leasings to mayntayne his truth and ryghtuousness withall... God not only permitteth and giueth leaue, but also executeth his will, both by the diuell and by wicked persons." 8 (Job 2:1-6), 34.a.13. *On allegue pour response, que quand les meschans font quelque mal, Dieu ne besongne point là: mais il permet, et donne simplement le congé. Or ayant l'authorité d'empescher et la puissance, quand il le permet, n'est-ce pas autant comme s'il le faisoit? C'est donc une excuse par trop frivole, et aussi Dieu n'a que faire de nos mensonges pour maintenir sa verité et sa isutice... Car que Dieu non seulement permette et donne le congé, mais aussi qu'il execute sa volonté et par Satan et par les meschans* [*CO* 33:106].

[135] 1 (Job 1:1), 1.b.32. *Mais cependant nous avons aussi à noter, qu'en toute la dispute Iob maintient une bonne cause, et son adverse partie en maintient une mauvaise. Or il y a plus, que Iob maintenant une bonne cause la deduit mal, et les autres menans une mauvaise cause la deduisent bien. Quand nous aurons entendu cela, ce nous sera comme une clef pour nous donner ouverture à tout le livre.* [*CO* 33:23].

[136] 1 (Job 1:1), 1.a.35. Fr. *patience* [*CO* 33:21].

[137] *Ibid.*, 1.a.44. *Resisté aux tentations et ont perseveré constamment en l'obeissance de Dieu* [*CO* 33:22].

[138] 2(Job 1:2-5), 5.a.55,59,64 [*CO* 33:33].

[139] 37 (Job 9:29-35), 170.b.41. *Il n'est pas question de trouver ici une dignité parfaite aux hommes, ne de dire que Dieu leur soit redevable, et qu'ils puissent contester avec lui, qu'ils ont bien merité qu'il ne trouve que redire en eux et en leur vie* [*CO* 33:456-457].

[140] 1 (Job 1:1), 1.b.39. *C'est qu'il cognoist que Dieu n'afflige pas tousiours les hommes selon la mesure de leurs pechez: mais qu'il a ses iugemens secrets, desquels il ne nous rend pas conte, et cependant qu'il faut que nous attendions iusques à ce qu'il nous revele pourquoy il fait ceci, ou cela. Il a donc tout ce propos persuadé, que Dieu n'afflige point tousiours les hommes selon la mesure de leurs pechez, et de cela il en a tesmoignage en soy, qu'il n'estoit pas un homme reietté de Dieu, comme on luy veut faire à croire. Voila une cause qui est bonne et vraye, cependant elle est mal deduite* [*CO* 33:23].

[141] 1 (Job 1:1), 1.b.55. *Que Dieu punit tousiours les hommes selon la mesure de leurs pechez* [*CO* 33:23].

[142] 98 (Job 27:5-8), 460.b.11. *Mais quand Dieu aura fait la grace à un homme de le conduire non seulement pour un mois, mais pour un an, pour trois, pour dix, et qu'il aura vescu longuement en cognoissant que c'est de Dieu et de son salut: si puis apres il est rebelle et qu'il se revolte, qu'il ne poursuive point iusques au bout: et ne voila point une lascheté beaucoup plus grande, que si un homme qui n'auroit point encores prins bonne racine ni assez profonde, se destournoit, et qu'il fust desbauché par quelque legereté? Car si un homme a gousté que c'est du bien, et que tantost apres on l'en destourne, il est vrai que devant Dieu il ne sera pas excusable: mais encores on aura pitié de ce qu'il a esté ainsi diverti devant qu'avoir receu pleine instruction. Mais quand un homme aura long temps suivi le droit chemin, et qu'il semblera qu'il soit des plus fermes, si cependant il s'aliene, et quelle excuse y aura-il en cela?* [*CO* 34:460-461].

[143] 72 (Job 19:26-29), 338.b.32. *qu'elle n'ait point tant de distractions comme nous avons accoustumé d'avoir* [*CO* 34:133]. The nature of this definition is interesting, not least because it raises the vexed issue of the relationship between faith and the assurance of faith, in Calvin. Cf. Calvin's definition of faith in the *Institutes*: "Now we shall possess a right definition of faith if we call it a firm and certain knowledge of God's benevolence toward us, founded upon the truth of the freely given promise in Christ, both revealed to our minds and sealed upon our hearts through the Holy Spirit." III.ii.7. *Nunc iusta fidei definitio nobis constabit, si dicamus esse divinae erga nos benevolentiae firmam certamque cognitionem, quae gratuitae in Christo promissionis veritate fundata, per spiritum sanctum et revelatur mentibus nostris et cordibus obsignatur* [*CO* 2:403]. This, as has been pointed out by numerous scholars, is in apparent contrast to the developed Puritan definition of faith as given, for example, in Westminster Confession of Faith: "This infallible assurance doth not so belong to the essence of faith, but that a true believer may wait long, and conflict with many difficulties, before he be a partaker of it." (XVIII.iii). See Joel R. Beeke, *Assurance of Faith: Calvin,*

*English Puritanism, and the Dutch Second Reformation*, American University Studies, series VII, vol. 89 (New York, San Francisco, Bern, Frankfurt am Main, Paris, London: Peter Lang, 1991). The intricacies of this debate are beyond the bounds of this thesis, but it is crucial to distinguish what Calvin and later Puritanism (the Westminster Confession in this case) are doing: Calvin is defining *faith*, whilst the Confession is defining the *assurance* of faith.

[144] "God exercised his seruaunt Abraham after a strange fashion vnaccustomed among men. And wherefore? for he had also strengthened him by his holie spirite, and therefore he gaue him greate and verie rough assaultes." 6 (Job 1:13-19), 25.a.35. *Nous voyons que Dieu a exercé son serviteur Abraham d'une façon estrange, et non accoustumee entre les hommes* [*CO* 33:83]. Cf. where God is said to "punish" Job, "not in that measure by reason of his misdeedes, but to trye the faith and patience of his serua[n]t." 118 (Job 31:35-40), 555.a.31. *Il ne le punit point en telle mesure pour avoir transgressé: mais il a voulu esprouver la foy et la patience de son serviteur, il a voulu aussi qu'il fust en exemple à tout le monde* [*CO* 34:714].

[145] See, *Institutes* III.ii.15,16,17 [*CO* 410-413].

[146] 155 (Job 40:7-19), 730.a.21. *Car voila aussi en quoi nostre foi se demonstre: c'est qu'au milieu de nos miseres nous puissions contempler les graces que Dieu nous a promises* [*CO* 35:459]. Cf. "What is the foundation of our faith? the free promises that God hath giuen vs." 138 (Job 35:12-16), 648.a.13. *Quel est le fondement de nostre foy? Ce sont les promesses gratuites que Dieu nous donne* [*CO* 35:242]. Cf. "Nowe then let vs learne to serue God in spirit and truth, and faith wil be a good guide therevnto, when we haue our eyes fastened vpon Gods worde, which will lead vs always to our Lord Iesus Christ, who is the heaue[n]ly patterne and the mirrour wherin we must behold the will of God his father, to frame ourselues thereafter." 3 (Job 1:2-5), 12.a.57. *Ainsi donc apprenons de servir Dieu en esprit et en verité, et la foy sera une bonne guide à cela, quand nous aurons nos yeux fichez sur la parole de Dieu, laquelle nous conduira tousiours à nostre Seigneur Iesus Christ, qui est la patron celeste, et auquel il faut que nous contemplions quelle est la volonté de Dieu son pere, pour nous y ranger* [*CO* 33:51].

[147] 35 (Job 9:16-22), 162.b.56. *Car la foy est une semence incorruptible en nos ames* [*CO* 33:436].

[148] 68 (Job 18:12-21), 320.b.51. *Esiouissez vous (dit nostre Seigneur Iesus à ses disciples [Luc. 10,20]) car vos noms sont escrits au registres de Dieu, et de vostre salut eternel. Ne voila point pour nous contenter? Nous ne sommes par comme ces fols, qui n'ont autre immortalité que de faire parler d'eux. Or cela est par trop maigre: mais nous savons que Dieu a enregistré nos noms en son livre, qu'il y a ce testament qu'il a escrit, voire de sa propre main, c'est à dire, en son conseil eternel (car la main de Dieu est ceste ordonnance qu'il a faite immuable) et puis il a ratifié le tout par le sang de nostre Seigneur Iesus Christ* [*CO* 34:85].

[149] 72 (Job 19:26-29), 338.a.39. *Car si nous pouvions recevoir les promesses de Dieu en vraye foy, n'auroyent-elles point assez de vertu pour nous faire surmonter toutes ces tentations qui dominent ainsi sur nous?* [*CO* 34:132]. Calvin earlier in the paragraph refers to Christ as the "mirrour and substance" of God's "goodly promises." 338.a.32. *belles promesses… le miroir et la substance en nostre Seigneur Iesus Christ* [*CO* 34:131].

[150] 7 (Job 1:2-22), 28.a.59. *Car si nous ne sommes patiens, il faut que nostre foy s'esvanouisse* [*CO* 33:93].

[151] 50 (Job 13:11-15), 236.b.47. *… la foy domine par dessus nos passions. Quand nous esperons en Dieu, quand nous l'invoquons, ce n'est pas que nous n'ayons tousiours des combats: mais il faut que la foy soit victorieuse* [*CO* 33:629-630].

[152] Thus "God dealeth with his seruaunts according to the measure of fayth which he hath distributed vnto them." 6 (Job 1:13-19), 24.b.30. *Dieu besongne envers ses serviteurs selon la mesure de foy qu'il leur a distribuee* [*CO* 33:82]. For "weake" faith and "greater strength," see, *Ibid.*, 24.b.53,54. *Car les uns demeurent infirmes et les autres ont une plus grande vertu beaucoup* [*CO* 33:82].

[153] 38 (Job 10:1-6), 178.a.26. *Voila donc comme la foy des enfans de Dieu sera bien establie, non point en orgueil ny en arrogance, mais en droite humilité* [*CO* 33:475]. Calvin can add: "Faith can neuer be without obedie[n]ce: it must needes be answereable to that which God hath ordeyned." 3 (Job 1:2-5), 11.a.22. *La foi ne peut iamais estre sans obeissance, il faut qu'elle responde à ce que Dieu aura institué* [*CO* 33:48].

[154] "… he will not fayle to keepe his promise, and that forasmuch as our welfare is in his hand, we are sure that no… enemie shall preuaile against vs." 157 (Job 42:1-5), 738.a.26. *Nous sommes asseurez que nul mal ne nous peut advenir: s'il nous a en sa protection, nous sommes aussi tout persuadez que nous serons invincibles contre nos ennemis* [*CO* 35:479].

[155] 35 (Job 9:16-22), 162.a.11. *Mais Dieu nous donne comme une estincelle de clarté, il nous donne quelque sentiment de foy, ouy sans que nous le cognoissions et le puissions discerner* [*CO* 33:434]. In the same chapter, Calvin speaks of faith being "stifled (*estouffee*)" *Ibid.*, 162.b.6 [*CO* 33:435].

[156] 41 (Job 10:18-22), 193.b.4. *Que nous ne sentions tousiours son amour paternel, duquel il use envers nous, afin de moderer nostre tristesse et de l'adoucir* [*CO* 33:515].

[157] In fact, even within the *Institutes*, Calvin can refer to this very phenomenon at various places: first, in delineating the purpose of the sacraments. Thus, baptism is to produce in us "the singular fruit of assurance and spiritual joy which is to be gathered from it… how sweet is it to godly minds to be assured, not only by word, but by sight, that they obtain so much favour with the Heavenly father…" *Institutes* IV.xvi.32. *Nempe ut singularem fiduciae et spiritualis gaudii fructum… ac de bonitatis etiam divinae gloria tantundem delibet* [*CO* 2:1001]. Similarly in the Lord's Supper, it is a means of grace whose purpose is that "we may dare assure ourselves

that eternal life... is ours." *Institutes* IV.xvii.2. *Hinc sequitur ut nobis secure spondere audeamus, vitam aeternam nostram esse, cuius ipse est haeres* [*CO* 2:1003]. Secondly, Calvin writes on several occasions of the nature of spiritual experience, suggesting that believers are "shaken by gravest terrors. For so violent are the temptations that trouble their minds as not to seem quite compatible with that certainty of faith." Calvin recognises the very tension implicit in his definition of faith and the experience of faith and goes on: "Accordingly we shall have to solve this difficulty if we wish the above-stated doctrine to stand. Surely, while we teach that faith ought to be certain and assured, we cannot imagine any certainty that is not tinged with doubt, or any assurance that is not assailed by some anxiety. On the other hand, we say that believers are in perpetual conflict with their own unbelief. Far, indeed, are we from putting their consciences in any peaceful repose, undisturbed by any tumult at all." *Institutes* III.ii.17 [*CO* 2:411-413]. Similar expressions on the fact that faith can sometimes appear weak occur in *Institutes* III.ii.4 [*CO* 2:399-400]. Cf. III.ii.37 [*CO* 2:413]. Thirdly, similar expressions are found in the *Institutes* in relation to Calvin's descriptions of the nature and effects of conflict, both internally, *Institutes* III.ii.4, [*CO* 2:399-401], and externally, *Institutes* III.ii.18, 20.[*CO* 2:576, 577-578]. Fourthly, even for Calvin, a place existed for the use of the practical syllogism: sanctification could and should be used as an encouragement to assurance. Thus he writes: "The saints quite often strengthen themselves and are comforted by remembering their own innocence and uprightness, and they do not even refrain at times from proclaiming it." *Quod autem innocentiae integritatisque suae memoria saepiuscule sancti se confirmant ac consolantur, nec etiam ab ea praedicanda interdum abstinent* [*CO* 2:576]. He adds, "... the saints by innocence of conscience strengthen their faith and take from it occasion to exult." *Institutes* III.ii.19. *Quum igitur a conscientiae innocentia fidem suam confirmant sancti, et exsultandi materiam sumunt, nihil aliud quam a fructibus vocationis se in filiorum locum a Domino cooptatos esse reputant* [*CO* 2:577]. Calvin explains very carefully that this is not a denial of salvation by grace: a conscience that is erected on grace "is established also in the consideration of works, so far, that is, as these are testimonies of God dwelling and ruling in us . . . Therefore, when we rule out reliance upon works, we mean only this: that the Christian mind may not be turned back to the merit of works as to a help toward salvation but should rely wholly on the free promise of righteousness. But we do not forbid him from undergirding and strengthening this faith by signs of the divine benevolence toward him . . . the grace of good works shows that the Spirit of adoption has been given to us. " *Institutes* III.xiv.18. *Quare, dum operum fiduciam excludimus, hoc volumus duntaxat, ne mens christiana ad operum meritum, velut ad salutis subsidium, reflectatur, sed penitus resideat in gratuita iustitiae promissione. Non vetamus autem ne divinae erga se benvolentiae signis hanc fidem fulciat et confirmet. Nam si, dum memoria repetuntur quaecunque in nos dona Deus contulit, sunt nobis quodammodo instar radiorum divini vultus, quibus illuminemur ad summam illam bonitatis lucem contemplandam; multo magis bonorum operum gratia, quae spiritum adoptionis nobis datum commonstrat* [*CO* 2:576-577]. The so-called tension between Calvin and later Puritan treatments of assurance seems less than some have advocated. A. N. S. Lane, for example, has insisted that "there is a sharp contrast between Calvin and the Westminster Confession in the matter of assurance of salvation." A. N. S. Lane, "The Quest for the Historical Calvin," *The Evangelical Quarterly* 55 (1983), 103; cf. A. N. S. Lane, "Calvin's Doctrine of Assurance," *Vox Evangelica* 11 (1979), 42-4; R. T. Kendall, *Calvin and English Calvinism to 1649* (Oxford, 1979), conveniently abridged in his "The Puritan Modifications of Calvin's Theology," in W. S. Reid (ed.), *John Calvin: His Influence in the Western World* ed. W.S. Reid (Grand Rapids, MI: Zondervan, 1982), 199-214; David. C. Lachman, *The Marrow Controversy* (Edinburgh: Rutherford House, 1988), 373-381. For a refutation of Lachman's position, which advocates that a change took place in seventeenth-century understanding of assurance, distancing itself from Calvin's position, see P. Helm, "Calvin, English Calvinism and the Logic of Doctrinal Development," *Scottish Journal of Theology* 34 (1981), 179-85; and *Calvin and the Calvinists* (Edinburgh: Banner of Truth, 1982); W. Cunningham, *The Reformers and the Theology of the Reformation* (London: Banner of Truth, 1967), 395-402; R. W. A. Letham, *Saving Faith and Assurance in Reformed Theology: Zwingli to the Synod of Dordt* (Ph.D. thesis, University of Aberdeen 1979); A. T. B. McGowan, *The Federal Theology of Thomas Boston (1676-1732)* (Carlisle, Cumbria: Paternoster Press/Edinburgh: Rutherford House, 1997), 185-202; Joel R. Beeke, *Assurance of Faith: Calvin, English Puritanism, and the Dutch Second Reformation*, American University Studies, series VII, vol. 89 (New York, San Francisco, Bern, Frankfurt am Main, Paris, London: Peter Lang, 1991).

[158] R. H. Tawney, *Religion and the Rise of Capitalism* (Harmondsworth: Penguin, 1938), 109. See also, M. Weber, *The Protestant Ethic and the Spirit of Capitalism* (London: Allen & Unwin, 1930). English Translation by T. Parsons of the German original published in 1905: *Die protestantische Ethik und der Geist das Kapitalismus.*

[159] *Hebrews and I and II Peter*, trans. W. B. Johnston, 240. *Docet enim, hoc christianae ecclesiae regimen ab initio divinitus fuisse constitutum, ut crux praeparatio esset ad triumphum: et mors, transitus ad vitam* [*CO* 55:217].

[160] 20 (Job 5:11-16), 89.b.13. ...*mais il est impossible que les enfans de Dieu vivent en ce monde, que tousiours ils ne soyent en beaucoup de perils* [*CO* 33:247].

[161] Cf. *Hebrews and I and II Peter*, trans. W. B. Johnston, 298. *... mors eius typus sit modo ac exemplar mortificationis nostrae* [*CO* 55:271].

[162] Ronald Wallace, *Calvin's Doctrine of the Christian Life*, 51.

[163] "there is a two-fold mortification." *Galatians, Ephesians, Philippians and Colossians*, 347. ...*duplicem esse mortificationem.* [*CO* 52:119].

[164] 66 (Job 17:6-16), 310.b.6. *Voila quelle est en somme la vie des fideles,*

*c'est assavoir, qu'il ne seront iamais sans beaucoup de tentations. Et sur tout d'autant que nous sommes assubiettis à tant de miseres, cependant que nous sommes en ce pelerinage terrien, que ceux qui taschent de servir le mieux à Dieu, ne laissent pas d'estre pressez souvent de beaucoup de maux, et de beaucoup d'afflictions. Mais quoy? Quand nous serons estonnez, comme il ne se peut faire que nous ne trouvions cela bien estrange du premier coup, que nous combations contre telles tentations, que nous persistions au droit chemin sans nous desbaucher: et combien que nous sentions beaucoup de difficultez en nous, prions Dieu qu'il nous donne une telle vertu et si invincible, que nous continuions iusques à la fin à son service, combien que Satan tasche de nous en divertir [CO 34:56-57].* Citing Job 13:19, "Though he slay me, yet will I trust him," Calvin adds in his commentary on Isaiah 26:8, "It is the true test of sincere godliness, when not only while God bestows his kindness upon us, but while he withdraws his face, and afflicts us, and gives us every sign of severity and displeasure, we place our hope and confidence in him. Let us learn to apply this doctrine to our own use, whenever we are hard pressed by the calamities of the present life; and let us not cease to trust in him, even when our affairs are in the most desperate condition." *Isaiah,* vol. 2, 219. *Proinde haec vera solidae pietatis probatio est, ubi non solum quum nos beneficentia sua prosequitur Deus, sed quum subducit faciem suam, nosque affligit, omniaque irae et severitatis signa praebet, in ipso spem fiduciamque nostra locamus. Discamus accommodare hanc doctrinam in usum nostrum, quoties nos urgent praesentis vitae calamitates: nec desinamus, etiam desperatissimis in rebus, in eum sperare [CO 36:431].*

[165] 54 (Job 14:5-12), 255.b.31. *Or le principal combat que nous ayons à faire c'est contre nous-mesmes, et contre nos vices: et c'est où il nous faut efforcer* [CO 33:679].

[166] 158 (Job 42:6-8), 741.b.44. *Notons bien donc que la vraye penitence emporte la haine du peché, voire iusques au bout: tellement que l'homme se reprouve, et se haysse d'autant qu'il ne se trouve pas tel qu'il devroit: et qu'aimant la iustice de Dieu il condamne tout ce qui est en lui, et ne cerche sinon d'estre despouillé de ceste vieille peau dont il est enveloppé. Voila comme nous approuverons nostre penitence* [CO 35:489].

[167] 55 (Job 14:13-15), 258.a.45. *Car la foy n'est iamais sans combats, il faut bien qu'elle soit bien exercee. Et comment cela se fait-il? Quand le diable nous propose beaucoup de matieres d'incredulité. Voila donc la vraye approbation de nostre foy* [CO 33:686].

[168] 98 (Job 27:5-8), 462.b.29. *Donc apprenons de nous assuiettir à Dieu et que nous ne soyons point si pervers et forcenez de nous vouloir exempter de la suiettion de celuy qui nous a creez et formez... Quand un homme se pourra ainsi assuiettir à Dieu en toute humilité et reverence, et renoncer à soy-mesme, pour dire, il faut que ton Createur gaigne par dessus toy, et qu'il ait toute maistrise: voila un bon commencement* [CO 34:466-467]. Cf. Sermon 122: "Whensoeuer we come to be taught in the name of God, if we

see that the doctrine which is offered vs is right, there must be no more replying: for wee shall winne nothing by it: but if there be reason, it behoueth vs to submit our selues to it. Furthermore this ought not to hinder vs from setting Gods maiestie before our eyes. For wee must not iudge of the doctrine that is set forth vnto vs, according to our owne wit and fancie. Therefore two things had neede to be matched here together. The one is, that wee fully determine to be ready to obey God, concluding in ourselues that our maker ought to haue all soueraintie ouer vs, and that we ought to be subiect vnto him. This is the preparatiue that must be made aforehand. And afterward we must enter into iudgement, that is too say, we muste examine the doctrine, howbeit not with pryde, nor with an opinion that we be wyse ynough of our selues, but praying vnto God to gouerne vs with his holy spirite, that we may follow the doctrine which he shall haue shewed vs. 122 (Job 33:1-7), 577.b.49...*toutes fois et quantes que nous venons pour estre enseignez au nom de Dieu, quand nous voyons que la doctrine qu'on nous presente est droite, il ne faut plus repliquer. Car nous ne gaignerons rien en plaidant: s'il y a raison, il s'y faut assuiettir. Au reste cela ne doit point empescher que la maiesté de Dieu ne nous vienne devant les yeux: car il ne faut point que nous iugions de la doctrine qu'on nous propose, selon nostre sens et phantasie. Il faut donc qu'il y ait ici deux choses meslées: l'une c'est, Que nous ayons tout conclud, que nous sommes prests d'obeir à Dieu, que nous ayons prins ceste conclusion en nous, O il faut que nostre Createur ait toute maistrise, et que nous luy soyons suiets. Voila le preparatif qui doit estre. Et puis, que nous entrions en iugement, c'est à dire que nous examinions la doctrine, voire non point avec une fierté, non point en cuidant estre assez sages, mais prians Dieu qu'il nous y gouverne par son sainct Esprit, pour suivre la doctrine qu'il nous aura monstree* [CO 35:51-52].

[169] 27 (Job 7:1-6), 125.a.41. *Et bien Seigneur, nous sommes en ta main, ce n'est pas à nous de t'imposer loy, de te sommer à heure presente, pour dire tu feras ceci ou cela: mais puis que tu nous as declaré que tu sauras bien mettre fin à nos maux, voire une fin heureuse et desirable, Seigneur nous attendrons patiemment ce que tu nous as promis* [CO 33:339].

[170] 7 (Job 1:20-22), 29.a.53. *Et n'y a rien plus difficile que de nous moderer tellement, que nous tenions reigle et compas* [CO 33:94].

[171] 51 (Job 13:16-22), 241.b.3. *Nos passions sont comme bestes sauvages lesquelles nous iettent contre Dieu* [CO 33:642].

[172] 51 (Job 13:16-22), 241.b.13. *Nos passions soyent reprimees, et nous les faut tenir en bride, voire qu'il nous les faut comme enchainer, c'est à dire qu'il nous faut faire tous efforts pour abbatre ceste impetueuse phrenesie qui est là* [CO 33:642].

[173] 47 (Job 12:14-16), 222.a.57. *Car nous tentons Dieu manifestement si nous voulons passer nos limites* [CO 33:590]. Calvin criticised David's expression of grief at the death of Saul and Jonathan as "excessive." John Calvin, *Sermons on 2 Samuel: Chapters 1-13* trans. Douglas Kelly (Edinburgh: Banner of Truth Trust, 1992), 32. "*excessif*" [SC 1:19.22). Earlier

in the sermons on 2 Samuel, Calvin had indicated, "how well he controlled his feelings," adding a little later, "David still kept himself under control," "... *moderé ses affections...*" [*SC* 1:5.1]; "*Mais cependant si tient il mesure.*" [*SC* 1:6.4].

[174] Peter Leithart, "Stoic Elements in Calvin's Doctrine of the Christian Life. Part III: Christian Moderation," *Westminster Theological Journal* 56 (1994) 59-85.

[175] 7 (Job 1:20-21) 29.a.4. *...si nous estions comme un tronc de boi, ou une pierre, il n'y auroit nulle vertu en nous... les bestes brutes quelquefois ne sentent rien, mais elles ne sont pas vertueuses pour cela* [*CO* 33:93]. Cited by Leithart, *op. cit.*, 60. See further examples on the emotional responses of Joseph and Paul cited by Leithart, 60-61.

[176] *Institutes* III.viii.10. *Sanctis enim tolerantiae laudem defert scriptura, dum ita malorum duritia afflictantur ut non frangantur nec concidant; ita amaritudine punguntur, ut simul perfundantur spirituali gaudio; ita premuntur anxietate, ut Dei consolatione exhilarati respirent. Interim versatur in eorum cordibus illa repugnantia, quod naturae sensus, quae sibi sentit adversa, refugit atque horret; pietatis autem affectus ad obedientiam divinae voluntatis etiam per has difficultates contendit* [*CO* 2:521].

[177] Thus, two emotions are experienced in prayer: Christians "groan under present ills and anxiously fear those to come, yet at the same time take refuge in God, not at all doubting he is ready to extend his helping hand." *Institutes* III.xx.11. *Ex utroque ergo affectu emergat pii hominis oratio convenit, utrumque etiam contineat et repraesentet; nempe ut malis praesentibus ingemat, et a novis sibi anxie timeat; tamen confugiat simul ad Deum, minime dubitans quin auxiliarem ille manum porrigere sit paratus* [*CO* 2:635].

[178] 28 (Job 7:7-15), 128.b.59. *Nous voyons maintenant comme les hommes estans considerez en eux mesmes, n'ont rien que defaillance... Que est-ce donques des hommes? un vent, une fumée: mais d'autant que Dieu nous a inspiré une vertu permanente, voila pourquoy nous sommes immortels* [*CO* 33:348-349]. T. F. Torrance, citing this passage, speaks of life as "borrowed" and then suggests that "Calvin has nothing to do with second causes." This seems unwarranted. Calvin denies the equal ultimacy of second causes, but not their power. See T. F. Torrance, *Calvin's Doctrine of Man*, 63.

[179] 17 (Job 4:20-5:2), 76.a.1. *Nous devons donc cognoistre à veuë d'oeil que nostre vie nous eschappe et s'escoule* [*CO* 33:212]. Cf. Calvin's letter to Madame de Coligny, August 5, 1563, "We ought to learn to have one foot raised to take our departure when it shall please God." *Letters*, ... *nous debvons apprendre davoir ung pied levé pour desloger quant il plaira a Dieu.*[*CO* 20:129].

[180] 53 (Job 14:1-4), 249.a.35. *Nostre vie s'escoule en un moment, regardons d'où cela procede, c'est assavoir, du peché* [*CO* 33:661-662].

[181] 72 (Job 19:26-29), 337.b.49. *Il est vray que ie voy que mon corps s'en va en decadence: s'il y a quelque vigueur, elle diminue de iour en iour, et ie contemple la mort sans l'aller chercher dix lieuës loin* [*CO* 34:130].

Interestingly, Calvin, with possibly a reference to his own age, says at one point: "True it is that a man may liue fiftie or threescore yeares." 31 (Job 8:7-13), 143.b.66. This is incorrectly cited as sermon 30 in Bouwsma, 245n138. *Il est vray qu'on vivra cinquante ou soixante ans* [*CO* 33:387]. Calvin was forty-five years old when he said this.

[182] 41 (Job 10:18-22), 190.b.68. *Car combien qu'il y ait des miseres infinies dont les hommes sont accablez: si est-ce qu'il nous faut mettre en la balance cest honneur que Dieu nous fait, quand il nous constitue par dessus ses creatures, qu'il veut que nous dominions icy bas comme ses enfans, qu'il se fait sentir pere envers nous: et au reste qu'il ne nous met point en ce monde sinon pour tendre plus haut, c'est assavoir, à ceste vie celeste, de laquelle il nous donne quelque sentiment et apprehension* [*CO* 33:508].

[183] 24 (2 Tim.3:16-17), 937.b.16. *Quand donc l'expose l'Escriture saincte, il faut que ie me regle tousiours là, c'est que ceux qui m'oyent, reçoivent profit de la doctrine que ie propose, qu'ils en soyent edifiez à salut. Si ie n'ay ceste affection-là, et que ie ne procure l'edification de ceux qui m'oyent, ie suis un sacrilege, prophanant la parole de Dieu* [*CO* 54:287].

[184] 95 (Job 26:1-7), 446.b.26. *Ainsi donc notons bien que quand nous traittons la parole de Dieu, il faut que nous ayons un certain but, pour ne point vaguer çà et là: mais que nous tranchions droit, sachans à quelle fin nous parlons, afin que nos propos ne soyent point extravagans, qu'ils ne s'esgarent point çà et là: car autrement nous pourrions bien dire beaucoup de bonnes choses: mais ce bien-la dequoy servira-il?* [*CO* 34:424].

[185] 62 (Job 16:1-9), 290.b.41. *Car il faut manier l'un autrement que l'autre* [*CO* 34:5].

[186] 78 (Job 21:1-6), 366.a.57 [*CO* 34:206].

[187] Cf. Charles Partee's assertion that union with Christ is the key element of Calvin's theology, in "Calvin's Central Dogma Again," *The Sixteenth Century Journal* 18 (1987), 191-199.

## Chapter 2

## The Incomprehensible Righteousness of God

The problem of theodicy is at bottom the problem of man in his lostness, the problem of the prodigal son (G. C. Berkouwer, *The Providence of God*, 260).

But wee must alwayes beare in minde that which I haue touched: that as long as we go no further but to the degree and state of creatures: there shall be a perfection in the Angels, verily such perfection as may in creatures. But come we once vnto God: the sayd perfection is as it were swallowed vp, like as the Starres appeere not any more when the Sunne giues his light (16 [Job 4:12-19], 74.a.51).

*[M]ais il nous faut tousiours retenir ce que i'ay touché, c'est assavoir que quand on demeure aux degrez et au reng des creatures, il y aura aux Anges une perfection, voire comme aux creatures: mais quand ce vient à Dieu, ceste perfection-la est comme engloutie ainsi que les estoiles n'apparoissent plus quand le soleil donne sa clarté* [CO 33:208].

It is no longer plausible to offer a theological portrait of Calvin apart from the late medieval tradition.[1] The medieval era is much more complex than we have been given to understand, and Calvin's relationship to it is one of enormous interest.[2] Calvin reveals that he was acutely aware of the issues of his medieval, scholastic background. Sometimes, he dismisses issues out of hand, as though aware of the pitfalls. Other times, Calvin displays a remarkable boldness, even when he knows that theological dangers are at hand. Nowhere is this more apparent than his treatment of the "double" righteousness of God in his sermons on Job.[3] The issue at stake is summed up this way: how can God's righteousness be maintained in view of the fact that Job suffers as a "righteous" man? The issue is exacerbated by testimony to his "righteousness" being given both by the author of Job (Job 1:1) and by God himself as bookends to the work (Job 1:8; 42:8).[4] That Job was not sinless is a point Calvin stresses in the exegesis of the book; but Job had "a good case."[5] How, then, can the righteousness of God be sustained in the face of such testimony? The issue depends upon the integrity of Job's claim to "innocence"; but it is a claim concerning which Calvin is ambivalent.

Similar tensions to those which arise in his exegesis of Job are to be found in Calvin's view of providence outlined in the *Institutes*. These tensions include the maintenance of God's justice, the nature of his power,[6] the extent of his self-revelation,[7] and the reality of suffering. In this chapter, however, we will major on a specific idea adduced by Calvin in the Joban sermons to counter the accusation that God's dealings with Job were unjust. If we grant the validity of Job's claim to personal righteousness (though this was problematic for Calvin), it becomes difficult to maintain God's integrity—how can it be right for him to allow the righteous to suffer? Calvin's solution is to resort to the idea of "double justice": that there is in God a righteousness apart from the revealed righteousness of the Law,[8] a *secret* righteousness before which even the angels are unsafe. For Susan Schreiner, this raises the spectre of medieval notions of "absolute power" (*potentia absoluta*).[9] At this point, at least, Calvin reveals himself a son of the medieval theologians.[10] This reading of Calvin needs evaluating in the light of what Calvin has to say about God's omnipotence and its relationship to his will in the Joban sermons. Here, Calvin is concerned to relate his doctrine of God with intensely personal issues of pain and suffering in the lives of his listeners. The issue is not hypothetical, but acutely personal.

In the third book of the *Institutes* (III.xxiii.2) Calvin attacks the distinction between the absolute and the ordained power of God as speculative. It involves a distinction between God's power and justice that potentially transforms God into a tyrant.[11]

The issue of suffering becomes problematic for those who, like Calvin, insist upon divine providence. "Ignorance of providence," he wrote in the *Institutes*, "is the ultimate of all miseries; the highest blessedness lies in the knowledge of it."[12] In the Joban sermons, Calvin is giving expression to what he had discussed more formally in Book I of the *Institutes*. In Job, Calvin discovers a world that he knew only too well: fragile, hazardous and intensely complicated, a world in which morality and theology are fully tested. In the interchange of ideas and arguments that unfold in the Joban Dialogues, the theology of providence is rigorously evaluated. In the face of Job's suffering— the suffering of a righteous man—is it possible to maintain God's government of the world *and* his justice?[13]

To examine these issues it is necessary for us to examine two further issues: first, Calvin's understanding of the nature of human righteousness in a believer, and second, Calvin's distinctive understanding (in the *Sermons on Job*) of the nature of the righteousness of God.

## The Believer's Righteousness

A tension develops in the exegesis of Job between the claim of Job's righteousness on the one hand, a claim made by the author of Job (1:1), by God himself (1:8; 42:7) and repeatedly by Job himself (9:15, 12:4, 13:16-18, 16:17, 23:7, 23:10-12, 27:5-6, 29:14-25), and, on the other hand, the integrity (justice/righteousness/power) of God in Job's suffering. The problem is three-fold: first, granting the validity of Job's initial claims to integrity, what are we to make of Job's repeated attributions of injustice in God's handling of him in such passages as 3:1-23, 9:22-25, 19:6-7 and 21:7-33? In addition, how are we to understand Job's confession of sin and repentance in the final chapters (see 39:33 (40:4)[14] and 42:1-6)?[15] Is a consistent claim to "innocent suffering" possible, particularly since Job himself uttered a statement confirming original sin, "Who can make clean one conceived of unclean seed?" (Job 14:4, Vulgate)?[16] Second, if it be maintained that Job sinned, not so much before, but during the trial, does this not mean that "Satan must have won the wager with God recounted in the Prologue?"[17] Job's own confession of sin in such passages as 7:20-21, 9:20-21, 14:4, 14:16-17, 31:33-34 seem decisive. If so, the entire theology of Job and Calvin's doctrine of providence are jeopardised. Third, if a consistent argument can be made for Job's righteousness (at least, prior to the onset of his suffering), how can God's righteousness be sustained in the face of what appears to be the suffering of an "innocent" man. If God's government of the universe be sustained in the way Calvin describes in the *Institutes*, does not his power take on overtures of the tyrannical and arbitrary, a medieval concern of which Calvin was acutely aware?

## Innocent Suffering

Taking these issues in order, we need to examine, in the first place, the possibility of "innocent suffering". Calvin is eager to endorse the biblical testimony with regard to Job's character. In the opening sermon he gives eloquent testimony to Job's godliness:

> It is sayd, that *He was a sound man*. This word *sound* in the Scripture is taken for a *playnnesse*, when there is no poynte of fayning, counterfayting, or hypocrisie in a man, but that he sheweth himself the same outwardly that he is inwardly, and specially when he hath no starting holes to shift himself from God, but layeth open his heart, and all his thoughts and affections, so as hee desireth nothing but to consecrate and dedicate himself wholly vnto God. The sayde worde hathe also bene translated *perfect*, as well by the Greekes as by the Latins. But for as muche as the woorde *perfect*, hath afterwarde bene misconstrued: it is much better for vs to vse the worde *sound*. For manie ignorant persones, not knowing howe the sayde *perfection* is to bee taken, haue thoughte thus: Beholde heere a man that is called perfect, and therefore it foloweth, that it is possible for vs to haue perfection in oure selues, euen during the tyme wee walke in this presente life. But they deface the grace of God, whereof wee haue neede continually. For euen they that haue liued moste vprightly, muste haue recourse to Gods mercie: and except their sinnes be forgiuen them, and that vphold them, they must needs all perishe.[18]

Rejecting "perfect" for "sound" in his comments on Job 1:1, Calvin adds:

> So then although that they whiche haue vsed the worde *perfect*, haue ment well: yet notwithstanding for as muche as there haue ben some that haue wrested it too a contrarie sense, (as I haue sayd) lette vs kepe still the word *Sound*. Then looke vpon Iob, who is called *Sound*. And how so? It is bicause ther was no hypocrisie nor dissimulation, nor any doublenesse of heart in him.[19]

Throughout his exegesis, Calvin upholds this defence of Job's character against the view taken by Job's counsellors, who maintain that Job's suffering is due to specific sin (or sins) on his part. A case for "innocent suffering," then, can be made. It is interesting, for example, since Calvin often compares Job with David, to note how he comments on David's plea in Psalm 7:8[9], "Judge me, O God, according to my righteousness, and according to the integrity that is in me." He writes:

> But it is asked, how can David here boast of his own integrity before God, when in other places he deprecates God entering into judgment with him? The answer is easy, and it is this: The subject here treated of is not how he could answer if God should demand from him an account of his whole life; but, comparing himself with his enemies, he maintains, and not without cause, that, in respect of them, he was righteous. But when

each saint passes under the review of God's judgment, and his own character is tried upon its own merits, the matter is very different, for then the only sanctuary to which he can betake himself for safety, is the mercy of God.[20]

In the opening sermon on Job, Calvin insists upon Job's "good case."[21] The immediate cause of Job's suffering must not be seen as retribution for personal guilt on Job's part. Taking up Job's protest in Job 9, Calvin remarks:

> Thus yee see what Job ment by saying that he was wounded without cause: that is to witte, as if a man shoulde haue demaunded of him, knowest thou any euident cause in thy selfe why God punisheth thee? I see none. For Job was handled after a very straunge fashion... Iob therefore sawe not to what ende God did this: there was no reason in it, as to his knowledge. That is true: for he speaketh not in hypocrisie.[22]

The theology of instant retribution is an inappropriate measurement of suffering, then. It is the canon of Job's friends to be sure, but it is one that Calvin consistently repudiates. Speaking of war and hostility, Calvin says:

> Ye shal see sometimes that a whole Citie or a whole Countrie is put to hauocke: yee see all is put to the fire and swoord, yea euen the little babes in whom was nothing to bee seene but innocencie.[23]

But Calvin grows weary of defending Job's "good case." In the *Institutes*, Calvin can say:

> There never existed any work of a godly man which, if examined by God's stern judgment, would not deserve condemnation.[24]

And again, in the first sermon on Job 23, Calvin writes:

> What is man in himself? A mortall enimie of God and all goodnesse. So then we haue no shift to discharge ourselues against God, if he leaue vs to ourselues, but contrariwise we shall do nothing else but prouoke his wrath. And again, whe[n] he graunteth vs the grace by his Holie spirit, to loue the things that is good, and therwithall putteth such a woorkfulnesse in vs as our life becommeth a mirrur and example of holinesse: yet do we fayle so many wayes, that if we be able to answer God to one point, we be giltie in a thousand points for it. Yea and (which more is) wee neuer do any good, wherein there is not some blemish insomuch that we shuld be

faultie in al respects before God, if he listed to handle vs vigorously. Howbeit, when God is so graciouse to vs as to gouerne vs by his holie spirit, he accepteth the goodnesse that he hath put in vs, notwithstanding that it bee vnperfect… Iob knew well ynough that he was a wretched sinner, and he was not so blinded with pryde, as too beare himself in hand that he was throughly rightouse, and that God did but byte at him without cause.[25]

That Job knew well enough he was a "wretched sinner" may well be true, but it was more than Job was himself saying. Clearly, Calvin is ill at ease defending the notion of "innocent" suffering. In another sermon, Calvin can say:

But euen when a man is gouerned by Gods Spirite, and by hys grace doth walke in goode woorkes: yet are all his good works unperfecte, and God myght cast them off: yea and they are so farre off from any woorthynesse or deseruing (as the Papistes imagin) as there is nothing but fylthynesse in them.[26]

In the penultimate sermon, though Calvin is making another point, differentiating the godly believer from the hypocrite, he expresses his view that godliness, encapsulated as it is by the "fear of God," is present with imperfection:

Looke (I say) upon a man that feareth God, and is rightly and purely minded too gyue hymselfe to well doing: and yet notwithstanding he shall haue many infirmities: hee halteth, hee staggereth, he reeleth, yea and sometimes falleth flat downe. Yea but his faultes which hee doth are forgiuen hym, and God doth stil reach him his hande to lift him vp, insomuch that all falleth out to his benefite, because the marke that hee ameth at, is to goe vnto God, and his minde leadeth hym styll thitherwarde.[27]

In the *Institutes*, Calvin reveals his opposition to perfectionism; human righteousness, even in its highest form, is defective. What appears in the *Sermons on Job* is in entire accord with what Calvin wrote in the *Institutes*:

The best work that can be brought forward from them (viz. Believers) is still always spotted and corrupted with some impurity of the flesh, and has, so to speak, some dregs mixed with it.[28]

This discomfiture with "innocent suffering" finds expression in what, for Calvin, becomes emblematic of godliness. Picking up the phrase used by Job in 40:4, Calvin expounds on the necessity to have one's mouth "shut" before God:

> Heere then we bee warned of a vice that is great, wicked and hurtfull: which is, that we will needes be sharpe witted in pleading agaynst God, and set forth ourselues with a brauerie, to the end to cloke our wantes with vaine excuses… For when our tongue is venemous and altogither soked in lying and falsehoode: at the last it bursteth out [eue] against God.[29]

Given this ambivalence in Calvin's interpretation of Job, that Job has a "good case," but that his pleas of "innocence" were misplaced, Calvin could have interpreted Job's suffering as retribution. However upright Job was, he was not perfect. Calvin could have joined the three counsellors (if not Eliphaz) and resorted to the theology of instant retribution.

## Instant Retribution

Citing Augustine's *City of God*, Calvin remarks early in the *Institutes*, "If now every sin were to suffer open punishment, it would seem that nothing is reserved for the final judgement. Again, if God were now to punish no sin openly, one would believe that there is no providence."[30] Few statements could be further from the mind-set of Job's friends. When asked to explain Job's suffering, they unanimously explained it in terms of instant retribution: Job received what he deserved; God was punishing him for sin.[31] Calvin rejects this view. It is an "euill case".[32]

When asked to explain Job's suffering, Bildad, Eliphaz and Zophar were of one mind: Job's pain was the result of God's immediate retribution, rendering to men and women, here and now, what they deserve; rewarding good with blessing, evil with punishment. Since Job was suffering, he must have sinned; God was displeased with Job. For Calvin, this is the "key" that unlocks the Book of Job:

> Job maynteying a good quarell, did handle it ill, and that the other setting foorth an vniust matter, did conuey it well. The vnderstanding of this, will be as a key to open vntoo vs all this whole booke.[33]

God's justice, Calvin insists, belongs to his very essence.[34] Calvin insists that God is a Judge who cannot be "brybed and corrupted, as wee see mortall men are."[35] Calvin continues:

> For, his being Iudge of the worlde, is not by good happe, or by electio[n] at auenture, or by sute, or by purchace: but it is incident to him by nature, he is no sooner God, but he is immediately iudge therwithal.[36]

The very history of the world, providence, records God's judgements:

> At all times since men dwelt vpon the earth, it hath bene Gods will that there should alwayes be some recordes of his iudgeme[n]ts and therefore that wee must not bee so dull and blockish as not to consider the things that God hath done for our instruction.[37]

Such judgments serve as,

> warnings too shewe vs that hee is the iudge of the world: we must learne to stande in awe of him, and to walke warely, that the punishments which he hath executed vpon the wicked may be lookingglasses for vs.[38]

These judgements belong to God's "ordinary righteousness."

> ...when God punisheth whoremoongers, theeues, and drunkards: euen that also is his ordinarie rightuousnesse. If wee see a wicked man that shall haue fleeced his neyghbours, and playd the cruell beaste in eating vp and deuouring other mennes goods, and God bloweth vpon his substance, so as nothing remaineth to him: the same is a true shewe of Gods Iustice, and an assured warrant that euill gotten goods waste away: and it maketh vs too acknowledge that God is a iudge. Again when murtherers be punished likewise, we consider how it is written, that the cruell man shall not liue out half his dayes, and so is it also with other misdooers.[39]

But, is it always possible to discern the justice of God in his judgements, for they are sometimes "secret"?

> For sometimes God punisheth the sinnes that are notorious to the worldward....[40]

And again:

> Also Gods iustice is knowne in his secret iudgements, when wee see God smite and torment such folke as had no notable faults in them, but rather they had some vertues in them.[41]

And again:

> Gods iudgments are not executed ordinarily in this present lyfe, although we haue now and then some signes of them, and that is all.[42]

It follows that the interpretation of providence becomes troublesome and without incentive or hope:

> For wee shall thinke it but lost time that is spent in doing good, seing that God hath no regard of men, to guide them, but leaueth then as it were at randon [sic].[43]

Furthermore, 'God seemeth to gouerne things confuzedly to this day.'[44] And Calvin continues, a little later:

> Iustice and vprightnesse consist of two partes: wherof the one is the punishing of euill folke, and the other is the releeuing of good folke and the mayntayning of them in their rightuous and sounde conuersation. Therefore if God punish the wicked: he muste also on the contrarie part maintayne the good, so as he keepe them vnder his tuicion, and suffer them not to be troubled or torme[n]ted, but that they may feele his succour so soone as they crie vnto him. Howbeit (as we see) the good are punished, not for a day or twoo, but with lingering paynes all their life long, so that in stead of shewing any signe that he is minded to help them, it seemeth that God taketh vengeance of them and is purposed to plunge them into the bottomlesse pit.[45]

But, says Calvin, we must not cavil at this seeming injustice:

> Let vs marke well, that they be two diuerse maners of speech to say, God is righteous, for he punisheth men according to their desert, and too say, God is righteous, for howsoeuer hee handle men, yet must wee always keepe our mouthes shet and not grudge agaynst hym bycause we cannot gayne any thing thereby.[46]

How, then, are we to assess the judgements of God?

> We must come vp higher, [and saye] that God is alwayes righteous howsoeuer he handle men.[47]

For the present, then, God may appear to delay in the execution of his justice:

> Our Lorde may well delay the corrections that he intendeth to sende, and on the other side the time may seeme long vnto vs: buy yet must we restreyne our mindes, and holde them short, knowing that God wil not punish all the sinnes of the worlde presently, and he knoweth why: there is reason good ynough why he should do so, as I haue sayd alreadie.[48]

But such delay is not to be interpreted as acquittal:

> Let vs marke then that God punisheth not men as soone as they haue done amisse: and yet it followeth not that they are therfore acquit, and shall neuer be called to account. Nay rather, it is bicause God giueth vs respite here to returne to his mercie, and to beseech him to receiue vs to mercie.[49]

Indeed, in one sense, for Calvin, sin is always accompanied by God's wrath in some form. "Wherever sin is..." he wrote in the *Institutes*, "It is accompanied by the wrath and vengeance of God."[50] God may come suddenly in judgement:

> For although they [the wicked] were lifted vp to heauen or reached vp to the clowdes with their heads: yet should they not co[n]tinue, but God would throw them downe out of hand.[51]

On the other hand, God is patient, tempering his wrath in this world:

> ...at length he will shew that although he wayted for their repentance, yet he forgat not their misdedes, but registred them before him, and packed them vp vpon a great heap, to increase the terror of his wrath. Their delay therefore shall be dearly solde vnto them, when they shall haue so abused gods pacience, who forbare to punish them at the first, to the ende they shoulde haue leysure to knowe their faults, & to amend them.[52]

In other words, "We see that God worketh not alwayes after one rate."[53]

> If God execute his iudgements after a visible maner: let vs marke them, that wee may take good by them. If wee see them not: well, let vs vnderstand that he hath reserued the vtterance of them till the last day, for the triall of our fayth.[54]

But we are never to lose sight of the possibility of immediate retribution:

> For when God mindeth to put men so to destruction, hee leaueth them destitute of all meanes of help and succoure.[55]

Adding:

> Therfore when God doth so shewe vs his iudgementes, lette vs quake at them, and lette vs stande in feare and awe of him, submitting ourselues wholly too that which he sayeth and vttereth.[56]

In part, then, the doctrine of immediate retribution is correct: God does sometimes judge the sin immediately.[57] Such immediate retribution is a token of that which is to come.

> True it is that they are not vtterly consumed for the present tyme, howbeeit they are tokens of the horrible vengeance that is prepared for them at the latter day. Yee see then that many men are touched with Gods hand, which notwithstanding are accursed. For they begin their hell alredye in this world, according as wee haue examples in all such as amend not their wicked lyfe when God sendeth afflictions vpon them…[58]

Sometimes, the different "rate" of punishment manifests itself in the principle enunciated in the second commandment (Exod. 20:4-6; Deut.5:8-10):

> And there is a double manner of punishing the wickednesse of the fathers vpon their children. For sometymes God sheweth mercie to the children, and yet notwithsta[n]ding cesseth not to chastize the vnrightuousnesse of their fathers in the persones of theyr children.[59]

Because of the difference in "rate" as to God's judgements, we are to be careful in our interpretation of providence. On the one hand, we are not to engage in crass moralistic assessments. Immediate retribution is a "token" of that which is to come, and since we are told specifically in Job's case that his suffering was not due to his sin as such, Calvin balks at the unilateral application of this doctrine by the counsellors. In the penultimate sermon on Job, Calvin returns to this theme, which preoccupied him throughout:

> Therefore let vs eschew rashnes when we see god afflict any man roughly, & let vs not be too swift of iudgeme[n]t to say that he is worthie to be so handled, & to comed [condemn] such as liue at their ease, as though they were better beloued of God: for that were too unaduised a iudging, so it were.[60]

On the other hand, we are to discern a difference between this life and the one that is to come. Justice, for Calvin, matures eschatologically.

> For there are promises that belong but too the presente lyfe: and wee see not those promises perfourmed alwayes after one rate, but after as GOD knoweth them too bee expedient for vs. As touching the Spirituall

promises, that belong too the welfare of our soules, they bee certayne, and it behoueth vs too conclude, that God will neuer disappointe vs of them. So then let vs put a difference betweene the things that concerne this transitorie life, and the things that co[n]cerne the heauenly life and the euerlasting kingdome of God.[61]

The doctrine of delayed punishment was, for Calvin, an intensely pastoral one, to be viewed within the canons of God's incomprehensible providence. We are to recall that we are "wayfarers and wanderers."

> Verely if God plucke the wicked mens goodes out of their hands: let vs vnderstand that he fulfilleth the threat whiche wee heare spoken of in this place. And if he do not: let vs marke that he reserueth the execution of hys iustice vntill the last day, and that he wil not bring things to perfection as now, bycause he will nurrish oure hope still, and not haue vs wedded to this world, nor seeke our felicitie heere bylow as in a Paradise of pleasure, but too lift vp our eyes aloft, and to passe as lightly through thys world as through a iourney, knowing ourselues too be wayfarers and wanderers in this world, and that therefore it behoueth vs too trauell continually too the heauenly and euerlasting heritage.[62]

Thus, God's judgements are to be viewed with the end in mind. Calvin again exhorts the righteous:

> Assure yourselues that seing you haue not had your rest vpon earthe, God prepareth it for you in heaue[n]. Again on the other side if it be a thing that standeth vpon Gods justice, that the wicked shuld be punished according to their deserts, and yet notwithstading we see it not doone in this world: assure yourselues, that in your aduersities, troubles and miseries, God doeth as it were in a glasse shewe you, that you shall one day come vnto him: and that also is the verie thing whervnto your hope must be referred.[63]

We are to "tarie," waiting for God's justice to be revealed in the end:

> True it is that the Sunne doth for a time shine vpon the wicked as well as vpon the good, and the one of them liueth as well as the other: But tarie a while, for the wicked are not heyers of the worlde: and although that as now they receyue that which belongeth not to them, and haue their eies open to receiue the light of the Sunne: yet shall they be vtterly bereft of it in the end.[64]

Such a posture will relieve us of the burden of envy that destroys the soul:

*The Incomprehensible Righteousness of God*

> Then seing it is so: let vs tarie till our Lord vncase the wicked: and then we shall haue no more cause to enuy them, nor to ouershoote ourselues with them. If it be sayd, that it is a common thing to vs all to go to dust, and there to rotte: it is true. Howbeit we haue good companie, inasmuch as we haue walked in the feare of God during our life. For we knowe that if we yeeld our soules into his hands, he will keepe them well and faythfully. We shal bee well accompanied inasmuchas we knowe that the verie Angelles of God (as the Scriptrue telleth vs) shall receyue our soules to put them into this sayd good and safe keeping, vntill we rise againe intoo the heauenly glorie. Albeeit then that to outward apperance, euery one of vs be cut of from the world, and from the companie of men, and laid in our graues: Yet shall we be well accompanied to Godward, when we haue walked in the feare of him.[65]

God's justice is then incomprehensible to us. "Shall mortall men dare saye," asks Calvin, "that they are able too comprehende the measure of Gods rightuouesnesse? What a folly were that?"[66] Having rejected the simplistic, "evil" theology of the counsellors, Calvin resorts to another explanation for suffering; he raises the idea of "secret justice."[67]

## Double Justice

Schreiner offers a useful starting point for this concept: "Briefly, the concept of double justice posits a higher, hidden justice in God that transcends the Law and could condemn even the angels."[68] But in order to understand fully all the nuances in Calvin's concept of God's justice,[69] we need to look closely at his own arguments.

A lengthy allusion to this idea comes in a sermon on Job 9:29, "If I bee wicked, why labour I in vaine?":

> For we must always beare in minde, that Gods Maiestie is hidden from vs, and that in the same Maiestie there is a certaine rightfulnesse whiche wee comprehende not. True it is that God hath well giuen vs a patterne and image of rightfulnesse in his lawe, howebeit, that is but according too our capacitie. But it behoueth vs too knowe, that oure reason is so grosse, as it can not mounte so high, as to conceyue perfectly what is in God. So then the verie rightuousnesse whiche is conteyned in Goddes lawe, is a rightuousnesse that is bounded within the measure of mans capacitie. Wee doo rightly call it perfect rightuousnesse, and so maye wee name it: yea and the Scripture tearmeth it perfect rightuousnesse: howebeeit but in respect of vs, that is too saye in respect of creatures. I meene not in respect of vs as wee bee sinners, and as we bee all cursed in Adam: but in respect of vs as wee bee Gods creatures: yea and (too take

> away all difficultie) euen in respect of the Angelles. This rightuousnesse then is suche a rightuousnesse, as Angelles and men ought too yeelde vntoo God, by obeying him and pleasing him, yea euen in asmuche as they bee his creatures. But yet for all this, there is another higher rightuousnesse in God: that is to say a perfect rightuousnesse, wherevntoo wee bee not able too attayne, neyther can wee bee able too come any whitte neere it vntill wee bee made like vntoo him, and haue the function of the glorie that is hid from vs as yet, and which we see not but as it were in a glasse and darkely.[70]

Several things of crucial importance emerge from this citation. First, there are two standards of justice: one is contained in, and revealed by, the Law; the other is "higher" and "secret."[71] This means that it is impossible to claim an adequate righteousness by obedience to the Law.

> Wee shoulde all of vs be confounded and damned, were it not that hee goeth on further, and setteth his mercie before vs. Otherwyse wee shoulde all abyde accursed, notwythstanding that wee had performed all the things that are conteyned in his lawe.[72]

Second, there is an incomprehensibility to all of God's attributes; we cannot expect to understand fully the extent of God's justice. In that respect, it is "hidden" or "secret." Third, there belongs to us as "creatures" an "unrighteousness" in comparison with God's Majesty.[73] And fourth, this "creaturely liability"[74] is shared by the angels. It is just here, in connection with the idea of creatureliness, that Calvin first introduces the idea of "double justice." Responding to the words of Eliphaz, "Behold, he fyndeth no steadfastnesse in his servants, and he hathe put vanitie in his Angels," (Job 4:18), Calvin makes the following remarks:

> But let vs put the cace, that Iob were as an Angell, and that he were able too go through to Godwarde according too the righteousnesse of the lawe: yet shoulde he alwayes find himselfe behinde hande in respect of the secrete rightfulnesse that is in God.[75]

And why should he always "find himselfe behinde"? Partly, as we have seen, because of Calvin's ambivalence regarding "innocent suffering". No one is so spotless as to pass the scrutiny of God's judgement:

And sith the case standeth so, that if God lifted to iudge his angels with rigor, he should find fault ynough in the[m]: what then should become of them which are so vnable to say any thing for themselues, as they haue nothing in the[m] but vanitie?[76]

On this basis, God may proceed "with rigour."

Nor will it do to suggest that this view is unique to the Joban sermons; it finds its way directly into the *Institutes*. In the 1539 edition of the *Institutes*, Calvin translates Job 4:18, "Shall man be justified in comparison with God? Or shall he be purer than his maker? Behold, they that serve him are not faithful and even in his angels he finds wickedness."[77] In the 1559 edition, Calvin considerably adds to this reference, citing in addition the passage from Job 15:15-16, "Behold, among his saints none is faithful, and the heavens are not pure in his sight. How much more abominable and unprofitable is man, who drinks iniquity like water?" Calvin concludes:

> Indeed, I admit that in The Book of Job mention is made of a righteousness higher than the observance of the law, and it is worth-while to maintain this distinction. For even if someone satisfied the law, not even then could he stand the test of that righteousness which surpasses all understanding. Therefore, even though Job has a good conscience, he is stricken dumb with astonishment, for he sees that not even the holiness of angels can please God if he should weigh their works in his heavenly scales. Therefore, I now pass over that righteousness which I have mentioned, for it is incomprehensible.[78]

Another, equally crucial reference occurs in Calvin's commentary on Colossians 1:20. Commenting on Paul's words regarding Christ "reconciling all things unto himself," Calvin adds:

> Between God and angels the relationship is very different, for there was there no revolt, no sin and consequently no separation. It was, however, necessary for two reasons for angels also to be set at peace with God; for being creatures, they were not beyond the risk of falling, had they not been confirmed by the grace of Christ. It is of no small importance for the perpetuity of peace with God to have a fixed standing in righteousness, so as no longer to fear fall or revolt. Further, in that very obedience which they render to God, there is not such absolute perfection as to satisfy God in every respect and without pardon. And this, without doubt, is the sense of that statement in the Book of Job, 'He will find iniquity in his angels' (4:18). For if it is expounded of the devil, what would be the point

of it? But the Spirit declares there that the greatest purity is soiled, if measured by the righteousness of God. We must, therefore, lay it down that there is not in the angels so much righteousness as would suffice for full union with God. They have, therefore, need of a peace-maker, through whose grace they may wholly cleave to God.[79]

Aquinas, too, dealt with this issue. In the *Summa Theologiae*, he asks, "Can there be moral evil in angels?"[80] Referring directly to Job 4:18, Aquinas cites the challenge, "We read in *Job, He found wickedness in his angels.*"[81] Aquinas' reply underlines the dependence of the unfallen angels upon the "grace" of God:

> Any creature endowed with intelligence, whether angel or not if considered simply in its nature, can act wrongly; and if any be found impeccable, this is a gift of grace, it cannot be due to the creature's nature alone.[82]

Calvin, then, is treading well-worn ground here. Both Aquinas and Calvin are positing something about the nature of the angels who have not sinned. With them, it is not so much their sinfulness that poses a problem; it is their creatureliness, Calvin suggests:

> But if wee wist what the righeousnesse of God is: wee should not maruevle that the Angels themselues are fou[n]d to bee faultie, if he should co[m]pare them with himselfe. For we must alwayes come backe to this poynt, that the good things that are in all creatures, are small in estimation of that which is in God which is vtterly infinite.[83]

And again:

> And heere ye see also why we say in our prayer, Thy will be done in earth as it is in heaven. For there is no gaynsaying, God is obeyed fully, and he reigneth in Heauen. Then do wee desire to be conformable to the Angels, and that ought to be ynough for us: for then shall he haue such a perfection as ought to be in creatures. Yea but is that as much to say, as the Angels haue a righteeouesnesse that may fully match and be compared with the righteousnesse of God? There is as great oddes betwixt them, as there is distance betweene heauen and earth. Although the righteousnesse of the Angels be perfect in respect of creatures: yet is it nothing but smoke when it commeth beefore the infinite maiestie of God.[84]

Calvin's conclusion is terse and, at first glance, chilling:

But out of all doubt, if God shoulde vse all the rigour that were possible, against a man that were like the Angels of heauen, and walked in all foundnesse and perfection: [I say] if God shoulde vtter all his rigour against him: yet should he be iust and rightuous still. Yea verily: and yet were that without cause.[85]

Is Calvin suggesting in these quotations that the unfallen angels may suffer the retribution of God? Is this the spectre of absolute power? Not according to Paul Helm.

A crucial question here is what Calvin means by God finding fault with the unfallen angels. Does he mean blame them? I suggest not, but rather that God recognises that the unfallen angels are not self-sufficiently righteous but, being liable to fall are, compared with God himself, 'faulty'. Faulty in this sense means liable to fail, or capable of failure, not actually failed.[86]

Corroboration of this view can be gained from several passages in the Joban sermons, including the following:

We see the Angels are neere vnto God, and behold his glorie, and are wholy giuen to his seruice: and yet for all that, there is no stedfastnesse in them, further than they be vphild by the grace of God: They might fade and vanish awaye of themselues, were it not that God of hys meere goodnesse mainteyned them.[87]

And again:

Therefore wee neede not too woonder though there be nothing else but infirmitie in men, seing that the Angels which are so neere vnto God, haue not so exquisite a perfection, but that God may condemne them if hee list to enter into iudgement with them.[88]

And further evidence is forthcoming from a comment Calvin makes in a sermon on 1 Timothy 6:16:[89]

So then it is true that the Angels are immortall Spirites, and that this qualitie also agreeth to our soules, but it is not naturall: For whatsoeuer had a beginning may haue an ende, and maye come to decay, yea and to perish vtterly. And as the Angels were made, so wee say that they haue not an abiding state of nature as though they could not change, but this stedines whiche they have to continue and abide still in obedience to GOD, is a gift giuen them from an other, and so is also immortallitie.[90]

Creaturely righteousness is inherently liable to fall. As Calvin stated in the commentary on Colossians 1:20 regarding angels, "being creatures, they were not beyond the risk of falling." According to Calvin's understanding, then, creaturely righteousness is a derived righteousness. The angels, of whom Calvin says that they are not "subiect to euill lustes as wee bee, there is no temptation in them to thrust them out of the way,"[91] sustain their position only because God sustains them.[92] Thus Calvin writes in the *Institutes*, in a section that underlines the incomprehensibility of God's righteousness by a reference to Romans 9:20-21, "Who are you, O man, to argue with God? Does the molded object say to its molder, 'Why have you fashioned me thus?' Or does the potter have no capacity to make from the same lump one vessel for honor, another for dishonor?":

> If the execution of judgment properly belongs to God's nature he loves righteousness and abhors unrighteousness. Accordingly, the apostle did not look for loopholes of escape as if he were embarrassed in his argument but showed that the reason of divine righteousness is higher than man's standard can measure, or than man's slender wit can comprehend... Monstrous indeed is the madness of men, who desire thus to subject the immeasurable to the puny measure of their own reason! Paul calls the angels who stood in their uprightness "elect" [1 Tim. 5:21]; if their steadfastness was grounded in God's good pleasure, the rebellion of the others proves the latter were forsaken. No other cause of this fact can be adduced but reprobation, which is hidden in God's secret plan.[93]

Calvin is dealing here with election—the *testificatio* of God to election in God's effectual call through preaching. In so doing, Calvin gives expression to what is at the heart of this chapter: that no creature is inherently righteous before God, for all creaturely righteousness is derived. Apart from God's providence, "God may condemn them if hee list to enter into iudgement with them."[94] Thus, it is a perilous, fatal course to go to law with God, "to dispute" as Job desired (Job 9:3,14,19). It is necessary for us now to examine the connection between righteousness and the Law.

## Righteousness and the Law

God's Law is "a full and certaine rule whereby to liue well."[95] Obedience to this law is "reckened for righteous before God in all perfection and goodnesse;"[96] but yet, there can be no room for boasting:

It is of his owne free sauoure that he saith, he that doth these things shall liue in them. For God might exact what he listeth at oure hande, and yet notwithstanding we can neuer say that we be not in his dette. For wee bee his, and what soeuer we bring vnto him he will not accepte it excepte he list, Although wee take it to be as righteouse as any thing can bee, and that (to oure seeming) there be no faulte in it. Yet will not God voutsafe to cast his eye vpon it, except he list: that is to saye, exepte his owne meere grace and bountifulnesse do moue him to do it.[97]

By the standards of the revealed Law, there is no one who attains righteousness in the sight of God.

There is no finding of any perfect rightuousnesse heere in men, neyther is it to be sayde, that God is beholding to them, and that they may go to law with him, or that they haue deserued well at his hand, and that he cannot find any fault in them or in their lyfe.[98]

It is folly, then, to consider going to law against God:

For if thou wilt go to lawe with thy God, it behoueth thee to be well armed to answer him. And what wilt thou say to him? Seing thou haste nothing but wretchednes & cursednesse in thee, would it not sta[n]d thee in ha[n]d to submit thyself to him with all obedience and humilitie?[99]

We may attain a certain conformity to the demands of the Law, but only by the aid of the Holy Spirit:

till God gouerne vs with his spirite, all the holynesse that men perceyue in vs, is but hypocrisie and vntruth.[100]

The Law is "a patterne and image of rightfulnesse"[101] that is "bounded within the measure of mans capacitie."[102] To obey the revealed Law would still mean that Job would be "behinde hande in respect of the secrete rightfulnesse that is in God."[103] In the Law, God shows us a "double goodnesse... when he both giueth vs his law and also plucketh vs out of the damnation whereinto the same casteth vs."[104] Without this mercy,

wee shoulde all of vs be confounded and damned, were it not that hee goeth on further, and setteth his mercie before vs. Otherwyse wee shoulde all abyde accursed, notwythstanding that wee had performed all the things that are conteyned in his lawe.[105]

Condemnation, then, is inevitable apart from God's intervention:

For he considereth, that if he be wicked, the lawe of God shal condemne him: and that if he be righteous, there is yet another righteousnesse aboue that, whereby he shal not misse to be co[n]demned.[106]

Not even in the garden of Eden could Adam boast:

> Here, then, is the course that we must follow if we are to avoid crashing into these rocks: when man has been taught that no good thing remains in his power, and that he is hedged about on all sides by most miserable necessity, in spite of this he should nevertheless be instructed to aspire to a good of which he is empty, to a freedom of which he has been deprived.... At the time when man was distinguished with the noblest marks of honor through God's beneficence, not even then was he permitted to boast about himself. How much more ought he now to humble himself, cast down as he has been—due to his own ungratefulness—from the loftiest glory into extreme disgrace! At that time, I say, when he had been advanced to the highest degree of honor, Scripture attributed nothing else to him than that he had been created in the image of God [Gen. 1:27], thus suggesting that man was blessed, not because of his own actions, but by participation in God.[107]

Thus, *mutatis mutandis*, with the angels. Their "vanitie" consists, not in their disobedience to the Law, but in their very creatureliness. Their problem is ontological, not moral. Theirs is a liability to fall, apart from the beneficence of God. Their righteousness is not *a se*. To cite the sermon on the ninth chapter of Job again:

> ...there is another higher rightuousnesse in God: that is too say a perfect rightuousnesse, wherevntoo wee bee not able too attayne, neyther can wee bee able too come any whitte neere it, vntill wee bee made like vntoo him, and haue the function of the glorie that is hid from vs as yet, and which we see not but as it were in a glasse and darkely.[108]

**Universal Mediatorship (or Ontological Mediation)**
The references to Job 4:18 and Colossians 1:20 in Calvin raise another issue, one that occupied Calvin for several years—the issue of the eternality of Christ's mediatorship.[109] Responding to Francesco Stancaro,[110] Calvin affirmed the eternality of Christ's mediatorship:

> Thus we understand first that the name of Mediator applies to Christ not only because he took on flesh or because he took on the office of reconciling the human race with God. But already from the beginning of creation he was truly Mediator because he was always the Head of the

Church and held primacy even over the angels and was the first-born of all creatures. (Eph. 1:2; Col. 1:15ff; Col. 2:10). Whence we conclude that he began to perform the office of Mediator not only after the fall of Adam but insofar as he is the Eternal Son of God, angels as well as men were joined to God in order that they might remain upright.[111]

This theme is one that is repeated almost verbatim in Calvin's exposition of Job 4:18, in which the angels are charged with "vanitie."

> ...the Angels haue their stedfastnesse in the grace of our Lorde Iesus Christ, forsomuch as he is the mediator betwene God & his creatures. True it is that Iesus Christ redemed not the Angels, for they needed not to be raunsomed from death whervnto they were not yet falne: but yet was he theyr mediator. And howso? to the intent to ioyne the[m] vnto god in all perfection, and afterward to mainteyne them by his grace, that they may be preserued fro[m] falling.[112]

It is to be noted that in this citation, Calvin is distinguishing Christ's mediation as reconciliation and mediation as sustenance.[113] Whatever we may think of Calvin's view here—and it is difficult not to draw universalistic implications from this doctrine of universal mediatorship—it is interesting to note that, once again, Calvin leans on the doctrine of incomprehensibility here. In the same sermon, he adds a few sentences after raising this issue:

> True it is that we vnderstand not his mightie power as apperteyneth: but the Angels (which are now much neerer to him than we bee, and which beholds his face) haue no such perfection but that some fault may be found in them, if hee list to examine them with rigor.[114]

Given our present "weaknesse" in comparison with the angels, will the situation be different in the world to come? Does Calvin suggest that, eschatologically, redeemed man will attain to this secret righteousness? To examine this in some detail, we need to look at what Calvin had to say about eschatological righteousness in the Joban sermons.

## Eschatological Righteousness

For Calvin, there remains an ontological gulf between the Creator and his creatures. It is forever fixed. Not even the angels can surmount it. There is in God a righteousness that is *a se*, which can never be attained by any of his creatures. Two questions arise for our consideration. First: is Calvin's understanding of righteousness in God arbitrary at this point? Putting it another way, what is the connection between God's righteousness and his power? Second: to what extent can we ever expect to understand God's righteousness and its outworking in practice?

On the first question we should note that recent interpretations of Calvin on Job suggest a less than happy view of his understanding of the relationship between God's righteousness and power. Indeed, these interpretations would have us believe that Calvin was capable of the most blatant contradictions over the entire corpus of his writing, preaching and teaching. Consider, for example, what Calvin had to say by way of a comment on Luke 1:37, the words of the angel to Mary about her own and Elizabeth's conception.

> There is however one axiom always to bear in mind, that it is wilful aberration to speculate on anything that might occur within the power of God, beyond His Word. We must so consider His infinity that we give ourselves ground for hope and confidence. It is not only rash, it is quite useless to discuss what may be possible for God without reckoning on His will.[115]

Clearly, Calvin bids us to be cautious. No more so than in the *Institutes*:

> When, therefore, one asks why God has so done, we must reply: because he has willed it. But if you proceed further to ask why he so willed, you are seeking something greater and higher than God's will, which cannot be found. Let men's rashness, then, restrain itself, and not seek what does not exist, lest perhaps it fail to find what does exist. This bridle, I say, will effectively restrain anyone who wants to ponder in reverence the secrets of his God... And we do not advocate the fiction of "absolute might"; because this is profane, it ought rightly to be hateful to us. We fancy no lawless god who is a law unto himself.[116]

Turning to the Joban sermons, we discover more than one problem. There is, in the first place, Calvin's own opposition to "tyrannical" power. But, secondly, Calvin's own view is often complicated by his faithful expressions of Job's view, a view that Calvin tries sometimes to defend, sometimes to condemn.[117]

God's power is infinite: no one is able to "bring any power that shall be able to match his."[118] Calvin's concern with God's omnipotence is a pastoral one. As a preacher he needed something to say to his beloved people in pain.

> Wee muste acknowledge the power of God to be so greate, as he is able too succour those that are as it were ouerthrowen, and that he is able too quicken them againe although they were alreadie dead. But we must not apply this doctrine onely to our neighbours: wee must also practize it eche one of vs in himselfe[119]

In Job, God has given us a "proof"[120] of his power. Nor need we look far to find this evidence of his majesty:

> We needed not too go out of ourselues: for wee shuld find presidents ynow bothe of his power and of his will, so as we should behold bothe his myghtinesse and his goodnesse within vs, without going any further.[121]

God's power belongs, for Calvin, with those things that are incomprehensible and hidden from us.

> Gods power is not subiect too any humane or worldely meanes: but that he worketh after such a fashion, as is incomprehensible and secret vntoo vs.[122]

Calvin finds proof of God's power in the final dénouement of the Joban narrative: the Leviathan and Behemoth.[123] Here, as we shall see later, is the Joban test: will Job be subject to God's power even when it *appears* incomprehensible, even unjust? In Sermon 146, Calvin refers to God's omnipotence over and over, concluding:

> …a man can neuer haue a good cace in maynteyning himself to be ryghtuouse and wise, but must first of all be vtterly disabled, and acknowledge that God hath all myght, power, and ryghtuousenesse in him, and that we cannot be but ouerwhelmed in our owne nature.[124]

But at the same time Calvin wants to avoid the notion of *potentia absoluta*, the "tyrrannicall or lawlesse" power of the nominalist tradition:

> Although God haue all power ouer vs: yet notwithstanding hee iudgeth vs with such vprightnesse, as there is no fault to bee founde in it… God hath no such lawlesse power… but as his power is infinite, so are all his doings indifferent and rightfull.[125]

It is clear that Calvin's opposition to tyrannical power as outlined in the *Institutes*, for example, continues in the Joban sermons, despite his attempts to defend Job. As we have already seen, Calvin sometimes regards Job's defence as blasphemous. If we look at the wider context, we will grasp why this is so. Thus, commenting on Job 23:6, "Would he debate the matter with me by force?," Calvin adds:

> How, meeneth he that God wil not deale with him by force? It were to go too lawe with him if he would giue him the hearing. Iob then presupposeth that God vseth an absolute or lawelesse power (as they terme it) towards him: as if he should say, I am God, I will doo what I list, although there be no order of Iustice in it but plaine lordly ouerruling. Herein Iob blasphemeth God: for although Gods power bee infinite, yet notwithstanding, to imagin it to bee so absolute and lawlesse is as much as to make him a Tirant, which were vtterly contrarie to his maiestie. For our Lord wil not vse might without right, nother is he lesse rightfull than mightful: his rightfulnesse and mightfulnesse are things inseparable. Therefore Iobs saying is euill.[126]

In similar fashion, and even more pointedly:

> And undoutedly wheras the doctors of Sorbon say that God hath an absolute or lawlesse power, it is a diuelish blasphemie forged in hell, for it ought not once to enter into a faithfull mannes head. Therfore we must say that God hath an infinite or endlesse power, whiche notwithstanding is the rule of all righteousnesse. For it were a rending of God in peeces, if we shuld make him almightie without being alrighteous. True it is, that his righteousnesse shall not always be apparant vnto vs, but yet ceasseth it not too continue euermore sounde and vnappayred.[127]

Similarly:

> the maner of dealing whiche God vseth towards him, is so high and profound, as mans reason can neuer reach vnto it. And it is a very true saying, so it bee well applied: but Iobs fault is, that forasmuch as he perceiueth not the reason of Gods doings, hee imagineth him too vse an absolute or lawlesse power (as they terme it) that is too say, that God woorketh at his owne pleasure withoute keeping any order or rule, and that hee doth as he listeth, like a Prince that will not be ruled by reason, but foloweth his owne liking. In so saying Iob blasphemeth God: howbeit, that is bycause of the suddaine pangs of his passions…[128]

In the next sermon, Calvin returns to the theme again, referring to Job's allegations as to God's power as "ouermuch"[129] adding, "But he surmizeth a lawlesse power that hath nother rule nor measure with it, wherein he doth God wrong."[130] Haunted as Calvin may be by Job 2:3, which states that God acted "without cause,"[131] Calvin is equally insistent that though the cause may be hidden to us, it is part of the incomprehensible knowledge of God. Schreiner seems unnecessarily reticent when she attributes to Calvin the following:

> Although he (Calvin) argues that Job would be guilty before this secret justice, Calvin will not say that Job was punished because of his sins before this higher standard. Consequently, he is forced to admit that while God can "act" according to this secret justice, God cannot "judge" according to it.[132]

Given Calvin's opposition to the *potentia absoluta*, it emerges that in those passages where notions of "lawlesse power" emerge, the exegete is being faithful to views expressed by Job in the rage of his passions.[133] That consistency of response from Job is not forthcoming is hardly surprising; later, we shall examine the emotional responses of Job to suffering, arguing that there is evidence of extreme contrasts, both in his reasoning and sentiment. That God has a "secrette" justice need not be interpreted as the ghost of late medieval nominalism; rather, as we shall see, it is yet another instance of Calvin's resort to incomprehensibility in the character and ways of God. We cannot expect to fully understand or justify the ways of God. There is another reason for suffering, one which is known fully to him, but is hidden from us, and even more so from Job himself to whom the Prologue was unknown.

There remains the second important question arising from Calvin's discussion of the righteousness of God. This concerns God's comprehensibility—to what extent can we ever expect to understand God's righteousness and its outworking in providence? The answer to this question seems to lie for Calvin in an oft-cited reference to 1 Corinthians 13:9-12 and to the fact that even though we may now know only in part, *then* (eschatologically considered) we shall know in some degree of fullness. To cite Calvin:

> Yet muste we honour his secrete and incomprehensible iudgements, and gather our wittes too vs in all humblenesse, too say, Beholde, it is true

that as now this seemeth too vs to bee able to preuayle against God. And so without any further replying, we must holde it for a sure conclusion, that God is rightuous. For asmuche then as wee see nowe but in parte, yea euen as it were in a glasse and darkley: lette vs wayte for the day wherein we shall see Gods glorie face to face, and then shall we comprehende the thing that is hidden from vs now.[134]

We shall deal later with the question as to how far Calvin is a sure guide at this point. It might be argued, for example, that no such promise is given of comprehensive understanding of the righteousness of God even in the eschatological dimensions of the world to come. If God is ontologically incomprehensible, as Calvin seems to have been arguing, consistency would argue that he remains so even when all aspects of sin are removed in the perfect world to come. This, at least, seems a minor caveat in Calvin's treatment of the righteousness of God, which we shall have to take up again in the following chapters.

Two issues raised in this chapter call for comment. The first has to do with "double justice." Though we have argued for caution in the scope that was given to his idea, some problems remain. If Calvin can appeal to incomprehensibility to escape the charge of nominalism, a pastoral problem emerges of huge proportions since the "innocent" sufferer can never be assured of final acceptance. On this score the Book of Job would turn out to be a message of despair rather than an incentive to the victory of faith.

Secondly, Calvin's resort to ontological/universal mediation is also problematic. Apart from the questionable exegesis of Job 4:18, other, more theological, considerations are in order. Calvin's opposition to any idea of an incarnation apart from the Fall (his oppositon to Osiander, for example[135]), appears to be at odds with the fact that he was prepared to consider the necessity of a Mediator for the unfallen condition. If unfallen humanity is need of a mediator, Christ in his human nature would also necessitate such mediation. This is a path, down which Calvin would not wish to travel.

## References

[1] See William J. Bouwsma, *John Calvin: A Sixteenth Century Portrait* (Oxford, New York: Oxford University Press, 1988), 2-5; Heiko A. Oberman, *The Dawn of the Reformation: Essays in Late Medieval and early Reformation Thought* (Grand Rapids, Michigan: William B. Eerdmans Publishing Company, 1986); Alister E. McGrath, *A Life of John Calvin: A Study in the Shaping of Western Culture* (Oxford UK, Cambridge USA: Blackwell Publishers, 1991); Alister E. McGrath, *Iustitia Dei: A History of the Christian Doctrine of Justification*, 2 vols. (Cambridge: Cambridge University Press, 1986).

[2] In distinguishing Calvin from the Scholastic, medieval background, commentators have pointed out that he was, after all, a student of Scripture; he did not engage in the speculative and uncertain exegetical method of the medieval writers; he did not seek the four-fold sense of Scripture (the so-called *quadriga*), but engaged in grammatico-historical exegesis, commenting sparingly on the text. Calvin's interests are practical rather than abstract, a mind-set drawn as a result of his view of Scripture as theologically sufficient. Turning, as the Reformers did, to the text of Scripture itself and to its own interpretation of itself—the Reformation hermeneutical principle *Sacra Scriptura sui ipsius interpres*—their concerns were to find the "literal" interpretation of Scripture. In doing so, their interests were practical rather than theoretical.

The *quadriga* is the term used for medieval exegesis that sought to detect four "senses" of a given text of Scripture: the literal or historical, the tropological or moral, the allegorical or doctrinal, and the analogical or ultimate, eschatological meaning. Though less rigid than Origen, Augustine distinguished the literal, moral, pneumatic and doctrinal or "psychical" meaning in his *On Christian Doctrine*, a volume that became the basic hermeneutical manual for the Middle Ages. For an in-depth analysis, see Richard A. Muller, *Dictionary of Latin and Greek Theological Terms: Drawn Principally from Protestant Scholastic Theology* (Grand Rapids, Michigan: Baker Book House, 1985), s.v. "quadriga." Muller notes that Calvin "used hermeneutic of promise and fulfilment to present the direct address of the Old Testament to his own time—paralleling the interest of the allegorical and analogical reading of the text." *Op. cit.*, p.255. For an analysis of Calvin's expository method, see T. H. L. Parker, *Calvin's Preaching* (Louisville, Kentucky: Westminster/John Knox Press, 1992), 79-91. See also Parker's companion volumes, *Calvin's Old Testament Commentaries* (Edinburgh: T. & T. Clark, 1986), *Calvin's New Testament Commentaries* (Edinburgh: T. & T. Clark, 1971). Calvin comments on the frivolity of searching for the allegorical meaning of Scripture: "It seems to me far too frivolous to search for allegories" *Comm.*, Dan. 8:25; cf. his comment about the "natural and simple meaning of Scripture" *Comm.*, Gal. 4:22 (against Origen), and "a most disastrous error" and the "source of many evils," *Comm.*, 2 Cor. 3:6. See also, G. C. Berkouwer, *Holy Scripture* (Grand Rapids, Michigan: William B. Eerdmans, 1975), 105-138. Susan Schreiner concludes: "Calvin tries to find what Aquinas called the historical or literal sense of the text: the meaning that allows the 'things signified by the words' to become clear." Susan Schreiner, *Where Shall Wisdom Be Found* (Chicago, London: The University of Chicago Press, 1994), 91.

[3] Parker himself cites a date for the start of the Joban sermons beginning in the last week of February 1554, *ibid.*, 151.

[4] "...there was no hypocrisie nor dissimulation, nor any doublenesse of heart in him." *Sermons on Job*, 1 (Job 1:1), 3.a.67. ...*c'est pource qu'il n'y a eu nulle hypocrisie, ne fiction en lui, qu'il n'a point eu le coeur double* [*CO* 33:28]. Cf. Job "was as a mirrour of pacience." *Ibid.*, 28 (Job 7:7-15), 130.b.19. ...*comme un miroir de patience* [*CO* 33: 353].

[5] "Job maynteineth a good case..." 1 (Job 1:1), 1.b.33. *Iob maintient une bonne cause...* [*CO* 33:23]. For the consistency with which Calvin maintains this argument in his understanding of Job, see the similar comment in 129 (Job 34:4-10), 607.a.4 [*CO* 35:131].

[6] See David Steinmetz, "Calvin and the Absolute Power of God," in *Calvin in Context* (New York, Oxford: Oxford University Press, 1995), 40-52. François Wendel, *Calvin: Origins and Development of His Religious Thought* (Durham, N.C.: Labyrinth Press, 1963, 1987), 126-29.

[7] I have in mind here the doctrine of God's incomprehensibility, which Calvin refers to in almost every sermon on Job. On the similarity with Luther's *Deus Absconditus*, see Brian Gerrish, "'To the Unknown God': Luther and Calvin on the Hiddenness of God," *The Old Protestantism and the New* (Chicago: University of Chicago Press, 1982). For Calvin, as opposed to Aquinas, the book of Job is as much about God's invisibility, his secret ways and acts, as anything else. See Schreiner, *Where Shall Wisdom be Found?*, 9. For a similar view, see William J. Bouwsma, *op. cit.*, 42.

[8] Calvin uses several expressions to describe this created justice, including *iustice ordinaire, notoire, manifeste*.

[9] As to whom Calvin has in mind when he castigates the defenders of *potentia absoluta*, see Stauffer, *op. cit.*, 116, "La question reste donc ouverte." Since then (1977), research has been more narrowly done on the origins and background to Calvin's thought. McGrath, for example, points out that the debate over *potentia absoluta* and the *potentia ordinata* arose out of the dialectic between the two powers of God between the *via moderna* and the *schola Augustiniana moderna*. Underlining, as the dialectic does, the principle known as Ockham's razor, not to multiply entities beyond necessity—*quia frustra fit per plura quod potest equaliter per pauciora* (In *II Sent.* Qq. 14-15 O)—theologians of both schools attempted to limit the discussion. The distinct issue for consideration here related to how God could be said to act reliably without simultaneously implying that he acted of necessity. In the interests of defending God's freedom, one school of thought (e.g., the Parisian Averroists) claimed that reliability was an admission of external constraint upon God. The "solution" came in the form of a discussion between the hypothetical and the actual. As McGrath puts it, "In

that God is omnipotent, he is able to do anything, provided that logical contradiction is not involved... However, God did not actualize each and every possibility: only a subset of the initial set of possibilities was selected for actualization. A careful distinction must therefore be drawn between two distinct subsets: the subset of actualized possibilities, and the subset of actualized possibilities which, although hypothetically possible, will never now be actualized. In other words, God must be thought of as possessing the *ability* to do many things which he does *will* to do, in the past, present or future. God's freedom in relation to the initial set of actualizable possibilities is designated as the sphere of his 'absolute power (*potentia absoluta*)', and in relation to the subset of actualized possibilities his 'ordained power (*potentia ordinata*)' — and it is the dialectic between these two powers of God which permits both the divine reliability and freedom to be upheld... God is totally reliable, in that having established the ordained order as an act of divine creative will, he remains faithful to that order. To act contrary to it would imply a contradiction within the divine will, which is unthinkable." Alister E. McGrath, *The Intellectual Origins of the European Reformation* (Oxford: Blackwell Publishers, 1987), 78-79. Cf. also his *Iustitia Dei*, vol. 1, 119-28. On the influence of 'Ockhamism' on Calvin, and the theories of Karl Reuter (that Calvin was introduced to 'Scotist theology' during his time at Paris) in *Das Grundverständis der Theologie Calvins* (Neukirchen, 1981), and the denial of it by A. Ganoczy, in *Le jeune Calvin: genèse et évolution de sa vocation réformatrice* (Wiesbaden, 1966), see McGrath, *The Intellectual Origins of the European Reformation*, 99-106. See also Thomas F. Torrance, "La philosophie et la théologie de Jean Mair ou Major (1469-1550)," *Archives de philosophie* 32 (1969), 531-47; 33 (1970), 261-94; Torrance, "Intuitive and Abstractive Knowledge from Duns Scotus to John Calvin," in *De doctrina Ioannis Duns Scoti: Acta tertii Congressus Scotistici Internationalis* (Rome, 1972), 291-305; François Wendel, *Calvin: Origins and Development of His Religious Thought* (Durham, N.C.: Labyrinth Press, 1963, 1987), 127-128.

[10] Schreiner, *Where Shall Wisdom be Found?*, 110-120. "Frankly," Schreiner concludes, "the sovereignty of Job's God scared even Calvin; the ruler of history cannot be a God who afflicts pain 'without cause' or by a will unformed by goodness or justice. This fear of an unreliable or tyrannical God haunts Calvin's use of the idea of double justice as a hermeneutical device throughout the sermons. The further he read into the text, the more Calvin saw Job facing the inscrutability of providence and the darker side of God's nature. Just when the darkness became unbearable, Calvin quickly rooted God's freedom in God's unchangeable promises and in the inseparable nature of the divine essence," 119-120. Earlier, Schreiner makes the observation that "Calvin develops a theory of justice that draws rather loosely on the Scotist-nominalist vocabulary of his day: the radical freedom of God," 106. On the complexity and non-homogeneous nature of this late medieval background, see Alister McGrath, *The Intellectual Origins of the European Reformation*, 75-85. On

the problem of defining nominalism, see the same work, 70-72. McGrath concludes, "there is an increasing recognition that the term 'nominalism' must be abandoned, in that it appears to be an unusable historical concept," 70. McGrath's conclusion is that Calvin shows closer links with the voluntarist tradition, deriving from William of Ockham and Gregory of Rimini, "in relation to which Scotus marks a point of transition," 105. See also William C. Placher, *A History of Christian Theology: An Introduction* (Philadelphia, PA: Westminster Press, 1983), 162-180.

[11] For an analysis of this issue outside the Joban material, see David Steinmetz, "Calvin and the Absolute Power of God," in *Calvin in Context* (New York, Oxford: Oxford University Press, 1995), 40-52.

[12] *Institutes* I.xvii.11. "*Ducem ergo et exercitum denuntiat Deus se hamo suo capturum, et tracturum quo volet. Denique, ne hic diutius immorer, facile, si animadvertas, perspicies, extremum esse omnium miseriarum, providentiae ignorationem; summum beatitudinem in eiusdem cognitione esse sitam.*" [*CO* 2:164].

[13] See Ian McPhee, "Conserver or Transformer of Calvin's Theology? A Study of the Origins and Development of Theodore Beza's Thought, 1550-1570" (Ph.D. thesis, Cambridge University, 1979), 60-66.

[14] In the section on Job 38:38-41:34, Calvin follows the versification of the Vulgate.

[15] Recent scholarship on Job often points out that the object of the verb נחם, often translated "repent" in Job 42:6 is unspecific. Thus, Norman C. Habel, for example, concludes that "the implied object of the verb *m's*, "reject/retract," is apparently Job's suit." He goes on, "Job does not negate the words he has spoken, but withdraws his case against Shaddai now that Yahweh has spoken with Job face to face." Norman C. Habel, *The Book of Job: A Commentary* (Philadelphia: The Westminster Press, 1985), 582. Cf. John C. L. Gibson, *Job*, The Daily Study Bible Series (Philadelphia: The Westminster Press, 1985), 260-261; S. R. Driver and G. B. Gray, *A Critical and Exegetical Commentary on the Book of Job*, 2 vols. (New York: Charles Scribner's Sons, 1921), 2:348. For a composite interpretation, see H. H. Rowley, *Job*, The Century Bible (New Series) (London: Thomas Nelson and Sons Ltd, 1970), 342. According to Rowley, "Whether Job is despising himself for the things he has said or recanting the things he has said... does not need to be decided, since the one would involve the other." For an interpretation that sees Job as recanting, "withdraw[ing] his avowal of innocence," see John E. Hartley, *The Book of Job* (Grand Rapids, MI: Eerdmans, 1988), 537. Calvin, on the other hand, takes the view that Job 42:6 is a confession of sin on Job's part. Commenting on verse 8 and the implication that, contrary to his friends, Job had spoken what was right, Calvin remarks, "How was that? For God notwithstanding condemned him as an ignorant, ouerweening and vnpatient person. And where is then the said rightnesse (I haue told you heeretofore how Iob had vndertaken a good case, howbeit hee proceeded amisse in it. Iob therefore ouershot himselfe in the following of his matter,

but yet for all that his case was good stil[)]." 158 (Job 42:6-8), 743.a.60. *Comment cela? Toutes fois Dieu l'a condamné comme un ignorant, comme un outrecuidé, comme un homme impatient. Et où est ceste droiture? Nous avons declaré ci dessus que Iob a demené une bonne cause, combien qu'il y ait mal procedé: Iob donc a failli en la procedure qu'il tenoit, mais cependant sa cause estoit bonne* [CO 35:493-494].

[16] "...like as God created all mankynd after his owne image in the persone of Adam: even so also through Adams sin, not only Adam himself, but consequently also all his offspring were depryved and shut out from the grace that had bene bestowed upon him. And whereof commeth that? Bycause wee were all inclosed within his persone, according to the will of God." 53: (Job 14:1-4), 248.b.49. ...*comme Dieu en la personne d'Adam avoit creé à son image tout le genre humain: ainsi Adam par le peché n'est pas seulement privé et banni des graces qui lui estoient conferees: mais tout son lignage par consequent. Et d'où procede cela? Pource que nous estions tous enclos en sa personne, selon la volonté de Dieu* [CO 33:660-661].

[17] Schreiner, *Where Shall Wisdom be Found?*, 107.

[18] 1 (Job 1:1), 3.a.40. *Il est dit,* Qu'il estoit un homme entier. *Or ce mot en l'Escriture se prend pour une rondeur, quand il n'y a point de fiction, ne d'hypocrisie en l'homme, mais qu'il se monstre tel par dehors comme il est au dedans, et mesmes qu'il n'a point d'arriere boutique pour se destourner de Dieu, mais qu'il desploye son coeur, et toutes ses pensees et affections, qu'il ne demande sinon de se consacrer à Dieu, et s'y dedier du tout. Ce mot ici a esté rendu Parfaict, tant par les Grecz que par les Latins: mais pource qu'on a mal exposé puis apres le mot de Perfection, il vaut beaucoup mieux que nous ayons le mot d'Integrité. Car beaucoup d'ignorans, qui ne savent pas comment se prend ceste perfection, ont pensé, Voila un homme qui est appelé parfait, il s'ensuit donc qu'il y peut avoir perfection en nous, cependant que nous cheminons en ceste vie presente. Or ils ont obscurci la grace de Dieu, de laquelle nous avons tousiours besoin: car ceux qui auront cheminé le plus droitement, encores faut-il qu'ils ayent leur refuge à la misericorde de Dieu: et si leurs pechez ne leur sont pardonnez, et que Dieu ne les supporte, les voila tous peris* [CO 33:27-28].

[19] 1 (Job 1:1), 3.a.62. *Ainsi donc combien que ceux qui ont usé du mot de Perfection, l'ayent bien entendu, toutesfois d'autant qu'il y en a eu qui l'ont destourné à un sens contraire (comme i'ay dit) retenons le mot d'Integrité. Voici donc Iob, qui est nommé entier. Comment? c'est pource qu'il n'y a eu nulle hypocrisie, ne fiction en lui, qu'il n'a point eu le coeur double:...*[CO 33:28].

[20] *Commentary on the Book of Psalms*, trans. James Anderson, vol. 1, in *Calvin's Commentaries, Vol. IV, Joshua-Psalms 1-35* (Grand Rapids, MI: Baker Book House, 1981), 84. *Sed quaeritur quomodo suam integritatem iactet coram Deo David, qui alibi deprecatur eius iudicium. Solutio facilis est, quia hic non agitur quomodo respondeat, si exigat ab eo Deus totius vitae rationem: sed se hostibus suis comparans, non frustra se eorum*

*respectu iustum esse asserit. Ubi autem pro se quisque sanctorum in Dei iudicium prodit, longe diversa est ratio: quia tunc unicum illis asylum superest in misericordia Dei* [CO 31:83]. On the comparison of Job and David, see Schreiner, *Where Shall Wisdom be Found?*, 95-105.

[21] 1 (Job 1:1), 1.b.33. *...une bonne cause...*[CO 33:23].

[22] 35 (Job 9:16-22), 163.b.13. *Voila comme Iob dit qu'il a esté navré sans propos: c'est assavoir, si on me demande, Cognois-tu une raison evidente en toy, pourquoy Dieu t'afflige? Ie n'en voy point. Car Iob esoit traité d'une façon bien estrange: nous avons veu qu'il estoit là comme un miroir d'un homme reprouvé, qu'il sembloit que Dieu voulust desployer toute son ire et sa fureur contre luy. Iob donc ne voit point pourquoy Dieu fait cela: il n'y a point de raison, voire quant à luy. Et cela est vray: il ne parle point par hypocrisie.*[CO 33:438].

[23] 35 (Job 9:16-22), 163.a.59. *Il y aura aucunesfois un sac d'une ville, ou d'un pays, voila tout qui est mis au feu, et à l'espee, voire iusques aux petis enfans, là où on ne voyoit qu'innocence* [CO 33:438].

[24] III.xiv.11. "*Nullum unquam exstitisse pii hominis opus quod, si severo Dei iudicio examinaretur, non esset damnabile.*" [CO 2:571]. Even in his comments on the man blind from birth (John 9:1ff.), in which Jesus insists that the cause of suffering lies outside of this man's (or his parents') sin, Calvin nevertheless adds: "What we have just said now is undoubtedly true, that all our distresses arise from sin." John Calvin, *The Gospel According to St. John,* Part One, 1-10, trans. T. H. L. Parker, ed. David W. Torrance and Thomas F. Torrance (Grand Rapids, MI: Eerdmans, 1993), 237. "*Primo, quum testatur scriptura aerumnas omnes, quibus obnoxium est genus humanum, ex peccato provenire...*" [CO 47:217].

[25] 88 (Job 23:1-7), 413.a.46. *Qu'est ce que l'homme en soy? Un ennemi mortel de Dieu, et de tout bien. Ainsi donc nous n'avons garde de nous acquiter envers Dieu quand il nous laissera tels que nous sommes: au contraire, nous ne ferons que provoquer son ire. Et puis quand il nous fait la grace par son sainct Esprit d'aimer le bien, et que mesmes il met une telle vertu en nous, que nostre vie soit comme un miroir et exemple de saincteté: si defaillons-nous en tant de sortes, que nous sommes coulpables en mille articles quand il y en aura un que nous pourrons proposer à Dieu. Qui plus est, iamais nous ne faisons rien de bien, où il n'y ait quelque tache, en sorte que nous serions coulpables en tout et par tout devant Dieu s'il nous vouloit traitter à la rigueur. Mais il y a que Dieu quand il nous fait la grace de nous gouverner par son sainct Esprit, accepte le bien qu'il a mis en nous, combien qu'il soit imparfait...Iob cognoissoit bien qu'il estoit un povre pecheur, il n'estoit pas si aveuglé d'orgueil, qu'il se fist à croire qu'il estoit du tout iuste, et que Dieu n'eust que mordre sur lui:...*[CO 34:334-335]. Even in Calvin's interpretation of Job's own claim to innocence, Calvin becomes increasingly anxious to avoid notions of perfection: "We must always holde this grounde, that Iob doth not here take the righteous and vnrighteous, as they bee founde to be before God. For where is the righteous

when wee come there? But he taketh rightuous and vnrightuous according to our perceyuing." 35 (Job 9:16-22), 164.b.53. *Or il nous faut tousiours retenir ce principe, c'est assavoir que Iob ne prend point ici l'inique et le iuste pour ceux qui se trouveront tels devant Dieu. Car où est le iuste quand nous venons-là? Mais il prend le meschant et le iuste, selon que nous le pouvons appercevoir* [*CO* 33:442]. And again, "Nowe, there is no man that performeth so much as any one thing, I meane that performeth it with a pure and perfect mind. And therefore it foloweth that God maye damne vs all." 40 (Job 10:16-17), 187.b.33. *Or il n'y a nul qui en accomplisse une seule: ie di accomplisse d'une affection pure et entiere. Il s'ensuit donc que Dieu nous peut tous condamner* [*CO* 33:500]. And again, "Let vs learne not too flatter our selues at such time as wee bee in rest: but let vs dayly thinke vpon the daye of Gods wrath, and preuent it: namely by trembling continually before oure iudge, praying him to receyue vs too mercie, bycause we be so greatly indetted vnto him: and let vs keepe our mouthes shet when it commeth too the mainteyning of our cace." 77 (Job 20:26-29), 363.b.64. *Apprenons donc de ne nous point flatter du temps que nous sommes en repos, mais pensons tousiours à ce iour de l'ire de Dieu, et prevenons-le: voire en tremblant iournellement devant nostre Iuge, le prians qu'il nous reçoive à merci, pource que nous lui sommes tant redevables: et que nous ayons la bouche close quand il sera question de maintenir nostre cause* [*CO* 34:200]. Similarly, in Sermon 89, commenting on Job's desire to go to law against God, Calvin remarks that Job is "grossely ouerseene in this behalfe. For if God had listed to haue punished him for the sinnes that he had committed: he might iustly haue done it: and in that he doth it not, it is of his meere free goodnesse. Iob therefore doth not discerne aright betweene God and his own person. For he shuld haue said, Lord it is true that thou chastizest me, and I know and thou mightest do it eve[n] by thy law: and it is true also that I haue indeuered to walke before thee in as great soundnesse as was possible for me to do. Neuerthelesse there hath alwayes bin somewhat amisse, and therfore thou shalt find all my works to be sinfull." *Iob faut lourdement en cela: car encores que Dieu l'eust voulu punir des transgressions qu'il avoit commises, il le pouvoit faire: et ce qu'il ne le fait point, cela est de sa pure liberalité. Ainsi Iob ne discerne point assez entre l'intention de Dieu, et sa personne de lui: car il devoit cognoistre, Seigneur il est vrai que tu me chasties, sachant que tu le pourrois faire, mesmes selon la Loi: il est vrai que i'ai mis peine à cheminer devant toi en la plus grande integrité qu'il m'a esté possible: mais si est-ce qu'il y a tousiours à redire: tu trouveras donc toutes mes oeuvres vicieuses.* 89 (Job 23:8-12), 419.a.57 [*CO* 34:351].

[26] 40 (Job 10:16-17), 187.b.19. *Mais encores quand un homme sera gouverné par l'Esprit de Dieu, et qu'il chemine en bonnes oeuvres par la grace d'iceluy: si est-ce que toutes les bonnes oeuvres qu'il fait sont imparfaites, et Dieu les peut repousser: tant s'en faut qu'il y ait dignité ou merite (comme les Papistes imaginent) qu'il n'y a qu'infection* [*CO* 33:499]. Note the following remark, after having accused Job of blasphemy, "bycause of the

suddaine pangs of his passions." Calvin continues, "and the mo[re] defences and excuses that wee thinke wee haue, so muche the more must oure sinfulnesse needes increace." 89 (Job 23:8-12), 417.b.3. ...*c'est d'autant qu'il a des passions soudaines...il faudra que nous soyons tous condamnez, et d'autant plus que nous cuiderons avoir les defenses et excuses, il faudra que nos pechez s'augmentent* [*CO* 34:345].

[27] 158 (Job 42:6-8), 743.b.50. *Voila, di-ie, un homme qui craindra Dieu, et aura une affection et droite et pure de s'addonner à bien faire. Or cependant il y aura beaucoup d'infirmitez, il cloche, il fleschist, il decline, il tombe quelquefois. Voire mais les fautes qu'il commet lui sont pardonnees, et Dieu lui tend tousiours la main pour le relever: et mesme le tout est à son profit, d'autant que c'est son but qui lui est proposé d'aller à Dieu, et que son affection le mene là.*[*CO* 35:495]. There are times when Calvin can sound like the comforters themselves: "Therefore if God scourge vs and sende vs afflictions: we must blame our sinnes for it." 31 (Job 8:7-13), 142.b.11. *Il faut donc imputer à nos pechez si Dieu nous persecute, s'il nous envoye des afflictions* [*CO* 33:383].

[28] *Institutes* III.xiv.9. "*Quod optimum ab illis proferri potest, aliqua tamen semper carnis impuritate respersum et corruptum esse, ac tanquam aliquid faecis admixtum habere.*" [*CO* 2:570].

[29] 153 (Job 39:36-40:6), 724.a.8. *Nous sommes donc ici advertis d'un vice qui est grand, et bien mauvais et pernicieux: c'est que nous voulons estre trop subtils pour plaider contre Dieu, et nous venons vanter afin de couvrir nos povretez par vaines excuses...Car quand nous avons une langue ainsi venimeuse, et laquelle est du tout confite en mensonge et en fausseté, en la fin elle se desborde à l'encontre de Dieu* [*CO* 35:443]. Cf. "we shall neuer profite, till wee haue learned to holde our peace." 128 (Job 33:29-34:3), 604.a.16. ...*nous ne profiterons iusques à ce que nous ayons apprins de nous taire* [*CO* 35:124]. "Neuerthelesse if we wist how too profit ourselues by the things that are conteyned in this doctrine: it would be ynough to teache vs lowelinesse, so as wee should no more open our mouthes to grudge against God or too complayne of him when hee doeth not things to our lyking." 143 (Job 38:4-11), 693.a.42. *Tant y a que si nous savions faire nostre profit des choses qui sont contenues en ceste doctrine, elle seroit assez suffisante pour nous instruire à humilité, en sorte que nous n'aurions plus la bouche ouverte pour murmurer contre Dieu, ne pour plaider contre luy, quand il ne fait point les choses à nostre appetit:...* [*CO* 35:363]. And again, "And that is the sobrietie wherunto it behoueth the faithfull to be brought by the Gospel, that they may simply giue glory vnto God by confessing themselues to knowe nothing." 157 (Job 42:1-5), 740.a.44. *Et c'est la sobrieté à laquelle il faut que tous fideles se reduisent par l'Evangile, pour donner gloire simplement à Dieu, confessans qu'ils ne savent rien* [*CO* 35:485].

[30] Augustine, *City of God* I. viii. Migne, J. P., *Patrologiae cursus completus*, series Latina 41:20; tr. *A Select Library of the Nicene and Post-Nicene Fathers*, second series. See *Institutes* I.v.10 [*CO* 2:48].

[31] See Derek Thomas, "Doctrine of Immediate Retribution," *Reformed Theological Journal* (November 1995), 57-74.
[32] 1 (Job 1:1), 1.b.34 [*CO* 33:23].
[33] 1 (Job 1:1), 1.b.35. *Mais cependant nous avons aussi à noter, qu'en toute la dispute Iob maintient une bonne cause, et son adverse partie en maintient une mauvaise. Or il y a plus, que Iob maintenant une bonne cause la deduit mal, et les autres menans une mauvaise cause la deduisent bien. Quand nous aurons entendu cela, ce nous sera comme une clef pour nous donner ouverture à tout le livre* [*CO* 33:23].
[34] "When he sayeth that God is not vnryghteouse: hee sheweth that his righteousnesse is a thing inseparable from his being." 136 (Job 35:1-7), 640.a.67. *Quand il dit, Dieu n'est point iniuste, il monstre que c'est une chose inseparable de l'essence de Dieu, que sa iustice* [*CO* 35:222].
[35] 30 (Job 8:1-6), 138.a.61. *Or il n'est point Iuge à la façon de ceux qui sont corrompus, comme on voit les hommes mortels qui seront bien eslevés en estat et authoritié, et cependant ils en abuseront souventes-fois...*[*CO* 33:372-373].
[36] 30 (Job 8:1-6), 138.a.64. *Ce qu'il est Iuge du monde n'est point par acquisition, ou qu'il ait esté esleu à l'adventure, et qu'il ait brigué son office, ou qu'il l'ait acheté: mais de nature cela luy compete, il n'est pas Dieu sinon qu'il soit iuge quant et quant* [*CO* 33:373].
[37] 73 (Job 20:1-7), 343.a.53. *...que de tout temps, et depuis que les hommes habitent en terre, Dieu a voulu qu'il y eust tousiours quelques tesmoignages de ses iugemens: et ainsi qu'il ne faut point que nous soyons si eslourdis et hebetez, que nous ne cognoissions ce que Dieu fait pour nostre instruction* [*CO* 34:145].
[38] 73 (Job 20:1-7), 343.b.13. *...n'a cessé de tousiours nous donner quelques advertisemens pour monstrer qu'il est Iuge du monde, que nous apprenions de le craindre, et de cheminer en solicitude, et que les punitions qu'il a faites sur les meschans nous soyent autant de miroirs, et autant de brides pour nous retenir* [*CO* 34:146].
[39] 97 (Job 27:1-4), 456.a.4. *...quand Dieu punit les paillars, les larrons, les yvrongnes, voila aussi sa iustice ordinaire. Nous verrons un meschant, qui aura pillé ses prochains, qui aura esté comme une beste cruelle pour manger et devorer la substance d'autruy: et bien, Dieu souffle dessus sa substance, il ne luy demeure rien: cela nous est une vraye monstre de la iustice de Dieu, et un certain tesmoignage que nous voyons que le bien mal acquis s'escoule: et cela nous fait cognoistre, O Dieu est Iuge. Apres, quand les meurtriers sont aussi bien punis, nous regardons, O il est escrit (Ps. 55, 24) que les hommes cruels n'acheveront point le cours de leur vie* [*CO* 34:448].
[40] 105 (Job 9:16-22), 163.a.46. *Car aucunesfois Dieu punira les pechez qui sont tout notoires aux hommes* [*CO* 33:437].
[41] 105 (Job 9:16-22), 163.a.56. *La iustice de Dieu se cognoist aussi en ses iugemens secrets, quand nous voyons des personnes où il n'y avoit quelques vertus: Dieu les afflige et les tormente* [*CO:* 438].

[42] 100 (Job 27:13-19), 468.b.64. *...pource que les iugemens de Dieu ne s'executent pas ordinairement durant ceste vie presente: nous en avons bien quelque signe, mais c'est tout* [CO 34:483].

[43] 67 (Job 18:1-11), 313.a.58. *...car nous cuiderons que c'est temps perdu de bien faire, veu que Dieu n'a nul regard aux hommes pour les conduire, mais les laisse comme à l'abandon* [CO 34:65].

[44] 36 (Job 9:23-28), 165.b.45. *Or est-il ainsi que Dieu reserve beaucoup de choses: et voila pourquoy il semble qu'il gouverne auiourd'huy en confus* [CO 33:444].

[45] 36 (Job 9:23-28), 165.b.59. *...la iustice et l'equité a deux parties: l'une c'est que les meschans soyent punis: et l'autre que les bons soyent soulagez, qu'ils soyent maintenus en leur droit et integrité. Si donc Dieu punit les meschans, il faut aussi à l'opposite qu'il maintienne les bons, qu'il les ait en sa garde, qu'il ne permette point qu'ils soyent affligez ne tormentez, mais si tost qu'ils crieront à luy ils sentent son secours. Or est-il ainsi que les bons sont affligez (comme nous le voyons) non point pour un iour ni pour deux, mais ils languissent tout le temps de leur vie, il semble que Dieu se venge d'eux, qu'il les vueille mettre en abysme, au lieu de monstrer quelque signe qu'il les veut aider* [CO 33:444].

[46] 103 (Job 9:1-6), 151.a.64. *Notons bien donc que ce sont deux façons de parler diverses, de dire: Dieu est iuste, car il punit les hommes selon qu'ils l'ont deservi: et de dire, Dieu est iuste, car comment qu'il traite les hommes, si faut-il que nous ayons tous la bouche close, et que nous ne murmurions point à l'encontre de luy, pource que nous n'y pourrons rien gagner* [CO 33:407].

[47] 103 (Job 9:1-6), 151.b.49. *Il faut venir plus haut, que Dieu est tousiours iuste comment qu'il traite les hommes* [CO 33:407]. Therefore we must not accuse God of being "asleep," "For we shall see many which imagin that God is asleepe in heauen. Howbeit his Godhead not a vayne imaginacion, but it importeth the things which I haue spoken concerning the gouerment and souereyne dominion of the world: namely that like as hath created all things so also bothe man and beast and all things else, are in his hand and protection, and all things must be brought to a good end for their sakes which are his: & that although things be out of order here bilowe, yet in the meane whyle, as in respect of himself, there is nothing at all out of order: and that although he suffer things to be otherwise disposed than wee would haue them, yea and appoint many confuzions also, yet can he well skill to set all things in perfect state agayne." 136 (Job 35:1-7), 640.b.6. *...car nous en verrons beaucoup qui imaginent Dieu comme endormi au ciel. Or sa deité n'est pas une phantasie vaine: mais elle emporte ce que i'ay touché du gouvernement et de l'empire du monde, Que Dieu, comme il a tout creé, aussi tout est en sa main et protection, et hommes et bestes, qu'il faut que pour les siens tout soit amené à bonne fin. Et combien qu'ici bas les choses soyent ainsi confuses, que cependant envers luy il n'y a iamais rien de desbordé: et s'il permet que les choses soyent autrement disposees que nous ne voudrions*

*pas, qu'il ordonne mesmes qu'il y ait beaucoup de confusions, il saura bien remettre le tout en son entier* [*CO* 35:222-223].

⁴⁸ 36 (Job 9:23-28), 166.b.31. *Nostre Seigneur pourra bien differer les corrections qu'il veut faire, et le temps nous semblera long d'autre costé: mais si faut il que nous restraignions nos esprits, que nous les tenions en bride courte, sachans qu'auiourd'huy Dieu ne veut point punir tous les pechez du monde, et il sait pourquoy* [*CO* 33:446].

⁴⁹ 36 (Job 9:23-28), 166.b.21. *Notons donc que Dieu ne punit pas si tost les hommes quand ils ont failli: mais ce n'est pas à dire, que pour cela ils soyent absous, et qu'ils ne doivent iamais rendre conte. Plustost c'est que Dieu nous baille ici espace de retourner à sa misericorde, et de luy demander qu'il nous reçoive à merci* [*CO* 33:446]. Cf. Calvin's words in the 186th sermon on Deuteronomy, "Therefore if our sinnes bee hidden as nowe from the worlde, so as wee be not accused of them nor no man rebuketh vs for them, insomuch that we doe as it were fall asleepe in them: let vs not therefore forbeare continually to mourne for them before God, and to enter into account, and to quicken vp ourselves, knowing well that the Registers must bee layd open, when the sentence shall bee giuen, and that as then our indictment must needes bee framed. We shall not bee made priuie to it aforehand, but as soone as the Trumpet shall haue sounded, and our Lorde is set vppon the benche, there shall neede neither Register nor Secretarie to reade it, but euery mans conscience must accuse himselfe, and euery man must lay open his owne shamefull dealings." *Sermons on Deuteronomy* 186 (Deut. 32:32-35), 1155.b.10. "*Si donc auiourd'huy nos pechez sont cashez selon le monde, que nous n'en soyons point accusez, que nul ne nous redargue, et mesmes que nous soyons comme endormis: que nous ne laissions pas pourtant de tousiours gemir devant Dieu, et d'entrer en conte, et qu'un chacun se sollicite, sachant bien qu'il faudra que les registres soyent publiez quand la sentence se donnera, qu'il faudra alors que nostre procez soit fait: on n'en savoit rien auparavant, mais quand la trompette aura sonné, et que le Seigneur sera assis, là il ne faudra point de greffier ne de secretaire pour lire, mais il faudra que nos consciences s'accusent d'elles-mesmes, et plustost qu'un chacun soit son tesmoin, qu'un chacun descouvre ses turpitudes.*" [*CO* 29:47].

⁵⁰ *Institutes* III.xi.2. "*Proinde ubicunque peccatum est, illic etiam se profert ira et ultio Dei*" [*CO* 2:533].

⁵¹ 73 (Job 20:1-7), 343.b.19. *Encores qu'ils fussent eslevez au ciel, qu'ils dressassent la teste iusques aux nues, si est-ce qu'ils ne consisteront point, Dieu les renversera bien tost* [*CO* 34:146].

⁵² 130 (Job 34:10-15), 612.a.2. ...*mais tant y a qu'en la fin Dieu, apres avoir differé long temps, et avoir prolongé le terme aux meschans, leur monstrera que s'il les a attendus à repentance, il n'a pas oublié leurs forfaits, que tout a esté enregistré devant lui, et mesmes qu'ils se sont amassé un plus grand thresor de son ire. Le terme donc leur sera bien cher vendu, quand ils auront ainsi abusé de la patience de Dieu, qui n'a pas voulu du premier*

*coup les punir, afin qu'ils eussent loisir de cognoistre leurs fautes, et de se corriger d'eux-mesmes* [*CO* 35:145-146]. Calvin continues: "God doth not so recompence euerie man according too his workes, but that hee also beareth with them whome hee punisheth, and sheweth them some fauour, although that on the one syde hee bee rigorous too them, and make them feele that hee is their Iudge.... Hee shoulde not sende vs diseases, wantes, and suche other things: but hee shoulde thunder vppon vs, and ouerwhelme vs at the first blowe, so as wee shoulde not feele some terrible punishment, but hee shoulde arme himselfe in his mightie Maiestie too confounde and ouerwhelme vs." 612.a.41. *...n'entend pas que Dieu rende telllement à chacun selon ses oeuvres, qu'il ne supporte ceux qu'il punit, et qu'il ne monstre quelque bonté envers eux, combien que d'un costé il leur soit severe, et qu'il leur face sentir qu'il est leur Iuge... Il ne nous envoyeroit point de maladies, des povretez et choses semblables: mais nous serions abysmez et foudroyez du premier coup, tellement qu'il ne seroit point question seulement de sentir quelque punition horrible, mais il faudroit qu'il s'armast en sa maiesté puissante pour nous confondre et abysmer* [*CO* 35:146].

[53] 33 (Job 9:1-6), 154.a.68. *Nous verrons bien que Dieu ne besongne point à toutes les fois d'un mesme cours* [*CO* 33:414]. Cf. "God executeth not his temporall punishments after one egall rate in this worlde, but reserueth the cheef to himselfe till the latter day." 100 (Job 27:13-19), 473.a.10. *Mais c'est pour nous monstrer que Dieu n'execute point d'un fil egal les punitions temporelles en ce monde, et cependant qu'il se reserve le principal au dernier iour* [*CO* 34:493-494]. Cf. 136 (Job 36:1-7), 652.a.5 [*CO* 35:253-254].

[54] 68 (Job 18:12-21), 318.b.21. *Mais si Dieu execute ses iugemens d'une façon visible, notons-les pour en faire nostre profit: si nous ne les voyons pas, et bien, sachons qu'il a reservé la manifestation iusqu'au dernier iour, afin d'esprouver nostre foy* [*CO* 34:79].

[55] 18 (Job 5:3-7), 83.a.14. *Car quand Dieu veut mettre ainsi les hommes à perdition, il les destitue de tous moyens de secours et d'aide* [*CO* 33:230].

[56] 18 (Job 5:3-7), 83.b.30. *Quand donc Dieu nous monstre ainsi ses iugemens, que nous tremblions dessous, et que nous soyons comme tenus captifs sous sa crainte, nous assubiettissans du tout à ce qu'il dit et prononce* [*CO* 33:232].

[57] Cf. Calvin's comment on Acts 5:5, on the death of Ananias and Sapphira: "But as God poured out visible graces on His Church in the beginning, so that we may know with assurance that he will be present with us by the secret virtue of His Spirit, and, furthermore, showed openly by external signs what we realize inwardly by the experience of faith, so He has demonstrated by the visible punishment of two persons, how horrible a judgment awaits all hypocrites, who have held Him and the Church in derision." *Calvin's Commentaries: The Acts of the Apostles 1-13*, trans. John W. Fraser and W. J. G. McDonald, ed. David W. Torrance and Thomas F. Torrance (Grand Rapids, MI: William B. Eerdmans, 1965), 135-136. *Sed quemadmodum visibiles initio gratias in ecclesiam suam Deus effudit, ut certo sciamus illum arcana*

*spiritus sui virtute nobis adfuturum: imo palam externis signis exhibuit, quod nos intus fidei experimento sentimus: ita visibili duorum poena testatus est, quam horribile hypocritas omnes iudicium maneat, qui derisui ipsum et ecclesiam habuerint* [CO 48:100].

[58] 21 (Job 5:17-18), 95.a.10. *Or il est vray qu'ils n'en sont point consumez du tout pour le present: mais ce sont autant de signes de ceste horrible vengeance qui leur est apprestee au dernier iour. Voila donc comme beaucoup sont touchez de la main de Dieu, lesquels toutesfois sont maudits: car ils commencent desia leur enfer en ce monde selon que nous en avons les exemples en tous ceux qui ne changent point leur mauvaise vie, quand Dieu leur envoye quelques afflictions...* [CO 33:261].

[59] 18 (Job 5:3-7), 82.b.21. *Or il y a double façon de punir l'iniquité des peres sur les enfans: car aucunesfois Dieu fait misericorde aux enfans, et ne laisse pas toutesfois de chastier en leurs personnes l'iniquité des peres* [CO 33:229]. Cf. "For if the children be well examined, they shall finde themselues guiltie on their owne behalfe: yea (say I), euen though they were but newly borne, and had neuer done any open fault that were knowen to the worlde. For what manner of ofspring are wee? What bring wee with vs by nature but vtter naughtinesse? Yee see then that euen infantes are sinners aforehande: they bee condemned before GOD being yet in their mothers wombes. The euill is not yet preceiued: but yet for all that their nature is sinfull and frowarde, they bee alreadie in condemnation, because of the originall sinne that is come from Adam vpon all mankinde.

"Now seeing that the little babes are not exempted from the wrath and curse of GOD, in so much that if hee punishe them it is not without cause, neither can men saye but that hee proceedeth always vprightlye as a good Iudge: much lesse canne they that are men frowen auowe themselues to be innocent but they shall much rather bee found guiltie." *Sermons on Deuteronomy*, 32 (Deut. 5:8-10), 189.b.44. Cf. 81 (Job 21:16-21), 382.b.7. *Car les enfans de leur costé se trouveront coulpables, quand ils seront bien examinez: ie di encores qu'il ne fissent que sortir du ventre de la mere, qu'ils n'eussent point commis des fautes manifestes, et qui fussent cogneues du monde: car quelle race sommes nous? Qu'apportons-nous de nature, sinon toute malice? Voila donc les enfans qui desia sont pecheurs, estans dedans le ventre de la mere, ils sont condamnez devant Dieu. On n'apperçoit point le mal encores: mais tant y a que leur nature est vicieuse et perverse, ils ont une semence cachee, et à cause de ce peché originel qui est venu d'Adam sur tout le genre humain, les voila desia en condamnation. Or puis qu'ainsi est que les petis enfans ne sont point exemptez de l'ire et de la malediction de Dieu: il est certain que s'il les punit, ce ne sera pas sans cause, et que tousiours on ce cognoisse qu'il y a procedé equitablement, comme bon iuge: par plus forte raison, ceux qui desia sont grands, ne se peuvent pas dire innocens: mais on les trouvera beaucoup plus coulpables* [CO 26:262].

[60] 158 (Job 42:6-8), 743.b.28. *Gardons-nous donc de temerité, quand nous*

*voyons que Dieu tormente rudement quelqu'un: que nous n'ayons point un iugement volage, pour prononcer contre lui qu'il est digne d'estre ainsi manié, et pour priser ceux qui sont à leur aise, comme s'ils estoyent mieux aimez de Dieu, car c'est iuger par trop à l'estourdie, que cela* [CO 35:494].

[61] 100 (Job 27:13-19), 470.b.60. *Or nous ne verrons point ces promesses-là tousiours accomplies d'un fil esgal, mais selon que Dieu cognoit qu'il est expedient. Touchant des promesses spirituelles qui appartiennent au salut de nos ames, elles sont certaines, il faut conclure que Dieu ne nous y defaudra iamais. Ainsi donc distinguons entre ce qui est de ceste vie caduque, et ce qui est de la vie celeste, et du royaume eternel de Dieu* [CO 34:488].

[62] 100 (Job 27:13-19), 471.b.26. *...voire, si Dieu arrache le bien de la main des meschans, cognoissons qu'il accomplit ceste menace dont nous oyons ici parler: s'il ne le fait pas, notons qu'il se reserve l'execution de son iugement iusques au dernier iour, et qu'il ne veut pas amener les choses maintenant à perfection, afin de nourrir nostre esperance: et que nous ne soyons point addonnez à ce monde, que nous ne cerchions point nostre felicité ici bas comme en un paradis: mais que nous ayons nos yeux eslevez en haut, et que nous passions tant plus legerement par ici bas comme par un chemin, et que nous cognoissions que nous sommes voyagers et vagabons en ce monde, et pourtant qu'il nous faut tousiours aspirer à cest heritage celeste et permanent* [CO 34:490].

[63] Ibid., 66 (Job 17:6-16), 312.b.30. *...cognoissez que Dieu vous a appresté vostre repos au ciel, puis que vous ne l'avez point eu en la terre. Et au reste, si c'est une chose convenable à la iustice de Dieu, que les meschans soyent punis selon qu'ils l'ont desservi, et que toutes fois nous ne voyons point cela en ce monde: cognoissez que Dieu comme en un miroir parmi vos afflictions, vos troubles et miseres, vous declare que nous viendrez une fois à lui: et c'est là aussi où il faut que vostre attente se remette* [CO 34:63].

[64] 149 (Job 38:12-17), 701.a.21. *Il est vray que pour quelque temps le soleil esclaire les meschans comme les bons, il y a une vie commune à tous: mais attendez, dit-il: car les meschans ne sont pas heritiers du monde: et combien qu'auiord'huy ils reçoivent ce qui ne leur appartient point, et ayent les yeux ouverts pour avoir la clarté du soleil: toutes fois en la fin ils en seront privez du tout* [CO 35:383-384]. Hence Calvin concludes, commenting on Psalm 73, in which Asaph had complained at the prosperity of the wicked and the trouble of the righteous: "men never form a right judgment of the works of God; for when they apply their minds to consider them, all their faculties fail, being inadequate to the task... Whenever we are dissatisfied with the manner of God's providence in governing the world, let us remember that this be traced to the perversity of our understanding." *Commentary of the Book of the Psalms*, trans. James Anderson, 3:150-151, in *Calvin's Commentaries*, vol. V (Grand Rapids, Michigan: Baker Book House). "*Etsi enim verum est quod ante diximus, homines de operibus Dei nunquam rectum iudicium facere, quia in illis considerandis deficiunt omnes eorum sensus:... Caeterum quoties non placebit nobis consilii Dei ratio in mundi*

*The Incomprehensible Righteousness of God* 133

*gubernatione, meminerimus id sensus nostri privitate fieri."* [*CO* 31:686].

[65] 74 (Job 20:8-15), 348.b.31. *Puis qu'ainsi est donc attendons que nostre Seigneur despouille les meschans, et alors nous n'aurons plus d'occasion de leur porter envie, ni de nous desbaucher avec eux. Si on dit, que cela est commun à tous, c'est assavoir, que nous allions en la poudre, et que nous y pourrissions: il est vrai: mais nous avons une bonne compagnie, quand nous aurons cheminé durant nostre vie en la crainte de Dieu, car nous saurons qu'en lui remettant nos ames entre ses mains, il en sera bon gardien et fidele: nous aurons une bonne compagnie, quand nous cognoistrons que les Anges de Dieu mesmes (comme l'Escriture le monstre) recevront nos ames pour les mettre en ceste garde bonne et seure, iusques à ce que nous ressuscitions en la gloire celeste. Combien donc que selon l'apparence il faille qu'un chacun de nous soit retranché de ce monde, et de la compagnie des hommes, et que nous soyons iettez au sepulchre: si est-ce que nous serons bien accompagnez selon Dieu, quand nous aurons cheminé en sa crainte* [*CO* 34:160].

[66] 35 (Job 9:16-22), 164.a.68. *Les hommes mortels oseront-ils dire qu'ils soyent capables de mesurer la iustice de Dieu? quelle folie sera-ce?* [*CO* 33:440-41]. Earlier in the sermon, Calvin had said: "Gods iustice consisteth not in the knowledge that wee haue of it, or that can enter into mans brayne." *...que la iustice de Dieu ne consiste pas en la cognoissance que nous en avons, et qui puisse entrer au cerveau des hommes* [*CO* 33:440]. Cf. "Therefore whensouer GOD openeth his chestes, hee will finde terrible manners of vengeance, which are incomprehensible to vs as nowe." *Sermons on Deuteronomy*, 186 (Deut.32:32-35), 1155.b.44. "*Quand donc Dieu ouvrira ses coffres, il trouvera de terribles façons de vengeance, lesquelles nous sont auiourd'huy incomprehensibles.*" [*CO* 29:47].

[67] Stauffer, *Op.cit.* 116-124; Stauffer concludes, "*Une autre application de la conception de la double justice se rencontre dans la prédication lorsque Calvin aborde le problème de la souffrance des iusts. Le Réformateur estime alors que, quand Dieu punit un méschant, cette punition procède de la justice ordinaire, mais qu'en revanche, quand il frappe l'innocent, son châstiment de sa justice secrète.*" 119. See also, Susan Schreiner, *Where Shall Wisdom be Found?*, 105-120; This book is an expansion on "Exegesis and Double Justice in Calvin's Sermons on Job," *Church History* 58 (1989): 322-38; see also, unpublished paper by Paul Helm, "Calvin Among the Angels," read at the Edinburgh Dogmatics Conference, 1992.

[68] Schreiner, *Where Shall Wisdom be Found?*, 105.

[69] For a passing reference to this issue as it relates to Calvin's concept of accommodation, see David F. Wright, "Calvin's Accommodating God" *Sixteenth Century Journal* (1997), 19.

[70] 37 (Job 9:29-35), 171.b.12. *Car nous avons tousiours à retenir, que Dieu a sa maiesté cachee, et qu'en ceste maiesté-la, il y a une iustice que nous ne comprenons point. Il est vray que Dieu nous a bien baillé en sa Loy un patron et une image de sa iustice, mais c'a esté selon nostre capacité. Or*

*savons-nous que nostre entendement est si rude, qu'il ne peut monter si haut, que de concevoir ce qui est en Dieu en perfection. Ainsi donc la iustice mesme qui est contenue en la Loy de Dieu, est une iustice qui est compassee à la mesure des hommes. Nous l'appellerons bien iustice parfaite, et la pourrons nommer ainsi: et l'Escriture la nomme iustice parfaite: voire au regard de nous, c'est à dire, au regard des creatures. Ie ne di pas au regard de nous, selon que nous sommes pecheurs, et que nous sommes tous maudits en Adam: mais selon que nous sommes creatures de Dieu: ou bien au regard des Anges, afin d'oster toute difficulté. Ceste iustice-la donc est une iustice que les Anges et les hommes doivent rendre à Dieu, pour luy obeir et complaire, voire entant qu'ils sont ses creatures. Mais tant y a qu'il y a encores une iustice plus haute en Dieu, c'est à dire une perfection, à laquelle nous ne pouvons pas attaindre, et de laquelle nous ne pouvons pas approcher, iusques à ce que nous soyons faits semblables à luy, et que nous ayons contemplé ceste gloire, qui maintenant nous est cachee, et que nous ne voyons sinon comme en un miroir, et par obscurité* [CO 33:458-59].

[71] Calvin uses a variety of expressions, *iustice cachee, secrette,* variously translated in these sermons as "higher", "secret", "double", "another."

[72] 37 (Job 9:29-35),174.a.47 ...*il faut que nous demourions tous confus et condamnez, sinon qu'il passe plus outre, et qu'il nous propose sa misericorde. Autrement nous demourerions tousiours maudits, encores que nous ayons accompli toutes les choses qui sont contenues en la Loy* [CO 33:465].

[73] Cf. Bouwsma's remark, "For Calvin there appears, then, to be a kind of satisfaction owed by creature to Creator that is neither moral nor possible. He saw guilt in creatureliness itself, guilt shared even by human beings created in God's image before the Fall, guilt toward the Father even on the part of his good children, guilt in *existing*." *John Calvin: A Sixteenth Century Portrait*, 42. Cf. the remarks of Suzanne Selinger, "Matter in itself, as much as the fall, seems to be the trouble." Suzanne Selinger, *Calvin Against Himself: An Inquiry in Intellectual History* (Hamden, Connecticut: Archon Books, 1984), 68.

[74] Cf. Schreiner's remark, "For Calvin, the Book of Job teaches that all creaturely perfection, even that of the angels, is 'accepted' by God only insofar as God 'contents' himself with the lower, median, or created justice revealed in the Law." *Where Shall Wisdom be Found*, 112.

[75] 37 (Job 9:29-35),172.a.22. *Mais prenons le cas, que Iob fust comme un Ange, qu'il peust suffire envers Dieu selon la iustice de la Loy: si est-ce que selon ceste iustice secrette qui est en Dieu, il se trouveroit tousiours redevable* [CO 33:460].

[76] 17 (Job 4:20-5:2), 75.a.12. *Or est-il ainsi, que si Dieu vouloit iuger de ses Anges à la rigueur, il y trouveroit à redire: que sera-ce donc de ceux qui sont si fragiles, pour dire en un mot, qu'ils n'ont en eux que vanité* [CO 33:209].

[77] *Institutes* III.xii.1. (1539): "*Perundum sane mox sit omnibus, ut alibi*

*scribitur (Iob.4,17 [sic]): numquid homo Dei comparatione iustificabitur, aut purior erit factore suo? ecce qui serviunt ei non sunt fideles, et in angelis suis reperit pravitatem."* [*CO* 1:747]. This section was expanded in the 1559 edition of the *Institutes* to explain the reference to Job 4:18 in the 1539 edition. See Susan Schreiner, *Where Shall Wisdom be Found?*, 106.

[78] *Institutes* III.xii.1. *"Fateor quidem in libro Iob mentionem fieri iustitiae, quae excelsior est observatione legis, atque hanc distinctionem tenere operae pretium est; quia etiamsi quis legi satisfaceret, ne sic quidem staret ad examen illius iustitiae, quae sensus omnes exsuperat. Itaque etiamsi Iob bene sibi conscius sit, attonitus tamen obmutescit; quia videt ne angelica quidem sanctitate posse Deum placari, si ad summam trutinam revocet eorum opera. Ego igitur iustitiam illam quam attigi, quia incomprehensibilis est, nunc omitto..."* [*CO* 2:554]. The reference is especially noteworthy, for it focuses again on three issues: the reference to Job 4:18, double justice and the idea of incomprehensibility, viz., the hiddenness of God.

[79] *The Epistles of Paul The Apostle to the Galatians, Ephesians, Philippians and Colossians*, ed. David W. Torrance and Thomas F. Torrance, trans. T. H. L. Parker (Grand Rapids: Eerdmans, 1965), 313. *"Inter Deum et angelos longe diversa ratio. Illic enim nulla defectio, nullum peccatum: ideoque nullum divortium. Sed tamen duabus de causis angelos quoque oportuit cum Deo pacificari. Nam quum creaturae sint, extra lapsus periculum non erant, nisi Christi gratia fuissent confirmati. Hoc autem non parvum est momentum ad pacis cum Deo perpetuitatem, fixum habere statum in iustitia, ne casum aut defectionem amplius timeat. Deinde in hac ipsa oboedientia, quam praestant Deo, non est tam exquisita perfectio, ut Deo omni ex parte et citra veniam satisfaciat. Atque huc procul dubio spectat sententia ista ex libro Iob (4, 18), In angelis suis reperiet iniquitatem. Nam si de diabolo exponitur, quid magnum? Pronuntiat autem illic spiritus summam puritatem sordere, si ad Dei iustitiam exigatur. Constituendum igitur, non esse tantum in angelis iustitiae, quod ad plenam cum Deo coniunctionem sufficiat. Itaque pacificatore opus habent, per cuius gratiam penitus Deo adhaereant."* [*CO* 52:88-89]. The Colossian commentary was written between late 1546 and early 1548, revised in 1551 and then thoroughly revised for the 1556 edition. See Parker, *New Testament Commentaries*, 21, 168.

[80] St Thomas Aquinas, *Summa Theologiae* (New York: Mcgraw-Hill Book Company; London: Eyre & Spottiswoode, 1963), vol. 9, Ia.63,1, 247. On the influence of Aquinas on Calvin's thought, see Alister E. McGrath, *A Life of John Calvin* (Oxford: Oxford University Press, 1990), 36-38. For opposing views, see Alexandre Ganoczy, *The Young Calvin*, trans. David Foxgrover and Wade Provo (Philadelphia: Westminster Press, 1987); Heiko A. Oberman, *Initia Calvini: The Matrix of Calvin's Reformation* (Amsterdam: Koninklijke Nederlandse Akademie van Wetenschappen, 1991), 10-19, 42-43. For other influences on Calvin, see François Wendel, *Calvin: The Origins and*

*Development of His Religious Thought*, trans. Philip Mairet (New York: Harper and Row, 1963), 19; T. F. Torrance, *The Hermeneutics of John Calvin* (Edinburgh: Scottish Academic Press, 1988), 3-11, 72-95; Susan Schreiner, *Where Shall Wisdom be Found?*, 8-18.

[81] The Vulgate translation reads: "*Ecce qui serviunt ei, non sunt stabiles, et in angelis suis reperit pravitatem.*" The "instability" of the angels was interpreted by Gregory and Aquinas to suggest that the angelic nature was mutable. For Gregory, see *Moralia in Iob, cura et studio Marci Adriaen, Corpus Christianorum: Series Latina* 143, 143A, 143B (Turnhout: Brepols, 1979-85), 5.38.68. For Aquinas, see *Expositio super Iob ad litteram, in Opera Omnia*, iussu Leonis XIII P.M. edita, cura et studio Fratrum Praedicatorum, vol. 26 (Rome, 1965), 4:18. Schreiner maintains that Calvin departs from this medieval exegesis of Job 4:18, reading instead, "*Voici il ne trouve point fermeté en ses serviteurs, et a mis vanité en ses Anges,*" *Where Shall Wisdom be Found?*, 112. Schreiner's point is that by suggesting the angels are full of *vanité*, Calvin argues that it is as true of the unfallen angels as it is of the fallen. The charge of Job 4:18, then, is not of apostasy or rebellion, but vanity. It is curious that Theodore Beza, Calvin's friend and successor at Geneva, makes no reference to this interpretation whatsoever in his own commentary on Job. The work is singularly imbalanced: the first half of the work covers the first six chapters of Job whilst the other thirty-six chapters are summed up in the second half. Alluding in the preface to his indebtedness to Calvin's sermons on Job (he adds the names of John Oecolampadius and John Mercer, "three divines of most happie memorie"), his translation of Job 4:18 reads: "Beholde (God) relyeth not vpon those his seruants, although he hath put light into those his messengers." The comment that follows (which is only a few lines) makes no allusion whatsoever to Calvin's unfallen angels idea. See Theodore T. Beza, *Jobus commentario et paraphrasi ilustratus* (Geneva, 1583). English Translation: *Iob expounded by Theodore Beza, partly in manner of a commentary, partly in manner of a paraphrase. Faithfully translated out of Laitine into English* (Cambridge, 1589). See also J. Raitt, "Beza, Guide for the Faithful Life (Lectures on Job, Sermons on Song of Songs, 1587)," *Scottish Journal of Theology* 39 (1986) 83-87.

[82] *Summa Theologiae*, Ia.63,1. Aquinas concludes, "I grant there is no potentiality (*Ad primum ergo dicendum quod...*) in an angel's natural being; but there is in his intellectual capacity, which can turn to this or to that object; and this makes evil a possibility (*potest*) for him."

[83] 16 (Job 4:12-19), 74.a.16. *...mais si nous cognoissons que c'est de la iustice de Dieu, il ne se faut point esbahir que les Anges mesmes soyent trouvez coulpables, quand il les voudroit accomparer à luy: car il nous faut tousiours revenir à ce point, que les biens qui sont aux creatures sont en mesure petite au pris de ce qui est en Dieu, qui est du tout infini* [*CO* 33:207].

[84] 40 (Job 10:16-17), 186.a.37. *Car il n'y a point de contredit, Dieu est là obei pleinement, il a son regne au ciel. Nous demandons donc d'estre*

*conformez aux Anges: et cela nous doit bien suffire, car alors nous aurions une perfection telle qu'elle doit estre aux creatures. Voire, mais assavoir si les Anges ont une iustice qui se puisse egaler et accomparer à celle de Dieu? Il y a aussi longue distance, qu'entre le ciel et la terre. La iustice des Anges combien qu'elle soit parfaite au regard des creatures, si est-ce que ce n'est rien, ce n'est que fumee quand on voudra venir devant la maiesté infinie de Dieu* [*CO* 33:496]. In an interesting allusion to Abraham, Calvin goes on to remark in the same sermon, "But let us come to the highest degree of this righteousnesse. Let vs take Abraham, or the other holy fathers that haue walked in suche perfection, as if they had bin Angels. Is it too bee sayde that these menne haue fulfilled the law? No. There is none of them all but hee shall fynde himselfe blamewoorthie when hys lyfe is examined before God." 40 (Job 10:16-17), 186.b.58. *Or venons au plus grand degré qui soit de ceste iustice. Prenons ou Abraham, ou les saincts Peres, qui ont cheminé en telle perfection qu'ils estoyent comme Anges: ceux-la assavoir s'ils ont accompli la Loy? Nenny, il n'y a celuy qui ne se trouve coulpable, quand sa vie sera examinee devant Dieu* [*CO* 33:497-498].

[85] 35 (Job 9:16-22), 163.b.38. *Or il est vray, que si Dieu exerce tout ce qu'il est possible de rigueur à l'encontre d'un homme qui ressemblera aux Anges du ciel, d'un homme qui cheminera en toute integrité, et perfection: si Dieu desploye sa rigueur contre celuy-la, encores sera-il iuste. Et voire: mais c'est sans propos* [*CO* 33:439].

[86] Paul Helm, *op. cit.* 11.

[87] 17 (Job 4:20-5:2), 75.a.34. *Voila les Anges qui sont prochains de Dieu, et contemplent sa gloire, ils sont du tout adonnez à son service: et toutesfois il n'y a point de fermeté en eux, sinon d'autant qu'ils sont soustenus par la grace de Dieu: ils porroyent mesmes s'escouler, et s'esvanouir n'estoit que Dieu les conservast par sa pure bonté* [*CO* 33:209-210]. Speaking of the angels again, Calvin says, "For if God should leave them to themselves, what woulde become of them?" 29 (Job 7:16-21), 135.b.4. *Car si Dieu les laissoit-là, que devien-droyent-ils?* [*CO* 33:365]. Cf. Aquinas's conclusion, 'It belongs to an angel's nature [*naturale*] to turn to God in love as to the source of his nature's existence [*principium naturalis esse*]; but to turn to him as the source of a supernatural happiness, this comes of a love received as a grace [*ex amore gratuito*]; and such love could be rejected, sinfully [*a quo averti potuit peccando*]. Summa Theologiae Ia.63,1.

[88] 17 (Job 4:20-5:2), 75.a.49. *Il ne se faut point donc esbahir, si aux hommes il n'y a que toute povreté, veu que les Anges qui sont si prochains de Dieu n'ont pas une perfection tant exquise que si Dieu vouloit entrer en iugement avec eux, ilne les condamnast* [*CO* 33:210]. In a similar passage, at a later stage in the exposition, Calvin remarks, "…let us take the Angels for a mirrour. Behold, the Angels indeuer to serve God: they are not tempted with euill affections as we bee: there is no rebelliousnesse nor sin in them: and yet notwithstanding, although the obedience which they yeeld vnto God bee pure in respect of vs: it ceasseth not to bee imperfect if it be compared with

the infinite maiestie of God. Now, then, God (if he listed) could vse vs after an extraordinarie maner: that is to say, although there were no lawe to rule vs by, yea, or although wee had performed all that is conteyned in the lawe: yet might he iustly condemne vs, but he will not do it. And why? He is contented with the rule that he hath giuen, shewing that he pitieth his poore creatures." 88 (Job 23:1-7), 414.a.30. *Et pour mieux comprendre cela, que nous prenions les Anges pour un miroir. Voila les Anges qui taschent de servir à Dieu: ils ne sont point tentez de mauvaises affections comme nous, il n'y a point de rebellion en eux, ne de peché: mais si est-ce que l'obeissance qu'ils rendent à Dieu, combien qu'elle soit pure selon nostre regard, ne laisse point d'estre imparfaite, si on l'accompare à la maiesté de Dieu infinie. Or maintenant Dieu, quand bon lui sembleroit, nous pourroit bien traitter d'une façon extraordinaire, c'est à dire que combien qu'il n'y eust point de regle de la Loy, ou mesmes quand nous aurions accompli tout, ce qui est là contenu, encores nous pourroit-il condamner: mais il ne le veut pas faire. Et pourquoy? Il se contente de ceste regle qu'il a donnee, monstrant qu'il a pitié de ses povres creatures. Et voila pourqouy les Anges sont purs et reputez iustes devant lui.* [*CO* 34:336-337].

[89] Calvin's sermons on 1 Timothy began on Sunday morning, 16 September 1554, and were to continue until the middle of April 1555, there being 54 sermons in all. [See *CO* 53:1-658]. For much of the time, Calvin's sermons on 1 Timothy ran contemporaneously with the Joban sermons. An English translation appeared in 1579, translated by L.T. (Laurence Tomson). *Sermons of M. Iohn Caluin, on the Epistles of S. Paule to Timothie and Titus.* Translated out of the French into English, by L.T. at London. Imprinted for G. Bishop and T. Woodcoke. 1579. (Hereafter, *Sermons on Timothy and Titus*).

[90] *Sermons on Timothy and Titus*, 52 (1 Tim. 6:15-16), 621.b.26. "*Vray est donc que les anges sont espirits immortels, que ceste qualité aussi convient à nos ames, mais cela n'est point de nature: car tout ce qui a eu commencement, peut avoir fin, et peut aller en decadence, voire perir du tout. Or est-il ainsi que les anges sont creez: ainsi de nature nous ne dirons pas qu'ils ayent un estat permanent, et qu'ils ne puissent changer, mais ceste constance qu'ils ont de persister en l'obeissance de Dieu, est un don qui leur procede d'ailleurs, et aussi d'immortalité.*" [*CO* 53:620]. Calvin refers to this passage in a sermon on Job 3, "When Sainct Paule sayth that there is none Immortall but onely God: it is certaine that hee excludeth all creatures. And yet we know that the Aungels are immortall spirites. For God hath created them of purpose, that they should not any more return to nothing, no more than the soule of man may at any time die. Howe then shall we make these sentences agree, that the Aungells are created to liue euerlastingly: and that there is none immortall but onely God? The solution is verie easie. For the Aungels are immortall, bicause they bee sustayned by power from aboue, and bycause God mainteyneth them, who beeing the immortall nature itselfe and the verie founatine of life, is in them, as it is sayde in the psalme. O Lorde, the fountaine of lyfe dwelleth in thee, and thy light shall we see

light." 16 (Job 3:12-19), 73.b.36. *Quand sainct Paul dit (1. Tim. 6, 16), qu'il n'y a que Dieu seul immortel, il est certain qu'il exclud toutes creatures: et toutesfois nous savons que les Anges sont esprits immortels: car Dieu les a creez à ceste condition-la pour n'estre iamais aneantis, non plus que l'ame des hommes ne doit iamais perir. Comment donc accorderons nous ces passages, que les Anges sont creez pour vivre à iamais, et qu'il n'y a que Dieu seul immortel? La solution est bien aisee. Car les Anges sont immortels, entant qu'ils sont soustenus par la vertu d'enhaut, et que Dieu les maintient, luy qui est immortel de nature, et la fontaine de vie est en luy: comme il est dit Pseaume 36 (v. 10): Seigneur la fontaine de vie gist en toy, et en ta clarté nous verrons clair* [CO 33:206]. Commenting on Job 15:15, "Behold, he findeth no stedfastnesse in his saints, nother are the heauens cleane in his sight," Calvin adds, "It is onely bycause they shoulde not haue the constancie too continue in goodnesse, vnlesse God preserued them by his power." 58 (Job 15:11-16), 272.b.52. *Ce n'est point seulement pource qu'ils n'auroient pas de constance de persister en bien, n'estoit que Dieu les preservast par sa vertu*...[CO 33:725].

[91] 58 (Job 15:11-16), 272.b.61....*car nous voyons qu'ils n'ont autre affection que d'obeir à Dieu, ils ne sont point subiets à mauvaises cupiditez, comme nous sommes, il n'y a nulle tentation en eux pour les divertir* [CO 33:725].

[92] A corollary of this viewpoint is that, for Calvin, providence is predestinarian; that, to cite David F. Wright, "predestination is woven inextricably into the warp and woof of all Calvin's theologizing." "Calvin's Accommodating God," 19.

[93] *Institutes* III.xxiii.4. "*Ad Dei naturam si proprie pertinet iudicium facere, iustitiam igitur naturaliter amat, iniustitiam aversatur. Proinde non, quasi deprehensus foret, apostolus ad cuniculos respectavit; sed indicavit altiorem esse iustitiae divinae rationem quam ut vel humano modo metienda sit, vel ingenii humani tenuitate possit comprehendi... Ac prodigiosus est hominum furor, dum ita rationis suae modulo subiicere appetunt quod immensum est. Angelos, qui steterunt in sua integritate, Paulus electos vocat (1 Tim. 5, 21); si eorum constantia in Dei beneplacito fundata fuit, aliorum defectio arguit fuisse derelictos. Cuius rei causa non potest alia adduci quam reprobatio, quae in arcano Dei consilio abscondita est.*" [CO 2:701-702].

[94] Cf. the citation above (footnote 88) on 17 (Job 4:20-5:2), 75.a.52 [CO 33:210].

[95] 40 (Job 10:16-17), 186.a.52. *Notons bien donc que quand la Loy nous a esté donnee, ç'a bien esté une regle certaine de bien vivre*...[CO 33:496]. It is of interest to note at this point that the theologians of the *via moderna*, from whom Calvin seems to have learned much, developed the concept of the reliability of *potentia ordinata* with reference to the notion of a 'covenant' or 'contract' (*pactum*) between God and man. To cite McGrath, "It is this *pactum* established unilaterally by God, which constitutes the turning point of the doctrines of justification associated with the *via moderna*. God is

understood to have imposed upon himself a definite obligation, embodied in the *pactum*, to reward the man who does *quod in se est* with the gift of justifying grace. If man meets the minimal precondition for justification (in other words, if he does *quod in se est*...) God is under a self-imposed obligation to justify him.... God may therefore be said to justify such a man of necessity, provided that this is understood as a 'necessity of consequence (*necessitas consequentiae*)' rather than 'absolute necessity (*necessitas absoluta*)'." *The Intellectual Origins of the European Reformation*, 81.

[96] 40 (Job 10:16-17), 186.a.54. ...*alors nous serions tenus et reputez pour iustes devant Dieu en toute perfection, ouy bien*...[*CO* 33:496].

[97] 40 (Job 10:16-17), 186.a.58. *C'est de pure grace quand il dit, Qui fera ces choses il vivra en icelles. Car Dieu pourroit exiger de nous tout ce que bon luy semblera, et cependant nous ne pourrons iamais dire que nous ne luy soyons redevables. Car nous sommes siens, et s'il veut, encores n'acceptera-il point ce que nous luy apporterons, combien que nous le tenions tant iuste que rien plus, et qu'il nous semble qu'il n'y ait que redire: Dieu ne daignera pas le regarder d'un bon oeil s'il ne veut, c'est à dire, qu'il ne soit esmeu de sa pure grace et liberalité à ce faire* [*CO* 33:496].

[98] 37 (Job 9:29-35), 170.b.41. *Il n'est pas question de trouver ici une dignité parfaite aux hommes, ne de dire que Dieu leur soit redevable, et qu'ils puissent contester avec lui, qu'ils ont bien merité qu'il ne trouve que redire en eux et en leur vie* [*CO* 33:456-457].

[99] 137 (Job 40:20-41:25), 735.a.23. *Car il faut que tu ayes de quoy pour respondre à ton Dieu si tu le veux tirer en plaid et en procez. Et qu'est ce que tu monstreras? Puis que tu n'as sinon toute povreté et malediction en toy: ne faut-il point que tu te submettes à luy en toute obeissance et humilitié?* [*CO* 35:471].

[100] 37 (Job 9:29-35), 170.b.27. ...*iusques à tant que Dieu nous gouverne par son sainct Esprit, il est certain que toute ceste saincteté que les hommes apperçoivent n'est qu'hypocrisie et mensonge* [*CO* 33:456].

[101] 37 (Job 9:29-35), 171.b.16. ...*un patron et une image de sa iustice*...[*CO* 33:458].

[102] 37 (Job 9:29-35), 171.b.22. ...*qui est compassee à la mesure des hommes* [*CO* 33:459].

[103] 37 (Job 9:29-35), 172.a.25. ...*si est-ce que selon ceste iustice secrette qui est en Dieu, il se trouveroit tousiours redevable* [*CO* 33:460].

[104] 37 (Job 9:29-35), 174.a.25. ...*que Dieu use envers nous d'une double bonté, quand il nous a donné sa Loy, et puis qu'il nous retire de ceste condamnation en laquelle elle nous met* [*CO* 33:465].

[105] 37 (Job 9:29-35), 174.a.47. ...*il faut que nous demourions tous confus et condamnez, sinon qu'il passe plus outre, et qu'il nous propose sa misericorde. Autrement nous demourerions tousiours maudits, encores que nous ayons accompli toutes les choses qui sont contenues en la Loy* [*CO* 33:465].

[106] 40 (Job 10:16-17), 185.a.65. *Car il considere que s'il est meschant, la*

*Loy de Dieu le condamne: s'il est iuste, il y a encores une iustice par dessus, et en laquelle il faudra qu'il demeure confus* [*CO* 33:494]. Cf. Calvin's comments in the sermon on Deuteronomy 5:21, "In deede there is a righteousness of God (as wee haue seene in the Booke of Iob) which surmounteth the righteousnesse of the lawe. But though the Angels of heauen giue themselues neuer so much to the keeping of Gods lawe: surely the vttermost that they can doe, is but to frame themselues, though they haue not had any wicked thing presented before them..." *The Sermons of M. Iohn Calvin vpon the Fifth Booke of Moses called Deuteronomie*, trans. Arthvr Golding (London: Henry Middleton, 1583). Facsimile edition (Edinburgh, Carlisle: Banner of Truth, 1987), 41. (Deut. 5:21), 245.b.54. "*Il est vray qu'il y a une iustice de Dieu (comme nous avons veu en Ioj) qui surmonte celle de la Loy: mais si les Anges de paradis s'appliquent à observer la Loy de Dieu, il est certain que c'est tout ce qui se pourra faire, que de se conformer à ceste reigle qui nous est ici donnee.*" [*CO* 26:380-81].

[107] *Institutes* II.ii.1. "*Ad hos ergo scopulos ne impingamus, tenendus hic cursus erit, ut homo nihil boni penes se reliquum sibi esse edoctus, et miserrima undique necessitate circumseptus, doceatur tamen ad bonum quo vacuus est, ad libertatem qua privatus est, aspirare, et acrius ab ignavia excitetur quam si summa virtute fingeretur instructus. Hoc secundum quam necessarium sit, nemo non videt. De priore video a pluribus dubitari quam conveniebat. Nam hoc extra controversiam posito, nihil homini de suo adimendum esse, quantopere intersit ipsum falsa gloriatione deiici, palam constare debet. Nam si ne tum quidem hoc homini concessum fuit, ut in se gloriaretur, quum Dei beneficentia summis ornamentis esset insignitus, quantum nunc humiliari convenit, ubi ob suam ingratitudinem ab eximia gloria in extremam ignominiam deturbatus est? Pro eo, inquam, tempore quo in summum honoris fastigium evectus erat, scriptura nihil aliud ei tribuit quam quod creatus esset ad imaginem Dei: quo scilicet insinuat, non propriis bonis sed Dei participatione fuisse beatum.*" [*CO* 2:185-186].

[108] 337 (Job 9:29-35), 171.b.34. ... *Mais tant y a qu'il y a encores une iustice plus haute en Dieu, c'est à dire une perfection, à laquelle nous ne pouvons pas attaindre, et de laquelle nous ne pouvons pas approcher, iusques à ce que nous soyons faits semblables à luy, et que nous ayons contemplé ceste gloire, qui maintenant nous est cachee, et que nous ne voyons sinon comme en un miroir, et par obscurité* [*CO* 33:459].

[109] See W. Duncan Rankin, "Carnal Union with Christ in the Theology of T. F. Torrance" (Ph.D. diss., University of Edinburgh, 1997), 212-13.

[110] An Italian Unitarian, Francesco Stancaro (1501-1574) taught Hebrew in Königsberg, conflicting with Andreas Osiander (1498-1565). Stancaro, who had suggested that Christ was only a mediator with God in his human nature, had claimed, by way of support, John Calvin. Leading Polish churchmen sought Calvin's opinion on the matter. See Calvin, "To John Lusen," dated 9 June 1560, *Tracts and Letters*, col. 7, 112-114 [*CO* 18:100-101]; Joseph Tylenda, "Christ the Mediator: Calvin versus Stancaro," *Calvin Theological Journal*

8 (1973): 5-16; and Tylanda [sic], "The Controversy on Christ the Mediator: Calvin's Second Reply to Stancaro," 131-157, which gives full English translations of Calvin's two treatises against Stancaro. See also, Rankin, *op. cit.*, 212n141.

[111] *CO* 9:338, quoted and translated by David Willis, in *Calvin's Catholic Christology*, vol. 2 of *Studies in Medieval and Reformation Thought*, ed. H. A. Oberman (Leiden: E. J. Brill, 1966), 70.

[112] 16 (Job 4:12-19), 74.a.60. *...que les Anges ont leur fermeté en ceste grace de nostre Seigneur Iesus Christ, entant qu'il est Mediateur de Dieu et des creatures. Il est vray que Iesus Christ n'a point esté Redempteur des Anges: car ils n'ont point besoin d'estre rachetez de la mort, en laquelle ils ne sont iamais tombez: mais il a bien esté leur Mediateur. Et comment? afin qu'il les conioigne à Dieu en toute perfection: et puis il faut qu'il les maintiene par sa grace, et qu'ils soyent preservez afin de ne point tomber* [*CO* 33:208]. This theme of the eternal Son's mediatorship and headship over angels and men is not unknown elsewhere, e.g., Calvin, *Institutes* (1559) II.xii.4 (467) [*CO* 2:255-256]; Calvin, *Galatians*, 129-130 (Eph. 1:8-10) [*CO* 51:150-51] and 310-313 (Col. 1:17-20) [*CO* 52:86-89]; Calvin, *Sermons on the Epistle to the Ephesians*, 63-64 (Eph. 1:7-10) [*CO* 51:149-51]; John Calvin, "Sermon on 1 Corinthians 11:2-3," in *Men, Women, and Order in the Church*, trans. Seth Skolnitsky (Dallas, TX: Presbyterian Heritage Publications, 1992), 18-19 [*CO* 49:472-75]; John Calvin, *Commentaries on the First Book of Moses called Genesis*, 2:429, in *Calvin's Commentaries* (Grand Rapids, MI: Baker Book House, 1989) [*CO* 23:226-227]; Calvin, *Harmony of Moses*, 1:61; George Smeaton, *Christ's Doctrine of the Atonement* (1870; reprint ed., Edinburgh: Banner of Truth Trust, 1991), 43. Calvin limits this eternal mediatorship and headship to angels and the elect, when he claims it does not apply to devils or the ungodly. See Calvin, *Galatians*, 313 (Col. 1:20) [*CO* 52:88-89].

[113] For a cogent discussion of Calvin's uses of the term "Mediator" before and after the incarnation, see Willis, 67-71. Willis points to three periods in which Calvin uses the term (pre-Fall, post-incarnation, and in-between) and two nuances of meaning (mediation as reconciliation and mediation of sustenance). On Christ's mediation of sustenance, Willis concludes: "When he uses mediation to refer to Christ's eternal sustaining of the order of the world, he applies the term in a new way to a function which the tradition held belonged to Christ but which the tradition did not usually describe as mediation." Willis, *op. cit.*, 71.

[114] 16 (Job 4:12-19), 74.b.31. *Il est vray que nous n'apprehendons point sa vertu puissante, comme il appartient: mais les Anges qui sont maintenant plus prochains de luy, et qui contemplent sa face n'ont point encores une telle perfection qu'il n'y trouvast à redire s'il les vouloit examiner à la rigueur* [*CO* 33:208]. Calvin's point is to suggest that if the angels may not stand this test, much less shall we, considering our "weaknesse." "What shall become of our vertues, if we would compare them with the Angels which are so noble and excellent creatures?" 16 (Job 4:12-19), 74.b.36. *...que*

*sera-ce de nos vertus, quand nous les voudrons accomparer à celles des Anges, qui sont creatures si nobles et si excellentes?* [*CO* 33:209].

[115] *A Harmony of the Gospels: Matthew, Mark and Luke*, Vol.1, trans. A. W. Morrison, ed. David W. Torrance and Thomas F. Torrance (Grand Rapids, Michigan: Eerdmans, 1972), 30. "*Quanquam semper tenendum est axioma, perverse eos vagari, qui de potentia Dei imaginantur extra verbum, si quid visum est: quia sic consideranda est eius immensitas, ut spei et fiduciae nobis sit materia. Iam vero non temere solum et inutiliter, sed etiam periculose disputatur, quid sit Deo possibile, nisi simul occurrat, quid ipse velit.*" [*CO* 45:32-33]. On Calvin's understanding of God's omnipotence generally, see Richard Stauffer, *op. cit.*, 112-116. For the influence of Duns Scotus on Calvin, see François Wendel, *Calvin: The Origins and Development of His Religious Thought*, trans. Philip Mairet (New York: Harper and Row, 1963), 92-94.

[116] *Institutes* III.xxiii.2. "Ubi ergo quaeritur cur ita fecerit Dominus, respondendum est, quia voluit. Quod si ultra pergas rogando cur voluerit, maius aliquid quaeris, et sublimius Dei voluntate, quod inveniri non potest. Compescat igitur se humana temeritas, et quod non est ne quaerat, ut ne forte id quod est non inveniat. Hoc, inquam, fraeno bene continebitur quisquis de arcanis Dei sui cum reverentia philosophari volet.... Nenque tamen commentum ingerimus absolutae potentiae: quod sicuti profanum est, ita merito detestabile nobis esse debet. Non fingimus Deum exlegem, qui sibi ipsi lex est" [*CO* 2:700]. Cf. "Therefore, with reference to the sentiments of the Schoolmen concerning the absolute or tyrannical will of God, I not only repudiate, but abhor them all, because they separate the justice of God from his ruling power." *Calumniae nebulonis cuiusdam de occulta providentia Dei*, trans. H. Cole, *Calvin's Calvinism* [1856], 266. On Calvin's opposition to the distinction between *potentia dei absoluta* and *potentia dei ordinata*, see David Steinmetz, *Calvin in Context*, 40-50. Here in Book III of the *Institutes*, Calvin attacks the distinction as a speculative doctrine that separates the omnipotence of God from his justice. Later Reformed theologians were to disagree with Calvin. William Ames drew the distinction routinely, see *Medulla Theologiae* I.vi.16-20. English translation by John Dystra Eusden, *The Marrow of Theology* (Grand Rapids: Baker Books, 1977). Francis Turretini attempts to salvage Calvin, suggesting that Calvin did not object to the distinction, only its abuse by certain unnamed medieval scholastics. See *Institutio Theologiae Elenchticae* loc.III q.21 a.3-5 (Edinburgh: John D. Lowe, 1847). English translation by George Musgrave Giger, ed. James T. Dennison, Jr. (Philipsburg, New Jersey: Presbyterian and Reformed Publishing, 1992, 1994, 1997), 3 vols.

[117]Sometimes Calvin is sympathetic to Job's plight. "We haue seene how he was as it were a mirrour of a castaway, and how it might seeme that God was minded too vtter all his anger and wrath against him. Iob therefore sawe not to what ende God did this: there was no reason in it, as to his knowledge. That is true: for he speaketh not in hypocrisie." 35 (Job 9:16-22), 163.b.18.

...*nous avons veu qu'il estoit là comme un miroir d'un homme reprouvé, qu'il sembloit que Dieu voulust desployer toute son ire et sa fureur contre luy. Iob donc ne voit point pourquoy Dieu fait cela: il n'y a point de raison, voire quant à luy. Et cela est vray: il ne parle point par hypocrisie* [*CO* 33:438]. Cf. Calvin's attempt in Job 27:2, "God... who hath taken away my ryght," to argue that Job is *not* accusing God of tyrannical power. 97 (Job 27:1-4), 454.b.14 [*CO* 34:443]; and again at 455.a.28 [*CO* 33:446]. Cf. Sermon 110 (Job 30:21-31), 517.a.22, [*CO* 34:611], in which Calvin says that Job expresses his "grief and the excesse of the miserie wherin he was." And again, 118, in which Calvin says that Job is "not without cause" that he should "make that wish to suggest his suffering was not for his sinnes." 118 (Job 31:35[36 *Fr.*]-40), 555.a.9 [*CO* 34:714]. And again, in Job 33:9, Elihu has heard Job saying, "I am pure and without sinne. I am cleane and there is no unrighteousnesse in mee," to which Calvin ambivalently suggests that Elihu "doth falsifie the woordes that he had heard," adding "it seemed then that he ment to accuse God of some tyrannie: not that he concluded so in himselfe, but that he was tempted so to do," adding by way of explanation a little later that Job was "caried away with his affections, as there scaped many disordered woordes by fits, which are not to be excused." 123 (Job 33:8-14), 578.b.62. ...*falsifie les propos qu'il a ouy*...[*CO* 35:54], 579.a.45. *Il sembloit donc qu'il voulust accuser Dieu de quelque tyrannie*...[*CO* 35:55], and 579.b.43. ...*transporté en ses passions, en sorte qu'il lui est sorti par bouffees des rebellions lesquelles ne sont point à excuser*...[*CO* 35:56].

In other places, Calvin is less happy to defend Job. In Sermon 88, Calvin accuses Job of blasphemy, 88 (Job 23:1-7), 413.b.66. ...*Or en cela Iob blaspheme Dieu*...[*CO* 34:336] and *evil* 414.a.5. *Ainsi le propos de Iob est mauvais*...[*CO* 34:336]. In the next sermon, Calvin says that Job "offended in saying that the righteouse and iust dealing man may pleade his cace before God." 89 (Job 23:8-12), 417.a.38. *Et ainsi donc nous voyons comme Iob a failli en disant, Que l'homme iuste et droit pourroit plaider sa cause devant Dieu* [*CO* 34:345]. And in the next sermon again, Job "did amisse in imagining that God vsed a lawlesse power, and in that he could not imagin otherwise." 90 (Job 23:13-17), 422.b.30. *Vray est que Iob a failli... d'autant qu'il a imaginé que Dieu usoit d'une puissance desreglee*...[*CO* 34:360]. Again, in Sermon 129, Calvin says repeatedly that Job "exceeded measure in his passions," "did amisse," and "ouershotte himself" in his outbursts. 129 (Job 34:4-10), 606.b.60, 66. ...*mais tant y a qu'il a excedé mesure en ses passions*...*Iob a failli*... [*CO* 35:131]. And in Sermon 157, for example, he has Job suggesting that "God therfore is almightie. As how? For looke what he purposeth in his mind, he can execute it by & by without any let. But it shuld seem that Iob here confesseth not all that he ought to do..." 157 (Job 42:1-5), 737.a.66. *Dieu donc peut toutes chose. Et comment? Car ce qu'il arreste en son conseil il le peut executer tantost, sans que nul l'empesche* [*CO* 35:478]. See also Schreiner, *Where Shall Wisdom be Found?*, 114.

[118] 154 (Job 39:36-40:6), 725.b.17....*pour monstrer qu'ils ne pourront*

*apporter nulle vertu qui soit pareille à la sienne* [*CO* 35:447]. Cf. "For all the power whych he hathe giuen to mortall men, there is no whit abated from himselfe." 32 (Job 8:13-22), 148.b.16. ...*mais sachons que ce qu'il a donné de pouvoir aux hommes mortels, il ne se l'est point osté à luy-mesme* [*CO* 33:399].

[119] 15 (Job 4:7-11), 67.a.25. ...*nous cognoissions la vertu de nostre Dieu estre si grande, qu'il pourra secourir à ceux qui sont comme accablez, qu'il les pourra vivifier combien que desia ils soyent en la mort. Mais il ne nous faut point seulement appliquer ceste doctrine à nos prochains, il faut que nous la pratiquions chacun de nous en soy* [*CO* 33:190].

[120] 109 (Job 30:11-21), 514.b.46. *approbation* [*CO* 34:604].

[121] 156 (Job 40:20-41:25), 735.b.38. ...*il ne nous faudroit point sortir hors de nous: car nous trouverions assez d'advertissemens de ce que Dieu peut et de ce qu'il veut aussi*...[*CO* 35:473].

[122] 109 (Job 30:11-21), 514.a.40. ...*que la vertu de Dieu n'est point suiette à quelques moyens humains, et de ce monde: mais qu'il besongne d'une façon qui nous est incomprehensible, voire en secret* [*CO* 34:603]. And in the same sermon, Calvin says, "are we able to inclose it in our brayne? It is vnpossible." 514.a.67. *Or quand nous voudrons comprendre ceste puissance et ceste vertu-la, ie vous prie, le pourrons-nous enclorre à nostre cerveau? Il est impossible* [*CO* 34:603-604].

[123] In the English translation, Golding consistently refers to it as the "elephant" and the "whale." For "Behemoth," at Job 40:15 [40:19 in the sermon text] Calvin says initially, "*et est parlé comme d'une seule beste,*" but concludes due to its size: "*ce soit un elephant à cause de la grosse masse de corps qui est en ceste beste-la... voila un elephant.*" 155 (Job 40:7-19), 730.b.54 [*CO* 35:460-461]. As for "Leviathan," at Job 41:1 [40:20 in the sermon text] Calvin alludes to the "whale" ("*balesne,*" "*baleine*"). 156 (Job 40:20-41:25), 732.a.8 [*CO* 35:464-465].

[124] 156 (Job 40:20-41:25), 734.a.63. *Le mot donc de* subsister *emporte que l'homme ne pourra iamais avoir bonne cause en se maintenant iuste et sage: mais qu'il faut qu'il soit en premier lieu du tout aneanti, et qu'il cognoisse que Dieu a toute puissance, vertu, et iustice, et que nous ne pouvons estre sinon abysmez en nostre nature* [*CO* 35:469].

[125] 129 (Job 34:4-10), 606.a.64. ...*combien que Dieu ait toute puissance sur nous, neantmoins qu'il nous iuge en telle equité, qu'il n'y a que redire... Dieu donc n'a pas une puissance absoluë... mais sa puissance est tellement infinie qu'il est tousiours equitable et iuste en ce qu'il fait* [*CO* 35:130-131].

[126] 88 (Job 23:1-7), 413.b.60. *Comment entend-il que Dieu ne debatra point avec luy par force? Ce seroit vouloir entrer en iustice, quand il luy voudroit donner audience. Iob donc presuppose que Dieu use envers luy d'une puissance absolue qu'on appelle: pour dire, Ie suis Dieu, ie feray ce que bon me semblera, encores qu'il n'y ait point de forme de iustice, mais comme une domination excessive. Or en cela Iob blaspheme Dieu: car combien que la puissance de Dieu soit infinie, si est-ce que de la faire ainsi*

*absolue, c'est imaginer en luy une tyrannie, et cela est du tout contraire à sa maiesté, car nostre Seigneur ne veut point estre puissant qu'il ne soit iuste: et ce sont choses inseparables, que sa iustice et sa puissance. Ainsi le propos de Iob est mauvais non pas que son intention soit (comme nous avons traitté) de blasphemer Dieu...* [CO 34:336].

[127] 88 (Job 23:1-7), 415.a.43. *Et de fait, quand ces docteurs Sorboniques disent, que Dieu a une puissance absoluë, c'est un blaspheme diabolique qui a esté forgé aux enfers: car il ne faut point que cela entre au cerveau de l'homme fidele. Il faut donc dire que Dieu a une puissance infinie, laquelle toutes fois est la regle de toute iustice: car c'est deschirer Dieu par pieces, quand nous le voudrons faire puissant, et qu'il ne sera plus iuste. Vrai est que sa iustice ne nous sera pas tousiours en son entier.* [CO 34:339-340]. Cf. the following: "We see many fantasticall persons, who when they talk of Gods almightines, fal to gazing at this and that, saying: If God be almightie why doth hee not such a thing? If God be almightie, then can hee do this. Yea, but wee must not range abrode so after our own imaginations, gods alimghtines ameth not at our dotages nor at any comon thing. Wherat then? Gods almightines & his wil are things inseparable. God is almighty: but is to do whatsoeuer ma[n] hath forged in hys braine? No fie: but it is to accomplish whatsoeuer he hath ordeyned in his own purpose. So the[n] let vs learne to knit these two thinges together, namely his almightines & his will." 157 (Job 42:1-5), 737.b.53. *Nous en voyons beaucoup de phantastiques, que quand ils parlent de la puissance de Dieu, ils speculent ceci et cela, O si Dieu est tout puissant, pourquoy ne fait-il telle chose? si Dieu est tout-puissant, cela est possible. Voire, mais il ne nous faut pas ainsi extravaguer en nos imaginations: la puissance de Dieu ne s'adresse point à nos resveries, et n'y a rien de commun. Quoy donc? Ce sont choses inseparables, que la puissance de Dieu et sa volonté. Dieu est tout-puissant: est-ce pour faire ce que l'homme aura basti en son cerveau? fy: mais c'est pour accomplir ce qu'il a ordonné en son conseil.* [CO 35:479]. Cf. also, "When wee speake of his power, or his iustice, or his wisedome, or his goodnesse: we speake of himself: they are things inseparable, and cannot be seuered (that is to say, they cannot be taken away from his Being): for they are so ioyned togither, as the one of them cannot be without the other.... His mightinesse defeateth not his goodnesse, nor yet his iustice....not that his greatnesse is onely in power, but also that with his greatnesse of power, there is infinite iustice, infinite wisdom, & al others things infinite in him." 123 (Job 33:8-14), 581.a.21.

*Quand nous parlons de sa puissance, ou iustice, ou sagesse, ou bonté, nous parlons de lui-mesme: ce sont choses inseparables, et qui ne se peuvent point discerner de son essence, c'est à dire pour en estre ostees. Car elles sont tellement coniointes, que l'une ne peut estre sans l'autre. Dieu-est-il puissant? Aussi il est bon. Sa puissance ne desrogue point à sa bonté, ni à sa iustice. Quand donc Eliu dit ici, que Dieu est plus grand que l'homme, il n'entend pas qu'il soit grand seulement pour pouvoir: mais il entend qu'avec ceste grandeur et vertu il a aussi une iustice infinie, une sagesse infinie, que tout est infini en lui. Et qui sommes-nous en comparison?* [*CO* 35:60]. For a similar reference to "tyrannical power" as a "blasphemie," see 90 (Job 23:13-17), 423.b.2 [*CO* 35:362]. For a similar reference to the inseparability of God's attributes, Calvin remarks, "Let vs assure ouselues that Gods almightinesse is not a tirannicall or inordinate power, but is ioyned in vnseparable band with hys righteousnesse, so as he doth all thinges after an vpright maner." 75 (Job 20:16-20), 354.b.30. *...cognoissons que Dieu n'a point une puissance tyrannique ou desordonnee, mais qu'elle est coniointe d'un lien inseparable avec sa iustice, et qu'il fait tout d'une façon equitable* [*CO* 34:175]. And again, "And it woorthy to be marked well, that whensoeuer we thinke of Gods mightie power, we must not take it to be a tirannicall power, to say, Beholde God may do with vs what he listeth, we are his Creatures: he seeth that there is nothing but fraylie in vs, and yet notwithsta[n]ding he ceaseth not to vexe vs without cause. When we speake after that fashio[n], it is not only outrage but also cursed blasphemie. And therfore let vs match Gods mighty power with rightfulnesse, saying: true it is that the power of my God is terrible vnto me, & I am wholly dismayde at it: but yet doth not my God ceasse to be righteous: he doth al things rightfully." 123 (Job 33:8-14), 580.b.37. *Et ceci est bien digne d'estre noté, Que quand nous pensons à la puissance de Dieu, il ne faut pas que nous lui attribuons une puissance tyrannique pour dire, O voila, Dieu fera de nous tout ce qu'il voudra, nous sommes ses creatures: il voit bien qu'il n'y a que fragilité en nous, et cependant il ne laisse pas de nous tormenter sans propos. Quand nous parlons ainsi, il n'y a point seulement de l'excez, mais ce sont des blasphemes execrables. Et pourtant conioignons la iustice de Dieu avec sa vertu et puissance. Il est vrai que la vertu de Dieu m'est espouvantable, m'en voila tout troublé: mais si est-ce que mon Dieu ne laisse point d'estre iuste: c'est avec iustice qu'il fait toutes choses* [*CO* 35:59]. And again, "Let vs assure ourselues that God vttereth not such power without cause, but that he doeth it through his iustice." 132 (Job 34:21-26), 620.b.47. *...cognoissons que Dieu ne desploye point une telle vertu sans propos, mais qu'il fait cela par sa iustice* [*CO* 35:169]. Stauffer cites other sermons in which Calvin states something similar, including the 69th sermon on II Samuel, after having raised the point that God has as much liberty, at the very least, as a potter may have over the clay as he fashions his pots, he adds that God does not exercise an absolute power that the "papistes" assign to him. See Stauffer, *op. cit.*, 116. Cf. 138 (Job 23:1-7), 415.a.43 [*CO* 34:339].

[128] 89 (Job 33:8-12), 417.a.61. *...que la façon de laquelle Dieu use envers lui est si haute et si profonde, que l'esprit humain ne pourroit parvenir iusques là. C'est une sentence bien vraye, moyennant qu'elle soit bien appliquee: mais la faute est, que Iob quand il n'apperçoit point la raison de ce que Dieu fait, imagine qu'il n'y a qu'une puissance absoluë (qu'on appelle) c'est à dire, que Dieu besongne à son plaisir, sans tenir nul ordre, nulle regle, et qu'il en fait comme bon lui sembe, ainsi qu'un prince quand il ne voudra point se regler par raison, mais voudra suivre son appetit. Iob*

*en cela blaspheme contre Dieu, mais c'est d'autant qu'il a des passions soudaines...* [*CO* 34:345].

[129] 90 (Job 33:13-17), 421.b.56. *excessif* [*CO* 35:357].

[130] 90 (Job 33:13-17), 421.b.60. *Or il imagine une puissance exorbitante, et qui n'a ne regle ne mesure: en cela il fait iniure à Dieu* [*CO* 34:357]. Cf. "God speaketh not of an absolute or lawlesse power... but of a power that is matched with rightfulnesse." 155 (Job 40:7-19), 728.b.4. *...que Dieu ne parle pas d'une puissance absoluë (comme nous avons dit) mais il parle d'une puissance coniointe avec sa iustice* [*CO* 35:454].

[131] Cf. "Wherfore let vs be sure, that our da[m]nation shall be the greater, if we be not quiet in our afflictions, but fall to grudging, and that although our mouth speake not a woorde, yet we be so ful of hartburning within, that we play the Mule which chaweth vpo[n] his bit. Now then, whe[n] we have such bitternesse in vs against God: it is asmuch as if wee accused him of picking couert quarrels to vs, to punish vs without cause." 123 (Job 33:8-14), 580.b.4. *Advisons donc que nostre condamnation sera beaucoup plus grande quand nous ne serons point du tout paisibles en nos afflictions, mais qu'il nous adviendra de murmurer, encores que la bouche ne sonne mot, quand nous aurons là dedans des angoisses, que nous serons comme si une mule rongeoit son frain. Quand donc nous aurons ainsi ces amertumes à l'encontre de Dieu, c'est autant comme si nous l'accusions d'avoir cerché des couvertures frivoles sans qu'il nous affligeast iustement* [*CO* 35:58].

[132] Schreiner, *Where Shall Wisdom be Found?*, 115.

[133] For example, it is Job's use of a notion of absolute power that Calvin is representing in Sermon 89, which he clearly speaks of as "Job's fault.". See, 89 (Job 23:8-12), 417.a.66 [*CO* 34:345]. See also, the earlier remark that Job "doth euill" in attributing to God a lawless power. 89 (Job 23:8-12), 417.a.2 [*CO* 34:344].

[134] 30 (Job 8:1-6), 138.b.17. *...toutesfois il nous faut adorer ses iugemens incomprehensibles et secrets, en recueillant tous nos esprits en ceste humilité pour dire, Voici il est vray que maintenant ceci nous semble tout contraire à toute raison: mais quoy? nous ne gaignerons pas nostre cause contre Dieu: et puis sans avoir autre replicque, il nous faut tenir ceste conclusion-la, qu'il est iuste. D'autant donc que maintenant nous ne voyons qu'en partie, voire comme en un miroir, et par obscurité: attendons le iour que nous puissions contempler face à face la gloire de Dieu: et alors nous comprendrons ce qui nous est maintenant caché* [*CO* 33:373]. Cf. a similar remark in Sermon 33, in which Calvin exhorts his hearers to be content to live in the light of the revelation already received, "and that is a far greater and better wisdome, than to be inquisitive of all things without exception," knowing that the "day of the full reuelatio[n]" is yet to come. 123 (Job33:8-14), 582.a.42,24. *...iour de pleine revelation...et que voila une sagesse plus grande et meilleure beaucoup, que s'ils vouloyent s'enquerir du tout indifferemment* [*CO* 35:63-64]. A similar statement is found again in Sermon 88. Speaking to the issue of election, and how some "wretched fooles, or

rather madde men, can not fynde in their hearts to stoup so low as to say: In dede it is a verie strange case, that God hauing created me, wil not also save th[em] al[l]," Calvin goes on: "but the day will come that our Lorde will make vs able to understand the things that are hidde[n] from vs as now. It is sayde that we know but partly & darkly: but whe[n] we become like to him, we shall not only see him as he is, but also we shal perfectly vndersta[n]d the things that are not yet disclosed vnto vs. These drunken sots that are sotted in their ouerweening, cannot abide to yeld God so much glorie, as to submit themselues wholly vnto him." 88 (Job 23:1-7), 415.b.33,38. *Or ces povres fols, ou plustost enragez, ne se peuvent humilier iusques là, de dire. Il est vrai que nous trouvons ces choses estranges, que Dieu ait creé des hommes qu'il ne vueille point sauver: mais cognoissons que la iustice de Dieu est trop haute et trop profonde pour nous: le iour viendra que nostre Seigneur nous rendra capables de cognoistre ce qui nous est maintenant caché. Il est dit (1. Cor. 13, 9 s.; 1. Iean 3, 2), que nous cognoissons en partie et en obscurité: mais quand nous serons semblables à lui, non seulement nous le verrons tel qu'il est, mais nous cognoistrons en perfection les choses qui maintenant ne nous sont point revelees. Ces yvrongnes ici qui sont enyvrez de leur outrecuidance, ne peuvent donner ceste gloire à Dieu...* [CO 34:341].

[135] *Inst.*, ii.xii.5 [CO 343-344].

# Chapter 3

# The Incomprehensibility of God

Behold, God is great, and we know him not…(Job 36:26).

His essence is incomprehensible; … his divineness far escapes all human perception (*Institutes* I.v.1).

In the secret mysteries of Scripture, we ought to play the philosopher soberly and with great moderation; let us use great caution that neither our thoughts nor our speech go beyond the limits to which the Word of God itself extends. For how can the human mind measure the measureless essence of God according to its own little measure, a mind as yet unable to establish for certain the nature of the sun's body, though men's eyes daily gaze upon it? Indeed, how can the mind by its own leading come to search out God's essence when it cannot even get to its own? Let us then willingly leave to God the knowledge of himself. For as Hilary says, he is the one fit witness to himself, and is not known except through himself (*Institutes* I.xiii.21).

Between God and us there stands the hiddenness of God, in which He is far from us and foreign to us except as He has of Himself ordained and created fellowship between Himself and us—and this does not happen in the actualising of our capacity, but in the miracle of his good-pleasure (Karl Barth, *Church Dogmatics*, II/1,182).

"When we come to conceiue the incomprehensible maiestie and inestimable highnesse that is in God, wee must needes bee so abashed as to humble our selues, and be no more puffed vp as we were."[1] In this way, Calvin highlights a major doctrinal theme and its consequent pastoral application. According to Harold Dekker, commenting on Calvin's preaching on the Book of Job,

> The final dimension of God's sovereignty for Calvin was not his revealed will but the unrevealed, and there was hardly a sermon in which this perspective was not present. One of the most distinctive features of Calvin's entire pastoral theology is his accent on the hidden in God, and the final mystery of all His dealings with His children. He has no better

comfort to offer to troubled spirits than the unrevealed purposes of a God of sovereign grace.[2]

Some have taken the idea to the extreme. Karl Barth, emphasising a radical transcendence, could write of "the God to whom there is no way and bridge, of whom we could not say or have to say one single word, had he not of his own initiative met us as *Deus revelatus*."[3] Contrast this with the judgement of Brian Gerrish: "Striving after clarity in the concept we should entertain of God" is "a fundamental mark of the Calvinistic mind."[4] The place given to the *incomprehensibilitas Dei* in theology is a matter of interest in itself but is beyond the scope of this present work.[5]

This is the assessment that we will now be evaluating, with particular reference to Calvin's Sermons on Job.[6] Calvin sees two dangers to be shunned in his presentation of Christian theism. On the one hand, he avoids the danger of *rationalism* by stressing that at no point are we to understand the revelation of God in the Scriptures as in any way indicating the full measure of his reality. God limits what we may know of him, accommodating himself to us. Calvin's chief concern is to limit theological triumphalism by urging his listeners to trust in the God who is beyond our grasp. On the other hand, Calvin equally desires to avoid the danger of *mysticism*. God reveals himself but a little, truly and not other than he is. Scriptural exegesis requires restraint; we can never fully understand the mind and being of God truly, but to the extent that God has made himself known to us, to that extent we may understand assuredly.[7]

Barth's concern is to avoid "irrelevant speculation."[8] This appears to have been Calvin's own concern, particularly in the writing of the *Institutes*. On over twenty occasions, particularly in Books I and III, Calvin has recourse to the doctrine of God's incomprehensibility.[9]

**Establishing criteria to justify the conclusion that the doctrine of God's incomprehensibility is central in the Joban sermons.**

There are four strands of evidence which suggest the conclusion that God's incomprehensibility provided Calvin with an important interpretative key for unlocking the meaning of the Book of Job. The first strand is his use of the doctrine in both the *Institutes* and the Commentaries. An examination of this usage will enable us to take a wider persepective on Calvin's understanding of God's incomprehensibility. We will discover that his stress on this doctrine was not fashioned solely by the Book of Job.

As we examine this material in some detail, we will note Calvin's conviction that the incomprehensibility of God arises from both metaphysical and harmartological considerations. Due to our finitude, our capacity to comprehend the infinite God is necessarily limited. In addition, our capacity to comprehend has been radically affected by the Fall. Sin renders us unwilling to acknowledge the revelation of himself that God gives. As we shall see, these two factors are intertwined in Calvin's treatment of our ability to comprehend God.

A second line of evidence is Calvin's use of God's incomprehensibility in the interpretation of the Joban sermons themselves. Here we shall make the statistical observation that Calvin employs the idea of God's incomprehensibility throughout the sermons. Thus, in over sixty of the sermons (almost 40%), Calvin directly resorts to an analysis of this issue, sometimes to explain why some suffer more than others, sometimes to defend God's providence against attack, sometimes to indicate what is at the heart of Christian piety: a submission in quiet, humble reverence to the God whose ways we may not comprehend. In some of these sermons, the references are numerous as we shall indicate in our analysis that follows. It is also of interest that Calvin seems to have blocks of sermons where he continues the theme of incomprehensibility (e.g. Sermons 1-11, 17-23, 30-40, 80-90, 100-103, 146-150). These would have provided, in some instances, a sustained emphasis lasting for several weeks of exposition.

Thirdly, we should note the regularity with which Calvin gives expression to this doctrine whenever he provides summary statements of the principal themes of the Book of Job. Even in the opening sermon, Calvin prepares us for what lies ahead. Responding to the apparent dilemma caused by Job's godliness and suffering, Calvin reminds his listeners that there exist "secret judgments" which God may enter into that we know nothing about.[10] At the very outset, Calvin is preparing us for a sustained agenda in which the incomprehensibility of God is to be prominent. Then again, in Sermon 157, almost at the very conclusion of the expositions, Calvin asks: "What is the first point of teachablenesse?" The answer? "It is that we take hym for our master and obey him fully in any thing that he shall list to teach vs." Calvin goes on to urge upon his listeners a view that does not attempt to comprehend those things which are beyond them. "How shall we comprehende what God is?" he asks.[11]

Fourthly, Calvin resorts to the incomprehensibility of God even when he has no compelling exegetical reason to do so. Thus, in the contributions of the three friends, even though Calvin is critical of their position, he nevertheless finds opportunity to formulate lessons as to the nature and character of the incomprehensible God. We shall show that Calvin is capable of a hermeneutical method in which he can draw positive lessons from material with which he is in essential disagreement. That he resorts to the incomprehensibility of God in such material shows how essential this is to his understanding of the Book of Job.

Having indicated the reasons for reaching the judgment that God's incomprehensibility is a key interpretative instrument in Calvin's understanding of the Book of Job, we must now define the meaning and significance of the incomprehensibility of God as Calvin uses this expression.

Despite the assertions of the Neo-Platonist, Plotinus, that nothing positive could ever be affirmed about God (we can only ever define God by what he is not—the *via negationis*), Calvin and others still maintained it proper to speak of the incomprehensible God without thereby sliding into agnosticism. Calvin insists that there are things about God that we are able to know. God may, in this sense, be apprehended. Writing in the *Institutes*, Calvin affirms:

> His essence, indeed, is incomprehensible, utterly transcending all human thought; but on each of his works his glory is engraven in characters so bright, so distinct, and so illustrious, that none, however dull and illiterate, can plead ignorance as their excuse.[12]

God is thus knowable and unknowable.

As we shall see, Calvin often uses the Lutheran language of "the hidden God" (*Deus absconditus*) in describing the incomprehensibility of God. The language was Aquinas' long before it became part of Luther's theological vocabulary. Though Luther stops short of Aquinas' natural theology, he does affirm the tenets that God can only be known in so far as he reveals himself, and what is revealed is partial and never complete.[13] There was, in fact, an official precedent for the language of incomprehensibility from the Fourth Lateran Council (November, 1215). Its opening statement, *On the Catholic Faith*, declares:

> We firmly believe and simply confess that there is only one true God, eternal and immeasurable, almighty, unchangeable, incomprehensible and ineffable.[14]

Aquinas discusses the issue at some length in the early sections of the *Summa Theologiae*. Having outlined the nature of Christian theology and arguments in favor of the existence of God, Aquinas pauses to reflect on two questions: is there any kinship between our finite minds and the infinite reality of God, and, if so, do the words of human thought truthfully describe it.[15] In the course of a discussion of Augustine, Aquinas affirms: "…it is impossible for any created mind to understand God infinitely; impossible, therefore, to comprehend him."[16] This implies incomprehensibility at the ontic, rather than the post-fallen level.

Interestingly, the Scots Confession of 1560 contains an affirmation of God's incomprehensibility in its first article:

> We confess and acknowledge ane onelie God, to whom only we must cleave, whom onelie we must serve, whom onelie we must worship, and in whom onelie we must put our trust. Who is Eternall, Infinit, Unmeasurable, Incomprehensible, Omnipotent, Invisible....[17]

In the next century, *The Westminster Confession* (1647) contains a similar statement in chapter 2:

> There is but one only, living and true God, who is infinite in being and perfection, a most pure spirit, invisible, without body, parts, or passions; immutable, immense, eternal, incomprehensible, almighty, most wise, most holy, most free, most absolute....[18]

From this time forth, Barth can say of this designation of incomprehensibility that "with varying degrees of emphasis the *incomprehensibilitas Dei* could be fairly regularly mentioned and discussed as one of the properties of God in the older Protestant dogmatics."[19]

We need to ask at this point whether our inability to comprehend God is an ontological necessity due to our creatureliness, or is something conditioned by our fallenness. According to John Baillie, it is this very issue that divides Luther and Aquinas, in that "for the former, as for St. Augustine, it was the sinful corruption of human nature that rendered impossible the naked vision of the divine essence, whereas for the latter it was the original constitution of human nature itself—so that even an unfallen human knowledge of God must have been only inferential in character."[20]

It is now time to consider Calvin's view on this issue and its practical application. He took the view that God's incomprehensibility is a consequence both of our creatureliness and our sinfulness. For the Reformer, the incomprehensibility of God is a doctrinal statement, an assertion about the limited extent of our knowledge of God. Thus, for example, in Sermon 85, in the context of an assertion about God's "incomprehensible majestyie," Calvin can say "if this doctrin wer wel printed in our harts, the world shuld be purged of al superstitios that haue always reigned in it."[21]

## The Doctrine of God's Incomprehensibility in the 1559 Edition of the *Institutes*.

The first mention of the issue, in the 1559 edition of the *Institutes*,[22] comes in Calvin's treatment of the knowledge of God in the created universe.[23] This is that "seed of religion" [*religionis semen*] which God has sown in men's minds. Since, however, "God's essence is incomprehensible...his divineness far escapes all human perception,"[24] he has "engraved unmistakable marks of his glory [*suis certas gloriae suae notas insculpit*]" in his work of creation. The universe is God's garment [*ornatu*][25] whereby God reveals himself; it is the "mirror [*speculi*][26] in which we can contemplate God, who is otherwise invisible."[27]

Calvin's denunciation of the use of images as representations of God is partly based on the fact that they contradict his being.[28] From time to time, to be sure, God did represent himself by signs, but they "clearly told men of his incomprehensible essence. For clouds and smoke and flame [Deut. 4:11], although they were symbols of heavenly glory, restrained the minds of all, like a bridle placed on them, from attempting to penetrate too deeply."[29] Citing Isaiah 44:12-17, in which the prophet denounces Israel for making an idol from the trunk of a tree, Calvin says that "there is nothing less fitting than to wish to reduce God, who is immeasurable and incomprehensible, to a five-foot measure!"[30] His "infinity ought to make us afraid to try and measure him by our senses. Indeed, his spiritual nature forbids our imagining anything earthly or carnal of him." And this is so, "because he is incomprehensible."[31]

God's incomprehensibility ought to make us wary of philosophy according to Calvin:

> ...we ought to play the philosopher soberly and with great moderation; let us use great caution that neither our thoughts nor our speech go beyond the limits to which the Word of God itself extends. For how can the human mind measure off the measureless essence of God according to its own little measure, a mind as yet unable to establish for certain the nature of the sun's body, though men's eyes daily gaze upon it? Indeed, how can the mind by its own leading come to search out God's essence when it cannot even get to its own? Let us then willingly leave to God the knowledge of himself.[32]

The limitations[33] of our comprehension of God's majesty as he is in himself ought, therefore, to induce reverence and godly fear:

> We know the most perfect way of seeking God, and the most suitable order, is not for us to attempt with bold curiosity to penetrate to the investigation of his essence, which we ought more to adore than meticulously to search out, but for us to contemplate him in his works whereby he renders himself near and familiar to us, and in some manner communicates himself.[34]

Not only is God incomprehensible to us in himself (in his essence), he is also incomprehensible in his works. Calvin mentions in the unfolding of Book I of the *Institutes*, the "incomprehensible brightness" of creation[35] and the "incomprehensible wisdom" of God's providence as he "disposes it to his own end."[36] Similarly, in a section in which Calvin seeks to apply the doctrine of providence,[37] he cites Psalm 36:6 and uses one of his favourite expressions, "the abyss."[38] "But if they do not admit," he writes, "that whatever happens in the universe is governed by God's incomprehensible plans, let them answer what end Scripture says that his judgments are a deep abyss."[39]

In Book II of the *Institutes*, we find Calvin alluding to incomprehensibility on four occasions. The first occurs in his rebuttal of Servetus' denial that Christ was called "Son of God" before he appeared in the flesh. Calvin implies somewhat cautiously that Proverbs 30:4, in which Solomon indicates "immeasureable loftiness... that both God and his son are incomprehensible,"[40] is just such a case.

In Calvin's unfolding of the three-fold offices of Christ as prophet, priest and king, the so-called *munus triplex*, he reminds us that "outside Christ there is nothing worth knowing."[41] "Why did [Christ] take the person of the Mediator? He descended from the bosom of the Father and from incomprehensible glory that he might draw near to us."[42] Citing Augustine on John 3:16, Calvin speaks of the love of God as "incomprehensible and unchangeable."[43] And what is the extent of this love? It is in Calvin's interpretation of the "descent into hell" clause of the Apostles' Creed that he once again resorts to incomprehensibility. In opposition to those whom he calls "untutored wretches,"[44] and possibly as direct response to Sebastian Castellio,[45] Calvin defends his understanding of the clause as a spiritual suffering borne by Christ on the cross in which he felt "that invisible and incomprehensible judgment" in which "he paid a greater and more excellent price in suffering in his soul the terrible torments of a condemned and forsaken man."[46]

Calvin's dependence upon Augustine for his use of the idea of incomprehensibility is worth pursuing a little. In the opening section of *The Confessions of St. Augustine*, the question is posed as to the nature of God. The answer:

> Most high, most excellent, most potent, most omnipotent; most piteous and most just; most hidden [*secretissime*] and most near; most beauteous and most strong, stable, yet contained of none [*incomprehensibilis*]; unchangeable, yet changing all things; never new, never old; making all things new, yet bringing old age upon the proud and they know it not; always working, yet ever at rest; gathering, yet needing nothing; sustaining, pervading, and protecting; creating, nourishing, and developing; seeking, and yet possessing all things.[47]

Similarly in his work on the Trinity, *De Trinitate*, Augustine uses the word six times. Five of these references occur in the same passage, in which Augustine notes that God, although incomprehensible, "is ever to be sought."[48]

> For things incomprehensible must so be investigated, as that no one may think he has found nothing, when he has been able to find how incomprehensible that is which he was seeking. Why then does he so seek, if he comprehends that which he seeks to be incomprehensible, unless because he may not give over seeking so long as he makes progress in the inquiry itself into things incomprehensible, and becomes ever better and better while seeking so great a good, which is both sought in order to be found, and found in order to be sought.[49]

Further references to incomprehensibility occur in Book III of the *Institutes*. The first reference occurs in Calvin's polemic against Osiander,[50] who held that Christ is justified only with respect to his divine nature and not his human nature. Calvin insists otherwise, drawing from his understanding of the sacraments, which draw attention to his flesh. "They teach that the matter both of righteousness and of salvation resides in his flesh; not that as mere man he justifies or quickens by himself, but because it pleased God to reveal in the Mediator what was hidden and incomprehensible in himself."[51] The need for a mediator lies in the nature of God's righteousness and our sin, something to which Calvin alludes in chapter 12 of Book III. In the opening section in which Calvin proves the point that there is no one who is righteous in God's sight, mention is made of the case of Job. We have seen elsewhere[52] that Calvin alludes to a particular understanding of Job 4:18 in which Calvin understands the verse to mean that even the angels who have not sinned are impure before the "secret righteousness" or 'double justice" of God.[53] There is a righteousness that is revealed in the law; but there is a secret righteousness, "higher than the observance of the law" which is "incomprehensible."[54]

The limitations of our comprehension of God's majesty, not only as it exists in him, but as seen in his works of creation and providence, ought again to induce reverence and godly fear. Commenting on the function of the Book of Job in his discussion of God's "secret providence," Calvin remarks: "In the Book of Job is set forth a declaration of such sublimity as to humble our minds."[55]

The issue of incomprehensibility arises again in Calvin's discussion of the relationship between providence, God's will and prayer. On the one hand, Calvin desires to make the point that prayer ought to be offered according to "the rule of the Word."[56] On the other hand, God hearkens even to defective prayer.[57] How can this be? Because God "tempers the outcome of events according to his incomprehensible plan."[58] This is in keeping with the nature of God, for the first petition of the Lord's Prayer, whilst we are reminded that he is "Our Father," yet, he is "Our Father ... *in heaven*" (Matt. 6:9):

> By this expression he is lifted above all chance of either corruption or change... it signifies that he embraces and holds together the entire universe and controls it by his might. Therefore it is as if he had been said

to be of infinite greatness or loftiness, of incomprehensible essence, of boundless might, and of everlasting immortality.[59]

In this way, too, God's "incomprehensible plan" is fulfilled even when Satan declaims against him.[60]

Predictably, Calvin alludes to incomprehensibility in relation to the doctrines of election and reprobation. In a summary, he concludes: "We assert that, with respect to the elect, this plan was founded upon his freely given mercy, without regard to human worth; but by his just and irreprehensible but incomprehensible judgment he has barred the door of life to those whom he has given over to damnation."[61] To balk at the doctrine of reprobation is a sign of "insolence." It is "unbearable if it refuses to be bridled by God's Word, which treats of his incomprehensible plan that the angels themselves adore."[62] God's decree is greater "than man's slender wit can comprehend."[63] "The history of Job as well as the prophetic books proclaim God's incomprehensible wisdom and dreadful might."[64] Calvin denies the sophistry that a distinction exists between God's will and God's permission.[65] We are fully accountable for our actions and cannot blame God's will for our corruption. "Accordingly, we should contemplate the evident cause of condemnation in the corrupt nature of humanity—rather than seek a hidden and utterly incomprehensible cause in God's predestination."[66]

A similar recourse to incomprehensibility occurs in Calvin's treatment of the unity of God's will. Referring to Job 1:21 and the statement, "As it pleased God, so was it done," Calvin understands the sovereignty of God in such a way so as to encompass evil:

> God's will is not therefore at war with itself, nor does it change, nor does it pretend not to will what he wills. But even though his will is one and simple in him, it appears manifold to us because, on account of our mental incapacity, we do not grasp how in divers ways it wills and does not will something to take place.[67]

The limitations[68] of our comprehension find expression, too, in Calvin's explanation of the purpose of the sacraments. In particular, Calvin's *virtualism*[69]—the power of the Holy Spirit operating in the sacrament as an explanation for the "mystery of Christ's secret union with the devout"—gives rise to incomprehensibility.[70] Indeed, it is a failure to "believe that it is through his incomprehensible power that we come to partake of Christ's flesh and blood"[71] that accounts for the error of the medieval church's understanding of the Lord's Supper.[72]

All this places upon us an obligation. "We must walk, we must advance, we must grow, that our hearts may be capable of those things which we cannot yet grasp."[73] Calvin hints at an eschatological knowledge out of all proportion to that which we currently know.[74] This, too, will be a recurring theme in the Joban sermons, as we shall see. For now, "let us not be ashamed to be ignorant of something in this matter, wherein there is a certain learned ignorance (*docta ignorantia*)."[75] Calvin continues:

> Rather, let us willingly refrain from inquiring into a kind of knowledge, the ardent desire for which is both foolish and dangerous, nay, even deadly. But if wanton curiosity agitates us, we shall always do well to oppose to it this restraining thought: just as too much honey is not good, so for the curious the investigation of glory is not turned into glory [Prov. 25:27]. For there is good reason for us to be deterred from this insolence which can only plunge us into ruin.[76]

Calvin seems in the *Institutes* eager to avoid two pitfalls: first, the overly rash pontificating of detractors who reveal a lack of modesty and a lack of submission to that which God has revealed of himself and his ways; and second, a fatalistic nominalism[77]

## The Incomprehensibility of God in Calvin's Commentaries

In a prefatory argument to his commentary on Genesis,[78] Calvin mentions the doctrine of incomprehensibility in the very first paragraph. Having suggested that God's "infinite wisdom is displayed in the admirable structure of heaven and earth," Calvin goes on to explain how difficult it is to expound on the subject

> in terms equal to its dignity. For while the measure of our capacity is too contracted to comprehend things of such magnitude, our tongue is equally incapable of giving a full and substantial account of them.[79]

In the commentary proper, Calvin refers to the use of רוח (*ruach*) in Genesis 3:8, rendered in the Authorised Version of the next century (1611), "in the cool of the day." Calvin, however, takes it to mean a "wind," and suggests that by it, God gave "some extraordinary sign of his approach." He then adds: "For, since he is in himself incomprehensible, he assumes, when he wishes to manifest himself to men, those marks by which he may be known."[80]

It is in the discussion of the repentance of God in Genesis 6 that Calvin has recourse once again to refer to God's incomprehensibility. Commenting on the words: "And it repented the Lord that he had made man on the earth" (Gen. 6:8), Calvin denies that genuine repentance takes place in God, defending the doctrine of impassibility. He explains: "For since we cannot comprehend him as he is, it is necessary that, for our sake, he should, in a certain sense, transform himself...the Spirit accommodates himself to our capacity."[81] In the same chapter (Genesis 6), alluding to the size and design of the ark, Calvin comments that in the account of the flood, "many wonderful things are here related, in order that hence the secret and incomprehensible power of God, which far surpasses all our senses, may be the more clearly exhibited."[82]

In the covenant with Abram in Genesis 15, God is said to appear to Abram "in a vision" (Gen. 15:1). Commenting on the use of the compound Divine name אדוני יהוה, Calvin adds: "Not that God appeared as he really is, but only so far as he might be comprehended by the human mind."[83] When, later, Sarah laughed at the promise of a child, the angel chided her, saying: "Is anything too hard for the Lord?" (Gen. 18:14). Calvin defends the translation, suggesting that what the angel meant was that, "the power of God ought not to be estimated by human reason,"[84] adding, "he who does not expect more from God than he is able to comprehend in the scanty measure of his own reason, does him grievous wrong."[85] Similarly, in the same chapter, the cry of Sodom and Gomorrah is said to be great. Genesis 18:21 records God as saying, "I will go down now, and see whether they have done, altogether according to the cry of it, which is come unto me; and if not, I will know." Calvin makes an allusion to the way in which God sometimes defers his judgements, adding, "Since however, such forbearance of God cannot be comprehended by us, Moses introduces Him as speaking according to the manner of men."[86] Commenting on the judgement of Sodom and Gomorrah, Calvin says, "whatever we are not able to comprehend by the limited measure of our understanding, ought to be submitted to his secret judgment."[87]

It is a pastoral insight of immense proportions that, for Calvin, we are called upon to trust in a God who is more powerful than we can imagine. Nowhere is this more apparent than in the way in which Abraham was asked to sacrifice his son, Isaac (Gen. 22:1-18). Emerging, as Abraham did, "from the labyrinth of temptation," he demonstrated his willingness to "depend upon the incomprehensible power of God."[88]

In the vision of God to Isaac (Gen. 26:24), something designed to make Isaac "listen more attentively," Calvin is eager to point out:

> God did not fully manifest his glory to the holy fathers, but assumed a form by means of which they might apprehend him according to the measure of their capacities; for the majesty of God is infinite, it cannot be comprehended by the human mind, and by its magnitude it absorbs the whole world.[89]

Similarly, in Jacob's dream (Gen. 28:13), God disclosed himself as יהוה, teaching, "that he is the only Creator of the world…but since his majesty is in itself incomprehensible, he accommodates himself to the capacity of his servant, by immediately adding, that he is the God of Abraham and Isaac."[90] In a further comment, Calvin adds: "the immense majesty of God cannot be comprehended even by angels, but rather absorbs them; were his glory to shine on us it would destroy us, and reduce us to nothing, unless he sustained and protected us.[91]

The Joseph story provides Calvin with another example of how God's judgements elude our comprehension: God uses the unjust in the execution of his incomprehensible judgements.[92] Even Satan is overruled by God: "whatever poison Satan produces, God turns it into medicine for his elect."[93]

The command to follow the ark, even to the brink of the river Jordan (Joshua 3:2), provides Calvin with an example of faith:

> This, indeed, is the special characteristic of faith, not to inquire curiously what the Lord is to do, not to dispute subtlety as to how that which he declares can possibly be done, but to cast all our anxious cares upon his providence, and knowing that his power, on which we may rest, is boundless, to raise our thoughts above the world, and embrace by faith that which we cannot comprehend by reason.[94]

The slaying of the sons of Achan, on account of the sin of their father, finds Calvin asking, "what here remains for us, but to acknowledge our weakness and submit to his incomprehensible counsel?"[95] Likewise the unfolding hostility of the Canaanites (Josh. 11:19) provided the Israelites with "a ground for prosecuting the war," and this, on the basis that God's "incomprehensible wisdom" was at work ensuring that Israel's enemies "justly suffered the punishment of their own temerity."[96]

The prophets provide Calvin with a plethora of examples to comment on God's providence, particularly in chastisement and judgement. Commenting on Hosea 13:11, Calvin says: "His purpose is not always apparent to us: it is, however, our duty reverently and with chastened minds to admire and adore those mysteries which surpass our comprehension."[97] Seeing a reference to a bodily resurrection in Hosea 13:14, Calvin adds: "though the judgment of nature rejects the truth, yet God is endued with that incomprehensible power by which he can raise us from a state of putrefaction."[98]

Calvin finds the Joel prophecy of Pentecost, when old men are to dream dreams and young men are to see visions (Joel 2:28), "hyperbolical language" designed to suit our "stupidity" and "torpidity" because "we can never sufficiently comprehend the grace of God."[99] God "accommodates his manner of speaking or his discourse to the comprehension of his people, for he knew whom he addressed."[100] Calvin addresses the issue of incomprehensibility again when dealing with the prophet Micah. Commenting on chapter 5:2: "His goings forth are from eternity," he adds: "with God there is nothing new," all "is overruled by his secret and incomprehensible providence."[101] In this way, God's will can never be thwarted. The incomprehensibility of God should, then, lead to thanksgiving,[102] as well as reverence. In a lengthy discussion of this theme in his commentary on Zephaniah 3:6-7, Calvin takes up the issue:

> It may be asked, whether men so frustrate God that he looks for something different from what happens. I have already said, that God speaks after the manner of men, and in a language not strictly correct: and hence we ought not here to enter or penetrate into the secret purpose of God… For what is more absurd than to conclude that there is a twofold will in God, because he speaks otherwise with us than is consistent with his incomprehensible majesty? God's will then is one and simple, but manifold as to the perceptions of men; for we cannot comprehend his hidden purpose, which angels adore with reverence and humility. Hence the Lord accommodates himself to the measure of our capacitie.[103]

The crossing of the Red Sea and the River Jordan,[104] as well as the destruction of Ninevah[105] and Jerusalem,[106] provide yet more examples of God's incomprehensible work.[107]

On the subject of creation, Calvin finds Zechariah prompting him to speak to the same issue:

> Since then God exceeds all that men can comprehend in the very creation of the world, what should hinder us from believing even that which seems to us in no way probable? For it is not meet for us to measure God's works by what we can understand, for we cannot comprehend, no, not even the hundredth part of them, however attentively we may apply all the powers of our minds.... Since then experience proves to us the power of God, which is not yet seen by our eyes, why should we not expect what he promises, though the event may appear incredible to us, and exceed all that we can comprehend.[108]

Yet another example is found in the exposition afforded to Habakkuk 2:20, "But the Lord is in his holy temple:"

> The God of Israel was indeed the creator of heaven and earth; but he had made himself known by his law, he had revealed himself to men, so that his majesty was not hidden; for when we speak of God, we are lost except he comes to us; for the capacity of our understanding is not so great that it can penetrate above all heavens. Hence the majesty of God is in itself incomprehensible to us; but he makes himself known by his works and by his word.[109]

When Isaiah refers to Zion as "the place of the name of the Lord" (Isa. 18:7), Calvin insists that God is not "limited to a place," but that the expression is used "on account of the ignorance of the people, who could not otherwise comprehend his majesty."[110] Again, when the prophet refers to God's "counsels which have been already decreed of old" (Isa. 25:1), the Reformer once more explains that "since we do not understand those secret decrees, and our powers of understanding cannot rise so high, our attention must therefore be directed to the manifestation of them; for they are concealed from us, and exceed our comprehension, till the Lord reveal them by his word, in which he accommodates himself to our weakness; for his decree is unsearchable (ἀνεξέυρητον)."[111] Similarly, there is a "disorderly passion" about us that makes our hearts either wander astray, or sink into indolence, so that they do not freely rise to God; for the essence of God is hidden from us, this makes us more sluggish in seeking him. From his hidden and incomprehensible essence, therefore, the Prophet draws our attention to the name of God, as if he enjoined us to rest satisfied with that manifestation of it which is found in the word, because there God declares to us, as far as is necessary, his justice, wisdom, and goodness, that is, himself.[112]

Insisting that God can only be worshipped "through Christ," Calvin again comments on a passage in Isaiah to the following effect:

> It is certain that we cannot comprehend God in his majesty, for he "dwelleth in unapproachable light," (1 Tim. 6:16) which will immediately overpower us, if we attempt to rise to it; and therefore he accommodates himself to our weakness, gives himself to us through Christ, by whom he makes us partakers of wisdom, righteousness, truth, and other blessings (1 Cor. 1:30).[113]

The language of accommodation again recurs in the eschatological description of "the kingdom of Christ" in Isaiah 30:25, where the prophet tells us: "And there shall be upon every high mountain, and upon every high hill, rivers and streams of water." Calvin insists,

> These expressions are allegorical, and are accommodated by the Prophet to our ignorance, that we may know, by means of those things which are perceived by our senses, those blessings which have so great and surpassing excellence that our minds cannot comprehend them.[114]

Similarly, commenting on the destruction of the reprobate in Isaiah 30:33, "the pile of it is fire," Calvin adds:

> He speaks metaphorically… which otherwise we cannot sufficiently comprehend, in the same manner as we do not understand the blessed and immortal life, unless it be shadowed out by some figures adapted to our capacity.[115]

Similar emphases abound in the New Testament commentaries. In the angel's benediction of Mary, "the small degree of our intelligence makes our minds too small to grasp the unmeasured greatness of the works of God."[116] Again, "the measure of faith is not adequate to comprehend the infinite greatness of the power and goodness of

God."[117] God cannot be "contained within any spatial limits."[118] In the miracles of Christ, God "often sets before us things that contradict our reason."[119]

Since, according to Calvin, we cannot ever attain to a knowledge of God in his essence, we must seek to know him as he discloses himself to us in his Word, works of creation and providence.[120] But, it is especially in his Son that God makes himself known. What is true of God's majesty is true of the glory of Christ. Thus, when Paul encountered Christ on the Damascus Road, Calvin suggests that "men's powers of perception cannot grasp the divine glory of Christ, as it is in itself, but just as God often adopts forms, by which to manifest Himself, so Christ now gave evidence of His divinity to Paul, and, indeed, gave a sign (*specimen*) of His presence which might strike Paul with terror."[121] Similarly, commenting on the expression in Hebrews 1:3, "Who being... the very image of his substance," Calvin elaborates: "while God is incomprehensible to us in Himself, yet His form appears to us in the Son."[122] Central to Calvin's understanding of the role of the Mediator is a metaphysical as well as an ethical dimension.[123] On the one hand, the problem has to do with our finitude: "For in His face God the Father, otherwise hidden far away, appears to us, so that the naked majesty of God shall not engulf us with its infinite brightness."[124] In this respect, Calvin is adhering to the philosophical principle: *finitum non capax infiniti*.[125] On the other, it has to do with the noetic effects of sin.[126]

Alluding to Paul's preaching in Athens of the resurrection and the judgment to come, Calvin urges preachers to follow his example, despite the hostility it may provoke: "Surely it is no wonder that this part of Paul's speech was scoffed at in Athens. For it is a mystery about which not an inkling ever entered the heads of even the greatest philosophers. And it can only be grasped by us when we lift up eyes of faith to the immense power of God."[127]

In the commentary on Romans, Calvin picks up the twin ideas of labyrinth and incomprehensibility in his understanding of providence.[128]

> In the law God shows us what is pleasing to Him. Those, therefore, who wish to examine properly how far they agree with God, test all their purposes and practices by this standard. Although nothing is done in this world except by the secret governing providence of God, to use this as an excuse and say that nothing happens without His approbation is intolerable blasphemy. What foolishness it is to seek in a deep labyrinth

for the distinction between right and wrong which the law has plainly and distinctly set before our eyes. The Lord, as I have said, does indeed have His own hidden counsel, by which he orders all things as he pleases; but because it is incomprehensible to us, we should know that we are debarred from a too curious investigation of it.[129]

In the same volume, Calvin insists that "we cannot fully comprehend God in His greatness, but that there are certain limits within which men ought to confine themselves, even as God accommodates to our limited capacity every declaration which He makes of himself."[130] On the theme of divine election in Romans 9-11, Calvin again has cause to refer to the divine mystery. Commenting on Romans 9:22, he adds:

It was unfitting that the things which are contained in the secret counsel of God should come under the censure of men. That mystery would not be explained. He therefore keeps us from inquisitively examining those matters which elude human comprehension. In the meantime, however, he shows that as far as God's predestination manifests itself, it reveals true righteousness.[131]

Indeed, "the cause of eternal reprobation is hidden from us, that we can do nothing else but wonder at the incomprehensible counsel of God."[132] Thus, when Paul has cause to exclaim, "O the depth of the riches both of the wisdom and the knowledge of God" (Rom. 11:33), Calvin adds:

If, therefore, we enter at any time on a discourse concerning the eternal counsels of God, we must always restrain both our language and manner of thinking, so that when we have spoken soberly and within the limits of the Word of God, our argument may finally end in an expression of astonishment. We ought not to be ashamed if our wisdom does not surpass his who, having been borne into the third heaven, had seen mysteries unutterable to man. And yet he had been able to find no other purpose here than that he should humble himself in this way.[133]

The fear of idolatry is again a feature of Calvin's commentary on Acts 17: 24:

The first approach to proper knowledge of God is this, if we go out of ourselves and do not measure Him by our own mental capacity, and what is more, do not form any mental pictures of Him according to our carnal understanding, but set Him above the world, and distinguish Him from created things.[134]

A verse to which Calvin often alludes is 1 Timothy 6:16, where God is said to dwell "in light unapproachable."[135] "While we are circumscribed by this mortal flesh, we shall never penetrate into the heart of God's deepest secrets so completely that nothing is hidden from us."[136]

What emerges in these commentaries is a two-fold cause of our inability to comprehend God. The first is a metaphysical reason: we are finite, our capability to comprehend anything is limited.[137] The second is a culpable reason: we are sinners; God's majesty has been impugned by our rebellion and we are suffering its consequences in terms of a divinely imposed covenantal curse. In his commentary on Hebrews 5:9, Calvin distinguishes the two:

> God deals with us so plainly and unambiguously that His Word is truly called our light. Its brightness is dimmed by our darkness. This happens partly through our dullness, and partly through our folly. Though we are more than dull in our understanding of the teaching of God, there is added to this vice the depravity of our affections.[138]

## The Incomprehensibility of God in Calvin's Sermons on Job

Now that we have seen that God's incomprehensibility forms a fundamental motif in both the *Institutes* and the commentaries, we can turn to the *Sermons on Job*. Here I shall prove that Calvin makes the incomprehensibility of God not only a theme in the organic development of the sermons, but its unifying tenet. It forms the basis for understanding the Book of Job.[139] Previous writers have not always realised this point.[140] In his doctoral thesis, for example, Peter Miln mentions the theme in passing, but fails to make the connection with the rest of Calvin's writings.[141] There appears to be a consistency in Calvin's allusions to God's incomprehensibility from the first edition of the *Institutes* in 1536 to the preaching of the Joban sermons in 1554-1555.

In the very opening sermon, Calvin sets the theme for what is to follow. God's judgements are beyond our grasp; to realise this is the key to a quiet and godly life and an entrance into the meaning of the Book of Job:

God dothe not euer punishe menne according to the measure of their sinnes, but hath his secrete iudgementes, whereof he maketh not vs priuie, and therfore that it behoueth vs to wayte till he reuele vnto vs for what cause he dothe this or that.[142]

Similarly, in the fifth sermon, Calvin outlines a general conclusion from the Joban material about how the Christian life ought to be lived:

It behoueth vs to humble ourselues, and to wayte till the day come that we may better conceyue Gods secretes which are incomprehensible to vs at this day, & therfore we must learne to magnifie them, and to honour Gods iudgements, hauing them in reuerence and admiratio[n], vntill they may be better knowne vnto vs.[143]

At one point, Calvin cites a common proverb, *Mitte arcana Dei*: "such as vnderstand no woorde of latine (to the intent to play the beasts) speake thus in latin: *Mitte arcana Dei*: the meening whereof is, that they must not inquire of Gods secretes."[144] None of this, of course, is to be interpreted as a diatribe against doctrine as such. For Calvin, it is "verie madnesse, when a man shutteth the dore agaynst all good doctrine, and weeneth himselfe to be so wise, as hee hath no more neede to be taught, but refuseth all things, and setteth a barre before him, as if he woulde say, God shall come no nerer me."[145]

In the Joban sermons, just as in the other writings of Calvin, God is, in himself, incomprehensible. It is in the revelation of his attributes that we comprehend him, and then but a little.[146] In particular, his majesty, or greatness, eludes our comprehension.[147] The category of sovereignty is paramount.[148] In an allusion to God's power, Calvin writes: "It is infinite, and a power that passeth our capacitie."[149] It leads to "reuerence the things that wee knowe not, confessing that the Maiestie of God is ouer hie for vs."[150] "A man durst not come neere a mortall Prince who is but a dead carkasse: and how shall we preace before the maiestie of our maker?"[151] In what is perhaps the most important sermon dealing with this theme, Sermon 138, Calvin elaborates on the knowledge of God:

Wee must beholde him in the glasse that he offereth vs that is to saye, in his worde and in his woorkes, and wee must walke in suche sobrietie, as wee must not bee desirouse too seeke more than is lawefull or than hee giueth vs leaue to do. There is then one maner of seeing God which is good and holy: which is to behold him so farre forth as it pleaseth him to shew himselfe vnto vs, and to distrust oure owne vnderstanding, so as wee desire to bee inlightned by his holy spirit, and not ouercurious and presumptuous to know more than he permitteth. But if we wil looke God in the face, and not suffer any thing to be hidde from vs, but will enter intoo his incomprehensible determinations, euen too the verie bottome of these depthes: it is an intollerable pride, and men do vtterly confounde themselues by it. Then let vs learne what meane we must holde too see God. We must not go to it with ouermuch hast, but we must be sober, knowing the small measure of our vnderstanding, and the infinite highnesse of Gods Maiestie.[152]

Calvin is deeply suspicious of anything "forged in our own brain,"[153] mainly because of man's propensity to idolatry.[154] God, then, must not be "disguised" by human reason.[155] He may work in ways that seem opposed to human reason.[156] God's "spirituall Secretes... outreache the common order of nature."[157] There is no obligation on God's part to explain.[158] And this, because of the fires of trial.[159] God appeared to Job "in a whirlwind and dark cloud" (cf. Job 38:1) precisely to discourage curiosity.[160] God may conceal his secrets, but that is not to say they are hidden to God himself: God is omnisicient.[161] The veiling is to guard us from becoming too bold.[162] Calvin was therefore opposed to the speculations that so ordered everything that no room was left for mystery and the rationally unexplainable. In this way, Calvin opposed the humanistic tendency to rhetoric. The majesty of God forbade it: "Then must all babling and all retorike ceasse when we come before the heauenly throne."[163] God, therefore, need not work according to human appointment.[164]

In the Joban sermons, too, God accommodates himself to communicate with us. Continuing to outline the theme of incomprehensibility and the way in which providence is often mysterious to us, Calvin alludes, in Sermon 34, to the way the stars appear small to us. This is because they are distant from us. Similarly, *mutatis mutandis*, the providence of God: "And God speaketh vnto vs of these things, according to our perceyuing of them, and not according as they be."[165] In only the second sermon, Calvin outlines what will become a motif in the Joban sermons: God's providences are "a bottomlesse depe:"

We comprehend not the greatnesse and heygth of Gods dooings, further than it pleaseth him to giue vs some tast of them, at least wyse according to our capacitie: which it ouersmall. None knoweth Gods workes but himselfe alone: they are a bottomlesse depe... and we haue no means to attain to them, insomuch that all they which wil search them shal be confou[n]ded except they goe too it with all reuerence and lowlynesse.[166]

Thus, for Calvin, "Gods goodnesse is a botomlesse pit,"[167] as are the works of election and providence,[168] as is the fate of the wicked.[169] Citing Jeremiah 5:22, Calvin at one point speaks of the sea as threatening to "abysm" the land: "the sea seemeth to threaten to drowne the earth, and it seemeth that the earth should bee swallowed vp at the rushing forth of euerye waue."[170] The biblical text, rather than any humanistic agenda, seems to be the conduit of Calvin's use of language here.

### The Quiet, Submissive Servant

According to Calvin, those who question God's incomprehensibility set themselves up in judgement of God. There must be no "gaynsaying."[171] For Calvin, this would be "a peruerting of the order of nature."[172] The goal of God's secret counsels is to "shut our mouths" lest by a spirit of undue inquiry and irreverence we impugn his integrity.[173]

> If Gods workes come in discourse, euery man thynkes himselfe a competent iudge too speake his verdite vppon them: yea and wee will bee bold inough (or rather ouerbolde) too controll them. For if God woorke not after our fashion, we wil bee full of grudging, and wee will saye, wherefore did he not this, and why went suche a matter so? What is the cause of suche ouerboldnesse, that men are so saucie with God as too holde plea agaynst him, and specially as to make themselues his iudges? It is bycause they haue not considered howe greate and incomprehensible his woorkes are.[174]

In Sermon 78, Calvin discourses on how our mouths can often betray our understanding of the nature of God:

> Gods woorks out passe our vnderstanding, so as we know not why he disposeth the things so which wee see: what is too bee doone? Wee must lay our hand vppon our mouth, that is too say, wee must not be so bold as too prattle of them... True it is that we must always haue our

mouth open after one sorte: that is, to glorifie God. But when we presume too bring him vnder the compasse of our vnderstanding, and would haue him to reserue nothing too himselfe: whither go we then? Is it not an open despiting of God? He intendeth to hyde the thing from vs. And why? Too the intent wee should knowe our owne ignorance, and yet not ceasse to acknowledge him to be rightuouse, and to honour his woonderfull and incomprehensible ordinance... But if God hyde the reason of his woorks from vs, and that it be to hygh for vs to reach vnto: Let vs shet our mouth, that is to say, let vs not be talkatyue to babble after our owne fancie: but let vs glorifie God, and not be ashamed to be ignorant. For the verye wisdome of the faythfull is to knowe no more than it hath pleased God to shewe them. Therfore let vs make silence vntoo God after what sort so euer he work, till the last day of discouerie be come, when we shall see him face to face in his glorie and maiestie.[175]

The issue for Calvin here is reverence:[176]

If we acknowledge God to be an incomprehensible *Beeing* [sic], so as we can say that God hath all maiestie in himself: and yet in the meane whyle rob him of that which is peculiar to him, and can[n]ot be separed [sic] fro[m] him: we make him but an ydol and a dead thing.[177]

We must learn to "cast downe our head."[178]

According to Calvin, it is because of an inadequate view of sin and God's majesty that the doctrine of justification has been so misunderstood.[179] From a consideration of God's incomprehensibility in the works of providence, Calvin draws an inference with respect to God's "greater" works:

"If there be infinite wisedome in those works of God which are the smallest and basest: what is there in the greatest sorte, and in such as surmount all our capacitie? Specially when the case concerneth our redemption, and when it concerneth Gods sealing vp of the recorde of our adoption in vs by his holie Spirite: it is a matter that surmounteth the common order of nature."[180]

The attempt to unravel what God has hidden from us Calvin denounces as "madde presumptuousnesse."[181] Thus, the very gospel has features that are incomprehensible:

But if wee come too the doctrine of the Gospell: there is a wisedome that surmounteth all mans vnderstanding: yea and is woonderfull euen too the verie Angelles.They bee the verie secretes of heauen which are conteyned in the Gospell. For it concerneth the knowing of God in the person of his sonne. And although oure Lorde Iesus Christ came downe heere beneath: yet must wee comprehende hys godly Maiestie, or else we cannot grounde and settle oure fayth in him. I say it concerneth the knowledge of things that are incomprehensible to mans nature.[182]

In a sermon on Job 22:12-17, Calvin alludes to Isaiah 66:1, "Heaven is my throne, and the earth is my footstool." Calvin emphasises both God's transcendence and immanence: "God then is not enclosed in Heauen... there is in heauen as it were such a marke of maiestie and glory, that when we lift vp our eyes thither, we must needes be moued therewith."[183] Is God's majesty seen in the work of creation? Certainly, but "we are not touched with suche a reuerence whe[n] we haue walked about here and ther beneath, as whe[n] we looke vp to heauen, bycause there is a marke and print of the maiestie and glory of God."[184]

### The Hidden Ways of God

Not only is God himself incomprehensible; his works also elude our understanding. God is called "maruellous" (Job 10:16), Calvin suggests, because "Gods secrete iudgements, which man cannot reach vnto... do farre passe his vnderstanding and wit."[185] Thus, the work of creation also displays the attribute of incomprehensibility.[186] And, in particular for the understanding of the argument of the Book of Job, God's works of providence are equally incomprehensible.[187] Thus, for example, we may find ourselves at death's door, but we are not to limit the possible ways by which God may save us.[188] Nor must we view providence in a simple way as though God works in the same way and with equal swiftness with each individual: "Gods iudgements must not be esteemed all after one rate... sometimes God doth things that are to vs incomprehensible."[189] This means that we are to learn patience, knowing that whilst the reason may be hidden from us, it is not hidden to God.[190]

As we have seen,[191] Calvin has recourse to suggesting that God's righteousness is incomprehensible to us. There is in God a double-justice. There is the righteousness that is revealed in the law, but there is also a secret righteousness that we cannot comprehend.[192] Not that we need to consider God's incomprehensible majesty in order to be humbled; the revealed law is sufficient to do that.[193] But, there is something peculiarly apposite about God's incomprehensibility, the veiling of his wisdom, that should keep us humble and submissive.[194]

It is Calvin's contention that Job, whilst having a just case, maintained it badly, ignoring the respect he owed to the majesty of God. In a critical sermon at the end of his Joban discourses, Calvin begins to draw some conclusions as to the nature of Job's conflict with the Almighty. When the silence is broken and God finally answers Job, the reply comes in the form of a rebuke (Job 38:1-4). And why? "For speaking to hastly of things that outreached his capacitie."[195]

All this underlines the importance of incomprehensibility as a *pastoral* issue for Calvin. In the Joban sermons his intent is to encourage perseverence in trial by assuring Christians that, though they may not comprehend what is happening, God certainly does. "He not only hath a way too deliuer vs from death, but also hath wayes which are incomprehensible too vs," he writes. "When wee bee locked vp so as there seemeth no way for vs to scape, God will finde one for vs, yea after his owne fashion, that is too say, aboue the vnderstanding and opinion of the fleshe."[196] Though lengthy, a citation from one of the closing sermons on Job sums up the importance of both the doctrine and the pastoral implication of God's incomprehensibility:

> What shal we do to his incomprehensible secretes, and to his priuie and hidden determinations, when both generally and particularly hee worketh after such a fashion, as seemeth straunge too vs, and farre outreacheth all our capacitie? Becommeth it vs to presume in that cace too iudge at all aduenture, and to giue our verdit vpon it as though wee were able to comprehende the things that he doth so beyonde our wit and capacitie? He sendeth many aduersities and miseries: One man loseth his goodes, another is smitten with sicknesse, another falles into reproch and slaunder, and another is wronged and beaten. It might be thought that God is farre ouerseene in handling men so roughly. No, not so. In all these things it behoueth vs to learne to confesse, that God is always righteous, and that he knoweth cause why to handle vs so, and that the same cause is good and rightfull though it be vnknowne to vs. And if we acknowledge not this, yet forasmuch as we be still in his hande, we shall gaine nothing by all our grudgings. Do wee see the wicked and vngodly haue their full scope in this worlde? Do wee see the dispisers of God liue at their ease? Do wee see them in credit and authoritie, and too bee as the maisters and Lords of the worlde? Do wee see that they spite God dayly, and yet notwithstanding are not punished at the first brunt? Do we see on the

contrarie part, that wee are faine to indure one while shame, another while trouble, and another while to be intrapped by treason, and that god succoureth vs not so soone as we would haue him? Let vs wayt paciently till God deliuer vs, as who knoweth what is expedient for vs. And therewithall let vs vnderstande, that if we wonder at the things which he doth here bilow euen in our owne persons, and in the things that we may beholde as it were before our feete: much more reason is it that we should wonder at, yea and honour the secrecie that surmounteth euen the capacitie of the Angelles. And therefore let these lower things teach vs to settle ourselues to the magnifying and glorifying of our God and so long as we shal be in this world, let vs suffer ourselues to be guided and gouerned by his holy Spirite, to the end he may order vs after his good pleasure.[197]

God's incomprehensibility teaches us to glorify God! We are to be teachable and submissive;[198] the "phantassicalnesse" in us is to be challenged.[199]

**Growing in the Knowledge of God**
Every now and then, Calvin hints that the veil of mystery will be lifted in the world to come. We have already noted how this occurs in the *Institutes*. In the Joban sermons, too, the Reformer looks forward to a day when we shall understand more than we currently do of the secret ways of God. "We must reuerence these great secretes," Calvin writes, "which are far aboue our capacitie, vntill such time as we may comprehend that which is hidden fro[m] vs as now."[200] And again, "the day will come that all shall be reuealed vnto vs to the full."[201] Whatever may be the knowledge we attain to in heaven, here, in this life, we are to seek to advance in our knowledge of God.[202] Learning to know God better is part of the discipline of providence. Through the trials and tribulations of life, we have cause to discern a sovereign hand and a hidden purpose. The proper response then must be to fall before the majesty of God in a spirit of awe and wonder:

> It is a liuely feeling when wee once vnderstande that it is God that hath created vs, and that wee are of him, and that whether we looke vpwarde or downwarde, all things are in his hand, and that there is in him a wonderfull rightuousnesse, there is in him a wisdome that is hid from vs, there is in him an incomparable goodnesse. If wee knowe all these things, it cannot bee but we must needes bee astonyed, and abashed in our selues, so as we shall vtterly abace ourselues before him, and honour his

hyghnesse whiche is infinite. So then let vs learne to know better what God is, to the ende wee may bee trayned to all modestie and sobernesse, and therewithal also let vs examin what we ourselues are. When we see our owne fleshe doth tickle vs to like well of ourselues, so as wee bee inclyned too flatter ourselues, and seeke to stande in our owne conceyte: let vs stirre vp ourselues to say, whence commeth this vice? It is bycause thou hast not yet knowne thyselfe. Consider who thou art, do but enter intoo thy selfe, and bee iudge of thyne owne state. There we shall finde that we haue a bottomlesse gulfe of sinfulnesse in vs, and that we bee wrapped in such ignorance as is horrible to beholde, which is as it were so thicke a darknesse, as it vtterly choketh and strangleth vs: and so farre off are wee from hauing our eyes open to know God: as we see not the thing that is before our noze. Therefore when men shall haue bethought themselues in that wize, it is certaine that they shall be so touched with the Maiestie of God, that whereas it was seene that they were full of pride, and as it were harebrayned in speaking of God, so as there was no reuerence nor modestie in them at all: then the feare of God shall fall vpon them. In steede of the great and straunge rashenesse that is too bee seene in the worlde, men shall finde the reuerent awe of God. And why? For... when wee haue once conceyued what God is: wee shall stoope vnder him.[203]

## References

[1] 85 (Job 22:12-17), 398.b.44. *Quand donc nous venons à concevoir ceste maiesté incomprehensible qui est en Dieu, ceste hautesse inestimable: il faut que nous soyons estonnez pour nous humilier, et n'estre plus ainsi eslevez comme nous estions* [*CO* 34:294].

[2] Harold Dekker, *Sermons from Job*, selected and trans. by Leroy Nixon (Grand Rapids, Michigan: Baker Book House, 1979), xxx. Interestingly, the Dutch theologian Herman Bavinck, in his treatment of the doctrine of God, begins with an assertion of the *incomprehensibilitas Dei*: "Mystery is the vital element of Dogmatics." *The Doctrine of God* (Grand Rapids, Michigan: Baker Book House, 1977), 13. *The Doctrine of God* is an English translation of volume 2 of *Gereformeerde Dogmatiek*. Cf. Barth, *CD* II/1,186. For a modern assessment of the issue, see John Frame, *The Doctrine of the Knowledge of God* (Phillipsburg, New Jersey: Presbyterian and Reformed Publishing Company, 1987), 18-49; Donald Bloesch, *God The Almighty* (Downer's Grove, Illinois: InterVarsity Press, 1995), 31-102; Bruce A. Demarest, *General Revelation: Historical Views and Contemporary Issues* (Grand Rapids, Michigan: Zondervan Publishing House, 1982), 43-60; B. B. Warfield, *Calvin and Augustine*, ed. Samuel G. Craig (Philadelphia, PA: The Presbyterian and Reformed Publishing Company, 1971), 151; see also, Richard A. Muller, *Christ and the Decree: Christology and Predestination in Reformed Theology*

*from Calvin to Perkins* (Grand Rapids, Michigan: Baker Book House, 1986), 17-22; Ronald S. Wallace, *Calvin's Doctrine of the Word and Sacrament* (Tyler, Texas: Geneva Divinity School Press, 1982), 1-10; Jacobus de Young, *Accommodatio Dei: A Theme in K. Schilder's Theology of Revelation* (Kampen: Dissertatie-Uitg. Mondiss., 1990); Brian Gerrish, *The Old Protestantism and the New: Essays on the Reformation Heritage*, 131-149. The doctrine of God's incomprehensibility was the occasion of an ecclesiastical disagreement within the Orthodox Presbyterian Church in 1948. The major opponents were Cornelius Van Til (1895-1987) and Gordon H. Clark (1902-1985). Van Til, eager to preserve the Creator–creature distinction even within epistemology, argued that the nature of God's thoughts about any given issue were different from man's. Clark, fearing scepticism, maintained that the difference was quantitative, but not qualitative. For an in-depth discussion of this debate, see Fred Klooster, *The Incomprehensibility of God in the Orthodox Presbyterian Conflict* (Franeker: T. Wever, 1951), and especially, John M. Frame, *The Doctrine of the Knowledge of God: A Theology of Lordship* (Philipsburg, New Jersey: Presbyterian and Reformed Publishing Company, 1987), 18-61. See also Cornelius Van Til, *An Introduction to Systematic Theology*, Westminster Theological Seminary Classroom Syllabus (1971), 159-173.

[3] *Church Dogmatics* I/1, 368.

[4] B. A. Gerrish, *Grace and Gratitude: The Eucharistic Theology of John Calvin* (Minneapolis: Fortress; Edinburgh: T. & T. Clark, 1993), 81.

[5] For an analysis of its historical roots, see, for example, Barth, *Church Dogmatics* II/1, 179-204. Barth cites a range of sources, including Eusebius, Justin Martyr, Augustine, Athanasius and Anselm. Curiously, however, he makes no mention of Luther's doctrine of *Deus absconditus* and only mentions Calvin in passing. Given its formulation within the major Reformed Confessions, e.g. The Westminster Confession of Faith II:I, "There is but one only, living and true God, who is... incomprehensible...," it is evidence of how little attention Barth gives to the Westminster Confession. Cf. the reference to the *extra Calvinisticum* in Q.48 of the Heidelberg Catechism (1563): "But are not the two natures in Christ separated from each other in this way, if the humanity is not wherever the divinity is? *Answer*: Not at all; for since divinity is incomprehensible and everywhere present, it must follow that the divinity is indeed beyond the bounds of the humanity which it has assumed, and is nonetheless ever in that humanity as well, and remains personally united to it." The Westminster Assembly's initial attempts at producing a catechism were put into the hands of Herbert Palmer (1601-1647), who, in 1642, had already produced *A Short Catechisme Containing the Principles of Religion Very profitable for all Sorts of People*. It contains a question, "*The nature of God is infinite and incomprehensible, how then may we conceive of him?*" to which is given the answer: "By his properties and by his works." Alexander F. Mitchell, *Catechisms of the Second Reformation* (London: James Nisbett and Co, 1886), 69. Samuel Rutherford

(1600-1661), in his *Ane Catachisme conteining The Soume of Christian Religion* (c.1639), contains an unnumbered question in section 2, "Of the Godhead and the Blissed Treinitie": "What is God in his nature?" to which is given the answer: "Jehovah having life and being of himself, and infinite and incomprehensible in all his properties, one God (1 Cor. Viii.6; Deut. Vi. 4; Deut. xxxii. 39) in nature; and three in persones, the father, Sone, and ane holie Spirit (Math. Iii. 16, 17; 2 Cor. Xiii. 4; 1 John v. 7)." *Ibid.*, 62.

[6] No entry, for example, is found in the *Index Theologicus* of the *Ioannis Calvini opera quae supersunt omnia*, ed. Joann Wilhelm Baum, August Eduard Cunitz, and Eduard Reuss (1863-1900), under "incomprehensibilis," "absconditus," "accommodatio," or similar searches under the entry for "Deus" despite, as we shall see, the copious references in Calvin's writings.

[7] One contemporary writer has suggested that "the dangers of speculating about God's immanent reality are so enormous that [Calvin] avoids the task of giving specific content to God's eternal identity and being." This is to take Calvin in the direction of mysticism. Unfortunately, the writer fails to give specific detail to the charge. See Serene Jones, *Calvin and the Rhetoric of Piety*, Columbia Series in Reformed Theology (Lousiville, Kentucky: Westminster John Knox Press, 1995), 199. For a more restrained reading of Calvin's use of rhetoric, see F. L. Battles, "God Was Accommodating Himself to Human Capacity," in *Interpreting John Calvin: Ford Lewis Battles*, ed. Robert Benedetto (Grand Rapids, Michigan: Baker Book House, 1996), 117-18.

[8] *Church Dogmatics* I/1, 301. Barth's concern is wider still, suggesting that both the doctrine of Scripture and the doctrine of God may be lost apart from a consideration of the central significance of the revealed doctrine of the Trinity. See Geoffrey W. Bromiley, *Introduction to the Theology of Karl Barth* (Edinburgh: T. & T. Clark, 1979), 13-14.

[9] For a brief discussion of this issue in Calvin, see Kenneth S. Kantzer, "John Calvin's Theory of the Knowledge of God and the Word of God" (Ph.D. thesis, Harvard, 1950), 54-99.

The theocentric stress of the Joban sermons lends weight to the idea expressed early in this century amongst Calvin scholars that the majesty of God lies at the heart of Calvin's theology. See Paul Tillich, *A History of Christian Thought*, ed. Carl Braaten (New York: Harper & Row, 1968), 263. Williston Walker has argued a similar line, suggesting the centrality of God's agency, *John Calvin: The Organiser of Reformed Protestantism, 1509-64* (New York: Schoken Books, 1969), 138, 148. A similar stress occurs in Ronald Wallace's treatment of Calvin, in which he argues for an (Augustinian) theocentric focus, *Calvin's Doctrine of the Christian Life* (Grand Rapids: Wm. B. Eerdmans, 1952), *passim*. Others have argued differently. Thus, T. F. Torrance has urged us to see grace, *Calvin's Doctrine of Man* (London: Lutterworth Press, 1952), 18; Wilhelm Niesel has written of the Christological focus, *The Theology of Calvin*, trans. Harold Knight (Philadelphia: Westminster Press, 1956), 246-50; François Wendel and, more recently, Brian Gerrish cautiously agree that Christology plays a large part in Calvin, but not to the detriment of all other points of focus. See Calvin: *Sources et évolution de sa pensée religieue* (Paris: Presses Universitaires de France, 1950), 200-201, and *Reformers in Profile* (Philadelphia: Fortress Press, 1967), 144.

Recently, Calvin scholarship has been loathe to speak of any centre or core to his theology, arguing that contradictions and tensions abound. See John Leith, "Calvin's Theological Method and the Ambiguities in his Theology," in *Reformation Studies*, ed. F. H. Littell (Richmond: John Knox, 1962), 108-113. Some have argued that his commitment to "biblicism" accounts for the lack of consistency in Calvin's thought. See Richard Stauffer, "Dieu, la Création et la Providence dans l'oeuvre homilétique de Calvin," in *La Revue Réformée* 27-28 (1977): 196-203; a similar point is made by Jack Forstman suggesting that his "exegetical techniques" account for the lack of homogeneity, *Word and Spirit: Calvin's Doctrine of Biblical Authority* (Stanford: University Press, 1962), 36. Mary Potter Engel has written of her agreement of a perceived lack of coherence, but has argued for "perspectivalism" as a means of integration: "Although his 'system' does not lend itself to a rigid rational analysis, it is definitely consistent due to the employment of shifting perspectives." See *John Calvin's Perspectival Anthropology* (Atlanta, Georgia: Scholars Press, 1988), xv.

[10] *Sermons on Job*, 1 (Job 1:1), 1.b.40 [*CO* 33:23].

[11] For a full citation and reference, see footnote 188 of this chapter.

[12] *Inst*. I.v.i. *Essentia quidem eius incomprehensibilis est, ut sensus omnes humanos procul effugiat eius numen; verum singulis operibus suis certas gloriae suae notas in sculpsit, et quidem adeo claras et insignes ut sublata sit quamlibet rudibus et stupidis ignorantiae excusatio* [*CO* 2:41].

[13] For a discussion of Luther's view, see John Baillie, *Our Knowledge of God* (New York: Charles Scribner's Sons, 1939), 191-198.

[14] *Firmiter credimus et simpliciter confitemur, quod unus solus est verus Deus, aeternus et immensus, omnipotens, incommutabilis, incomprehensibilis et ineffabilis.* See, Norman P. Tanner, ed., *Decrees of the Ecumenical Councils*, Vol. 1 "Nicea 1 to Lateran V" (Sheed & Ward/ Georgetown University Press, 1990), 230. The Athanasian Creed contains the threefold assertion of "The Father incomprehensible: the Son incomprehensible: and the Holy Ghost incomprehensible." The original Latin text uses the word *immensus* here rather than *incomprehensibilis*. See, *The Creeds of Christendom With a History and Critical Notes*, ed. Philip Schaff, Vol. II "The Greek and Latin Creeds" (Grand Rapids: Baker Books, 1983), 66.

[15] St Thomas Aquinas, *Summa Theologiae* 60 vols. (New York: McGraw-Hill Book Company/ London: Eyre & Spottiswoode, 1963), Vol. 3.

[16] *Ibid*., 25. ...*impossibile est quod aliquis intellectus creatus Deum infinite cognoscat; unde impossibile est quod Deum comprehendat.*

[17] G. D. Henderson, ed., *The Scots Confession 1560* (Edinburgh: The Saint Andrew Press, 1960), 33. In the Gifford Lectures of 1937 and 1938, commenting on this portion of the Scots Confession, Karl Barth could say: "If we do not wish to end up by really defining ourselves, when we think that we are

defining God, we can only... hold fast to the *incomprehensible* majesty of His person as Father, Son and Holy Spirit." Karl Barth, *The Knowledge of God and the Service of God*, trans. J. L. M. Haire and Ian Henderson (London: Hodder and Stoughton, 1938), 33.

[18] WCF 2:i.

[19] Karl Barth, *Church Dogmatics* II.i: The Doctrine of God, ed. G. W. Bromiley and T. F. Torrance (Edinburgh: T & T Clark, 1957), 185. Barth goes on to lament the decline in "the older theologies" of this doctrine, applauding its re-emergence in Herman Bavinck's *Gereformeerde Dogmatiek* of 1918.

[20] *Op. cit.*, 195-196.

[21] 85 (Job 22:12-17), 399.a. 43, 51 [*CO* 34:296]. *...si ceste doctrine estoit bien imprimee en nous, le monde seroit purge de toutes les superstitions qui y a ont tousiours regné*. And a little further: *et sa maiesté incomprehensible*.

[22] Mention here ought to be made of the relationship between the 1536 edition of the *Institutes* and the subsequent editions. Following the introductory sentence in 1536: "Nearly the whole of sacred doctrine consists in these two parts: knowledge of God and of ourselves," he adds: "Surely, we ought for the present to learn the following things about God. To hold with sure faith, first that he is infinite wisdom, righteousness, goodness, mercy, truth, power and life." *Institutes of the Christian religion embracing almost the whole sum of piety, and whatever is necessary to know of the doctrine of salvation: A work most worthy to be read by all persons zealous for piety, and recently published*, trans. Ford Lewis Battles (Grand Rapids: Eerdmans Publishing Company, 1975), I:i.15. *Summa fere sacrae doctrinae duabus his partibus constat: Cognitione Dei ac nostri* [*CO* 1:27]. In a passage reflecting II.xiv.6 of the final edition, the 1536 edition treats the deity of Christ, commenting that "Jesus Christ is One with the Father, of the same nature and substance or essence, not otherwise than distinct as to the person which he has as his very own, distinct from the Father." He adds, "It is fitting that anything there is of human wisdom be here submitted and as it were held captive. And neither prattling inquisitively nor hesitating will advance the worship of such mysteries at all, which far surpasses all the capacity of human understanding." II.xi.50. *Quidquid autem est humanae sapientiae, hic submitti ac velut captivum teneri decet, nihilque aut curiose argutando, aut haesitando huiusmodi mysteria adorari, quae omnem humani sensus captum longe superant* [*CO* 1:64]. On the doctrine of election, Calvin comments: "We indeed cannot comprehend God's incomprehensible wisdom nor is it in our power to investigate it so as to find out who have by his eternal plan been chosen, who condemned [Rom. 11:1-36]." II.xxiii.59. *Comprehendere quidem non possumus incomprehensibilem Dei sapientiam, nec eam excutere nostrum est: ut nobis constet, qui aeterno eius consilio electi, qui reprobati sint* (Rom. 11) [*CO* 1:74]. Alluding to Job 2:10, Calvin comments on providence in a similar manner: "We should also so receive all adverse things with calm and peaceful hearts, as if from his hand, thinking

that his providence so also looks after us and our salvation while it is afflicting and oppressing us." II.xx.49. *Omnia, adversa quoque, aequis placidisque animis, quasi ex eius manu suscipiamus, cogitantes eius providentiam sic quoque nobis ac saluti nostrae prospicere, dum affligit et tribulat* [*CO* 1:63]. Then again, in a passage reflecting III.xx.40 of the 1559 edition, Calvin comments on prayer, and alluding to Isaiah 66:1, "Heaven is [God's] seat, and the earth, his footstool," Calvin adds: "By this he obviously means that he is not confined to any particular region but is diffused through all things. But our minds, so crass are they, could not have conceived his unspeakable glory otherwise." III.16 (78). *Coelum suam sedem esse, terram autem scabellum pedum suorum (Act 7.17). Quo scilicet significat, non certa aliqua regione se limitari sed diffundi per omnia* [*CO* 1:92]. Finally, using the term "*incomprehensibilis*", Calvin comments on the second commandment, thus: "He is incomprehensible, incorporeal, invisible, and so contains all things that he can be enclosed in no place." I.10 (20). *Qui cum sit incomprehensibilis, incorporeus, invisibilis, sicque omnia contineat, ut nullo loco concludi possit* [*CO* 1:32].

[23] The section, I.v.1, begins: "The final goal of the blessed life, moreover, rests in the knowledge of God." *Ad haec, quia ultimus beatae vitae finis in Dei cognitione positus est...* [*CO* 2:41]. Cf. I.i.1; I.x.2.

[24] I.v.i. *Essentia quidem eius incomprehensibilis est, ut sensus omnes humanos procul effugiat eius numen...* [*CO* 2:41]. The wording in the 1560 French edition was as follows: *Son essence est incomprehensible, tellement que sa maiesté est cachée bien loin de tous nos sens* [*CO* 3:59]. The earlier, 1541, French edition was simpler: *de nature il soit incomprehensible et caché à intelligence humaine* [*CO* 3:59 subtext beneath sections 59-60]. The 1539 Latin text shows Calvin using Luther's terminology of the *Deus absconditus*: *Nam quum sit natura incomprehensibilis, et ab humana intelligentia procul absconditus, certas suae maiestatis notas, quibus, pro tenuitatis nostrae modulo, comprehendi queat, singulis suis operibus impressit* [*CO* 1:286].

[25] The 1560 French edition reads *paré* [*CO* 3:60].

[26] Cf. I.v.11, "the Lord represents both himself and his everlasting Kingdom in the mirror of his works with very great clarity." *Atqui quantacunque claritate et se et immortale suum regnum Dominus in operum suorum speculo repraesentet* [*CO* 2:49].

[27] I.v.1. *Speculi... in quo invisibilem alioqui Deum contemplari liceat* [*CO* 2:42].

[28] "God's majesty is sullied by an unfitting and absurd fiction, when the incorporeal is made to resemble corporeal matter, the invisible a visible likeness, the spirit an inanimate object, the immeasurable a puny bit of wood, stone, or gold." I.xi.2. *ut doceat indecora et absurda fictione foedari Dei maiestatem, dum incorporeus materia corporea, invisibilis visibili simulacro, spiritus re inanimata, immensus exigui ligni, papidis, vel auri frusto assimilatur* [*CO* 2:75].

[29] "...*de incomprehensibili eius essentia. Nubes enim et fumus et flamma, quanquam symbola erant coelestis gloriae, quasi iniecto fraeno cohibebant omnium mentes ne penetrare altius tentarent*" [*CO* 2:76].

[30] I.xi.4. "*Quando scilicet nihil minus consentaneum, quam velle Deum, qui immensus est ac incomprehensibilis, redigere ad quinque pedum mensuram*" [*CO* 2:77]. In the same passage, Calvin adds: "All we conceive concerning God in our minds is an insipid fiction." *Quidquid proprio sensu concipimus de Deo, insipidum esse figmentum* [*CO* 2:77]. These emphases on idolatry find expression in vivid form in Sermon 85 on Job. 85 (Job 22:12-17), 399.a.4ff [*CO* 34:295-296].

[31] I.xiii.1. "*Nam certe eius immensitas terrere nos debet, ne eum sensu nostro metiri tentemus; spiritualis vero natura quidquam de eo terrenum aut carnale speculari... ut est incomprehensibilis*" [*CO* 2:89-90]. We shall, of course, return to the issue of how Calvin's use of incomprehensibility relates to the philosophical principle: *finitum non capax infiniti*.

[32] I.xiii.21. The section is cited by Barth, *CD* I/1, 301. Barth is attempting to show a contradiction in Calvin's own methodology, placing the discussion of the Trinity of God after the prolegomena of the doctrine of the Word of God. For Barth, the place and function of Scripture in theology is subsumed in the context of the Triune God's revelation of himself.

[33] Our incapacity to comprehend God is due to at least two factors, according to Calvin: depravity and creatureliness. Alluding to John's prologue, Calvin comments on the saying, "Life was in God from the beginning and that life was the light of men; this light shines in the darkness, but the darkness comprehended it not" (John 1:4-5). "[John] shows that man's soul is so illumined by the brightness of God's light as never to be without some light or flame or at least a spark of it; but even with this illumination it does not comprehend God. Why is this? Because man's keenness of mind is mere blindness as far as the knowledge of God is concerned... Flesh is not capable of such lofty wisdom as to conceive God and what is God's, unless it be illumined by the Spirit of God." II.ii.19. *Indicat quidem hominis animam fulgore divinae lucis irradiari, ut nunquam plane vel exigua saltem eius flamma, vel saltem scintilla destituatur, sed ea tamen illuminatione Deum non comprehendere. Cur id? quia eius acumen, quantum ad Dei notitiam, mera est caligo... non esse tam sublimis sapientiae capacem carnem, ut Deum, et quod Dei est, suscipiat, nisi Dei spiritu illuminetur* [*CO* 2:201]. On the other hand, even with the Spirit's illumination, only "a tiny portion of that truly divine wisdom is given us in the present life... the immeasurable cannot be comprehended by our inadequate measure and with our narrow capacities." III.ii.20. *Quam tenuis in praesenti vita illius vere divinae sapientiae portiuncula nobis detur... innuit tamen modula nostro et angustiis quod immensum est non posse comprehendi* [*CO* 2:414]. Elsewhere, however, Calvin can say: "As we cannot come to Christ unless we be drawn by the Spirit of God, so when we are drawn we are lifted up in mind and heart above our understanding. For the soul illumined by him, takes on a new

keenness, as it were, to contemplate the heavenly mysteries, whose splendour had previously blinded it. And man's understanding thus beamed by the light of the Holy Spirit, then at last truly begins to taste those things which belong to the Kingdom of God, having formerly been quite foolish and dull in tasting them." III.ii.34. *Quemadmodum ergo nisi spiritu Dei tracti, accedere ad Christum nequaquam possumus, ita ubi trahimur, mente et animo evehimur supra nostram ipsorum intelligentiam. Nam ab eo illustrata anima novam quasi aciem sumit, qua coelestia mysteria contempletur, quorum splendore ante in se ipsa perstringebatur. Atque ita quidem spiritus sancti lumine irradiatus hominis intellectus tum vere demum ea quae ad regnum Dei pertinent gustare incipit, antea porsus ad ea delibanda fatuus et insipidus* [CO 2:426-427]. Cf. commentary on Hebrews 8:11, "The right knowledge of God is a wisdom which far exceeds what can be comprehended by human understanding, and therefore no one can attain it except by the secret revelation of the Spirit." *Nam recta Dei cognitio sapientia est, quae humani ingenii captum longe exsuperat: ideo eam adipisci nemo potest, nisi arcana spiritus revelatione. The Epistle of Paul The Apostle to the Hebrews and The First and Second Epistles of St Peter*, trans. William B. Johnston, ed. David W. Torrance and Thomas F. Torrance (Grand Rapids, Michigan: Eerdmans, 1989), 112 [CO 55:104].

[34] I.v.9. *Unde intelligimus hanc esse rectissimam Dei quaerendi viam et aptissimum ordinem; non ut audaci curiositate penetrare tentemus ad excutiendam eius essentiam, quae adoranda potius est, quam scrupulosius disquirenda; sed ut illum in suis operibus contemplemur, quibus se propinquum nobis familiaremque reddit ac quodammodo communicat* [CO 2:47]. On Calvin's use of *familiaremque*, see T. F. Torrance, *Calvin's Doctrine of Man* (Grand Rapids: Eerdmans, 1957), 30.

[35] I.xiv.1. Latin: "*inaestimabili*" [CO 2:118]. Calvin adds that the purpose of the scriptural account of creation is to "restrain the wantonness that tickles many and even drives them to hurtful speculations," forgetting the God "whose wisdom, power, and righteousness are incomprehensible." *Haec non minus gravis quam severa admonitio compescat lasciviam, quae multos titillat, adeoque impellit ad pravas et noxias speculationes. Denique meminerimus, Deum illum invisibilem et cuius incomprehensibilis est sapientia, virtus et iustitia* [CO 2:117]. Calvin refers to Augustine's tale of the shameless fellow who mockingly asked a pious old man what God had done before the creation of the world. His reply: that he had been building hell for the curious.

[36] I.xvi.4. *disponat ad suum finem* [CO 2:148].

[37] I.xvii.2 [CO 2:155-156].

[38] Latin: *abyssum*. Used four times in this section. See William J. Bouwsma, *John Calvin: A Sixteenth Century Portrait* (Oxford, New York: Oxford University Press, 1988), 46.

[39] I.xii.2. *Verum nisi admittant, incomprehensibili Dei consilio quidquid in mundo accidit gubernari, respondeant quorsum dicat scriptura, eius*

*The Incomprehensibility of God*                                                                   185

*iudicia profundam esse abyssum?* [*CO* 2:155].

⁴⁰ II.xiv.7. *de immensa Dei altitudine disserens, tam filium eius, quam ipsum incomprehensibilem affirmat* [*CO* 2:359].

⁴¹ II.xv.2. *nempe extra ipsum nihil esse utile cognitu* [*CO* 2:362]. On Calvin's treatment of the *munus triplex*, see J. F. Jansen, *Calvin's Doctrine of the Work of Christ* (London: James Clarke & Co., Ltd., 1956), 20-38. Jansen argues for a rejection of the prophetic office in Calvin, saying that his movement from a two-fold to a three-fold office in the 1559 edition of the *Institutes* was "peripheral" and "artificial." This has been rejected by a host of writers, including Robert Peterson, G. C. Berkouwer, Benjamin Charles Milner and E. David Willis. See Robert A. Peterson, *Calvin's Doctrine of the Atonement* (Phillipsburg, New Jersey: Presbyterian and Reformed Publishing Co., 1983), 27-39; G. C. Berkouwer, *The Work of Christ* (Grand Rapids, Michigan: Eerdmans, 1965), 61-63; Benjamin Charles Milner, *Calvin's Doctrine of the Church*, Studies in the History of Christian Thought, vol. 5 (Leiden: Brill, 1970), 164; E. David Willis, *Calvin's Catholic Christology: The Function of the So-called 'Extra-Calvinisticum' in Calvin's Theology*. Studies in Medieval and Reformation Thought, vol. 2 (Leiden: Brill, 1966), 86.

⁴² II.xv.5. *Quia ideo mediatoris induit personam ut e sinu patris et incomprehensibili gloria descenderes ad nos appropinquaret* [*CO* 2:366]. Since "God is comprehended in Christ alone," Calvin tentatively approves of the difficult statement of Irenaeus, "that the Father, himself infinite, becomes finite in the Son, for he has accommodated himself to our little measure lest our minds be overwhelmed by the immensity of his glory." II.vi.4. *Patrem, qui immensus est, in filio esse finitum, quia se ad modulum nostrum accommodavit, ne mentes nostras immensitate suae gloriae absorbeat* [*CO* 2:252].

⁴³ II.xvi.4. *Incomprehensibilis, inquit, ac immutabilis est Dei dilectio* [*CO* 2:370]. Continuing to cite from Augustine's commentary on John's Gospel, Calvin continues: "For it was not after we were reconciled to him through the blood of his Son that he began to love us. Rather, he has loved us before the world was created, that we also might be his sons along with his only-begotten Son—before we became anything at all." *Non enim ex quo ei reconciliati sumus per sanguinem filii eius, coepit nos diligere, sed ante mundi constitutionem dilexit nos, ut cum eius unigenito etiam nos filii eius essemus, antequam omnino aliquid essemus. Ibid.* Cf. Augustine, *John's Gospel*,cx. 6 (*Patrologiae cursus completus, series latina*, ed. J. P. Migne, 35. 1923 f.; trans. Select Library of Nicene and Post Nicene Fathers, VII.411).

⁴⁴ II.xvi.12. "*nebulones*" [*CO* 2:378].

⁴⁵ Sebastian Castellio (1515-1563) was a humanist scholar and an advocate of religious toleration. Having embraced the Reformation in Lyon, France, he moved to Strasbourg where, initially, he gained Calvin's confidence. When Calvin refused to admit him into the ministry, the relationship between the two soured, and Castellio moved to Basel. It was Castellio's writings against capital punishment for religious beliefs that gained the opprobrium of Calvin.

See Peter Barth and W. Niesel, *Calvini Opera Selecta* (*OS*), III, 497, note 1 for the view that Castellio is unlikely to be in the context of this discussion. Calvin had written to Viret in March 1544 about Sebastian Castellio's objection to this interpretation. Castellio argued that Calvin was placing *before* what belonged *after* his death. *Selected Works of John Calvin: Tracts and Letters*, ed. Henry Beveridge and Jules Bonnet, vol. 4, *Letters*, part 1 1528-1545, ed. Jules Bonnet, trans. David Constable (Grand Rapids, Michigan: Baker Book House, 1983), 409 [*CO* 12:688].

[46] II.xvi.10. *invisibile illud et incomprehensibile iudicium ... aliud maius et excellentius pretium fuisse, quod diros in anima cruciatus damnati ac perditi hominis pertulerit* [*CO* 2:377].

[47] "The Confessions of St. Augustine," *A Select Library of the Nicene and Post-Nicene Fathers of the Christian Church*, ed. Philip Schaff, vol. I (Grand Rapids, Michigan: Wm. B. Eerdmans, 1956), 46. *Summe, optime, potentissime, omnipotentissime, misericordissime et justissime, secretissime et praesentissime, pulcherrime et fortissime, stabilis et incomprehensibilis; immutabilis, mutans omnia; nunquam novus, nunquam vetus; innovans omnia, et in vetustatem perducens superbos, et nesciunt: semper agens, semper quietus; colligens, et non egens; portans, et implens, et protegens; creans, et nutriens, et perficiens; quaerens, cum nihil desit tibi. Confessiones* I.iv.4 [CD-ROM] (Cambridge: Chadwyck-Healey Inc., 1993-95).

[48] *De Trinitate*, XV.i.2.

[49] "St. Augustine on the Trinity," trans. Rev. Arthur West Haddan, *A Select Library of the Nicene and Post-Nicene Fathers of the Christian Church*, ed. Philip Schaff, Vol. III (Grand Rapids, Michigan: Wm. B. Eerdmans, 1956), 199-200. *Sic enim sunt incomprehensibilia requirenda, ne se existimet nihil invenisse, qui quam sit incomprehensibile quod quaerebat, potuerit invenire. Cur ergo sic quaerit, si incomprehensibile comprehendit esse quod quaerit, nisi quia cessandum non est, quamdiu in ipsa incomprehensibilium rerum inquisitione proficitur, et melior meliorque fit quaerens tam magnum bonum, quod et inveniendum quaeritur, et quaerendum invenitur? Nam et quaeritur ut inveniatur dulcius, et invenitur ut quaeratur avidius. De Trinitate*, XV.2.2.

[50] Andreas Osiander (1498-1552) was Professor of Theology at Königsberg and a major Lutheran controversialist. In 1550 he opposed Melanchthon's doctrine of imputation of Christ's righteousness, positing instead the giving and crass mixing of the essential divine righteousness of Christ with believers. The role of Christ's human nature in our justification, a crucial dogmatic point for Calvin, was the issue of controversy between Calvin and Osiander. See Calvin, *Institutes* II.xii.4-7 [*CO* 2:342-347] and III.xi.5-12 [*CO* 2:536-545]. See Jaroslav Pelikan, *The Christian Tradition*, vol. 4, *Reformation of Church and Dogma (1300-1700)*, (Chicago: University of Chicago Press, 1984), 151-152; Niesel, *Theology of Calvin*, 133-134; W. Krusche, *Das wirken des Heiligen Geistes nach Calvin* (Göttingen: Vanden Hoeck & Ruprecht, 1957), 268-270.

## The Incomprehensibility of God

[51] III.xi.9. *simul tamen iustitiae et salutis materiam in eius carne residere docent. Non quod a se ipso iustificet aut vivificet merus homo, sed quia Deo placuit, quod in se absconditum et incomprehensibile erat, in mediatore palam facere* [CO 2:540]. Calvin immediately adds: "I usually say that Christ is, as it were, a fountain, open to us, from which we may draw what otherwise would lie unprofitably hidden in that deep and secret spring, which comes forth to us in the person of the Mediator." *Christum esse nobis quasi expositum fontem, unde hauriamus quod alioqui sine fructu lateret in occulta illa et profunda scaturigine, quae in mediatoris persona ad nos emergit* [CO 2:540].

[52] In the chapter: "The Incomprehensibile Righteousness of God."

[53] III.xii.1 [CO 2:553-554]. Without recourse to a double righteousness, Calvin can occasionally allude to the "higher" nature of God's righteousness: "The reason of divine righteousness is higher than man's standard can measure, or than man's slender wit can comprehend." III.xxiii.4. *Esse iustitiae divinae rationem quam ut vel humano modo metienda sit, vel ingenii humani tenuitate possit comprehendi* [CO 2:701].

[54] *Iustitiae, quae excelsior est observatione legis...quia incomprehensibilis est* [CO 2:554].

[55] I.xvii.2. *Huius quoque altitudinis elogium ponitur in libro Iob, quod mentes nostras humiliet* [CO 2:155].

[56] III.xx.15. *ad verbi praescriptum* [CO 2:640].

[57] Calvin mentions Samson's prayer in Judges 16:28f as a prayer that had mixed in with it "a burning and hence vicious longing for vengeance." ...*fervida tamen atque ideo vitiosa cupiditas vindictae. Idem.*

[58] *Quia pro sua incomprehensibili consilio* [CO 2:641].

[59] III.xx.40. *Deinde hac loquendi formula supra omnem aut corruptionis aut mutationis aleam evehitur. Demum universum orbem complecti et continere suaque potentia moderari significatur. Quare hoc perinde est ac si dictus esset infinitae magnitudinis aut sublimitatis, incomprehensibilis essentiae, immensae potentiae, aeternae immortalitatis* [CO 2:665].

[60] III.xx.43. *incomprehensibili suo consilio...* [CO 2:668].

[61] III.xxi.7. *Hoc consilium quoad electos in gratuita eius misericordia fundatum esse asserimus, nullo humanae dignitatis respectu; quos vero damnationi addicit, his iusto quidem et irreprehensibili, sed incomprehensibili ipsius iudicio, vitae aditum praecludi* [CO 2:686]. Cf. Alluding to the thought that "the Lord has created those whom he unquestionably foreknew would go to destruction," Calvin adds: "this has happened because he has so willed it. But why he so willed it, it is not for our reason to inquire, for we cannot comprehend it." III.xxiii.5. *Esse a Domino creatos, quos in exitium ituros sine dubitatione praesciebat, idque ita factum quia sic voluit. Cur autem voluerit, non esse nostrum rationem exigere, qui comprehendere non possumus* [CO 2:702].

[62] III.xxiii.1. *Nec vero tolerabilis est hominum protervia, si Dei verbo fraenari se non sustinet, ubi agitur de incomprehensibili eius consilio,*

*quod angeli ipsi adorant* [*CO* 2:698].

[63] III.xxiii.4. *vel ingenii humani tenuitate possit comprehendi* [*CO* 2:701].

[64] III.xxiii.5. *quod de incomprehensibili Dei sapientia et terribili potentia tam historia Iob quam prophetici libri praedicant* [*CO* 2:702]. Calvin goes on to cite some words from Augustine: "Ignorance that believes is better then rash knowledge." *Melior est fidelis ignorantia quam temeraria scientia.* Augustine, *Sermons* xxvii. 3. 4; 6. 6; 7. 7 (*Patrologiae cursus completus, series latina*, ed. J. P. Migne, 38. 179-182).

[65] Calvin mentions the Pelagians, Manichees, Anabaptists and Epicureans. III.xxiii.8 [*CO* 2:705].

[66] *Idem. Quare in corrupta potius humani generis natura evidentem damnationis causam, quae nobis propinquior est, contemplemur, quam absconditam ac penitus incomprehensibilem inquiramus in Dei praedestinatione.* On the issue of whether or not to keep silence over predestination because of its essential incomprehensibility, Calvin cites Augustine again: "Must that which is manifest be denied because that which is hidden cannot be comprehended?" For Calvin, the answer is a negative one. Calvin, *Institutes* III.xxiii.13. *Numquid ideo negandum est quod apertum est, quia comprehendi non potest quod occultum est?* [*CO* 2:709]. Augustine, *On the Gift of Perseverance* xiv. 37 (*Patrologiae cursus completus, series latina*, ed. J. P. Migne, 45. 1016; trans. Select Library of Nicene and Post Nicene Fathers, V. 540).

[67] I.xviii.3. *Neque tamen ideo vel secum pugnat, vel mutatur Dei voluntas, vel quod vult se nolle simulat; sed quum una et simplex in ipso sit, nobis multiplex apparet: quia pro mentis nostrae imbecillitate, quomodo idem diverso modo nolit fieri et velit, non capimus* [*CO* 2:171]. Thus Calvin can make what appears to be a logical contradiction—that God can will what he forbids and yet his will is simple—on the basis of human incapacity (*imbecillitas*). Commenting further on our mental "sluggishness" (*hebetudinem*), he adds: "when we do not grasp how God wills to take place what he forbids to be done, let us recall our mental incapacity, and at the same time consider that the light in which God dwells is not without reason called unapproachable (1 Tim. 6:16), because it is overspread with darkness." *Ubi non capimus quomodo fieri velit Deus quod facere vetat, veniat nobis in memoriam nostra imbecillitas, et simul reputemus, lucem quam inhabitat, non frustra vocari inaccessam, quia caligine obducta est* [*CO* 2:171].

[68] Calvin is not always careful to point out the limitations of knowledge. Thus, in commenting on the self-authenticating (*autopiston*) nature of Scripture, he has cause to say: "only those to whom it is given can comprehend the mysteries of God (cf. Matt, 13:11)." I.vii.5. *non alios comprehendere Dei mysteria nisi quibus datum est* [*CO* 2:61]. This ambivalence is something we shall see again when we examine the Joban sermons.

[69] Calvin uses the term *virtutem* in describing the mysterious "power" (*virtus*), the power of the Holy Spirit, in the sacrament of the Lord's Supper. Interestingly, Calvin alludes to the mind's inability to comprehend the truths

that lie behind the sacrament of the Lord's Supper in a later section in Book IV: "Even though it seems unbelievable that Christ's flesh, separated from us by such great distance, penetrates to us, so that it becomes our food, let us remember how far the secret power of the Holy Spirit towers above all our senses, and how foolish it is to wish to measure his immeasurableness by our measure. What then, our mind does not comprehend, let faith conceive: that the Spirit truly unites things separated in space." IV.xvii.10. *Etsi autem incredibile videtur in tanta locorum distantia penetrare ad nos Christi carnem ut nobis sit in cibum, meminerimus quantum supra sensus omnes nostros emineat arcana spiritus sancti virtus, et quam stultum sit eius immensitatem modo nostro velle metiri. Quod ergo mens nostra non comprehendit, concipiat fides, spiritum vere unire quae locis disiuncta sunt* [CO 2:1009]. Cf. IV.xvii.11, *virtutem* [CO 2:1010]; IV.xvii. 18 [CO 2:1016-1017]. See Brian Gerrish, *Grace and Gratitude: The Eucharistic Theology of John Calvin* (Edinburgh: T & T Clark/Minneapolis, MN: Augsburg Fortress, 1993), 177-178; R. Wallace, *Calvin's Doctrine of the Word and Sacrament* (Tyler, Texas: Geneva Divinity School Press, 1982), 218-221.

[70] IV.xvii.1. *Quoniam vero mysterium hoc arcanae Christi cum piis unionis natura incomprehensibile est...*[CO 2:1002]. John T. McNeill, in a footnote on this section in the McNeill/Battles edition of the *Institutes*, implies that "'mystery' is not treated by Calvin as an intellectual puzzle. "It is indeed inexplicable, but the emphasis is on the effectual transformation of the believer, through union with Christ." John Calvin, *The Institutes of the Christian Religion*, The Library of Christian Classics, vol. XXI, ed. John T McNeill, trans. Ford Lewis Battles (Philadelphia: The Westminster Press, 1975), 1361 note 5. The full text, however, reads: "Since, however, this mystery of Christ's secret union with the devout is by nature incomprehensible, he shows its figure and image in visible signs best adapted to our small capacity (*aptissimis*). Indeed, by giving guarantees and tokens he makes it as certain for us as if we had seen it with our own eyes. For this very familiar comparison penetrates into even the dullest minds (*crassissimas quasque mentes*)." The accommodation due to our inability to comprehend is also in view here. In a later section, commenting on the "mystery" of the Lord's Supper, something "I do not even sufficiently comprehend with my mind," he adds: "I urge my readers... to strive to rise much higher than I can lead them. For, whenever this matter is discussed, when I have tried to say all, I feel that I have as yet said little in proportion to its worth. And although my mind can think beyond what my tongue can utter, yet even my mind is conquered and overwhelmed by the greatness of the thing. Therefore nothing remains but to break forth in wonder at this mystery, which plainly neither the mind is able to conceive nor the tongue to express." IV.xvii.7. *Quin potius lectores hortor, ne intra istos nimium angustos fines, mentis sensum contineant; sed multo altius assurgere contendant, quam meo ductu possint. Nam ego ipse, quoties hac de re sermo est, ubi omnia dicere conatus sum, parum adhuc mihi pro eius dignitate dixisse videor. Quanquam autem cogitando animus plus valet,*

*quam lingua exprimendo, rei tamen magnitudine ille quoque vincitur et obruitur. Itaque nihil demum restat nisi ut in eius mysterii admirationem prorumpam, cui nec mens plane cogitando, nec lingua explicando par esse potest* [*CO* 2:1007].

[71] IV.xvii.33. ...*nisi credimus fieri incomprehensibili eius virtute ut cum carne et sanguine Christi communicemus* [*CO* 2:1033].

[72] For Calvin's view of the Lord's Supper, particularly in relation to the doctrine of transubstantiation, see *Institutes* IV.xvii.11-20 [*CO* 2:1010-1019]. See also B. A. Gerrish, *Grace and Gratitude*, 10,137,146,184; Ronald S. Wallace, *Calvin's Doctrine of the Word and Sacrament*, 221-223; W. Niesel, *The Theology of Calvin*, 211-228; Joseph N. Tylenda, "A Eucharistic Sacrifice in Calvin's Theology?" *Theological Studies* 37 (1976), 456-466; Joseph N. Tylenda, "Calvin and Christ's Presence in the Supper - True or Real," in *Scottish Journal of Theology* 27 (1974), 65-75; Auguste Lecerf, "The Liturgy of the Holy Supper at Geneva in 1542," trans. by Floyd D. Shafer, *Reformed Liturgics* 3 (1966), no page numbers.

[73] III.xxi.2. *Ambulandum est, proficiendum est, crescendum est: ut sint corda nostra capacia earum rerum, quas capere modo non possumus* [*CO* 2:680].

[74] See chapter 4, references 288, 289. Also reference 133 in chapter 2.

[75] *Ibid.* The expression is Augustine's. *Letters* cxxx.15.28 (MPL 33.505; tr.FC 18.398). It formed the title to an important philosophical study of the knowledge of God by Nicholas of Cusa, *De docta ignorantia* (1440). Nicholas of Cusa (1401-1464), was a doctor of canon law at Cologne, dean of St. Florin's, Koblenz (1431), and later still, a papal emissary in Germany. He eventually became bishop of Brixen (1450). He spent his final years as camerarius of the Sacred College of Rome where he was to write *De docta ignorantia* (1440). He also made contributions in mathematics, cartography and legal history.

[76] *Ibid. Neque vero nos pudeat aliquid in ea re nescire, ubi est aliqua docta ignorantia. Quin potius libenter ab eius scientiae inquisitione abstineamus, cuius est cum stulta, tum periculosa, atque adeo exitialis affectatio. Quod si nos sollicitat lascivia, semper illud, quo retundatur, opponere expediet, sicut nimium mellis non bonum est, ita investigationem gloriae non cedere curiosis in gloriam (Prov. 25,27). Est enim cur ab ea audacia absterreamur, quae nihil quam in ruinam praecipitare nos potest* [*CO* 2:680-681].

[77] Cf. "Indeed, what is the beginning of true doctrine but a prompt eagerness to hearken to God's voice?" I.vii.5. *Etenim quodnam verae doctrinae initium est nisi prompta alactritas ad audiendam vocem Dei?* "He is shown to us not as he is in himself, but as he is toward us; so that this recognition of him consists more in living experience than in vain and high-flown speculation." I.x.2. *Quibus nobis describitur non quis sit apud se, sed qualis erga nos; ut ista eius agnitio vivo magis sensu, quam vacua et meteorica speculatione constet* [*CO* 2:73].

[78] The Genesis commentary was published in 1554, the same year in which Calvin began his preaching on the Book of Job.

*The Incomprehensibility of God* 191

[79] John Calvin, *Commentaries on the First Book of Moses*, 1:57, in *Calvin's Commentaries* Vol. 1 (Grand Rapids, Michigan: Baker Book House, 1981). *Quum immensa Dei sapientia in hoc admirabili coeli et terrae opificio reluceat, multum abest quin possit conditi mundi historia pro dignitate sua rite explicari, nam et exiguus nimis est ingenii nostri modulus, ut tantam capiat rerum amplitudinem: tantum abest ut lingua ad plenam solidamque earum enarrationem sufficiat* [*CO* 23:5-6].

[80] *Ibid.*, 161. *Nam quum sit incomprehensibilis, dum se hominibus manifestare vult, induit eas notas unde possit agnosci* [*CO* 23:65].

[81] *Ibid.*, 249. *Quia enim eum apprehendere non possumus qualis est: necesse est ut se quodammodo nostra causa transfiguret... ideo se spiritus ad captum nostrum format* [*CO* 23:118]. On the use of "accommodation" in Calvin, see David F. Wright, "Calvin's Accommodating God," in *Calvinus Sincerioris Religionis Vindex*, Sixth International Congress on Calvin Research, 1994, ed. W. H. Neuser and B. G. Armstrong (Kirksville, MO: Sixteenth Century Journal Publications, 1997), 3-19; Ford Lewis Battles, "God Was Accommodating Himself to Human Capacity," *Interpretation* 31 (1977): 19-38; reprinted in Donald K. McKim, ed., *Readings in Calvin's Theology* (Grand Rapids, Michigan: Baker Books, 1984), 21-42; reprinted in Robert Benedetto, ed., *Interpreting John Calvin: Ford Lewis Battles* (Grand Rapids, Michigan: Baker Book House, 1996), 117-138; and also in Richard Gamble, ed., *Articles on Calvin and Calvinism* (New York, London: Garland, 1992), 6:13-32; and more recently, Randall C. Zachman, "Calvin as Analogical Theologian," *Scottish Journal of Theology* 51 (1998), 162-187. According to Zachman, the language and concept of accommodation necessarily takes place in Calvin's theology because "language is the image of the mind (*Lingua est character mentis*)." Commentary on Jer. 5:15, *Calvin's Commentaries*, vol. IX, 286 [*CO* 37:626].

[82] *Ibid.*, 257. *Multa hic referri prodigia, ut potius inde melius refulgeat arcana illa et incomprehensibilis Dei virtus, quae sensus omnes nostros longe superat* [*CO* 23:123].

[83] *Ibid.*, 401. *Non quod Deus qualis est apparuerit, sed quatenus capi poterat humano sensu* [*CO* 23:209].

[84] *Quod scilicet non debeat ex hominum sensu aestimari Dei facultas.* *Ibid.*, 475 [*CO* 23:255]. Cf. 139 (Job 36:1-7), 655.a.55. "Wee shall neuer knowe God to bee righteous and mightie in himselfe as wee ought to do, if wee consider him but by our naturall wit." *Dieu ne sera point cognu en soi iuste et puissant comme il le merite, si nous le voulons contempler selon nostre sens naturel* [*CO* 35:262].

[85] *Ibid.*, 476. *Gravissimam Deo iniuriam facit qui non plus ab eo sperat quam sensus sui modulo comprehendere potest* [*CO* 23:255]. Commenting on Zechariah 8:6 and the suggestion that God's power is confined to that which we can comprehend, Calvin insinuates: "when God promises anything, doubts immediately creep in—'Can this be done?' If a reason does not appear, as the thing surpasses our comprehension, we instantly conclude

that it cannot be. We thus see how men pretending to wonder at God's power entirely obliterate it." John Calvin, *Commentaries on the Twelve Minor Prophets*, 5:197, in *Calvin's Commentaries*, Vol. XV (Grand Rapids, Michigan: Baker Book House, 1981). *Si quid ergo Deus promittat statim obrepunt dubitationes, An hoc fieri poterit? Si non apparet ratio, statim, quoniam res superat modulum nostrum, statuimus hoc falsum esse. Videmus ergo ut homines dum se mirari potentiam Dei simulant, prorsus exinaniant* [*CO* 44:237-238]. In a further comment on Zechariah 8:7-8, he adds: "God then does here exalt himself, that we may learn to exalt his power, and not to judge of it according to our own comprehension... The Prophet then... applies what he had just said of God's infinite and incomprehensible power, which men absurdly attempt to inclose in their own brains, and to attach to earthly instrumentalities" (199-200). *Deus ergo hic sese attollit, ut discamus virtutem eius magnificare, non autem aestimare ex sensu nostro... Ergo nihil hic novum adiungit propheta, sed applicat in verum usum quod nuper dixit de immensa et incomprehensibili virtute Dei, quam perperam homines includunt in suo cerebro, vel affigunt terrenis mediis* [*CO* 44:239].

[86] *Genesis*, 485. *Quoniam autem talis Dei tolerantia a nobis comprehendi non potest, eum humano more loquentem inducit Moses* [*CO* 23:261].

[87] *Ibid.*, 513. *Deinde quidquid iudicii nostri modulo metiri non possumus, arcano eius iudicio debere subiici* [*CO* 23:278].

[88] *Ibid.*, 564. *Ex tentationis labyrintho emergit* [*CO* 23:313]. On the use of the word "labyrinth" in Calvin, see William J. Bouwsma, *John Calvin: A Sixteenth Century Portrait* (New York, Oxford: Oxford University Press, 1988), 45-48, 100, 173.

[89] Calvin, *Genesis*, vol. II, 70. *Caeterum gloriam suam non in solidum patefecit Deus sanctis patribus, sed formam induit, ex qua eum pro captus sui modulo agnoscerent: nam ut immensa est Dei maiestas, neque humano sensu comprehendi potest, et sua magnitudine totum mundum absorbet* [*CO* 23:365].

[90] *Ibid.*, 114. *Unicum esse mundi opificem... sed quia per se incomprehensibilis est eius maiestas, ut se ad captum servi sui accommodet, statim addit se esse Deum Abrahae et Isaac* [*CO* 23:392]. Cf. Calvin's comment on the expression, "the God of Abraham" in Acts 3:13, "Moreover, God had taken this title to Himself, to distinguish Himself by some indication from idols. For we do not comprehend God in His essence, which is invisible and infinite. He therefore uses such means as are appropriate to us (*rationem ergo nobis congruam attemperat*) to lead us to the knowledge of Himself." *The Acts of the Apostles 1-13*, Calvin's New Testament Commentaries, trans. W. J. G. McDonald, ed. David W. Torrance and Thomas F. Torrance (Grand Rapids, Michigan: Eerdmans, 1989), 97. *Hunc porro sibi titulum indiderat Deus, ut nota aliqua se discerneret ab idolis. Neque enim Deum in sua essentia, quae invisibilis et infinita est, comprehendimus. Rationem ergo nobis congruam attemperat qua nos deducat in sui notitiam* [*CO* 48:68].

[91] Commentary on Genesis 32:30, *ibid.*, 202. *Imo quum ne ab angelis quidem capi possit immensa Dei maiestas, quin eos potius absorbeat, simul ac*

*nobis affulserit eius gloria, totos evanescere ac in nihilum redigi necesse erit, nisi nos sustentet ac protegat. Quamdiu praesentem non sentimus Deum superbe nobis placemus* [CO 23:446]. Cf. God's "incomparable lenity whereby in manifesting Himself to His elect, He does not altogether absorb and reduce them to nothing." *Harmony of the Pentateuch*, 3:324, in *Calvin's Commentaries*, Vol. II (Grand Rapids, MI: Baker, 1979). *In eo igitur se prodit incomparabilis Dei clementia, dum se electis suis manifestans, non prorsus eos absorbet, ac in nihilum redigit* [CO 25:77].

[92] Commentary on Genesis 42:28, *ibid.*, 348. *Tamen incomprehensibili modo* [CO 23:536].

[93] Commentary on Genesis 50:20, *ibid.*, 488. *Ita quidquid veneni concipit Satan, Deus in medicinam electis suis temperat* [CO 23:619]. Calvin adds: "If human minds cannot reach these depths, let them rather suppliantly adore the mysteries they do not comprehend, than, as vessels of clay, proudly exalt themselves against their Maker." *Si ad tantam altitudinem non perveniant humanae mentes, mysteria quae non capiunt, suppliciter potius adorent quam figulina vascula superbiant contra suum opificem* [CO 23:620].

[94] John Calvin, *Commentaries on the Book of Joshua*, 59, in *Calvin's Commentaries*, Vol. IV (Grand Rapids, Michigan: Baker Book House, 1981). *Atqui hoc praecipuum est fidei caput, non inquirere curiose quid facturus sit Deus, nec subtiliter disceptare quomodo fieri possit pronunciat: verum curas omnes quibus angimur, reiicere in eius providentiam: et quoniam immensa est eius potentia, ut in eam recumbamus, sensus nostros attollere supra mundum, et fie amplecti quod ratione non capimus* [CO 25:447].

[95] *Ibid.*, 117. *Quid nobis hic reliquum nisi ut infirmitatis nostrae conscii, incomprehensibili eius consilio cedamus* [CO 25:480]. Calvin adds the remark: "It may be that death proved to them a medicine; but if they were reprobate, then condemnation could not be premature." *Fieri potest, ut mors illis ad medicinam profuerit. Quod si reprobi erant, non potuit immatura esse eorum damnatio*. Cf. Commentary on Jonah 1:14, "For thou, Jehovah, hast done as it hath pleased thee": "his counsels be secret and cannot be comprehended by us." John Calvin, *Commentaries on the Twelve Minor Prophets*, 3:62, in *Calvin's Commentaries*, Vol. XIV (Grand Rapids, Michigan: Baker Book House, 1981). *Etiamsi arcana sint eius consilia, et non possint captu nostro comprehendi* [CO 43:228].

[96] *Ibid.*, 174. *Incomprehensibili sapientia... merito dederunt suae temeritatis poenas* [CO 25:511].

[97] John Calvin, *Commentaries on the Twelve Minor Prophets*, 1:471, in *Calvin's Commentaries*, vol. XIII (Grand Rapids, Michigan: Baker Book House, 1981). *Atqui causa non semper nobis apparet: nostrum tamen est reverenter et sobriis animis suspicere et adorare mysteria quae captum nostrum superant* [CO 42:489].

[98] *Ibid.*, 479. Using *inaestimable*: *Deum praeditum esse illa virtute inaestimabili, ut nos excitet a putredine* [CO 42:493]. Similarly, in his

concluding prayer on this section of Hosea, Calvin is recorded as saying: "O grant, that we may ever by faith direct our eyes towards heaven, and to that incomprehensible power, which is to be manifested at the last day by Jesus Christ our Lord, so that in the midst of death we may hope that thou wilt be our Redeemer, and enjoy that redemption, which he completed when he rose from the dead." *Ibid.*, 487. Cf. Calvin's prayer at the end of the exposition of Amos 5:8-13: "Grant, Almighty God, that as we cannot see with our eyes thy infinite and incomprehensible glory, which is hid from us, we may learn at least by thy works what thy great power is, so as to be humbled under thy mighty hand, and never trifle with thee as hypocrites are wont to do..." *Commentaries on the Minor Prophets*, 2:272, in *Calvin's Commentaries*, vol. XIV (Grand Rapids, MI: Baker, 1979).. These prayers at the end of the sermons and *praelectiones* are not included in the *Calvini Opera*, partly because the editors found a certain sameness in them. The prayers are found in the earlier Latin edition of the works of Calvin published in Geneva in 1576, with a foreword by Theodore Beza, entitled *Tractatus theologici omnes, nunc primum in unum volumen, certis classibus congesti*. The *praelectiones* prayers were translated in the Calvin Translation Society edition of the Old Testament Commentaries. For an anthology, see Charles E. Edwards, *Devotions and Prayers of John Calvin* (Grand Rapids: Baker, 1960); *The Piety of John Calvin: An Anthology Illustrative of the Reformer*, trans. and ed. Ford Lewis Battles (Grand Rapids: Baker, 1978), 117-118. See also T. F. Torrance, "Legal and Evangelical Priests: The Holy Ministry as Reflected in Calvin's Prayers," in *Calvin's Books*, Festschrift (Peter de Klerk), ed. Wilhelm H. Neuser, Herman J. Selderhuis and Wilhelm van't Spijker (Heerenveen: Groen, 1997), 63-74.

[99] John Calvin, *Commentaries on the Minor Prophets*, 2:94, in *Calvin's Commentaries*, vol. XIV (Grand Rapids, Michigan: Baker Book House, 1981). *Et simul tenendum est, prophetam hyperbolice extollere Dei gratiam: quia tantus est stupor noster, et tarditas, ut nunquam satis apprehendamus Dei gratiam, nisi quum nobis proponitur sub figuris loquendi hyperbolicis* [*CO* 42:567].

[100] *Ibid.*, 95. *Sed accommodat stylum vel sermonem ad captum populi sui* [*CO* 42:569].

[101] John Calvin, *Commentaries on the Minor Prophets*, 3:300-301, in *Calvin's Commenatries*, vol. XIV (Grand Rapids, Michigan: Baker Book House, 1981). *Quia scilicet Deo nihil sit novum... sed hoc totum occulta et incomprehensibili eius providentia gubernari, quod populus pessum ibit* [*CO* 43:369]. Cf. the comment on Jeremiah 18:7-8, speaking of God's "hidden predestination (*arcana Dei praedestinatione*), in which Jeremiah is said to "accommodate" his doctrine, adding, "God determined, before the creation of the world, what he pleased respecting each individual; but his counsel is hid, and to us incomprehensible." *Commentaries on Jeremiah*, 2:398, in *Calvin's Commentaries*, vol. IX (Grand Rapids, MI: Baker, 1979). *Sed hoc est arcanum eius consilium, et nobis incomprehensibile* [*CO* 38:298].

## The Incomprehensibility of God

[102] In a comment on Psalm 139:13-14, Calvin, having expressed God's wonders as incomprehensible, continues: "The knowledge he means, therefore, is not that which professes to comprehend what, under the name of wonders, he confesses to be incomprehensible, nor of that kind which philosophers presumptuously pretend to, as if they could solve every mystery of God, but simply that religious attention to the works of God which excites to the duty of thanksgiving." *Commentaries on the Psalms*, 5:215, in *Calvin's Commentaries*, vol.VI (Grand Rapids, MI: Baker, 1979). *Non ergo hic ponitur cognitio quae sensibus nostris subliiciat quod David sub miraculi nomine confessus est non posse comprehendi (sicut philosophos inflat sua arrogantia ut nihil Dei occultum relinquant) sed tantum pia attentio notatur, quae nos ad reddendam Deo gloriam expergefaciat* [*CO* 32:381].

[103] John Calvin, *Commentaries on the Minor Prophets*, 4:276-277, in *Calvin's Commenatries*, vol. XV (Grand Rapids, Michigan: Baker Book House, 1981). *Nunc quaeritur an Deum homines frustrentur quasi aliud exspectet quam quod accidit. Iam dixi Deum loqui humano more et improprie: ideoque hic non debemus ingredi, vel penetrare usque ad arcanum Dei consilium... Quid enim stultius est quam colligere duplicem esse Dei voluntatem, si aliter loquitur nobiscum quam ferat incomprehensibilis eius maiestas? Una ergo et simplex est Dei voluntas, sed multiplex est quoad sensum hominum: quia non possumus capere arcanum illud consilium, quod angeli adorant cum reverentia et humilitate. Ideo Dominus sese accommodat ad modulum ingenii nostri* [*CO* 44:56]. In a similar comment on Acts 13:27, that the Jews in their condemnation of Christ fulfilled what had been written, Calvin adds: "He directs the perverse efforts of the ungodly towards a different end than they thought and intended, so that they may do nothing but what he has willed. As far as they are concerned those men indeed act against His will, but the outcome is according to the will of God, in some sort of incomprehensible way. Since this procedure is contrary to nature, it is no wonder if it is not visible to carnal wisdom." *The Acts of the Apostles 1-13*, Calvin's New Testament Commentaries, trans. W. J. G. McDonald, ed. David W. Torrance and Thomas F. Torrance (Grand Rapids, Michigan: Eerdmans, 1989), 373. *Sic perversos impiorum conatus occulta virtute in diversum quam putabant ac volebant finem dirigit, ne quidquam faciant nisi quod voluit. Ipsi quidem, quoad se, contra eius voluntatem faciunt: sed mod quodam incomprehensibili succedit pro Dei voluntate. Quum hic cursus sit praeter naturam, non mirum, si carnis prudentiae non sit visibilis* [*CO* 48:297].

[104] *Minor Prophets*, 4:168-169, in *Calvin's Commentaries* vol. XV (Grand Rapids, MI: Baker, 1979). Latin: *incredibilis Dei potentiae* [*CO* 43:584].

[105] Commentary on Nahum 2:11-12. Calvin, *Commentaries on the Minor Prophets* 3:473, in *Calvin's Commentaries*, Vol. XIV (Grand Rapids, Michigan: Baker Book House, 1981). *Incomprehensibile opus Dei* [*CO* 43:470].

[106] *Commentary on Jeremiah and Lamentations*, 5:429, in *Calvin's Commentaries* vol. XI (Grand Rapids, MI: Baker, 1979). *Incomprehensibile*

*Dei iudicium* [*CO* 39:589].

[107] Calvin vilifies those who "scorn all threatenings." "They are very wrong," he writes, "who judge of him, or measure him, by men." *Commentaries on the Twelve Minor Prophets*, 1:403, in *Calvin's Commentaries* vol. XIII (Grand Rapids, MI: Baker, 1979). (Hosea 11:8-9). *Et perperam eos facere, qui aestimant eum, vel metiuntur humano more* [*CO* 42:443].

[108] John Calvin, *Commentaries on the Twelve Minor Prophets*, 5:341-342, in *Calvin's Commentaries*, vol. XV (Grand Rapids, Michigan: Baker Book House, 1981). (Zech. 12:1) *Quum ergo Deus omnem humani ingenii captum superet in ipso mundi opificio, quid iam impediat quominus credamus quod tamen videtur minime esse consentaneum? neque enim metiri convenit Dei opera sensu nostro, quando ne centesimam quidem eorum partem capimus, utcunque applicemus ad considerationem quidquid est in nobis... Quum ergo experientia nobis demonstret virtutem Dei, quae tamen non est oculis conspicua, cur non exspectabimus quae promittit, etiamsi eventus nobis incredibilis videtur et omnes sensus nostros excedit?* [*CO* 44:322].

[109] John Calvin, *Commentaries on the Twelve Minor Prophets*, 4:130, in *Calvin's Commentaries*, vol. XV (Grand Rapids, Michigan: Baker Book House, 1981). *Maiestas ergo Dei per se nobis est incomprehensibilis: sed per opera sua, et per verbum sese declarat* [*CO* 43:562].

[110] John Calvin, *Commentary on the Book of the Prophet Isaiah*, 2:45, in *Calvin's Commentaries*, vol.VII (Grand Rapids, Michigan: Baker Book House, 1981). *Per locum nominis Domini, non intelligit essentiam Dei illic esse inclusam... idque ob ruditatem populi, qui aliter eius maiestatem comprehendere non poterat* [*CO* 36:326-327].

[111] *Ibid.*, 191. *Nos enim latent et comprehensionem nostram exsuperant, donec ea Dominus patefaciat verbo suo, quo se ad imbecillitatem nostram attemperat: quia consilium ipsius* ἀνεξεύρητον *est* [*CO* 36:414].

[112] Commentary on Isaiah 26:8. *Ibid.*, 219-220. *Quum autem essentia Dei nobis abscondita sit, eo fit ut tardiores simus ad ipsum quaerendum. Ideoque ab occulta essentia et incomprehesibili ad nomen eius nos revocat propheta: ac si iuberet manifestatione quae in verbo occurrit nos esse contentos: quia illic Deus quoad expedit, iustitiam, sapientiam et bonitatem suam et sese nobis declarat* [*CO* 36:431-432].

[113] *Ibid.*, 202. *Certum est Deum in sua maiestate a nobis non posse comprehendi: quia lucem inaccessam habitat, qua protinus obreumur, si ad eam conscendere velimus. Ergo sese ad imbecillitatem nostram demittit, se nobis per Christum communicat, per quem sapientiae, iustitiae, veritatis aliorumque beneficiorum participes facit* [*CO* 36:421]. Cf. the comment on Acts 7:32, referring to Stephen's reference to the Abrahamic covenant as a "covenant of grace" (*gratuito foedera*). Calvin continues: "Since the majesty of God is infinite, if we wish to grasp it, what happens rather is that it swallows up our thoughts; if we try to mount up to it, we vanish away. He therefore clothes and adorns Himself with titles under which He can be grasped by

us." *The Acts of the Apostles 1-13,* Calvin's New Testament Commentaries, trans. W. J. G. McDonald, ed. David W. Torrance and Thomas F. Torrance (Grand Rapids, Michigan: Eerdmans, 1989), 192. *Ut infinita est Dei maiestas, si eam comprehendere volumus, potius sensus nostros absorbet: si ad eam adscendere conamur, evanescimus. Se ergo titulis ornat et vestit, sub quibus comprehendi a nobis queat* [*CO* 48:146].

[114] Commentary on Isaiah 30:25. *Ibid.,* 375. *Sed allegoricae sunt istae loquutiones, quibus propheta sese ad ruditatem nostram accommodat, ut iis quae sensibus nostris percipiuntur maiora et praestantiora, quam quae ingeniis nostris comprehendi possint, intelligamus* [*CO* 36:525].

[115] *Ibid.,* 387-388. *Metaphorice loquitur de exitio reproborum, quod satis alioqui mente complecti non possumus, quemadmodum nec beatam et immortalem vitam percipimus, nisi sub figuris quibusdam ingenio nostro accommodatis adumbretur...* [*CO* 36:532]. Cf. commentary on Isa. 32:19, "they borrow their metaphors from an earthly kingdom, because our ignorance would make it almost impossible for us to comprehend, in any other way, the unspeakable treasure of blessings." *Ibid.,* 424. *Nam similitudines suas a terreno regno mutuantur, quod alioqui inaestimabilem bonorum thesaurum assequi pro nostra ruditate vix possemus* [*CO* 36:554].

[116] Comment on Luke 1:28, *Harmony of the Gospels,* vol. I, trans. A. W. Morrison, 22. *Et certe quum pro tenui intelligentiae suae modulo magis angustae sint nostrae mentes, quam ut immensam operum Dei magnitudinem capiant, optimum hoc remedium est, quum eas ad meditandam gratiae eius infinitatem erigimus* [*CO* 45:25].

[117] *The Acts of the Apostles 1-13*, Calvin's New Testament Commentaries, trans. W. J. G. McDonald, ed. David W. Torrance and Thomas F. Torrance (Grand Rapids, Michigan: Eerdmans, 1989), 70. *Est enim angustior fidei mensura quam ut immensam divinae potentiae et bonitatis amplitudinem capiat* [*CO* 48:44].

[118] Commentary on Acts 7:49. *Ibid.,* 209. *Sed quia immensus est, negat se ullis locorum spatiis contineri* [*CO* 48:160].

[119] *The Gospel According to John Part One,* 119. *Ergo ut nos sibi morigeros reddat, ea saepe obiicit quae cum ratione nostra pugnant* [*CO* 47:106]. He adds that we show our "teachableness when we follow the bare word with our eyes shut, though it does not seem worth our while." *Tunc ergo demum docilitatem nostram probamus, ubi clausis oculis sequimur nudum verbum, etiamsi nullum operae pretium videmur nobis facturi.*

[120] "Although by nature the knowledge of God is engraven on the hearts of all men, yet it is so confused and dark, and entangled by many errors, that, if the light of the word be not added to it, by knowing they know not God, but wander miserably in darkness." *Commentary on Isaiah,* 4:164. *Quamvis enim omnium animis naturaliter impressa sit notitia Dei, tamen adeo confusa et obscura est, variisque deliriis involuta, ut nisi accedat lux verbi Deum noscendo non agnoscant, sed misere errent in tenebris* [*CO* 37:287]. And again: "For God cannot be apprehended by the human mind. It is necessary

that he reveal himself to us by his Word; and it is as he descends to us that we on our side rise up to heaven." *Daniel 1-6*, 118 (Dan. 3:7). *Deus enim non potest apprehendi humano sensu: sed necesse est ut se nobis patefaciat verbo suo, et quemadmodum ad nos descendit, ita etiam vicissim nos attollamur in coelum* [*CO* 40:620]. For Calvin's use of Scripture as "God's liuely image," see *Sermons on Job*, 122 (Job 33:1-7), 574.b.6. *Qu'il veut que sa parole soit son image vive* [*CO* 35:42].

For references to creation, see: "In respect of his essence, God undoubtedly dwells in light that is inaccessible; but as he irradiates the whole world by his splendour, this is the garment in which He, who is hidden in himself, appears in a manner visible to us." *Commentaries on the Psalms*, 4:145 (Psa. 104:1), in *Calvin's Commentaries* vol. VI (Grand Rapids, MI: Baker, 1979). *Si de essentia eius agitur, habitat certe lucem inaccessam: sed dum irradiat totum mundum suo fulgore, haec vestis est in qua visibilis quodammodo nobis apparet qui in se ipso erat absconditus* [*CO* 32:85].

For references to providence, see: "When therefore we seek to comprehend what God is, or how to attain the knowledge of him, let us direct all our thoughts, and eyes, and minds to his works." *Commentary on Jeremiah and Lamentations*, 5:228 (Jer. 51:23), in *Calvin's Commentaries* vol. XI (Grand Rapids, MI: Baker, 1979). *Ubi ergo comprehendere cupimus Deum, hoc est, qua via perveniamus ad eius notitiam, sensus omnes nostros et oculos et mentes nostras dirigamus in eius opera* [*CO* 39:459]. It is the work of God's providence that emerges as crucial in the Joban sermons.

[121] Commentary on Acts 9:3. *Ibid.*, 257. *Non potest quidem divinam Christi gloriam, qualis est, capere hominum sensus: verum sicuti Deus formas saepe induit, quibus se manifestaret, ita nunc Christus suam divinitatem Paulo testatam fecit, ac praesentiae quidem suae specimen dedit, quod Paulo terrorem incuteret* [*CO* 48:200].

[122] *The Epistle of Paul The Apostle to the Hebrews and The First and Second Epistles of St Peter*, trans. William B. Johnston, ed. David W. Torrance and Thomas F. Torrance (Grand Rapids, Michigan: Eerdmans, 1989), 8. *Nam quum Deus per se nobis sit incomprehensibilis, in filio demum eius forma nobis apparet* [*CO* 55:12]. In an illuminating passage in the sermons on Deuteronomy, Calvin reveals his understanding of the importance of the Mediator in the revelation of God: "Beholde, God doth not onely report himself to be the Maker of heauen and earth; but also because he is incomprehensible, and his maiestie passeth all our vnderstanding, he will haue vs to looke vpon him in his liuely image, that is to wit in our Lord Iesus Christ." 79 (Deut 11:26-32), 485.b.45. *Voici Dieu qui non seulement se dit createur du ciel et de la terre: mais pource qu'il est incomprehensible, que sa maiesté surmonte tous nos sens, il veut que nous le contemplions en son image vive, c'est assavoir en nostre Seigneur Iesus Christ* [*CO* 27:144]. See Calvin's attack on those who "fly to God's incomprehensible divinity," but are ashamed of Christ's humiliation." *The Gospel According to St John, Part 2 and The First Epistle of John*, trans. T. H. L. Parker, 74. (John 14:1).

*Incomprehensibile Dei numen evolant* [*CO* 47:322].

[123] As we shall see, Calvin is preparing himself here for a wider use of the expression "mediator" to cover its necessity for unfallen man, an idea that comes into play in the Joban sermons when Job, though not sinless, insists upon his innocence. Calvin, at least initially, gives Job a great deal of sympathy.

[124] *Gospel According to St John*, trans. T. H. L. Parker, part one, 127. (John 5:22). *In eius facie Deus pater qui alioqui procul esset absconditus nobis apparet, ne nuda Dei maiestas immenso suo fulgore nos absorbeat* [*CO* 47:114]. The ethical and metaphysical are combined in a comment on 1 Peter 1:21: "we cannot believe in God except through Christ, in whom in a manner makes Himself little (*quodammondo parvum facit*), in order to accommodate Himself to our comprehension (*ut se ad captum nostrum submittat*), and it is Christ alone who can make our consciences at peace, so that we may dare to come in confidence to God." *Commentaries on Hebrews, I and II Peter*, trans. W. B. Johnston, 250. *Hinc apparet, non posse nos Deo credere, nisi per Christum, in quo se Deus quodammodo parvum facit, ut se ad captum nostrum submittat: et qui solus tranquillas reddit conscientias, ut familiariter ad Deum accedere audeant* [*CO* 55:227]. Cf. "God dwells in light inaccessible; how great, then, is the distance between us and him? Except Christ, then, presents himself to us as a middle person, how can we come to God?" *Commentaries on The Twelve Minor Prophets*, 1:134 (Hos. 3:2), in *Calvin's Commentaries* vol. XIII (Grand Rapids, MI: Baker, 1979). *Nam Deus lucem inaccessam habitat: deinde quanto spatio nos ab ipso distamus? Ergo nisi Christus se medium nobis offerat, qua via possemus ad Deum accedere?* [*CO* 42:264]. Cf. *Commentary on Jeremiah and Lamentations*, 5:422 (Lam. 3:33), in *Calvin's Commentaries*, vol. XI (Grand Rapids, MI: Baker, 1979). ...*non potest concipi in sua incomprehensibili gloria humano sensu* [*CO* 39:584]; *Commentary on the Book of Psalms*, Vol. 3, 500 (Psa. 92:8) [*CO* 32:13]; Vol. 4, 313 (Psa. 111:2) [*CO* 32:167-168]. On the use of "mediator" in Calvin, see David Willis, *Calvin's Catholic Christology*, 67-78. Willis makes no reference to the Joban sermons in this material, but a fascinating instance occurs in Sermon 16 of Calvin's *Sermons on Job*. Commenting on Colossians 1:20, Calvin says: "the Angels haue their stedfatnesse in the grace of our Lorde Iesus Christ, forsomuch as he is the *mediator* betwene God & his creatures. True it is that Iesus Christ redemed not the Angels, for they needed not to be raunsomed from death whervnto they were not yet falne: but yet was he theyr mediator." 16 (Job 4:12-19), 74.a.60. *Que les Anges ont leur fermeté en ceste grace de nostre Seigneur Iesus Christ, entant qu'il est Mediateur de Dieu et des creatures. Il est vray que Iesus Christ n'a point esté Redempteur des Anges: car ils n'ont point besoin d'estre rachetez de la mort, en laquelle ils ne sont iamais tombez: mais il a bien esté leur Mediateur* [*CO* 33:208]. On a related issue, Calvin sees the problematic implications of the ontological aspects of the incarnation, refusing in the *Institutes* to divorce incarnation from sin and the Fall. Thus, *Inst.* II.xii.2 [*CO* 2:341]. Willis points to three periods in which Calvin uses

the term "Mediator" (pre-Fall, post-incarnation, and in-between) with two shades of meaning (mediation as reconciliation and mediation as sustenance). On Christ's mediation as sustenance, Willis concludes: "When he uses mediation to refer to Christ's eternal sustaining of the order of the world, he applies the term in a new way to a function which the tradition held belonged to Christ but which the tradition did not usually describe as mediation." Willis, 71. For other instances of Calvin's idea of Christ's mediatorship over angels, see Calvin's correspondence with the Italian Unitarian, Francesco Stancaro (1501-1574) in Calvin, *Tracts and Letters*, vol. 7, 113 [*CO* 9:338], cited by Willis, 70; *Galatians*, 129-130 (Eph. 1:8-10) [*CO* 51:150-151] and 310-313 (Col. 1:17-20) [*CO* 52:86-89]; Calvin, *Sermons on the Epistle to the Ephesians*, 63-64 (Eph. 1:7-10) [*CO* 51:149-151]; George Smeaton, *Christ's Doctrine of the Atonement* (1870; reprint ed., Edinburgh: Banner of Truth, 1991), 43; John Calvin, *Commentaries on the First Book of Moses called Genesis*, in *Calvin's Commentaries* (Grand Rapids, MI: Baker Book House, 1989), 2:429 (Gen. 16:6) [*CO* 23:226-227]. For a similar and related comment on the views of the puritan John Owen and his dependence on Calvin at this point, see Carl Trueman, *The Claims of Truth* (Carlisle, Cumbria: Paternoster Press, 1998), 63.

[125] See Karl Barth *CD* I/1, 272; E. David Willis, *Calvin's Catholic Christology*, 2-7, 74-78; Heiko A. Oberman, "The 'Extra' Dimension in the Theology of Calvin," *Journal of Ecclesiastical History* vol. XXI, No. 1 (1970), 60-62; Richard A. Muller, *Christ and the Decree: Christology and Predestination in Reformed Theology from Calvin to Perkins*, Grand Rapids, Michigan: Baker Book House, 1986), 20. According to Oberman, this formula does not occur in the works of Calvin. (60). A similar claim is made by G. C. Berkouwer, *The Person of Christ* (Grand Rapids, Michigan: Eerdmans, 1954), 282. Oberman further alludes to the fact that it is this very principle that, according to Friedrich Loofs (1858-1928), who is himself drawing upon Alexander Schweizer, accounts for the Nestorian tendencies in Calvin and Calvinistic theology. The claim that the expression originated with Nestorius himself is regarded by Oberman as "not convincing." The claim is made by Werner Elert, in "Uber die Herkunft des Statzes 'Finitum infiniti non capax'," Festschrift Carl Strange, *Zeitschrift für Systematische Theologie*, xvi (1939), 503. Muller points out that *finitum non capax infiniti* "provides a key to our understanding of the *extra calvinisticum* and of Calvin's views on *kenosis* and *communicatio idiomatum*," and despite the "spatial categories" evoked by the word *capax*, the word can mean "ability to grasp." In this sense, the expression supplements the issue of the incomprehensibility of God, a theme of which Calvin never tires. *Op. cit.*, 20.

[126] Contrast what Calvin writes about the pre-fallen noetic condition: "Therefore God provided man's soul with a mind, by which to distinguish good from evil, right from wrong... Man in his first condition excelled in these pre-eminent endowments, so that his reason, understanding, prudence, and judgments not only sufficed for the direction of his earthly life, but by

them men mounted up even to God and eternal bliss." *Institutes* I.xv.8. *Ergo animam hominis Deus mente instruxit, qua bonum a malo, iustum ab iniusto discerneret, ac quid sequendum vel fugiendum sit, praeeunte rationis luce videret... His praeclaris dotibus excelluit prima hominis conditio, ut ratio, intelligentia, prudentia, iudicium, non modo ad terrenae vitae gubernationem suppeterent, sed quibus transscenderent usque ad Deum et aeternam felicitatem* [*CO* 2: 142]. Cf. "Yee see then that Adam was formed after the image of God, to haue vnderstanding of all things that pertayned to him, in such wise as he could not wishe anything more, if he had had a modest and well ruled desire. But what? Satan blowed him in the eare, that he should be like vnto God in knowing all things. Therevpon he ouershot himself, and playd the horse that is broken loose... Whereof commeth it that the sense of man comprehendeth nothing of Gods misteries, and that if God call vs on the one side, wee shrinke backe on the other side, or else are so lazie, as we cannot finde in our hearts to come to him? whereof commeth this? It is the payment of Adams pryde." 102 (Job 28:10-28), 481.b.30. *Voila donc Adam qui est formé à l'image de Dieu, pour avoir intelligence de tout ce qui luy appartenoit, tellement qu'il ne pouvoit rien souhaitter, s'il eust eu un desir modeste et bien reglé. Mais quoy? Voila Satan qui luy souffle en l'aureille, qu'il sera semblable à Dieu, cognoissant toutes choses. Là dessus il se desborde, et fait du cheval eschappé... D'où vient cela que l'homme sensuel ne comprend rien des mysteres de Dieu, et que si Dieu nous appelle d'un costé, nous reculons de l'autre, ou bien que nous sommes si lasches, que nous ne pouvons pas approcher de luy? D'où procede cela? C'est le payement de cest orgueil qui a esté en Adam* [*CO* 34:515].

[127] *The Acts of the Apostles 14-28*, Calvin's New Testament Commentaries, trans. W. J. G. McDonald, ed. David W. Torrance and Thomas F. Torrance (Grand Rapids, Michigan: Eerdmans, 1989), 127. *Nec vero mirum est derisam fuisse Athenis hanc Paulinae concionis partem. Est enim mysterium humanis mentibus absconditum, de quo ne summis quidem philosophis aliquid unquam in mentem venit. Nec aliter comprehendi a nobis poteit quam dum fitei oculos ad immensum Dei potentiam attollimus* [*CO* 48:422-423].

[128] Cf. footnote 88, above; cf. 102 (Job 28:10-28), 482.b.66 [*CO* 34:516].

[129] *Romans*, Calvin's New Testament Commentaries, trans. Ross McKenzie, ed. David W. Torrance and Thomas F. Torrance (Grand Rapids, Michigan: Eerdmans, 1989), 162. *In lege enim ostendit quid sibi placeat: ideo qui rite examinare volunt quam bene cum Deo sibi conveniat, sua omnia consilia et studia ad hanc normam exigant. Etsi enim nihil in mundo agitur nisi moderatrice arcana Dei providentia, hoc praetextu nihil nisi eo approbante fieri dicere, intolerabilis est blasphemia: quod hodie phrenetici quidam cavillantur. Recti enim et iniqui discrimen, quod palam et distincte ante oculos nostros lex statuit, in profundo labyrintho quaerere, cuius vecordiae est: Habet quidem abditum (ut dixi) suum consilium Dominus, quo universa pro nutu dispensat: sed quia incomprehensibile nobis est sciamus a nimis curiosa eius investigatione arceri* [*CO* 49:143].

[130] *The Epistles of Paul to the Romans and the Thessalonians*, trans. R. MacKenzie, 31. (Rom. 1:19). *Quo verbo significat, Deum, quantus est, minime posse mente nostra capi: sed aliquem esse modum intra quem se cohibere debeant homines: sicuti Deus ad modulum nostrum attemperat quidquid de se testatur* [*CO* 49:23]. Adding: "only fools, therefore, seek to know the essence of God." *Delirant ergo quicunque scire appetunt quid sit Deus.*

[131] *Ibid.*, 210-211. *Nam et indignum erat ut quae arcano Dei consilio continentur, venirent sub hominis censuram: et mysterium illud inexplicabile futurum erat. Quae ergo humanam intelligentiam fugiunt, ab iis curiose excutiendis nos arcet: interim ostendit, quatenus se profert Dei praedestinatio, in ea meram iustitiam apparere* [*CO* 49:187]. Anticipating the Joban material, we note Calvin's words on Romans 11:35 in Sermon 156: "God choze whom he listed to be heires of euerlasting lyfe, and also that he forsooke whom he listed. If a man should demaund the reason why: it is not for vs to knowe it, nother is it lawful for vs to seeke any further than his will, which ought to bee insted of al reason vnto vs. Not that he doeth anything vniustly: but bycause the secretes of his mynd are hidden and incomprehensible to vs, and his ways are vnknown to vs." 156 (Job 40:20-41:1-25), 734.b.52. *Il monstre que Dieu choisist ceux que bon luy semble pour estre heritiers de la vie eternelle: qu'il reprouve aussi ceux qu'il veut. Si on luy demande la raison pourquoy, ce n'est pas à nous de la savoir, et ne nous est point licite de nous enquerir plus outre, sinon que sa volonté nous doit estre pour toute raison: non pas qu'il face rien iniustement: mais tant y a que les secrets de son conseil nous sont cachez et incomprehensibles, ses voyes ne nous sont point cognues* [*CO* 35:470-471].

[132] Commentary on Romans 11:7. *The Acts of the Apostles 14-28*, Calvin's New Testament Commentaries, trans. W. J. G. McDonald, ed. David W. Torrance and Thomas F. Torrance (Grand Rapids, Michigan: Eerdmans, 1989), 244. *Imo aeternae reprobationis ita abscondita est causa, ut nihil aliud nobis supersit quam admirari incomprehensibile Dei consilium* [*CO* 49:216].

[133] *Ibid.*, 259. *Neque enim pudere nos debet si non sapimus supra eum, qui in tertium usque coelum raptus viderat mysteria homini ineffabilia: neque tamen alium hic finem reperire poterat quam ut se ita humiliaret* [*CO* 49:230]. Cf. Commentary on 1 Timothy 1:17, again alluding to Romans 11:33, "He wants us to behold the immense and incomprehensible wisdom of God with such reverence that, if His works overwhelm our minds, still wonder may hold us fast." *The Second Epistle of Paul to the Corinthians, and the Epistles to Timothy, Titus and Philemon*, trans. T. A. Smail, ed. David W. Torrance and Thomas F. Torrance (Grand Rapids, Michigan: Eerdmans, 1989), 199-200. *Quam abscondita sunt Dei consilia? Quam inscrutabiles viae eius? Vult enim immensam ac incomprehensibilem Dei sapientiam ita reverenter a nobis suspici, ut, si opera eius sensus nostros superant, admiratio tamen nos contineat* [*CO* 52:261].

[134] *The Acts of the Apostles*, II, trans. John W. Fraser, 113. *Hic primus est aditus in rectam Dei notitiam, si extra nos egredimur, nec ipsum metimur*

*mentis nostrae captu: imo nihil de eo pro sensu carnis nostrae imaginamur: sed statuimus eum supra mundum, et a creaturis discernimus* [*CO* 48:411].

[135] We shall have more to say about this passage in the material on the Joban references that follow.

[136] *The Second Epistle of Paul to the Corinthians, and the Epistles to Timothy, Titus and Philemon*, trans. T. A. Smail, ed. David W. Torrance and Thomas F. Torrance (Grand Rapids, Michigan: Eerdmans, 1989), 280. *Quamquam verum est, nunquam, dum hac mortali carne circumdamur, nos eousque penetrare in ultima adyta Dei, ut nihil nos fugiat* [*CO* 52:332]. Earlier, he adds, "God is hidden from us... because of the weakness of our perception... the dullness of our minds." 280. *Deum nobis esse absconditum... quibus propter imbecillam mentis aciem, vel hebetudinem potius* [*CO* 52:332].

[137] For further examples, see the comment on Psalm 77:14: "He does not speak of the hidden and mysterious essence of God which fills heaven and earth, but of the manifestations of his power, wisdom, goodness, and righteousness, which are clearly exhibited, although they are too vast for our limited understandings to comprehend." *Commentary on the Book of Psalms*, 3:219-220, in *Calvin's Commentaries*, vol. V (Grand Rapids, MI: Baker, 1979). *Magnitudinem Dei probans ab operum miraculis, ac si diceret se non loqui de abscondita Dei essentia, quae coelum et terram implet, sed de virtutis, sapientiae, bonitatis, iustitiae documentis, quae palam apparent, licet modum intelligentiae nostrae excedant* [*CO* 31:718].

[138] *Hebrews*, 67. *Et certe ita clare semper nobiscum agit Dominus, et extra omnes ambages, ut eius verbum merito vocetur lux nostra: sed eius splendor tenebris nostris suffocatur* [*CO* 55:64]. Calvin adds: "We would rather apply our minds to vanity than to the truth of God. We are continually hindered either by our rebelliousness, or by the cares of this world, or by the lusts of our flesh." 67. *Nam ad vanitatem potius adiicimus animos quam ad veritatem Dei. Et nos vel contumacia, vel huius mundi curis, vel carnis cupiditatibus subinde impedimur* [*CO* 55:65]. According to Kenneth Kantzer, the metaphysical dimension, as opposed to the ethical, "is only incidental." On the basis of the evidence here, and particularly in the Joban sermons, the metaphysical aspects of man's finitude are a central feature of the Reformer's pastoral polemic. "John Calvin's Theory of the Knowledge of God and the Word of God" (Ph.D. diss. Harvard University, 1950): 59. Cf. the comment on Isaiah 55:9: "Are men, who are corrupted and debased by sinful desires, not ashamed to compare God's lofty and uncorrupted nature with their own, and to confine what is infinite within those narrow limits by which they feel themselves to be wretchedly restrained? In what prison could any of us be more straitly shut up than in our own unbelief?" *Isaiah*, 4:169, in *Calvin's Commentaries*, vol. VIII (Grand Rapids, MI: Baker, 1979). *Annon pudet homines pravis cupiditatibus corruptos ac refertos excelsam Dei et incorruptam naturam cum sua conferre, ac restringere quod immensum est ad augustias quibus se misere constringi ipsi quoque sentiunt? Quo enim ergastulo*

*arctius includi quisque nostrum posset quam propria infidelitate?* [*CO* 37:290]. For the language of bodily imprisonment limiting our knowledge of God, see Calvin's comment on Moses glimpsing the "back parts" of God, *Harmony of the Four Last Books of the Pentateuch*, 3:382. (Exod 33:21), in *Calvin's Commentaries* vol. III (Grand Rapids, MI: Baker, 1979). *Ita nos corporibus tanquam ergastulis inclusi, non possumus recto et libero intuitu cognoscere Dei gloriam* [*CO* 25:111].

[139] Susan Schreiner, whilst mentioning aspects of God's hiddenness in Calvin's preaching on Job, does not allude to incomprehensibility as such. See, Susan Schreiner, *Where Shall Wisdom be Found?*, 94, 102, 119-20, 122, 127-28, 135-38, 141, 148,153.

[140] For example, T. F. Torrance, in *Calvin's Doctrine of Man*, makes numerous references to the Joban sermons in chapters 9 and 10. He accents Calvin's understanding of the noetic effects of sin, but he only hints at the issue of incomprehensibility. Cf. "The knowledge of God is an operation of grace beyond the natural capacity of the human mind." T. F. Torrance, *Calvin's Doctrine of Man* (Westport, Connecticut: Greenwood Press Publishers, 1977), 128.

[141] Peter Miln, "Hommes D'une Bonne Cause: Calvin's Sermons on the Book of Job," (Ph.D. diss., Nottingham University, 1989). "For Calvin, God's unrevealed Will is the final dimension of God's sovereignty." *Ibid.*, 142. "The present writer is of the opinion that the incomprehensibility of God and the final inscrutability to man of all His doings constitute the leading thought in Calvin's preaching on Job." 156. Miln devotes but a few pages of his thesis in elaboration of this "leading thought." 155-159. Cf. Richard Stauffer's use of the word "*déspatialise*" to describe this aspect of God's infinity. Richard Stauffer, *Dieu. La création et la Providence dans la prédication de Calvin*, 111.

[142] *Sermons on Job*, 1 (Job 1:1), 1.b.40. *Dieu n'afflige pas tousiours les hommes selon la mesure de leurs pechez: mais qu'il a ses iugemens secrets, desquels il ne nous rend pas conte, et cependant qu'il faut que nous attendions iusques à ce qu'il nous revele pourquoy il fait ceci, ou cela* [*CO* 33:23].

[143] *Ibid.*, 5 (Job 1:9-12), 22.b.26. *Il nous faut humilier, voyant que l'Escriture en parle ainsi, et attendre le iour que nous concevions mieux les secrets de Dieu, lesquels nous sont auiourd'huy incomprehensibles, et que pourtant il faut que nous apprenions à les magnifier, que nous adorions les iugemens de Dieu, qu'ils nous soyent admirables, iusques à ce qu'ils nous soyent mieux cognus* [*CO* 33:77].

[144] *Ibid.*, 103 (Job 28:10-28), 484.a.35. *Et nous voyons que ceux qui n'ont point entendu un seul mot de latin, afin de s'abbrutir ainsi parlent latin,* Mitte arcana Dei, *c'est à dire, qu'il ne se faut point enquerir des secrets de Dieu* [*CO* 34:522].

[145] 131 (Job 34:16-20), 616.b.59. *Car c'est bien une espece de rage, quand on ferme la porte à toute bonne doctrine, et qu'on pense estre si sage,*

*qu'on n'ait plus besoin d'instruction, mesmes que nous repoussons tout, que nous mettons là une barre pour dire, Dieu n'approchera point de nous* [*CO* 35:159]. Cf. Calvin's cautionary words in Sermon 78: "When euerie man shootes foorth his bolt vpon a doctrine before hee haue throughly examined it: is not suche rashnesse worthie too bee double condemned?... it is certayne that Gods doctrine is much more precious than mennes persons." 78 (Job 21:1-6), 367.a.23. *Comme si quelqu'un devant qu'avoir bien examiné une doctrine, en dit sa ratelee: ie vous prie, ceste temerité-là n'est elle pas à condamner au double?... il est certain que la doctrine est beaucoup plus precieuse que ne sont pas les personnes* [*CO* 34:208].

[146] "Lo how God wold haue vs to comprehend what he is. Not that we can attaine to the vttermost depth of that wisdome for it is too deepe a gulfe: but yet for al that, it behoueth vs to be diligent, and to do our indeuoure that we may prooue good scholers in Gods schoole, according to our abilitie." 46 (Job 12:3-16), 215.b.30. *Voila Dieu qui veut que nous comprenions quel il est: non pas que nous puissions venir iusques au bout de ceste sagesse (car c'est un abysme trop profond) mais tant y a que selon nostre mesure il nous faut estre diligens, et mettre peine que nous soyons bons escoliers de Dieu* [*CO* 33:572].

[147] 34 (Job 9:7-15), 156.b.20. "God's maiestie which is incomprehensible." *Maiesté de Dieu qui est incomprehensible* [*CO* 33:420].Cf. 50 (Job 13:11-15), 234.a.8. As we have already suggested in the Introduction, Bouwsma's characterisation of Calvin's high view of God's majesty as nominalistic seems misplaced. Rather than the distinctives of nominalism versus determinism, Calvin research of late seems to have emphasised his affinity to biblical rather than philosophical categories.

[148] William J. Bouwsma presents Calvin's presentation of God's majesty as part of his troubled ambivalence, or "anxiety"; one time emphasising natural order, another highlighting God's sovereignty. See William J. Bouwsma, *John Calvin: A Sixteenth Century Portrait*, 33. But this is a troubled and deeply flawed thesis. It has been criticised by T. H. L. Parker. See T. H. L. Parker, *Calvin: An Introduction to His Thought* (Louisville, Kentucky: Westminster/ John Knox Press, 1995), 11, footnote 7. Parker alleges that Bouwsma's "programme is based on Kant's claim (by implication) to know Plato better than Plato knew himself." For Parker, Bouwsma's reading of Calvin in relation to humanism spells "the end of meaningful commerce with the past."

[149] 81 (Job 21:16-21), 381.a.18. *Infinie, une puissance que nous ne concevons pas* [*CO* 34:246]. Cf. "God doth euermore hold such a superioritie ouer vs, as he maye dispose of hys owne as hee listeth hymselfe." 7 (Job 1:20-22), 31.b.24. *Voyans donc comme Dieu doit avoir ceste maistrise, non seulement sur ce que nous possedons* [*CO* 33:100]. Cf. Commentary on Amos 3:6, "There is no evil in the city which God hath not done," where Calvin adds: "the government of this world is administered by God, and that nothing happens except through his power... nothing happens but by the will of God." *Administrari imperium mundi huius a Deo, et nihil accidere nisi ab*

*eius manu... nihil accidit nisi volente Deo* [*CO* 43:43]. Cf. Commentary on Psalm 121:1: "He holds the whole world in his hand, and governs it as it seemeth good in his sight." *Quia totus mundus in eius manu est, eiusque arbitrio regitur* [*CO* 32:300].

[150] 101 (Job 27:19-28:9), 476.a.39. *Mais adorons ce qui nous est incognu, confessans que la maiesté de Dieu est trop haute par dessus nous* [*CO* 34:501]. On a similar point relating to God's providence, cf. 19 Job 5:8-10), 87.a.34. "Let vs vndersta[n]d therwithal that we must reuerence the works of God. And howe? To comprehende the infinite wisdome, righteousnesse, and power that is conteyned in the[m], according to our finall capacitie, assuring ourselues that God doth not anything without reason, no not although the same be not know[n]e vnto vs at the first dash." *Mais au reste sachons quant et quant que nous devons adorer les oeuvres de Dieu. Et comment? Pour comprendre, selon nostre petite mesure, la sagesse, et iustice, et vertu infinie qui est là contenue, que nous sachions que Dieu ne fait rien sans raison, voire combien que cela ne nous soit point manifesté du premier coup* [*CO* 33:241-242].

[151] 44 (Job 11:13-20), 207.b.38. "Preace" is an obsolete form of "press." See *The Oxford English Dictionary* (Oxford: Clarendon Press, 1970), vol. VIII, 1237. *On n'osera point approcher d'un prince mortel, qui n'est qu'une charongne: et comment viendrons-nous devant la maiesté de nostre Createur?* [*CO* 33:552].

[152] 138 (Job 35:12-15), 648.b.64. *Et cependant aussi nous le devons contempler au miroir qu'il nous presente, c'est assavoir en sa parole, et puis en ses oeuvres, et cheminer en telle sobrieté que nous vueillions point nous enquirir plus qu'il ne nous est licite, et qu'il ne nous le permet. Il y a donc une façon de regarder Dieu qui est bonne et saincte, c'est que nous le contemplions d'autant qu'il luy plaist se manifester à nous, et nous defians de nostre intelligence, que nous luy demandions d'estre illuminez par son sainct Esprit, et que nous n'ayons point une curiosité trop grande ni presomption de savoir plus qu'il ne nous permet. Mais quand nous voulons regarder Dieu en face, que nous ne voulons point que rien nous soit caché, que nous voulons entrer en ses conseils incomprehensibles iusques au plus profond des abysmes: voila une arrogance insupportable, et les hommes alors se confondent du tout. Apprenons donc quel moyen nous avons à tenir pour voir Dieu: que ce n'est pas d'y aller avec une hastiveté trop grande: mais qu'il nous faut estre sobres cognoissans la petite mesure de nostre esprit, et la hautesse infinie de la maiesté de Dieu* [*CO* 35:245].

[153] *Ibid.*, 17 (Job 4:20-5:2), 78.b.38. "Therefore let vs learne to mislyke whatsoeuer thing men haue forged of their owne braine, and let vs holde vs to this simplicitie, namely that we must not couet too knowe ought, sauing that which God hath declared too vs with his own mouth." *Apprenons donc de detester tout ce que les hommes auront forgé en leur cerveau, et nous tenons à ceste simplicité, que nous ne devons appeter de rien savior, sinon ce que Dieu nous a declaré de sa propre bouche* [*CO* 33:219].

[154] Cf. *Institutes*, I.xi.8. "Man's nature... is a perpetual factory of idols." *L'esprit de l'homme est une boutique perpetuelle et de tout temps pour forger idoles* [*CO* 3:129]. Cf. 146 (Job 37:14-24), 687.b.50. "All the vnaduised wordes which we shoote foorth concerning God, and all the wandring imaginations which we conceyue in our braynes, are as it were grudgings that are made in huckermucker." *Que tous les propos temeraires que nous tenons de Dieu, toutes les phantasies extravagantes que nous concevons en nos cerveaux, sont comme des murmures qui se font en cachette* [*CO* 35:348]. The expression, "hucker-mucker," later known as "hugger-mugger," has the meaning "conceal" or "secret.' *The Oxford English Dictionary* (Oxford: Clarendon Press, 1970), vol. IV, 440. Cf. Calvin commentary on John 4:22: "By it we are taught that we are not to essay anything in religion rashly or unthinkingly. For unless there is knowledge present, it is not God that we worship but a spectre or ghost." Calvin, *John*, 98. (John 4:22). *Qua docemur nihil in religione temere vel fortuito esse tentandum, quia, nisi assit scientia, non iam Deus, sed phantasma vel spectrum colitur* [*CO* 47:87].

[155] *Sermons on Job*, 19 (Job 5:8-10), 86.a.30. "God doth exceeding great and incomprehensible things, his doings are wonderfull and without ende. When we vnderstand that Gods workes are exceeding great and incomprehensible: shall wee not be forced to lift vp our myndes, and to perceyue that wee must not disguyse him, nor surmize anything of him after oure naturall reason, but that wee muste mounte vp higher?" *Dieu fait des choses grandes et incomprehensibles, ses actes sont admirables, et sans fin. Quand nous aurons cognu que les oeuvres de Dieu sont grandes et incomprehensibles, ne serons-nous pas contraints d'eslever nos esprits, et de sentir qu'il ne faut point que nous deguisions Dieu, ne que nous imaginions rien de luy selon nostre sens naturel, mais qu'il faut monter plus haut?* [*CO* 33:239]. Cf. 36 (Job 9:23-28), 166.a.67., "It becometh vs not to taske him so to our ordinarie maner of proceeding, for he hath iudgements that are inco[m]prehensible to vs." *Il ne faut pas que nous le vueillions ici renger à nostre façon ordinaire, car il a des iugements qui nous sont incomprehensibles* [*CO* 33:445-446]. Later in the same sermon, he adds: "When wee shall haue searched to the vttermost, and made great circuites and discourses: in the ende wee shall be dazeled and not see any reason why God doth this or that. What is to bee done then? wee muste honour this iustice of God which is vnknowne to vs." 168.b.4. *Nous aurons beau à enquerir, et faire de grands circuits et discours, en la fin nous demourerons esblouys, et ne verrons nulle raison pourquoy Dieu fait ceci ou cela* [*CO* 33:451].

[156] 36 (Job 9:23-28), 165.a.56. "For he hath his secrete iudgements, which are incomprehensible to vs, in so much that wee cannot but be abashed and amazed when God shall doo things that seeme to bee quite against reason." *Car il a ses iugements secrets, et qui nous sont incomprehensibles, en sorte que nous ne pouvons estre sinon esbahis et estonnez, quand Dieu fera des choses qui nous semblent estre du tout contre raison* [*CO* 33:443]. Cf. 40 (Job 10:16-17), 188.a.49. God's "secrete iudgements, which man cannot reach

vnto, by reason that the same do farre passe his vnderstanding and wit." *Ces iugements secrets de Dieu, lesquels l'homme ne peut comprendre: la raison est, pource que cela outrepasse son sens et son esprit* [CO 33:501]. Cf. 66 (Job 17:6-16), 311.a.12. "Inquire a ma[n] neuer so much, & trauell he neuer so much, yet shal he be neuer the neerer, bycause Gods judgeme[n]ts are secret and inco[m]prehensible." *Qu'on s'enquiere, qu'on y travaille beaucoup, on y demeurera confus, d'autant que les iugemens de Dieu sont secrets et incomprehensibles* [CO 34:58].

[157] 149 (Job 38:12-17), 702.a.54. *Conseils spirituels...qui surmonte toutes creatures* [CO 35:387].

[158] 123 (Job 33:8-14), 582.a.2. "When he executeth the office of a scholemaster towards vs, it is not to open vnto vs al things that we would doubt of, or whereof we would be inquisitiue." *Mais cependant notons quand il fait office de maistre envers nous, que ce n'est pas pour nous reveler toutes choses dont nous pourrions douter, et dont nous pourrions nous enquerir* [CO 35:63].

[159] 50 (Job 13:11-15), 236.a.11. "There haue beene some which in their disputations, would fayne alwayes conclude after the maner of the Philosophers, that al things are so put in order, as there is no disagreement, but a certaine league or couenant throughout all things: but such men neuer knew what it is to haue beene sifted by God, and to haue passed through his iudgements. And why? For... God handleth vs after such a straungue fashion, that all things are confounded in that cace. And in good sooth there are things in vs also which can neuer be made to agree. For sometimes we be desirous to liue, and sometymes wee woulde fayne die: and these are things contrarie." *Il y en a qui voudroient en leurs disputes faire tousiours des conclusions à la façon des Philosophes, que tout fust mis par ordre, tellement qu'il n'y eust point diversité, et qu'il y eust paction par tout: mais telles gens n'ont iamais cognu que c'est d'avoir esté maniez de Dieu et d'avoir passé par ses iugemens. Et Pourquoy? Comme i'ay dit, Dieu nous traite d'une façon si sauvage que tout y est confus. Et de fait aussi il y aura en nous des choses comme incompatibles. Car aucunesfois nous desirerons de vivre, et aucunesfois nous desirerons de mourir: et ce sont choses contraires* [CO 33:627]. Cf. Bouwsma, "For Calvin, too, there were more things in heaven and earth than are dreamt of in philosophy." *John Calvin: A Sixteenth Century Portrait*, 161.

[160] Cf. Calvin's words in a sermon on Deuteronomy 4:11: "We must not inquire of his maiestie further than he giueth vs leaue... God shewed not himselfe in any visible shape, least it might bee thought that his essence or being had some shape... We knowe how curious and ouerbolde men are, for they woulde faine knowe what Gods being or substance is, and search our euery whit of him by inchmeale, and that so presumptuously as though they would pushe vp their hornes into heauen." 22 (Deut. 4:10-14), 130.a.25. *Qu'il ne nous faut point enquerir de sa Maieste plus que il ne nous est licite. Dieu ne s'est point monstré en forme visible, à ce qu'on pensast son essence eust*

*quelque figure, comme il en sera que traitté demain au plaisir de Dieu... Nous savons quelle est la curiosite, et aussi l'audace des hommes: car ils voudroyent savoir quelle est l'essence de Dieu, et esplucher tout par le menu, voire avec une presomption telle, qu'ils viendront hurter des cornes iusques au ciel* [CO 26:139-140].

[161] 157 (Job 42:1-5), 738.b.54. "God may conceale his secrets: howbeit, that is with knowlege, for he is not ignorant of anything, neither is it because he is not able to shew vs why he doth this or that: but because we be not able to co[n]ceiue the things which as now are incomprehensible to vs." *Voila donc Dieu qui cachera le conseil, mais c'est avec science: car de luy il n'est ignorant de rien, et ce n'est pas qu'il ne nous peust monstrer pourquoy il fait ceci et cela: voire, si nous estions assez habiles pour comprendre ce qui nous est maintenant incomprehensible* [CO 35:481].

[162] 102 (Job 28:10-28), 480.b.43. "It is in that men are desirous to knowe more than God hath appoynted: and too bee short, that they woulde be wise whether God woulde or no, whereas God onely is the fountayne of wisedome... yet will men bee inquisitiue of that whiche is not lawfull for them." *C'est que les hommes veulent plus savoir tousiours que Dieu ne leur ordonne: bref, ils veulent estre sages en despit que Dieu en ait: et c'est Dieu qui est la fountaine de toute sagesse... les hommes veulent quoi qu'il en soit s'enquerir de ce qui ne leur est point permis* [CO 34:513]. See Bouwsma, *John Calvin: A Sixteenth Century Portrait*, 157.

[163] 35 (Job 9:16-22), 161.a.2. *Donc que tout babil et toute rhetorique cesse, quand nous venons devant le siege celeste* [CO 33:431]. Cf. Bouwsma, *John Calvin: A Sixteenth Century Portrait*, 108.

[164] "God must not doo things at our appointment... if wee finde anything in the Scripture which is straunge to our vnderstanding: let vs assure ourselues that we must not leane so to our owne reason, that God should do what wee thinke ought to be done... let his will reygne and let men stoupe vnto it: For he ought not to aske counsell of vs." 135 (Job 34:33-37), 635.b.16. *Que Dieu face les choses de par nous... quand nous trouverons quelque chose en l'Escriture qui sera estrange à nostre sens, que nous conclusions qu'il ne faut point tellement nous ranger à nostre raison que Dieu face ce que nous iugeons devoir estre fait... que sa volonté domine, et que les hommes ayent la teste baissée, car ce n'est point à nous qu'il doit demander conseil* [CO 35:209]. Cf. in the same passage: "That men should haue the libertie to say, this must bee done: and that God shoulde haue the souereyntie to gouerne vs, as he listeth: are twoo things that cannot stand together. And why? We agree with God, as fire with water. 635.b.58. *Il y a deux choses incompatibles, que les hommes ayent liberte de dire, Cela se doit faire et que Dieu ait la maistrise pour gouverner comme bon lui semble. Et pourqoui? Nous sommes accordans avec Dieu, comme le feu avec l'eau* [CO 35:210]. And again: "Our desires are corrupt and so are al our affections and thoughts. So then, how should we agre with God, who is the infinite and incomprehensible wisdome, and vnto whose righteousnesse it behoueth vs to be subiect?

Seing there is such a contrarietie betweene God and men..." 635.b.66. *Nos appetits sont corrompus, et toutes nos affections et pensees. Ainsi donc comment accorderons-nous avec Dieu, lui qui est la sagesse infinie et qui nous est incomprehensible, lui qui a son equité à laquelle il nous faut estre suiets? Puis qu'il y a une telle contrarieté entre Dieu et les hommes* [CO 35:210].

[165] 34 (Job 9:7-15), 157.b.39. *Or Dieu nous parle de ces choses selon que nous les appercevons, et non pas selon qu'elles sont* [CO 33:423]. Similarly, when God asks Satan what he had been doing (Job 1:7), Calvin remarks: "Our rudenesse and the small measure of our vnderstandding comprehend not these things: it behoueth vs... that there be such a declaration as is agreeable to vs... bicause we canot attayne vnto him, nor mount so high: he humbleth himself to vs, and as it were transformeth himself." 4 (Job 1:6-8), 16.b.50. *Nostre rudesse, et en une si petite mesure, comme elle est en nostre sens, il faut (comme i'ay dit) qu'il y en ait une declaration qui nous soit convenable. Et en cela voyons-nous la bonté de Dieu, de ce qu'il se conforme à nous, d'autant que nous ne pouvons point parvenir à luy, que nous ne pouvons pas monter si haut, il se rend familier, il est comme transguré, afin que nous cognoissions ce qui nous est bon et propre* [CO 33:62-63]. In the same sermon, Calvin continues (17.a.1): "His meaning is, not onely to instruct the great Clerkes, and such as are very suttle and well exercysed in schooles: but also to apply himself vnto vs that are of the rudest and unskilfullest sort, that can be... God hath applied himself vnto vs." 17.a.1. *Dieu nous monstre qu'il ne veut pas seulement instruire les grands clercs, et ceux qui seront bien subtils, et qui auront esté exercez à l'escole, mais qu'il se veut accomoder iusques aux plus rudes idiots qui soyent... Dieu s'accommode à nous* [CO 33:63]. In a similar passage of the eighth sermon, Calvin remarks on Satan's appearance before God: "The Scripture speaketh so, too applye itselfe to oure rudenesse, bycause wee conceyue not howe all thyngs are presente afore God, and that he is of suche a power and preeminence, as nothing is hidde[n] from him... it teacheth vs by such meane as is most conuenient for vs, and moste agreeable to our vnderstanding." 8 (Job 2:1-6), 35.a.26. *Mais l'Escriture parle ainsi, s'accommodant à nostre rudesse pource que nous ne concevons pas que toutes choses sont presentes à Dieu, et qu'il a une telle puissance et maistrise que rien ne luy est caché. Quand cela nous est exprimé, il faut recognoistre, que l'Escriture s'accommode à nostre raison, et qu'elle nous enseigne par tel moyen, qu'il est convenable à nostre sens* [CO 33:109].

[166] 8 (Job 2:1-6), 33.b.15. *Nous ne comprenons point la grandeur et la hautesse des oeuvres de Dieu, sinon d'autant qu'il luy plaist nous en donner quelque goust, voire selon nostre mesure qui est bien petite. Il n'y a que Dieu seul qui cognoisse ses oeuvres, c'est un abysme profond (comme dit l'Escriture [Pse. 36:7]) et nous n'avons nul moyen d'y parvenir, tellement que tous ceux qui s'en voudront enquerir, demeureront confus, sinon qu'ils y procedent en toute reverence et humilité* [CO 33:105]. Calvin, in this

allusion to the "*abysme profond*," is, of course, citing Psalm 36:6, "His judgments are like a great and bottomless abyss." The reference is crucial to Calvin's understanding of providence, and twice, he cites it in the *Institutes*, at I.xvii.2 and III.xxiii.5. In both these passages, Calvin alludes to Job: "The Book of Job is set forth a declaration of such sublimity as to humble our minds" (I.xvii.2); *Ceste hautesse nous est aussi bien preschée au livre de Iob, pour humilier nos esprits* [3:252, 1560 French edition]; "Why does not some fear at least restrain you because the history of Job... proclaim God's incomprehensible wisdom and dreadful might" (III.xxiii.5); *Comment ce qui est escrit de sa sagesse incomprehensible de Dieu et de sa vertu espovantable, tant en l'historie de Iob... ne vous bride-il de quelque crainte et frayer* [4:492, 1560 French edition]. In both sections, Calvin uses the language of *abysme* (four times in I.xvii.2 and twice in III.xxiii.5). Interestingly, the Commentary on the Psalms was begun in the same year (1553) that Calvin began preaching on Job. See T. H. L. Parker, *Calvin's Old Testament Commentaries*, 31. Since it took him four years to compile, ending in 1557, the commentary on Psalm 36 may well have been written simultaneously, or shortly after the material on Job. It is also of interest to note that Calvin draws two meanings from the language of *abysme* in the Psalms commentary: having noted its meaning, "that to whatever side we turn our eyes, and whether we look upward or downward, all things are disposed and ordered by the just judgment of God," Calvin then goes on to suggest another meaning: "that the judgments of God far exceed our limited capacity, and are too mysterious for our being able to comprehend them," adding that "the similitude of an abyss is not inappropriate." John Calvin, *Commentary on the Book of Psalms*, 2:9, in *Calvin's Commentaries* vol. V (Grand Rapids, Michigan, Baker Book House, 1979). *Quod scilicet iudicia Dei captum nostrum longe superent, sintque magis abscondita quam ut eorum ratio apprehendatur, nec inepte huc aptatur similitudo abyssi* [*CO* 31:362]. Calvin elaborates, however, to suggest that the language of the psalmist is to be understood in a far more extensive sense, namely that however great the depths of wickedness may be, "the depth of God's providence" is greater. 9. *Maiorem tamen esse providentiae Dei abysum* [*CO* 31:362]. Cf. *Commentary on Ezekiel*, 2:60-61, in *Calvin's Commentaries* vol. XI (Grand Rapids, MI: Baker, 1979). (Ezek. 14:9). *Iudicia antem Dei sunt abyssus profunda* [*CO* 40:311]. Bouwsma attempts a somewhat unhelpful subjective, di-polar use of the word "abyss" in Calvin's writings, one being positive, and suggesting "infinity"; the other being negative, suggesting "his own horror and to induce horror in others." *John Calvin: A Sixteenth Century Portrait*, 46. It is interesting that the McNeill-Battles edition of the *Institutes* does not even list "abyss" in the index! See the review of Bouwsma's work on Calvin in "Between the 'Labyrinth' and the 'Abyss'," *Reformed Journal* (April 1997), 21-28, and Bouwsma's reply, *Reformed Journal* (July 1997), 8-9.

[167] 9 (Job 2:7-10), 42.a.41. *Car c'est un abysme de la bonté de Dieu* [*CO* 33:128].

[168] 40 (Job 10:16-17), 188.b.14. God shows that he is "maruellouse" in his "election, in hys prouidence, and in all the things that he doth aboue our vnderstanding. Behold a part of Gods secretes which are as a bottomlesse pit vnto vs ward." *Prenons l'example en l'election de Dieu, en sa providence, et en tout ce qu'il fait par dessus nostre sens. Car voila une partie des secrets qui nous sont comme un abysme* [CO 33:502]. Cf. Calvin's warnings about "human curiosity" (*hominum curiositas*) in discussing predestination in *Institutes* III.xxi.1 [CO 2:680]; and the use of the word "labyrinth" in his commentary on Romans 9:4: "The predestination of God is truly a labyrinth from which the mind of man is wholly incapable of extricating itself. But the curiosity of man is so insistent that the more dangerous it is to inquire into a subject, the more boldly he rushes to do so." Calvin, *Romans*, 202. (Romans 9:14). *Est enim praedestinatio Dei vere labyrinthus, unde hominis ingenium nullo modo se explicare queat: atqui adeo importuna est hominis curiositas, ut quo periculosior est cuiusque rei inquisitio, eo audacius perrumpat* [CO 49:180].

[169] 26 (Job 6:24-30), 119.b.6 [CO 33:324]. Cf. 73 (Job 20:1-7), 345.a.12. "God will find meanes well ynough to throw them downe, yea and to sink them euen intoo hell." *Que Dieu trouvera bien les moyens de les abaisser, voire et de les abysmer iusques aux enfers* [CO 34:150].

[170] 96 (Job 26:8-14), 451.a.22. *Il semble que la mer menace la terre de l'abysmer, et ne se iette vague qu'il ne semble que la terre doive estre engloutie* [CO 34:435].

[171] 156 (Job 40:20-41:25), 735.b.9. "If we meete with a thing that seemeth straunge to vs, yet let vs consider that God hath spoken it, and therfore we must receiue it without gaynsaying. Furthermore if God let a thing alone and tel vs it not: it behoueth vs too stoppe there without going any further, and we must not be inquisitiue after our owne fancie." *Si nous cognoissons, Dieu l'a ainsi prononcé, il le faut recevoir sans contredit. Mais au reste, quand Dieu nous laissera là, ne nous disant point la chose, il nous faut retenir tout court, et ne passer point outre: et ne faut point que nous vueillions estre subtils à nostre phantasie* [CO 35:472].

[172] 147 (Job 38:1-4), 692.b.52. "For is it not a peruerting of the order of nature, that a mortall man which is nothing, should incroche vpon his maker, and cause audience to be giuen to himself, and God in the meane while should hold his peace? What a dealing is that? And yet notwithstanding wee doo it as oft as wee murmure against God, or teare his woord in peeces, or cast foorth woords at random to say: Thus and thus doeth it seeme to me. What is the cause hereof, but that wee would put God too silence, and haue ourselues heard aboue him? Is not this a starke madnesse? Therefore too correct this statelinesse that is in vs, let vs learne, not too presume too answer our God, knowing that when wee come before him, he hath authoritie too examine vs, yea euen according too his owne will, and not after our lyking and appointment, and that it shal be toto [sic] much to our shame when he shal haue stopped our mouth and begone to speak himself." *Car*

*n'est-ce point pervertir l'ordre de nature, que l'homme mortel qui n'est rien anticipe sur son Createur, et se face donner audience, et que Dieu cependant se taise? Ou est-ce aller?Et c'est neantmoins ce que nous faisons, toutes fois et quantes que nous mumurons contre Dieu quand nous descirons sa parole par pieces, que nous iettons des propos à la volee pour dire, Voila ce qui m'en semble. Qui est cause de cela, sinon que nous voulons que Dieu nous face silence et que nous soyons ouis par dessus luy. Ne voila point une pure rage? Ainsi donc que pour corriger ceste arrogance qui est en nous, nous apprenions de ne presumer point de respondre à nostre Dieu: sachans que quand nous viendrons devant luy, il aura ceste autorité de nous examiner: voire selon sa volonté, et non point à nostre appetit: et à nostre poste: et que quand il nous aura clos la bouche, et qu'il aura commencé à parler, nous serons plus que confus* [CO 35:362].

[173] 37 (Job 9:29-35), 173.b.25. " We must reuerence his secretes, which are incomprehensible too vs: and so wee must euerye way haue our mouth shet [sic], and not say, If I might reason the matter, I shoulde preuayle in the cace." *Là nous le devons glorifier, et s'il se cache, qu'il nous faut adorer ses secrets qui nous sont incomprehensibles. Et ainsi en toutes sortes que nous ayons la bouche close, et que nous ne disions point, Si ie disputoye, i'auroye mon procez gagné* [CO 33:464]. Cf. 138 (Job 35: 12-15), 649.a.65. "wee must brydle our tongues, and holde our thoughtes as prisoners, assuring our selues that God intendeth to keepe vs in humilitie by concealing the reason of all his woorkes from vs." *Mais nous faut brider nos langues, et tenir nos pensees captives, sachans que Dieu nous veut tenir en humilité, quand il ne nous monstre point la raison de toutes ses oeuvres* [CO 35:246]. Cf. the opening words of Sermon 148 (Job 38:4-11), 693.a.40 [CO 35:363].

[174] 19 (Job 5:8-10), 86.a.42. *Quand on traitera des oeuvres de Dieu, chacun s'estime estre iuge suffisant pour en dire sa rastelee: et mesmes nous serons assez hardis (ou plustost audacieux) de le controller: car si dieu ne besonge à nostre guise, nous serons pleins de murmures: nous dirons. Pourquoy ceci ne se fait-il? Et pourquoy une telle chose va elle ainsi? Qui est cause d'une telle audace, que les hommes a'attachent ainsi à Dieu, qu'ils intentent proces contre iuy, et mesmes qu'ils se constituent comme ses ouges? C'est d'autant que iamais ils n'ont senti combien les oeuvres sont grandes et incomprehensibiles* [CO 33:239]. The citation continues: "But if the workes of God bee incomprehensible: haue we a measure that is great inoughe to declare what is in them? What is oure witte? When wee haue stretched it out too the vttermoste length and breadth that maye bee: is it able too comprehende the hundreth parte of Gods woorkes, and of his determination whiche is so highe as all of it is hidden from vs? Wee muste goe out of our selues, if wee mynde but only too taste the wonderfull and infinite wisedom that appeereth in Gods woorkes. Nowe if we must mount aboue all our owne wittes, too gette but a little taste of them: what shall become of vs when wee will incloze all, and when wee will know all that is in them too the vttermoste? I pray you, can we attayne therevnto? We see

then howe men are worse than mad when they bee so presumptuouse as too desyre too determine of Gods woorks which are incomprehensible. For true it is that wee cannot gage the bottom of Gods woorks, too comprehend the reason of them: but yet God keepeth a good way to giue vs such a knowledge of them, as hee knoweth too be for our behoof. And so we note, that Gods woorks are incomprehensible in themselues: that is to say, that if we will search out al that euer is in them by parcelmeale, wee shall neuer bee able too atteyne too the depth of them...wee cannot atteyne too the secrets that are in them." *Or si les oeuvres de Dieu sont incomprehensibles, avons-nous une mesure assez grande pour en declarer ce qui en est? Qu'est-ce que nostre sens? Quand nous l'aurons estendu au long, et au large, pourra-il comprendre en soy la centime partie des oeuvres de Dieu, et de son conseil qui est si haut, que tout cela nous est caché? Il faut que nous sortions hors de nous-mesmes, si nous voulons seulement gouster que c'est de la sagesse admirable et infinie qui apparoist aux oeuvres de Dieu. Si pour en gouster seulement un peu il faut que nous surmontions tous nos sens, et que sera-ce quand nous voudrons tout enclorre, que nous voudrons savoir tout ce qu'en est iusques au bout? Ie vous prie, y pourrons-nous parvenir? Nous voyons donc que les hommes sont plus qu'enragez quand ils presument ainsi de vouloir deliberer des oeuvres de Dieu, lesquelles sont incomprehensibles. Or il est vray que nous ne pourrons nullement sonder les oeuvres de Dieu pour comprendre quelle en est la raison: mais si est ce que Dieu tient un bon moyen pour nous en donner une cognoissance telle qu'il cognoist nous estre utile. Et ainsi notons que les oeuvres de Dieu sont incomprehensibles de soy, c'est à dire que si nous voulons esplucher par le menu tout ce qui y est, iamais nous ne pourrons atteindre iusques au bout. Il faut donc que nous soyons comme accablez sous ceste grandeur-là, et que nous sachions que si nous voulons estre iuges des oeuvres de Dieu, nous avons à clorre les yeux d'autant que nous ne pouvons point atteindre iusques aux secrets qui sont là contenus* [CO 33:239-240].

[175] 78 (Job 21:1-6), 369.b.5. *Que nous cognoissions donc nostre faculté, afin de ne nous point esgarer à travers champs: mais que nous suivions tousiours le droit chemin. Pour ce faire il faut que nous sachions seulment ce qui nous est donné: comme S. Paul aussi nous ramene à ceste regle, de ne point plus savoir que iusques là où Dieu nous conduit (Rom. 12,3). Cependant qu'il nous tend la main, allons hardiment: mais quand nous n'avons point de conduite de Dieu, il faut demeurer là, et que nous soyons comme muets. Il est vrai que nous devons tousiours avoir la bouche ouverte en une sorte, c'est assavoir, pour glorifier Dieu: mais quand nous presumerons de tout assubiettir à nostre sens, et que nous ne voudrons pas que Dieu se reserve rien, où sera-ce aller cela? N'est-ce point despitter Dieu manifestement? Il nous voudra cacher une chose. Et pourquoy? Afin que nostre ignorance nous soit cognue, et que nous ne laissions pas cependant de recognoistre qu'il est iuste, et d'adorer son conseil admirable, et incomprehensible. Ainsi donc (comme i'ay desia touché) quand Dieu*

*nous monstrera la raison de ses oeuvres, et bien remercions sa bonté, pour dire, Seigneur, tu descens bien bas à nous povres creatures, quand tu daignes bien nous declarer pourquoy tu fais ceci, ou cela: ta bonté merite bien d'estre magnifiee par nous, quand tu la communiques si priveement à ceux qui ne le valent pas. Mais si Dieu nous cache la raison de ses ouevres, et que cela nous soit trop haut: que nous ayons la bouche close, c'est à dire, que nous ne soyons point legers pour babiller à nostre phantasie, mais que nous glorifions Dieu, et que nous n'ayons point honte d'estre ignorans, car c'est la vraye sagesse des fideles, de ne point savoir sinon ce qu'il plaist à Dieu de leur monstrer. Que donc nous facions silence à Dieu en quelque sorte qu'il besongne, iusques à ce que le dernier iour de revelation soit venu, quand nous le verrons face à face en sa gloire et en sa maiesté* [*CO* 34:215-216].

[176] Alluding to the rhetoric of blasphemy, Calvin, in Sermon 11, has recourse to comment on the abuse of language in referring to God: "In blaspheming of God, men haue a certayne naturall Rhetorike, and are so cunning in the art, as there is no lacke in them... if men will go too blaspheming: then yee shall see them as eloquent as may bee deuysed, and there is not the man that may not seeme to haue bene at schoole to learne fine Rhetorike." 11 (Job 3:2-10), 51.a.56. *Au reste, nous voyons que les hommes en blasphemant dieu, ont comme une rhetorique naturelle, qu'ils sont rhetoriciens, qu'il n'y a que redire... mais quand les hommes veulent blasphemer, alors les voila tant elegans que rien plus, il n'y a celuy qu'il ne semble avoir esté à l'escole pour avoir belle faconde* [*CO* 33:150-151]. Cf. Bouwsma, *John Calvin: A Sixteenth Century Portrait*, 95. Bouwsma's footnote appears to be astray. Cf. also Calvin's comment on Lamentations 3:36-38: "Let us then learn not to subject God to our judgment, but adore his judgments, though they surpass our comprehension; and since the cause of them is hid from us, our highest wisdom is modesty and sobriety." *Commentary on Jeremiah and Lamentations*, 5:429-430, in *Calvin's Commentaries* vol. XI (Grand Rapids, MI: Baker, 1979). (Lam. 3:36-38). *Ergo discamus non subiicere Deum nostro iudicio, sed adoremus eius iudicia, dum nos figunt, hoc est, dum eorum causa nos latet ac fugit: haec est vera sapiendi ratio, nempe modestia et sobrietas* [*CO* 39:589]; *Commentaries on the Psalms*, 4:314 (Psa. 111.2), in *Calvin's Commentaries* vol. VI (Grand Rapids, MI: Baker, 1979). *Sed utcunque incomprehensibilis sit sapientiae, aequitatis, iustitae, virtutis, misericordiae immensitas in Dei operibus, notitiam tamen delibant fideles quae ad Deum glorificandum sufficiat* [*CO* 32:168].

[177] 79 (Job 21:7-12), 372.a.47. *Si nous cognoissons Dieu estre une essence incomprehensible, pour dire, Dieu a toute maiesté en soy, et cependant que nous le despouillions de ce qui lui est propre, et qui ne peut estre separé de lui: nous en faisons une idole, et une chose morte* [*CO* 34:222]. Cf. 82 (Job 21:22-34), 384.a.34. "Wee must with all humilitie reuerence the secrets of God and his incomprehensible iudgements: and shal mortal man, that is but duste and ashes, take vpon him to search them out, and to know a reason thereof?"

*Or il faut qu'en toute humilité ils adorent les secrets de Dieu, et ses iugemens incomprehensibles: et l'homme mortel qui n'est que pourriture entreprendra-il de les sonder, et en vouloir savoir la raison?* [*CO* 34:254]. Cf. 157 (Job 42:1-5), 739.b.38. "Lette vs neuer speake nor thinke of Gods secrets but with all reuerence and humilitie." *Et par ainsi que nous ne parlions iamais, et ne pensions de ses secrets qu'avec toute reverence et humilité* [*CO* 35:484].

[178] "When we behold his maiestie, the spite of our teeth wee must learne too cast downe our head, and to reuerence the infinite highnesse that is in him." 85 (Job 22:12-17), 398.b.33. *Et quand nous contemplons sa maiesté, en despit de nos dents il faut alors que nous apprenions de baisser la teste, et d'adorer ceste hautesse infinie qui est en lui* [*CO* 34:294].

[179] 33 (Job 9:1-6), 152.b.3. "Wee must know the incomprehensible maiestie of God. Therefore let euery man thinke thereof, and then shall all of vs be wakened, to withdrawe ourselues out of our follies, and wee shall haue no mo [sic] of these vaine imaginacions and dotages that haue bin wont to rocke sinners asleepe. Had this bin obserued: there shoulde be none of the debates that are nowe adayes in christendome about the righteousnesse of faith." *Il nous faut cognoistre la maiesté incomprehensible de Dieu. Qu'un chacun donc pense-là, et alors nous serons tous resveillés, pour nous retirer de nos folies, nous n'aurons plus ces vaines imaginations et resveries qui ont accoustumé d'endormir les pecheurs. Si cela eust esté observé, auiourd'huy on n'auroit point les debats en la Chrestienté, qu'on a touchant la iustice de la foy* [*CO* 33:409].

[180] 19 (Job 5:8-10), 86.b.35. *Or si ainsi est, que aux oeuvres de Dieu qui semblent les plus petites et basses il y a une sagesse infinie, que sera-ce de ce qui est plus grand, et qui surmonte toute nostre capacité? Et sur tout quand il est question de nostre redemption, quand il est question de ce que Dieu seelle en nous par son S. Esprit, ce tesmoignage de nostre adoption: cela surmonte l'ordre commun de nature* [*CO* 33:240].

[181] 150 (Job 38:18-32), 706.b.43. *folle presomption* [*CO* 35:398].

[182] 120 (Job 32:4-10), 566.b.68. *Maintenant si nous venons à la doctrine de l'Evangile, voila une sagesse qui surmonte tout sens humain, mesmes qui est admirable aux Anges: voila les secrets du ciel qui sont contenus en l'Evangile: car il est question de cognoistre Dieu en la personne de son Fils: et combien que nostre Seigneur Iesus soit descendu ici bas, si est-ce qu'il nous faut comprendre sa maiesté divine, ou nous ne pouvons pas nous fonder, et reposer nostre foy en luy. Il est question, di-ie, que nous cognoissious ce qui est incomprehensible à la nature humaine* [*CO* 35:23]. Cf. 147 (Job 38:1-4), 692.a.26. "When we treate of his woord, and of the doctrine of our saluation, and of the holie Scripture, euerye one falls to it at aduenture, and euery man shoots forth his verdit, as though they reasoned but of moone shyne in the water. They be such things as passe al vnderstanding of man, and yet notwithstanding it is manifest that we be bolder too treate of Gods so hygh mysteries, which ought to rauish our witts

to wonder at them, and which we ought to honour with a lawfulnesse, I say wee be bolder to babble of them, than if a man spake but of a matter of fiue shillings valew, or of some trifle I wote not what. And what is the cause hereof, but that men haue not considered howe God hydeth and ouercasteth his owne secret determinations, and hath in his holye Scripture vttered vnto vs his will wherevnto it behoueth vs to be subiect." *Quand on traitte de sa parole, et de la doctrine do nostre salut, et de toute l'Escriture saincte, un chacun ira à la volee: si on en devise à l'ombre d'un pot, chacun en dira sa rastelee. Voila des choses qui outrepassent tout entendement humain: et toutes fois on voit que nous serons plus hardis à traitter des mysteres de Dieu si hauts, et qui nous devroyent ravir en estonnement, et lesquels nous devrions adorer avec toute solicitude: nous serons, di-ie, plus hardis à en babiller, que si on traittoit d'un proces de cinq sols vaillant, ou ie ne say quoy. Et qui est cause de cela, sinon que les hommes n'ont point regardé que Dieu nous cache et obscurcit son conseil et qu'en l'Escriture il nous a desployé sa volonté à laquelle il nous falloit assuiettir?* [CO 35:360]. Cf. 149 (Job 38:12-17), 702.b.46. "For in the Lookingglasse of his Gospell he maketh vs to beholde the secretes of heauen, so farre forth as is expedient for vs. Yea, I say so farre as is necessarie for vs: for it is not for vs to followe our owne foolish and inordinate lustes: but we must content ourselues with that which God openeth vnto vs, and not be curious in searching beyonde his worde." *Car il nous a fait contempler au miroir de son Evangile les secrets du ciel, tant qu'il nous estoit expedient. Or ie di entant qu'il nous estoit necessaire: car il n'est pas question de suivre nos appetits fols et desbordez: mais contentons nous de la revelation que Dieu nous donne (et ne soyons point curieux pour nous enquerir outre sa parole) contentons nous qu'il nous illumine par son sainct Esprit, afin que nous puissions iuger de ses oeuvres comme il appartient* [CO 35:388].

[183] 85 (Job 22:12-17), 398.b.59. *Dieu donc n'est point enclos au ciel: mais ce n'est pas sans causes toutes fois que l'Escriture en parle ainsi. Pourqoui? Il y a comme une marque de maiesté et de gloire telle au ciel, que quand nous eslevons là les yeux, il faut que nous soyons esmeus* [CO 34:294-295]. In an almost identical comment upon Isaiah 66:1 in his commentary on Isaiah, Calvin adds: "The Scripture often teaches that God is in heaven; not that he is shut up in it, but in order that we may rise our minds above the world, and may not entertain any low, or carnal, or earthly conceptions of him; for the mere sight of heaven ought to carry us higher and transport us into admiration." *Commentary on the Book of the Prophet Isaiah*, 409-410. (Isa. 66:1), in *Calvin's Commentaries*, vol. VIII (Grand Rapids, MI: Baker, 1979). *Saepe docet scriptura, Deum esse in coelo, non quod illic inclusus sit, sed ut mentes extra mundum evehamus, nec quidquam humile aut carnale aut terrenum de ipso cogitemus* [CO 37:436].

[184] *Ibid.*, 398.b.66. *...[mais] pource que nous ne sommes point touchez d'une telle reverence, quand nous aurons circui çà et là ici bas, comme quand nous regardons au ciel, pource que là il y a une marque et impression*

*de la gloire et de la maiesté de Dieu* [*CO* 34:295]. Calvin continues: "It is said that God dwelleth in the heaue[n]s, to the end we shuld know that it lieth not in our power to inclose him in this world, and to conceiue what he is (for we can neuer co[m]prehe[n]d him: our senses haue to smal a measure), but rather that we shuld lern to reuere[n]ce him with al humilitie." 399.a.11. *Il est dit, Dieu habite és cieux, afin que nous sachions que ce n'est point à nous de l'enclorre en ce monde pour concevoir quel il est (car nous ne le comprendrons iamais, nos sens ont une trop petite mesure) mais plustost que nous apprenions de l'adorer en toute humilité* [*CO* 34:295].

[185] 40 (Job 10:16-17), 188.a.49. *Ces iugements secrets de Dieu, lesquels l'homme ne peut comprendre... que cela outrepasse son sens et son esprit* [*CO* 35:501].

[186] 102 (Job 28:10-28), 480.b.21. "But if men come too the creation, it is so woonderfull a thing, as they muste needes be abashed, and reuerence the infinite wisedome of God, and confesse themselues vnable too comprehende it." *Mais si on vient à la creation, c'est une chose si admirable, qu'il faut que les hommes s'esbahissent, et qu'ils adorent la sagesse infinie de Dieu, et confessent qu'elle leur est incomprehensible* [*CO* 34:512]. Further references to God's incomprehensible power in creation occur at 148 (Job 148:4-11), 695.a.23, 68 [*CO* 35:367, 368]; and to the same power exhibited in the Sea, 697.a.64; 697.b.2 [*CO* 35:374]. Bouwsma engages in psychoanalysis of Calvin's relationship to the created order. "Calvin's anxiety..." he writes, "found radical expression in his ambivalence about the order of nature. He clung, at times with frantic tenacity, to the conception of a natural order that had traditionally helped human beings to feel comfortable in the world. But this conception was also antithetical to his deep sense of the incomprehensibility of God and the contingency of the world. There were... psychologically and culturally not one but (at least) two Calvins." William J. Bouwsma, *John Calvin: A Sixteenth Century Portrait*, 33. For an alternate view, see Susan Schreiner, *The Theater of His Glory* (Grand Rapids, Michigan: Baker Book House, 1991), 28-31.

[187] 70 (Job 19:13-16), 330.a.1. "Let vs not esteeme our life nor our welfare by that which we behold, and may bee discerned by eyesight, or by our mother witte: but let vs vndersta[n]d that God inte[n]deth to preserue vs by a meane which we are not able to comprehend." *N'estimons point donc nostre vie ne nostre salut par ce que nous voyons, et qui se peut iuger à l'oeil, ou de nos sens naturels: mais cognoissons que Dieu nous veut conserver d'un moyen qui nous est incomprehensible* [*CO* 34:109].

[188] 31 (Job 8:7-13), 142.b.30. "God hath wo[n]derfull meanes and inco[m]prehensible to vs, to augment that which seemeth to be very small: and notwithstanding that wee were as good as at deathes doore, so as it might seeme we should neuer bee plucked out of our miseries : yet shall God well finde some good way out of them." *Au contraire il est dit, que Dieu a des façons admirables, et qui ne nous sont point comprehensibles pour augmenter ce qui semble estre bien petit comme il est dit, Encores que nous*

*fussions comme pressez en la mort, qu'il ne semblast pas que nous deussions iamais estre retirez de nos miseres, que Dieu trouvera bien quelque bonne issue* [*CO* 33:384].

[189] 75 (Job 20:16-20), 354.b.43. *Or il ne faut pas que tous les iugemens de Dieu soyent estimez d'une mesme mesure. Et pourquoy? Comme i'ay dit, Dieu quelquefois fera des choses qui nous seront incomprehensibles* [*CO* 34:175-176].

[190] Hence, says Calvin, it teaches us to pray: "O my God, thy determinations are incomprehensible, and forasmuch as I am not able as now to know any more by reason of the rudenesse and infirmitie of my vnderstanding: I will wayte paciently till thou make mee to perceyue the cause why." 123 (Job 33:8-14), 579.b.16. *O mon Dieu, tes conseils sont incomprehensibles, i'attendray patiemment que tu me faces cognoistre pourquoy, quand ie ne puis pour le present cognoistre d'avantage pour ma rudesse, et l'infirmité de mon Esprit. Ainsi, Seigneur, apres que i'auray demeuré ici comme un povre aveugle, tu m'ouvriras les yeux, tu me feras sentir où ces choses tendent, quelle en doit estre l'issue, et i'y profiterai mieux qu'à present* [*CO* 35:56].

[191] See chapter 2, "The Incomprehensible Righteousness of God."

[192] Thus, in addition to the references given, see 39 (Job 10:7-15), 181.b.46 [*CO* 33:484].

[193] 40 (Job 10:16-17), 187.a.32. "Then let vs inure our selues to consider well Gods true and peculiar righteousnesse which is incomprehensible to vs, and let vs honour him in all his secrets, and let vs not conceiue the things that are in him, after our owne witte: for we see our owne smalnesse...Truely, for the condemning of our selues, wee neede not to climbe so high as to say, God hath a righteousnesse whiche cannot bee comprehended by creatures, and wherevnto mans witte cannot reach. Wee haue not too do with this for the condemning of oure selues: for the lawe will be ynough for that matter, as hath bin shewed already. As often then as a man shall be so proude as to thinke he can maintaine himselfe before God by his owne works, let him bethinke him selfe well, and looke vpon Gods lawe." *Exerçons nous donc à bien considerer la vraye iustice de Dieu, laquelle nous est incomprehensible, et que nous l'adorions en tous ses secrets: que nous ne concevions point ce qui est en luy selon nostre sens, car nous voyons nostre petitesse. Et en somme que nous faut-il faire? Il est vrai que pour nous condamner tous, il ne faut point que nous venions iusques là de dire, Dieu a une iustice, laquelle ne se comprend point par les creatures, et à laquelle le sens humain ne peut atteindre. Nous n'avons que faire de cela pour nous condamner, car la Loy nous suffira: comme desia il a esté demonstré. Toutes fois et quantes donc qu'un homme aura cest orgueil de cuider qu'il pourra estre maintenu devant Dieu en ses propres oeuvres: qu'il pense bien à sa vie, et qu'il regarde á la Loy de Dieu* [*CO* 33:498-499]. Cf. 88 (Job 23:1-7), 416.a.22. "There is always in him an incomprehensible rightfulnesse which it behoueth vs too honour though we perceyue it not." *Qu'il y a tousiors une iustice*

*incomprehensible en lui, laquelle il nous faut adorer, quand nous ne l'appercevons pas* [*CO* 34:342]. For Calvin's denial of absolute power, see especially references in 89 (Job 23:8-12), 417.a.50, 61 [*CO* 34:345-346]. I have examined this theme at length in chapter 2, "The Incomprehensible Righteousness of God."

[194] 146 (Job 37:14-24), 687.b.37. "Seeing then that Gods wisdome which of itselfe is incomprehensible too vs, protesteth that hir delight and pleasure is to dwell with vs, and to be familiar with vs: I pray you, haue we not cause to be of good cheere, and to be watchfull to take profite of the things that God sheweth vs, howbeit with such sobernesse and modestie, as wee may not couet to knowe ought but that which he teacheth vs, and to glorifie him, by yeelding him his deserued prayse?" *Quand donc la sagesse de Dieu (qui de soy nous est incomprehensible) proteste que ses delices et son plaisir est d'habiter avec nous, et de nous estre familiere: ie vous prie, n'avons-nous point occasion d'estre consolez en nous, et d'estre vigilans pour profiter en ce que Dieu nous monstre, voire avec une telle sobrieté et modestie, que nous n'appetions de savoir sinon ce qu'il nous enseigne, et de le glorifier pour luy rendre la louange qu'il merite?* [*CO* 35:347-348].

[195] 147 (Job 38:1-4), 691.b.57. The citation continues: "For although he had excellent gifts of grace: yet ought he always to haue humbled himself with acknowledgement of his infirmities, and also to haue brydled himself, sith he was wel neere out of his wittes, and wist not what to think of Gods judgements. And forasmuch as he felt himself at such an afterdeale, he should haue had an eye to the feblenesse of his own vnderstanding, and acknowledging himself to be a mortal man, he shuld haue said, Alas there is nothing but ignora[n]ce and folishnesse in mee. Herewithal he shuld also haue loked vp to the inestimable maiestie and inco[m]prehensible purpose of God: and that should haue meekened him." *D'autant qu'il avoit trop hastivement parlé de ce qui excedoit sa mesure: car combien qu'il eust des graces excellentes: si est-ce qu'il devoit tousiours s'humilier, cognoissant son infirmité: et se devoit aussi tenir en bride quand il estoit comme au bout de son sens, qu'il ne savoit que penser des iugemens de Dieu: et se sentant ainsi confus, il devoit regarder à la foiblesse de son esprit: et se cognoissant homme mortel il devoit dire, Helas! il n'y a qu'ignorance et sottise en moy. Cependant il devoit aussi regarder à la maiesté inestimable de Dieu, et à son conseil incomprehensible: cela le devoit rendre humble* [*CO* 35:359].

[196] 22 (Job 5:19-27), 100.a.28. *Comme il est dit qu'il n'a point seulement une issue pour nous delivrer de la mort, mais il a les issues qui nous sont incomprehensibles. Quand nous serons affligez d'un costé, Dieu nous fera sentir de l'autre qu'il nous assiste: quand nous serons enserrez, qu'il n'y aura nul moyen d'eschapper ce semble, Dieu en trouvera, voire à sa façon, c'est à dire par dessus le sens et opinion de la chair* [*CO* 33:274].

[197] 148 (Job 38:4-11), 697.b.25. *Que sera-ce de ses secrets incomprehensibles, de ses conseils estroits et cachez: quand il besongne, tant en general, qu'en particulier, d'une façon qui nous semble estrange, et qui sermonte*

*The Incomprehensibility of God* 221

*toute nostre capacité? Faut-il que là nous presumions de iuger à la volee, et d'en donner nostre arrest, comme si nous pouvions comprendre ce qu'il fait ainsi outre nostre sens, et apprehension? Il nous envoyera beaucoup d'adversitez, et beaucoup de maux: l'un perdra ses biens, l'autre sera affligé par maladie, l'autre sera en ignominie et opprobre, l'autre sera outragé, et batu. On pourroit estimer que Dieu est excessif, en traittant les hommes si rudement. Mais quoy? Si faut-il qu'en tout cela nous apprenions de confesser que Dieu est tousiours iuste, et qu'il sait la raison pourquoy il nous traitte ainsi: et qu'elle est bonne et iuste: combien qu'elle nous soit incognue. Que si nous ne cognoissons cela, si est ce, d'autant que nous sommes en sa main, que nous ne gaignerons rien pour tous nos murmures. Voyens-nous les meschans et iniques avoir la vogue en ce monde? Voyons nous les contempteurs de Dieu estre à leur aise? Les voyons-nous en credit et authorité, et estre comme maistres et seigneurs du monde? Voyons-nous qu'ils despitent Dieu iournellement, et toutes fois qu'ils ne soyent point punis du premier coup? Voyons-nous au contraire, qu'il nous faille endurer maintenant opprobre, maintenant fascherie, maintenant qu'on nous prenne par trahison: et que Dieu ne nous secoure point si tost que nous voudrions? Que nous attendions patiemment que Dieu nous delivre, comme il sait qu'il nous sera expedient. Et que cependant nous cognoissions, que si nous avons en admiration ce qu'il fait ici bas mesmes à nos personnes, et en ce que nous pouvons regarder comme à nos pieds: que par plus forte raison il faut bien que nous admirions, voire adorions ce conseil qui surmonte mesme la capacité des Anges. Et ainsi apprenons à estre addressez par ces choses basses, à magnifier et glorifier nostre Dieu: et cependant que nous serons en ce monde, que nous souffrions d'estre conduits et gouvernez par son sainct Esprit, afin qu'il dispose de nous à son bon plaisir* [CO 35:375-376].

[198] 157 (Job 42:1-5), 740.b.32. "What is the first point of teachablenesse? It is that we take hym for our master and obey him fully in any thing that he shall list to teach vs. For whe[n] a yong child comes first to schoole, if hee wyll needes choose his bookes after his owne liking, to say I will learne such a science, or I wil be taught such a thing or such a thing, before hee haue gone to his Abcee, so as hee will bee a great Doctor, before he haue the meane whereby to be taught, or become to the place where learning is to be had: I pray you is that as scholerlike modestie?" *Et la premiere docilité quelle est elle? C'est qu'il soit maistre, et qu'il soit obei pleinement en ce qu'il voudra nous enseigner. Car quand un enfant viendra à l'escole, et qu'il voudra choisir les livres à son appetit, pour dire, Ie veux savoir une telle science, ie veux estre enseigné en ceci et en cela, devant qu'il soit à l' A B C, s'il veut estre grand docteur devant qu'il soit venu au lieu et à l'endroit où il doit estre enseigné: ie vous prie, est-ce une modestie d'escolier, que cela?* [CO 35:486].

[199] "We should not curiously gad astray as we are wont to do. For we see that men are so ticklish as nothing can bee more: and when they speake of God, they dispute of him to no purpose or reason and without all modestie,

saying: yea, but how is this? And how is that? And when they reason of God, it seemeth they do not only speake of him as of theyr companion, but as of some one that were inferior vnto them. We see then such diuelish boldnesse in men, that they will enter into the deepest secrets of God, and they will turne vp all things, and leaue him nothing vnremoued. To be shorte, God must be as it were subiecte vnto them. See wherto we are now come. For this cause holy Scripture saith vnto vs, that God hath the darke cloudes as places to hide himselfe in. And whereto saith it so? It is to mocke at the phantasticalnesse that is in vs... Will we comprehend his secrets?... How shall we comprehende what God is?... For we cannot comprehende him... God then cannot be knowne of vs.... So then men of their selues cannot approche vnto God: but hee must approch vnto vs, and we must conceiue him to be suche as he doth offer himselfe by his word, contenting oureselues with that which is there conteined." 85 (Job 22:12-17), 400.a.66. *Sinon afin que nous ne soyons point exorbitans en nos curiositez, comme nous avons de costume? Car nous voyons les hommes estre si fretillans que rien plus: et quand on parle de Dieu, ils en disputent sans propos ne raison, et sans modestie aucune. Et voire, mais qu'est-ce ceci? Qu'est-ce cela? Et quand ils disputent de Dieu, il semble que non seulement ils en parlent comme de leur compagnon, mais de ie ne say quoy qui est inferieur à eux. Nous voyons donc ceste audace diabolique aux hommes, qu'ils veulent entrer aux plus profonds secrets de Dieu, ils veulent remuer tout, et ne lui rien laisser: bref il faudra que Dieu soit comme suiet à eux. Voila où nous en sommes. Pour ceste cause l'Escriture saincte nous dit, Que Dieu a les nuees obscures comme des cachettes. Et comment cela? C'est pour se mocquer d'une telle phantasie qui est en nous... Voulons nous comprendre tous ses secrets?... comprendrons-nous que c'est de Dieu?... car nous ne le pouvons pas comprendre... Dieu donc ne peut pas estre cognu de nous... Ainsi donc les hommes d'eux-mesmes ne peuvent approcher de Dieu: mais il faut qu'il approche de nous, et que nous le concevions tel qu'il se presente par sa parole, nous contentans de ce qui est là contenu* [CO 34:299-300].

[200] *Ibid.*, 26 (Job 9:23-28), 166.a.41. *Mais que nous adorions ses grands secrets qui surmontent toute nostre capacité, iusques à ce que nous puissions comprendre ce qui nous est caché auiourd'huy* [CO 33:445]. Cf. 82 (Job 21:22-34), 384.b.23. "Wee may then desire of God that he would shewe vs the cause of his workes: yea so farre foorth as it is expedient for vs: but we must also come with all humilitie, not taking vpon vs to make God subiect to our iudgement, to say, that he must disclose vnto vs in euery poynt wherefore he doth this or that. No: but let vs tarie paciently vntill he declare vnto vs, that which we know now but partly. And forasmuch as wee cannot atteyne to the full knowledge of Gods workes and to the causes of the same, vntil we be transformed into his image." *Nous pourrons bien donc demander à Dieu qu'il nous declare la raison de ses oeuvres: ouy, entant qu'il nous est expedient: mais il faut aussi que nous y aillions en toute humilité, ne presumans pas d'assuiettir Dieu à nostre sens, pour dire qu'il nous deschiffre*

*en tout et par tout pour-quoi il fait ceci ou cela. Nenni: mais attendons en patience iusques à ce qu'il nous declare ce qui nous est maintenant cognu seulement en partie. Et d'autant que nous ne pouvons point pleinement cognoistre ce que c'est des oeuvres de Dieu, et la raison d'icelles, iusques à ce que nous soyons transfigurez en son image* [*CO* 34:255-256]. Cf. "For asmuch then as wee see nowe but in parte, yea euen as it were in a glasse and darkely: lette vs wayte for the day wherein we shall see Gods glorie face to face, and then shall wee comprehende the thing that is hidden from vs as now." 30 (Job 8:1-6), 138.b.23 [*CO* 33:373]. For similar references, see 8 (2:16), 33.b.33 [*CO* 33:105]; 21 (Job 5:17-18), 97.b.3 [*CO* 33:267]; 23 (Job 9:1-6), 151.b.28 [*CO* 33:407]; 37 (Job 9:29-35), 171.b.14 [*CO* 33:459]; 123 (Job 33:8-14), 582.a.22 [*CO* 35:63]. Calvin is ambivalent on this theme. At one point, commenting on 1 John 3:2, he is insistent: "the perfection of glory will not be so great in us that our seeing will comprehend God totally, for the diversity of proportion (*longa distantia proportionis*) between us and Him will even then be very great." *The Gospel According to John, Part Two and The First Epistle of John*, trans. T. H. L. Parker, 267-268. (1 John 3:2). *Sed inde probat nos divinae gloriae fore participes, quia nisi spiritualis, et coelesti beataque immortalitate praedita esset natura, ad Deum nunquam tam prope accederet* [*CO* 55:331]. At another, he seems to hold out a greater illumination: "It becomes us too to be satisfied with apprehending the judgments of God only in some imperfect measure while we remain upon earth, and leaving him to defer the fuller discovery of them to the day of *complete* revelation." *Commentary on the Book of Psalms*, 3:483, in *Calvin's Commentaries* vol. V (Grand Rapids, MI: Baker, 1979). (Emphasis mine). (Psa. 91:8). *Adde quod sufficere nobis debet, si iudicia sua Deus ex maiori parte in diem plenae revelationis differens, aliquem nunc gustum praebeat* [*CO* 32:4]. See chapter 4, "Interpreting the Hand of God."

[201] 40 (Job 10:16-17), 188.b.56. *Mais c'est attendant le iour que le tout nous soit revelé* [*CO* 33:503]. Calvin continues (the context is the doctrine of election): "He could well giue vs the full and perfect light at this day: but he seeth it is not for our profite, and therefore hee giueth vs but a certaine portion, and he applieth (*s'accommode*) himselfe vnto vs. And therefore, let it not greeue vs too haue this knowledge of God as yet by measure, as it is giuen vs in the Scripture, and to wait till he haue bereft vs of this mortall body, and specially till he haue wholly refourmed our mindes that they maye bee no more wrapped in these wordlinesse, and earthlinesse, and specially in the sinfulnesse that proceedeth of the sinne of Adam." 189.a.57. *Il nous pourroit bien bailler une clarté entiere et parfaite auiourd'hui: mais il voit que cela ne nous est point utile: et pourtant il nous en donne quelque portion certaine, il s'accommode à nous. Et ainsi qu'il ne nous face point mal d'avoir maintenant par mesure ceste cognoissance de Dieu, comme elle nous est donnee en l'Escriture, attendans qu'il nous ait despouillez de ce corps mortel, qu'il ait mesmes du tout reformé nos ames, qu'elles ne soyent plus ainsi enveloppees de ce qui est de l'homme, et de la terre, et*

*mesmes de ce qu'il y a des vices procedans du peché d'Adam* [CO 33:504].

[202] In the "argument" that begins Calvin's commentary on Genesis, the Reformer urges his readers thus: "It becomes us to press towards this mark during our whole life, that (even in extreme old age) we shall not repent of the progress we have made, if only we have advanced ever so little in our course." *Commentary on Genesis*, 57-58. *Atque ad hunc scopum ita nos eniti tota vita convenit, ut nos (etiam in ultima senectute) profectus minime poeniteat, modo aliquantum simus a carceribus progressi* [CO 23:5-6].

[203] 50 (Job 13:11-15), 234.a.10. *Voila une apprehension vive quand une fois nous aurons entendu, Voila Dieu qui nous a creez, nous sommes à lui: et regardons haut et bas, il n'y a rien qui ne soit en sa main, il y a en lui une iustice admirable, il y a une sagesse qui nous est cachee, il y a une bonté incomparable. Quand nous aurons cognu toutes ces choses, il est impossible que nous ne noyons là comme estonnez, estans abbatus en nous-mesmes, pour nous abaisser du tout devant lui, et adorer sa hautesse qui est infinie. Ainsi donc apprenons de cognoistre mieux que c'est de Dieu, afin que nous soyons instruits à toute modestie et sobrieté: et cependant examinons aussi qui nous sommes. Quand nous voyons que nostre chair nous chatouille pour nous applaudir, que nous sommes enclins à nous flatter, que nous cerchons à nous complaire: que nous nous incitions nous-mesmes pour dire, Et d'où vient une telle faute? C'est que tu ne t'es pas encores cognu: regarde qui tu es, entre seulement là dedans, et que tu sois iuge de ta condition. Là nous trouverons qu'il y a un abysme de pechez en nous, que nous sommes enveloppez en tant d'ignorances que c'est un horreur: ce sont comme des tenebres si espesses qu'elles nous suffoquent du tout, et nous estranglent: tant s'en faut que nous ayons les yeux ouverts pour cognoistre Dieu, que ce qui est devant nostre nez nous ne le voyons pas. Quand donc les hommes auront ainsi pensé à eux, ô il est ceratin qu'alors ils seront touchez de la Maiesté de Dieu, tellement que sa craint tombera sur eux, au lieu qu'on les voyoit pleins d'orgueil, et qu'ils estoyent comme esgarez quand il estoit question de parler de Dieu, qu'il n'y avoit ne reverence ne modestie qui soit. Au lieu donc d'une temerité si grande et si estrange qu'on la voit au monde, on y trouvera une reverence de Dieu. Et pourquoi? Car (comme i'ai dit) quand nous concevrons que c'est de Dieu, nous serons abbatus sous lui* [CO 33:622-623].

# Chapter 4

# Interpreting the Hand of God: Calvin's Pastoral Understanding of Job

As yet, we know not what will be the event. But since it appears as though God would use your blood to sign His truth, there is nothing better than for you to prepare yourselves to that end, beseeching Him so to subdue you to His good pleasure, that nothing may hinder you from following whithersoever he shall call. For you know, my brothers, that it behoves us to be thus mortified, in order to be offered to Him in sacrifice (John Calvin, "Letter to the Five Prisoners of Lyons, 15 May 1553," *Selected Works of John Calvin: Tracts and Letters*, vol. 5, 405).

Wee see then, that if wee had our eyes open to beholde Gods prouidence, and the order of nature that is set afore vs: the same woulde serue too teache vs too put our whole trust in him (John Calvin, *Sermons On Job*, 144 [Job 37:1-6], 677.a.33). *Nous voyons donc, que si nous avions les yeux ouverts pour contempler la providence de Dieu, et l'ordre naturel qui nous est proposé, cela nous devroit servir d'instruction pour mettre pleinement nostre fiance en lui* [*CO* 35:320].

For it is not right for men unrestrainedly to search out things that the Lord has willed to be hid in himself, and to unfold from eternity itself the sublimest wisdom, which he would have us revere but not understand, that through this also he should fill us with wonder. He has set forth by his Word the secrets of his will that he decided to reveal to us. These he decided to reveal insofar as he foresaw that they would concern us and benefit us (*Institutes* III.xxi.1) [*CO* 2:680].

For Calvin, God is completely in charge of his world. His hand may be hidden, but his rule is absolute. "Nothing happened without his prouidence," Calvin remarks.[1] We have examined the nature of Calvin's doctrine of providence elsewhere; here, we are concerned with investigating the pastoral implications of this doctrine in the unfolding of Job's trial. For Calvin, theology is not a doctrine of the tongue but of life. It is not apprehended by the understanding and memory alone, as other disciplines are, but it is received only when it possesses the whole soul, and finds a seat and resting place in the inmost affection of the heart.[2]

In fact, Calvin finds multiple applications for his understanding of the doctrine of providence. He ranges over the entire scope of the Christian life as he unravels the story of Job's trial. One lesson, however, receives consistent emphasis: providence is essentially incomprehensible, and that, because God himself is incomprehensible to us. Just as we know God only in part, so we understand God's ways in part.

Whereas in the *Institutes* Calvin could concern himself with the profound issues of the relationship of divine providence and sin, Calvin's overriding concern in the sermons is that we "learn from,"[3] "profit from"[4] and "apply"[5] God's providence.[6] Sometimes, he compares man to beasts,[7] unable to discern the hand of God in all things. Consequently, it is possible to "misread" providence. Equally, Calvin insists that afflictions do no good unless God works in our hearts by the Holy Spirit.[8] That is why Job needed wisdom to discern the misplaced counsel that he received from his friends suggesting that his afflictions were judgements from God.[9] Calvin complains, at one point, that, "Iob turneth Gods prouidence quite vpside downe, and that in steade of co[m]forting and cheering himself therewith, he would fayne that God were farre of."[10] Similarly, he complains at Bildad's simplistic and mono-thematic interpretation of God's works of providence, insisting as he does that Job's suffering is a judgement from God.[11] A measure of discernment[12] is necessary, Calvin insists, in order to interpret God's providence correctly.

Whilst Calvin is consistently critical of the advice of Bildad, Eliphaz, and Zophar, he is generally supportive of the contribution of Elihu.[13] According to Susan Schreiner, "There are few people in the Bible Calvin admires more than Elihu."[14] Schreiner continues:

> Elihu understood the sinfulness of human nature, the impossibility of merit, the justice of all suffering, and the inability of any human being to plead against God.... Like Calvin, Elihu knew that God's will is the rule of justice. The verses about divine transcendence, so frequent in these chapters, prove that Elihu understood the infinite distance between God and humans and between divine and human justice. Elihu also understood

the inseparability of the divine attributes, a principle that allowed him to recognise that God's justice and power are inseparable from God's goodness. Because he understood the inseparability of the divine attributes, Calvin's Elihu rightly charged Job with wrongly accusing God of acting according to an absolute or tyrannical power.[15]

In particular, Elihu sees adversity as educative[16] rather than necessarily retributive. Adversity is often pedagogic, for "sometymes it is his will too trie the obedience of good men,"[17] Calvin observes, as he contemplates the nuances of Elihu's contribution.

In Sermon 140 (Job 36:6-14), drawing on Elihu's distinctive contribution, Calvin brings to the surface the various pedagogic inferences of suffering. Thus, affliction serves several ends: it is "the true schoolemistresse to bring men to repentance";[18] it weans us from dependence on the things of this world;[19] it provokes us to prayer.[20] Significantly, afflictions are the voice of God and a sign of his providence.[21] They are by God's appointment;[22] they are God's "archers,"[23] his artillery.[24] Afflictions are a part of God's "double means" whereby he humbles us (the other being his Word).[25] Yet, at the same time, they are "stirred up" by Satan.[26] Applications of this nature underline the importance of Elihu for Calvin. It forms the basis upon which Calvin understands the entire book of Job and the lessons that are to be learned throughout the book.

Thus, Calvin can draw a myriad of lessons from afflictions throughout these sermons. It is an interesting feature of Calvin's exegesis that he can draw positive lessons even from passages where the application to Job himself may be doubtful. One obvious example is the connection in the Book of Job between suffering and sin. Calvin is careful to relieve Job of the charges made by his friends, at least for a while; but he nevertheless finds general points of application even in these passages. Thus, in Sermon 3, after highlighting Job's godliness, Calvin can still make an application about the need for lifelong repentance.[27] In Sermon 19, Calvin draws attention to an insufficient repentance that may result from conviction of sins as a result of trials.[28]

Significantly, following the opening lines of the *Institutes*,[29] afflictions serve us in knowing God[30] and knowing ourselves.[31] Though Calvin accepts Job's innocence to a degree, he is not averse to the suggestion that our sins well deserve afflictions.[32] Thus, afflictions show us our sins[33] and cause us to flee in repentance.[34] But in the main, Calvin is concerned in Job to allude to other features of afflictions, lessons that emerge from the mysterious and unexplained occurrence of diverse providences. Hence, whilst afflictions are "blessed,"[35] "good,"[36] and for our "profit,"[37] we are not always "privie" to their purpose.[38] They therefore should humble us,[39] and cause us to be more reverent before God.[40] Afflictions also drive us to desire more of God's help,[41] provoking us to return to him,[42] by drawing us to him,[43] taming us,[44] and teaching us to pray.[45] Furthermore, Calvin insists that the afflictions of the godly last only for a time,[46] and that God afflicts the believer no more than he can bear.[47]

These are some of the lessons that Calvin would have us learn from the knowledge that God can "dispose of his creatures at his owne pleasure..."[48] In addition, Calvin adds that such providences are unavoidable.[49] They "light upon" everyone,[50] at God's "good pleasure."[51] None are too "insignificant" to avoid God's attention.[52] They are the voice of God. We can, therefore, learn as much from the trials of others as of ourselves.[53] Trials are periods of peculiar temptation that require God to "moderate our afflictions."[54] Not that everyone experiences equal measures of trial, for there are degrees of suffering;[55] not everyone is afflicted alike.[56]

Trials, then, are to be welcomed by God's children as a privilege.[57] There is a reason for suffering; providence is intelligent and purposive.[58] As we have already seen, the distribution of trials is not whimsical or arbitrary.[59] The purpose of the trial may be hidden to us, but not to God.[60] God has "another will which may be compared to a deep abyss."[61] In this respect, God's providences are essentially incomprehensible to us.[62] There are "secrete and incomprehe[n]sible iudgements."[63] There are "hygh mysteries,"[64] which are "aboue our ordinarie capacitie."[65] In our comprehension of certain providences, we ought to be content to limit ourselves to that which God has revealed about them.[66] The information necessary to decipher certain providences is withheld at God's behest.[67] Consequently, we ought not to fret about the means of our deliverances.[68] It is this perception—that a Fatherly hand guides our lives, even as the source of trials—that makes it possible for the believer to view all affliction as a joy, rather than a sorrow.[69] We are not to judge God harshly just because we fail to see the reason that lies behind certain providences.

## Providence and Sin

Whilst it is true that there is an aspect to providence that ever remains a mystery to us, Calvin would have us learn that some providences are meant to be clear in their instructive qualities. For example, in Sermon 5, Calvin, speaking in general terms and not necessarily here about Job, alludes to the "two purposes" that afflictions serve: firstly, to mortify visible sins; secondly, to bring to the surface those sins that are not immediately apparent.[70] Thus, providence ought to cultivate self-examination.[71] It facilitates the conviction of known sin,[72] and the drawing out of otherwise hidden vices within us.[73] This explains why, for Calvin, providence is to be praised. Providence is proof of God's interest in us. "And so," Calvin writes, "the greatest mishappe that can lyght vpon vs, is when God suffereth vs too welter in our owne wickednesse."[74] However, Calvin insists that blessing is not automatically derived from providence; some do not profit by affliction.[75] Some, despite the variety of providences, still reveal a scant knowledge of their sinfulness.[76] But others are deeply affected by a sight of their sins.[77] For Calvin, such conviction of God's wrath against our sins is the greatest of all afflictions.[78] There are "secret sinnes" that continue to lurk within the heart, which providence ought to bring to the surface that we might acknowledge them.[79] Dark providences, or trials, no matter how great their intensity, do not sanctify by any power inherent within them.[80] It is possible to disdain trials and thereby despise "the chastening hand" of God.[81] In this way, men are like anvils, "the beating vpon them is not able to chaunge their nature, for wee see how they beate backe the blowes again."[82] Thus, trials may "blind" us and make us incoherent.[83]

Trials are profitable only for those who are exercised to piety as a result of them. Unless the Holy Spirit works in us, trials will only harden and destroy.[84] This is the Holy Spirit's "second grace,"[85] which makes "his roddes and his corrections too auayle, and cause the holie Ghost too woork in such wyse in the hart, as a man may no more bee hardened too aduaunce himself against God, but may haue the care too think vpon his owne sinnes, and be rightly tamed and humbled."[86] Without this effectual work of the Spirit, men resist God's overtures in providence.[87]

## Subjection

All of this calls forth our submission to God's providence.[88] We have already noted Calvin's alluding to the two-fold aim of affliction in mortifying visible sins and bringing to the surface those sins that are not immediately apparent.[89] Calvin also speaks of two further aims of affliction: bringing the godly to obedience, whilst confirming the wicked in their unbelief.[90] God uses affliction to make the reprobate "vnexcusable."[91]

Calvin is fond of using the expression, we "play the horses that are broken looce" to convey the notion of an unwillingness to yield to God's rule.[92] We are to "honour" God's judgements and not fight against them even when they are incomprehensible to us.[93] Trials of this kind are meant to wean us from our dependence on all but God himself;[94] they serve the goal of consecration. Seeing trials as of divine origin ought to make us teachable. In a tone of seeming exasperation, Calvin observes the tendency to immodesty in his own students:

> And what is the first point of teachablenesse? It is that we take hym for our master and obey him fully in any thing that he shall list to teach vs. For whe a yong child comes first to schoole, if hee wyll needes choose his books after his owne liking, to say I will learn such a science, or I will be taught such or such a thing, before hee haue gone to his ABCee, so as hee will bee a great Doctor, before he haue the meane whereby to be taught, or be come to the place wher learning is to be had: I pray you is that a scholer-like modestie? But if a scholer that takes a ma[n] to teache him, ought to submit himself wholy to him: what ought we to do to god? What comparison is there in that case? So then let vs marke wel, that if we desire vnfeignedly too be taught of God, we wil not follow our own lusts, to say that he should show vs whatsoeuer wee haue conceiued in our owne head: but wee will hold vs contented with that which hee knoweth to bee for our welfare: and to discerne that it belongeth vnto hym.[95]

Thus, God's mysterious providence calls forth two things in particular: meekness and reverence.

## Meekness and Reverence

For Calvin, meekness is an essential quality of every Christian.[96] What is meekness? It is that teachable spirit that receives what God says to us.[97] Trials ought to cultivate sincerity and openness before God.[98] It is an expression of our reverence[99] and honor.[100] Thus, all religion is summarized by the fear of God.[101] The providences of God should make us "quake."[102] Understanding Job as a model,[103] Calvin differentiates godly fear from servile fear.[104] Godly fear, Calvin suggests, is a response to the goodness of God as much as it is to his majesty.[105] Fear and awe is the response of the soul to God's omniscience,[106] steadfastness,[107] and power.[108] Does this mean that we ought never to be afraid of God? No for Calvin, such would border on presumption. The judgments of God are meant to make those afraid who have cause to be afraid.[109] Such godly fear explains Job's initial response to the trial.[110] The judgments of God should provoke in the godly a similar response.[111] Contemplation of providence ought to induce a sympathy towards others in adversity.[112] Such fear involves having a right understanding of God and his works, a mind and heart that are not given over to speculation.[113] Godly fear reveres Scripture and desires to profit from it.[114] Such godly fear in response to God's providences ought, writes Calvin, to "shut our mouths,"[115] cause us to renounce ourselves,[116] prevent us from presumption,[117] "over-boldness" and "vanitie,"[118] and result in true joy, "the true marke whereby to discerne Gods flocke from all the wilde beastes that raunge abroad."[119] Adversity, in particular, is suited to the cultivation of the fear of God since it underlines our frailty and insecurity apart from God's fatherly hand upon us.[120] Nor is this godly fear known by any, save those who are in Christ.[121]

Thus, it becomes clear that, for Calvin, man's chief end is to render homage to God, and this through adversity as well as blessing. The most important lesson that we can learn is to glorify God in every providence.[122]

**Patience**
Another consequence of the sometimes dark and mysterious providences of God is to teach us patience. We are called to be patient in our adversities.[123] Without it, no service can please God.[124] In Sermon 7, Calvin gives an interesting definition of patience. Insisting that it does not mean insensitivity to pain, he goes on to amplify it in this way: "…when they can moderate themselues, and hold suche a measure, as they cease not to glorifye God in the middest of all their miseries."[125] Calvin accepts that Job was a patient man, but cautions on the misuse of James' commendation.[126] Job was deeply troubled

by his "passions" during the course of his trial, thereby causing him at times to become impatient.[127] Impatience is more than a dislike of adversity; it is a passionate and willful opposition.[128] Impatience manifests itself in striving against God and finding fault with him,[129] in making ourselves "equal" with God.[130] Citing Elihu favourably, Calvin insists that impatience gains us nothing,[131] and that those who exercise it are "stark fooles."[132] Furthermore, unrepented impatience will add to the rigor of our final judgment![133]

Trials are intended, then, to induce patience.[134] When all we have are the promises of God, and providence seems to call them into question, trials call forth our trust in the sovereignty of God.[135] Again, Calvin takes an opportunity to introduce the idea of God's incomprehensibility. It belongs to the nature of providence, as ultimately incomprehensible to our finite brains, that we cannot possibly expect to unravel all its details so as to satisfy our curiosity. It follows that we are called upon to believe in God's goodness to us in our hearts.[136] The measure of God's goodness is not always immediately apparent; we are to judge by faith and not by sight, trusting in the promises of God.[137] And Calvin is eager to underline that if Job fell into mistrust, how much more are we likely to do the same?[138] There is the ever-present danger of "weak faith."[139] Adversity often encourages us to grow in faith, leaning more and more upon God and not ourselves.[140] In this way, God tests each one differently.[141] Some, who know greater degrees of the Holy Spirit's enablement, can expect to be tested all the more.[142]

### Joy

Providence may also teach us about joy, or contentment. There is an "inordinate" joy, which we ought to avoid.[143] Commenting upon Zophar's words in Job 20:1-7, Calvin outlines the contrasting views that believers and unbelievers have towards material prosperity. Drawing from Philippians 4:14, Calvin relates why believers know how to have "abundance" even in scarcity. "Thus," he concludes, "the mirth of Gods childre[n] differeth greatly from the mirth of the vnbeleeuers and worldings."[144] And why is this so? Because, Calvin explains, unbelievers "reioyce in the things that they hold in hand...," whereas believers are led to "the acknowledging of Gods goodnesse in that he hath made them feele him more than a father towardes them."[145]

## Prayer

It is hardly surprising that Calvin makes mention of prayer several times in the Joban sermons. Job's cries are, after all, cries to God. Trials force us to cry unto God.[146] Prayer, then, is an expression of our utter dependence upon God: it is a corollary of providence.[147] Prayer is also expressive of our communion and "closeness" to God, a response to the revelation of Fatherly goodness to us.[148] Thus, for Calvin, the Christian life *is* prayer; it is the greatest privilege we know.[149] Prayer thus expresses the (subjective) act of believing *and* the (objective) focus of what we believe. It is an expression of our belief in God's sovereignty. The *need* for prayer is our frailty; our tendency to collapse under pressure thus calls from us a cry for help from God.[150] In this way, adversity encourages prayer when, perhaps, prayer has become neglected. Interestingly, Calvin reiterates in the Joban sermons something that he made explicit in the final edition of the *Institutes*: that prayer be made according to the tenor of the covenant of grace.[151] The *pactum* of his ordained will[152] provides the limitations of allowable prayer. Thus Calvin can insist "That wee request nothing which is not agreeable to his will."[153] In this way, Calvin links prayer with God's promises.[154] Thus Calvin is scathing on those who subject God to their own demands whatever they may be.[155]

As to the manner of prayer, Calvin again insists upon sincerity. "Let vs rather lay open our hartes before God ... so as we haue nothing wrapped vp in them."[156] Prayer is thus part of a spiritual battle, one in which we need the assistance of the Holy Spirit to enable us to persevere in prayer[157] and to keep us from stumbling.[158] In this way, prayer is a microcosm of the Christian life. In the same way that we struggle with adversity in life, so we struggle with it in prayer. What seems to be "unanswered" prayer calls forth from us both patience[159] and perseverance.[160] In this way, prayer is a means of grace in adversity.

## Self-denial

Trials, the onset of dark providences, may bring out the worst in us. They manipulate the affections in a way that is inappropriate. Our affections, therefore, need to be tamed.[161] According to Calvin, the godly must respond to providence by learning self-denial.[162] The proper response to cross-bearing is a true repentance.[163] In the person of

Job, then, we have both a positive and a negative model: positive, in that Job appears to Calvin again and again to be a model of the pious life; but negative, too, in that Job's excessive "passions" sometimes get the better of him.[164] There is a need for us to learn to put "both feet upon our affections" lest we be guilty of an intemperate response to providence.[165] Our affections blind us;[166] they rob us of our understanding;[167] they make us ungovernable.[168] A due sense of God's majesty and greatness should encourage us to temper our response.[169] Calvin calls on us to "mistrust" our affections,[170] even to repress them.[171] We are to learn to mistrust ourselves.[172] In an illuminating pastoral insight, Calvin remarks: "if he giue his excessiue passions head, the same must needes rebounde backe vpon himselfe or agaynst himselfe."[173] In this way, Calvin treats Job's lapses into melancholy as expressions of "the passions of the fleshe."[174]

**The Spiritual Battle**
The Joban sermons provide Calvin with an opportunity to speak with great clarity as to the nature of providence, which believers like Job can expect in this world. Thus, God may treat us "roughly," as certain physicians might in order to cure us from some ill.[175] It may appear as though God picks us up and throws us down again.[176] God may "dispose of his creatures at his owne pleasure ..."[177] Though Calvin is careful not to suggest that Job is being punished for his sins, thereby falling into the trap of his counsellors who seem only to possess an "instant retribution" theology of suffering, he does, nevertheless, allow for general comments about chastisement throughout the sermons. Such chastisement is painful.[178] His wrath kindles our sins like tinder wood.[179] God need but raise his hand and we would all perish.[180] That is why providence ought to teach us to be humble before God, recognising that apart from his grace and mercy we would all know greater affliction than we do.[181] We shall examine elsewhere the degree to which Calvin maintains Job's innocence.

God may make us feel his displeasure as he did in the case of Hezekiah (2 Kings 20:1-11; 2 Chron. 32:24-26; Isa. 38:1-22),[182] but the affliction we receive is never more than we are able to bear.[183] God sustains us even if we do not comprehend his working.[184] God does not cease to love us even when he afflicts.[185] In the midst of affliction, he makes us taste his goodness.[186]

Painful experiences of providence have a bearing on our relationship to others, Calvin suggests. We may learn to profit from affliction in learning sensitivity to others who likewise experience trials.[187] In this way, providence cultivates our experience of the communion of saints.[188]

We have already noticed that prayer is a microcosm of the Christian life, reflecting in its struggle the difficulties encountered with providence. Calvin elaborates in many of the Joban sermons on the nature of this struggle: that the Christian life is meant to be a fight all the way. As we shall see later, this is in harmony with Calvin's overall portrayal of the Christian life, particularly in his exegesis of Romans 6–8. In the Joban sermons Calvin faces this issue head on. Sensitive to Job's great loss, the emotional, psychological trauma he experienced and, in addition, his physical sickness, Calvin insists that none of these is equal in intensity to the spiritual struggle within Job's soul.[189] Prayer, then, prepares us for this battle.[190] The nature of the Christian life is a race requiring us to persevere with all diligence.[191] Calvin emphasises the imagery of pilgrimage and conflict, the holy war in which the believer is inevitably engaged. In a remarkable passage in Sermon 66, Calvin muses on the possibility of a quietist view of the Christian life:

> Were we as it were in a faire medow, that we might runne along the riuers side in the shadowe, and that there might be nothing but pleasure and joy in al our whole life: who could vaunt that he had serued God with good affection? But when God sendeth vs things cleane contrarie to our desire, and that we must be fayne one whyle to enter into a quaqmyre, another whyle to marche vpon rugged stones, and anotherwyle too be combered with bryers and thornes: whe[n] we must be fayne to meete with hedges and diches and to leape ouer them, and when we shall haue traueled a greate whyle, it shall still seeme that we haue gone verie little or nothing foreward, and yet we see no end of our journey: behold, it is a troublesome temptation to vs that couet to walk according to Gods wil. And whyso? Bycause we haue not vtterly renou[n]ced our selues. He hath not yet lerned to tame his affections, and to subdue his will to the seruing of God, notwithsta[n]ding that it be hard for him to doo: knoweth not yet in good earnest what it is to liue well and faythfully. So the[n] let vs practize that which is spoken here of holding on our wayes, that is to say, of knowing that if we be desirouse to rule our life according to Gods lawe, the way is verie difficult, and it wil not be doone without many lets and hinderances: and yet we must be firme and constant to hold on our way still....[192]

For Calvin, Job is proof that the experience of strife and opposition is not indicative of some spiritual malfunction or the lack of faith; suffering is to be expected, opposition is normative. We ought to "prepare ourselues too battaile."[193]

The conflict is internal and subjective as well as external and objective. Internally, Satan knows the sin that lies within our hearts. He makes full use of it.[194] Thus in the Joban sermons, Calvin sees affliction as a means of enabling mortification.[195] Satan does not understand that as believers we are no longer in bondage to the flesh or to him.[196] But, since Job's suffering is not directly related to any indwelling sin as such[197]—Calvin's acceptance of Job's "good case"— the focus of opposition in Job is not so much the world or the remaining corruption within Job's heart; the opposition is primarily the result of Satanic intrusion. Satan seeks, comments Calvin in the *Institutes*, "to drive the saint to madness by despair."[198] Though Calvin insists that Satan is ultimately powerless,[199] what power he has, he has by virtue of God's decree[200] and permission.[201] The "devils are God's hangmen."[202] Satan is the destroyer,[203] the hinderer,[204] the devourer,[205] and the seducer.[206] With his wiles[207] he accuses,[208] he tempts,[209] he deceives—convincing us that he is our friend and ally and that God is our real enemy;[210] but it is the Devil who is our real enemy.[211] He may even drive us to despair.[212] Without God's continual supervision, Satan would overpower and destroy us.[213] But in all this, God overrules Satan's activity for our good, using the bitterness of the providence as medicine for the cure of our souls.[214] In some, God permits Satan to wreak greater havoc than in others.[215] And in some, God allows Satan to do his worst, thus reminding us that, apart from God's grace, we are altogether without hope.[216]

The conflict in which we are engaged bears also an external nature: it is a consequence of the fact that we live *in the world*. Believers are called upon to wrestle against the inevitable tensions and conflicts that result from our union with Christ,[217] on the one hand, and our life in this world, on the other.[218]

## Service

It is against such opposition we are called upon to live out our Christian lives. Nowhere is this call to Christian piety defined more succinctly than in Sermon 66:

Lo what the lyfe of the faythfull is in effect: that is to wit, that they shall neuer bee without manye temptations: and specially that we be subiect to so many miseries during the tyme that we be in this earthly wayfaring, that such as indeuer too serue God best, ceasse not to be often ouerpressed with many inconueniences, and manye afflictions. But what for that? Whe[n] we be astonished, (as it cannot be but wee must think it straunge at the first brunt) let vs fight against such temptations, and let vs holde on in the right way without starting out of it. And although we fine much hardnesse in ourselues, let vs pray God to giue vs such an inuincible strength, as we may continue in his seruice euen to the end, nowithstanding that Satan labour too thrust vs out of it.[219]

Continuing "in his service" was something Calvin desired to preach to his congregation in Geneva. Though they were surrounded by many difficulties, beyond the city there were friends in greater distress and need. Calvin sought to encourage his listeners against the malaise of despair and dysfunctionalism. God orders his rule in such a way as to encourage new areas of service for us to perform.

For Calvin, God's providential ordering of trials is also a means of cultivating and encouraging usefulness in the kingdom. In the very opening sermon on Job, Calvin sees in the patriarch a model of pious service rendered to God.[220] In that sense, Job exemplifies the role for which we were created.[221] Every detail of God's self-revelation to us is in order that we might know him and serve him better.[222] And our chief service? It is to praise God in every circumstance.[223]

**Wisdom**
For such accomplishments, there will be the need for wisdom to respond in such a way as will glorify God. Such wisdom is a gift of God.[224] As we have already noted, this concern is reflected in Calvin's opening statement in the 1559 edition of the *Institutes*, "Nearly all the wisdom we possess, that is to say, true and sound wisdom, consists of two parts: the knowledge of God and of ourselves."[225] Afflictions are, then, God's providential manner of making us wise by a reverent and submissive response.[226] We have need to pray that we might profit wisely from providence.[227] And what is this wisdom that ought to mark us? Submission to God's ways and thoughts.[228] In Sermon 103, Calvin devotes an entire sermon to wisdom, in which he begins by pointing out man's dependence upon God's revelation for wisdom. Without it, men "become brutish" and lack modesty, seeking to know

what is unknowable to them.[229] Men pry into "God's secrets" with no sense of humility.[230] There are boundaries over which we dare not pass, limits set by God that should keep us in subjection to God.[231] It is our wisdom, then, "to fear God."[232] The fear of God is the "chiefe poynt."[233] This leads us once more to our contention that integral to Calvin's understanding of Job is the concept of God's incomprehensibility. True wisdom is an acknowledgement that we know God only insofar as he has been pleased to reveal himself to us. To go beyond that is idle speculation and dangerous impiety.[234] It is to be overbold,[235] and it is "madde presumptuousnesse."[236]

Providence teaches us that we must accept a thing as from God, whatever that may be.[237] It beckons us to be teachable[238] and reverent before God.[239] Referring to the doctrine of election as one of God's "secrets," Calvin calls "wretched dogge[s]" those who think they can pry into the reason for God's choosing.[240] God's wisdom far exceeds our own capacity to comprehend it.[241] Incomprehensibility lies at the very heart of the gospel itself, and God's providence facilitates our appreciation of this mystery.[242] Once again, Calvin's pastoral interpretation of Job leads him to God's incomprehensibility. We may not know the cause of affliction, or for that matter, its purpose and aim; but we are to understand that whatever its nature, it is just.[243] As we have seen already, this calls forth patience on our part. God's judgments are often incomprehensible,[244] and we are too often "dullheaded."[245] Calvin urges that we do not rush into an interpretation of any event, particularly a dark providence, for God can change the situation before we know it.[246] They are "aboue our ordinarie capacitie."[247] Nor is this incomprehensibility something that time will erase, as though God's providence may be fully understood so long as we wait long enough.[248] Even when God is "fayne to play the schoolemaister,"[249] we often fail to profit. We ought, in such circumstances, to "bethinke vs of Gods maiestie which is incomprehensible, so as wee may be mooued to honour him, and to submit our selues vnto him as we ought to doe."[250] Thus, in the opening sermon, Calvin has recourse to incomprehensibility, urging his listeners that we must oftentimes wait patiently[251] before the cause of the trial be made known to us.[252] We are to be content with that which God has been pleased to reveal to us regarding our plight, and not speculate into things that cannot be known.[253] We must refrain from bringing God down to us, but rather, we ought to lift up our minds towards him.[254] We may find ourselves at death's door, with no means of escape known to us; but God may find some avenue for our escape incomprehensible to us.[255] We are to trust the wisdom of God's ways even when we cannot fully, or even partly, discern it.[256]

Incomprehensibility applies to redemptive and soteriological issues as much as it does to God's providence.[257] And this, because whilst God is not incomprehensible to himself,[258] he is incomprehensible to us.[259] This should call forth our deepest reverence.[260] Calvin argues at one point in the Joban sermons that fundamental errors over the nature of sin, faith and justification arise due to a lack of appreciation for God's incomprehensible majesty.[261] "The least offence that wee committe, trespasseth againste the maiestie of God."[262]

God's incomprehensibility should "shut our mouths."[263] In fact, for Calvin the Joban sermons appear to reflect the quintessential nature of the Christian life: living with incomprehensibility. In a moving passage in Sermon 78, Calvin writes:

> Gods woorks out passe our vnderstanding, so as we know not why he disposeth the things so which wee see: what is too bee doone? Wee must lay our hand vppon our mouth, that is too say, wee must not be so bold as too prattle of them. Wherefore let vs lerne to knowe our owne abilitie, that we fling not our selues astray ouer all the feelds: but rather follow always the right way. For the dooing hereof, wee neede to knowe no more but what is giuen vs: according also as Sainct Paule bringeth vs to the same rule, namely, to knowe no more than God leadeth vs vnto. So long as he reacheth vs his hand, let vs go boldly: but when he leadeth vs no further, we must stop there, and be as dumbe. True it is that we must alwayes haue our mouth open after one sorte: that is, to glorifie God. But when we presume too bring him vnder the compasse of our vnderstanding, and would haue him to reserue nothing too himself: whither go we then? Is it not an open despising of God? He intendeth to hyde the thing from vs. And why? Too the intent wee should knowe our owne ignorance, and yet not ceasse to acknowledge him to be rightuouse, and to honour his woonderfull and incomprehensible ordinance... But if God hyde the reason of his woorks from vs, and that it bee to hygh for vs to reach vnto: Let vs shet our mouth, that is to say, let vs not be talkatyue to babble after our owne fancie: but let vs glorifie God, and not be ashamed to be ignorant. For the verye wisdome of the faythfull is to knowe no more than it hath pleased God to shewe them. Therfore let vs make silence vntoo God after what sort so euer he work, till the last day of discouerie be come, when we shall see him face to face in his glorie and maiestie.[264]

In Sermon 138, Calvin devotes the entire message to God's incomprehensibility. It is an intolerable pride to suggest that we can know God to a greater depth than he has been pleased to allow.[265]

**Eschatological Lessons**

Calvin interjects an eschatological lesson from afflictions in the Sermons on Job.[266] We may not be able to perceive any value whatsoever in our present trials; but that is to lack a vision for what God may intend to do in the future. The afflicted are to recall that in the world to come, there will be no pain.[267] Afflictions can make us long for heaven. In contrast to the rest of creation, Calvin suggests, man has no excuse but to recognise that "this lyfe is but a wayfaring."[268] But, that is not to suggest that we disdain life here and now; it, too, is a gift of God and afflictions only prove God's interest and love for us as he prepares us for the world to come.[269] In a moving passage, Calvin comments:

> Truly in winter time the trees seeme to be dead, we see how the raine doth as it were rotte them, they are so swolne that they bee readie to burst, and thus ye see well one kynde of rottennesse: Afterwarde commeth the frost, as it were to seare them, and to drie them vp. We see all these thynges, and wee see not so muche as one floure: and thys is a cutting vs off. Beholde heere a kynde of death, which lasteth not for a daye or twayne, but for foure or fiue monethes. Neuerthelesse although the life of the trees be vnseene: yet is their sap in their roote, and in the hart of the wood. Euen so is it with vs, that our life also is hidden, howbeit not in our selues. For that were a poore kinde of hiding. There should neede no great frost to sterue it vp, nor greate wet to marre it. For we carrie fire and frost ynough in our selues to consume it. But our life is hidden in God, he is the keeper of it and wee knowe that Iesus Chist (sic) is the partie from out of whome we drawe all our life.[270]

Calvin thus urges his listeners to see a medicinal aspect to God's providence;[271] we are to ask: to what end does this providence aim?[272]

One such end is the contemplation of,[273] and preparation for, death[274] and the eventual certainty of death.[275] Providences, particularly dark providences, provoke us to consider the possibility of death.[276] Death should not take us by surprise.[277] Life is at best uncertain,[278] and even the memories of the great ones fade after a time.[279] Providence forces us to consider that death is nearer than we care to think.[280] The very thought of it should humble us[281] and make us sombre[282] and not drive us to melancholy as it does some.[283] Referring to Bildad's phrase, that death is "the King of terrors" (Job 18:14), Calvin remarks, "The wicked are threatened to be driuen into such a terrible and exessiue feare, that all the feares in the worlde which the godly do conceyue, are nothing to it."[284] Commenting upon one of Job's mournful laments, wishing that he had not been born, Calvin observes the lawfulness of desiring death.[285] Mary Potter Engel has drawn attention to the vertical dimension of eschatology in Calvin, as well as the horizontal.[286] In a dramatic way, Calvin says,

> Although this life bee full of much wretchednesse, and is as it were a Sea of all miseries: yet must we set store by it, bycause God hath set vs in it, and preserueth vs in it, to the intent we should knowe him to bee our Creator and father, according as indede the end why we were created, and why we be mainteyned in this transitorie life: is that we should know how it is God that interteyneth vs here, and that we should feele his fatherly goodnesse, in that it pleaseth him to haue a care of vs and to gouerne vs. So then our life ought to be deare vnto vs in that respect.[287]

Another lesson that emerges from the persistence of trials is the value of looking to Christ and gaining help from him.

> The miseries that are in our nature, are as it were a maze: and yet for all that, if wee holde our selues by our Lorde Iesus Christ, who is the band betweene God and vs, and looke vpon him as the partie that knitteth vs too God his father: There shall be nothing to hinder vs that we shoulde not bee alwayes merie.[288]

An interesting question emerges from Calvin's treatment of God's incomprehensibility in the Joban sermons. Given that we are incapable of discerning particular providences here and now, will this always be so? Will we know the pedagogic reason behind a certain providence in, say, the world to come? On several occasions Calvin seems to imply that we will, and this despite his insistence that incomprehensibility is a derivative of our *human* (and thus, created) nature. For example, in Sermon 30, Calvin cites 1 Corinthians 13:9-12 to justify his claim that in the eschaton, "then shall wee comprehende the thing that is hidden from vs as now."[289] Similarly, in Sermon 40, Calvin affirms that a day will come when the fullness of God's revelation will be ours.[290]

## Knowing God through adversity

As Calvin alludes to these many pedagogic lessons of adversity, one appears to emerge again and again: that through adversity, we come to know God better. Through adversity, we grow in our understanding and appreciation of God, expanding from a knowledge of God as Creator to a knowledge of God's justice,[291] goodness,[292] greatness,[293] righteousness[294] and love.[295] Of particular interest is the way Calvin draws attention to God's "fatherly" love in the midst of trials.[296] In particular, adversity enables us to appreciate the immensity and mystery of God; that he is beyond our grasp, hidden from us, and in many ways incomprehensible to us.[297] "It behoueth vs to humble ourselues," says Calvin, "and to wayte till the day come that we may better conceyue Gods secretes which are incomprehensible to vs at this day."[298]

We know him only "in parte."[299] God often appears as though he hides his face from us.[300] Early in the exposition of Job, Calvin is drawn to the conclusion that "there is nothing better than to submit all things to Gods maiestie."[301] It is of a piece with Calvin's claim that a lack of submission is the underlying cause of irreligion and error. Commenting on Jeremiah's denunciations of idolatry in Jeremiah 7:21-24, Calvin makes the trenchant observation that "the basis of true religion is obedience."[302] Similarly, Calvin begins a sermon on Job 13, reminding his hearers of the previous sermon, the essence of which was that "the Scripture sheweth vs many things which our vnderstanding cannot brooke."[303] Continuing in the same sermon, Calvin reminds them that God is of "another maner of one than they haue imagined him to bee: for they haue not had an eye to the infinite glorie that is in him."[304] We do not have the mental capacity to grasp God adequately: God's judgements are "too deepe a dungeon for vs to go downe intoo."[305] In summary, therefore, Calvin urges: "wee must know the incomprehensible maiestie of God."[306]

*Interpreting the Hand of God...* 243

## References

[1] 5 (Job 1:9-12), 23.b.14. *Que rien n'estoit advenu sans sa providence* [*CO* 33:79]. For a comprehensive treatment of Calvin's doctrine of providence, see H. Strohl, "La Pensée de Calvin sur la Providence divine," *Revue d'Histoire et de Philosophie religieuses* 22 (1942), 154-169.

[2] *Non enim linguae est doctrina, sed vitae; nec intellectu memoriaque duntaxat apprehenditur, ut reliquae disciplinae, sed tum recipitur demum ubi animam totam possidet, sedemque et receptaculum invenit in intimo cordis affectu. Institutes* III.vi.4 [*CO* 2:504]. Cf. II.ii.36. See Ronald Wallace, *Calvin, Geneva and the Reformation*, (Edinburgh: Scottish Academic Press, 1988,1990), 233-235.

[3] See e.g., 3 (Job 1:5), 12.a.57 [*CO* 33:51]; 17 (Job 4:20-5:12), 78.b.38 [*CO* 33:219]; 19 (Job 5:8-10), 84.b.25. *Iamais nous ne serons instruits à vraye humilité...* [*CO* 33:235]; 29 (Job 7:16-21), 136.b.47. *apprenions* [*CO* 33:369]; "There needeth no great lerning nor skill too vnderstand what is sayd heere." 39 (Job 10:7-15), 183.a.15. *Il ne faut point avoir ne lettres ne grand savoir pour comprendre ce qui est ici dit* [*CO* 33:488].

[4] See e.g., "Therefore let vs beare this doctrine well in minde, considering that it is so muche for our profite: and furthermore aboue all, let vs aduise oure selues too practise it at oure neede." 20 (Job 5:11-16), 88.b.66. *Or donc retenons bien ceste doctrine, veu qu'elle nous est si utile: et au reste advisons sur tout de la pratiquer au besoin* [*CO* 33:246]; 20 (Job 5:11-16), 89.b.30 [*CO* 33:248]; 22 (Job 5:19-27), 101.a.59. *"bien utile."* [*CO* 33:277]. Some, clearly, do *not* profit from God's providence: "Wee see then before our eyes, that many men are the more vnhappie for being chastized at Gods hand, bycause they profit not in his schoole, nor yet take any good by his corrections." 21 (Job 5:17-18), 95.a.29. *Nous voyons donc à l'oeil comme beaucoup de gens sont d'autant plus malheureux d'estre chastiez de Dieu, pource qu'ils ne profitent point en son escole, ils ne font point leur profit de ses verges...* [*CO* 33:262]. Cf. Calvin's comment in his sermon on 2 Timothy 3:16-17, "Therefore if we be diligent to read Holy Scripture, we shall perceiue there is nothing couched in it, but is good and fit for vs, and whereof we may reap some commoditie *Quand donc nous serons diligens à lire l'Escriture saincte, nous sçaurons que Dieu n'a rien la couché que ne nous soit bon et propre, et dont nous ne recueillions quelque usage* [*CO* 54:285].

[5] 33 (Job 9:1-6), 152.a.40. *appliquions* [*CO* 33:408].

[6] Examples in the *Institutes* where Calvin deals with the relationship of providence and sin are numerous, including: I.xvi.8ff [*CO* 2:151-152]; I.xvii.1ff [*CO* 2:153-154]; 1.xviii.1ff.[*CO* 2:167-168]. Also II.iii.5 [*CO* 2:213-14]; II.iv.1ff [*CO* 2:224-225]; II.v.1ff [*CO* 2:229-230]; III.xxiii.4ff [*CO* 2:701-703], and especially III.xxiii.7 [*CO* 2:704-705]; III.xxiv.12ff [*CO* 2:229-230]. On Calvin's use of Job as an "example," see M. H. Woudstra, "The Use of 'Example' in Calvin's Sermons on Job," in *Bezield Verband*, ed. by J. Bouma, et al.(Kampen: Uitgeverij Van den Berg, 1964), 344-51.

[7] See e.g., 40 (Job 10:16-17), 189.a.16 [*CO* 33:503]; 112 (Job 31:5-8), 529.a.36

[*CO* 34:645]. Calvin even compares childhood this way, suggesting that "our childhod is such, that they which are in it, differ little or nothing from brute beastes (*les bestes brutes*), 17 (Job 4:20-5:2), 75.b.21 [*CO* 33:211]. Elsewhere, he adds, "Though beasts are destitute of reason and understanding, still they are capable of being taught; to such an extent, at least, as to recognise those who feed them... Nor ought we to wonder at this; for beasts frequently observe the order of nature more correctly, and display greater kindness, than men themselves." *Commentary on the Book of the Prophet Isaiah*, 1:41, in *Calvin's Commentaries*, vol. VII (Grand Rapids, MI: Baker Books, 1979). *Illae enim quamvis mente et ratione careant, sunt tamen dociles: ea saltem parte, quod agnoscunt eos a quibus pascuntur... Nec profecto mirum: saepe enim bestiae naturae ordinem melius sequuntur, et plus humanitatis prae se ferunt quam homines ipsi* [*CO* 36:30]. Cf. the comment on Job 32:7-8, "True it is, that generally God hath made vs all reasonable Creatures (*creatures raisonnables*): and that is the thing wherein we differ from the brute beastes." 120 (Job 32:4-10), 566.b.15 [*CO* 35:22].

[8] "For it is not ynough for God too stryke vs with his hand, except he touche vs within also by his holie spirit." 21 (Job 5:17-18), 94.b.36. *Car ce n'est point assez que Dieu frappe de sa main, sinon qu'il nous touche là dedans par son sainct Esprit...* [*CO* 33:260].

[9] See, e.g., 34 (Job 6:8-14), 111.a.3. "...*ou qu'ils s'efforcent de ce faire, il nous faut bien garder de nous aller atacher à eux.*" [*CO* 33:302].

[10] 29 (Job 7:16-21), 133.b.65. "... *Iob tourne tout au rebours la providence de Dieu, qu'au lieu qu'il se devoit consoler et resiouyr en icelle, il voudroit que Dieu fust bien loin.*" [*CO* 33:361].

[11] "... it behoueth vs also to haue skill to discerne betweene Gods workes as neede requireth. As how? Ye see how Bildad is vtterly co[n]founded in his owne matter. For he sayeth that bicause God hath created the world in settled order, and mayntenyeth it in the same: therefore it foloweth that his iudgements are al certeyne, & that men may see them and know them. But that is an ill co[n]seque[n]ce [sic]. Why? Gods wil is that the sunne should rize and go downe, and thereby we be assertayned that he will giue vs al things necessary for the preseruatio[n] of our life, euen to the worldes ende. When we see the vines, the trees, & the earth yeelde fruite, well, God sheweth vs that he hath a care of this present life, notwithstanding that it be flightful & drooping. But his so doing is as it were to take vs by the hand to lift vs vp to heaue[n] vnto himself. God the[n] wil haue vs to know this most certenly, & so comaundeth vs: but as touching his iudgemets, that is another cace." 67 (Job 18:1-11), 315.a.10. ...*mais il faut aussi que nous sachions discerner entre les oeuvres de Dieu comme il appartient. Comme quoy? Voici Bildad qui est confus du tout en son propos. Car il dit, Dieu ayant creé le monde à un ordre certain, lequel est maintenu par lui: il s'ensuit donc que ses iugemens sont tous certains, et qu'on les peut voir et cognoistre. Or la consequence est mauvaise. Pourqouy? Dieu veut que le soleil se couche et se leve, et que par cela nous soyons advertis que iusques en la fin du monde*

*il nous donnera les choses qui nous sont necessaires pour nous preserver ici. Quand nous voyons les vignes, et les arbres, et la terre qui fructifie, et bien, c'est Dieu qui nous monstre qu'il a le soin de ceste vie, combien qu'elle soit mortelle et caduque: mais c'est comme s'il nous prenoit par la main pour nous eslever là haut au ciel à soy. Dieu donc veut bien que nous cognoissions cela tout priveement, et nous le commande: mais quant à ses iugemens, il y a une autre raison* [CO 34:69].

[12] "For the holy Scirpture putteth a difference betweene the outward things that are done, and the purpose of God which is not knowne but to the faythfull, which lift vp themselues aboue their owne reason and aboue all their naturall wittes. For we shall neuer attayne to the knowledge of Gods Maiestie, except we be caried vp aboue all our owne abilitie." 5 (Job 1:9-12), 23.b.19. *Car l'Escriture saincte discerne entre les choses exterieures qui se font et le conseil de Dieu, qui ne se cognoist point sinon des fideles, qui s'eslevent par dessus toute leur raison, et tous leurs sens naturels. Car nous ne parviendrons iamais à la cognoissance de la maiesté de Dieu, si ce n'est que nous soyons eslevez par dessus toutes nos facultez* [CO 33:80].

[13] As we have seen, and will continue to do so, Calvin finds pedagogic lessons from suffering in the counsel of Bildad, Eliphaz and Zophar also, despite his assessment of their "bad case." Even if what they say is misplaced as far as Job is concerned, Calvin still finds occasion to make application of their remarks to those for whom the counsel is pertinent. In the very opening counsel of Eliphaz in chapter 4, Calvin, having dismissed Eliphaz's case against Job as "evil," nevertheless continues, "Surely the principles that are sette downe here, are drawne out of Gods pure truthe. By reason whereof it is as much as if the holie Ghost had pronounced this saying..." 15 (Job 4:7-11), 66.b.34. *Tant y a donc que les principes qui sont ici mis en avant, sont tirez de la pure verité de Dieu. Parquoy c'est autant comme si le sainct Esprit avoit prononcé ce mot...* [CO 33:188].

For a summary of Calvin's interpretation of Elihu, see Susan Schreiner, *Where Shall Wisdom be Found?*, 131-135. The judgement is based in part upon the interpretation of 38:2, when God says, "Who is that man wrapping his opinion in ignorant speeches?" For Calvin, this is addressed to Job and not to Elihu. 147 (Job 38:1-4), 690.b.55. *Dieu en premier lieu se mocque ici de Iob...*[CO 35:356]. Schreiner cites that both Gregory (in his *Moralia in Iob*) and Aquinas (in his *Expositio super Iob ad Litteram*) had taken this as a rebuke of Elihu. See Schreiner, *op.cit.*, 244n.61. Schreiner's analysis of Elihu needs some clarification, for Calvin is not uniformly uncritical of Elihu as her evaluations might seem to suggest. For example, commenting upon the Joban author's remarks in 33:2 that Elihu "became very angry with Job for justifying himself rather than God," Calvin insists that Elihu is misjudging Job. "Truly his intent was not so, and he would rather a hundred times that the earth had swallowed him vp, or that he had neuer ben borne into the world, than to haue thought such a blasphemie. And truly I haue told you, that as often as ouershot himselfe, it was not to conclude fully so, but it was through the raging of his passions, according as it is verie harde for men to staye themselues, but that many passions shall oftentimes escape them." 119 (Job 32;1-3), 560.b.66. *Vray est que son intention n'a pas esté telle, et il eust mieux aimé cent fois que la terre l'eust englouti, ou n'avoir iamais esté nay au monde, que d'avoir pensé un tel blaspheme. Et defait, nous avons dit, toutes fois et quantes qu'il s'est desbordé, que ce n'a pas esté pour faire une conclusion, mais il a ietté ses bouillons: comme il est difficile aux hommes de se retenir, qu'il ne leur eschappe beaucoup de passions souventesfois* [CO 35:7].

[14] *Where Shall Wisdom be Found?*, 131. Cf. "The sermons on chapters 32-37 provide a summary of Calvinist theology." 133. Whereas Aquinas believed that Elihu "abused" Job's words, Schreiner adds, "Calvin disagress; in his view, Elihu was right." 133.

[15] *Ibid.*, 133.

[16] Cf. "he teacheth vs to receyue his grace, sometimes by the chastisements which he giueth vs, and sometimes by afflictions and great stripes of his roddes. And if he see that we be dull and slowe, he striketh the harder, so as we are co[m]pelled to come vnto him, bicause we be vtterly quayled and can holde out no longer." 128 (Job 33:29-34:3), 601.a.45. *Or le moyen nous a esté declaré: c'est qu'il nous apprend à recevoir sa grace, maintenant par chastimens qu'il nous donne, maintenant par afflictions, et avec grands coups de verges: et s'il voit que nous soyons durs et tardifs, il renforce les coups, tellement que nous sommes contraints de venir à lui, comme estans du tout defaillis, et que nous n'en puissions plus* [CO 35:116].

[17] ...*mais cependant si est ce que quelquefois qu'il voudra esprouver l'obeissance des bons,* 121 (Job 32:11-22), 569.b.57 [CO 35:30]. Commenting upon Elihu's observation that the righteous are afflicted (36:6), Calvin observes, "For God hath some iuste reason to do it, which wee be not able too conceue as at the firste brunt. But lette vs tarrie with pacience, and wee shall knowe that God will make such afflictions to do vs good, and that they tende to a good ende." 140 (Job 36:6-14), 658.a.29. *Car Dieu a iuste raison, laquelle nous ne pouvons pas voir du premier coup: mais attendons en patience, et nous cognoistrons que Dieu fera profiter telles afflictions, et qu'elles tendent à bonne fin* [CO 35:269].

[18] "For affliction is the true schoolemistresse to bring men to repentance, to the ende they may condemne themselues before God, and being so co[n]demned learne to hate their sinnes wherein they weltered afore. Therefore, when wee knowe the frute of the chastizements that God sendeth vs, wee will beare them with a meelder and quietter minde than wee do." 140 (Job 36:6-14), 658.b.9. ...*car l'affliction est la vraye maistresse pour amener les hommes à repentance, afin qu'ils se condamnent devant Dieu, et s'estans condamnez aprenent à hayr leurs fautes, ausquelles auparavant ils se baignoyent. Quand donc nous aurons cognu le fruict des chastimens que Dieu nous envoye, nous les porterons en plus grande douceur et d'un courage plus paisible que nous ne faisons pas* [CO 35:270].

[19] 658.b.54 [*CO* 35:271].

[20] "Howbeit forasmuch as wee be dull vpon the spurre, or (which more is) wee bee vtterly stubborne and deafe vnto all the warnings that he giueth vs: It behoueth vs to pray him too perce our eares, and to open them in such wise to his instructions, as the same may turne to our profite: and that he suffer not the ayre onely to be beaten, without touching of our heart: but that he moue vs too come and returne vnto him." 659.a.10. *Mais d'autant que nous sommes durs à l'esperon, qui plus est, que nous sommes du tout rebelles, que nous sommes sourds à toutes les admonitions qu'il nous fait: il le faut prier qu'il nous perce l'aureille, et qu'il nous donne telle ouverture à ses instructions, qu'elles nous profitent: qu'il ne permette point que l'air seulement en soit batu, sans que le coeur en soit touché: mais que nous soyons esmeus de venir et retourner à luy* [*CO* 35:272].

[21] "It is apparant what a number are afflicted and tormented, and it is euident that Gods scourges are occupied eueryewhere nowadayes. But how fewe are there that thinke vpon them? Yee shall see a whole Realme oppressed with warres till they can no more: and yet shall ye scarce find a dozen men among a hundred thousand, that heare God speake. Behold, the yerkes and lashes of his whippes do sounde and roare in the ayre: there is horrible weeping and wayling eueryewhere: menne crie out alas and wo is mee: and yet of all the whyle they looke not too the hande that smyteth them... Wee see the lyke in plague times and dearth." 659.b.36. *On voit combien il y en a qui sont affligez et tormentez, on voit que les verges de Dieu sont auiourd'huy espandues par tout. Mais combien y en a il qui y pensent? On verra tout un peuple qui sera pressé de guerres tant qu'il n'en pourra plus: mais entre cent mille hommes à grand' peine en trouvera-on une douzaine qui escoutent Dieu parler. Voila les coups de fleaux qui resonnent et retentissent en l'air, les pleurs et les gemissemens seront horribles par tout, les hommes crieront assez helas: mais cependant ils ne regardent point à la main qui frappe... Nous voyons le semblable en peste et en famine* [*CO* 35:273-274].

[22] "... our afflictions befall vs not without his good pleasure." 27 (Job 7:1-6), 124.b.13. ... *et que les afflictions ne nous adviennent point sans son bon plaisir* [*CO* 33:337]; cf. (Job 1:9-12), 21.a.28,42 [*CO* 33:73]; 63 (Job 16:10-17), 295.b.65 [*CO* 34:18]; 71 (Job 19:17-25), 331.a.1 [*CO* 34:112].

[23] 63 (Job 16:10-17), 296.a.9. ...*les archiers de Dieu* [*CO* 34:18].

[24] 150 (Job 38:18-32), 704.b.62. ...*Comme s'il estoit dit, que ce sont ses artilleries, ses lances, ses espees, quand il veut combatre contre ses ennemis.*" [*CO* 35:393].

[25] "And therefore is sta[n]deth vs the more in hand to labour for humilitie betimes, and to resort to this comfort that God giueth vs when he sayeth, that hee teacheth vs by double meanes. For on the one side he maketh his woord to bee preached vnto vs: & on the otherside he beateth vs with his roddes, to the end that euery of vs in his own behalfe should me moued to returne into the right way." 140 (Job 36:6-14), 660.b.32. *Et d'autant plus nous*

*faut-il efforcer de nous humilier de bonne heure, et venir à ceste consolation que Dieu nous donne, quand il dit qu'il nous instruit en double sorte: car d'un costé il fait que sa parole nous soit preschee: et d'autre costé entant que nous sommes batus de ses verges, un chacun de nous en son endroit est induit à retourner au bon chemin* [CO 35:276].

[26] "… the diuell also stirreth them vp in vs…" 1 (Job 1:1), 1.a.66. *…toutesfois que le diable cependant nous les suscite…*[CO 33:22].

[27] "Euery one of vs must haue an eye to his owne poorenesse and vncleannesse, and be displeased with himselfe for it, and therewithall also desire our Lorde Iesus Christ to washe vs and make vs cleane with his bloud." 3 (Job 1:5), 10.a.54. *C'est qu'un chacun regarde à ses povretez, et pollutions, et qu'il s'y desplaise, et cependant que nous demandions à nostre Seigneur Iesus Christ, qu'il nous lave, et nettoye de son sang, à ce que nous puissions apparoistre devant la face de Dieu son Pere, comme purs.*[CO 33:46].

[28] "We may see some man that is sufficientlye conuinced of his sinnes, who notwithstandyng goeth on styll, and followeth his owne swynge: and if he bee reproued, or else otherwyse feele remorse in hys owne conscience, hee passeth it ouer, and taketh no greate greefe for it, and why so? Bycause hee hath not his eye vppon God." 19 (Job 5:8-10), 84.b.55. *Voila un homme qui est assez convaincu de ses pechez: mais tant y a qu'il marche tousiours et poursuit son train: si on le redargue, ou bien qu'il ait autrement remors en la conscience, il passe outre, et n'en fait pas grand scrupule: et pourquoy? car il n'a point son regard à Dieu* [CO 33:235]. Cf. Calvin's statement on repentance in the *Institutes*: "…it is the true turning of our life to God, a turning that arises from a pure and earnest fear of him; and it consists in the mortification of the flesh and of the old man, and in the vivification of the Spirit." III.iii.5. *…esse veram ad Deum vitae nostrae conversionem, a sincero serioque Dei timore profectam, quae carnis nostrae veterisque hominis mortificatione et spiritus vivificatione constet* [CO 2:437]. Cf. Ronald S. Wallace, *Calvin's Doctrine of the Christian Life* (Edinburgh: Oliver and Boyd, 1959), 95f.

[29] *Institutes* I.1.i. "Nearly all the wisdome we possess, that is to say, true and sound wisdom, consists of two parts: the knowledge of God and of ourselves." *Tota fere sapientiae nostrae summa, quae vera demum ac solida sapientia censeri debeat, duabus partibus constat, Dei cognitione et nostri* [CO 2:31].

[30] Note, for example, how Calvin begins his series on Job by pointing out that the "storie here written, sheweth vs howe we be in Gods hande, and that it lyeth in him to determine of our lyfe, and to dispose of the same according to his good pleasure." 1 (Job 1:1), 1.a.15. *Or l'histoire qui est ici escrite nous monstre, comme nous sommes en la main de Dieu, et que c'est à luy d'ordonner de nostre vie, et d'en disposer selon son bon plaisir* [CO 33:21].

[31] 20 (Job 5:11-16), 88.b.55. "…*nous cognoistre afin…*," [CO 33:246].

[32] "For we are sure that iniquitie is as a water cloud, and that as euery man

feeleth it particularly in himselfe, so are wee al of vs infected with vices in common." 63 (Job 16:10-17), 298.b.23. *Cognoissons que l'iniquité est comme un deluge, et que si en particulier chacun s'en sent, nous sommes aussi tous entachez des vices du commun* [*CO* 34:26].

[33] 21 (Job 5:17-18), 95.a.67. ... *c'est assavoir que Dieu nous afflige à cause de nos pechez...* [*CO* 33:262]; Cf. 64 (Job 16:18-22), 300.a.63. ...*c'est pour nos pechez* [*CO* 34:30]; 140 (Job 36:6-14), 658.a.48. ...*leurs pechez* [*CO* 35:269].

[34] 142 (Job 36:20-24), 667.a.37 [*CO* 35:294].

[35] 18 (Job 5:3-7), 81.a.17 [*CO* 33:225].

[36] 5 (Job 1:9-12), 21.b.37 [*CO* 33:74]; 159 (Job 42:9-17), 749.a.19 [*CO* 35:508].

[37] 21 (Job 5:17-18), 96.a.2 [*CO* 33:262]; 128 (Job 33:29-34:3), 602.a.10 [*CO* 35:118].

[38] "God will not alwayes make vs priuie why he executeth his iudgements, but we shall be blynd in that behalf." 132 (Job 18:21-26), 623.b.14. ...*que Dieu ne nous fera pas tousiours cognoistre pourquoi c'est qu'il exerce ses iugemens, nous y serons aveugles* [*CO* 35:176]. "Sometimes for som other secrete cause vnknowne to vs" 158 (Job 42:6-8), 743.b.27. ...*aucunesfois il y a des causes secrettes, qui nous sont incognues* [*CO* 35:494].

[39] 121 (Job 32:11-22), 569.b.29. "...*pour les humilier,*" [*CO* 35:29]; "that wee be beaten downe and humbled vnder his hand...," 140 (Job 36:6-14), 659.a.69. *nous soyons abbatus et humiliez sous sa main* [*CO* 35:273]; 123 (Job 33:8-14), 579.a.19 [*CO* 35:54]; "wee on our side are dull vppon the Spurre, and not easie too be brought in subiection, and therefore wee haue neede of great violence to abate the pride that is in vs by nature...," 154 (Job 39:36-40:6), 723.a.5. *nous ne sommes pas aisément assuiettis: et ainsi il faut qu'il y ait une violence grande pour abbatre l'orgueil qui est en nous de nature* [*CO* 35:440]. Cf. In Calvin's third sermon on 'the Song of Hezekiah' (Isaiah 39:15-17), the Reformer concludes that God makes use of trials to humble us: "One must know that the principle virtue of the faithful, when God punishes and afflicts them, is to become as nothing." *La principale vertu des fideles, quand Dieu les afflige et les punit, c'est d'estre comme aneantis* [*CO* 35:555].

[40] 7 (Job 1:20-21, 30.a.20 [*CO* 33:96].

[41] 20 (Job 5:11-16), 92.a.63 [*CO* 33:255].

[42] 21 (Job 5:17-18), 94.a.52 [*CO* 33:259].

[43] 38 (Job 10:1-6), 179.b.23 [*CO* 33:478].

[44] 141 (Job 36:15-19), 662.a.47. *il les veut rendre inexcusables,*" [*CO* 35:280]; 20 (Job 5:11-16), 88.a.59. "*il nous afflige pour estre domtez,*" [*CO* 33:245].

[45] 4 (Job 1:6-8), 19.a.5 [*CO* 33:68]; 140 (Job 36:6-14), 659.a.10 [*CO* 35:272].

[46] 5 (Job 1:9-11), 22.b.56. *quand Dieu permet une telle vogue à Satan sur ses fideles ce n'est que pour peu de temps...* [*CO* 33:77].

[47] 21 (Job 5:17-18), 97.b.14 [*CO* 33:268].

[48] 2 (Job 1:2-5), 7.a.44 [*CO* 33:37].

[49] "It is impossible that Gods children should liue in this world and not be in many perils continually." 20 (Job 5:11-16), 89.b.13. ...*mais il est impossible que les enfans de Dieu vivent en ce monde, que tousiours ils ne soyent en*

*beaucoup de perils* [*CO* 33:247].

⁵⁰ "Afflictions lyght vpon all men without exception." 31 (Job 5:17-18), 94.b.4. *...car cependant nous voyons que les afflictions sont communes à tous* [*CO* 33:260].

⁵¹ "Our afflictions befall vs not without his good pleasure." 27 (Job 7:1-6), 124.b.13. *...et que les afflictions ne nous adviennent point sans son bon plaisir* [*CO* 33:337].

⁵² Calvin observes Job's mistaken surprise that God should try us so, seeing we are so insignificant: "If men (who are but woormes of the earth) can well skill to alledge, that it is not comely for them too beare malice to those that are farre their inferiors: there is farre greater reason too thinke that God seemeth too magnifie men ouer much, when hee matcheth himselfe agaynst them. For who are they? What is their state? God therefore ought too set light by them, [and to say:] Tushe, well yee are but woormes, yee are but vermine; and shall I chalenge you too go fight with you? That were greatly too the defacing of my glorie and Maiestie." 29 (Job 7:16-21), 133.a.46. *Si les hommes (qui ne sont que vers de terre) savent bien alleguer cela, que ce n'est pas chose decente, qu'ils s'attachent à ceux qui sont inferieurs de beaucoup: par plus forte raison, quand Dieu se vient ainsi adresser aux hommes, il semble qu'il les magnifie par trop. Car qui sont-ils? quelle est leur condition? Dieu donc les devroit mespriser. Et bien, vous n'estes que des vers, vous n'estes que des vermines: et que ie m'aille attacher à vous pour y avoir combat? Cela seroit par trop deroguer à ma gloire et à ma maiesté* [*CO* 33:360]. Calvin goes on to observe that here, Job "turneth Gods prouidence quite vpside downe, and that in steade of co[m]forting and cheering himself therewith, he would fayne that God were farre of." 133.b.65. *...Iob tourne tout au rebours la providence de Dieu, qu'au lieu qu'il se devoit consoler et resiouyr en icelle, il voudroit que Dieu fust bien loin* [*CO* 33:361]. Calvin also notes that this is in opposition to the eighth Psalm: whereas Job is surprised that God should try us so, seeing we are so insignificant, the psalmist is surprised that God should bless and honour us so, seeing that we are but creatures. 133.a.58 [*CO* 33:360].

⁵³ "If God teach vs at another mans cost, so as hee chastizeth other men before our eyes: let the same touch vs, and let vs applie such examples to our owne instruction, to the intent to preuent the matter, that God be not compelled to fall vpon vs bycause we haue not profited by the chastizementes whyche hee hathe shewed vs in the person of others." 33 (Job 9:1-6), 152.a.38. *Si Dieu nous instruit aux despens d'autruy, qu'il corrige les autres devant nos yeux: car cela nous touche, que nous appliquions tels exemples à nostre instruction, afin de prevenir, que Dieu ne soit point contraint de se ruer sur nous, d'autant que nous n'aurons point fait nostre profit des chastimens qu'il nous a monstré en la personne des autres* [*CO* 33:408].

⁵⁴ "True it is that God doth sometimes beare vp his seruants in their infirmitie, so long till he cut of the edge of the wicked mens prosperitie, according also as it is sayd in the Psalme, that if we should be alwaies in aduersitie without

any release, wee might reache out our hande too do euill: that is too say, wee bee so frayle, that although wee called vpon God, and were desirous too serue him: yet might wee be tempted too breake square, if God did not both moderate our afflictions and also represse the wicked by giuing the[m] such blowes as should beate them downe to the g[r]ound." 67 (Job 18:1-11), 315.b.58. *Vrai est que Dieu supporte les siens en leur infirmité iusques-là, que souvent il coupe la broche à la prosperité des meschans: comme aussi il en est parlé au Pseaume (125, 3), que si nous estions tousiours en affliction sans avoir nulle relasche, nous pourrions estendre nos mains à malfaire: c'est à dire, comme nous sommes fragiles, encores que nous invoquions Dieu, et que nous desirions de le servir, si pourrions-nous estre tentez à nous desbaucher, n'estoit que Dieu moderast nos afflictions, et qu'il reprimast les meschans, et leur donnast de tels soufflets, qu'ils fussent abbatus* [*CO* 34:72].

[55] "When God presseth vs with his iudgment, it is but for a small while if wee compare our selues with the holy persons that haue incountred agaynst the sorrowes of death and hell." 23 (Job 6:1-9), 105.a.11. ...*mais quand Dieu nous presse de son iugement, cela n'est que pour un peu, si nous faisons comparaison de nous avec ces saincts personnages qui ont combatu contre les douleurs de la mort, et d'enfer* [*CO* 33:287].

[56] "God dealeth with his seruaunts according to the measure of fayth which he hath distributed vnto them." 6 (Job 1:13-19), 24.b.30. ...*Dieu besongne envers ses serviteurs selon la mesure de foy qu'il leur a distribuee* [*CO* 33:82].

[57] "Therefore let vs assure our selues, that when God maketh vs too feele his hand, so as wee are humbled vnder the same: hee dooth vs a speciall good turne, and it is a priuiledge which he giueth too none but too his owne children." 21 (Job 5:17-18), 95.a.34. *Cognoissons donc que Dieu nous fait un bien special, et que c'est un privilege qu'il ne donne qu'à ses enfans, quand il nous fait sentir sa main pour nous humilier sous icelle* [*CO* 33:262].

[58] E.g., 5 (Job 1:5-12), 20.a.7 [*CO* 33:69]; 68 (Job 18:12-21), 319.a.43 [*CO* 33:81]; 90 (Job 23:13-17), 425.a.10 [*CO* 34:366]; 125 (Job 33:18-25), 588.a.55 [*CO* 35:80]; 141 (Job 36:15-19), 662.a.46 [*CO* 35:281].

[59] See the discussion of God's power and justice.

[60] "My comfort is to pray God to giue me eyes, not only to behold presente things, but also to know those things by faith which are hidden from me as now." 27 (Job 7:1-6), 126.b.11. *Voire: mais où est ma consolation cependant? C'est, que ie prie Dieu qu'il me donne des yeux, non point pour contempler les choses presentes: mais afin que par foy ie puisse cognoistre ce qui m'est maintenant caché* [*CO* 33:342].

[61] *Institutes*, 1.xvii.2. *Sequitur profundae abysso conferri aliam voluntatem absconditam*... [*CO* 2:155].

[62] In the very opening sermon on Job, Calvin sets the agenda for his interpretation of providence. "It is in that hee knoweth, that God dothe not euer punishe menne according to the measure of their sinnes, but hath his

secrete iudgmentes, whereof he maketh not vs priuie, and therfore that it behoueth vs to wayte till he reuele vnto vs for what cause he dothe this or that."1 (Job 1:1), 1.b.39. ...*c'est qu'il cognoist que Dieu n'afflige pas tousiours les hommes selon la mesure de leurs pechez: mais qu'il a ses iugemens secrets, desquels il ne nous rend pas conte, et cependant qu'il faut que nous attendions iusques à ce qu'il nous revele pourquoy il fait ceci, ou cela* [*CO* 33:23]. And again, "God doth exceeding great and incomprehensible things, his doings are wonderfull and without ende. When we vnderstand that Gods workes are exceeding great and incomprehensible: shall wee not be forced to lift vp our myndes, and to perceyue that wee must not disguyse him, nor surmize anything of him after oure naturall reason, but that wee muste mounte vp higher?" 19 (Job 5:8-10), 86.a.30. *Dieu fait des choses grandes et incomprehensibles, ses actes sont admirables, et sans fin. Quand nous aurons cognu que les oeuvres de Dieu sont grandes et incomprehensibles, ne serons-nous pas contraints d'eslever nos esprits, et de sentir qu'il ne faut point que nous deguisions Dieu, ne que nous imaginions rien de luy selon nostre sens naturel, mais qu'il faut monter plus haut?* [*CO* 33:239].

[63] 30 (Job 8:1-6), 138.b.18. *...ses iugemens incomprehensibles et secrets...* [*CO* 33:373]. Cf. "Inquire a ma[n] neuer so much, & trauell he neuer so much, yet shal he be neuer the neerer, bycuse Gods judgemets are "secret and incomprehensible." 66 (Job 17:6-16), 311.a.12. *...la raison n'en sera pas evidente: qu'on s'enquiere, qu'on y travaille beaucoup, on y demeurera confus, d'autant que les iugemens de Dieu sont secrets et incomprehensibles* [*CO* 34:58]; "For he hath his secrete iudgements, whiche are incomprehensible to vs." 36 (Job 9:23-28), 165.a.56. *Car il a ses iugements secrets, et qui nous sont incomprehensibles* [*CO* 33:443]. "They shall neuer attayne to the great secrets of God, for they surmount all their capacitie and reach." 89 (Job 23:8-12), 417.a.57. *...ils ne viendront iusques aux grans secrets de Dieu: car ils surmontent toute leur portee et faculté* [*CO* 34:345]. "But when we enter into the doctrine of saluation, and into Gods works, and fall to disputing of his prouidence and wil [sic] then must we not go to it so unaduysedly, for we do but wrap vp or intangle *secrets* in vnskilfull words." 147 (Job 38:1-4), 691.b.51. *Mais quand nous entrons en la doctrine de salut, que nous entrons aux oeuvres de Dieu, et que nous disputons de sa providence, et de sa volonté: alors il n'est pas question d'y aller ainsi à l'estourdie: car nous enveloppons, ou entortillons le conseil en des propos sans science* [*CO* 35:359].

[64] 147 (Job 38:1-4), 692.a.32. *...des mysteres de Dieu si hauts...* [*CO* 35:360].

[65] 40 (Job 10:16-17), 188.a.58. *...desia cela est par dessus nostre mesure...* [*CO* 33:501].

[66] "Therefore let vs learne to mislyke whatsoeuer thing men haue forged of their owne braine, and let vs holde vs to this simplicitie, namely that we must not couct too knowe ought, sauing that which God hath declared too vs with his owne mouth." 17 (Job 4:20-5:2), 78.b.38. *Apprenons donc de detester tout*

*ce que les hommes auront forgé en leur cerveau, et nous tenons à ceste simplicité, que nous ne devons appeter de rien savoir, sinon ce que Dieu nous a declaré de sa propre bouche* [*CO* 33:219].

[67] "He teacheth vs that which he knoweth to bee expedient for vs at this time." 82 (Job 21:22-34), 384.b.36. ...*qu'il cognoist nous estre expedient pour cest heure...*[*CO* 34:256].

[68] "...God hath wo[n]derfull meanes & inco[m]prehensible to vs, to augment that which seemeth to be very small: and notwithstanding that wee were as good as at deathes doore, so as it mighte seeme we should neuer bee plucked out of our miseries: yet shall God well finde some good way out of them." 31 (Job 8:7-13), 142.b.30. ...*que Dieu a des façons admirables, et qui ne nous sont point comprehensibles pour augmenter ce qui semble estre bien petit comme il est dit, Encores que nous fussions comme pressez en la mort, qu'il ne semblast pas que nous deussions iamais estre retirez de nos miseres, que Dieu trouvera bien quelque bonne issue* [*CO* 33:384].

[69] "So then wee perceyue, that they whom God chastyzeth are happie, notwithstanding that wee shunne aduersitie as much as wee possibly can." 21 (Job 5:17-18), 95.b.9. *Ainsi donc voila comme nous cognoissons, que ceux que Dieu chastie sont bien heureux, nonobstant que nous fuyons, entant qu'il nous est possible, les adversitez* [*CO* 33:262]. It is this perception that Calvin notes in his exegesis of Romans 5:3, "We glory in our tribulations also": "They are... rightly said to glory, because in their grief and sorrow they are greatly consoled by the thought that all their sufferings are dispensed to their good by the hand of a most indulgent Father... We learn, therefore, from this, what is the purpose of our tribulations..." *The Epistle of Paul the Apostle to the Romans and to the Thessalonians*, trans. Ross Mackenzie, ed., David W. Torrance and Thomas F. Torrance (Grand Rapids, MI: Wm. B. Eerdmans Publishing Company, 1973, 1991), 106. *Quod autem dicit sanctos in tribulationibus gloriari, non ita est intelligendum ac si res adversas non extimescerent et refugerent, vel nulla earum acerbitate premerentur ubi incidunt: (nam nec patientia inde nasceretur, nisi esset amaritudinis sensus), sed quia dolendo ac gemendo ingenti tamen consolatione non carent, quod sibi indulgentissimi patris manu in suum bonum, quidquid ferunt, dispensari reputant, merito dicuntur gloriari. Ubicunque enim profectus est salutis, illic non deest gloriandi materia. Hinc ergo docemur quis sit tribulationum nostrarum finis: si quidem filios Dei praestare libet* [*CO* 49:90].

[70] "...for to those two purposes do afflictions serue: that is to wit, God killeth the vices that are in vs. For when he punisheth vs, then are we tamed, and he commaundeth vs to withdrawe our selues from the worlde, and not to be giuen to our pleasures and fleshly delights. But there is yet a further thing: that is to wit, that like as in a furnace gold is tried to knowe whither it haue any drosse in it: so also God sheweth what we be, by afflicting vs. For men knowe not themselues before they haue bene so proued. Before wee haue passed through the siue, we seeme to our selues to feare God, and that

there is nothing to be mislyked in vs: and yet all the whyle there be many vices in vs, that we know not of. ... then finde we what our infirmitie is. Now if God make the afflictions of his faythfull ones to serue them as a mirror wherein to behold themselues." 5 (Job 1:9-12), 20.a.7. ...*car les afflictions servent à ces deux usages: c'est que Dieu mortifie les vices qui sont en nous, quand il nous afflige, nous sommes domtés, il nous commande de nous retirer de ce monde, de n'estre plus adonnez à nos voluptez et delices charnelles. Mais il y a plus: c'est que tout ainsi qu'en la fournaise l'or est esprouvé, pour savoir s'il y a de l'escume, aussi Dieu monstre quels nous sommes, quand il nous afflige: car les hommes mesmes ne se cognoissent point devant qu'avoir esté ainsi esprouvez: devant qu'avoir passé par l'estamine, il nous semblera que nous craignons Dieu, qu'il n'y a que redire en nous, et cependant il y aura des vices, qui nous sont incognus. Dieu nous les monstre, il nous les fait sentir, quand il nous envoye quelque trouble, quelque fascherie, et alors nous sentons quelle est nostre infirmité. Or si Dieu fait servir les afflictions à ses fideles comme d'un miroer, auquel ils se contemplent* [*CO* 33:69-70].

[71] ". . . but euery man must enter into himselfe, and examin his owne state and life: and when we finde any fault in our selues, wee must condemne it." 18 (Job 5:3-7), 80.a.39. ...*mais qu'un chacun doit entrer en soy, et examiner son estat et sa vie: et quand nous trouverons du mal en nous, il nous le faut condamner* [*CO* 33:223]. Cf. Ronald S. Wallace, *The Christian Life* (Tyler, TX: Geneva Divinity School Press, 1959,1982), 228. See also D. Foxgrover, "Self-Examination in John Calvin and William Ames," in *Later Calvinism* vol. XXII, Sixteenth Century Essays and Studies, ed. by W. F. Graham (Kirksville, MO: Sixteenth Century Journal Publishers, 1994), 451-70.

[72] "Ye see wherefore he trieth vs: namely too the intent that euery of vs should knowe himselfe, not onely too say yeauerely I perceyue well that I am a sinner: but also too haue a liuely feeling of our sinnes, that wee may bee vtterly ashamed of them before him." 19 (Job 7:16-21), 136.b.10. *Voila pourquoy il nous examine: c'est afin qu'un chacun de nous se cognoisse, non seulement pour dire, Et voila ie sen bien que ie suis pecheur: mais que nous ayons un sentiment vif de nos fautes, pour estre plus que confus devant luy* [*CO* 33:368].

[73] "When an offender hath acknowledged his crymes and euill dooings before an earthly iudge, a man demaundeth no more at his hande: but God is a spirituall iudge, and will bring vs too the inwarde knowledge of our sinnes." 19 (Job 7:16-21), 136.a.68. *Quand un malfaicteur aura cognu ses crimes, et ses malefices devant un Iuge terrien, on ne demande plus rien de luy: mais Dieu est Iuge spirituel, qui nous veut amener à une cognoissance interieure de nos pechez* [*CO* 33:368].

[74] 21 (Job 5:17-18), 95.b.26. *Et ainsi le plus grand malheur qui nous puisse advenir, c'est quand Dieu nous laisse croupir en nos iniquitez: car il faut en la fin que nous y pourrissions du tout* [*CO* 33:263].

[75] "Wee see then before our eyes, that many men are the more vnhappie for

being chastized at Gods hand, bycause they profit not in his schoole, nor yet take any good by his corrections." 21 (Job 5:17-18), 95.a.29. *Nous voyons donc à l'oeil comme beaucoup de gens sont d'autant plus malheureux d'estre chastiez de Dieu, pource qu'ils ne profitent point en son escole, ils ne font point leur profit de ses verges...* [*CO* 33:262].

[76] "Looke vpon a whorehunter that hath haunted the stewes halfe a score yeares: Looke vpon a blasphemer that ceasseth not to raile at God and to spite hym: Looke vpon a villaine that despiseth God and all religion. Looke vpon an vnthrifte or an vnconscionable person that seeketh nought else but to be catching withoute faithfulnesse or honest dealing: and such doggs will saye it is true that they be sinners before God, for no manne is righteouse. They go no further with their faults but so, which are so hideous as may be, but shrowde themselues vnder the cloadke of naturall infirmitie, saying that there is no manne that can bee equall with God. They thinke they haue doone very muche in yelding suche a confession." 33 (Job 9:1-6), 152.a.10. *Voila un paillard qui aura hanté le bordeau par l'espace de dix ans: voila un blasphemateur qui ne cesse de maugreer et despiter Dieu: voila un vilain contempteur de Dieu, et de toute religion: voila un desbauché, un homme sans conscience qui ne demande que d'en avoir, sans foy, sans loyauté: telles canailles diront qu'il est vray qu'ils sont pecheurs devant Dieu: car nul n'est iuste. Ils laisseront là leurs fautes qui sont si enormes que rien plus, et se cacheront sous ce manteau de l'infirmité humaine: et diront qu'il n'y a nul homme mortel qui puisse estre egalé à Dieu. Il leur semble qu'ils ont beaucoup fait de passer une telle confession* [*CO* 33:408].

[77] "For whosoeuer is touched rightly and too the quicke, shall feele himselfe as it were in hell when hee bethinketh him of his sinnes, and specially if God sommon him before his seate, and make him feele howe gyltie hee is." 38 (Job 10:1-6), 175.b.25. *Car quiconques est vrayement touché, et au vif, celuy-la se pourra bien sentir comme aux enfers quand il pense à ses pechez: et sur tout si Dieu l'adiourne devant son siege, et qu'il lui face sentir combien il est coulpable* [*CO* 33:468].

[78] "For we take our selues for stoute men of warre and too haue beene tried too the vttermost, when wee haue indured some sicknesse, or some other aduersitie: and wee thinke then that God ought not too begin newe againe with vs, but that we be quite discharged, and are become stout chapions. And yet notwithstanding, all the bodily afflictions that wee can indure are nothing in respect of the distresse that a poore sinner is in when he perceyueth that God is as it were a partie agaynst him, and persecuteth him, so as hee can finde no meanes to come too attonement and agreement with him. Therefore when our sinnes come after that sort before vs, and the diuell maketh vs too feele Gods wrath, and againe on the other side oure owne conscience reproueth vs, so as God seemeth too be vtterly angrie with vs: that (say I) is a farre greater and dreadfuller anguish, than all the miseries are, that we can indure in our flesh." 41 (Job 10:18-22), 193.a.3. *Car il nous semble que nous soyons vaillans gensdarmes, que nous avons esté esprouvez*

*iusqu'au bout: quand nous aurons enduré quelque maladie, ou quelque autre affliction, il nous semble alors que Dieu ne doive point recommencer: mais que nous sommes quittes, que nous sommes vaillans champions. Et toutesfois ce n'est rien de tout ce que nous pourrons souffrir d'afflictions corporelles, au prix de ceste destresse en laquelle est un povre pecheur, quand il apprehende que Dieu est là comme sa partie adverse, qu'il le persecute, qu'il n'y a nul moyen de trouver accord avec luy ne d'appointer. Quand donques nos pechez nous viennent ainsi au devant, et que le diable nous fait sentir l'ire de Dieu, et puis que d'autre costé nostre conscience nous redargue, que Dieu se monstre là comme courroucé: voila (di-ie) une angoisse qui est plus grande et plus espouvantable, que ne sont pas tous les maux que nous pouvons endurer en nostre chair* [CO 33:513-514].

[79] Referring to Psalm 19:13 and to the use of "secret sinnes," Calvin comments, "For it behoueth vs to knowe our sinnes, or else we cannot confesse them to be sinnes... God seeth more cleerly than we do." 23 (Job 9:1-6), 153.b.51. *Car il faut que nos pechez soyent cognus, ou nous ne les pouvons pas confesser pour pechez* [CO 33:413].

[80] "Afflictions cannot alwayes tame and subdue men..." 90 (Job 23:13-17), 425.a.31. *...les afflictions ne peuvent pas tousiours domter et matter les hommes...*[CO 34:366]. Cf. Calvin's reference to Pharaoh in Sermon 21: "What auayled all the roddes that Pharao felt, sauing that they made him the more vnexcusable, bycause hee continewed stubborne and vnable too bee amended..." 21 (Job 5:17-18), 94.b.8. *Que est-ce qu'ont profité toutes les verges que Pharao a senti, sinon que ç'a esté pour le rendre plus inexcusable à cause qu'il est demeuré rebelle et incorrigible envers Dieu iusques en la fin?* [CO 33:260]. "For it is not ynough for God too stryke vs with his hand, except he touche vs within also by his holie spirit. If God soften not the hardnesse of our harts, it will fall out with vs as it did with Pharao." 21 (Job 5:17-18), 94.b.36. *Car ce n'est point assez que Dieu frappe de sa main, sinon qu'il nous touche là dedans par son sainct Esprit: il en seroit autant de nous comme de Pharao, sinon que Dieu amollist la durté de nos coeurs* [CO 33:260-261].

[81] For Calvin's use of Hebrews 12:15 and the warning given about "the root of bitterness" that can sometimes accompany trials, see 21 (Job 5:17-18), 96.a.45 [CO 33:264]. Cf. Calvin's commentary on Hebrews 12:16: "Since men become profane in various ways, greater care must be taken that there is no opening given to Satan to defile us by his corruption, and as there is no true religion without consecration we must always progress in the fear of God, in the mortification of the flesh, and in the whole practice of piety." *The Epistle of Paul the Apostle to the Hebrews and The First and Second Epistles of St Peter*, trans. William B. Johnston, ed. by David W. Torrance and Thomas F. Torrance (Grand Rapids, MI: Wm. B. Eerdmans Publishing Company, 1963), 197. *Quoniam autem variis modis profanescunt homines, eo maior danda est opera ne Satanae rima pateat ad nos suis corruptelis inquinandos. Et quemadmodum sine consecratione nulla est vera religio, semper in timore*

*Dei, mortificatione carnis, totaque pietatis exercitatione proficiendum est* [*CO* 55:179].

[82] 21 (Job 5:17-18), 94.b.41. *Car les hommes sont semblables à des enclumes: quand on frappe dessus, ce n'est pas pour changer leur nature, car nous voyons qu'elles repoussent les coups* [*CO* 33:261]. Cf. "And for the better vnderstanding of this streyne: let vs marke, that God dooth oftentymes afflict those that are wilfull and harde harted. But what? Their minde is neuer the more humbled for all that. For they beate backe all Gods iudgements, as an Anuylde beateth backe the hammer." 23 (Job 6:1-9), 105.b.15. *Or pour mieux comprendre ce passage, notons que souvent Dieu affligera ceux qui sont obstinez et endurcis. Mais quoy? Leur esprit n'est point humilié pourtant: car ils repoussent tous les iugemens de Dieu, comme l'enclume repoussera le marteau* [*CO* 33:288].

[83] "Whensoeuer wee haue any trouble, straightwayes withoute regarding what it is, our eyes are dazeled at it, so as wee cannot discerne betweene redde and greene, but wee babble out this and that too no purpose." 24 (Job 6:8-14), 111.b.28. *...toutes fois et quantes que nous avons quelque fascherie sans regarder à rien qui soit, nos yeux sont esblouis que nous ne discernons plus entre le rouge et le verd: mais nous decliquons et ceci et cela sans propos* [*CO* 33:304].

[84] "... Till God haue touched vs with his holie spirit, it is vnpossible that his chastyzements should serue to bring vs backe to repentance, but rather they shall make vs too wex woorse, and woorse." 21 (Job 5:17-18), 94.b.54. *Apprenons donc que iusques à ce que Dieu nous ait touchez par son sainct Esprit, il est impossible que ses chastimens nous servent pour nous induire à repentance, mais plustost il nous feront empirer* [*CO* 33:261].

[85] 21 (Job 5:17-18), 96.a.8. *"seconde grace"* [*CO* 33:264].

[86] 21 (Job 5:17-18), 96.a.9. *...voire quand il adiouste ceste seconde grace, c'est assavoir, qu'il fait valoir ses verges et ses corrections, que le sainct Esprit besongne dedans le coeur, telement que l'homme n'est plus endurci pour s'eslever contre Dieu, qu'il a ceste sollicitude de penser à ses pechez, et qu'il est vrayement domté et humilié* [*CO* 33:264].

[87] "For it is a deadly plage when wee shall be so headstrong and wilfull in the matters that wee take in hand. It is all one as if wee should shet the gate against God, and say hee shall not come in, and that although he visit vs, and although he be desyrous to shewe vs that which is greatly for our welfare: yet notwithstanding, wee will repulse that grace." 26 (Job 6:24-30), 118.a.34. *Car c'est une peste mortelle, quand nous aurons ceste obstination, et que nous serons opiniastres en nos entreprinses: c'est comme si nous fermions la porte à Dieu, pour dire, qu'il n'aura point d'entrée, et combien qu'il nous visite, combien qu'il nous vueille monstrer ce qui est bon pour nostre salut, que toutesfois nous repousserons ceste grace-la* [*CO* 33:320].

[88] "So long as men are forepossessed with pride, so as they weene themselues worth anything, yee shall see them so locked vp as the grace of God can neuer enter intoo them." 28 (Job 7:7-15), 129.b.44. *...cependant que*

*les hommes sont preoccupez d'orgueil, qu'ils cuident valoir quelque chose, les voila enserrez, que iamais la grace de Dieu ne pourra entrer à eux* [*CO* 33:351]. Calvin notes, for example, on 2 Corinthians 12:9-10 that Paul was reconciled to his "thorn in the flesh": "The man who is too ashamed to glory in this way shuts the door against Christ's grace and in a way drives it from him, for we make room for Christ's grace when with a resigned mind we feel and confess our own weakness. The valleys are watered with rain to make them fruitful while the summits of lofty mountains remain dry. A man must become a valley if he wants to receive the heavenly rain of God's spiritual grace." *The Second Epistle of Paul to the Corinthians and the Epistles to Timothy, Titus and Philemon*, trans. T. A. Small, ed., David W. Torrance and Thomas F. Torrance (Grand Rapids, MI: Wm. B. Eerdmans Publishing Company, 1964, 1991), 161-162. *Ergo quem pudet huius gloriae, is ianuam Christi virtuti claudit, et eam quodammodo a se repellit. Tunc enim locum damus Christi gratiae, dum vera animi submissione infirmitatem nostram sentimus et confitemur. Valles pluvia rigantur ad foecunditatem, quum interea summi altorum montium vertices sicci manent. Valli sergo fiat, qui coelestem spiritualis Dei gratiae pluviam vult suscipere* [*CO* 50:142].

[89] See fn. 70.

[90] "For in afflicting men, he ameth at twoo endes. As for the reprobates, he purposeth to make them vnexcusable: and as for the godly, hee intendeth to tame them in such wise, as they may returne to him with a lowly mind." 141 (Job 36:15-19), 662.a.45. ...*car quand il afflige les hommes, il tend à double fin: quant aux reprouvez, il les veut rendre inexcusables: et quant aux bons, il les veut tellement matter que d'un coeur humble ils retournent à luy* [*CO* 35:280-281]. Cf. Calvin's comment in Sermon 128: "Obedience pleaseth him best of all things." 128 (Job 33:29-34:3), 604.a.21. ... *l'obeissance luy plaist sur tout* [*CO* 35:124].

[91] 141 (Job 36:15-19), 662.a.46. ...*il les veut rendre inexcusables*...[*CO* 35:280]. Cf. "there be many hypocrytes which cannot be knowne nor discouered vntill God sende aduersitie." 5 (Job 1:9-12), 19.b.67. *Et ainsi il y a aura beaucoup d'hypocrites, qui ne seront point cognus ne descouverts, sinon que Dieu les afflige. Car cependant qu'ils sont à leur aise, et en repos, ils ne monstreront point la rebellion qui est en eux, elle sera cachee* [*CO* 33:69].

[92] 36 (Job 9:23-28), 167.b.4. ... *nous faisons des chevaux eschappez* [*CO* 33:448]; Cf. 37 (Job 9:29-35), 172.a.45. ... *nous viendrions faire des chevaux eschappez* [*CO* 33:460].

[93] 30 (Job 8:1-6), 138.b.18 [*CO* 33:373].

[94] "Then let vs vndersta[n]d that God intendeth here to exercise our obedience, by trying vs to the vttermost so as we can indure no more, no nor somuch as drawe our brethe, but seeme to be vtterly choked. Therfore when our Lord bringeth vs too that point, it is to the end to knowe whether we be wholly his, and whether we can abyde to be gouerned by his hand or no." 125 (Job 33:18-25), 588.a.54. *Cognoissons donc que Dieu veut ici exercer*

*nostre obeissance, quand il nous examine iusques à l'extremité, et que nous n'en pouvons plus, non pas mesmes ravoir nostre halaine, qu'il s'emble que nous soyons suffocquez du tout. Quand donc nostre Seigneur nous amene du tout iusques là, c'est afin de savoir si nous sommes du tout siens, et si nous pourrons souffrir d'estre gouvernez par sa main* [CO 35:80].

[95] 157 (Job 42:1-5), 740.b.31. *Et la premiere docilité quelle est elle? C'est qu'il soit maistre, et qu'il soit obei pleinement en ce qu'il voudra nous enseigner. Car quand un enfant viendra à l'escole, et qu'il voudra choisir les livres à son appetit, pour dire, Ie veux savoir une telle science, ie veux estre enseigné en ceci et en cela, devant qu'il soit à l'A B C, s'il veut estre grand docteur devant qu'il soit venu au lieu et à l'endroit où il doit estre enseigné: ie vous prie, est-ce une modestie d'escolier, que cela? Or si un escolier quand il prend un homme pour l'instruire, se doit du tout assuiettir à lui: que devons-nous à Dieu? Quelle comparison y a il? Ainsi donc notons bien, que si sans feintise nous interroguons Dieu pour estre enseignez, nous ne voudrons pas le ranger à nos appetits, pour dire qu'il nous monstre tout ce que nous aurons conceu: mais il nous suffira de savoir ce qu'il cognoist nous estre utile: et c'est à lui de discrener* [CO 35:486-487].

[96] "if wee will bee Gods children, we must haue the spirit of meeknesse." 26 (Job 6:24-30), 118.a.41. ...*qu'il nous faut avoir l'esprit de mansuetude, si nous voulons estre enfans de Dieu* [CO 33:320].

[97] "to haue a meeke mynd [*espirit debonnaire*]," is for Calvin, "To receyue what is sayd vntoo vs." 26 (Job 6:24-30), 118.b.52 [CO 33:322]. Cf. "Would we then shewe how wee profite in Gods woorde? It behoueth vs aboue all things to haue a meeke and gentle spirite [*espirit debonnaire et paisible*]." 128 (Job 33:29-34-3), 603.a.57 [CO 35:122].

[98] "But Iob sayeth here, that when we shall haue chosen our words, and told a goodly painted tale that might amaze our hearers, God will not passe a whit for it. Then must all babling and all retorike ceasse when we come before the heauenly throne. For tunges are not heard there: Mens thoughts muste come to light there: these bookes must be opened there." 35 (Job 9:16-22), 160.b.67. *Or Iob dit ici, que quand nous aurons choisi paroles qu'il y aura eu des propos bien fardez, qui seroyent pour estonner ceux qui nous oyent, que Dieu ne s'esmouvera point pour cela. Il faut donc que tout babil et toute rhetorique cesse, quand nous venons devant le siege celeste. Car là les langues ne seront point ouyes: il faut que les pensees des hommes viennent en clarté, les livres seront ouverts...*[CO 33:431].

[99] "But we must reuerence these great secretes which are far aboue our capacitie, vntill such time as we may comprehend that which is hidden fro[m] vs as now." 36 (Job 9:23-28), 166.a.41. ...*mais que nous adorions ses grands secrets qui surmontent toute nostre capacité, iusques à ce que nous puissions comprendre ce qui nous est caché auiourd'huy* [CO 33:445], adding: "...he hath iudgements that are inco[m]prehensible to vs." 166.a.68. ...*car il a des iugemens qui nous sont incomprehensibles* [CO 33:446].

[100] "When wee shall haue searched to the vttermost, and made great circuites

and discourses: in the ende wee shall be dazeled and not see any reason why God doth this or that. What is to bee done then? wee muste honour this iustice of God which is vnknowne to vs." 36 (Job 9:23-28), 168.b.4. *...nous aurons beau à enquirir, et faire de grands circuits et discours, en la fin nous demourerons esblouys, et ne verrons nulle raison pourquoy Dieu fait ceci ou cela. Que faut-il donc? Que nous adorions ceste iustice qui nous est incognue* [*CO* 33:451].

[101] "Thus you see, how that vnder this *fearing of God*, here is comprehended all religion: that is to wit, all the seruice and honoure whiche the creatures owe vntoo their God." 1 (Job 2:11-13), 4.b.45. *Voila comme sons ce mot de crainte de Dieu, toute la religion est comprinse, c'est à savoir tout le service, et l'hommage que les creatures doivent à leur Dieu* [*CO* 33:31]. For an in-depth analysis of Calvin's use of 'piety' [*pietas*], see Sou-Young Lee, "Calvin's Understanding of *Pietas*," in *Calvinus Sincerioris Religionis Vindex: Calvin as Protector of the Purer Religion*, ed. by Wilhelm H. Neuser and Brian G. Armstrong. Sixteenth Century Essays and Studies, vol. XXXVI. (Kirksville, MO: Sixteenth Century Journal Publishers, Inc., 1997), 225-239. For Calvin, Lee argues, the fear of God and piety are terms used synonymously. *Ibid.*, 227.

[102] 19 (Job 5:8-10), 83.b.31. ...*tremblions*...[*CO* 33:232].

[103] See, e.g., "For in the person of Iob, the holy Ghoste hath set oure frailtie before our eyes as it were in a glasse. I meane the frailtie of mind and not of body [*ie di fragilité de sens, et non point du corps*]. 27 (Job 7:1-6), 123.a.46 [*CO* 33:334]. Calvin also refers to Job as a "mirror": "And herein we see vpon what condition God hath set vs in this world, namely that we should be here as mirrors of his vertue. For when he giueth vs the grace to gouerne our selues by his holie Spirite, he setteth vs as it were vpon a scaffold, to the end that his gracious goodnesse and mercie should be knowne in vs, and therevpon he himselfe might be glorified against Satan in our persones. And sure the honor is inestimable which God doeth vnto vs, when he choozeth vs, I say when he choozeth vs poore wormes of the earth, to be glorified in vs against Satan, and to make his triumphes by vs." 4 (Job 1:6-8), 17.b.25. *Et en cela voyons-nous à quelle condition Dieu nous a mis au monde, c'est que nous soyons ici comme miroirs de sa vertu: quand il nous a fait ce bien de nous gouverner par son sainct Esprit, il nous met comme sur un eschaffaut, afin que sa bonté et misericorde se cognoisse en nous, et sur cela il se glorifie contre Satan en nos personnes. Or c'est un honneur inestimable que Dieu nous fait, quand il nous choisit, nous povres vers de terre, pour estre glorifié en nous contre Satan, et qu'il fait ses triomphes sur nous* [*CO* 33:65].

[104] "we haue to vnderstand, that it is not a slauish feare (as men terme it:) but it is so termed in respect of the honour which we owe him." 1 (Job 1:1), 4.b.32. *Notons donc que iamais nous ne pourrons ordonner nostre vie comme il appartient, si nous n'avons les yeux fichez en Dieu, et à nos prochains* [*CO* 33:31].

[105] "to feare God it behoueth vs to be sure of his goodnesse." 103 (Job

28:10-28), 486.a.34. ... *pour craindre Dieu nous soyons certifiez de sa bonté...* [*CO* 34:528].

[106] Calvin has in mind that "Gods Registers are full of our woorkes, woordes, and thoughts ... This knowledge then must holde vs in awe." 29 (Job 7:16-21), 136.a.39,60. ...*les registres de Dieu sont pleins de toutes nos oeuvres, de nos paroles, de nos pensees... Ceste cognoissance donc nous doit retenir...*[*CO* 33:367-368].

[107] Thinking of God's steadfastness in preserving the creation, Calvin responds: "What is to be done then, but only to woorship our God, confessing ourselues to come farre short of so houge greatnesse, and so incomprehensible wisdome? For of a truthe it is good reason that we should walk in all humblenesse and feare, when we come to the considering of Gods woonderfull woorks, which shewe themselues euery where in the order of nature." 148 (Job 38:4-11), 695.a.65. *Que nous reste-il donc, sinon d'adorer nostre Dieu, confessans que nous defaillons du tout sous une telle grandeur, et sous une telle sagesse, et si incomprehensible? Car à la verité, c'est bien raison que nous cheminions en humilité et crainte, quand il est question de contempler les oeuvres admirables de Dieu, comme elles se demonstrent en tout l'ordre de nature* [*CO* 35:368].

[108] 88 (Job 33:1-7), 415.b.7 [*CO* 34:339].

[109] "...that in considering God iudgments, wee muste looke higher than our ownes wittes can reach vnto: for that is the cause why we feare not God so much as we ought to do. Yet notwithstanding we diminishe not his power, in not fearing the highnesse that is in him, which ought too make vs afrayd." 142 (Job 36:20-24), 666.a.52. ...*qu'en considerant les iugemens de Dieu, il nous les faut comprendre plus haut que nostre esprit ne monte: car voila qui est cause que nous ne craignons point Dieu tant que nous devons. Tant y a que nous aneantissons sa vertu, en ne craignant la hautesse qui est en lui, laquelle nous doit effrayer* [*CO* 35:292]; Cf. "It is with vs as it is with little children: for as long as they be not afrayd they sport and play, and runne euerywhere. But if they bee scared with any feare, a man shall not get them out of their mothers lap. The little chickens would neuer gather themselues so hastily vnder their dames winges, as when they be scared and put in feare. Wee be so witlesse, that if wee knowe there is no daunger for vs, wee play the stray beasts. And therefore our Lorde to drawe vs home too him, sendeth vs such feare, as wee be fayne spite of our teeth to acknowledge that our lyfe is vnsure, if it be not garded by God." 118 (Job 18:12-21), 319.a.45. *C'est de nous comme des petis enfans: car s'ils ne craignent, ils s'esgayent, ils se iettent de costé et d'autre: mais s'il y a quelque crainte qui les espouvante, on ne les peut faire sortir du giron de leurs meres. Les petis poulsins mesmes ne se rassemblent point si facilement sous les ailes de leurs meres, sinon qu'ils soyent effarouchez, et qu'ils craignent. Nous sommes tant despourveus de sens, que si nous ne savons qu'il y a danger pour nous, nous faisons des bestes esgarees. Et nostre Seigneur pour nous retirer à soy nous envoye des craintes, tellement qu'il faut qu'en despit de nos dents,*

*nous cognoissions que nostre vie est mal asseuree, sinon qu'elle ait Dieu pour sa garde* [*CO* 34:81]. Cf. John Murray's response to the question: Is it right to be afraid of God? "The only proper answer is that it is the essence of impiety not to be afraid of God when there is *reason* to be afraid." *Principles of Conduct* (London: The Tyndale Press, 1957,1971), 233.

[110] "If we bee giuen to the feare of God, wee shall haue a firme and well settled state." 17 (Job 4:20-5:2), 77.a.27. *...quand nous serons adonnez á la crainte de Dieu, nous aurons une condition ferme, et bien establie* [*CO* 33:215].

[111] "Therfore when God doth so shewe vs his iudgementes, lette vs quake at them, and lette vs stande in feare and awe of him, submitting our selues wholly too that which he sayeth and vttereth." 18 (Job 5:3-7), 83.b.30. *Quand donc Dieu nous monstre ainsi ses iugemens, que nous tremblions dessous, et que nous soyons comme tenus captifs sous sa crainte, nous assubiettissans du tout à ce qu'il dit et prononce* [*CO* 33:232].

[112] "That such as haue no pitie vpon the poore wretched creatures which are in aduersitie, haue giuen ouer the feare of God... That to proue our selues to haue the feare of God, it behoueth vs to labour to doo good to the afflicted... wee must be softened by the syght of euery one that is in distresse." 25 (Job 6:15-23), 113.b.22,50. *Que ceux qui n'ont nulle pitié des povres miserables qui sont en affliction, que ceux-là ont delaissé la crainte de Dieu... que pour approuver que nous avons la crainte de Dieu, il faut que nous taschions bien faire aux affligez* [*CO* 33:308-309].

[113] Citing Proverbs 1:4 and 14:27, that "the fear of the Lord is the beginning of wisdom," and "a fountain of life," Job adds, "such as are edified to feare and obey God, are men of right vnderstading: and that the same is thing wherevpon we must set our mindes, and not vpon wandring speculatio[n]s ." 103 (Job 28:10-28), 485.a.39. *...que ceux qui sont edifiez à craindre Dieu et à luy obeir, sont vrayement entendus, et que c'est là où il nous faut appliquer nostre estude, et non point à des speculations volages* [*CO* 34:525].

[114] Linking "fear" and "wisdom," Calvin lashes out at the spirit that refuses to submit to the revelation of God: "Therefore let vs marke well that it not ynough for vs to haue a good desire to profite in the holy Scripture: but also that we must come to it with all reuerance, and desire nothing but to imbrace all that is contayned there, not hauing our tongues filed with prattle with God, nor bringing our doctrine or disputations against the pure doctrine of the Scripture, but concluding generally , and saying : "looke, whatsoeuer is sayde to vs here, or whatsoeuer wee reade here, wee know it to be the truth of God." 103 (Job 28:10-28), 486.b.42. *Ainsi donc notons bien que ce n'est point assez que nous ayons affection de profiter en l'Escriture saincte: mais sachons qu'il nous y faut venir avec toute reverence, que nous ne demandions sinon d'embrasser tout ce qui est là contenu, que nous n'ayons point un bec affilé pour iaser à l'encontre de Dieu, que nous n'apportions point des doctrines ne disputations contraires à la pure doctrine de l'Escriture, mais que nous ayons ceste conclusion generale, Tout ce qui*

*nous est dit, et que nous lisons en particulier, cognoissons-nous que c'est la verité de Dieu?* [*CO* 34:529].

[115] 37 (Job 9:29-35), 173.b.27. *la bouche close* [*CO* 33:464]; cf. 138 (Job 35:12-15), 649.a.21,65 [*CO* 35:245]; 148 (Job 38:4-11), 697.b.24 [*CO* 35:374].

[116] "... we cannot go forwarde in the feare of God, but by renouncing our selues. For what haue wee else in our nature but a Sea and bottomlesse pitte? But we must cast off all that geare, and learne to exercise our selues in the things that God sheweth vs by his woorde..." 103 (Job 28:10-28), 487.b.60. *...que nous ne pourrons profiter en la crainte de Dieu, sinon en renonçant à nous-mesmes. Car qu'est-ce que nous avons en nostre nature, sinon une mer et un abysme de tout mal? Or il faut que nous reiettions tout cela, et que nous apprenions de nous exercer en ce que Dieu nous monstre par sa parole...* [*CO* 34:532].

[117] "Wee see then the madde presumptuousnesse that is in men, to be desirous to co[n]ceyue in their brayne the things that are not graunted to them, and to enter into Gods secretes whither he will or no." 150 (Job 38:18-32), 706..b.43. *Voila une admonition bien propre, attendu d'un costé la nonchalance qui est aux hommes, et de l'autre costé leur folle presomption: car si Dieu nous veut cacher ses secrets, il semble qu'en despit de luy nous appetions de les savoir* [*CO* 35:398].

[118] "For there are two vyces in men which are harde too correct. The one is ouerboldenesse [*l'audace*], and the other foolishe vanitie [*fole vanité*]. As touching the Ouerboldnesse, it is in that men are desirous to knowe more than God hath appoynted; and too bee short, that they woulde be wise whether God woulde or no, whereas God onely is the fountayne of wisedome." 102 (Job 38:10-28), 480.b.41. *Car il y a deux vices aux hommes qui sont difficiles à corriger: l'un est l'audace, l'autre est une fole vanité. Or quant à ceste audace, c'est que les hommes veulent plus savoir tousiours que Dieu ne leur ordonne: bref, ils veulent estre sages en despit que Dieu en ait: et c'est Dieu qui est la fontaine de toute sagesse* [*CO* 34:513].

[119] 103 (Job 28:10-28), 487.a.20. *Voila di-ie, la vraye marque pour discerner le troupeau de Dieu d'avec toutes les bestes sauvages qui se desbordent* [*CO* 34:530].

[120] "Wherefore let vs bethinke vs well to walke in such feare, that vpon knowledge of our owne feeblenesse, wee may not be blinded with any presumption, but rather pray God to guyde vs and hold vs with his mightie hand, and not suffer vs in any wise to fall: And that if he happen to suffer vs to swarue, he neuerthelesse so hold vs vp, as we may not come to the full poynt of iniquitie, but that as soone as we shall haue done amisse, we may by and by be sorie, and flee to his mercie." 141 (Job 36:15-19), 663.b.14. *Avisons bien donc de cheminer en telle solicitude, que cognoissans la foiblesse qui est en nous, nous n'ayons nulle presomption que nous aveugle: mais plustost que nous prions Dieu qu'il nous quide et nous tienne la main forte, et ne permette pas que nous tombions en façon que ce soit. Et s'il advient qu'il nous laisse decliner, que toutes fois il nous retienne, en sorte*

*que nous ne venions point iusques au comble d'iniquité: mais que si tost que nous aurons failli, nous gemissions pour recourir à sa misericrode* [*CO* 35:284]. Cf. "God hathe had iust cause to set vs in suche state... to the ende to hold vs in awe and subiection vnto hym." 28 (Job 7:7-15), 128.a.66. ...*que Dieu a en iuste cause de nous mettre en telle condition, que nous soyons enserrez de tous maux, et de toutes afflictions* [*CO* 33:347]. And again: "Therefore when wee bee afflicted, lette vs pray God so to hold vs in awe, as we may glorify him, and that if any toyes come in our heads too grudge againste him, they may be beate[n] downe, knowing that we cannot speake one word of ourselues, but the same shall prouoke Gods wrath more and more." 89 (Job 23:8-12), 419.b.15. *Ainsi donc prions Dieu qu'il nous retiene quand il nous afflige, tellement que nous le puissions glorifier: et si des choses nous viennent en phantasie pour murmurer contre lui, que cela soit rabbatu, sachans que nous ne pouvons pas dire un seul mot de nous-mesmes, que ce ne soit pour provoquer l'ire de Dieu d'advanatge* [*CO* 34:351].

[121] "...the feare of God will neuer be in vs, till we be come to the poynt that we spake of: which is, that we know Gods mercie as it is offered vs in our Lord Iesus Christe: Namely that wee be drawne vnto him by his goodnesse, where through he allureth vs, and that we haue the boldnesse to call vpon him as our father, so as wee returne vnto him euen when wee bee vtterly dismayed." 103 (Job 28:10-28), 487.a.54. ...*que la crainte de Dieu ne sera iamais en nous, iusques à tant que nous soyons venus là où i'ay dit, c'est que nous cognoissions la misericorde de Dieu selon qu'elle nous est offerte en nostre Seigneur Iesus Christ: c'est que nous soyons attirez à luy par sa bonté, par laquelle il nous convie, et que nous ayons ceste hardiesse de l'invoquer comme nostre Pere, que quand nous serons confus nous retournions à luy* [*CO* 34:531].

[122] "But the chiefest assault wherewith he will exercise vs, is that wee may giue him glorie, notwithstanding that it seeme he is minded to thunder downe vpon us." 26 (Job 9:23-28), 165.a.17. *Mais le principal assaut où il nous veut exercer, c'est que nous luy donnions gloire, cependant qu'il semble qu'il nous vueille du tout foudroyer* [*CO* 33:442].

[123] "But by the way wee bee here new againe warned too prepare ourselues to pacience, not onely for some one kind of aduersitie, but for all that euer can betyde vs, according as wee see howe menne are borne too diuers afflcitions." 22 (Job 5:19-27), 100.a.35. *Or cependant nous sommes ici advertis derechef de nous preparer à patience, non pas seulement pour une espece de mal, mais pour tout ce qui nous peut advenir: comme nous voyons que les hommes sont nais à diverses afflicitions* [*CO* 33:274-275].

[124] "If we be not pacie[n]t when God scourgeth vs: all the seruice that we do vnto him wil be no great matter." 5 (Job 1:9-11), 20.a.62. ...*si nous ne sommes patiens quand Dieu nous afflige, tout le service que nous luy ferons ne sera pas grand chose* [*CO* 33:71].

[125] The full defintion is as follows: "...this word *Pacient*, or *Pacientnesse* betokeneth not that me[n] should become blockish, so as they should haue

no heauinesse at al, nor be combered with any griefe when they feele aduersities: but the vertue is when they can moderate themselues, and hold suche a measure, as they cease not to glorifye God in the middest of all their miseries: nor be so ouercombred and swallowed vp with sorrowe and anguish, as to quaile altogither: but fight against their owne passions, vntil they maye be able to frame themselues to the good will of God, and to conclude as Job doth here, and finally to say that he is righteous in all respects." 7 (Job 1:20-22), 29.a.14. *Ainsi donc notons que le mot de Patience ne signifie pas que les hommes soyent eslourdis, qu'ils n'ayent nulle tristesse, qu'ils ne soyent point faschez quand ils sentiront quelque affliction: mais la vertu est, quand ils se pourront moderer, et tenir telle mesure, qu'ils ne laisseront point de glorifier Dieu au milieu de toutes leurs miseres: qu'ils ne seront point troublez d'angoisse, et tellement engloutis, que de quiter là tout: mais qu'ils batailleront contre leurs passions iusques à ce qu'ils se puissent renger à la bonne volonté de Dieu, et conclure comme fait ici Iob, et dire qu'il est du tout iuste* [CO 33:93-94].

[126] Commenting on the commendation of Job in James 5:11, Calvin remarks: "If, however, it be asked, Why does the Apostle so much commend the patience of Job, as he had displayed many signs of impatience, being carried away by a hasty spirit? To this I reply, that though he sometimes failed through the infirmity of the flesh, or murmured within himself, yet he ever surrendered himself to God, and was ever willing to be restrained and ruled by him. Though, then his patience was somewhat deficient, it is yet deservedly commended." [*Quaeritur tamen cur patientiam Iob tantopere commendet apostolus, quum tamen caeco impetu abreptus, multa impatientiae signa edat. Respondeo: etiamsi vel interdum carnis infirmitate labascat, vel secum tumultuetur: semper tamen huc redire ut se totum Deo permittat, seque ipsi fraenandum ac regendum offerat.*] *Commentaries on the Catholic Epistles*, trans. John Owen, in *Calvin's Commentaries*, vol. XXII (Grand Rapids, MI: Baker Book House, 1981), 351-352 [CO 55:428]. It is now common to suggest that the Greek *hupomone* is better understood as meaning "perseverance" or "endurance" rather than "patience." See, for example, Peter Davids, *The Epistle of James: A Commentary on the Greek Text* (Exeter: The Paternoster Press, 1982), 186-187. Such considerations were unnecessary for Calvin, who saw no difficulty in applying the word "patience" to Job in a general way.

[127] "True it is that he was not vtterly destitute of pacience: but he ceassed not to bee tormented with horrible passions…" 30 (Job 8:1-6), 138.b.68. *Vray est qu'il n'a pas esté destitué du tout de patience: mais il n'a pas laissé d'estre tormenté d'horribles passions…* [CO 33:374]. Calvin admits that the best are impatient in some way. 123 (Job 33:8-14), 580.a.30 [CO 34:57].

[128] "It is not simply a greef conceyued of the mislyking of our aduersities when wee be werie of them: but it is an excessiue hartburning or stomaking against the[m], when we can[n]ot submit ourselues simply vnto God to dispose of vs at his pleasure." 67 (Job 18:1-11), 314.a.20. *Ce n'est pas une*

*simple passion, quand nous sommes faschez de nos maux, mais c'est un despit excessif, quand nous ne pouvons pas simplement nous assubiettir à Dieu afin qu'il dispose de nous à sa volonté* [CO 34:66-67].

[129] "... when wee be so foolish or madde as to runne rushing agaynst him." 153 (Job 39:22-35), 719.a.42. ...*quand nous serons si fols et enragez de venir heurter contre lui* [CO 35:431].

[130] "It is all one as if wee would first rob him of his right, & afterward make him our fellow and companion, so as he should haue no more authoritie nor superioritie ouer vs." 123 (Job 33:8-14), 581.b.8. ...*c'est autant comme si nous le voulions faire nostre pareil et compagnon, apres l'avoir despouillé de son droit, que nous voulussions qu'il n'eust plus de maistrise ne de superiorité par dessus nous* [CO 35:61].

[131] 146 (Job 37:14-24), 687.b.62 [CO 35:61].

[132] 152 (Job 39:22-35), 721.a.25. ...*insensez du tout* [CO 35:436].

[133] "Therfore let vs learne that whensoeuer we lift vp our neb [*le bec*, i.e., "beak," or "snout"] against God, we shall win nothing by it, but our woordes shall flip into the aire, and vanish away as smoke. Neuerthelesse let vs marke by the way, that our woords shall not fall to the ground, but must be registered to our greate and horrible confuzion. Then if our pride be suche as we dare murmure against God: such blasphemousenesse must needs come to a reckening, and not scape vnpunished." 146 (Job 37:14-24), 688.a.18. *Apprenons donc, toutes fois et quantes que nous leverons le bec à l'encontre de Dieu, que nous n'y gaignerons rien, que nos paroles s'escouleront en l'air, et s'en iront en fumee. Toutes fois notons cependant que nos propos ne tomberont point à terre, qu'il faudra qu'ils soyent enregistrez à nostre grande confusion et horrible. Quand donc nostre arrogance sera telle, d'oser murmurer contre Dieu: il faudra que tels blasphemes viennent en conte, et ils ne demeureront point impunis* [CO 35:348-349].

[134] "It behoueth us to conclude, O my God, thy determinations are incomprehensible, and forasmuch as I am not able as now to know any more by reason of the rudenesse and infirmitie of my vnderstanding: I will wayte paciently till thou make mee to perceyue the cause why. So Lord, when I shall haue taried in this forte like a poore blind soule, thou wilt open mine eyes, and make me perceyue wherevnto these things tende, and what shall be the ende of them, and I shall profite better by them, than I do now." 123 (Job 33:8-14), 579.b.16. ...*si faut-il conclurre, O mon Dieu, tes conseils sont incomprehensibles, i'attendray patiemment que tu me faces cognoistre pourquoy, quand ie ne puis pour le present cognoistre d'avantage pour ma rudesse, et l'infirmité de mon Esprit. Ainsi, Seigneur, apres que l'auray demeuré ici comme un povre aveugle, tu m'ouvriras les yeux, tu me feras sentir où ces choses tendent, quelle en doit estre l'issue, et i'y profiterai mieux qu'à present* [CO 35:56].

[135] "Too bee short, we must haue nothing left vs saue only the promis [*donne*] that God hath made vs, saying, I will be your Sauiour, when as notwithstanding he seemeth therwithall to turne his backe vpon vs, and that

he hath shaken vs off, yea and that he euen fauoreth our enimyes, and that he putteth the cudgell into their hand too strike vs with, and is altoogither against vs. I say when all this betydeth, yet neuerthelesse must be trust continually in him." 20 (Job 5:11-16), 93.a.29. ...*bref que nous n'ayons sinon le mot que Dieu nous donne pour dire, Ie seray vostre Sauveur, et que neantmoins cependant il semble qu'il nous tourne le dos, qu'il nous ait reiettez, qu'il semble mesme que Dieu favorise à nos ennemis, qu'il leur monstre le baston en la main, duquel nous soyons frappez, qu'il semble qu'il nous soit contraire. Quand tout cela sera, di-ie, si faut-il neantmoins que nous esperions tousiours en luy* [*CO* 33:257].

[136] "Gods wisedome is so infinite, as it can neuer be thoroughly comprehended. So long as men liue in this world, it is ynough that they haue some tast of it, and profite dayly more and more in it. On the otherside, let vs marke well, that when we haue learned any thing, wee keepe it ill, and forget it out of hand: and therefore wee had need to be put in minde of it: and God is so gratious vnto vs, as to set this mercie afore vs, to the end we should nor be vtterly as it were desperate and past hope of trusting in him. For the vnderstanding of a thing in our brayne, is not all that wee haue to do: but is must moreouer be printed in our hart." 128 (Job 33:29–34:3), 604.b.16. *Ainsi nous voyons que la sagesse de Dieu est si infinie, que iamais elle ne se comprendra du tout: cependant que les hommes vivent en ce monde, c'est assez qu'ils en ayent quelque goust, et y profitent iournellement. D'autre costé notons bien que quand nous aurons apprins une chose, nous la retenons mal, et nous l'aurions tantost oubliee. Il faut donc qu'elle nous soit ramenteuë: et Dieu nous fait ceste grace de nous proposer sa misericorde afin que nous ne demeurions point vuides, et comme desesperez pour n'avoir point d'esperance en luy. Car ce n'est point le tout que nous ayons entendu une chose en nostre cerveau: mais il faut qu'elle nous soit imprimee au coeur.*[*CO* 35:125].

[137] "Wee muste not measure the assistaunce of our God by our eyesight, but by the promisse of succour that is behighted vs from aboue..." This is for Calvin a "very important lesson." 22 (Job 5:19-27), 101.a.60. ...*mais selon le secours qui nous est promis d'enhaut...* [*CO* 33:278].

[138] 27 (Job 7:1-6), 125.a.1 [*CO* 33:338], Cf. 89 (Job 23:8-12), 419.b.10 [*CO* 34:351].

[139] Preaching on the ninth chapter of Job, Calvin notes that Job falls into near despair, losing faith in prayer and in God's even hearing him in his troubles (Job 9:16). Calvin draws the lesson, however, that even here, some "sparke of brightnesse" [*estincelle de clarté*] still remains. "He giueth vs some feeling of faith..." 35 (Job 9:16-22), 162.a.11. ...*il nous donne quelque sentiment de foy...* [*CO* 33:434]. Earlier, Calvin compares Job's cry with Christ's cry of dereliction in Matthew 27:46 and Jesus being enabled, even in his agony, to call upon God when he felt utterly forsaken. 161.b.56 [*CO* 33:434].

[140] Calvin, at one point in the Joban sermons, reminds us of the story of

Jacob in this regard. "Wee see what happened to Iacob: he wrestled with an Angell, and therefore is called Israell: that is to say, preuayling with God: but yet notwithstanding he halted, and was fayne to haue a lame hip as long as he liued: to the ende he might feele, that hee had not gotten that victory in suche wise as there was no feeblenesse in him. And that is an example and patterne for vs, that although God strengthen vs by his power, so as wee ouercome our temptations: yet the same is not done without some markes of our infirmity." 129 (Job 34:4-10), 607.a.28. *Nous voyons comme il en est advenu à Iacob: il a lutté avec l'Ange, et en est appellé Israel, c'est à dire victorieux avec Dieu: toutes fois si est-ce qu'il en cloche, et faut que sa hanche soit hors de son lieu tant qu'il vit, afin qu'il sente qu'il n'a point eu ceste victoire, tellement qu'il n'y ait eu de la foiblesse en luy. Et ce nous est un exemple et patron, Que combien que Dieu nous fortifie par sa vertu, tellement que nous venions au dessus de nos tentations, cela ne se fait point point qu'il n'y ait des marques de nostre infirmité* [*CO* 35:132].

[141] "According as a man shall bee weake, and as God shall not haue indewed him with so greate a grace of his holy spirite: so verily will he make him to feele is iudgement thereafter: howbeit hee will holde him vp, and make him to taste of his mercie in the middes (sic.) of his wrath, so as the same shall not vtterly dismaye him." 23 (Job 6:1-9), 104.b.63. ...*qu'un homme sera debile, et que Dieu ne l'aura point doué d'une si grande grace de son sainct Esprit: et bien, s'il lui fait sentir son iugement, ce sera en le supportant, il lui fera gouster sa misericorde au milieu de son ire, tellement qu'elle ne lui sera point espouvantable* [*CO* 33:287].

[142] "But as for him that hath receiued a more singular stre[n]gth, and whom God hath fortified with his holy spirite: hee must be faine to sustain greater brunts, and farre rougher assaults, than such as are feeble like little children." 23 (Job 6:1-9), 105.a.1. *Mais celui qui aura receu une force plus singuliere, et lequel Dieu aura fortifié par son S. Esprit, il faut que celui-la soustiene de plus grands hurts, et beaucoup plus rudes que ceux qui sont foibles comme petis enfans* [*CO* 33:287].

[143] "... a blinde reioycing, such as is among wordlings, which are caried away with their goods: so that they forget God, and remember no more their owne frailtie: but are exalted in themselues. This then is a frantike ioy, an inordinate ioy, a ioy that turneth vs away from God, and maketh vs so drunken, as we know not any more what we be." 115 (Job 31:24-28), 542.a.14. *Mais Iob parle ici d'une resiouissance aveugle, et telle qu'elle est aux hommes mondains, qui sont transportez de leurs biens, en sorte qu'apres avoir mis Dieu en oubli, il ne leur souvient plus de leur fragilité, mais ils s'eslevent en eux-mesmes. Voila donc une ioye enragee, une ioye desbordee, laquelle nous destourne de Dieu, et nous enyvre tellement, que nous ne savons plus qui nous sommes* [*CO* 34:680].

[144] 73 (Job 20:1-7), 344.a.42. *ioye des enfans* [*CO* 34:148]. In Sermon 99, Calvin, alluding to Luke 6:25, defines worldly mirth as "a cleane forgetting of themselues, and a turning away from God, according as wee see that most

men cannot bee merrie [*esiouir*], vnlesse they thrust God a good way off, and runne riot, and gyue themselues to such superfluitie [*intemperance*], as there remaineth no more wit nor reason [*sens ne raison*] in them." 99 (Job 27-8-12), 466.b.18. *C'est qu'ils se mettent en oubli, et se destournent arriere de Dieu: comme nous voyons que la plus part ne se peuvent esiouir sinon qu'ils reiettent Dieu bien loin, se desbordent, et s'adonnent à une telle intemperance, qu'il n'y ait plus ne sens ne raison en eux* [*CO* 34:477].

[145] 344.a.44,50. *Car ceux-ci se resiouissent en ce qu'ils tiennent à la main... qu'ils cognoistront la bonté de leur Dieu, quand il s'est fait sentir à eux plus que Pere...* [*CO* 34:148].

[146] "Wherefore sendeth he them so many aduersities, that they are fayne to sighe and grone, and wote not on which side too turne them? It is too make them too call vpon him, and too flee vnto him for refuge. We see then howe that by these afflictions we bee taught, first to knowe our selues, that we presume not anything of our selues, nor bee puffed vp with pride and statelynesse: and secondly not too take too muche pleasure in our owne lustes, but rather too forsake all worldly things, and finally to call vpon God, which is the principallest poynt of all." 19 (Job 5:8-10), 88.b.50. *Pourquoy est-ce qu'il leur envoye tant de maux, qu'ils souspirent et gemissent, ne sachans de quel costé se tourner? C'est afin qu'ils l'invoquent, qu'ils ayent leur refuge à luy. Nous voyons donc comme par les afflictions nous sommes enseignez premierement de nous cognoistre afin de ne rien presumer de nous, de n'estre point enflez de fierté et d'arrogance: et puis afin de ne nous point esgayer par trop en nos cupiditez, mais plustost renoncer aux choses de ce monde, et finalement invoquer Dieu: car c'est le principal que cela* [*CO* 33:245-246].

[147] "For the principall poynt is, that we referre all vnto God, acknowledging our selues to be wholy his, and that it is reason that our life & our death be offered vnto him in sacrifyze: that we worship him, that we do homage vnto him for the things that he hath giuen into our handes, that we confesse how he ought to haue all superioritie ouer vs, that we protest it by our prayers and requestes, and that we shewe how it is he that is our whole refuge, and how it is he to whom we are beholding for all things." 4 (Job 1:6-8), 18.a.51. *Or il y a le principal, que nous rapportions le tout à Dieu, sachans que nous sommes siens, et que c'est raison que nostre vie, et nostre mort luy soit offerte en sacrifice, que nous l'adorions, que nous luy facions hommage de ce qu'il nous a mis entre les mains, que nous protestions qu'il doit avoir toute superiorité sur nous, que par prieres et requestes nous confessions cela, que nous declarions que c'est de luy que nous tenons tout* [*CO* 33:66-67].

[148] "God is absent from vs as in respecte of eyesight. And although he dwell in vs by his power, and make vs to fele his grace: yet notwithstanding we be as it were separated from him, to outward appearaunce. Neuerthelesse, by prayer we mount vp into heauen, and present ourselues before his maiestie, and (to be short) are ioyned vnto him. Ye see then that here is a

band of familiarity betweene God and men, in this libertie which he giueth vs to call vpon him. But yet can we not pray vnto him as we ought to do, except we knowe his goodnesse, according as it is sayd in the fifth Psalme, Lord I will worship in thy temple, euen vpon the multitude of thy mercies. Vntill such time as our God hath certified vs that he is our father, it is not possible for vs to dare come vnto him: our mouth is shet, and our hart is locked vp, and to be short, wee are vtterly excluded from the priuiledge of calling vpo[n] him." 126 (Job 33:29), 595.b.48. *Voila donc un lien de privauté qui est entre Dieu et les hommes, en ceste liberté qu'il nous donne de l'invoquer. Or tant y a que nous ne le pouvons prier comme il appartient, sinon que nous ayons cognu sa bonté: comme il est dit au Pseaume cinquieme (v. 8), i'adoreray en ton temple, Seigneur, en la multitude de ta bonté. Iusques à tant donc que nostre Dieu nous ait certifiez qu'il nous est Pere, il n'est point possible que nous osions venir à luy: nostre bouche sera close, nostre coeur sera enserré: bref, nous serons du tout privez et exclus de ce privilege de l'invoquer [CO 35:101].*

[149] "The greatest honour that God requireth at our hands, is that we should call vpon him in all our aduersities." 70 (Job 19:13-16), 327.b.36. *Le plus grand honneur que Dieu demande de nous, c'est que nous l'invoquions en toutes nos adversitez [CO 34:103].*

[150] Thus in the opening sermon, Calvin can say: "Seing then that we be so easily caryed away: we ought the rather to pray vnto God, that when we haue a good case, he himselfe will voucsafe to guyde vs in all singlenesse by his holie spirit, so as we may not passe the boundes, which he hath set vs by his worde..." *Voyons donc que nous sommes ainsi aisement transportez, d'autant plus devons nous prier Dieu, que quand nous aurons bonne cause, il nous conduise par son Sainct Esprit en tout simplicité, que nous ne passions point les limites, qu'il nous a constituez par sa parole.* 1 (Job 1:1), 2.a.18 [*CO* 33:24].

[151] "...to pray rightly is a rare gift [*Unde sequitur singulare esse recte orandi donum.*]" *Institutes* III.xx.5 [*CO* 2:629]. For a defence of Calvin's covenantal theology, see A. A. Woolsey, "Unity and Continuity in Covenantal Thought: A Study in the Reformed Tradition to the Westminster Assembly," 2 vols. (Ph.D. diss., Glasgow University, 1988). See also P. Lillback, "The Binding of God: Calvin's Role in the Development of Covenant Theology" (Ph.D. diss. Westminster Theological Seminary, 1985).

[152] Cf. Schreiner, *Where Shall Wisdom be Found?* 118-119.

[153] 24 (Job 6:8-14), 108.b.17. *C'est que nous ne luy demandions rien qui ne soit accordant à sa volonté [CO 33:296].*

[154] "...let vs be well aduised that wee be sober minded when we fall in hande with praying vnto God, and that we haue well considered aforehand what thinigs God promiseth and permitteth." 24 (Job 6:8-14), 109.a.1. ...*que nous soyons sobres quand il est question de prier, et que nous ayons bien regardé devant la main ce que Dieu nous a promis ou permis [CO 33:297].* And again: "a man must not couet any thing which he might not be bolde to

aske at Gods hande, will bee a bridle too vs. And wee must not presume too aske any thing, but that whiche God hath graunted by hys worde." 24 (Job 6:8-14), 109.a.35. *...qu'il ne faut point que l'homme appete rien, sinon ce qu'il osera demander à Dieu. Et il ne faut point que nous presumions de rien demander, sinon ce que Dieu a ottroyé par sa parole* [*CO* 33:297]. Calvin expands upon legitimate prayer in his commentary on Psalm 119:38: "Here we have briefly set forth the sole end and legitimate use of prayer, which is, that we may reap the fruits of God's promises... For we perceive the prophet allows not himself to petition or wish any thing but what God has condescended to promise. And certainly their presumption is great, who rush into the presence of God without call from his word." *Commentary on the Psalms*, 4:428-29, in *Calvin's Commentaries* vol. (Grand Rapids, MI: Baker, 1979). *Hic breviter notatur legitimus et unicus precandi finis, ut promissionum Dei effectus ad nos perveniat, unde sequitur, perperam facere qui habenas temere suis votis laxant. Videmus enim ut propheta nihil petere vel optare sibi permittat nisi quod Deus promittere dignatus est* [*CO* 32:231]. For a similar analysis of John Owen's dependence on Calvin here, see Sinclair Ferguson, *John Owen and the Christian Life* (Edinburgh: The Banner of Truth, 1987), 225.

[155] "Beholde (say I) an vntollerable presumptuousnesse, when a mortall man will beare such sway, as God must be subiect to his demaundes." 24 (Job 6:8-14), 108.b.59. *Voila (di-ie) une arrogance, qui est intolerable, quand un homme mortel veut dominer tellement que Dieu soit subiect à ce qu'il luy demandera* [*CO* 33:297].

[156] 24 (Job 6:8-14), 109.a.18 [*CO* 33:298]. "We must not come vntoo God with our heade vpright, nor bee so bolde as too make so farre account of him, that hee shoulde do whatsoeuer wee haue conceyued in oure brayne." 109.a.28. *Quand nous en ferons ainsi, que nous penserons de nostre costé qu'il ne faut point que nous venions devant Dieu la teste levee, que nous soyons hardis iusques là de le sommer de faire ce que nous aurons conceu en nostre cerveau: mais qu'il faut que nous luy soyons subiets en tout et par tout* [*CO* 33:297].

[157] "...spirituall battelles, praying God to strengthen vs, for wee see how all mans strength fayleth in that behalfe, so as wee shall bee quickely ouerwhelmed if wee bee not propped vp from aboue, and lifted vp by GOD when wee bee falne, and set agayne in too the right way when we bee stepped out of it." 41 (Job 10:18-22), 193.a.20. *Et ainsi apprestons-nous à tels combats spirituels, et prions Dieu qu'il nous fortifie, puis que nous voyons que toutes les vertus des hommes defaudront en cest endroit, et que nous serions bien tost abysmez, si ce n'estoit que nous fussions soustenus d'enhaut, et que Dieu nous relevast quand nous sommes cheus, qu'il nous redressast au droit chemin quand nous en sommes esgarez* [*CO* 33:514].

[158] 141 (Job 36:15-19), 663.b.14 [*CO* 35:284]. See n.120.

[159] "Yet is it Gods pleasure too exercize his children after that maner by hyding himselfe from them, and by making no countenance of hearing them,

or of regarding the miseries that they indure. True it is that he hath promised too bee readie too helpe vs as soone as we desire him: yea and that hee will not tarie too bee sued vntoo, but will preuent our requestes. And that it is that maketh the temptation much greeuouser, namely when God seemeth too haue dallied with vs, and too haue giuen vs a vaine and frutelesse hope. But let vs vnderstande, that seeing he hath exercised his children so heretofore: we must not maruell though he do the like to vs nowadayes. Wherfore let vs wait paciently, and we shal see by the ende, that he hath not forgotten vs, ne [sic] ceasseth too heare vs, although he shewe not oute of hande in the open sight of the worlde, that hee hath his hande stretched out ouer vs. And out of doubt, if wee bee pacient, and able too continue in prayer: it is a token that God hath heard vs alreadie. For if he had not preserued vs after that maner, were it possible for vs to haue continued one minute of an houre, as hath beene declared?" 70 (Job 19:13-16), 327.a.33. *Tant y a que Dieu veut ainsi exercer les siens, c'est qu'il se cachera, et ne fera point semblant de les ouir, ne de regarder aux maux qu'ils endurent. Vray est qu'il a promis, que si tost que nous le requerrons, il sera prest pour nous aider: mesmes qu'il n'attendra pas d'estre solicité, mais qu'il previendra nos requestes. Et voila aussi quiaggrave ceste tentation beaucoup plus, quand il nous semble que Dieu s'est mocqué, et qu'il nous a donné une esperance frivole et inutile. Mais cognoissons puis qu'il a ainsi exercé les siens, qu'auiourd'hui il ne se faut point esbahir s'il fait le semblable envers nous. Ainsi attendons en patience, et nous verrons par l'issue qu'il ne nous a point mis en oubli, et qu'il ne laisse pas de nous exaucer, encores qu'il ne monstre pas si tost en evidence qu'il ait la main estendue sur nous. Et de fait, quand nous sommes patiens, et que nous pouvons persister en nos oraisons, c'est signe que desia Dieu nous a exaucez: car s'il ne nous avoit ainsi preservez, seroit-il possible que nous puissions durer une seule minute de temps, comme il a esté exposé?* [CO 34:101-102]. Cf. 18 (Job 5:3-7), 80.a.63 [CO 33:223].

[160] "To be shorte, Gods children continue in prayer, and haue the sayde perseuerance or holding out, insomuch that although God afflict them, and seeme to turne his backe to the[m], and to be deafe to their requests: yet neuerthelesse they hold on still, and neuer give ouer cleane. Contrariwise, if God graunt not the faithful [sic, read "faithlesse"] their request as soone as they pray vnto him, if he pleasure them not by and by, if hee perfourme not their desires withoute delay: they thinke they haue lost their time." 99 (Job 27:8-12), 466.a.11. *En somme les enfans de Dieu continuent à prier, et ont ceste perseverance-la, telement que combien que Dieu les tormente, et qu'il sembe qu'il leur ait tourné le dos, et soit sourd à leurs requestes, si continueront-ils neantmoins, et ne se lasseront iamais. Au rebours les incredules apres avoir prié si Dieu ne leur applaudit, et qu'il ne leur gratifie, et face tous leurs desirs, il leur semble qu'ils ont perdu leur temps* [CO 34:475]. Calvin continues a little further on, "But when we hauc sighcd and sobbed to day, if we feele no assuagement by it, let vs retourne to the same

remedie again tomorrow. In good faith, ye see that although a sick person perceiue not that his Phisition hath done him good at the first: yet will he not ceasse to beleeue his counsell stil." 99 (Job 27:8-12), 466.a.33. ...*mais quand auiourd'huy nous aurons gemi et souspiré, s'il advient que nous n'ayons point senti d'allegement, que demain nous retournions encores à ce remede. Et defait, voila un malade qui ne s'appercervra point du premier coup de quoy la medicine luy profite: il ne laissera point toutes fois de croire le conseil qu'on luy donnera* [CO 34:476]; cf. 109 (Job 30:11-21), 515.b.57 [CO 34:608].

[161] "we haue not vtterly renou[n]ced ourselues [*tout renoncé à nous-mesmes*]. He that hath not yet lerned to tame his affections, and to subdue his will to the seruing of God, notwithstanding that it be hard for him to doo: knoweth not yet in good earnest what it is to liue well and faythfully." 66 (Job 17:6-16), 309.b.53. *Car nous n'avons pas du tout renoncé à nous-mesmes. Celui qui n'a point encores apprins de dompter toutes ses affections, et d'assuiettir sa volonté au service de Dieu, combien qu'il lui soit difficile: celui-là ne sait pas encores à bon escient que c'est de vivre bien et fidelement* [CO 34:55].

[162] Cf. fn. 114. Ronald S. Wallace, *Calvin's Doctrine of the Christian Life*, 51-67.

[163] "If God holde their nozes to the gryndstone by some sicknesse or by some other crosse: then they make fayre promises. But assoone as Gods hande is withdrawen from them: they shewe playnly how there was nothing but dissimulation in them." 31 (Job 8:7-13), 142.a.30. *Si Dieu les tient serrez, ou en quelque maladie, ou en une autre affliction, ils feront de belles promesses: la main de Dieu est-elle retiree? Ils monstrent bien qu'il n'y a eu que feintise en eux* [CO 33:382].

[164] "And it is certeyne that in the persone of one faythfull and pacient man, God intended to giue vs a mirrour of oure inordinate affections, too the ende wee shoulde beware of them, and seeke too feele the succour and refreshment that are shewed vs heere." 29 (Job 7:16-21), 135.b.17. *Or il est certain qu'en la personne d'un homme fidele, et en la personne d'un homme patient Dieu nous a voulu donner un miroir de nos affections excessives afin que nous y prenions garde, afin que nous cerchions de sentir le secours et allegement qui nous est ici monstré* [CO 33:365-366]. In graphic language, Calvin adds in another sermon that Job "acknowledgeth that hee ought too holde his mouth shette. Neuerthelesse hee ceasseth not too haue his skumme, as a boyling pot that seetheth vp into great wallops muste needes spirt ouer on one side or other." 69 (Job 19:1-12), 325.a.63. *...qu'il ait la bouche close. Mais si ne laisse-il point d'avoir des escumes: comme quand un pot boult, et que les bouillons sont trop grans, il faut qu'ils se iettent de costé et d'autre* [CO 34:97].

[165] "Let vs beseech [God] that if we haue but one foote already vpon our wicked affections, we may set both vpon the[m], that we may so treade them downe, as they may neuer rise againe: and that when the Diuell commeth to

tempt and prouoke vs vnto euill, he may not bring it to passe, but that our wittes may alwayes ouer reach him: and… that Gods spirit may so reigne in our hearts, that although there be wicked affections there, yet they may be so brideled and fettered, as they may not lift vp themselues nor tosse vs hither and thither, but that wee may alwayes stand at a stay, and bee fully resolued to say: It is meete that our God shoulde gouerne vs, and that wee should folowe his holy will." 111 (Job 31:1-4), 523.b.15. *Que si nous le requerons, et que nous sentions que nous avons desia un pié par dessus nos meschantes affections: mettons y tous les deux, et qu'elles soyent tellement foulees, que iamais ne puissent estre relevees. Et quand le diable nous vient picquer pour nous soliciter à mal, qu'il ne viene point à bout de nous, mais que nous ayons tousiours nos sens par dessus: bref, que l'Esprit de Dieu domine tellement en nos coeurs, qu'encores qu'il y ait des affections meschantes, elles soyent là tenues comme bridees, voire enchainees, et qu'elles ne s'eslevent point, que ce ne soit point pour nous agiter ne çà ne là, mais que nous demeurions tousiours fermes, et soyons resolus pour dire, Il faut que nostre Dieu nous gouverne, et que nous suivions sa saincte volonté* [CO 34:630]. Cf. "haue brydeled our affections," 112 (Job 31: 5-8), 529.b.21. …*retenu nos coeurs en bride*…[CO 34:646].

[166] 12 (Job 3:11-19), 54.a.45 [CO 33:157].

[167] "*parlé sans y penser,*" 51 (Job 13:16-22), 241.a.40 [CO 33:641].

[168] Calvin speaks of our affections "boiling up" [*bouillantes*], 11 (Job 3:2-10), 51.b.29 [CO 33:149]; "we be so heddie [*violents*] in our affections, we cannot iudge Gods works with a settled mind [*sens rassis*]." 56 (Job 14:16-22), 261.b.40 [CO 33:695].

[169] "all our ouergreat and excessiue affections, all our murmurings [*nos affections trop grandes et excessives*], and all other such like things: proceede of this, that wee knowe not what God is, and that we spoyle him of his Maiestie, asmuch as lieth in vs." 123 (Job 33:8-14), 581.a.47 [CO 35:61].

[170] 136 (Job 35:1-7), 640.a.21, 58. …*qu'il y a lors des bouffees plus que vehementes en nous*… [CO 35:221].

[171] 65 (Job 17:1-5), 305.b.18 [CO 34:431].

[172] 110 (Job 30:21-31), 518.b.28 [CO 34:615-616].

[173] 38 (Job 10:1-6), 176.b.3. …*que s'il lasche la bride à ses passions excessives, il faudra que cela reviene sur soy, ou contre soy* [CO 33:470].

[174] 29 (Job 7:16-21), 134.b.46. …*passionné selon la chair*…[CO 33:363].

[175] "The Phisicion seeth weel ynough how it is too the weakening of a poore man and too the vnstrengethening of his veynes and sinewes: and specially when no gentler meanes will serue than letting of bloud, it is euen as much as too drawe the substance out of a mannes bodye, and yet must he needs vse suche violent meanes, too remedie such a maladie: Euen so is God fayne too woork with vs, howbeeit that the same bee an extraordinarie maner with him. For when we say wee bee happie too bee chastized at Gods hand: it must leade vs vntoo lowelinesse, seing that God cannot procure our salvation, but by shewing himself too bee against vs. Is it not too bee sayd iustly,

that there is a maruellouse corruptnesse in men, sith God cannot bee their Sauiour and father but by handling them roughly?" 21 (Job 5:17-18), 96.a.63. *Le medecin voit bien que c'est pour affoiblir un povre homme, pour luy debiliter veines et nerfs: mesmes quand il n'y aura qu'une saignee bien douce, c'est autant tirer de la substance d'un homme, mais il faut qu'une telle violence de face pour remedier à un tel mal. Ainsi faut-il que Dieu besongne en nous, combien que ce luy soit un moyen extraordinaire. Car quand nous disons que nous sommes bien-heureux estans chastiez de la main de Dieu, il faut que cela nous induise à humilité, voyans que Dieu ne peut procurer nostre salut sinon en se monstrant contraire à nous. Ne faut-il pas bien dire qu'il y ait une merveilleuse corruption aux hommes, que Dieu ne puisse estre leur Sauveur et leur Pere sinon en les traitent rudement?* [*CO* 33:265].

[176] "hee lifteth vs vp as if wee were little kinges, and that hee seemeth too haue a fatherly care of vs, and to preferre vs aboue all creatures: and afterwarde throweth vs downe as men in the picture of the wheele of fortune." 29 (Job 7:19-21), 133.a.19. ...*qu'il nous esleve comme si nous estions des petis Rois, qu'il fait semblant d'avoir un soin paternel de nous, et de nous preferer à toutes creatures: et apres il nous abbat, comme on a ceste peincture de le rouë de fortune* [*CO* 33:359].

[177] 2 (Job 1:2-5), 7.a.44. ...*qu'il disposer de ses creatures à son plaisir*...[*CO* 33:38].

[178] "We see how they that haue some goodly outward shew, become brutish: and therefore let vs be sure that God visiteth vs with his whippes bicause of our sinnes." 17 (Job 4:20-5:2), 79.a.4. *Nous voyons comme ceux qui avoyent quelque belle apparence s'abbrutissent: et ainsi sachons que Dieu nous visite par ses fleaux à cause de nos pechez* [*CO* 33:220]. Elsewhere, Calvin distinguishes the nature of adversity as chastisement to God's children and punishment to the wicked. 21 (Job 5:17-18), 94.b.3 [*CO* 33:260].

[179] "...for lyke as wood caryeth that nature and propertie in it, that hee receyueth fire and kindleth easily: so also standeth the case with vs. For we haue sin, which is as it were the wood and matter of all afflictions: wherevpon commeth the wrath of God, & so must we nedes be co[n]sumed." 19 (Job 5:8-10), 84.a.21. *Car tout ainsi que le bois porte en soy ceste nature et proprieté qu'il reçoit aisément le feu, et s'enflamme: ainsi en est-il de nous: car nous avons le peché qui est comme le bois et la matiere de toutes afflictions: l'ire de Dieu vient dessus, et il faut que nous en soyons consumez* [*CO* 33:233].

[180] "For what would become of vs, if God should stretch out his arme against vs? Alas, what creature were able too stande before him? Verily he needeth no more but to shewe one angrie looke, and beholde all the worlde shoulde perishe." 21 (Job 5:17-18), 97.b.17. ...*mesmes il ne faut sinon qu'il monstre sa face courroucée, et voila tout le monde peri: et encores qu'il ne face point cela, seulement qu'il retire son Esprit, et il faut que tout defaille...* [*CO* 33:268].

[181] 97.b.41 [*CO* 33:268].

[182] "Ezechias felte as much. For God not onely afflicted him with sickenesse as may commonly befall vnto us: but also besides that, he shewed him a token of his displeasure." 23 (Job 6:1-9), 104.b.33. *Ezechias en sent autant. Car Dieu ne l'afflige point de maladie seulement, comme il nous pourra advenir communement: mais outre cela il luy monstre un signe de son ire* [*CO* 33:286]. Cf. 23 (Job 6:1-9), 106.a.50 [*CO* 33:290].

[183] "According as a man shall bee weake, and as God shall not haue indewed him with so greate a grace of his holy spirite: so verily will he make him to feele his iudgement thereafter: howbeit hee will holde him vp, and make him to taste of his mercie in the middes (sic.) of his wrath, so as the same shall not vtterly dismaye him." 23 (Job 6:1-9), 104.b.63. ...*selon qu'un homme sera debile, et que Dieu ne l'aura point doué d'une si grande grace de son sainct Esprit: et bien, s'il lui fait sentir son iugement, ce sera en le supportant, il lui fera gouster sa misericorde au milieu de son ire, tellement qu'elle ne lui sera point espouvantable* [*CO* 33:287]. Commenting on 1 Cor. 10:13, Calvin says: "[God] supplies us with the resources we need, and sets a limit to the temptation... God mitigates temptations to prevent their overpowering us by their weight. For He knows how far our ability can go, when He Himself has given it to us, and He adjusts our temptations to that degree of ability." *The First Epistle of Paul The Apostle to the Corinthians,* trans. John W. Fraser, ed., David W. Torrance and Thomas F. Torrance (Grand Rapids, MI: Wm. B. Eerdmans Publishing Company, 1960, 1989), 214. *Dupliciter autem opitulatur nobis Deus ne opprimamur a tentatione: nam et vires nobis suppeditat et tentationi modum imponit. De posteriore modo hic maxime loquitur apostolus: priorem tamen non excludit, nempe Deum sublevare tentationes, ne suo pondere nos deiiciant. Novit enim facultatis nostrae quam ipse contulit modum: ad quem tentationes attemperat* [*CO* 49:463].

[184] "...euen in the things that are seene before our eyes, wee want sufficient iudgement to comprehend them: I pray you what shall wee doo on Gods narrowe and hidden secrets whereby he ordeyneth and appointeth what he listeth in heauen?" 148 (Job 38:4-11), 693.b.63. *Or puis qu'ainsi est, qu'en ce qui nous apparoist devant les yeux, nous n'avons pas iugement suffisant pour le comprendre: que sera-ce (ie vous prie) des conseils de Dieu estroits, et cachez, quand il ordonne et determine au ciel ce qui luy plaist?* [*CO* 35:364].

[185] "God in afflicting vs doeth not ceasse to loue vs..." 30 (Job 8:1-6), 139.a.26. *Dieu en nous affligeant ne laisse pas de nous aimer...* [*CO* 33:374]. "There is nothing that comforteth vs, but oure knowing that euen in the middes of our sorrowes wee bee still beloued of God, and that in the ende hee will haue pitie of vs and giue vs saluation and like by meanes of our Lorde Iesus Christ." 39 (Job 7:16-21), 132.b.56. *Il n'y a rien qui nous console, sinon quand nous savons qu'au milieu de nos miseres nous ne laissons pas d'estre aimez de Dieu, et qu'il aura pitié de nous en la fin, nous donnant salut et vie par le moyen de nostre Seigneur Iesus Christ* [*CO* 33:359].

[186] "God scourgeth vs, yet he ceasseth not too giue vs some taste of his goodnesse…" 13 (Job 3:11-19), 57.a.33. ...*quand Dieu nous afflige, qu'il ne laisse pas toutesfois de nous donner quelque goust de sa bonté...* [*CO* 33:164].

[187] "For if wee had God before our eyes, we would consider that he hathe set vs here to liue togither and to communicate one with another: wee would condier that he is the father of vs all: wee would consider how he hath made vs all of one kynd, to the end wee should one of vs haue care of another, and none of vs drawe away by himself alone…" 25 (Job 6:15-23), 113.b.39. *Car si nous avions Dieu devant nos yeux, nous cognoistrions qu'il nous a ici mis pour vivre ensemble, pour communiquer les uns avec les autres: nous cognoistrions qu'il est pere de tous: nous cognoistrions qu'il nous a fait d'une mesme nature afin que nous ayons soin les uns des autres: et qu'il ne faut point que nul se retire à part, sachans que nous avons besoin les uns des autres* [*CO* 33:309].

[188] 73 (Job 20:1-7), 345.b.20 [*CO* 34:152]. Calvin suggests in this passage that we triumph over our afflictions when we learn to appreciate that God has "knit us together" so that we may minister to one another.

[189] Thus in the opening sermon, Calvin can pinpoint the nature of the entire Book of Job as a spiritual battle: "Surely these spirituall battelles are farre more harder to be borne, than all the myseries and aduersities that we can suffer by any persecution" 1 (Job 1:1), 1.b.26. *Or ces combats spirituels sont beaucoup plus difficiles à porter; que ne sont pas tous les maux et toutes les adversitez que nous pouvons souffrir quand on nous persecute* [*CO* 33:23].

[190] "And therefore let vs prepare oure serlues too suche spirituall battelles, praying God to strengthen vs, for wee see how all mans strength fayleth in that behalfe, so as wee shall bee quickely ouerwhelmed if wee bee not propped vp from aboue…" 41 (Job 10:18-22), 193.a.19. *Et ainsi apprestons-nous à tels combats spirituels, et prions Dieu qu'il nous fortifie, puis que nous voyons que toutes les vertus des hommes defaudront en cest endroit, et que nous serions bien tost abysmez, si ce n'estoit que nous fussions soustenus d'enhaut...* [*CO* 33:514].

[191] "…according also as the Scripture exhorteth vs, shewing vs that this life heere is but as a race, and therefore wee may not go loyteringly, but euery man must cheere vp himselfe, and pricke and spurre forwarde himselfe." 17 (Job 4:20-5:2), 76.b.10. ...*comme aussi l'Escriture nous exhorte, monstrant que ceste vie ici n'est que une course, qu'il ne faut point que nous cheminions comme d'une façon lasche...* [*CO* 33:213].

[192] 66 (Job 17:6-16), 309.b.39. *Si nous avions comme une belle prairie, et que nous allissions tout au long d'une riviere, que nous eussions l'ombrage dessus, qu'il n'y eust que plaisir et esiouyssance en toute nostre vie: qui est-ce qui se pourroit vanter d'avoir servi à Dieu d'une bonne affection? Mais quand Dieu nous envoye les choses tout au rebours de nos souhaits, et qu'il faut que maintenant nous entrions en une fange, maintenant que*

*marchions sur des cailloux, maintenant nous trouvions des ronces et des espines qui nous empeschent, que nous rencontrions les hayes et les fossez, et qu'il nous faille sauter par dessus, et quand nous aurons bien travaillé qu'il semble encores que nous ayons avancé bien peu ou rien du tout, que nous ne voyons point d'issue: quand cela y est, voila une fascheuse tentation à nous qui aurons eu desir de cheminer selon Dieu. Et pourquoi? Car nous n'avons pas du tout renoncé à nous-mesmes. Celui qui n'a point encores apprins de dompter toutes ses affections, et d'assuiettir sa volonté au service de Dieu, combien qu'il lui soit difficile: celui-là ne sait pas encores à bon escient que c'est de vivre bien et fidelement. Ainsi donc, pratiquons ce qui est ici dit de retenir nos voyes, c'est à dire, de cognoistre que le chemin est fort difficile, quand nous voudrons regler nostre vie selon Dieu, et que cela ne sera pas que nous n'ayons beaucoup de contradictions et d'empeschemens: mais si faut-il que nous soyons fermes et constans pour retenir nos voyes* [*CO* 34:54-55].

[193] 22 (Job 5:19-27), 99.a.63. ...*apprester aux combats*... [*CO* 33:272].

[194] "For being wilie and politike as he is, he koweth full well on which side to assayle vs." 5 (Job 1:9-12), 19.a.67. *Car comme il est fin et rusé, il sait bien de quel costé il nous faut assaillir* [*CO* 33:69].

[195] See Calvin's use of the word "mortification" [*mortifie*] in 5 (Job 1:9-12), 20.a.8 [*CO* 33:69]; 13 (Job 3:20-26), 58.a.18 [*CO* 33:167]; 158 (42:6-8), 744.b.49 [*CO* 35:497], and especially, "*l'Escriture sainte lui attribue cest office de mortifier devant qu'il vivifie...*" 125 (Job 33:18-25), 588.a.52 [*CO* 35:80]. Thus afflictons serve to "bridle our tongues" and hearts, 28 (Job 7:7-15), 130.a.24 [*CO* 33:352]. They also urge us to be better disposed to seek the heavenly life, 159 (Job 42:9-17), 750.a.18 [*CO* 35:311].

[196] "But in the meane while he had no vndersta[n]ding of Gods grace, how strong and inuincible the same is in vs..." 5 (Job 1:9-12), 21.a.52. ...*or cependant, il n'apprehende point la grace de Dieu, combien elle est forte et invincible en nous...* [*CO* 33:73].

[197] Job's covenant with God as to the use he made of his eyes provides Calvin with an interesting explanation of how Satan may employ our faculties for his ends: "...oure eyes which were created to looke vpon Gods workes, to the end we might be taught to loue, reuerence and feare him: are become as it were the baudes [*maquereaux*, i.e., "pimp,"or "brothel-keeper"] of Satan, and are as it were inticers, whiche come to beguile vs and worke our destruction." 112 (Job 31:5-8), 529.a.14. ...*que nos yeux qui ont esté creez pour nous faire contempler les oeuvres de Dieu, afin d'estre instruits à son amour, à sa reverence et crainte, sont comme des maquereaux de Satan, ce sont comme des trompeurs qui nous viendront seduire, et nous faire perir* [*CO* 34:645].

[198] *Institutes* I.18.1. *Molitur satan sanctum virum desperatione adigere in furorem...* [*CO* 2:168]. Cf. "If the Deuill may winne that at our handes, he is well apayed: but if God wakeneth vs, then doth the diuell labour ro driue vs to dispayre." 90 (Job 23:13-17), 425.a.13. *Si le diable a gaigné cela sur nous,*

*il se contente: mais quand Dieu nous resveille, alors le diable tasche de nous mettre en desespoir* [*CO* 34:366].

[199] "... the Diuels of hell which are enimies and rebels to him to the vttermost of their power, which labour to subuert his Maiestie, and practyze to confound all things: so as they be forced (spite of their teeth) to be subiect vnto God and to yeeld him account of all their doings, and cannot do anything without his permission and leaue. Thus ye see in what wise Satan appeared among the Angels." 4 (Job 1:6-8), 15.a.46. *...mais aussi les diables d'enfer, qui luy sont ennemis et rebelles tant qu'il leur est possible, qui taschent de ruiner sa maiesté, qui machinent à brouiller tout: qu'il faut que ceux-la (en despit de leurs dents) soyent subiets à Dieu, et qu'ils lui rendent conte de tout ce qu'ils font, et qu'ils ne puissent rien attenter sans sa permission et son congé* [*CO* 33:58]. "For Satan also is subiect vnto God, and therefore it may not be surmyzed that Satan hath any authoritie, other than is giuen him by God." 4 (Job 1:6-8), 16.a.7. *Or Satan est aussi subiet à Dieu, d'autant qu'il ne faut point imaginer que Satan ait aucune principauté que celle qui luy est donnee de Dieu* [*CO* 33:60]. Cf. Calvin's comment on Hebrews 2:14: "The apostle means that the devil has been destroyed in so far as he had power to ruin us. His power is so called from its effect of being ruinous and deadly to us. He teaches us that not only has the tyranny of Satan been broken by the death of Christ, but that the devil himself has been so laid low as to be of no more account, as if he did not exist." *The Epistle of Paul the Apostle to the Hebrews and The First and Second Epistles of St Peter*, trans. William B. Johnston, ed., David W. Torrance and Thomas F. Torrance (Grand Rapids, Michigan: Wm. B. Eerdmans Publishing Company, 1963), 31.*Significat enim apostolus abolitum esse diabolum quatenus in nostrum exitium regnabat. Nam ab effectu sic vocatur, eo quod nobis sit exitiale et mortiferum. Non ergo tantum abrogatam morte Christi fuisse docet Satanae tyrannidem, sed ipsum quoque ita prostratum ut pro nihilo habendus sit ac si nullus foret* [*CO* 55:32].

[200] "God therefore knowing what the issue of Iobs afflictions should be had determined in his own purpose to scourge him, and so you may see he did it not at Satans instigation." 5 (Job 1:9-12), 21.a.68. *Ainsi donc Dieu cognoissant quelle seroit l'issue des afflictions de Iob, avoit determiné en son conseil de l'affliger, voire n'estant point incité à cela par Satan* [*CO* 33:74].

[201] "...the Diuell is hild short, and that how soeuer he play the mad feende against our saluation, yet can he do nothing, further than is permitted him from aboue." 4 (Job 1:16-18),16.a.47. *...le diable est tenu en bride, et quelque chose qu'il soit enragé contre nostre salut, que neantmois il ne peut rien faire sinon d'autant qu'il luy est permis d'enhaut* [*CO* 33:61]. Calvin draws a comparison with Ahab, thus: "Who is it that shall beguyle me Achab? Satan preue[n]ted not God in that cace, nother came he aforehand to say, If thou wilt giue me leaue to beguyle Achab, I will do whatsoeuer thou wilt haue me to do." 5 (Job 1:9-12), 21.b.46. *Qui est-ce qui me seduira Achab?*

*Satan n'anticipe point la, il ne vient point dire, Si tu me donnois congé pour decevoir Achab, ie ferois tout ce que tu voudrois...* [*CO* 33:75]. Cf. "...the deuill still kindleth the fire by Gods iust permission, in the hartes of them that regard not him." 75 (Job 20:16-20), 353.a.64. ...*et le diable allume tousiours le feu par une iuste permission de Dieu au coeur de ceux qui ne peuvent regarder à lui* [*CO* 34:172].

[202] "...the Diuelles are as it were Gods hangmen to execute his iudgeme[n]ts and the punishments which he will haue done vpon the wicked. Also they are as his roddes whereby he chastizeth his children. To bee short, it behoueth the Diuell to be the instrument of Gods wrath, and to execute his will." 5 (Job 1:9-12), 22.a.20. ...*que les diables sont sous la conduitte de Dieu, tellement qu'ils ne peuvent rien faire sans son congé. Mais il y a encores plus, c'est à savoir, que les diables sont comme bourreaux pour executer les iugemens de Dieu, et les punitions qu'il veut faire sur les meschans...* [*CO* 33:75].

[203] "... the Diuelles are always buzie to procure our destruction ." 4 (Job 1:6-8), 17.a.33. ...*les diables sont tousiours à procurer nostre perdition...*[*CO* 33:63]. And again, "We know he desireth nothing but our destruction." 16.a.36. *Nous savons qu'il ne demande que nostre perdition...* [*CO* 33:61].

[204] "And further, that for asmuch as we be continually beset with many stumblingblockes, and the Diuell practizeth to thrust vs out of the right way." 2 (Job 1:2-5), 5.a.61. *Et pource que nous sommes tousiours environnez de beaucoup de scandales, et que le diable machine de nous destourner du bon chemin...*[*CO* 33:33].

[205] "But behold, God telleth vs that Satan is like a roaring Lion which hath his throte euer open to swalow vs vp: and that we haue no weapons to resist him, except he giue vs them." 4 (Job 1:6-8), 16.b.9. *Voice Dieu qui nous declare que Satan est un lion bruyant, qui a tousiours la gueule ouverte pour nous engloutir: que nous n'avons point armures pour luy resister, sinon qu'il nous en donne:...* [*CO* 33:62].

[206] "Dauid the[n] being one of Gods children, was notwithstanding sometimes deliuered into the power of Satan, to be beguyled by him." 5 (Job 1:9-12), 22.b.48. *David donc estant du nombre des enfans de Dieu, ne laisse pas d'estre quelquefois mis en la puissance de Satan pour estre trompé* [*CO* 33:77].

[207] "For the wyles are infinite whiche he forgeth in his shop: and therefore it behoueth vs the more to stande vpon our garde." 4 (Job 1:6-8), 18.b.54. *Car il a des cautelles infinies, qui se forgent en sa boutique: et d'autant plus nous faut-il estre sur nos gardes* [*CO* 33:68]. Cf. "...the Diuell practizeth to thrust vs out of the right way..." 2 (Job 1:2-5), 5.a.63. ...*le diable machine de nous destourner du bon chemin...* [*CO* 33:33].

[208] Cf. Calvin's comments on Job 1:9 and 2:4-5. 5 (Job 1:9-12), 21.a.8 [*CO* 33:72], and 8 (Job 2:1-6), 36.a.36 [*CO* 33:14].

[209] "Wherfore, when we feele any wicked desire in our selues, so as we be caried, some to one lewde lust, & some to another: we must marke that it is the enimie that worketh so craftily. And thus we find by experience, that the

Diuelles are euer practicing against vs." 4 (Job 1:6-8), 17.a.43. *Parquoy quand nous sentirons quelque mauvais desir en nous, que l'un sera mené d'une concupiscence mauvaise, l'autre de ceci, l'autre de cela: notons que c'est l'ennemi qui besongne ainsi finement* [*CO* 33:64].

[210] "... the diuel commes to put a toy in our head, that God is our deadly enimie." 1 (Job 1:6-8), 1.b.18. ...*le diable nous vient mettre en phantasie, que Dieu nous est ennemy mortel*... [*CO* 33:23].

[211] "For hee is oure cheefe enemie whome wee haue cheefely too resist, that wee maye repulse all the practises and deuises whiche hee can attempt agaynst vs." 82 (Job 21:22-34), 386.b.6. ...*pource que c'est le principal ennemi et auquel il faut sur tout resister pour repousser toutes les pratiques et machinations qu'il pourra dresser contre nous* [*CO* 34:260-261]. It is a theme to which Calvin returns often in his preaching. Cf. Calvin's sermon on Amnon's violation of Tamar in 2 Samuel 13:15-25, "When men do us an injury, they are motivated by Satan; he is their guide and their master. Therefore, let us keep in mind our ultimate enemies, so as to be on guard against them." *Sermons on 2 Samuel Chapters 1-13*, trans. Douglas Kelly (Edinburgh: The Banner of Truth Trust, 1992), 637. *Car quand les hommes nous font quelque iniure, ilz sont poussez de Satan, c'est leur conducteur et leur maistre. Pensons donc a noz ennemys les plus principaux, a fin de nous en garder* [*SC* 1:369:30-32].

[212] "...it is one of Satans policies to driue vs to despayre..." 35 (Job 9:16-22), 163.a.5. *Car c'est l'astuce de Satan, de nous mettre en desespoir*... [*CO* 33:437]. Note how Calvin counsels his readers not to despair but to trust in God, 10 (Job 2:11-13), 46.b.52 [*CO* 33:139]; 128 (Job 33:29-34:3), 602.b.59 [*CO* 35:120].

[213] "But if God once withdrawe himselfe from vs, or do but onely slacke his hande a little, by and by we shall be ouercome by Satan." 5 (Job 1:9-12), 23.b.47. *Mais si Dieu s'est une fois eslongné de nous, qu'il nous ait seulement lasché la main, nous serons incontinent vaincus de Satan* [*CO* 33:80].

[214] "So then, when God giueth Satan leaue to tempt faithful ones: ordinarily it is to make them to be serued therewith as with a medicine. And herein we see Gods maruelous goodnesse, how he turneth the euill into good. For what can Satan bring but ranke poyson and venim? ... God findeth the meane that the euill which is in Satan, is turned to our welfare." 5 (Job 1:9-12), 23.a.3. *Ainsi donc ordinairement quand Dieu permet à Satan de tenter ses fideles, c'est pour leur faire servir le tout comme de medecine. Et en ceci voyons nous une bonté merveilleuse de Dieu, qu'il convertit le mal en bien: car qu'est-ce que peut apporter Satan sinon tout venin, et poison?...Or cependant Dieu trouvera le moyen, que le mal qui est en Satan nous sera converti à salut* [*CO* 33:78]. And again, referring to Paul's thorn in the flesh (2 Cor.12:8), "Out of doubt Satan ment to haue ouerwhelmed Paule, and his intent was to haue driuen him into wickednesse, to the end he should haue giuen ouer the seruice of God, and by little and little withdrawne himself from Christianitie, by reason of the wearisome troubles and miseries which he

endured without ceassing.... God vsed him not as a man of armes that fighteth in the fielde, to giue him a glorious vicotorie: but buffeted him like a boy to his shame and reproch.... Satan spitted in his face and wrought him many other villanies. We see then how God turneth the euill into good, when he maketh all Satans stinges to serue vs as medicines, wherby he purgeth vs of the vyces that lye hid in vs." 23.a.29. *Il est vray que Satan cuidoit abismer S. Paul, que son intention estoit bien de le desbaucher, afin qu'il quittast le service de Dieu, et qu'estant fasché des troubles et miseres qu'il enduroit incessammet, il se retirast un peu de la Chrestienté... que Dieu ne l'exerce pas comme un gendarme en un camp de bataille, pour luy donner une victoire glorieuse: mais il le soufflette avec ignominie et opprobre... qu'il luy crache au visage, qu'il luy face beaucoup d'ignominies. Nous voyons donc comme Dieu, convertit le mal en bien, quand il nous fait servir tous les aiguillons de Satan à medicine, et que par ce moyen-la il nous purge des vices qui sont cachez en nous* [CO 33:78-79].

[215] ". . but also for that he gyueth Satan full power ouer them, and letteth hym haue the brydle, too reygne in suche houses at his own pleasure." 18 (Job 5:3-7), 82.b.54. ...*mais aussi il permet toute puissance à Satan, et luy lasche la bride à ce qu'il domine en telles maisons* [CO 33:230].

[216] "...when the diuel poysoneth men, it is not by stinging them lightly, but by sheading his venim into the botto[m] of their hart, so as their witte and vnderstanding may conceyue nothing but euill. Lo how God punisheth such as haue despyzed him, and giuen themselues ouer to euill, so as they do dayly appayre and wex euer woorse and woorse. Hereby we see that it is not in mannes choyce to repent when he listeth, as these skoffers say, mocking God, with Tush, there needs but one good sigh at the end. But who shall giue them that sigh? Wherfore let vs beware that we welter not in our sinnes..." 78 (Job 20:8-15), 348.a.55. ...*que si le diable a empoisonné les hommes ce n'est point pour leur donner quelque petite pointure mais c'est pour leur fourrer son venin au plus profond du coeur, tellement qu'en leurs esprits, et en leurs sens ils conçoivent tout mal. Voila donc comme Dieu punit ceux qui l'auront mesprisé, et qui se seront ainsi iettez à mal, c'est qu'ils ne feront tousiours qu'empirer, et aller de mal en pis. Par cela voyons-nous que la repentance n'est point en la main des hommes, comme ces gaudisseurs disent, se mocquans de Dieu, O il ne faut qu'un bon souspir en la fin. Et qui est-ce qui le leur donnera? Parquoy apprenons de ne point crouppir en nos iniquitez:...* [CO 34:159]. Cf. Calvin's sermon on Ephesians 6:10-12, "For not only by one blow but a hundred thousand times we should be overwhelmed by the power of the devil, if our Lord did not uphold us." 45 (Eph. 6:10-12), *Sermons on The Epistle to the Ephesians*, trans. Arthur Golding (Edinburgh: The Banner of Truth Trust, 1973), 661. ...*et non seulement pour un coup, mais cent mille fois nous serions abysmez par la vertu du diable, sinon que nostre Seigneur nous supportast* [CO 51:822]. Earlier, in the same sermon, Calvin makes the following remark: "... therefore God has to waken us and say to us, Wretched creatures, would you not be lost a thousand

times, if I did not hold you by the hand? Now then, our Lord's leaving of infirmities in us is to draw us to himself and to subdue us to meekness that we may have matter for which to praise him, in that he does not permit our falls to be deadly; and again, that we should seek him every minute of time, knowing that if he did not lift us up again when we have fallen, and keep us on our feet, we should perish without any mercy. *Op. cit.*, 655-656. ... *et pourtant il faut que Dieu nous resveille, et qu'il nous monstre, Povre creature, si ie ne te tenoye la main, ne serois-tu pas cent mille fois abysmee? Ainsi donc, quand nostre Seigneur laisse des infirmitez en nous, c'est pour nous attirer á luy, et pour nous renger en modestie, que nous ayons argument de luy rendre louange de ce qu'il ne permet pas que nos cheutes soyent mortelles: et puis, que nous le requerions à chacune minute de temps, cognoissant que s'il ne nous relevoit quand nous sommes cheus, et qu'il ne nous tinst debout, que nous peririons sans aucune merci* [CO 51:816-817].

[217] According to David Willis-Watkins, "Calvin's doctrine of the union with Christ is one of the most consistently influential features of his theology and ethics, if not indeed the single most important teaching which animates the whole of his thought and his personal life." D. Willis-Watkins, "The Unio Mystica and the Assurance of Faith According to Calvin," in *Calvin: Erbe und Auftrag, Festschrift für W. H. Neuser*, ed. Willem van't Spijker (Kampen: Kok Pharos Publishing House, 1991), 78.

[218] "...that his afflicting of vs is, bicause we haue neede to be wounde out of this intangling worlde here." 18 (Job 2:3-7), 81.a.63. ...*et qu'il nous afflige d'autant que nous avons mestier d'estre desveloppez de ce monde ici...* [CO33:226].

[219] 66 (Job 17:6-16), 310.b.6. *Voila quelle est en somme la vie des fideles, c'est assavoir, qu'il ne seront iamais sans beaucoup de tentations. Et sur tout d'autant que nous sommes assubiettis à tant de miseres, cependant que nous sommes en ce pelerinage terrien, que ceux qui taschent de servir le mieux à Dieu, ne laissent pas d'estre pressez souvent de beaucoup de maux, et de beaucoup d'afflictions. Mais quoy? Quand nous serons estonnez, comme il ne se peut faire que nous ne trouvions cela bien estrange du premier coup, que nous combations contre telles tentations, que nous persistions au droit chemin sans nous desbaucher: et combien que nous sentions beaucoup de difficultez en nous, prions Dieu qu'il nous donne une telle vertu et si invincible, que nous continuions iusques à la fin à son service, combien que Satan tasche de nous en divertir* [CO 34:56-57]. Serene Jones has attempted a redefinition of Calvin's formulation of piety, criticizing the formulations of, amongst others, Edward Dowey and Richard Stauffer. See *Calvin and the Rhetoric of Piety*, 146-150. Sou-Young Lee argues that "*pietas* was his entire theological direction and goal, rather than merely one theme in his theology." *Op. cit.*, 226.

[220] "We must begin at the foresaid poynt, as I haue told you afore: and then to haue perfecte soundesse, it behoueth that our eyes, our hands, our feete,

our armes, and our legs be answering thervnto: so as in our whole life we may shewe that our will is to serue God, and howe that it is not in vayne that wee pretende a meaning to keepe the same soundness within." 1 (Job 1:1), 3.b.51. ...*que nous commencions par ce bout-la, comme i'ay dit: mais si est-ce que pour avoir bonne integrité, il faut que les yeux, et les mains, et les pieds, et les bras, et les iambes respondent, qu'en toute nostre vie nous declarions que nous voulons servir à Dieu, et que ce n'est point en vain que nous protestons, que nous voulons garder ceste integrité au dedans* [CO 33:29].

[221] "To the ende we may know, that we be created to his glorie, to serue him and to worship him. For although he haue no neede of vs as our neybours haue, nor is either the better or the worse for our seruice: yet is it his will to haue reasonable creatures which shuld know him, and in knowing him, yeeld him that whiche belongeth vnto him." 1 (Job 1:1), 4.b.25. *A fin que nous sachions que nous sommes creez à sa gloire, pour le servir et adorer: car combien qu'il n'ait pas affaire de nous, comme auront nos prochains, et que cela ne luy apporte ne chaud ne froid, si est-ce qu'il a voulu avoir des creatures raisonnables, qui le cogneussent, et l'ayans cognu, luy rendissent ce qu'il luy appartient* [CO 33:31].

[222] "When worldly folke speake of God, they can well say that he is the soueraine Creator of the world: but yet in the meane season they acknowledge not the thing that is propre vnto him, nor him in suche wise as it (is) (sic.) his will to manifest himselfe uvto vs: that is to wit in his Iustice, in his goodnesse, in his wisdome, and in all things whereby we may take taste to loue him, to honor him, and to serue him." 30 (Job 8:1-6), 138.a.4. *Quand les gens prophanes en parlent, il est vray qu'ils diront bien que Dieu est souverain Createur de monde: mais cependant ils ne cognoissent point ce qui luy est propre, et comme il se veut manifester à nous, c'est assavoir en sa iustice, et en sa bonté, et sagesse, et en toutes choses où nous pouvons prendre goust pour l'aimer, et pour l'honorer, et le servir* [CO 33:371].

[223] "But seing that the cheef service which God requireth of men, is to be praysed at their hands, and wee make none account of it, but (which woorse is) doo rob him of his honour, and disseate him of that which is his, in that we glorifie him not as he deserueth: surely wee shall pay deerly for it when it commeth to the reckening." 148 (Job 38:4-11), 696.a.29. ...*attendu que le principal service que Dieu requiert des hommes, c'est d'estre loué d'eux: et nous n'en tenons conte: qui pis est, nous luy ravissons son honneur, nous le frustrons de ce qui est sien, quand il n'est point glorifié par nous comme il le merite* [CO 35:370].

[224] "Wisdome is the singular gift of God, and a good and comendable thing: and in good soothe fro[m] whe[n]ce cometh it, but fro[m] the holie Ghost, who is the fountaine and welspring therof according also as the holie scripture sheweth vs?" 20 (Job 5:11-16), 91.b.9. *La sagesse est un don singulier de Dieu, et est une chose bonne et louable, et de fait d'où procede-elle, sinon du S. Esprit, qui en est la source et la fontaine, comme aussi l'Escriture*

*Interpreting the Hand of God...* 285

saincte le monstre? [*CO* 33:252].

[225] *Institutes* I.i.1. [*CO* 2:31]. See fn.29. The editors of the LCC edition of the *Institutes* draw attention in a footnote (36n.3) that Calvin may well draw from such sources as Clement of Alexandria, Augustine and Aquinas for this statement. Calvin, however, has given it a calibre all of its own.

[226] "Whensoeuer God afflicteth you, & that you light into temptations, assure your selues it is for your profit and welfare." 67 (Job 18:1-11), 314.a.40. *...estimez quand Dieu vous afflige, et que vous venez en des tentations, que c'est pour vostre profit et salut* [*CO* 34:67].

[227] "And this is a cause why wee ought to pray alwayes vnto God to giue vs skill and discretion too know how to apply that things [sic] rightly which we shall haue learned out of Gods woorde. For wee may turne that thing too euill, which might bee too our profite, according as wee see how a number abuse the holie Scripture crossely and ouerthwartly." 73 (Job 20:1-7), 341.a.42. *Voila pourquoy nous devons bien tousiours prier Dieu qu'il nous donne prudence et discretion, pour savoir appliquer droitement ce que nous aurons cognu de la parole de Dieu: car nous pourrions destourner à mal ce qui nous seroit utile: comme nous en voyons beaucoup qui abusent de l'Escriture saincte à tors et à travers.* [*CO* 34:139-140].

[228] "What is oure chief wisedom? Saint Iames sheweth it vs when he sayeth, that we ought to be slowe to speake, and willing too suffer our selues to bee taught. For when we haue the modestie too refrayne from hastie speaking; God will giue vs the grace to knowe the matters: and when wee knowe them, wee shall tell howe they stande. At a worde, wee shall haue profited greatly, when we haue learned too refrayne hastie iudgement." 78 (Job 21:1-6), 366.b.57. *Et pourtant quelle est nostre sagesse principale? Sainct Iaques nous le monstre, quand il dit (1, 19), Que nous soyons tardifs à parler, et que nous souffrions d'estre enseignez, car quand nous aurons usé de ceste modestie-là, de ne nous point haster en nos propos, Dieu nous fera la grace que nous cognoistrons les choses: et les ayant cognues, nous en parlerons comme il en va* [*CO* 34:207]. And again, "Let vs note then that there is nothing better than to bee wise, onely so farre foorth as it pleaseth God to instruct vs, and let vs knowe that too obey him, and too submit oure selues vntoo him in all things, is our true wisedome." 82 (Job 21:22-34), 385.b.2. *Notons donc qu'il n'y a rien meilleur, que d'estre sages seulement entant qu'il plaist à Dieu de nous instruire: et sachons que de lui obeir, et nous assuiettir à lui en tout et par tout, c'est nostre vraye sagesse* [*CO* 34:258].

[229] 103 (Job 18:10-28), 484.a.28. *Ils s'abbrutissent...* [*CO* 34:522].

[230] "And we see that such as vnderstand no woorde in latine (to the intent to play the beasts) speake thus in latine: *Mitte arcana Dei*: the meening whereof is, that they must not inquire of Gods secretes. See how men do retch their boundes continually, and cannot keepe a good meane." 484.a.35. *Et nous voyons que ceux qui n'ont point entendu un seul mot de latin, afin de s'abbrutir ainsi parlent latin, Mitte arcana Dei, c'est à dire, qu'il ne se faut point enquerir des secrets de Dieu. Voila comme les hommes excedent*

*tousiours leurs limites, ne pouvans tenir bon moyen* [CO 34:522].

[231] "...our Lord hath set vs bou[n]ds which we may not passe, and that such as will be wise and politike, must not stray at rouers, and giue the[m]selues to fond speculations and dotages, but hold the[m] first to this lesson of not coueting any thing which God sheweth them not. Lo what wisedome is: let that be alwayes our entraunce: and when we intend to shew our selues wise, let vs herke[n] to this voyce, namely that out Lord holdeth vs within such listes, as he will not haue vs to run out here and there, but to receyue that which he thinketh good to teach vs." 484.b.6. ...*nostre Seigneur nous a mis des bornes qu'il ne nous faut point exceder: et que ceux qui voudront estre sages et bien entendus, il ne faut pas qu'ils s'esgarent à travers champs, et s'appliquent à des folles speculations et resveries, mais qu'ils retiennent cest leçon en premier lieu, c'est assavoir de ne point appeter sinon ce que Dieu leur monstre. Voila nostre sagesse, que ce soit là tousiours comme nostre preface: et quand nous voudrons estre bien entendus, escoutons ceste voix, c'est assavoir, que nostre Seigneur nous tient en telle modestie, qu'il ne veut pas que nous trottions çà et là: mais que nous recevions ce que bon lui a semblé de nous enseigner* [CO 34:523].

[232] "It is our wisedome to feare God." 484.b.16. *C'est nostre sagesse de craindre Dieu* [CO 34:523].

[233] 485.a.27. ...*c'est pour monstrer que c'est le principal*...[CO 34:525]. "...such as are edified to feare and obey God, are men of right vnderstanding: and that the same is the thing wherevpon we must set our mindes, and not vpon wandring speculatio[n]s..." 485.a.39. ...*qui sont edifiez à craindre Dieu et à luy obeir, sont vrayement entendus, et que c'est là où il nous faut appliquer nostre estude, et non point à des speculations volages* [CO 34:525].

[234] "...Gods wisedome is so infinite, as it can neuer be thoroughly comprehended. So long as men liue in this world, it is ynough that they haue some tast of it, and profite dayly more and more in it. On the otherside, let vs marke well, that when we haue learned any thing, wee keepe it ill, and forget it out of hand: and therefore wee had neede to be put in minde of it: and God is so gratious vnto vs, as to set his mercie afore vs, to the end we should not be vtterly as it were desperate and past hope of trusting in him. For the vnderstanding of a thing in our brayne, is not all that wee haue to do: but is must moreouer be printed in our hart." 128 (Job 33:29-34-3), 604.b.16. ...*la sagesse de Dieu est si infinie, que iamais elle ne se comprendra du tout: cependant que les hommes vivent en ce monde, c'est assez qu'ils en ayent quelque goust, et y profitent iournellement. D'autre costé notons bien que quand nous aurons apprins une chose, nous la retenons mal, et nous l'aurions tantost oubliee. Il faut donc qu'elle nous soit ramenteuë: et Dieu nous fait ceste grace de nous proposer sa misericorde afin que nous ne demeurions point vuides, et comme desesperez pour n'avoir point d'esperance en luy. Car ce n'est point le tout que nous ayons entendu une chose en nostre cerveau. mais il faut qu'elle nous soit imprimee au coeur* [CO 35:125].

²³⁵ 102 (Job 28:10-28), 480.b.44. ... *l'un est l'audace, l'autre est une fole vanité* [*CO* 34:513].

²³⁶ 150 (Job 38:18-32), 706.b.43. ... *ceste presomption enragee* [*CO* 35:398].

²³⁷ "And if we meete with a thing that seemeth straunge to vs, yet let vs consider that God hath spoken it, and therfore we must receiue it without gaynsaying." 156 (Job 38:18-41:25), 735.b.9. *Et quand nous verrons quelque chose qui nous semblera estrange: si nous cognoissons, Dieu l'a ainsi prononcé, il le faut recevoir sans contredit* [*CO* 35:472].

²³⁸ In a sermon that has God's incomprehensibility as the main theme, Calvin goes on to say: "What is the first point of teachablenesse? It is that we take hym for our master and obey him fully in any thing that he shall list to teach vs." 157 (Job 42:1-5), 740.b.32. *Et la premiere docilité quelle est elle? C'est qu'il soit maistre, et qu'il soit obei pleinement en ce qu'il voudra nous enseigner* [*CO* 35:486].

²³⁹ "And so lette vs neuer speake nor thinke of Gods secrets, but with all reuerence and humilitie." 157 (Job 42:1-5), 739.b.38. *Et par ainsi que nous ne parlions iamais, et ne pensions de ses secrets qu'avec toute reverence et humilité* [*CO* 35:484].

²⁴⁰ "If a man should demaund the reason why: it is not for vs to knowe it, nother is it lawful for vs to seeke any further than his will, which ought to bee in sted of al reason vnto vs. Not that he doeth any thing vniustly: but bycause the secretes of his mynd are hidden and incomprehensible to vs, and his wayes are vnknowne to vs. Howbeeit forasmuchas it is hard for men to hold themselues quiet, when they heare that doctrine: (according as we see how these doggs bark against it nowdayes, and these gloriouse beggers intending to play the greate doctors, say they comprehend it not: and who art thou thou wretched dogge. Doest thou not comprehend it? Get thee vp vpon thy dinghill and learne to knowe what thou art)..." 156 (Job 40:20-41:25), 734.b.54. *Si on luy demande la raison pourqouy, ce n'est pas à nous de la savoir, et ne nous est point licite de nous enquerir plus outre, sinon que sa volonté nous doit estre pour toute raison: non pas qu'il face rien iniustement: mais tant y a que les secrets de son conseil nous sont cachez et incomprehensibles, ses voyes ne nous sont point cognues. Or pource qu'il est difficile aux hommes de se tenir coys, quand ils oyent ceste doctrine: comme nous voyons ces chiens qui abbayent auiourd'huy à l'encontre: ces glorieux belistres, quand ils veulent faire des docteurs, ils diront, O ie ne compren point cela. Et qui es-tu povre chien? Tu ne le compren pas? Et va-ten sur ton fumier, et cognois qui tu es...* [*CO* 35:470-471].

²⁴¹ "...let vs conclude, that God is righteous although wee see it not, and that whensoeuer wee finde his dooinges straunge, and are offended at them, we must thinke thus: wretched creature, thou hast eyes in deed, but they are to dimme, yea they are starke blinde, and although they God inlighten thee, yea eue[n] with some good portion, yet will he stil restrain theee, to the end thou maist do him the honor to confesse that he is righteous." 138 (Job 35:12-15), 649.b.57. *Concluons donc que Dieu est iuste, encores que nous ne*

*le voyons point: et toutes fois et quantes que nous trouvons estrange ce qu'il fait, pour en estre scandalisez: pensons, Et povre creature, il est vray que tu as des yeux: mais ils sont trop esblouis, mesmes ils sont aveugles du tout: et si ton Dieu t'illumine, voire en quelque portion, cependant il te veut retenir, afin que tu luy faces cest honneur de le confesser estre iuste* [CO 35:248].

[242] "...there is a wisedome that surmounteth all mans vnderstanding: yea and is woonderfull euen too the verie Angelles.They bee the verie secretes of heauen which are conteyned in the Gospell. For it concerneth the knowing of God in the person of his sonne. And although oure Lorde Iesus Christ came downe heere beneath: yet must wee comprehende hys godly Maiestie, or else we cannot grounde and settle oure fayth in him. I say it concerneth the knowledge of things that are incomprehensible to mans nature." 120 (Job 32:4-10), 567.a.1. ...*voila une sagesse qui surmonte tout sens humain, mesmes qui est admirable aux Anges: voila les secrets du ciel qui sont contenus en l'Evangile: car il est question de cognoistre Dieu en la personne de son Fils: et combien que nostre Seigneur Iesus soit descendu ici bas, si est-ce qu'il nous faut comprendre sa maiesté divine, ou nous ne pouvons pas nous fonder, et reposer nostre foy en luy. Il est queston, di-ie, que nous cognoissions ce qui est incomprehensible à la nature humaine* [CO 35:23]. Cf. "But when we enter into the doctrine of saluation, and into Gods works, and fall to disputing of his prouidence and wil, then must we not go to it so vnaduysedly, for we do but wrap vp or intangle *secrets* in vskilfull words." 147 (Job 38:1-4), 691.b.51. *Mais quand nous entrons en la doctrine de salut, que nous entrons aux oeuvres de Dieu, et que nous disputons de sa providence, et de sa volonté: alors il n'est pas question d'y aller ainsi à l'estourdie car nous enveloppons, ou entortillons le conseil en des propos sans science* [CO 35:359]. And again, "When we treate of his woord, and of the doctrine of our saluation, and of the holie Scripture, euerye one falls to it at aduenture, and euery man shoots forth his verdit, as though they reasoned but of moone shyne in the water. They be such things as passe al vnderstanding of man, and yet notwithstanding it is manifest that we be bolder too treate of Gods so hygh mysteries, which ought to rauish our witts to wonder at them, and which we ought to honour with all awefulnesse, I say wee be bolder to babble of them, than if a man spake but of a matter of fiue shillings valew, or of some trifle I wote not what. And what is the cause hereof, but that men haue not considered howe God hydeth and ouercasteth his owne secret determinations, and hath in his holye scripture vttered vnto vs his will wherevnto it beoueth vs to be subiect." 147 (Job 38:1-4), 692.a.26. *...quand on traitte de sa parole, et de la doctrine do [sic] nostre salut, et de toute l'Escriture saincte, un chacun ira à la volee: si on en devise à l'ombre d'un pot, chacun en dira sa rastelee. Voila des choses qui outrepassent tout entendement humain: et toutes fois on voit que nous serons plus hardis à traitter des mysteres de Dieu si hauts, et qui nous devroyent ravir en estonnement, et lesquels nous devrions adorer avec toute solicitude: nous*

serons, di-ie, plus hardis à en babiller, que si on trattoit d'un proces de conq sols vaillant ou ie ne say quoy. Et qui est cause de cela, sinon que les hommes n'ont point regardé que Dieu nous cache et obscurit son conseil et qu'en l'Escriture il nous a desployé sa volonté à laquelle il nous falloit assuiettir?* [*CO* 35:360]. Cf. similar thoughts expressed by Calvin on the nature of the created order. 148 (Job 38:4-11), 695.a.22 [*CO* 35:367], 695.b.2 [*CO* 35:368].

[243] "...though we know not wherefore God punisheth vs, we must alwayes acknowledge the same to be rightfull. But yet therwithall it behoueth vs moreouer to haue this lesson printed in our harts: namely that God loueth vs so tenderly, that he desireth nothing but to bring vs home againe, in so much that he spareth vs, and holdeth vs as it were in his lap, for so we see that the Scripture speaketh." 5 (Job 1:9-12), 21.b.24. *Vray est qu'il nous faut avoir cela pour resolu, quand nous ne cognoissons point pourquoy Dieu nous afflige, que nous le confessions tousiours estre iuste: mais cependant si faut-il encores que nous ayons ceste doctrine imprimee en nos coeurs, c'est à savoir que Dieu nous aime si tendrement, qu'il ne demande sinon à nous reduire, il nous espargne, il nous tient comme en son giron: car voila comme l'Escriture en parle* [*CO* 33:74].

[244] "Yet muste we honour his secrete and incompre[n]hensible iudgements, and gather our wittes too vs in all humblenesse, too say, Beholde, it is true that as now this seemeth too vs to bee able to preuayle against God. And so without any further replying, we must holde it for a sure conclusion, that God is rightuous." 30 (Job 8:1-6), 138.b.17. *...toutesfois il nous faut adorer ses iugemens incomprehensibles et secrets, en recueillant tous nos esprits en ceste humilité pour dire, Voici il est vray que maintenant ceci nous semble tout contraire à toute raison: mais quoy? nous ne gaignerons pas nostre cause contre Dieu: et puis sans avoir autre replicque, il nous faut tenir ceste conclusion-la, qu'il est iuste* [*CO* 33:373]. Cf. 35 (Job 9:16-22), 165.a.56 [*CO* 33:443]. And again: "but we must reuerence these great secretes which are far aboue our capacitie, vntill such time as we may comprehend that which is hidden fro[m] vs as now... It becometh vs not to taske him so to our ordinarie maner of proceeding, for he hath iudgements that are inco[m]prehensible to vs." 36 (Job 9:23-28), 166.a.41,67 *...mais que nous adorions ses grands secrets qui surmontent toute nostre capacité, iusques à ce que nous puissions comprendre ce qui nous est caché auiourd'huy... Il ne faut pas que nous le vueillions ici renger à nostre façon ordinaire, car il a des iugemens qui nous sont incomprehensibles* [*CO* 33:445-446]; cf. 38 (Job 10:1-6), 177.b.41 [*CO* 33:474]; 39 (Job 10:7-15), 181.b.46 [*CO* 33:484].

[245] "We see then that although God suffer thynges too bee confuzed in this worlde, so as good folke are tormented to the vttermost, and wicked folke aduaunced in triumph: yet wee bee so drouzie and so dulheaded, as wee cannot be moued to come vnto God, and to consider what he saith to vs: namely that oure life is hidden as yet, and that wee must tarrye till it bee reueled by the comming of Iesus Christe." 32 (Job 8:13-22), 150.a.29. *Nous*

*voyons qu'encores que Dieu laisse les choses confuses en ce monde, que les bons soyent tourmentez iusqu'au bout que les meschans soyent eslevez en triomphe: si est-ce que nous sommes ici assoupis, que nous sommes si stupides que nous ne pouvons pas estre touchez de venir à Dieu, et de regarder ce qu'il nous dit, assavoir, Que maintenant nostre vie est cachée, et qu'il nous faut attendre qu'elle soit revelée quand Iesus Christ apparoistra* [CO 33:403].

[246] "True it is that too mans expectation, all may be fordone: but God hath meanes (which are incomprehensible to vs) whereby to succour his seruants..." 15 (Job 4:7-11), 67.a.18. *Il est vray que selon les hommes tout sera perdu, mais Dieu a des moyens qui nous sont incomprehensibles pour secourir aux siens* ... [CO 33:189].

[247] 40 (Job 10:16-17), 188.a.58. *...dessus nostre mesure...* [CO 33:501].

[248] "Inquire a ma[n] neuer so much, & trauell he neuer so much, yet shal he be neuer the neerer, bycause Gods iudgeme[n]ts are secret and inco[m]prehensible." 66 (Job 17:6-16), 311.a.12. *...qu'on s'enquiere, qu'on y travaille beaucoup, on y demeurera confus, d'autant que les iugemens de Dieu sont secrets et incomprehensibles* [CO 34:58].

[249] 34 (Job 9:7-15), 156.a.68. *...face office de maistre...* [CO 33:419]. Cf. "...whe[n] he executeth the office of a scholemaster towards vs, it is not to open vnto vs al things that we would doubt of, or whereof we would be inquisitiue." 123 (Job 33: 8-14), 582.a.2. *Mais cependant notons quand il fait office de maistre envers nous, que ce n'est pas pour nous reveler toutes choses dont nous pourrions douter, et dont nous pourrions nous enquerir* [CO 35:63].

[250] 34 (Job 9:7-15), 156.b.19. *...nous pensions tant mieux à ceste maiesté de Dieu qui est incomprehensible, afin que nous soyons esmeus à l'adorer, et nous humilier sous luy comme nous devos* [CO 33:420].

[251] "...to wayte till the day come that we may better conceyue Gods secretes which are inco[m]prehensible to vs at this day, & ther[e]fore we must learne to magnifie them, and to honour Gods iudgements, hauing them in reuerence and admiratio[n], vntill they may be better knowne vnto vs. For we haue too small a capacitie to know them throughly as now." 5 (Job 1:9-12), 22.b.27. *...et attendre le iour que nous concevions mieux les secrets de Dieu, lesquels nous sont auiourd'huy incomprehensibles, et que pourtant il faut que nous apprenions à les magnifier, que nous adorions les iugemens de Dieu, qu'ils nous soyent admirables, iusques à ce qu'ils nous soyent mieux cognus. Car nous avons une trop petite mesure pour les cognoistre maintenant du tout* [CO 33:77]. Cf. "O my God, thy determinations are incomprehensible, and forasmuch as I am not able as now to know any more by reason of the rudenesse and infirmitie of my vnderstanding: I will wayte paciently till thou make mee to perceyue the cause why. So Lord, when I shall haue taried in this sorte like a poore blind soule, thou wilt open mine eyes, and make me perceyue wherevnto these things tende, and what shall be the ende of them, and I shall profite better by them, than I do now." 123 (Job 33:8-

14), 579.b.16. *O mon Dieu, tes conseils sont incomprehensibles, i'attendray patiemment que tu me faces cognoistre pourquoy, quand ie ne puis pour le present cognoistre d'avantage pour ma rudesse, et l'infirmité de mon Esprit. Ainsi, Seigneur, apres que i'auray demeuré ici comme un povre aveugle, tu m'ouvriras les yeux, tu me feras sentir où ces choses tendent, quelle en doit estre l'issue, et i'y profiterai mieux qu'à present* [*CO* 35:56].

[252] "It is in that hee knoweth, that God dothe not euer punishe menne according to the measure of their sinnes, but hath his secrete iudgmentes, whereof he maketh not vs priuie, and therfore that it behoueth vs to wayte till he reuele vnto vs for what cause he doth this or that." 1 (Job 1:1), 1.b.39. *...c'est qu'il cognoist que Dieu n'afflige pas tousiours les hommes selon la mesure de leurs pechez: mais qu'il a ses iugemens secrets, desquels il ne nous rend pas conte, et cependant qu'il faut que nous attendions iusques à ce qu'il nous revele pourquoy il fait ceci, ou cela* [*CO* 33:23].

[253] "Therefore let vs learne to mislyke whatsoeuer thing men haue forged of their owne braine, and let vs holde vs to this simplicitie, namely that we must not couet too knowe ought, sauing that which God hath declared too vs with his owne mouth." 17 (Job 4:20-5:2), 78.b.38. *Apprenons donc de detester tout ce que les hommes auront forgé en leur cerveau, et nous tenons à ceste simplicité, que nous ne devons appeter de rien savoir, sinon ce que Dieu nous a declaré de sa propre bouche* [*CO* 33:219].

[254] "God doth exceeding great and incomprehensible things, his doings are wonderfull and without ende. When we vnderstand that Gods workes are exceeding great and incomprehensible: shall wee not be forced to lift vp our myndes, and to perceyue that wee must not disguyse him, nor surmize anything of him after oure naturall reason, but that wee muste mounte vp higher?" 19 (Job 5:8-10), 86.a.30. *...Dieu fait des choses grandes et incomprehensibles, ses actes sont admirables, et sans fin. Quand nous aurons cognu que les oeuvres de Dieu sont grandes et incomprehensibles, ne serons-nous pas contraints d'eslever nos esprits, et de sentir qu'il ne faut point que nous deguisions Dieu, ne que nous imaginions rien de luy selon nostre sens naturel, mais qu'il faut monter plus haut?* [*CO* 33:239].

[255] 31 (Job 8:7-13), 142.b.31 [*CO* 33:384].

[256] "For if God woorke not after our fashion, we wil bee full of grudging, and wee will saye, wherefore did he not this, and why went suche a matter so? What is the cause of suche ouerboldnesse, that men are so saucie with God as too holde plea agaynst him, and specially as to make themselues his iudges? It is bycause they haue not considered howe greate and incomprehensible his woorkes are. But if the workes of God bee incomprehensible: haue we a measure that is great inoughe to declare what is in them? What is oure witte? When wee haue stretched it out too the vttermoste length and breadth that maye bee: is is able too comprehende the hundreth parte of Gods woorkes, and of his determination whiche is so highe as all of it is hidden from vs? Wee muste goe out of our selues, if wee mynde but only too taste the wonderfull and infinite wisedom that appeereth in Gods woorkes.

Nowe if we must mount aboue all our owne wittes, too gette but a little taste of them: what shall become of vs when wee will incloze all, and when wee will know all that is in them too the vttermoste? I pray you, can we attayne therevnto? We see then howe men are worse than mad when they bee so presumptuouse as too desyre too determine of Gods woorks which are incomprehensible. For true it is that wee cannot gage the bottom of Gods woorks, too comprehend the reason of them: but yet God keepeth a good way to giue vs such a knowledge of them, as hee knoweth too be for our behoof. And so we note, that Gods woorks are incomprehensible in themselues: that is to say, that if we will search out all that euer is in them by parcelmeale, wee shall neuer bee able too atteyne too the depth of them.. . . wee cannot atteyne too the secrets that are in them." 19 (Job 5:8-10), 86.a.47.

...*car si Dieu ne besongne à nostre guise, nous serons pleins de murmures: nous dirons, Pourquoy ceci ne se fait-il? Et pourqouy une telle chose va elle ainsi? Qui est cause d'une telle audace, que les hommes s'attachent ainsi à Dieu, qu'ils intentent proces contre luy, et mesmes qu'ils se constituent comme ses iuges? C'est d'autant que iamais ils n'ont senti combien les oeuvres sont grandes et incomprehensibles. Or si les oeuvres de Dieu sont incomprehensibles, avons-nous une mesure assez grande pour en declarer ce qui en est? Qu'est-ce que nostre sens? Quand nous l'aurons estendu au long, et au large, pourra-il comprendre en soy la centime partie des oeuvres de Dieu, et de son conseil qui est si haut, que tout cela nous est caché. Il faut que nous sortions hors de nous-mesmes, si nous voulons seulement gouster que c'est de la sagesse admirable et infinie qui apparoist aux oeuvres de Dieu. Si pour en gouster seulement en peu il faut que nous surmontions tous nos sens, et que sera-ce quand nous voudrons tout enclorre, que nous voudrons savoir tout ce qu'en est iusques au bout? Ie vous prie, y pourrons-nous parvenir? Nous voyons donc que les hommes sont plus qu'enragez quand ils presument ainsi de vouloir deliberer des oeuvres de Dieu, lesquelles sont incomprehensibles. Or il est vray que nous ne pourrons nullement sonder les oeuvres de Dieu pour comprendre quelle en est la raison: mais si est ce que Dieu tient un bon moyen pour nous en donner une cognoissance telle qu'il cognoist nous estre utile. Et ainsi notons que les oeuvres de Dieu sont incomprehensibles de soy, c'est à dire que si nous voulons esplucher par le menu tout ce qui y est, iamais nous ne pourrons atteindre iusques au bout. Il faut donc que nous soyons comme accablez sous ceste grandeur-là, et que nous sachions que si nous voulons estre iuges des oeuvres de Dieu, nous avons à clorre les yeux d'autant que nous ne pouvons point atteindre iusques aux secrets qui sont là contenus* [CO 33:239].

[257] "Thus wee see the two poynts that we haue to marke heere. But if there be infinite wisedome in those works of God which are the smallest and basest: what is there in the greatest sorte, and in such as surmount all our capacitie? Specially when the case concerneth our redemption, and when it concerneth Gods sealing vp of the recorde of our adoption in vs by his holie

Spirite." 19 (Job 5:8-10), 86.b.34. *Voila donc les deux poincts que nous avons à noter. Or si ainsi est, que aux oeuvres de Dieu qui semblent les plus petites et basses il y a une sagesse infinie, que sera-ce de ce qui est plus grand, et qui surmonte toute nostre capacité? Et sur tout quand il est question de nostre redemption, quand il est question de ce que Dieu seelle en nous par son S. Esprit, ce tesmoignage de nostre adoption...* [*CO* 33:240].

[258] "Behold, God dwelleth in lyght, so as he seeth, not only when the Sunne shyneth, as a mortall man doeth. For if a man walke at high nonedayes, he seeth his way: and when he giues himself to the doing of anie thing, [the light of the Sunne] is his guide and direction: and again if he intend to v[I]ew his grounds and possessions, he looketh round about him. God therfore not only hath that: but also dwelleth in so great and infinite light, that nothing is hidde[n] from him: al things are open vnto him: there is not time past nor time to come with him: he reacheth eue[n] into the depes & dungeo[n]s as we haue seene eheretofore." 146 (Job 37:14-24), 687.a.50. *Voila Dieu qui habite une clarté, tellement qu'il ne voit pas comme un homme mortel, seulement quand le soleil luist. Or est-il ainsi encores, qu'un homme quand il marche en plein midi, voit son chemin: et quand il s'applique à faire quelque chose, il a sa conduite et son adresse: et puis s'il veut regarder ses champs et possessions, il estend sa veuë. Dieu donc n'a point seulement cela: mais il habite une clarté si grande et si infinie, que rien ne luy est caché, toutes choses luy sont patentes: il n'y a ne temps passé, ne temps à venir en luy, il va iusques aux abysmes, comme nous avons veu par ci devant* [*CO* 35:346]. Cf. "Thus then ye see that god may conceale his secrets: howbeit, that is with knowlege, for he is not ignorant of any thing, neither is it because he is not able to shew vs why he doth this or that: but because we be not able to co[n]ceiue the things which as now are incomprehensible to vs." 157 (Job 42:1-5), 738.b.54. *Voila donc Dieu qui cachera le conseil, mais c'est avec science: car de luy il n'est ignorant de rien, et ce n'est pas qu'il ne nous peust monstrer pourquoy il fait ceci et cela: voire, si nous estions assez habiles pour comprendre ce qui nous est maintenant incomprehensible* [*CO* 35:481].

[259] Thus Calvin applies incomprehensibility to God's righteousness, 30 (Job 8:1-6), 137.b.63 [*CO* 33:371]; his judgements, 30 (Job 8:1-6), 138.b.18 [*CO* 33:373]; and his majesty, "wee shall neuer knowe God to bee righteous and mightie in himselfe as wee ought to do, if wee consider him but by our naturall wit." 139 (Job 36:1-7), 655.a.55. ...*Dieu ne sera point cognu en soi iuste et puissant comme il le merite, si nous le voulons contempler selon nostre sens naturel* [*CO* 35:262 ].

[260] "If we acknowledge God to be an incomprehe[n]sible *Beeing* so as we can say that God hath all maiestie in himself: and yet in the meane whyle rob him of that which is peculiar to him, & ca[n]not be separed fro[m] him: we make him but an ydol and a dead thing." 79 (Job 21:7-12), 372.a.47. *Si nous cognoissons Dieu estre une essence incomprehensible, pour dire, Dieu a toute maiesté en soy, et cependant que nous le despouillions de ce qui lui*

*est propre, et qui ne peut estre separé de lui: nous en faisons une idole, et une chose morte...* [*CO* 34:222]. Cf. 82 (Job 21:22-34), 384.a.34 [*CO* 34:254]; 88 (Job 23:1-7), 416.a.21 [*CO* 34:342]; 89 (Job 23:8-12), 417.a.44 [*CO* 34:345].

[261] "...wee must know the incomprehensible maiestie of God....and we shall haue no mo [sic] of these vaine imaginacions and dotages that haue bin wont to rocke sinners asleepe. Had this bin obserued: there shoulde be none of the debates that are nowe adayes in christendome about the righteousnesse of faith." 33 (Job 9:1-6), 152.b.3. ...*il nous faut cognoistre la maiesté incomprehensible de Dieu. Qu'un chaciun donc pense-là, et alors nous serons tous resveillés, pour nous retirer de nos folies, nous n'aurons plus ces vaines imaginations et resveries qui ont accoustumé d'endormir les pecheurs. Si cela eust esté observé, auiord'huy on n'auroit point les debats en la Chrestienté, qu'on a touchant la iustice de la foy* [*CO* 33:409].

[262] 88 (Job 23:1-7), 414.b.29. *La moindre offense que nous aurons commise, aura desia violé la maiesté de Dieu* [*CO* 34:338].

[263] 37 (Job 9:29-35),173.b.27. ...*la bouche close...*[*CO* 33:464]. For Calvin, every time we exclaim, "thus it seems to me" [*voila ce qui m'en semble*], we violate God's incomprehensibility, not being subject to that revelation of himself God has been pleased to give us. 147 (Job 38:1-4), 692.b.59 [*CO* 35:362].

[264] 78 (Job 21:1-6), 369.b.5. ...*Dieu outrepassent nostre sens, et que nous ne savons pas pourqouy c'est qu'il dispose les choses ainsi que nous les voyons, que faut-il faire? Que nous mettions la main à la bouche, c'est à dire, que nous n'ayons point ceste audace d'en babiller. Que nous cognoissions donc nostre faculté, afin de ne nous point esgarer à travers champs: mais que nous suivions tousiours le droit chemin. Pour ce faire il faut que nous sachions seulement ce qui nous est donné: comme S. Paul aussi nous ramene à ceste regle, de ne point plus savoir que iusques là où Dieu nous conduit (Rom. 12, 3). Cependant qu'il nous tend la main, allons hardiment: mais quand nous n'avons point de conduite de Dieu, il faut demeurer là, et que nous soyons comme muets. Il est vrai que nous devons tousiours avoir la bouche ouverte en une sorte, c'est assavoir, pour glorifier Dieu: mais quand nous presumerons de tout assubiettir à nostre sens, et que nous ne voudrons pas que Dieu se reserve rien, où sera-ce aller cela? N'est-ce point despitter Dieu manifestement? Il nous voudra cacher une chose. Et pourquoy? Afin que nostre ignorance nous soit cognue, et que nous ne laissions pas cependant de recognoistre qu'il est iuste, et d'adorer son conseil admirable, et incomprehensible. Ainsi donc (comme i'ay desia touché) quand Dieu nous monstrera la raison de ses oeuvres, et bien remercions sa bonté, pour dire, Seigneur, tu descens bien bas à nous povres creatures, quand tu daignes bien nous declarer pourquoy tu fais ceci, ou cela: ta bonté merite bien d'estre magnifiee par nous, quand tu la communiques si priveement à ceux qui ne le valent pas. Mais si Dieu nous cache la raison de ses oeuvres, et que cela nous soit trop haut: que nous ayons la bouche close, c'est à dire, que nous ne soyons point legers pour*

*babiller à nostre phantasie, mais que nous glorifions Dieu, et que nous n'ayons point honte d'estre ignorans, car c'est la vraye sagesse des fideles, de ne point savoir sinon ce qu'il plaist à Dieu de leur monstrer. Que donc nous facions silence à Dieu en quelque sorte qu'il besongne, iusques à ce que le dernier iour de revelation soit venu, quand nous le verrons face à face en sa gloire et en sa maiesté* [CO 34:214-216]. Cf. 138 (Job 35:12-15), 649.a.65 [CO 35:246]; 148 (Job 38:4-11), 697.b.25 [CO 35:374-375].

[265] "...wee must beholde him in the glasse that he offereth vs that is too saye, in his worde and in his woorkes, and wee must walke in suche a sobrietie [*sobreté*], as wee must not bee desirouse too seeke more than is lawefull or than hee giueth vs leaue to do. There is then one maner of seeing God which is good and holy: which is to behold him so farre forth as it pleaseth him to shew himselfe vnto vs, and to distrust oure owne vnderstanding, so as wee desire to bee inlightned by his holy spirit, and not ouercurious and presumptuous to know more than he permitteth. but if we wil looke God in the face, and not suffer any thing to be hidde from vs, but will enter intoo his incomprehensible determinations, euen too the verie bottome of these depthes: it is an intollerable pride, and men do vtterly confounde themselues by it. Then let vs learne what meane we must holde too see God. We must not go to it with ouermuch hast, but we must be sober, knowing the small measure of our vnderstanding, and the infinite highnesse of Gods Maiestie." 138 (Job 35:12-15), 648.b.64. ...*nous le devons contempler au miroir qu'il nous presente, c'est assavoir en sa parole, et puis en ses oeuvres, et cheminer en telle sobrieté que nous ne vueillions point nous enquerir plus qu'il ne nous est licite, et qu'il ne nous le permet. Il y a donc une façon de regarder Dieu qui est bonne et saincte, c'est que nous le contemplions d'autant qu'il luy plaist se manifester à nous, et nous defians de nostre intelligence, que nous luy demandions d'estre illuminez par son sainct Esprit, et que nous n'ayons point une curiosité trop grande ni presomption de savoir plus qu'il ne nous permet. Mais quand nous voulons regarder Dieu en face, que nous ne voulons point que rien nous soit caché, que nous voulons entrer en ses conseils incomprehensibles iusques au plus profond des abysmes: voila une arrogance insupportable, et les hommes alors se confondent du tout. Apprenons donc quel moyen nous avons à tenir pour voir Dieu: que ce n'est pas d'y aller avec une hastiveté trop grande: mais qu'il nous faut estre sobres cognoissans la petite mesure de nostre esprit, et la hautesse infinie de la maiesté de Dieu* [CO 35:245].

[266] Mary Potter Engel has written that "this eschatological structure is essential to the creation of human beings." See *John Calvin's Perspectival Anthropology*, 25. Calvin alludes to this in a sermon in which Calvin conjectures about Adam's future, had he not sinned. "For when God created man, it was not too the intent he shoulde haue beene mortall. True it is that wee shoulde haue liued euermore in this worlde in the same state that Adam was in. For God would haue chaunged vs intoo glorious immortalitie. But yet notwithstanding, wee shoulde not haue beene fayne to haue dyed, neyther

should our mortalitie haue needed to haue beene renued. The state of Adam should haue beene suche, as when hee had liued [his full tyme] in thys worlde, hee shoulde haue had his euerlasting heritage with God. But sinne stepped in, And beholde, God added death out of hande, yea euen a death wherein there is nothing but confuzion. And why? For thereby man coulde pereyue nothing but Gods curse vppon him, which hath after a sort cutte off man from the number of creatures." 41 (Job 10:18-22), 193.b.35. *Quand Dieu a creé l'homme, ce n'a pas esté à ceste condition, qu'il fust mortel. Il est vray que nous n'eussions pas tousiours vescu en ce monde en l'estat auquel estoit Adam. Car Dieu nous eust changez en immortalité glorieuse. Mais tant y a qu'il ne nous eust point fallu estre mortels, il n'eust point fallu que ce qui est mortel en nous eust esté renouvellé. La condition d'Adam estoit telle, qu'ayant vescu au monde, il avoit son heritage eternel avec Dieu. Or le peché est-il survenu? Voila la mort que Dieu adiouste quant et quant, voire une mort, où il n'y a que confusion. Et pourquoy? Car l'homme ne la pouvoit sentir, sinon que la malediction de Dieu fust dessus, laquelle a comme retranché l'homme du nombre des creatures* [CO 33:515].

[267] "For Gods promises will leade vs to the darknesse of death, and there given vs light to the intente to put vs always in some hope that we shall one day bee deliuered from our aduersities." 27 (Job 7:1-6), 125.b.5. *Car les promesses de Dieu nous conduiront aux tenebres de mort: et là elles nous esclaireront afin de nous donner tousiours quelque esperance que nous serons une fois delivrez de nos maux* [CO 33:340].

[268] 98 (Job 27:5-8), 462.b.57. *...ceste vie n'est qu'un passage* [CO 34:467]. Calvin goes on in this sermon to speak of the fragility (*fragilité*) of life and "the chiefest of all," which is "the heauenly life" (*la vie celeste*).

[269] "...that wee muste honor this present lyfe, bycause God hath set vs in it, to the intent it should be as a recorde to vs, that he taketh vs for his children, & wil be our father... so precious and noble a gift of God." 41 (Job 10:18-22), 192.b.3. *...c'est que nous honorions la vie presente, d'autant que Dieu nous y a mis, afin qu'elle nous fust comme un tesmoignage qu'il nous tient comme ses enfans, et qu'il nous veut estre Pere. Apres, que nous cognoissions, voila ce qui est en nous...* [CO 33:512].

[270] 32 (Job 8:13-22), 149.b.33. *Il est vray qu'en l'hyver il semblera que les arbres soyent morts, nous verrons la pluye qui sera là comme pour les pourrir, ils en seront tant pleins qu'ils en crevent: et bien voila une pourriture. Apres, la gelée viendra, comme pour les brusler et desseicher. Nous verrons toute ces choses, nous ne verrons point une seule fleur: cela est retranché. Voila donc une espece de mort, qui dure non point pour un iour ne pour deux, mais quatre mois ou cinq. Or tant y a que la vie des arbres est cachée, la verdure est en la racine, et au coeur du bois. Ainsi donc en est-il que nostre vie est cachée, non point en nous: car ce seroit encores une povre cachette: il ne faudroit point grande gelée pour la brusler, ne grande pluye pour la corrompre: car mesmes nous portons le feu et la gelée en nous pour la consumer: mais nostre vie est cachée en*

*Dieu, il en est le gardien. Et nous savons que Iesus Christ est celuy duquel nous tirons toute nostre vie* [CO 33:402].

[271] "For nothing can bring vs too yeeld him glorie, and too confesse that he afflicteth vs iustly and ryghtly, excepte wee feele that the presente afflications are auaylable to our saluation, and that God ruleth them in such wise, as they serue vs for medecynes." 136 (Job 35:1-7), 639.b.58. *Or il n'y a rien qui nous puisse amener à luy donner gloire, et confesser qu'il nous afflige iustement et en droiture, sinon que nous sentions que les afflictions presentes nous sont bonnes pour nostre salut, et que Dieu les modere en sorte qu'elles nous servent de medecine* [CO 35:221].

[272] "Therefore wee must haue an eye to the end, & not be to hastie to shoote foorth our verdit at the first dash, as they do which iudge at all auentures. Now then what is the ende of our afflictions? It is to make vs to perceyue our sinnes." 140 (Job 36:6-14), 658.a.44. *Il faut donc que nous regardions à la fin, et non pas de precipiter du premier coup nostre sentence, comme ceux qui iugent à l'estourdie. Or la fin de nos afflictions quelle est-elle? C'est de nous faire sentir nos pechez* [CO 35:270].

[273] "The one poynt is, that whatsoeuer wee doo, we should alwayes haue death before our eyes, and bee prouoked to thinke vpon it." 17 (Job 4:20-5:2), 76.a.7. *L'un est que quelque chose que nous facions, la mort nous soit tousiours devant les yeux, et que nous soyons solicitez d'y penser* [CO 33:212].

[274] "Then let vs marke, that it is great wisedom to prepare ourselues vnto death, & to passe through it cheerfully when we come at it." 77.b.39. *Notons donc que c'est une grande sagesse de nous preparer à la mort, et quand nous y sommes venus, de passer par là allegrement...*[CO 33:216]. Cf. "Let euery man dispose himself to die, assuring ourselues that God doth vs an inestimable grace in voutchsafing too deliuer vs from corruption by the meanes of death: and that although this transitorie lodging of our body bee destroyed, yet will he reare up a new buylding in vs which shall bee much more excellent, in asmuch as wee shall bee clothed with glorie and immortalitie." 68 (Job 18:12-21), 318.a.56. *Qu'un chacun se dispose à mourir, cognoissant que Dieu nous fait une grace inestimable, de ce qu'il luy plaist par le moyen de la mort nous delivrer de corruption: et combien que ceste loge caduque de nostre corps soit abbatue, qu'il redressera un edifice en nous, qui est beaucoup plus excellent, d'autant que nous serons revestus de gloire et d'immortalité* [CO 34:78]. And again, "So then it behoueth vs to vnderstande, that all mankinde is shet vp vnder this necessitie of dying." 76.b.22. *Ainsi donc il faut que nous cognoissions que tout le genre humain est enclos sous ceste necessité la de mourir* [CO 33:214].

[275] "...if we looke but to the order of nature: death dispatcheth all that euer is of any woorthinesse in men, in so much that all returneth intoo myre, and dirt, and earth." 39 (Job 10:7-15), 182.a.15. *...nous n'avons regard qu'à l'ordre de nature, la mort aneantit tout ce qui est de dignité aux hommes, tellement que le tout retourne en bouë et en fange, et en terre* [CO 33:485].

[276] "For our bodies are prisons, as darke to hinder vs from the beholding of God, as if we were already vnder the earth... Therefore wee neede not too woonder though there be nothing else but infirmitie in men, seing that the Angels which are so neere vnto God, haue not so exquisite a perfection, but that God may condemne them if hee list to enter into iudgement with them." 17 (Job 4:20-5:2), 75.a.43. *...car nos corps sont de prisons aussi obscures pour empescher que nous ne regardions à Dieu, comme si desia nous estions sous terre...Il ne se faut point donc esbahir, si aux hommes il n'y a que toute povreté, veu que les Anges qui sont si prochains de Dieu n'ont pas une perfection tant exquise que si Dieu vouloit entrer en iugement avec eux, il ne les condamnast* [*CO* 33:210].

[277] "So then let vs marke that the holye Ghoste intendeth too doo vs to vnderstande, that forasmuch as wee bee so flyghtfull, wee ought to haue death alwayes before our eyes, to the ende we should make hast thitherward, and not be attached with fearefulnesse when it shall please God to take vs out of this world..." 17 (Job 4:20-5:2), 76.b.66. *Ainsi donc notons, que le sainct Esprit nous veut admonester qu'estans ainsi caduques, nous devons tousiours avoir devant les yeux la mort, afin que nous y tendions, et que nous ne soyons point saisis de frayeur quand Dieu nous voudra retirer de ce monde...* [*CO* 33:214].

[278] "...and that a hundred thousande deathes manace vs in the cheefe lustinesse that we haue heere bylowe." 17 (Job 4:20-5:2), 75.b.35. *...et qu'il y a cent mille morts, qui nous menacent en la plus grande vigueur que nous ayons ici bas* [*CO* 33:211].

[279] 75.b.37 [*CO* 33:211].

[280] "...wee passe not a minute of oure lyfe, but it is as it were in approching vntoo death." 75.b.62. *...nous ne passons minute de nostre vie que ce ne soit comme pour approcher de la mort* [*CO* 33:212]. Cf. "So then it is not ynough for vs to knowe, that so long as wee bee in this worlde, wee bee consumed euerie minute of an houre." 76.a.35. *...nous cognoissions que vivans en ce monde nous sommes consumez à chacune minute de temps...*[*CO* 33:212]. "... therfore must we be the busier to bestow the time well that God giueth vs, bicause it is so short." 76.b.1. *...d'autant plus devons nous employer le temps que Dieu nous donne, veu qu'il est si bref* [*CO* 33:213]. "If wee considered well the shortnesse of our lyfe, how it glideth away as a shadow: it is certayne that wee would be so much the more diligent to inquire after things past." 31 (Job 8:7-13), 144.a.3. *Quand nous aurons bien cognu la briefveté de nostre vie, que tout le temps s'escoule tout ainsi qu'un ombrage: il est certain que nous serons tant plus diligens, à nous enquerir des choses passees* [*CO* 33:387]. "For what are afflictions? Signes of his wrath: and wee knowe that all diseases are the messengers of death, and that all the sorowes which we conceiue, are drownings of vs. But our Lord sendeth vs sorowes, sicknesses, and torments, and holdeth vs in them as vpon the rack, till we can no more, and till wee faynt in such wise as our life draweth to the graue." 125 (Job 33:18-25), 588.a.38. *Car que sont-ce que les afflictions? Signes de*

*son ire: comme nous savons que toutes maladies sont messages de mort: nous savons que toutes les tristesses que nous concevons sont pour nous abismer. Or nostre Seigneur nous amene à tristesses, à maladies, à tourmens, il nous tient là comme en torture, que nous n'en pouvons plus, que nous languissons en sorte que nostre vie approche du sepulchre...* [CO 35:80]. It is interesting that Calvin approves of the remembering of birthdays, despite the abuse of them by "the Heathen." They are useful, Calvin says, "too yeelde God thankes . . . to prouoke them selues to prayse God." 11 (Job 3:2-10), 49.a.45. ...*de rondre graces à Dieu... afin de s'induire à benir Dieu* [CO 33:145].

[281] "True it is, that it behoueth vs to bee humbled by death: that is to witte, that God should bereue vs all of glorie, and that wee shoulde bee brought as it were to nothing, to the ende wee might know that al our stedfastnesse and power proceedeth not from else where, than from the free goodnesse of our God: and to be short, that we liue, not in our selues, but bicause it pleaseth God to haue vs too come neere vntoo him, and that we should drawe out of the fulnesse that is in him, according as he hath giuen it vs in our Lord Iesus Christ." 77.b.2. *Il est vray qu'il faut que nous soyons humiliez par la mort, c'est à dire que Dieu nous despouille de toute gloire, et que nous soyons comme reduits à neant, afin de cognoistre que toute nostre fermeté et vertu ne procede d'ailleurs sinon de la bonté gratuite de nostre Dieu: bref que nous vivions non pas en nous, mais d'autant qu'il plaist à Dieu de nous approcher de soy, et que nous puisions de ceste plenitude qui est en luy, comme il nous l'a donnee en nostre Seigneur Iesus Christ* [CO 33:216].

[282] "And so they that thinke not vpon death, ne put the[m]selues in mind of it, ouershoot themselues as much as is possible for them. Yea they could finde in their hearts, to play the wilde Colts in forgetting themselues." 77.b.55. *Et ainsi ceux qui ne pensent point à la mort, et qui ne la reduisent point en memoire, ceux-la se transportent tant qu'il leur est possible: ils veulent faire des chevaux eschappez en se mettant en oubly* [CO 33:217].

[283] "For it is a melancholike matter, insomuch that if a man speake of death, euery man is greeued at it, & falles into his dumps." 77.b.45. ...*car c'est matiere de melancolie, tellement que si on parle de la mort, chacun se despite et se chagrigne* [CO 33:217].

[284] 68 (Job 18:12-21), 319.a.32. ...*car si Dieu nous envoye quelque occasion de souci et de frayeur, nous sommes faschez* [CO 34:80]. Cf. 98 (Job 27:5-8), 463.a.16 [CO 34:468].

[285] See 41 (Job 10:18-22), 191.b.10 [CO 33:510]. Calvin is not, of course, advocating the lawfulness of death by one's own hands here. He goes on to explain that pain reminds us of the difficulty of this present life and that we are all sinners — "it holdeth vs in the thraldome and prison of so manye infirmities that are contrarie to Gods wil." 191.b.27. *D'autant qu'elle nous tient en captivité, et en ceste prison de tant d'infirmitez, qui sont contraires à la volonté de Dieu* [CO 33:510]. Calvin is not, of course, suggesting that the suffering of Job is a punishment for his sin.

[286] *Calvin's Perspectival Anthropology*, 6. Engel is critical of both Ronald Wallace and T. F. Torrance for obscuring this distinction. She adds: "The now/not yet or above/ahead interpretation of humankind's participation in the eternal life in Calvin has led me to refer to this governing structure as eschatological rather than teleological." 26.

[287] 125 (Job 33:18-25), 589.b.55. *Combien que ceste vie soit pleine de beaucoup de povretez, et qu'elle soit comme une mer de toutes miseres: si est-ce que nous la devons estimer precieuse d'autant que Dieu nous y a mis et nous y conserve, afin que nous l'y cognoissions nostre Createur et nostre Pere: comme defait nous sommes creez à ceste fin-la, et sommes maintenus en ceste vie caduque, afin que nous cognoissions que c'est Dieu qui nous y entretient, et sentions sa bonté paternelle quand il luy plaist d'avoir le soin de nous, et de nous gouverner. Ainsi donc nostre vie nous doit estre precieuse pour ce regard-la* [CO 35:85].

[288] 41 (Job 10:18-22), 193.b.9. *C'est comme un labyrinthe des calamitez qui sont en nostre nature: mais tant y a que si nous avons nostre Seigneur Iesus Christ, qui soit le lien entre Dieu et nous, que nous le regardions comme celuy qui nous conioint à Dieu son Pere, il n'y aura rien qui nous empesche que tousiours nous n'ayons dequoy nous resiouir* [CO 33:515].

[289] "For asmuche then as wee see nowe but in parte, yea euen as it were in a glasse and darkely: lette vs wayte for the day wherein we shall see Gods glorie face to face, and then shall wee comprehende the thing that is hidden from vs as now." 30 (Job 8:1-6), 138.b.23. *D'autant donc que maintenant nous ne voyons qu'en partie, voire comme en un miroir, et par obscurité: attendons le iour que nous puissions contempler face à face la gloire de Dieu: et alors nous comprendrons ce qui nous est maintenant caché* [CO 33:373]. For similar references, see 8 (2:16), 33.b.33 [CO 33:105]; 21 (Job 5:17-18), 97.b.3 [CO 33:267]; 23 (Job 9:1-6), 151.b.28 [CO 33:407]; 37 (Job 9:29-35), 171.b.14 [CO 33:459]; 123 (Job 33:8-14), 582.a.22 [CO 35:63]. Cf. Schreiner, *Where Shall Wisdom be Found?*, 149, as she refers to 1 Cor. 13:12 as "the heuristic principle for interpreting the story."

[290] "Gods doings but in part, but the day will come that all shall be reuealed vnto vs to the full." 40 (Job 10:16-17), 188.b.56. *...en partie ce que Dieu fait mais c'est attendant le iour que le tout nous soit revelé* [CO 33:503]. Cf. 79 (Job 21:7-12), 372.b.68 [CO 34:224]; 82 (Job 21:22-34), 384.b.30 [CO 34:256]; 88 (Job 23:1-7), 415.b.39 [CO 34:341]; 97 (Job 27:1-4), 455.b.37 [CO 34:447]; 123 (Job 33:8-14), 582.a.22 [CO 35:63]; 149 (Job 38:12-17), 702.a.55 [CO 35:387].

[291] See Chapter 1 for a full discussion of Calvin's concept of divine justice in Job.

[292] "He setteth vs as it were vpon a scaffold, to the end that his gracious goodnesse and mercie shoulde be knowne in vs." 4 (Job 1:6-8), 17.b.28. *...il nous met comme sur un eschaffaut, afin que sa bonté et misericorde se cognoisse en nous, et sur cela il se glorifie contre Satan en nos personnes* [CO 33:65]. Cf. "And herein we see Gods maruelous goodnesse, how he turneth the euill into good." 5 (Job 1:9-12), 23.a.6. *Et en ceci voyons nous une*

*bonté merveilleuse de Dieu, qu'il convertit le mal en bien...* [*CO* 33:78]. And again, "he neuer vseth such sharpnesse towardes vs, but he will make vs feele his goodnesse and mercye therwithall." 21 (Job 5:17-18), 94.a.11. *...que iamais il n'use envers nous d'une telle rigueur, qu'il ne nous face sentir sa bonté et misericorde...* [*CO* 33:259].

[293] "Also it behoueth vs to acknowledge his dominion and superioritie ouer vs." 1 (Job 1:1), 4.b.42. *Il faut aussi que nous cognoissions la maistrise et superiorité qu'il a sur nous...* [*CO* 33:31].

[294] "Let vs conclude, that God is righteous although wee see it not, and that whensoeuer wee finde his dooinges straunge, and are offended at them, we must thinke thus: wretched creature, thou hast eyes in deed, but they are to dimme, yea they are starke blinde, and although thy God inlighten thee, yea eue[n] with some good portion, yet will he stil restrain theee, to the end thou maist do him the honor to confesse that he is righteous." 138 (Job 35:12-16), 649.b.57. *Concluons donc que Dieu est iuste, encores que nous ne le voyons point: et toutes fois et quantes que nous trouvons estrange ce qu'il fait, pour en estre scandalisez: pensons, Et povre creature, il est vray que tu as des yeux: mais ils sont trop esblouis, mesmes ils sont aveugles du tout: et si ton Dieu t'illumine, voire en quelque portion, cependant il te veut retenir, afin que tu luy faces cest honneur de le confesser estre iuste* [*CO* 35:248].

[295] "When worldly folke speake of God, they can well say that he is the soueraine Creator of the world: but yet in the meane season they acknowledge not the thing that is propre vnto him, nor him in suche wise as it [is] his will to manifest himselfe vnto vs: that is to wit in his Iustice, in his goodnesse, in his wisdome, and in all things whereby we may take taste to loue him, to honor him, and to serue him." 30 (Job 8:1-6), 138.a.4. *Quand les gens prophanes en parlent, il est vray qu'ils diront bien que Dieu est souverain Createur du monde: mais cependant ils ne cognoissent point ce qui luy est propre, et comme il se veut manifester à nous, c'est assavoir en sa iustice, et en sa bonté, et sagesse, et en toutes choses où nous pouvons prendre goust pour l'aimer, et pour l'honorer, et le servir* [*CO* 33:371]. Cf. Richard Stauffer, *Dieu. La création et la Providence dans la prédication de Calvin*, 105-124; B. B. Warfield, *Calvin and Augustine*, ed. Samuel G. Craig (Philadelphia: The Presbyterian and Reformed Publishing Company, 1971), 133-185.

[296] "And if wee doo thus, let vs not doubt but God will performe that which he hath promised vs: that is too witte, that after hee hath beaten vs, (howebeit with mens rods, keeping such measure as we shall not bee vtterly destroyed) he will withdraw his hande againe, and we shall feele him mercifull and fauourable in our Lorde Iesus Christ, as in whom he hath set foorth the riches of his goodnesse and fatherly loue towardes vs." 17 (Job 4:20-5:2), 79.b.5. *Et quand nous en serons ainsi, ne doutons point que Dieu n'accomplisse ce qu'il nous a promis, c'est assavoir qu'apres qu'il nous aura batus, voire de verges humaines, gardant telle mesure, que nous ne serons point du tout accablez, qu'encores retirera-il sa main de nous, et le*

*sentirons propice et favorable en nostre Seigneur Iesus Christ: comme c'est en luy qu'il a desployé les richesses de sa bonté, et de son amour paternelle envers nous* [*CO* 33:220]. Cf. "...hee lifteth vs vp as if wee were little kinges, and that hee seemeth too haue a fatherly care of vs, and to preferre vs aboue all creatures: and afterwarde throweth vs downe as men in the picture of the wheele of fortune." 29 (Job 7:19-21), 133.a.19. *...qu'il nous esleve comme si nous estions des petis Rois, qu'il fait semblant d'avoir un soin paternel de nous, et de nous preferer à toutes creatures: et apres il nous abbat, comme on a ceste peincture de le rouë de fortune* [*CO* 33:359]. And again, 27 (Job 7:1-6), 124.b.16 [*CO* 33:337]; 41 (Job 10:18-22), 193.b.4 [*CO* 33:515]; 73 (Job 20:1-7), 344.a.50 [*CO* 34:148].

[297] William J Bouwsma, in his psychoanalytical "portrait" of Calvin has suggested that this recourse to incomprehensibility is nominalist and at odds with other strands in Calvin's thought, viz., his attempts to justify the ways of God to man in, for example, the explanation for apparent divine judgements (something which Bouwsma refers to as "facile moralism"). See William J Bouwsma, *John Calvin: A Sixteenth Century Portrait* (New York, Oxford: Oxford University Press, 1988), 97. This analysis of incomprehensibility is, however, unacceptable, as this study of Calvin's use of the concept in the Joban sermons has sought to show; Calvin did not use incomprehensibility in the sense of God being completely unpredictable, but there are occasions when this is so. In Calvin's treatment on Job, for example, he has on many occasions agreed with the theology of instant retribution. It is its application to the case of Job that is problematic for Calvin, and not the idea itself.

[298] 5 (Job 1:9-12), 22.b.26. *...et attendre le iour que nous concevions mieux les secrets de Dieu, lesquels nous sont auiourd'huy incomprehensibles...* [*CO* 33:77].

[299] 123 (Job 33: 8-14), 582.a.22. *...en partie...*[*CO* 35:63].

[300] "...he hideth his face from vs, when he afflicteth vs, when things seeme straunge to vs, and when wee knowe no reason why he worketh after that sorte. Therefore when God holdeth vs so in ignorance, it is a hyding of his face from vs." 133 (Job 34:26-29), 629.a.28. *...il nous cache sa face, quand il nous afflige, quand les choses nous semblant estranges, et que nous ne savons point de raison pourqouy il besongne ainsi. Quand donc Dieu nous tient ainsi en ignorance* [*CO* 35:192].

[301] "There are very fewe that haue this consideration with them, to rest quietly vpon it, and to confesse that there is nothing better than to submit all things to Gods maiestie, and to acknowledge that if he should let vs folow our own sway, there were no way with vs but confusion: and that if hee gouerne vs according to his will, all will be to our profite and welfare." 7 (Job 1:20-22), 32.a.8. *Il y en a bien peu qui ayent ceste consideration là, tellement qu'ils demeurent là paisibles, et confessent qu'il n'y a rien meilleur sinon de s'assubiettir du tout à la maiesté de Dieu, et de recognoistre que s'il nous laissoit aller selon nos appetits, il n'y auroit que confusion: mais*

*quand il nous gouverne selon sa volonté, que c'est pour nostre profit et salut* [*CO* 33:101].

³⁰² *A Commentary on Jeremiah*, vol. 1 (Edinburgh: The Banner of Truth Trust, 1989), 395.... *nempe pietatem fundatam esse in obedientia...* [*CO* 37:692].

³⁰³ 50 (Job 13:11-15), 232.a.28. ...*c'est que l'Escriture nous monstre plusieurs choses, qui ne convienent point à nostre esprit* [*CO* 33:617].

³⁰⁴ 50 (Job 13:11-15), 234.b.5. *Cependant que les hommes aussi cognoissent qu'il est tout autre qu'ils ne l'ont imaginé: car ils n'ont point eu esgard à ceste gloire infinie qui est en lui* [*CO* 33:623].

³⁰⁵ 119 (Job 32:1-3), 561.b.37. ...*sont des abysmes trop profonds pour nous...* [*CO* 35:9].

³⁰⁶ 33 (Job 9:1-6), 152.b.3. ...*il nous faut cognoistre la maiesté incomprehensible de Dieu...* [*CO* 33:409].

# Chapter 5

# A Christological Focus?

There are, I think, two typical answers to this question [what is the centre of Calvin's theology], the one holding the field prior to World War I, the other predominant after. If the earlier answer was: the doctrine of God, and his sovereign predestinating will, the response of the latter has tended to be: the revelation of God in Jesus Christ. Where the former was inclined to see in Calvin both a rationalist and a legalist, the latter defines him as a Christ centred and confessional thinker (B. C. Milner Jr., *Calvin's Doctrine of the Church*, 2).

For many centuries no man was thought clever who lacked the cunning and daring to transfigure with subtlety the sacred Word of God. This was undoubtedly a trick of satan to impair the authority of Scripture and remove any true advantage out of the reading of it (John Calvin, *Commentary on Galatians* 4:22) [*CO* 50:236].

So far, our study of Calvin's Sermons on Job has noted the prominence given to the doctrine of providence, especially as this relates to the character of God. Since God is himself essentially incomprehensible to us, his ways in this world are also beyond our grasp. Consistently, Calvin has contended that Job's status as a creature prevented his grasping the significance of his ordeal. We have seen that this provides a key to an understanding not only of Calvin's exegesis but of his pastoral application of the doctrine of providence to the reality of suffering. We have also examined the range of pastoral issues that the Joban material evokes as Calvin expounds the text. We have also reflected upon one particular issue for the Reformer in this material: his understanding of the relationship between God's justice and power in the overall dogmatic schema. We have noted the Reformer's ambivilence, attempting on the one hand to distance himself from the absolutism of the nominalists, whilst on the other hand desiring to defend the notion of God's freedom to do whatever he wills.

One further issue is raised in the Joban sermons in relation to Calvin's christological focus. Quite simply: can it be said that the Reformer is governed by such an agenda? In his defence of the grammatico-historical exegetical method, does Calvin make any attempt to "bring the Book of Job into the New Testament"? Given the later accusations of rabbinical interpretation of Old Testament books, can anything at all be learned from the Joban material to help us appreciate Calvin's pastoral method in relation to the Old Testament? Our conclusion will prove somewhat surprising: Calvin is not at all preoccupied with a christological agenda. Apparently Calvin is quite prepared to exegete within the bounds of the given revelation, with only an occasional leap into the developed doctrine of the New Testament. This will be our study in this final chapter. But first we must set out the historical context for the debate over Calvin's exegetical method in relation to Christology.

There is something of an "old-school" and "new-school" understanding of the focus of Calvin's theology. Following Schweizer's significant and ground-breaking contribution in 1854, it became paradigmatic for Reformation scholars to view predestination as the *a priori* from which the entirety of Calvin's theology stemmed.[1] This image of Calvin has, of course, been fractured by the studies of Niesel, Wendel and Jacobs.[2] These studies prepared the way for a christological understanding, not simply of predestination (along the lines of the 1559 edition of the *Institutes*), but of the totality of Calvin's thinking. Some attempts have been made to modify this reactionary swing, giving a more prominent role to the dynamic of predestination in Calvin's thinking.[3] And Partee, Hall, Leith and McPhee, for example, have accused the "Barthian" interpreters of exaggerating their case.[4]

Be that as it may, Calvin's rearrangement of the doctrine of predestination in the final edition of the *Institutes*, where it occupies a place within the doctrine of soteriology rather than of God proper, still attracts the attention of Calvin scholars.[5] Whatever the rearrangement of the locus of predestination may have done to salvage Calvin from determinism, it did not, of course, do the same for the doctrine of providence.[6] Whereas providence had once enjoyed a status alongside the doctrine of predestination—indeed, providence was originally seen as the logical construct of predestination, as their conjunction in one chapter up until the 1554 edition demonstrates—in the final edition of the *Institutes*, providence is left bereft of christological underpinnings.[7] If Christ is the mirror of election, no such metaphor appears to be forthcoming to aid us in our understanding of providence.[8] Indeed, some have pointed out a growing "hardening" of Calvin's theology in the 1550s, the very time when the Reformer chose as a theme with which to engage his listeners, the book of Job and its concern with providence.[9] Wiley is even more to the point: providence is predestination historically realised.[10] Confirmation of this can be sustained, for example, in the way Calvin argues the doctrine of reprobation in the *Institutes*, using providence as the key.[11]

Calvin gave extensive consideration to this matter, as can be seen in his reply to Bolsec and, in particular, his earlier treatise against the Libertines in 1545, both of which provide us with further evidence of his thinking on the nature of providence.[12] Our concern in this chapter is to examine the extent to which Calvin's Christology affects his understanding of one particular feature of his ministry: preaching the Book of Job. If, as has been suggested, Christology is at the heart of Calvin's theology, how much of this is evidenced in these 159 *Sermons on Job*? It is interesting, for example, that in 1595, some three decades after Calvin's death, the Lutheran Aegidius Hunnius could make the charge that Calvin was no better than a "Judaizer" in his understanding of the Old Testament in a work entitled: *Calvin the Judaizer: Judaistic Glosses and Corruptions by Which John Calvin Did Not Shrink to Corrupt in a Detestable Manner, the Most Illustrious Places and Testimonies of Sacred Scripture Conerning the Glorious Trinity, the Deity of Christ and the Holy Spirit, including the Predictions of the Prophets concerning the Coming of the Messiah, His Birth, Passion, Resurrection, Ascension to Heaven, and Session at the Right Hand of God, in a Detestable Fashion.*[13] According to David Puckett, who has recently analysed Calvin's exegetical method with special reference to his use of the Old Testament, all this shows that "ambiguity and tension existed throughout the Christian era concerning the role of the Old Testament in the life and thought of the church."[14] Puckett's conclusion, following an exhaustive study of Calvin's Old Testament commentaries, is shared by Battles: that Calvin attempted to find a middle way between the opposing extremes of Jewish interpretation on the one hand and Lutheran, Christocentric interpretations on the other, with the result that he found himself "on the Christian end of any Jewish-Christian exegetical continuum."[15]

Puckett reaches this conclusion from examining the commentaries alone. However, it may be argued that the desire to reach christological conclusions is heightened in preaching, which requires careful exegetical work to be applied in a way that a commentary does not. It will be of interest, therefore, to uncover Calvin's methodology in the Joban sermons, to which Puckett does not refer.

Whilst this study will not greatly affect Puckett's conclusion, it may lend some weight to the observation that Calvin, at least in these sermons, is on the *Jewish* end of any Jewish-Christian exegetical continuum.[16] Hans Joachim-Kraus has uncovered eight exegetical principles in Calvin's use of the Old Testament, including this one: the principle of reading the Old Testament with the purpose of finding Christ there.[17] This, as we shall see, becomes a little difficult in Job, and Calvin shows little desire to engage in it. Indeed, the analysis shows that Calvin could frequently preach several sermons on Job in succession without ever mentioning Christ in any way. It is to this analysis that we must now turn.

## Allegory, typology and prophecy

Calvin seems preoccupied with two opposing trends with regard to Old Testament interpretation. On the one hand, Calvin sees the Roman Catholic tendency to interpret the New Testament in the light of the Old Testament as fundamentally flawed.[18] On the other hand, he was equally concerned by the opposing fault of the Anabaptists, Servetus in particular, who dismissed the historical base of the Old Testament (which we might today refer to as its redemptive-historical foundation) in preference for an almost Marcionite view in which the Old Testament has virtually no relevance at all.[19] For Calvin, the Old Testament forms the initial part of a unified story of redemption, one that finds its culmination and apex in the unfolding of the New Covenant in Christ. Thus, in commenting on Job 19:25-26, Calvin can make this observation:

> And lette vs make this comparison betweene Iob and our selues, that if Iob hauing not had such assurance of Gods goodnesse, nor so familiar teaching by the hundreth parte as wee haue, do notwithstanding say that hee shall and will beholde God: are wee to bee excused when wee fleete to and fro, specially seing that our Lorde Iesus Christe offereth himselfe vnto vs, in whom dwelleth the whole fulnesse of the glorie of the Godhead, and in whom the ful power of the holy Ghoste was shewed at suche time as hee was rayzed from the dead? And surely wee neede not too streyne our eye sight to looke far for him: for the Gospell is the cleere looking glasse wherein we see him face to face.[20]

Clearly, what was only partially glimpsed by Job is more clearly seen in the New Testament administration, or "gospel."[21] The word 'gospel' is "... a solemn proclamation of the grace revealed in Christ," and hence, "... the word denotes the New Testament."[22] Calvin insisted that the Anabaptists were separating the Old and New Testaments, depreciating the intrinsic value of the former in favour of the latter. The seriousness with which Calvin viewed this error can be seen in the fact that in the second edition of the *Institutes* (published in 1539 during a stay in Strasbourg, where he had extensive contacts with the Anabaptists) he added an entirely new chapter, which was later to be expanded into three chapters in the final edition of 1559. His aim was to refute the Anabaptist understanding of the relationship between the Old and New Testaments.[23]

For Calvin, then, Christ is present in the Old Testament. As we shall see, the entire ceremonial cultus (something that arises within the opening text of Job) both shadowed Christ and mediated him. In addition, the prophetic word predicted him.[24] Thus it is that Calvin, underlining the unity of God's covenant of grace, can say in the *Institutes*:

> Accordingly, apart from the Mediator, God never showed favour toward the ancient people, nor ever gave hope of grace to them.[25]

Similarly, Calvin can comment on the promise of the New Covenant in Jeremiah 31:31:

> Now, as to the new covenant, it is not so called, because it is contrary to the first covenant; for God is never inconsistent with himself, nor is he unlike himself, he then who once made a covenant with his chosen people, had not changed his purpose, as though he had forgotten his faithfulness... Let us now see why he promises to the people a new covenant. It being new, no doubt refers to what they call the form; and the form, or manner, regards not words only, but first Christ, then the grace of the Holy Spirit, and the whole external way of teaching. But the substance remains the same. By substance I understand the doctrine; for God in the Gospel brings forward nothing but what the Law contains. We hence see that God has so spoken from the beginning, that he has not changed, no not a syllable, with regard to the substance of the doctrine.[26]

It is more than just a matter of reading Christ back into the Old Testament; Calvin is insisting that Christ was actually present in the

Old Testament. Thus, in commenting on the exodus event, Calvin can say emphatically:

> ... our heavenly Father then led the Israelites only by the hand of his only-begotten Son. Now, since He is the eternal guardian of His Church, Christ is not less truly present with us now by His power, than he was formerly manifest to the fathers.[27]

In this way, Calvin can find himself saying that Christ is the *scopus omnium prophetarum*.[28] The whole of the Old Testament, in all of its details, points to Christ.

> Indeed every doctrine of the law, every command, every promise, always points to Christ. We are, therefore, to apply all its parts to him.[29]

And again:

> We must read Scripture with the intention of finding Christ therein. If we turn aside from this end, however much trouble we take, however much time we devote to our study, we shall never attain the knowledge of the truth. Again, can we be wise without the wisdom of God?[30]

It is precisely for this reason that the Jews could so disastrously misinterpret the Old Testament. They do not give attention to the Law's true "end."[31]

David Puckett, confining himself exclusively to the commentaries, thoroughly documents Calvin's opposition to Origen's allegorical method of exegesis.[32] In the Joban sermons also, Calvin voices his concerns over allegorical interpretation, principally because it ignores the historical context and meaning, favouring instead a higher, or spiritual, meaning. In Sermon 156, dealing with Leviathan (which Calvin interprets to be a whale), Calvin finds himself tempted to interpret the words of Job 41:25, "He is king ouer all the children of pryde," allegorically of Satan. He muses how "a man myght wel vse this similitude of the whales and the Elephants, to make men perceyue how greatly the power of the diuell ought to fray vs, seeing he is termed the prince of the aire and of the world."[33] But, this would be a mistake, ignoring as it does the "simplicitie" of the text:

> For it is an euill thing to dally with the holie scripture by transforming of it intoo allegories, nother ought allegories to be drawen but out of a naturall meening, as we see that Sainct Paule doth in the Epistle to the Galathians and in other places.[34]

A little further on in the same sermon, Calvin again berates allegorical interpreters who see in the figure of the elephant more than is intended:

> If we beare away this singlenesse, it will stand vs in better sted than all the curiouse expositions that can be deuysed, as when these Allegorimakers serched out his ribbes and backebones, and treated also of his skin and of this and that, and to be short, there was not that pece of him, wherin they found not some toy or other. But this is as it were to make the holie Scripture a noze of wax, by transforming it from the naturall sense.[35]

It has been argued, from a hermeneutical point of view, that the theoretical basis and rationale for Calvin's use of typology in his Old Testament exegetical work is that of the concept of accommodation.[36] But for Calvin, the justification of typology rests just as much on the authority of Scripture itself. Noting that Christ alludes to Psalm 110 as speaking of himself, Calvin can say:

> …we need not apply to any other quarter for the corroboration of this statement…It is acknowledged that the kingdom of Christ is typified in the person of David…[37]

There is, of course, little scope in the Joban material for typological interpretation other than with reference to Job himself. It is interesting, despite the charge that "Calvin would not be Calvin" without typology, that nowhere does Calvin specifically see Job as a type of Christ.[38] And this, despite the fact that on occasions, he does draw parallels between Job and David, whom he often sees as typological of Christ.[39] Interestingly, it is early in the exposition of Job that Calvin already resorts to drawing the parallel between Job's cry of anguish and that of David in Psalm 22. It is the citation of the words, "My God! my God! Why have you forsaken me?" by Christ on the cross (cf. Matt. 27:46) that provides Calvin with the pretext that the psalm is a prophecy of Christ.[40]

It is the offering of sacrifices by Job on behalf of his family, which occurs both at the beginning and at the close of the narrative (Job 1:5; 42:8), that occasions from Calvin an explanation that these are "figures" of the sacrifice of Jesus Christ.[41] For Calvin, a mere historical description of the offerings is insufficient. The sacrifices required under the Old Covenant were healpe before the coming of the Lorde Iesu[s] Christ, by reason of the rawenesse of the time. But now in these dayes we know, how we ought to haue recourse to the precious bloud of Gods sonne, which was shedde to wash vs withall. Therefore if we meane to be receyued for cleane before God: it behoueth vs to repayre to the bloud of our Lord Iesus Christ.[42]

They were *praeparatio ad evangelium*, "for there hath God discouered himselfe familiarly vnto vs."[43] They were "to betoken that if we wil obteine forguinesse of our sinnes, wee muste haue recourse to the Sacrifice that was offered vp once for al for our redemptio[n]."[44]

## Christ as the scope of the text?

In the opening sermon, Calvin makes four allusions to Christ. At one point he alludes to Matthew 7:12, that we should do unto others as we would have done unto ourselves, anticipating his criticism of Job's comforters as he outlines the general theme of the Book of Job for his listeners.[45] A little later, anticipating what is to come, Calvin alludes to 1 Corinthians 3:12 suggesting that Job's comforters were attempting to dislodge Job from the foundations of Christ.[46] Commenting on the phrase that Job "withdrew himself from evil," Calvin exhorts all Christians to engage in a similar fight against the world.[47] In a general remark, Calvin adds that "it is to no purpose to haue a gay life that pleaseth men, and is had in great estimation, vnlesse we be renued by the grace of God."[48]

Similar cases can be discovered whereby Calvin alludes to something that Jesus may have said or done during his exposition of the text of Job, without wishing to draw any specific christological ideas or New Covenant themes from the passage. Alluding to Job's riches in the second sermon, Calvin makes three allusions to the Gospels, where Jesus warns of the temptation that often accompanies wealth.[49] Several other sermons contain similar allusions to a New Covenant parallel. Thus, for example, in Sermon 25, Calvin appeals to the words of Jesus in Matthew 5:45 and 48 as having a bearing on the words of Job 6:14, "that a man forsaketh the feare of God when he hath not compassion on the afflicted."[50] In the next sermon, Calvin can again suggest that we need to receive correction and reproof, just as Jesus says the lambs hear their Master's voice (John 10:4-5).[51] A further fourteen sermons have similar allusions.[52]

## A Christological Focus

Sometimes, Calvin can set the entire revelation of Job against the "whole perfection of wisedome in the Gospell," as revealed in the New Testament. His argument is that those who despise or resist the "more excellent" revelation will be condemned by those (of Job's time) who received less.

> Shall they not vpbraid vs with the obedience whiche they yelded vnto Job, who in deede was a Prophet of God, but yet had no such record of his calling, as our Lord Iesus Christ hath giuen to those that preach his gospell in these dayes? And therefore let vs marke well this text. For like as it is said that the least in the kingdome of Heauen (that is to say of them that preach the gospel in these days) is more excellent in his ministrie, than Iohn Baptist and all the Prophets: so on the co[n]trary part, when we despise the doctrine that God sendeth, seeing that he commaundeth it to be so honoured: it is certaine that we shall be double giltie.[53]

Sometimes, it is to a New Testament text in one of the epistles of Paul that Calvin refers, opening it up in a christological fashion and bringing the conclusion to bear upon the Joban text in view. Thus in Sermon 43, Calvin makes an extensive application from a reference to Ephesians 3:18:

> And here ye may see why S. Paule meening to correct the foolishe and rashe curiositie that is in men, sheweth them whereto they ought to apply themselues: that is to wit, to know throughly what the loue is which God hath shewed vs in our Lord Iesus Christ, so as wee neede to do nothing els all our life long, than to seeke diligently the sayd grace that is shewed vs in our Lord Iesus Christ, as how we be rescued from Satans tyrannie, and set free from the bondage of sinne and death; howe that whereas wee were vtterly damned by nature, and wretched and lothely sinners before God: wee be now become rightuous before him, so as he receyueth vs and liketh well of vs: How wee be gouerned by his holy spirit, to the ende wee should fight against the lustes of our owne flesh: and how we be preserued vnder his hande and protection, so that although the Diuell practize to ouerthrowe vs euery minute of an hower, yet wee may be able to driue him backe, bicause we be in the shepefolde and keeping of the good shepeherd Iesus Christe, who hath promised that he will not suffer any of them to perish whom the father hath put into his hande.[54]

## Christological conclusions to the Joban Sermons

It is worth specifying how often Calvin attempts to close his sermon with a christological focus. Surprisingly, only 27 of the 159 sermons do so, approximately 17 per cent.[55] Some are mere allusions, as in Sermon 113, in which Calvin makes an appeal for humility, reminding us that:

> Wee see howe Iesus Christ the Lorde of glorie abaced himselfe so lowe, as too become the seruant of seruants.[56]

In an early warning as to the inevitability of trials, Calvin makes a trenchant plea at the close of the sixth sermon:

> For if Satan durst be so hardie as to offer battell to the Sauior of the world, according as we see how our Lord Iesus Christ was assailed: wee may be sure he will bee more hardie to runne vppon vs.[57]

Occasionally, the appeal is more extensive. At the end of Sermon 3, Calvin makes a pointed appeal, on the basis of Job's priestly action with regard to his sons, that we, too, ought

> to clenze ourselues by beleeuing in our Lord Iesu Christ, knowing that he is the onely wasshing whereby all our spottes may be made cleane. Will we then be acceptable vnto God? It behoueth vs to attayne to it by the meanes of our Lorde Iesus Christ, shrowding vs vnder the grace which he hath purchaced vs by his death and Passion, as who is the full perfection and accomplishment of the things that haue bene giuen forth in old time in figures and shadowes.[58]

Similarly, in Sermon 24, Calvin draws his discourse to a conclusion by appealing to Christ: to see in him the rest afforded to weary souls. Thus in Sermon 24, Calvin urges Christians to persevere,

> vntill they be gathered into the euerlasting rest, which is prepared for them in heauen, according as it hath bene purchased for vs by our Lorde Iesus Christ.[59]

Some are extensive applications:

> Thus ye see that the only remedy wherby we maye bee deliuered of the sayd fearefulnesse and astonishemente wherewith the wicked are

## A Christological Focus

dismaide, is for vs to beseech God to make vs heare the voice of the Gospell, where he telleth vs that he receyueth vs louingly, that he is our father, that he accepteth vs as righteouse for our Lord Iesus Christs sake, and that both in life and in death he will alwayes hold vs in hys hand. When this voice soundeth in our eares, so as we vnderstand it throughly, we shall not be dismaid at these deafe and blind skarings (sic), as the vnbeleeuers are but we shall be surely fenced against all the dismayings that can betide vs. Therefore if we haue our recourse vnto God, and he by his holy spirit giue vs the grace to rest vpon his promises: let vs not doubt but he wil stablish vs more and more in all the good things that he shall haue giuen vs, and so strengthen vs by his power, that in all the terrours of this world we shall euermore stand stedfast, vntill he haue taken vs into his eternal rest.[60]

In Sermon 27, Calvin's appeal is pointed to those in a weary condition:

Therefore we must pray him to hold vs in awe, if we wil haue oure minds to abide quiet and peasable in the midds of the troubles that may befall vs. And this also cannot be done except Iesus Christ be at hand with vs, that we may haue some solace in him, according as he himselfe sayth, come vnto me all ye that laboure and are ouerloden, and I will refresh you, and you shall finde rest for your soules.[61]

In the very next sermon, Calvin appeals to Christ's resurrection, seeing it as a mirror in which to behold our own:

What are men then? A wind: a smoke. Howbeeit forasmuch as God hath breathed a continuing power intoo vs: therefore wee bee immortall. Furthermore it behoueth God to stablishe that thing which he hath once put into vs: for if hee mainteyned it not by his grace, all would go too decay. And specially we must come to the *Highest poynt*, that is to witte, too the Resurrection which is promised vs. And where shall we finde that? Not in our owne nature. But wee muste stie vp aboue the worlde, and wee must vnderstande that there is none but onely Iesus Christ, whiche is the true mirror wherein to see that thing.[62]

Likewise, in Sermon 32, Calvin introduces an eschatologically focused idea: troubles cease, not in this world, but in the next:

So then let vs learne, not to put our trust in thys worlde, nor in any of the inferioure meanes heere belowe. But let vs leane vnto God, seeing that hee hathe gyuen vs oure Lorde Iesus Christ, too the ende that beeing graffed in hym, wee maye drayne suche strength and sap from hym, that although oure lyfe bee hydden, so as wee bee euen as it were in death: we maye not ceasse to continue still, and too bee mainteined in good and sure state, waiting tyll thys good GOD haue deliuered vs out of all worldlie miseries, and out of all the troubles whyche wee be fayne too suffer heere, vntill hee call vs and bring vs into the kingdome of heauen, and into the glorie which he hath purchaced by the preciouse bloud of our Lord Iesus Christ.[63]

A similar appeal is found at the close of Sermon 123, where Calvin alludes again to 1 Corinthians 13:12, that we see now "in a glasse darkly," adding:

> For although the Gospell be called the brightnesse of the noone day: yet notwithstanding the same is referred to our measure. God inlighteneth vs there sufficiently: we see his face in our Lord Iesus Christ: & we behold it to be tran[n]sfigured into the same: but howsoeuer the worlde go, we see not that which is prepared agaynst the latter day.[64]

In the following sermon, Calvin again pleads that we run to Jesus Christ for refuge:

> And so let vs assure ourselues that, there is none other meane to obteyne fauour before God and to haue our sinnes couered, (no not euen after we haue frankly confessed that there is nothing but filth and infection in vs) but by fleeing for refuge to our Lord Iesus Christ. For there shall the full and perfect ryghtuousnesse be founde, by the vertew whereof we shall be acceptable to God, and find him mercifull to vs.[65]

In Sermon 42, Calvin appeals to Christ as the one who alone has rendered obedience and whose righteousness alone can make us acceptable:

> ..another rightuousnesse which is not in men, and whereof there is not one drop to be fou[n]d there. Then must they be fayne to haue an other rightuousnesse, which is, that hauing condemned vs in our owne persons, should take vs too mercie for oure Lorde Iesus Christes sake: that by hys meane we may be acceptable and holy to him, forsomuch as the obedience which Iesus Christ yeelded vnto him, is set ouer vnto vs.[66]

Some forty sermons later, he ends in similar fashion, appealing to his listeners that they find in Christ alone the one who restores this fallen world:

*A Christological Focus*

It is true that in deth al things are turned vpsidedown: but God knoweth howe to bring all things into an order and perfect state: as it is sayd that at the comming of oure Lorde Iesus Christ, when hee shall appeare too iudge the worlde, then shall be the restoring of all things. If it be so then that Iesus Christ shall come to restore the worlde: It followeth that the worlde at this day is out of frame, and things therein are out of order: but in the meane season let our fayth surmount all these things here, and let vs paciently abide till God finish his worke, and find a remedie for all.[67]

In Sermon 90, Calvin finds himself referring to the theme of election and assurance, calling on his listeners to see God's determination in election as having a christological basis: we are not to view election outside of the revelation of Christ:

Ye see then that we ought to glorify God for that determination, forsomuche as it pleased hym too choose vs and too call vs too saluation, and to make vs heires of his kingdome. And thys determination hathe bin vttered too vs in oure Lorde Iesus Chryste: and if we be members of our Lord Iesus Christ, wee be sure of our adoptio[n]. The[n] neede we not to seeke the registers for it aloft in heauen, but let vs co[n]tent ourselues with the assurance that he hath giuen vs of it. For if man that hath but the copie of an autentike register, do content himselfe with it: ought not we when God hath declared his purpose concerning our saluation, oughte not we (I say) to rest vpon it?[68]

Calvin then closes the sermon with an appeal:

Therfore lette vs always repayre vntoo hym that hath wounded vs, assuring oure selues that hee is the soueraine Surgyon, who will helpe vs for oure Lorde Iesus Christes sake.[69]

In Sermon 106, Calvin finds himself commenting on the words of Job 29:14, "I was clothed with rightuousnesse," insisting that, "God declareth vnto vs… hee himselfe hath cloathed vs with his owne rightuousnesse."[70] Calvin then insists that this righteousness needs to be considered in two ways. First, wisdom is needed in order to live the Christian life in the face of temptations to compromise, and this, not only magistrates need, but "also them which haue no more to gouern but themselues, and theyr housholdes."[71] Second, Calvin adds:

Then if we be clothed with the rightuousnesse of oure Lorde Iesus Christ, and with the vprightnesse and wisedome which he will giue vs by his holy spirit: then shall wee bee garnished and decked conueniently to appeare before God. But forasmuch as in this present life, there will alwayes bee some imperfection in vs, and somewhat will alwayes bee amisse: our Lorde Iesus Christ must of his meere grace couer all our faultes, so as they may bee pardoned for his sake, and hee supplie our wantes, and therewithall continually increase the giftes of his holie spirite in vs more and more, and guide vs by the power of the same, vntill hee haue cleare ridde vs from all the infirmities and corruptions of our flesh, and that wee bee come to the marke wherevnto we be going.[72]

Sermon 111 finds Calvin ending with a call to seek Christ for the forgiveness of sins:

And therefore let vs pray our good God that when he hath looked vpo[n] the faults and sinnes which wee our selues cannot see: it may please him to blot them out, that by meanes thereof we may not repose the trust of our welfare and saluation in any other thing, than in his receyuing of vs to mercie for our Lord Iesus Christ sake, and also in our hauing of the washing wherewith he hath clensed vs, that is to say, the bloud which he hath shedde for our redemption.[73]

Suffering, of course, is central to the Joban message, as well as to Calvin's understanding of union with Christ. Consequently, we find him closing Sermon 141 by suggesting that all chastisements are for our instruction. They teach us, when we come to an end of ourselves,

that we be bereft of all meanes to scape Gods hand, and that we should of necessitie be vtterly consumed, but that he vseth pitie towardes vs: wee must vnderstand that he hath giuen vs a good remedie, in that it pleased him to offer vp his onely Sonne in sacrifize for vs: for then were we fully raunsomed, and that is a sufficient discharge to put away all our faults, so as the Diuell shall not haue any interest in vs. For although we were ouerwhelmed with the infinite multitude of our sinnes: yet notwithstanding if the bloud of Iesus Christ answere for vs, it is a sufficient satisfaction for all our offences, and ynough to appease the wrath of God.[74]

In addition, it is interesting that Calvin once again felt obliged to make an extensive christological application in the final sermon on Job. Just as in the opening sermons, particularly Sermon 3, Calvin has an opportunity in the last verses of Job to comment on Job's priestly role within his own family (Job 42:9-17; cf. 1:1-5). Having already alluded in Sermon 3 to the "rawnesse of the time" in which Job lived and the "healpes" that were necessary for them to appreciate the need for forgiveness and cleansing, Calvin makes a similar appeal in this final sermon.[75] Job's priestly role should remind us that "it is the office of Iesus Christ to giue vs accesse and to open to vs the gate."[76] That God accepted Job's prayer on behalf of his family should encourage us,

> seing our euerlasting aduocate who is entred in to the sanctuary of heauen, that is to wit, our Lord Iesus Christ, shal neuer be refused, nor we neither if we com to God his father by his means, holding euermore the way...[77]

In particular, having alluded to the possibility that some know Christ to be the Son but not the advocate and therefore do not go to him, Calvin adds:

> let vs be sure that now our Lord Iesus Christ will make vs to find God pitiful and fauorable towardes vs.[78]

Then Calvin seems to summarise his theology of suffering, by alluding to Romans 8:28, that in our infirmities:

> Whereas our Lord Iesus Christ is the liuely Image of al the faithful children of God, they bee made conformable to him... that in al our aduersities we bee shaped like to the image of our Lorde Iesus Christ, who is the eldest sonne in the house of God.[79]

It is just here that Calvin seems to come to his most intense christological allusion. Focusing on the cross apart from the resurrection will lead to despair. Equally, focusing on suffering apart from an appreciation of God's ultimate design in us is to find ourselves without hope:

> And truely if we looke but only vpon the crosse of Iesus Christ, it is cursed by Gods owne mouth: we shal see nothing there but shame and terrour: and to be short, it wil seeme that the very gulfe of hel is open to swallow vp Iesus Christ. But when we ioyne his resurrection to his death, behold wherewith to comfort vs, behold wherewith to asswage al our sorrowes, to the ende we be not ouer sorrowful whensoeuer it shal please God to aflict vs. And this was purposely fulfilled in our Lorde Iesus

Christ, to the intent we should know that this was not written for any one person onely: but to the intent that al of vs should vnderstande, that the sonne of God will make vs partakers of his life if we die with hym, and partakers of his glory, if wee beare al the shames and aduersities which it shal please God to lay vpon our shoulders.[80]

In this way, following his theology of suffering as outlined in the *Institutes*, Calvin can speak of Christ as our model in suffering:

> Againe, haue wee not Iesus Christ for oure guyde? Then let vs go to death. Doo wee not knowe howe it is the entrie whereby too come too the glorie of heauen? Seeing that the resurrection was ioyned too the death of Gods sonne, was not that also too assure vs that God will not suffer vs too continue in rottennesse?[81]

Calvin can even suggest a christological focus to Job's longevity, suggesting that our lives are shorter,

> bicause Iesus Christ is appeared vnto vs, and hath shewed vs that we are but strangers in this world, that we might run to the heritage whiche is purchased by his bloud.[82]

Adding:

> For seing that our Lord Iesus Christ hath died and is risen again, we need no long time in this worlde to know that God is our father, and that we bee sure of our saluation.[83]

It is in the closing words of the sermon, Calvin's appeal to Christology as the only source of peace in tribulation, that his understanding of the Joban narrative becomes clear. Christ is the pledge of God's love to us, no matter what the circumstances may be. He is the mirror of our security.

> Ye see then that we must always be satisfied with lyfe, seeing that god hath giuen vs so good a pledge of his loue in our Lord Iesus Christ, and we must not desire to haue our life prolonged here, to the end to haue a large confirmation thereof.[84]

Thus it is that Calvin can suggest the conjunction of joy and trial:

Thus ye see how it behoueth vs to apply all our mirth to this end, namely that there may be a melodie sounding in vs wherby the name of God may be blissed and glorified in our Lord Iesus Christe.[85]

### Shining New Testament light into the Old Testament

Every so often, Calvin discusses a theological issue that can only be adequately explained by reference to the fullness of revelation in Christ. Thus, on one level, Calvin can reprimand Eliphaz for suggesting that Job's words must have been inherently sinful since they were not received well by men. This reasoning would condemn Christ also.[86] Thus, in discussing the issue of trials that befall the seemingly innocent, Calvin makes a passing allusion to Christ:

> We see what befell too our Lorde Iesus Christe who is the Head, the Mirrour, and the Patterne of all Gods children.[87]

As we have discussed elsewhere in this volume, Calvin alludes to the doctrine of the *imago Dei*, finding in it a need to refer to Christ. In Sermon 4, commenting on the expression "the sons of God" in Job 1:4, Calvin says:

> True it is that men are very oftentymes called the *Children of God*, bycause he hath printed his image in them, specially in the faythfull, for asmuch as they be reformed to the likenesse of our Lord Iesus Christ, who is the liuely image of God his father, and also for that they haue receyued the spirit of adoption, which is a warrant vnto them that God beareth a fatherly loue towards them.[88]

Alluding to the possible reason for Job's suffering, Calvin refers to the pedagogic use of pain to make us desire all the more the grace that God gives in Christ:

> …it behooued God first too make [Job] feele hys sharpe and sore rigour, and afterwarde to comfort him againe… if wee mynde too receyue the grace that God giueth vs, and offereth too vs continually in oure Lorde Iesus Christ: we must first feele what wee oure selues are, and in what plight wee bee. Are wee desyrous (I say) too taste what the heauenly lyfe is? First wee muste knowe too what ende wee bee borne, yea euen according as wee bee sinners in Adam.[89]

In a passage reminiscent of the *Institutes*, Calvin refers to Christ as the mirror of our election:

they ca[n]not see the registers of heauen, to know whither they be written there or no. It is ynough for them that God hath giuen them a good copie of their election to looke vpon in our Lord Iesus Christ, insomuch that being his me[m]bers they doubt not but God will auow them to be his children.[90]

In Sermon 157, Calvin has recourse to comment upon God's power in the closing section of the Book of Job. For Calvin, God's self-disclosure as all-powerful is to the intent that we should be assured of our relationship to Christ.

> This (say I) is the cause for which we shuld mind gods almightiness, according as it is shewed vs where it is saide that no man shall plucke vs out of Christs ha[n]d who hath taken vs into his keeping. And why? For the father who hath committed vs to him, is stronger than all. Why, and to what end hath Iesus Christ alleaged to vs the inuincible power of God his father? It is to the end we should be quiet and not doubt but he will saue vs…[91]

We have already examined the issue of double justice as it occurs in these Joban sermons, whereby Calvin refers to a secret justice over and above that which is revealed in the law and before which we would be reckoned guilty even if we were able to fulfil all the demands of God's revealed justice. We have already examined in Chapter 2, Calvin's exegesis of Job 4:18, and the Christological basis for universal (or ontological) mediation. Thus Calvin is deeply disturbed by Job's statement that "the righteouse myghte go to lawe with God." Job "therfore doth amisse in this poynte," "is farre ouerseene in saying that a righteouse man may pleade hys cace," that "Job offended in saying that the righteouse and iust man may pleade his cace before God."[92]

> It standeth vs then in hand to haue Iesus Christ for our aduocate: and he in pleading our case alledgeth not our deserts, he setteth himselfe in our defence to say that God doth vs wrong in punishing vs: but he alledgeth the amends that he himselfe hath made, and that forsomuch as he hathe released vs our dets, we be now quit before God.[93]

Adding:

> Thus our comming vnto God, must not be to pretende any iustifying of our selues, nor to make any satisfaction: but to acknowledge our sinnes, and to beseech him to admit vs of his owne meere goodnesse and mercie,

and not to open our mouth to pleade our cace. For that manner of debating belongeth not to vs: it is the office that is giuen to our Lord Iesus Christ. Therefore let vs on our part hold our peace, and suffer Iesus Christ to be our spokesman and to make intercession for vs, that by that meanes our faultes may be buried and we be quitte in sted of being condemned.[94]

In Sermon 44, Calvin makes an extensive application regarding prayer:

> how Jesus Christ reacheth vs his hand: & that his office is to make intercessio[n] for vs: & that God also hath opened vs the gate, desiring nothing of vs fro[m] day to day, but that we should come vnto him.[95]

In Sermon 83, it is the subject of shallow repentance and conviction of sin that concerns the Reformer:

> Oure Lorde Iesus sayth not, Come vntoo mee all yee that say, I am a sinner, there are infirmities in mee: no hee sayth not so. But all yee that are loden and wearie, whose shoulders doo bende vnder the weight of your sinnes. These are they that bee called of Iesus Christ, too the ende they may finde mercie in him, and in his grace: and not they that so mocke with God, making a light confession, and beeing not once touched in their hartes.[96]

Speaking of peace in the midst of trouble, for example, Calvin also reminds us that true peace comes in knowing "that God is our father in our Sauiore Iesus Christ."[97]

In summary fashion, Calvin often returns to the idea of the fear of God as expressive of godliness. Commenting on Job 28:10-24, a passage that Calvin summarises as "our wisdome is to feare God," he explains:

> his meening is not to withdraw vs from fayth and fro[m] that which depenedeth therevpon, that is to wit, from knowing the infinite goodnesse of our God, to rest therevpon, so as we should not doubt but he is merciful vnto vs, bicause he pardoneth our sinnes for our Lord Iesus Christ sake, and also hath adopted vs & will loue vs as his children to procure our saluacio[n] vnto the end.[98]

For Calvin, the very revelation of the gospel is, in the nature of things, incomprehensible. There is in it a wisdom that surpasses anything that man can attain:

[I]f wee come too the doctrine of the Gospell: there is a wisedome that surmounteth all mans vnderstanding: yea, and is woonderfull euen too the verie Angelles. They bee the verie secretes of heauen which are conteyned in the Gospell. For it concerneth the knowing of God in the person of his Sonne. And although oure Lorde Iesus Christ came downe heere beneath: yet must wee comprehende hys godly Maiestie, or else we cannot grounde and settle oure fayth in him. I say it concerneth the knowledge of things that are incomprehensible to mans nature."[99]

## Christ and the Old Testament in general

Sometimes, it is not the Joban text, but other Old Testament passages Calvin introduces, that provide him with an opportunity to focus on Christ. Thus, commenting on Satan's appearance and opposition in the opening chapter of Job, Calvin refers his listeners to Zechariah 3:1ff, showing how the prophet introduces the figure of Satan setting himself up against the High Priest as the "head of the Churche and as a figure of our Lorde Iesus Christe."[100] Christ must be our refuge in all temptations. Interestingly, Calvin takes occasion to comment on the difference between our temptability and Christ's. Whereas Christ is tempted externally, because he had a "sound nature," we are also tempted from "inward affection," that is to say, a fallen nature.

I haue told you already, that our eyesight is a tempting of vs to follow the wicked lustes of our hart, when the euill is already conceyued within. Ye see then that sinne goeth formost: and so it must needes be concluded, that if the hart were not infected with corruption, our eyes should bee cleene. It is true: but yet for all that, it is true also that we are sometimes tempted without any inward affectio[n]: like as Iesus Christ himselfe was often tempted, and yet notwithstanding had not any vncleannesse in him: but was tempted after such manner, as a sound nature might be: he had outward sightes, but his will continued stedfast in goodnesse, for there was no corruptnesse at all in his senses. But it is otherwise with vs: for all our sences are corrupted by reason of sinne.[101]

Earlier in the same sermon, Calvin, commenting on the nature and function of angels, refers to Hebrews 1:16, which speaks of Christ having been "clothed himself with our nature and our substance." Calvin adds:

When we see that the Sonne of God is come so neere vnto vs, as to vouchsaue to be parttaker of mans nature, we may perceyue that his so

## A Christological Focus

doing is the verie welspring from whence proceedeth the other grace, that the Angels trauell and watch on our behalf, and also that it is their peculiar charge and vocation to procure our welfare.[102]

Calvin is fond of reminding us of the words of Jesus in John 10:29, to the effect that the Father has given us into the safe keeping of Jesus' hands. In Sermon 8, for example, Calvin then expands on this idea, comforting his listeners who may be in any trouble:

> For we shall haue strengthe inough, and we shall be sure of the victorie, if we rest vpon God, and leane vnto the grace of our Lorde Iesus Christe, whereof mention is made in the tenthe chapter of Iohn. The father (sayth he) whiche hath put you into my hande, is stronger than all. Feare ye not that Satan shall ouercome his maker. For God hath put vs into the handes of oure Lord Iesus Christ, to the intent that he shuld be the good and faythful keper both of our soules and of our bodies.[103]

Job's godliness can excite Calvin to urge him as a model for us. But the Reformer finds it necessary to remind his Christian listeners who have been "once baptized in the name of our Lorde Iesus Christe," that

> it behoueth vs to be holie both in bodie and mynde, and to bee giuen wholly vnto God, and dedicated to his seruice: whiche thing can not bee doone, but by withdrawyng our selues from the defylementes that may corrupt vs.[104]

Sometimes, as we have noted already, Calvin draws a parallel between Job, David and Christ, as he does in Sermon 12. Passing references can be made to Christ in the course of exposition, as when Calvin refers to Scripture as given "as well by his Prophetes, as by his sonne our Lorde Iesus Christe."[105]

Controversially, Calvin makes a lengthy reference to Christ as the mediator of angels, referring to Colossians 1:20 as support:

> True it is that Iesus Christ redemed not the Angels, for they needed not to be raunsomed from death whervnto they were not yet falne: but yet was he theyr mediator. And howso? To the intent to ioyne the[m] vnto god in all perfection, and afterward to mainteyne them by his grace, that they might be preserued fro[m] falling... The Angels (which are now much neerer to him than we bee and which beholde his face) haue no

such perfection but that some fault may be found in them, if hee list to examine them with rigor.[106]

Similarly, Calvin can on occasions pause to comment on the error of "the Papists" on this or that issue. In Sermon 33, it is their rejection of imputed righteousness by faith in Jesus Christ that he mentions in passing.[107] Again, in Sermon 40, Calvin returns briefly to the doctrine of justification by faith, adding:

> When wee saye that men are made ryghteous by fayth: it is as much too saye, as God forgyueth theyr sinnes, and cleerely acquiteth them for our Lorde Iesus Christes sake.[108]

## Christ: the Eschatological Focus

In his pastoral understanding of pain, the Reformer finds himself using Job as a model, urging those who find themselves in any trouble to "trust in the grace that is offered vs in our Lorde Iesus Christ," in order that, "wee may not ceasse to continue and holde out to the ende."[109] It is the doctrine of our union with Christ that affords the Reformer the greatest hope: that just as we are in union with Christ in his suffering and death, so are we in union with him in his resurrection and life.

> But let vs learne too fence oure selues with that whiche is shewed vs in the holy Scripture; namely, that wee shall haue matter of gladnesse ynough, when wee shall haue increased and profited in Iesus Christ as well too death as to life. Are wee then ioyned to Iesus Christ? Although our lyfe be more than miserable: yet shall it turne to our profite, so as if wee haue troubles in this world, the same shall be as many helpes to our saluation. Therfore whensoeuer it shall seeme that we be vtterly forlorne, let vs not therefore ceasse to call vpon our God, hoping not only that he will in the ende turne all our troubles into joy and glory: but also that he will continue his goodnesse towardes vs vntill he make vs feele it in all perfectnesse.[110]

We have noted Calvin's ending to Sermon 33, whereby he alludes to the future hope of delivery from all trials that is in Christ. Other sermons do something similar. Sermon 12, for example, finds Calvin alluding to our lives being hidden with Christ, yet another reference to Colossians 3:3.[111] Thus he can go on to suggest that "the faythful that are departed out of this world, are in joy with God, and do know, that forasmuch as they be Christes members, they can not perish."[112] In the very next sermon, Calvin makes a passing reference to the way in which a consideration of our weakness should spur us on to have "an eye to the lyfe that is prepared for vs in heauen, whyche shall bee fully shewed vpon vs at the coming of our Lorde Iesus Chryst."[113] In a reference to Job 5:22-23 and Hosea 2:18, Calvin anticipates the "league" between man and beast, adding that Christ is

> the vniuersall heire of all creatures, and all things are giuen into his handes: and if wee bee his members, we shall bee parttakers of all the benefites whiche the father hath committed too him in all perfection.[114]

Interestingly, Calvin can sometimes appeal to the dialogue of Romans 7 and 8 to underline the tension of living in the period between the two advents of Christ:

> Wretched man that I am (sayeth he) who will deliuer mee from the prison of my bodie? But by and by he yeeldeth thanks to God through our Lord Iesus Christ.[115]

Adding:

> But on our parte lette vs bee contented to languish and to haue our flesh payned, and our minde distressed during this life: for yet haue wee whereof to reioyce in God, bicause he promiseth to bee alwayes our father and Sauior. Doo wee die? Wee knowe that is our aduantage, as S. Paule sayeth, bicause that by that meanes God taketh vs out of the miseries of this worlde, too make vs parttakers of his riches and glorious immortalitie.[116]

Every now and then, Calvin inevitably raises the specter of future judgment, particularly since Job's counselors are intent on raising it. Thus, in Sermon 66 he commends us to look to Christ to acquit us.[117] In a similar vein, it is the advent of the future resurrection to glory that encourages us in the face of present opposition.[118] It is the doctrine of providence above everything else that affords us the possibility of viewing our present sufferings in the light of a greater and far more wonderful future. Thus, in Sermon 81, Calvin goes on at length to end his sermon on this high note:

> Therfore let vs so consider the vanities that are here beneath, as it may not greeue vs when we see ourselues certaine and sure of nothing here.

And why? For if we desire to be rooted here beneath, we shall renounce the kingdome of heave[n]. But whosoeuer knoweth that our life is with God, and that it shal be reueled vnto vs at the coming of our Lorde Iesus Christ: it shall not greeue him to be tossed in this world, and to see that there is nothing but chopping and changing, nor any thing certaine and sure, and that therfore we must long for the heaue[n]ly life, to the which God calleth and biddeth vs dayly by his woorde, yet in the meane season in the middest of all these worldly troubles, and things so disordered as we see: let vs not be ignora[n]t that God so guydeth and gouerneth the worlde by his prouidence, as nothing is done, here beneath without his will.[119]

It is the disordered nature of this life, with its trials and incomprehensible judgements that, for Calvin, makes the expectation of future judgement and re-creation all the more desirable. Thus, in an extensive section closing Sermon 92, Calvin can fuse together the twin themes of present suffering and future glory in a christological fashion. God's judgement is not yet fully apparent, and this should make us long for the coming of our Lord Jesus Christ:

and so muche the more hartely long for him as our Redeemer... Well Lorde, if all things were ordered as wee woulde wishe, wee shoulde no more hope for the coming of our Lorde Iesus Christ, nor for the Resurrection that is promised vs, nor for his heauenly kingdome: we should bee alreadie as in a Paradyse. But nowe that wee tossed as in a raging sea, and are in the middes of stormes, and whirlewyndes: it serueth well too teach vs to long for the rest that is prepared for vs in heauen, and which thou hast promised vs, too the ende wee may haue our sight alwayes fastened vpon the comming of oure Lorde Iesus Christ, thy Sonne, who shall gather vs all to himselfe, according as thou haste committed vs too his charge, protection and guiding.[120]

## Christ: The scope of Calvin's preaching

Where has all this brought us? Has Calvin showed us in these sermons that we ought to read Job "with the intention of finding Christ therein"? If we simply consider how often Calvin mentions the name of Christ in any way in these sermons, an astonishing fifty-eight sermons, 36.5 per cent of them, fail to do so.[121] In addition, a further three Sermons make no mention of Christ at all, but the recorded prayers do.[122] We have already seen that a mere 17 per cent aim to bring the sermon to a christological conclusion, and of these some are less forthright than others. Of course, it will be argued that few passages in Job have a specific christological import in any case and that we should not expect Calvin to interpret Job in such a way. Several passages, however, have been identified by some as having a christological significance, even if the precise meaning of these passages is greatly disputed. But even here, Calvin is deeply reticent in seeing too readily a christological import and, from one perspective at least, fails to do full justice to what might be considered a redemptive-historical interpretation. But this apart, does Calvin attempt to bring the sermons round to Christ in any way in order to see the bigger picture from the vantage point of the completed canon? Since Calvin could comment on John 5:39 that "the Scriptures should be read with the aim of finding Christ in them," can it be said that he interprets Job this way? Is there, for example, any attempt to bring the theology of the Book of Job to a christological focus, to shine the light of the gospel into these passages?

**Exegesis of specific Joban texts: A reluctant Christology?**
If the Joban material provides Calvin with little by way of direct allusions to an anticipated Redeemer, four particular passages in the text have been so interpreted. These are Job 9:33, 16:19, 19:25 and 33:23-24, in which the figure of a mediator, or arbitrator, appears, providing Job with assurance that his case will be heard and vindicated.[123] These passages are treated in Sermons 37, 64, 71, 72, 125, 126 and 127. What is surprising is the reticence with which Calvin treats these passages. Whilst he does have a christological hermeneutic at work in all these passages, Calvin is far less eager to interpret these texts from a New Testament, fulfillment point of view. We once again witness the desire of the Reformer to allow the text to interpret itself.

In Job 9:33, we find the Reformer almost at the end of the sermon before he attempts to deal with the verse, which asks: "Who is the vmper who will put his hande betwixt vs?"[124] Having mentioned God's "double goodness" in giving us his law and saving us from its penalty, he makes the interesting point that "if you fulfill my lawe, I will giue you euerlasting life in rewarde, notwithstanding that I mighte require it at youre hande withoute recompence."[125] He goes on to add that this is a requirement of the (pure, unfallen) angels in heaven, too, "for there is no respect too bee had too our owne nature as it is nowe sinfull and corrupted."[126] Raising the spectre of a secret righteousness again, Calvin warns that even if we were able to fulfil the law's demands perfectly, there is another law to which we have no access that would also condemn us. Calvin then takes up Job's plea for an "vmpire" (Hebrew, הוֹכִיחַ), understanding it in sin-reconciliation terms, rather than the demand for the justice of Job's case to be vindicated. Calvin adds:

> In steede of vmpers too heare oure matter debated: let vs seeke Iesus Christ that hee may bee our vmper to take vp the matter. Let vs not desire too haue a iudge too lay hande both vpon him and vs: but let vs beseech him, that there maye bee some meanes of attonement betweene vs and his Maiestie.[127]

Adding a little later:

> What remayneth more? That Iesus Christ put himselfe betwixt vs: Iesus Christ muste bee fayne too bee our dayesman, not too passe in iudgement vppon the Maiestie of God, nor too set God at the barre with vs: but too bee the meane too reconcyle vs vntoo God, and too drawe vs after him as oure heade, too knit vs in suche wyse vntoo God, as wee may bee all one in him.[128]

In Job 16:18-22, Job cries: "For euen now is my witnesse in heauen, and he that warranteth me is in the highest places." Here, one might have expected Calvin to continue the line adopted in the interpretation of Job 9:33 and see the "witnesse in heauen" as Christ in his capacity as Intercessor and High Priest. But Calvin does not see the verse in this way, instead implying, in a brief and closing remark in the sermon, that the witness in heaven is the "good case' that Job has argued.

> And he doubteth not to appeale vnto God, forasmuch as hee knowes his cace is good. True it is (as I haue sayde alreadie) that he missehandleth his cace: howebeit in so doing he had iust cause to mainteyne his owne soundnesse.[129]

The statement of Job in Job 19:25-26 is perhaps the most well known in the book. In it, Job exclaims: "I am sure that my redeemer liueth, and he shall at the last rise vp vpon the earth." The question that all interpreters must face is the identity of the redeemer (Hebrew: גֹּאֵל). Is this a reference to the as yet hidden Messiah? Is Job giving an expression of a belief in future resurrection based on the mediatorial work of Christ in his death and passion on our behalf, when he goes on to say, "Although after my skinne, the [wormes] destroy this [body: yet] I shall see God in my flesh" (Job 19:26)?

Again, Calvin's treatment of verse 25 comes at the end of sermon 71, and what is most significant about his comment is its brevity. Barely twenty lines of text follow, and although Calvin takes up the theme in the next Sermon, his comment is briefer still! Calvin's comment at the end of Sermon 71, in fact, suggests, "Verely this cannot be wholly expounded as now."[130] He then suggests that its meaning has to do with the integrity of Job's "good case." That God is alive (this is how Calvin later translates this verse) is the basis of Job's assurance that his case will not fall on deaf ears.[131]

> Wee knowe that men will laboure all that they can too excuse themselues, and that is, bycause they thinke not vpon God, it is ynough for them that the worlde likes well of them, and that they bee taken for honest men. Thus then do the hypocrisie ingender an unshamefastnesse. For if I knowe not God too bee my iudge, it will suffice me that men clap theyr handes at me, and haue me in good reputation. And what gayne I by that? Nothing at al. Is it not an exceeding great shamelesnesse, when although mine owne conscience accuse me, and I be conuicted to haue done amisse, yet for all that I will perke vp with my neb, and saye, whereof can any man accuse me? What haue I done? Haue I not a good cace? I will take faire colours to couer my skinne, and if I can bleare mens eyes, tush my cace shall then speede well ynough.[132]

This may be Calvin's most un-christological statement in these sermons. Far from seeing an allusion to Christ, Calvin sees an allusion to God as the one who will hear his un-hypocritical defense of his own good case.[133]

Calvin interprets Job 33:23-24, in which Elihu asks "If there be an eloquent messanger to shewe a man his righteousnesse," in a different way. The righteousness in view here might at first be expected to be Job's own moral integrity, the righteousness expressed by the author of the book of Job and by God's own testimony in the opening two chapters. This would be consistent with how Calvin has seen the allusions of Job 16:19 and 19:25. Instead, however, Calvin sees here a testimony to Job's imputed righteousness. That is, Elihu is seeking for ministers (the "eloquent messengers") who can show to Job the method of acquiring this imputed righteousness: by faith in the Christ of the gospel.

> True it is that Iesus Christ is the partie that hath let vs looce from the bondage of sin and euerlasting damnation, wherin wee were by nature: But yet hath he committed the same charge to all shepherds of his churche.[134]

Adding:

> Then are wee righteouse, not in our selues nor through our owne vertues, but bycause it pleaseth God to forgiue vs.[135]

An extensive paragraph follows on the nature of this imputed righteousness as opposed to a works righteousness:

> Wheron then shall our ryghteousnesse rest? On the free mercy of our God, bycause that when he hath once scoured awaye our spotts with the blood of his sonne, and discharged vs from death and damnation by the raunsome which our Lord Iesus Christ paid vpon the crosse, he wypeth out our sinnes, and layeth not our offences to our charge. Thus the ryghteousnesse which is preached vnto vs by Gods messengers, is that we be iustified or accepted for ryghteouse.[136]

Calvin develops this theme in the very next sermon. Continuing to allude to ministers, Calvin draws from such passages as Matthew 16 and 2 Corinthians 5 to make the point that "the office of such as preache the gospel, is to forgiue sinnes."[137] Commenting upon 1 Corinthians 5:18, he sees Paul as saying:

> The propertie of the gospell is, to be a message of attonement betweene God and man: which is, that Iesus Christ who knewe no sinne, but was the vnspotted lambe, did put himself vnder the curse of our sinnes, to the end that wee should find the ryghteousnesse of God in him, that is to say, after wee are washed in his bloud, and haue put ourselues vnder the sacrifice which he hath offered, wee bee taken and reputed for righteouse, bycause the sayd sacrifice had the power to put away all faultes and offences.[138]

## Conclusion

Aegidius Hunnius' criticism that Calvin was too "Jewish" in his interpretation of the Old Testament is oddly at variance with modern assessments of a christological focus to Calvin's thought.[139] Be that as it may, our studies in Calvin's preaching on the Joban text have

# A Christological Focus

uncovered some strange results: Calvin, in many instances, preached entire sermons, even successive sermons, without ever seeing a need to focus on Christ as the fulfillment and scope of Scripture. Over a third of these sermons fail to mention Christ at all. Barely over a fifth of the sermons find Calvin concluding his message with a christological focus. Seventeen sermons, just over a tenth, allude to passages of Scripture cited by Jesus in the Gospels. In fact, only a handful of sermons have what we might term an extensive christological focus.[140] Of the rest, as we have seen, Calvin is content to make brief, but often pointed, allusions to a christological fulfillment, in which the principle he is expounding finds its clearest realisation in Christ. Whilst it may be true to point out that the Joban material gives little scope for christological intepretation, Calvin remains reluctant even in those passages that have been interpreted christologically. It is particularly noteworthy that even where an exegete might have a good reason to discover a warrant for a Christian interpretation in passages of the Book of Job, Calvin has been acutely reticent to give an exposition that ignores the historical context, even though that leads him to some inconsistency in his interpretations of Job 9:33-34 and 33:23-24, as compared to those of Job 16:18-21 and 19:25-26.

All of this may lend some support to Battles' contention that Calvin deliberately set out to find a middle way between opposing extremes of interpretation, a view largely based on an examination of the *Institutes*.[141] Puckett has shown convincingly that this thesis can be extended to that of Calvin's Old Testament commentaries.[142] Puckett maintains that "Calvin unquestionably would have placed himself on the Christian end of any Jewish-Christian exegetical continuum."[143] *Unquestionably*? For Calvin's commentaries, this seems abundantly proven. But as we have seen in this chapter, the contention is difficult to prove as far as the sermons on Job are concerned.

On the other hand, for Bouwsma, Calvin betrayed a tension between his philosophical, rational side and his rhetorical, humanist side, with the latter triumphing in the end. Puckett does question Bouwsma's insistence on the clear victory of the rhetorical, but a study of Calvin's sermons on Job seems to question this a great deal further. Calvin seems as reluctant, if not more so, to be accused of christianizing the Old Testament.[144] As a result of our study, it might be more accurate to say that, here at least, Calvin locates himself almost entirely at the centre of this continuum.

At one level, this seems altogether surprising. It might be expected that in the freer style of preaching, Calvin would be less concerned with hermeneutical procedures than in the commentaries. It might be anticipated that the burden to come to Christ as the foundation and substance of the Old Covenant might prove, at the conscious level, so great that interpretative restraints might be relaxed. This does not appear to be the case. In fact, the Reformer's determination to demonstrate historico-grammatical sensitivity seems all the more apparent. Calvin did view history in terms of divine providence, and this greatly affects his exegetical methodology. Additionally, he viewed God as accommodating himself in human words, an idea central to his entire interpretation of Job's predicament. But whatever tensions may exist at points of detail, Calvin is primarily concerned to explain the text within the boundaries of historico-grammatical exegesis; the need to see Christ was given second place.

This conclusion bears directly on some current Calvin scholarship, which is determined to view the entire corpus of his deliberations from a christological, christo-monistic, point of view. The neo-orthodox agenda for our understanding of Calvin, for example, will find little by way of support in the Joban sermons. Since these sermons represent Calvin at the very peak of his powers, within a few years of his final and definitive edition of the *Institutes*, then it is proper to conclude that the Joban sermons are representative of his mature thought. As such, he seems less preoccupied with applying a Christ-centred agenda than we have been given to understand in certain studies. The Reformer consistently prioritises grammatico-historical considerations as he approaches the text of Scripture. His concern throughout is to adhere rigidly to the text before him, applying what he finds to the needs of folk who hear him as he deems it relevant. The hermeneutic from text to sermon seems to confirm the hypothesis that Calvin sought a middle ground between the extremes of Jewish and Christian interpretations. Calvin thereby fails to please many other interpereters of Old Testament Scripture, including, it has to be said, those who avidly follow his theology and exegesis in our time. The fact that Calvin was a Trinitarian theologian, and therefore Christian by inference, fails to uphold what many would consider to be a necessary emphasis in Old Testament interpretation and homiletics: that the text should come to Christ.

# References

[1] A. Schweizer, *Die protestantischen Centraldogmen in ihrer Entwicklung innerhalb der reformatierten Kirche*, 2 vols. (Zurich, 1854-56). A different approach was taken by H. Bauke in 1922, who drew attention to Calvin's ability to follow biblical themes through to their conclusion even when it resulted in a *complexio oppositorum. Die Probleme der Theologie Calvins* (Leipzig, 1922). It has been supported by A. Ganoczy, who refers to the dialectical structure "and profound bipolarity" of Calvin's thought. See *Le Jeune Calvin* (Weisbaden, 1966); *The Young Calvin*, trans. David Foxgrover and Wade Provo (Philadelphia: The Westminster Press, 1987), 181-187. Others, like W. J. Bouwsma, "The Quest for the Historical Calvin," *Archiv für Reformationsgeschichte* 77 (1986), 47-57, and B. G. Armstrong, "Duplex Cognitio Dei, or, The problem and relation of structure, form and purpose in Calvin's theology," in *Probing the Reformed Tradition*, ed. E. A. McKee and B. G. Armstrong (Louisville, 1989), 135-153, are both cautious over any attempt to formulate a systematic theology from Calvin's published writings. See also R. Gamble, "Calvin as Theologian and Exegete: Is There Anything New?" in *Calvin Theological Journal* 23(1988), 178-194.

[2] W. Niesel, *The Theology of Calvin*, trans. H. Knight (1956); F. Wendel, *Calvin: Origins and Development of His Religious Thought*, trans. P. Mairet (New York: Harper & Row, 1963); P. Jacobs, *Prädestination und Verantwortlichkeit bei Calvin* (Neukirchen Kr. Moers, Buchhandlung des Erziehungsvereins, 1937).

[3] Cf. D. N. Wiley, "Calvin's Doctrine of Predestination: His Principal Soteriological and Polemical Doctrine," (Ph.D. thesis, Duke University, 1971). Cf. G. M. Thomas, *The Extent of the Atonement: A Dilemma for Reformed Theology from Calvin to the Consensus (1536-1675)* (Carlisle, Cumbria: Paternoster Publishing, 1997), 12-15.

[4] C. Partee, *Calvin and Classical Philosophy*, Studies in the History of Christian Thought, no. 14. (Leiden: E. J. Brill, 1977), 84; B. Hall, "Calvin Against the Calvinists," in *John Calvin*, ed. G. E. Duffield (Leiden: E. J. Brill, 1966) 22-23; John H. Leith, "Calvin's Theological Method and the Ambiguity in his Theology," in *Reformation Studies* (1962), 108; Ian McPhee, "Conserver or Transformer of Calvin's Theology? A Study of the origins and Development of Theodore Beza's Thought, 1550-1570" (Ph.D. thesis, Cambridge University, 1979), 41-42. For Barth's criticism of Calvin's doctrine of providence as lacking a christological focus, see *Church Dogmatics* III/3:30. Barth takes Niesel to task for his assertion that Calvin's doctrine of providence is entirely based "on the revelation of God in Jesus Christ," adding: "I have not found this asssertion supported in the very slightest by the passages which Niesel quotes."

[5] *Institutes*, preface, [*CO* 2:9-30]. Cf. *Concerning the Eternal Predestination of God*, trans. J. K. S. Reid (London: James Clarke, 1961) [*CO* 8:270-366]. There is also a nineteenth-century translation by H. Cole, *Calvin's Calvin-*

*ism* (Grand Rapids: Eerdmans, 1956). A remarkable similarity of construction seems to have governed Calvin's writing of *De aeterna Praedestinatione Dei* in 1552 and the final shape of the *Institutes*, reflecting amongst other things, the profound effect the Bolsec controversy had on his thinking. *De aeterna* was a patch-work production, consisting in polemic against Pighius and Georgius, together with a separate piece on providence. Little is known of Georgius except that he wrote a commentary on Romans. On Pighius, see the introduction to Calvin's Latin title: *Defensio sanae et Orthodoxae Doctrinae De Servitute et Liberatione Humani Arbitrii Adversus Calumnias Alberti Pighii Campensis* [CO 6:225-404]. The work has been translated as, *The Bondage and Liberation of the Will: A Defence of the Orthodox Doctrine of Human Choice against Pighius*, trans. G. I. Davies, ed. A. N. S. Lane (Grand Rapids: Baker Books, 1996), xiii-xviii.

[6] The objections against Calvin on the grounds of perceived determinism were raised following the first edition of the *Institutes* in 1539. Similar charges were raised against Augustine by a friend of John Cassian (who may have been St Vincent of Lérins). See O. Chadwick, *John Cassian* (Cambridge: Cambridge University Press, 1968), 118.

[7] For successive editions of the *Institutes*, see F. Wendel, *Calvin: Origins and Development of His Religious Thought*, trans. P. Mairet (New York: Harper & Row:1963), 112-122. Responding to the attempts to explain Calvin's removal of predestination from Book I to Book III of the *Institutes*, Wendel has suggested that Calvin would have "put predestination immediately after the exposition on providence—even, indeed, before the chapters on the creation..." Richard Muller has taken this a step further, suggesting that "the positions of predestination and providence be reversed" in the logic of Calvin's system. Richard Muller, *Christ and the Decree* (Durham, NC: The Labyrinth Press, 1986), 24.

[8] *Institutes* III.xxiv.5. *Christus ergo speculum est in quo electionem nostram contemplari convenit, et sine fraude licet* [CO 2:716]. Wendel has noted that "predestination can in fact be regarded as in some respects a particular application of the more general notion of providence." F. Wendel, *Calvin: Origins and Development of His Religious Thought*, trans. P. Mairet (New York: Harper & Row, 1963), 178, 267.

[9] Wiley, *op. cit.* 129ff; McPhee, *op. cit.* 46f. Though Calvin makes few references to contemporary events, it does appear that his own personal trials were the catalyst that caused him to concentrate upon the doctrine of God as he discovered it in the Book of Job.

[10] Wiley, *op. cit.*, 175ff. Cf. "We make God the ruler and governor of all things, who in accordance with his wisdom has from the farthest limit of eternity decreed what he was going to do, and now by his might carries out what he has decreed." *Inst.* I.xvi.8. *Sed Deum constituimus arbitrum ac moderatorem omnium, qui pro sua sapientia, ab ultima aeternitate decrevit quod facturus esset, et nunc sua potentia, quod decrevit exsequitur* [CO 2:151].

[11] "Man falls according as God's providence ordains, but he falls by his own fault." *Institutes* III.xxiii.8. *Cadit igitur homo, Dei providentia sic ordinante: sed suo vitio cadit* [*CO* 2:705]. Cf. III.xxiii.3,9 [*CO* 2:700-701, 705-706].

[12] *Contre la secte phatastique et furieuse des Libertins qui se nomment spirituelz* (1545) [*CO* 7:145-252]. Here, Calvin distinguishes between three ways of God's government. Firstly, there is a universal operation by which all creatures function in accordance with their natures. Creatures retain liberty even though God works through them as instruments in his hands. Secondly, there is a general providence. God sends prosperity and adversity by means of the elements (wind, rain, etc.), or by men who function as *causes inférieures*. In this way, as the book of Job illustrates, even Satan and the wicked *sont executeurs de son vouloir* [*CO* 7:188]. It is here that Calvin speaks directly to the issue of the relationship of God to the origin of sin. Countering the allegation of the Libertines, who maintained that God was the sole cause of both good and evil, Calvin alleges that Satan and the wicked are not merely passive instruments; rather they act *selon la qualité de sa nature qu'il lui a donnée* [*CO* 7:188]. Thirdly, there is a government of the church by the Holy Spirit. For a full account of the Bolsec controversy, see P. Holtrop, *The Bolsec Controversy on Predestination from 1551 to 1555* (Lewiston, N.Y.: Edwin Mellen, 1993).

[13] Aegidius Hunnius, *Calvinus Iudaizans, Hoc est: Iudaicae Glossae et Corruptilae, Quibus Iohannes Calvinus illustrissima Scripturae sacrae loca & Testimonia, de gloriosa Trinitate, Deitate Christi, & spiritus sancti, eum primis autem vaticinia Prophetarum de Adventu Messiae, nativitate eius, passione, resurrectione, ascensione in coelos & sessione ad dextram Dei, detestandum in modum corrumpere non exhorruit. Addita est corruptelarum confutatio.* (Wittenberg, 1595). Aegidius Hunnius (1550-1603) studied theology under Jakob Andreae, Jacob Heerbrand, Johannes Brenz, and Erhard Schnepf at Tübingen (1565-1574), later taught at Marburg (1576-1592), and later still at the university of Wittenberg. See entry by William R. Russell in *The Oxford Encyclopedia of the Reformation*, ed. Hans J. Hillerbrand, vol. 2 (New York, Oxford: Oxford University Press, 1996), 276.

Jerome Friedman suggests that Calvin would not have been surprised by this charge since the term Judaizer was a frequent epithet of the times by all sides. "The Lutheran author Hunnius described John Calvin as a judaizer much as Calvin believed Lutheran liturgy was highly judaistic. On the other hand, Roman Catholic spokesmen thought Lutheran preoccupation with scriptural literalism was judaistic while both Reformed and Lutheran thinkers assumed Roman Catholic interest in ceremony and ritual reflected judaizing tendencies. Expressing a rare ecumenism, all agreed that Michael Servetus was a severe judaizer by any and all standards. For his part, Servetus lamented his being persecuted by judaizing Christians, Calvin in particular." Jerome Friedman, *The Most Ancient Testimony: Sixteenth-Century Christian-Hebraica in the age of Renaissance Nostalgia* (Athens, Ohio: Ohio

University Press, 1983), 182. On Calvin's view of Lutheran liturgy, see his letter to Guillaume Farel, April 1539 [CO 10:340]. See also, David Puckett, *John Calvin's Exegesis of the Old Testament* (Louisville, Kentucky: Westminster John Knox Press, 1995), 1-18.

[14] Puckett, *op. cit.*, 1-2.

[15] *Ibid.*, 140. See also, Ford Lewis Battles, *Calculus Fidei: Some Ruminations on the Structure of the Theology of John Calvin* (Grand Rapids: Calvin Theological Seminary, 1978). For an analysis of christological interpretations prior to Calvin, see James Samuel Preus, *From Shadow to Promise* (Cambridge, Massachusetts: Harvard University Press, 1969).

[16] Cf. Calvin's comment on Psalm 72:1: "We must always be careful not to give the Jews any reason to claim that we split hairs in order to find a reference to Christ in passages not directly related to him." *Deinde semper cavendum est ne Iudaeis obstrependi detur occasio, ac si nobis propositum esset sophistice ad Christum trahere quae directe in eum non competunt* [*CO* 31:664]. Cf. David L. Puckett, *John Calvin's Exegesis of the Old Testament*, 53. Calvin may well be objecting to the interpretation of Faber Stapulensis at this point. See Richard A. Muller, "Calvin's Exegesis of Old Testament Prophecies," in *The Bible in the Sixteenth Century*, ed. David C. Steinmetz (Durham, London: Duke University Press, 1990), 77. Cf. Jacobus Faber Stapulensis, "Introduction to Commentary on the Psalms," in *Forerunners of the Reformation*, ed. with introduction by Heiko A. Oberman (New York: Holt, Rinehart and Winston, 1966), 297-305.

[17] Hans Joachim-Kraus, "Calvins exegetische Prinzipien," *Zeitschrift für Kirchengeschichte* 79 (1968): 329-41; "Calvin's Exegetical Principles," trans. Keith Crim, *Interpretation* 31 (January 1977): 8-18. Kraus' assessment of Calvin's exegetical method stands in agreement with that of several others, including Henri Clavier, "Calvin commentateur biblique," in *Études sur le calvinisme*, ed. H. Clavier (Paris, 1936), 99-144; Wilhelm Vischer, "Calvin exégète de 'Ancien Testament," *La Revue Reformée* 18 (1967): 1-20; Benoit Girardin, *Rhetorique et Théologique. Calvin: Le Commentaire de l'Epître aux Romains* (Paris, 1979), 76-81; Alexandre Ganoczy and Stefan Scheld, *Die Hermeneutik Calvins: Geistesgeschichtliche Voraussetzungen und Grundzüge* (Weissbaden, 1983); T. H. L. Parker, *Calvin's Old Testament Commentaries* (Edinburgh: T & T Clark Ltd., 1986); *Calvin's New Testament Commentaries* (Edinburgh: T & T Clark Ltd., 1971,1993); Richard Gamble, "*Brevitas et facilitas*: Toward an Understanding of Calvin's Hermeneutic," *Westminster Theological Journal* 47 (1985): 1-17; "Exposition and Method in Calvin," *Westminster Theological Journal* 49 (1987): 153-65; "Calvin as Theologian and Exegete: Is There Anything New?" *Calvin Theological Journal* 23 (1988):178-94. T. F. Torrance's contribution to this field in *Calvin's Hermeneutic* (Edinburgh, 1988), that Calvin borrowed hermeneutical principles from Scotist and nominalist epistemology learned in Paris from John Major, has been challenged by Ganoczy in his *Le Jeune Calvin* (Weisbaden, 1966); *The Young Calvin*, trans. David Foxgrover and Wade Provo (Philadel-

phia: The Westminster Press, 1987).

Richard A. Muller has taken issue with Kraus' conclusions, suggesting that apart from one principle, that of "clarity and brevity," "not a single principle noted here separates Calvin definitively from the medieval exegete." Richard A. Muller, "Calvin's Exegesis of Old Testament Prophecies," in *The Bible in the Sixteenth Century*, ed. David C. Steinmetz (Durham, London: Duke University Press, 1990), 69. Cf. Henri Strohl, "La méthode exégétique des Réformateurs," in *Le probléme biblique dans le Protestantisme*, ed. J. Boisset (Paris, 1955), 98. Muller's point is that Kraus and others have drawn mainly from the *Institutes* rather than from the example of Calvin's hermeneutic in the exposition of the text. He does note, through an examination of Calvin's commentary on the Psalms, that Kraus has "come very close in places to a full sense of Calvin's mode of interpretation." In particular, he cites with approval Kraus' observation of Calvin's hermeneutic that "the Old Testament 'looks to the future for the fulfillment of promises and prophecies' in such a way that Christ, as fulfillment, focuses and unifies the whole of Scripture." "Calvin's Exegesis of Old Testament Prophecies," 76. Cf. Kraus, "Calvin's Exegetical Principles," 17.

[18] Anthony Baxter has described this as "Old Testament monism." See *John Calvin's Use and Hermeneutics of the Old Testament* (Ph.D. diss., University of Sheffield, 1987), 68.

[19] It is probably Servetus that Calvin has in mind in Sermon 78, when he closes with the unusually personal attack: "When our Lord hath executed so terrible iudgements as mens eares ought too glowe at them: a man needes not too speake of them: For these good defenders of the honour of Geneua make complaynt of it. I say, when a man speaketh of the man whom God would haue to be an horrible spectacle and a feare and terrour too all men, if a man bring that thing to rememberance, and shewe that the blasphemer which spited God and all religion, was as ye would say, straught [of his witts,] insomuch that the moother which bare him in hir wo[m]be, deposed that the diuell brought him in: they will say that men dishonour the citie. Behold these good men that are so zelous of the honour of Geneua, they could find in their harts that the Towne were sunken (it is well knowen who they bee, and a man needes not too poynt them out with his finger, nor too call them by their names, for they bee knowne wellynough) and yet for all that they pretend a desirousnesse too the honour of the citie: but it is well seene of what hart their dooings proceede." 78 (Job 21:1-6), 369.a.13. *Quand nostre Seigneur a fait des iugemens qui sont si espouvantables, que les aureilles en devroyent corner, il ne faut point qu'on en parle: car ces bons defenseurs de l'honneur de Geneve feront une queremonie là dessus. Quand, di-ie, on parlera de celui que Dieu a voulu estre en spectacle horrible, et en effroy et espouvantement à tous, quand on reduira cela en memoire, qu'on monstrera qu'un blasphemateur qui despitoit Dieu et toute religion a esté comme ravi, en sorte que la mere qui l'a porté au ventre depose que le diable l'en a emporté: ils diront qu'on deshonore la ville. Voila ces bons*

*zelateurs de l'honneur de la ville, qui voudroyent que Geneve fust abysmee (comme on cognoist bien quels ils sont, et ne les faut point monstrer au doigt, il ne les faut point nommer par leurs noms, car ils sont assez cognus) et cependant ils feront bien semblant de vouloir defendre l'honneur de la ville: mais on voit bien de quel coeur ils y procedent.* [*CO* 34:213-214].

[20] 72 (Job 19:26-29), 338.b.53. *Or faisons tousiours ceste comparaison entre Iob et nous, que si Iob n'ayant point un tel tesmoignage de la bonté de Dieu, n'ayant point une doctrine si familiere de la centieme partie comme nous avons, à toutes fois dit, qu'il contempleroit Dieu: et nous, serons-nous à excuser, quand nous aurons esté esgarez çà et là, voire attendu que nostre Seigneur Iesus Christ se presente à nous, auquel habite toute plenitude de gloire divine, et que toute la vertu du S. Esprit s'est monstree en lui, quand il est ressuscité des morts? Et mesmes il ne faut point que nous estendions nostre veuë bien loin pour le contempler: car l'Evangile est un beau miroir, où nous le voyons face à face* [*CO* 34:133].

[21] Cf. Calvin's comments in Sermon 107: "For... the doctrine of God was very darke in those days, and God sent it but as it were drop by drop, eue[n] as whe[n] there falleth a small deaw in the night. To be short, men are taught it but slightly in comparison of the abunda[n]ce of grace whiche God sendeth into the worlde in these days. For in the Gospell we haue infinite treasures of wisedome and knowledge, God sheweth himselfe familiarly vnto vs, he will haue vs to be filled, and throughly filled with all perfection of his doctrine, and he giueth so cleere and certain vnderstanding as can be possible." 107 (Job 29:18-25), 505.b.17. *Car...la doctrine estoit fort obscure, Dieu en bailloit comme goutte à goutte, ainsi que si la nuict il tomboit quelque petite rosee: bref, on n'estoit enseigné qu'à lesche doigt (comme on dit) en comparaison de ceste abondance de grace qu'auiourd'hui Dieu envoye au monde. Car en l'Evangile nous avons les thresors infinis de sagesse et d'intelligence, Dieu se declare priveement à nous: il veut que nous soyons remplis et rassasiez en toute perfection de sa doctrine: il nous en donne une intelligence si claire et si certaine que rien plus* [*CO* 34:581].

[22] John Argumentum [*CO* 47:vii]. Calvin never uses the word "gospel" to mean the Old Testament, just as he never uses the word "law" to mean the New Testament. Commenting on John 1:1, Calvin can agree that "gospel" can refer to the promises of mercy in the Old Testament, but this is an improper usage. "Holy Scripture does not speak thus of itself." *L'Escriture saincte n'use point de ce langage*...[*CO* 47:465]. Cf. *Insitutes* II.ix.2 "Now I take the gospel to be the clear manifestation of the mystery of Christ." *Porro evangelium accipio pro clara mysterii Christi manifestatione* ... [*CO* 2:310].

[23] Chapter 7 of the 1539 Latin edition of the *Institutes* was entitled *De similitudine ac differentia veteris et novi testamenti*. In 1543, this became chapter 11, and in the final edition of 1559, this material was expanded into chapters 9-11 of Book II. That Calvin has the Anabaptists in view is clear from the opening lines of this material, and the fact that the reference to Servetus is not found in any of the editions from 1539 to 1554 adds to the

idea that this may well have been on Calvin's mind in his expositions of Job: "Indeed, that wonderful rascal Servetus and certain madmen of the Anabaptist sect, who regard the Israelites as nothing but a herd of swine, make necessary what would in any case have been proftable for us." *Inst.* II.x.1. *Quin etiam, quod utilissimum alioqui futurum erat, necessarium nobis fecerunt prodigiosus nebulo Servetus et furiosi nonnulli ex Anabaptistarum secta, qui non aliter de israelitico populo sentiunt quam de aliquo porcorum grege, utpote quem nugantur a Domino in hac terra saginatum, citra spem ullam coelestis immortalitatis* [*CO* 2:313].

[24] See Calvin's comment on John 1:16: "All the godly, no doubt, who lived under the law, drew out of the same fullness; ... From the beginning of the world all the Patriarchs drew whatever gifts they had from Christ. For although the Law was given by Moses it was not from him that they obtained grace." *Commentary on the Holy Gospel of Jesus Christ According to John,* vol. XVII, 50-51. *Certum quidem est pios omnes qui sub lege vixerunt, ex fadem plenitudine hausisse...imo contextus non male hoc modo fluet, omnes ab initio mundi patres a Christo hausisse quidquid habuerint donorum: quia, tametsi lex per Mosen data esset, non tamen inde gratiam obtinuerint* [*CO* 47:17].

[25] II.vi.2 [*CO* 2:248]. Cf. *Ac proinde veteri populo nunquam se Deus ostendit propitium, nec spem gratiae unquam fecit absque mediatore.* Cf. Later in the same section: "...the blessed and happy state of the Church always had its foundation in the person of Christ." ... *beatum et felicem ecclesiae statum semper in Christi persona fuisse fundatum* [*CO* 2:248]. And again, by way of conclusion to this section: "From this it is now clear enough that, since God cannot without the Mediator be propitious toward the human race, under the law Christ was always set before the holy fathers as the end to which they should direct their faith." *Hinc iam satis liquet, quia non potest Deus propitius humano generi esse absque mediatore, sanctis patribus sub lege Christum semper fuisse obiectum, ad quem fidem suam dirigerent* [*CO* 2:250].

[26] *Commentaries of the Book of the Prophet Jeremiah and The Lamentations,* 4:126-127, in *Calvin's Commentaries,* Vol. X (Grand Rapids, MI: Baker, 1979) [*CO* 38:688]. *Iam quod ad novum foedus spectat, non sic vocatur quia aliud sit a primo foedere. Deus enim secum non pugnat: neque est sui dissimilis....Nunc videndum est cur promittat foedus novum populo. Non dubium est quin hoc referatur ad formam, sicuti loquuntur. Forma autem haec non tantum posita est in verbis, sed primum in Christo, deinde in gratia spiritus sancti, et tota docendi ratione externa: substantia autem eadem manet. Substantiam intelligo doctrinam, quia Deus in evangelio nihil profert, quod lex non contineat. Videmus ergo Deum ab initio sic loquutum esse, ne syllabam quidem postea mutaverit, quantum attinet ad doctrinae summam.* In the 1559 edition of the *Institutes,* Calvin expounds at length on this theme, suggesting that the Old Testament does not differ in substance from the New. What differences there are apply only to the mode of dispensation (*dispensatio*) and administration (*administratio*). For Calvin,

then, the Old and New Testaments form but two stages in the unfolding of the one covenant, which covenant bears witness to Christ. Cf. W. Niesel, *The Theology of Calvin*, 105. Cf. Hans Heinrich Wolf's remark, that "...the *substantia* and *res* of the covenant is a question of Christ himself." [*Es handelt sich bei substantia und res Bundes um Christus selbst.*] *Die Einheit des Bundes: Das Verhältnis von Altem und Neuem Testament bei Calvin* (Druck: Verlag der Buchhandlung des Erziehungsvereins Neukirchen Kreis Moers, 1958), 24.

[27] *Commentaries in the Four Last Books of Moses arranged in the Form of a Harmony* 1:232 (Exod. 13:21), in *Calvin's Commetaries* vol. 2 (Grand Rapids, MI: Baker, 1979) [*CO* 24:145]. Cf. Anthony G. Baxter, *John Calvin's Use and Hermeneutics of the Old Testament*, 361.

[28] Commentary on Matthew 17:3 [*CO* 45:486].

[29] Commentary on Romans 10:4. *Imo quidquid doceat lex, quidquid praecipiat, quidquid promittat, semper Christum habet pro scopo: ergo in ipsum dirigendae sunt omnes partes* [*CO* 49:196]. Calvin can go on to say: "... the law in all its parts has reference to Christ, and therefore no one will be able to understand it correctly who does not constantly strive to attain this mark." *Habemus autem insignem locum, quod lex omnibus suis partibus in Christum respiciat: itaque rectam eius intelligentiam habere nemo poterit, qui non ad hunc scopum perpetuo collimet.*

[30] [*CO* 47:125]. Cf [*CO* 45:817; 50:45]. Cf. W. Niesel, *The Theology of Calvin* (Philadelphia: Westminster Press, 1956), 27, 107-108.

[31] Cf. comment on Exodus 34:29, in which Calvin refers to Christ as "the soul of the Law." *Commentaries on the Four Last Books of Moses arranged in the form of a Harmony*, 3:394 (Exod. 34:29), in *Calvin's Commentaries* vol. III (Grand Rapids, MI: Baker Book House, 1979). *Donec ad Christum (qui legis est anima) Moses ab ipsis conversus fuerit* [*CO* 25:118].

[32] David C. Puckett, *John Calvin's Exegesis of the Old Testament* (Louisville, Kentucky: Westminster John Knox Press, 1995), 106-113. On Calvin's rejection of allegorical exegesis, see, Anthony G. Baxter, *op. cit.*, 144-169.

[33] 156 (Job 40:20-41:25), 733.a.7 ...*bien prendre ceste similitute des balaines, et des elephants, pour nous faire sentir combien la vertu du diable nous doit effrayer, veu qu'il est appellé le prince de l'air et du monde* [*CO* 35:465].

[34] 156 (Job 40:20-41:25), 733.a.34. ...*et les allegories ne doivent estre tirees sinon du sens naturel: comme nous voyons que sainct Paul en fait en l'Espistre aux Galatiens et en d'autres passages* [*CO* 35:466]. Calvin was not opposed to allegory if such could genuinely be proved to be the intention of the writer. An example can be seen in Calvin's commentary on Daniel 4:10-16, "the whole discourse being metaphorical." Allegory is for Calvin, in the nature of things, a form of God's accommodation of truth for the infancy of the church [*CO* 40:657]. Cf. Puckett, *op. cit.*, 110-113. See also Paul K. Jewett, "Concerning the Allegorical Interpretation of Scripture," *The Westminster Theological Journal* 17 (1954): 1-20; Patrick Fairbairn, *The Typology of Scripture* (Grand Rapids, Michigan: Zondervan Publishing House, 1965);

*The Interpretation of Prophecy* (London: Banner of Truth Trust, 1964).

[35] 156 (Job 40:20-41:25), 733.b.29. *Si nous avons retenu ceste simplicité-là, elle nous vaudra mieux que toutes les expositions subtiles qu'on pourra amener: comme quand ceux qui ont ici basti des allegories, ont espluché les os et les arestes des balaines, et ont aussi traitté de la peau, de cecy et de cela: bref, il n'y a rien où il n'y ait fallu trouver ie ne say quels menus fatras. Or c'est comme faire de l'Escriture saincte un nez de cire, la transfigurant hors de son sens naturel* [*CO* 35:467].

[36] On the relationship between typology and accommodation in Calvin, see Anthony G. Baxter, *op. cit.*, 243. On the use of "accommodation" in Calvin, see David F. Wright, "Calvin's Accommodating God," in *Calvinus Sincerioris Religionis Vindex*, Sixth International Congress on Calvin Research, 1994, ed. W. H. Neuser and B. G. Armstrong (Kirksville, MO: Sixteenth Century Journal Publications, 1997), 3-19; Ford Lewis Battles, "God Was Accommodating Himself to Human Capacity," *Interpretation* 31 (1977): 19-38; reprinted in *Readings in Calvin's Theology*, ed. Donald K. McKim (Grand Rapids, Michigan: Baker Books, 1984), 21-42; reprinted in *Interpreting John Calvin: Ford Lewis Battles*, ed. Robert Benedetto (Grand Rapids, Michigan: Baker Book House, 1996), 117-138; and also in *Articles on Calvin and Calvinism*, ed. Richard Gamble (New York, London: Garland, 1992), 6:13-32; and more recently, Randall C. Zachman, "Calvin as Analogical Theologian," *Scottish Journal of Theology* 51 (1998): 162-187. According to Zachman, the language and concept of accommodation necessarily takes place in Calvin's theology because "language is the image of the mind (*Lingua est character mentis*)." Commentary on Jer. 5:15, *Calvin's Commentaries*, vol. IX, 286 [*CO* 37:626].

[37] "*non aliunde quidem nobis quam ex eius ore petenda est certitude.... Fateor quidem in Davidis persona fuisse adumbratam effigiem regni Christi*" [*CO* 32:159].

[38] See Thomas M. Davis, "The Traditions of Puritan Typology," in *Typology and Early American Literature*, ed. Sacvan Berkovich (Amherst, Mass.: University of Massachusetts Press, 1972), 38. Cf. Jackson Forstman's comment: "Although he had a weakness for typology, he disclaimed allegory and was constantly seeking out the natural meaning of the text on the basis of the original sources." *Word and Spirit: Calvin's Doctrine of Biblical Authority* (Stanford, Calif.: Stanford University Press, 1962), 106. Cf. David Puckett's conclusion: "It should not be surprising that one who stresses the unity of scripture as strongly [as, *sic*] Calvin does would use typology extensively. *John Calvin's Exegesis of the Old Testament*, 114.

[39] 12 (Job 3:11-19), 52.a.62 [*CO* 33:153]. For similar parallels with David, see 9 (Job 2:7-10), 39.b.67 [*CO* 33:121]; 98 (Job 27:5-8), 463.b.19 [*CO* 34:468]; 159 (42:9-17), 749.b.40 [*CO* 35:510]. For an example of Calvin's typological understanding of David, see his commentary on Jeremiah 33:17, where he says: "what was David but a type of Christ [*Christi typus*] ...God then gave in David a living image of his only-begotten Son..." Comm. on Jer. 33:17 [*CO* 38:70].

[40] Cf. Calvin's appeal to Matthew 27:46, "Why hast thou forsaken me?" in Sermon 35: "We see this yet much better in the persone of our Lord Iesus Christ. He sayeth, Why hast thou forsake[n] me? And in deede he is there in extremitie, as the partie that beareth the burthen of al the sinnes of the world. Therefore it was requisite that for a while Iesus Christe should feele himselfe as it were forsaken of God his father. But yet neuerthelesse he had a co[m]fort to the co[n]trary as he shewed by saying, *My God my God.* So long as we ca[n] call vpon God, assuring our selues that he is our Sauiour, & that we may preace vnto him: so long doth faith beare sway, and thereby wee be perswaded that God hath not forsaken vs." 35 (Job 9:16-22), 161.b.56. *Nous voyons cela encore mieux en la personne de nostre Seigneur Iesus Christ. Il dit, Pourquoy m'as-tu laissé? Et de fait, il est là en extremité comme celuy qui porte le fardeau de tous les pechez du monde. Il faut donc, que Iesus Christ, pour peu de temps, se sente comme abandonné de Dieu son Pere. Or tant y a neantmoins qu'il a une consolation contraire, comme il le monstre en disant, Mon Dieu, mon Dieu. Cependant que nous pouvons invoquer Dieu, sachans qu'il est nostre Sauveur, et que nous avons accez à luy, la foy domine, et sommes lors persuadez que Dieu ne nous a point delaissez* [*CO* 33:434]. Cf. Gilbert Vincent in "Calvin, commentateur du Psaume XXII," *Bulletin du Centre Protestant d'Etudes et de Documentation* 293 (July-August 1984): 32-52.

[41] 3 (Job 1:2-5), 10.a.51. *les figures* [*CO* 33:45]; cf. 158 (Job 42:6-8), 745.b.14ff [*CO* 35:500]. For a similar use of the word "figure", see Sermon 2, in which Calvin, responding to the question of our acceptance by God, exhorts: "It beoueth vs to attayne to it by the meanes of our Lorde Iesus Christ, shrowding vs vnder the grace which he hath purchased vs by his death and Passion, as who is the full perfection and accomplishment of the things that haue bene giuen forth in old time in figures and shadowes. *Il nous y faut venir par le moyen de nostre Seigneur Iesus Christ, lui presentans la grace qu'il nous a acquise par sa mort et passion comme il est la perfection, et l'accomplissement, des choses, qui ont esté donnees anciennement en figure, et en ombrage.* 2 (Job 1:2-5), 10.a.12 [*CO* 33:46]. Calvin also sees the High Priest in the vision of Zechariah 3 as a "figure" of Christ. 4 (Job 1:6-8), 19.a.18. ...*comme figure de nostre Seigneur Iesus Christ* [*CO* 33:68].

[42] 3 (Job 1:2-5), 10.a.38. *Les Anciens ont eu certaines ceremonies, comme il a esté besoin devant la venue de nostre Seigneur Iesus Christ, qu'il y eust de telles aides pour la rudesse du temps. Auiourd'huy nous savons qu'il nous faut avoir nostre refuge au sang precieux du Fils de Dieu, qui a esté espandu pour nostre lavement. Il nous faut donc adresser au sang de nostre Seigneur Iesus Christ, si nous voulons estre receus comme nets devant Dieu.* [*CO* 33:45].

[43] 3 (Job 1:2-5), 10.b.35. *car là Dieu se revele privément à nous.*[*CO* 33:47].

[44] Referring to the sacrifices Job offered, Calvin comments: "And that was to betoken that if we wil obteine forgiuenesse of our sinnes, wee muste haue recourse to the Sacrifice that was offered vp once for al for our redemptio[n]."

For so long as Iesus Christ is not the meane betweene God and vs: we must co[n]tinue accursed, forlorn, & hopelesse." *Pour signifier que quand nous voudrons obtenir pardon de nos pechez, il faut avoir ceste adresse du sacrifice qui a esté une fois offert pour nostre redemption. Car cependant que Iesus Christ ne sera point au milieu de Dieu et de nous, il faut que nons demeurions maudits, perdus, et desesperez.* 158 (Job 42:6-8), 745.b.16. [*CO* 35:500].

⁴⁵ 1 (Job 1:1), 4.a.10 [*CO* 33:29].

⁴⁶ 1 (Job 1:1), 2.a.2 [*CO* 33:24].

⁴⁷ Calvin encourages "that we may suffer God to clenze vs from all our filthinesse and infection (according as he hath promised vs in the name of Iesus Christ,) vntill he haue pulled vs quite out of the soyle and vnclenesse of this world, to match vs with his Angels, and to make vs parttakers of that endlesse felicitie, for the which we must labour here continually." 1 (Job 1:1), 5.b.7. ...*mais que nous souffrions que Dieu nous purge de toutes nos ordures et infections, comme il nous l'a promis au nom de nostre Seigneur Iesus Christ, iusques à ce qu'il nous ait retirez des souillures et pollutions de ce monde, pour nous conioindre avec ses Anges, et nous faire participans de ceste felicité eternelle, à laquelle nous devons maintenant aspirer* [*CO* 33:33-34].

⁴⁸ 1 (Job 1:1), 3.b.61. ...*car ce ne seroit rien d'avoir une belle vie, qui pleust aux hommes, et qui fust en grand' estime, sinon que nous fussions renouvelez par la grace de Dieu* [*CO* 33:29].

⁴⁹ At 6.a.28 of Sermon 2 (Job 1:2-5), Calvin alludes to Matthew 13:22 in which Jesus calls riches "thornes." [*CO* 33:35]. Then he adds at b.24 a reference to Matthew 19:24, where Jesus suggests that it is easier for a camel to go through the eye of a needle than for a rich man to enter the kingdom of God [*CO* 33:36]. Finally, at 6.b.67, he mentions the case of Lazarus and the rich man in Luke 16:19 [*CO* 33:37]. Cf. Calvin's commendation of Job's generosity in Job 31:16, alluding to Jesus' praise of the widow's offering in Mark 12:41. 114 (Job 31:16-23), 538.a.13 [*CO* 34:669].

⁵⁰ 25 (Job 6:15-23), 113.b.3 [*CO* 33:308]; Golding edition has Matt 6:45, 48.

⁵¹ "Therefore let vs lerne too bee reproued, and too receyue correction whensoeuer it is brought vs: and generally let vs lerne too yeeld our selues too all things that wee knowe to bee good and of God." 26 (Job 6:24-30), 118.a.49. *Apprenons donc d'estre reprins, et de recevoir correction quand elle nous sera apportée: et en general apprenons de nous renger à tout ce que nous cognoistrons estre bon et de Dieu* [*CO* 33:320-321]. The English text has John 16:4-5, but the reference is to John 10. The point is repeated at 119.a.61 where the allusion to John 10 is again made [*CO* 33:323].

⁵² Thus, Sermon 30 cites the words of Jesus in Luke 23:30, 30 (Job 8:1-6), 140.b.8 [*CO* 33:378]; Sermon 32 cites John 15:1-2,5, 32 (Job 8:13-22), 147.b.5,22 [*CO* 33:396-397]; cf. 43 (Job 11:7-12), 200.b.42 [*CO* 33:533]; Sermon 36 alludes to Matthew 7:11, 36 (Job 9:23-28), 166.b.65 [*CO* 33:447]; Sermon 38 alludes to Luke 22:53, 38 (Job 10:1-6), 179.a.17 [*CO* 33:477]; Sermon 41 makes a refer-

ence to Jesus' condemnation of Judas, 41 (Job 10:18-22), 192.b.24 [*CO* 33:512]; Sermon 49 alludes to John 7:18 (twice), 49 (Job 13:1-10), 228.a.61 [*CO* 33:607] and 231.a.58 [*CO* 33:615]; Sermon 75 refers to Jesus' parable of the rich man in Luke 12:19ff., 353.b.14 [*CO* 34:172]; Sermon 83 refers to Jesus' words in Matthew 25:40 about giving to the poor, 83 (Job 22:1-8), 389.b.61 [*CO* 34:270]; Sermon 86 refers to Matthew 10:31, where Jesus says we are worth more than little sparrows, 86 (Job 22:18-22), 405.b.35 [*CO* 34:314]; Sermon 90 alludes to several of Jesus' words (Matthew 10:30; 13:52, and John 10:29), 90 (Job 23:13-17), 421.b.31 [*CO* 34:357]; 423.a.7 [*CO* 34:360]; 423.a.43 [*CO* 34:361]; Sermon 99 makes mention of Luke 11, where Jesus exhorts us to pray without ceasing, 99 (Job 27:8-12, 466.a.53 [*CO* 34:476]; Sermon 111 sees Calvin commenting on Job's words about having made a covenant with his eyes and cites Jesus' words from Matthew 5:28 to the effect that we must not think we have abstained from adultery by bodily abstention only, 111 (Job 31:1-4), 522.a.40 [*CO* 34:626]; Sermon 116 has a lengthy reference to Matthew 5:44 and the need to love our enemies, 116 (Job 31:29-32), 546.b.14 [*CO* 34:691]; b.3 [*CO* 34:692]; b.62 [*CO* 34:692], and the whole of 547 a.b.; 548.a; 549.a [*CO* 643-700]; and in Sermon 139, Calvin refers to the invitation "Come unto me..." of Matthew 11:28, referring to it not as Jesus' words, but God's, 139 (Job 36:1-7), 656.a.37 [*CO* 35:265].

[53] 107 (Job 29:18-25), 505.b.61. *...ne nous viendront-ils point là reprocher l'obeissance qu'ils ont rendue à Iob, qui estoit bien Prophete de Dieu, mais qui n'avoit point un tel tesmoignage de sa vocation, comme auiourd'hui Iesus Christ l'a donnee à ceux qui preschent son Evangile? Et pourtant notons bien ce passage: car comme il est dit que le moindre du royaume des cieux, c'est à dire, de ceux qui auiourd'huy preschent l'Evangile, est plus excellent en son ministere et que Iean Baptiste et que tous les Prophetes: aussi au contraire quand nous mesprisons la doctrine que Dieu nous envoye, veu qu'il commande qu'elle soit ainsi honoree, il est certain que nous serons coulpables au double* [*CO* 34:581-582]. Interestingly, Calvin concludes this sermon by charging ministers to deal gently with those who labour and are heavy laden (Matt 11:28) but roughly with those who "haue neede to be roughly handled." 506.b.25 [*CO* 24:584].

[54] 43 (Job 11:7-12), 201.b.52. *Et voila pourquoy sainct Paul voulant corriger ceste folle curiosité et temeraire qui est aux hommes, leur monstre (Eph. 3, 18) à quoy ils se doivent appliquer: c'est de bien cognoistre quel est l'amour de Dieu qu'il nous a monstré en nostre Seigneur Iesus Christ, qu'il ne nous faut point tout le temps de nostre vie autre chose, sinon de nous enquerir diligemment de ceste grace qui nous a esté manifestee en nostre Seigneur Iesus Christ, comme nous avons esté retirez de la tyrannie de Satan, et affranchis de la servitude du peché et de la mort: qu'au lieu que nous estions damnez pleinement de nature, et povres pecheurs detestables devant Dieu, nous sommes maintenant iustifiez devant lui, qu'il nous reçoit et lui sommes agreables: comme nous sommes gouvernez par son sainct Esprit, afin de batailler contre les cupiditez de nostre chair: comme nous sommes*

*A Christological Focus* 347

*preservez sous sa main et protection, combien que le diable machine de nous ruiner à chacune minute de temps, toutesfois que nous le pouvons repousser, d'autant que nous sommes en la bergerie et en la garde de ce bon Pasteur Iesus Christ, lequel a promis que de tout ce que le Pere lui a donné en main, il ne souffrira point que rien perisse* [*CO* 33:536-537]. Cf. his use of Colossians 3:1-5, see 54 (Job 14:5-12), 254.a.40 [*CO* 33:675]. Later in this same sermon, Calvin adds: "For he worketh wo[n]derosuly: insomuch that we through that power of his (saith he) whereby he made all things, are tra[n]sformed into the glory of our Lord Iesus Christ. And although our bodies be now weake, and subiect to so many necessities: yet shall they be taken into the heauenly glory." 54 (Job 14:5-12), 255.a.34. ...*car il besongne miraculeusement: voire, selon la puissance (dit-il) par laquelle il fait tout, nous sommes transfigurez en la gloire de nostre Seigneur Iesus Christ: et combien que nos corps soyent auiourd'hui debiles, subiets à tant de povretez, si est-ce qu'ils seront recueillis en la gloire celeste* [*CO* 33:678]; cf. "Let vs pray our Lorde to nurrish our roote beneath, that although we carie no outwarde shewe before men, yet we may not cease to haue our life hidden in Christe." 68 (Job 18:12-21), 320.a.44. The French is less clear than Golding's translation: *Que nostre Seigneur donc nourrisse tousiours nostre racine au dessous: et qu'encores que nous n'ayons point apparence devant les hommes, nous ne laissions point d'avoir nostre vie cachee en lui* [*CO* 34:83]; "Therefore let vs waite vpon that good God, and pray him to giue vs the grace to looke alwayes vnto him, till the time come that he discouer that which is now unknown." 70 (Job 19:13-16), 330.a.7. *Et ainsi attendons, et prions ce bon Dieu, qu'il nous face la grace de tousiours regarder à lui, iusques à ce que le temps soit venu qu'il revele ce qui est maintenant incognu* [*CO* 34:109]; "The life of Iesus Christ being in heaue[n] in that glorious bodie in the which he was raysed vp, is not made manifest vnto vs, for if we loke where Iesus Christ, or his kingdome is, we shall not perceyue by our naturall wit, what is become of him. Neuerthelesse seing our life is hidden in heaue[n] with Iesus Christ, we may be well assured of it." 86 (Job 22:18-22), 405.b.36. *La vie de Iesus Christ estat au ciel en ce corps glorieux auquel il est ressuscité, ne nous est pas manifestee: car si nous regardons, où est Iesus Christ? où est son royaume? Nous n'appercevrons point selon nostre sens naturel ce qui en est: mais tant y a quand nostre vie est cachee au ciel avec Iesus Christ, que nous en pouvons bien estre asseurez* [*CO* 34:314]; "Intend we then to be good schollers, and to profite in the doctrine of our Lorde Iesus Christ? Sith we see that we be plunged (ouer our heade and eares) in this worlde, and in these corruptible things: let vs labour too wade out, and let vs from day to day fight against our owne affections, that we may draw neere vnto God, and be made alone with our Lord Iesus Christ, according as Saint Paule sheweth vs in the thirde to the Collossians, that if wee minde to haue part in heauen, and to cleaue vnto Iesus Christ, who is gone vp aloft, and to bee made one with him: it behoueth vs to mortifie whatsoeuer is of the earth." 144 (Job 37:1-6), 679.b.10. *Ainsi donc voulons-*

*nous estre bons escoliers pour profiter en la doctrine de nostre Seigneur Iesus Christ? Que voyans que nous sommes comme plongez au monde, et en ces choses corruptibles, nous mettions peine de nous en retirer: et que de iour en iour nous combations contre nos affections pour approcher de Dieu, et estre unis à nostre Seigneur Iesus: comme sainct Paul le nous monstre au troisieme des Colossiens, qu'il faut que nous mortifions ce qui est de la terre, si nous voulons avoir part au ciel, et si nous voulons adherer à Iesus Christ qui est monté la haut, afin de nous unir à soy* [CO 35:326]; cf. 32 (Job 8:13-22), 149.b.27 [CO 33:402]. Cf. Calvin's reference to Philippians 3:20 in Sermon 73: "the heritage is prepared for vs there already, that we be already set in the heauenly places, namely in the persone of our head Iesus Christ, who hath knit and vnited vs to himself neuer to be separated." 73 (Job 20:1-7), 345.a.56 [CO 34:151]. For a similar comment on Ephesians 3:18, see Calvin's sermon on Job 28:10-24, where he adds: "True it is that many lighthedded persons ca[n] speake ynough of the grace of our Lord Iesus Christ, and of the rightuousnesse that is giuen vs in him, and can babble well of fayth: but yet they neuer tasted what it is to haue the grace of God, except they were rauished to come vnto him, and that in so doing they haue the sayde feare that is spoken of here." 103 (Job 28:10-24), 487.b.19. *Il est vray que beaucoup de gens volages parleront assez de la grace de nostre Seigneur Iesus Christ, et de la iustice qui nous est donnee en luy, ils pourront babiller de la foy: mais iamais n'ont gousté que c'est de l'avoir de Dieu, sinon qu'ils soyent ravis pour venir à luy, et qu'en y venant nous ayons ceste crainte de laquelle il est icy parlé* [CO 34:531-532]. Cf. similar allusions to Philippians 1:15-16 at 122 (Job 33:1-7), 576.a.5 [CO 35:46].

[55] These include Sermons 2, 6, 24, 27, 28, 32, 33, 42, 53, 54, 59, 64, 79, 81, 82, 90, 92, 94, 98, 106, 111, 113, 123, 134, 141, 158, and 159. In addition, Calvin makes a passing reference to "martyrs of Iesus Christ" at the close of Sermon 100 (Job 27:13-19), 473.a.16. *martyrs de Iesus Christ* [CO 34:494]. The death of such martyrs belong to those "iudgements as are hidden and incomprehensible as yet." *Iugemens cachez et incomprehensibles pour le iourd'hui.*

[56] 113 (Job 31:9-15), 534.b.33 [CO 34:660].

[57] 6 (Job 1:13-19), 28.b.9 [CO 33:92].

[58] 2 (Job 1:2-5), 10.a.9 [CO 33:46]. Cf. "seing he hath redeemed vs by the death and passion of his onely begotten Sonne, he hath well deserued too haue all souerainte ouer vs. And now that he hath purchased vs so dearly, we must no more be addicted to our ourselues, but be wholly dedicated to his seruice." 80 (Job 21:13-15), 377.a.26. *...d'autant qu'il nous a rachetez par la mort et passion de son Fils unique, qu'il merite bien d'avoir toute superiorité sur nous. Or nous ayant acquis si cherement, il ne faut pas que nous soyons plus addonnez à nous-mesmes, mais que nous soyons du tout dediez à son service* [CO 34:235]. Cf. Sermon 115, where Calvin, having cited Gregory, adds: "For wee say that our saluation is grounded vpon the free goodnesse of God, and vpon the death and passion of our Lorde Iesus

Christ, and that we be saued by faith only: and contrarywise the Pope will haue euerie man to be his owne sauiour." 115 (Job 31:24-28), 543.b.66. ...*car nous disons que nostre salut est fondé sur la bonté gratuite de Dieu, sur la mort et passion de nostre Seigneur Iesus Christ, que nous ne sommes point sauvez sinon par foy: et le Pape au contraire veut que chacun soit son sauveur* [*CO* 34:685].

[59] 24 (Job 6:8-14), 112.b.23. ...*iusques à ce qu'ils soyent recueillis en ce repos eternel, qui leur est appresté au ciel, comme il nous a esté acquis par nostre Seigneur Iesus Christ* [*CO* 33:306]. Cf. Sermon 64: "And in very deede we know hee hath giuen vs a good pane, and a good assurance of it in oure Lorde Iesus Christ, whome hee hath made oure iudge, too the intent wee might finde mercie in him, as in the partie that sheweth himselfe oure redeemer and aduocate." 64 (Job 16:18-22), 303.b.10. *Comme de fait nous cognoissons qu'il nous à donné de cela un bon gage, et une bonne asseurance en nostre Seigneur Iesus Christ, le constituant nostre Iuge, afin que nous trouvions merci envers lui, comme envers celui qui se monstre nostre Redempteur et Advocat* [*CO* 34:38].

[60] 59 (Job 15: 17-22), 279.a.32. *Voila donc le seul remede comme nous pourrons estre delivrez de cest affroi et estonnement dont les meschans sont esperdus: c'est assavoir, que nous demandions à Dieu qu'il nous face ouyr la voix de son Evangile, où il nous declare qu'il nous reçoit en son amour, qu'il nous est Pere, qu'au nom de nostre Seigneur Iesus il nous accepte comme iustes, que et en la vie et en la mort il nous tiendra tousiours en sa main. Quand donc ceste voix là sonnera à nos aureilles, qu'elle sera bien entendue de nous, nous ne serons point estonnez de ces effrois sourds et aveugles, comme sont les incredules: mais nous serons asseurez contre tous les espouvantemens qui nous pourront advenir. Pourtant quand nous aurons ainsi nostre recours à Dieu, qu'il nous fera la grace que par son sainct Esprit nous serons appuyez sur ses promesses, ne doutons point que de plus en plus il ne nous conferme en tous les biens qu'il nous aura eslargis, et qu'il ne nous fortifie par sa vertu, tellement que parmi tous les effrois de ce monde nous demeurerons tousiours fermes, iusques à ce qu'il nous ait recueillis en son repos eternel* [*CO* 33:742]. Cf. Sermon 61, where Calvin says that "it is not a common gift vnto all men to beleeue the Gospell." He adds: "We see the woord of God is preached, and should there be any gaynsaying if men were not wilfull and froward? Whereas God declareth himself to bee a father and a Sauyour, and aboue all thing whereas hee seeing vs full of sinnes giueth vs a warrant of our saluation in the persone of his Sonne, assuring vs that although we bee full of all iniquitie, yet notwithstanding our Lord Iesus Christe hath satisfied for vs, so that by the meanes of his death and passion we be set cleere and may appeere before Gods iudgementseate, and bee hiid there for righteouse and giltlesse: I pray you, if we were not vtterly brutish, which of vs would not giue eare too it with earnest desire?" 61 (Job 15:30-35), 285.b.29. *Nous voyons que la parole de Dieu se presche: or si les hommes n'estoyent bien corrompus et pervertis, y*

*auroit-il nulle contradiction? Quand Dieu se declare Pere et Sauveur, et sur tout que nous voyant pleins de pechez, il nous donne le gage de nostre salut en la personne de son Fils, qu'il nous declare, combien que nous soyons pleins de toute iniquité, neantmois que nostre Seigneur Iesus Christ a satisfait pour nous, tellement que nous sommes acquitez par le moyen de sa mort et passion, et que nous pouvons comparoistre devant le seige iudicial de Dieu, que là nous sommes tenus pour iustes et innocens: ie vous prie, si nous n'estions du tout abbrutis, qui est-ce qui ne l'escouteroit avec un desir ardent?* [CO 33:758-759]. For a similar reference to hope in death, see the conclusion of Sermon 98: "Seing then that wee knowe that God calleth vs to so happie a life, and giueth vs assurance of it in our Lorde Iesus Christe: wee neede not to shunne death, sith that thereby wee enter into the full possession of our saluation." 98 (Job 27:5-8), 463.a.40. *Quand donc nous cognoissons que Dieu nous appelle à une telle vie et si heureuse, et qu'il nous en donne le gage en nostre Seigneur Iesus Christ, il ne faut point que nous fuyons la mort, puis que par là nous entrons en possession parfaite de nostre salut.* [CO 34:468]. He adds a little later: "But for our parte, it behoueth vs to knowe, that God hath created vs after his owne image and likenesse, to the intent to gather vs vp to himselfe, and that we should be sure that he will do it, if wee referre ourselues wholly vnto him, following the example that our Lorde Iesus Christe sheweth vs." 463.b.3. *Or de nostre costé il faut que nous cognoissions que Dieu nous a creez à son image et semblance, afin qu'il nous recueille à soy: et que nous soyons certains qu'il le fera, quand nous-nous remettrons du tout à luy, suivant l'exemple que nous en monstre nostre Seigneur Iesus Christ* [CO 34:468]. Calvin concludes that in death we should repeat the prayer of David (a prayer that Jesus Christ also prayed), "Thou hast redeemed me, O Lord God of truth" from Psalm 31:6. 463.b.19 [CO 34:468-469]. Cf. Sermon 110: "For to what end came Iesus Christ into the world? Yea, why went he downe into hell, that is to say, why suffered he the anguishes that were due to all wretched sinners, but to deliuer vs from them? So then if men cannot now conceyue good hope to be co[m]forted in death: it is al one as if they would denie that our Lord Iesus Christ hath suffered it in his person. For whereas the Sonne of God abaced himself so farre, as to be subiect to our curse, and to feele Gods hand against him: that was to the end to deliuer vs from death, and to assure vs that the victorie which he hath purchased, is for vs...But we shal be rescued wel ynough, if we haue Iesus Christ for our redemer, who is ordeyned too be our pledge and warrant, & hath abolished the paynes of death, broke the ba[n]ds of Sathan, and burst open the brazen gates, to set vs free." 110 (Job 30:21-31), 518.b.62. *Car pourquoy est-ce que Iesus Christ est descendu en ce monde? pourquoy mesmes est'il descendu iusques aux enfers, c'est à dire, qu'il a souffert les angoisses qui estoyent deuës à tous povres pecheurs, sinon afin de nous en delivrer? Et ainsi donc ceux qui maintenant ne peuvent concevoir bonne esperance pour se resiouir en la mort, c'est comme s'ils vouloyent nier que nostre Seigneur l'ait souffert en sa personne. Car d'autant que le Fils de*

*Dieu s'est aneanti iusques là, qu'il a esté suiet à nostre malediction, et a senti la main de Dieu qui luy estoit contraire: ç'a esté afin de nous delivrer de la mort, et nous asseurer que la victoire qu'il a acquise, est pour nous...O nous serons secourus assez, quand nous aurons Iesus Christ pour nostre Redempteur, lequel s'est constitué plege et garant pour nous, qui a aneanti les douleurs de mort, qui a rompu les liens de Satan, qui a brisé les portes d'airain, afin de nous affranchir* [CO 34:616-617]. Cf. Sermon 156: "I pray you mark this general principle of our faith, to the end that the grace which is manifested to vs in our Lord Iesus Christ, may be knowne, & we haue our recourse thervnto, not looking eyther for the beginning or the full perfecting of our saluation elswhere, than in Gods voutsafing to work the same freely: that is to say, without any bynding of him too it on our side, or without bringing any thing of our owne in that behalfe. And that is the cause why he expresly addeth, *who wil preuent mee, and I will satisfie him*? As if he should say, that if wee will pleade against him, he must needes be in our det, and bee bound vnto vs, and we must haue some ryght and interest." 156 (Job 40:20-41:25), 734.b.27. *Voila, di-ie, le principe general de nostre foy, afin que ceste grace qui nous est manifestee en nostre Seigneur Iesus Christ soit cognue, et que nous y ayons nostre refuge, et que nous n'attendions ni commencement ni perfection de nostre salut, sinon en ce qu'il plaist à Dieu, de besongner gratuitement: c'est à dire sans que nous l'y obligions de nostre costé, ou que nous luy apportions rien qui soit du nostre.*

Et voila pouquoy il adiouste notamment, Qui est-ce qui me previendra, et ie luy satisferay? Comme s'il disoit, que si nous voulons plaider contre luy, il faut qu'il nous doive, qu'il soit obligé envers nous, que nous ayons quelque droit et quelque titre [CO 35:470].

[61] 27 (Job 7:1-6), 127.a.34*Il faut donc que nous le prions, qu'il nous retienne en bride, si nous voulons que nos esprits demeurent coys et paisibles au milieu des troubles qui nous pourront advenir. Et cela aussi ne se peut faire, que nous n'ayons Iesus Christ qui nous soit prochain, afin qu'en luy nous puissions avoir quelque soulagement, comme il dit, Venez à moy vous tous qui estes chargez, et qui travaillez, et ie vous soulageray, et vous trouverez repos à vos ames* [CO 33:344].

[62] 28 (Job 7:7-15), 129.a.2. *Que est-ce donques des hommes? un vent, une fumée: mais d'autant que Dieu nous a inspiré une vertu permanente, voila pourquoy nous sommes immortels.*

*Au reste il faut que Dieu conferme en nous ce qu'il y a mis une fois: car s'il ne le maintenoit par sa grace, tout s'en ioit decliner. Et mesmes il nous faut venir au degré souverain, c'est assavoir à ceste resurrection qui nous est promise. Et où est-ce que nous la trouverons? Ce ne sera pas en nostre nature: mais il nous faut monter par dessus le monde, et faut que nous sachions qu'il n'y a que Iesus Christ seul, qui en soit le vray miroir.* [CO 33:349]. Cf. Sermon 32: "Now then, what is our true resurrection and renewment? Euen that God shoulde reserue vs and set vs in hys kingdome: that when hee hath made vs to wayfare through thys worlde, and to passe through fire and water and all other afflictions: we maye in the ende be exempted from all the miseries of thys world, and be made partakers of hys lyfe and glorie. And let vs beare in mynde howe sainte Paule sayth vnto vs, that our life is hydden in Iesus Christe, and that wee shall not see the true and perfect manifestation of it, vntill our Lord Iesus come from heaven. To be short, let vs marke one other similitude which we ought to bee well acquainted with. Truly in winter time the trees seeme to be dead, we see how the raine doth as it were rotte them, they are so swolne that they bee readie to burst, and thus ye see well one kynde of rottennesse: afterwarde commeth the frost, as it were to feare them, and to drie them vp. We see all these thynges, and wee see not so muche as one floure: and thys is a cutting vs off. Beholde heere a kynde of death, whiche lasteth not for a daye or twayne, but for foure or fiue monethes. Neuerthelesse although the life of the trees be vnseene: yet is their sap in their roote, and in the hart of the wood. Euen so is it with vs, that our life is also hidden, howbeit not in our selues. For that were a poore kind of hiding. There should neede no great frost to sterue it vp, nor greate wet to marre it. For we carrie fire and frost ynough in our selues to consume it. But our life is hidden in God, he is the keeper of it and wee knowe that Iesus Christ is the partie from out of whome we drawe all our life. So then let vs content our selues with the saide heddinesse." 32 (Job 8:13-22), 149.b.21. *Quelle est donc nostre vraye resurrection et renouvellement? assavoir, que Dieu nous reserve et mette en son royaume: quand il nous aura pourmenez par ce monde, qu'il nous aura fait passer par eau et par feu, et par toutes afflictions, qu'en la fin nous soyons exemptez de toutes miseres de ce monde, et qu'il nous face participans de sa vie, et de sa gloire. Et ainsi retenons ce que nous dit sainct Paul (Colos. 3,3), Que nostre vie est cachée en Iesus Christ, et que nous n'en verrons point la vraye manifestation et parfaite, iusques à ce que nostre Seigneur Iesus viene du ciel. Bref, regardons à une autre similitude qui nous doit estre assez familiere. Il est vray qu'en l'hyver il semblera que les arbres soyent morts, nous verrons la pluye qui sera là comme pour les pourrir, ils en seront tant pleins qu'ils en crevent: et bien voila une pourriture. Apres, la gelée viendra, comme pour les brusler et desseicher. Nous verrons toutes ces choses, nous ne verrons point une seule fleur: cela est retranché. Voila donc une espece de mort, qui dure non point pour un iour ne pour deux, mais quatre mois ou cinq. Or tant y a que la vie des arbres est chachée, la verdure est en la racine, et au coeur du bois. Ainsi donc en est-il que nostre vie est cachée, non point en nous: car ce seroit encores une povre cachette: il ne faudroit point grande gelée pour la brusler, ne grande pluye pour la corrompre: car mesmes nous portons le feu et la gelée en nous pour la consumer: mais nostre vie est cachée en Dieu, il en est le gardien. Et nous savons que Iesus Christ est celuy duquel nous tirons toute nostre vie. Ainsi donc contenons nous de ceste cachette-la* [CO 33:402].

[63] 32 (Job 8:13-22), 150.b.46. *Ainsi donc apprenons de ne point mettre nostre appui en ce monde, ni en tous les moyens inferieurs d'ici bas: mais*

*ayons nostre appuy en Dieu, voire, d'autant qu'il nous a donné nostre Seigneur Iesus Christ, afin qu'estans plantez en luy nous en tirions vertu et substance telle, que encores que nostre vie soit cachée, que nous soyons mesme comme en la mort: nous ne laissions pas de subsister, et d'estre maintenus en bon estat et ferme, voire attendans que ce bon Dieu nous ait delivrez de toutes les miseres de ce monde, et de toutes les tribulations qu'il nous y faut souffrir, iusques à ce qu'il nous appelle et introduise au royaume celeste, et en ceste gloire qu'il nous a acquise par le precieux sang de nostre Seigneur Iesus Christ* [CO 33:406].

[64] 123 (Job 33:8-14), 582.a.24 *Car combien que l'Evangile soit appellé une clarté de plein midi: toutes fois cela se rapporte à nostre mesure. Dieu nous esclaire là suffisamment, nous voyons sa face en nostre Seigneur Iesus Christ, et la contemplons pour estre transfigurez en icelle: mais quoi qu'il en soit, nous ne voyons pas auiourd'hui ce qui nous est appresté au dernier iour* [CO 35:63].

[65] 33 (Job 9:1-6), 155.b.20. *Et ainsi, sachons qu'il n'y a autre moyen pour obtenir grace devant Dieu, et faire que nos pechez soyent couverts, voire apres avoir confessé franchement qu'il n'y a que toute ordure et infection en nous, sinon que nous ayons nostre refuge à nostre Seigneur Iesus Christ. Car là se trouvera une pleine iustice et parfaicte, en vertu de laquelle nous serons agreables à Dieu, et le trouverons propice envers nous* [CO 33:418].

[66] 42 (Job 11:1-6), 199.a.11. ...*à une autre iustice qui n'est point aux hommes, et ne s'y en trouvera point une seule goutte. Il faut donc qu'ils ayent une autre iustice: c'est que Dieu nous ayant condamnez en nos personnes, nous prenne à merci au nom de nostre Seigneur Iesus Christ: que nous luy soyons agreables par ce moyen, et que nous luy soyons sanctifiez, d'autant que l'obeissance que Iesus Christ a rendue, nous est imputee* [CO 33:529].

[67] 82 (Job 21:22-34), 386.a.16. *Il est vray qu'en la mort tout est confus, mais Dieu saura bien tout ramener en ordre et en estat de perfection: comme il est dit, qu'à la venue de nostre Seigneur Iesus Christ, quand il apparoistra pour iuger le monde, ce sera la restauration de toutes choses. Si ainsi est donc que Iesus Christ viendra pour restaurer le monde, il faut que le monde soit auiourd'huy comme dissipé, que les choses y soyent en confus: mais cependant que nostre foy passe outre ces choses ici, et que nous attendions en patience que Dieu parface son oeuvre, et qu'il remedie à tout* [CO 34:259].

[68] 90 (Job 23:13-17), 423.b.60. *Voila donc comme il faut que nous glorifions Dieu en ce decret, quand il lui a pleu nous choisir et nous appeller à salut, et nous constituer heritiers de son royaume. Or ce decret ici nous a esté declaré en nostre Seigneur Iesus Christ: et si nous sommes membres de Iesus Christ: nous sommes asseurez de nostre adoption. Il ne faut point donc que nous allions visiter les registres de Dieu là haut au ciel: contentons-nous du tesmoignage qu'il nous en a rendu. Car si un homme qui pourra seulement avoir une copie authentique du registre, se contente de cela: et ne faut-il pas quand Dieu nous a declaré son conseil touchant nostre salut, ne faut-il pas (di-ie) que nous y acquiescions?* [CO 34:363].

[69] 90 (Job 23:13-17), 425.b.41. *Que nous venions donc tousiours à celui qui a fait les playes, sachans qu'il est le souverain medecin qui nous en garentira au nom de nostre Seigneur Iesus Christ* [CO 34:368].

[70] 106 (Job 29:13-17), 501.b.18. *...voicy Dieu qui nous declare...il nous couvrira luy-mesme quand nous serons revestus de iustice* [CO 34:569-570].

[71] 106 (Job 29:13-17), 501.b.33. *mais ceux qui ont à gouverner seulement leurs maisons* [CO 34:570].

[72] 106 (Job 29:13-17), 501.b.45. *Si donc nous sommes revestus de la iustice de nostre Seigneur Iesus Christ, et de la droiture et prudence qu'il nous distribuera par son sainct Esprit: voila comme nous serons deuëment ornez et parez pour comparoistre devant Dieu. Mais d'autant qu'en la vie presente il y aura tousiours de l'imperfection en nous, qu'il y aura tousiours à redire: il faut que nostre Seigneur Iesus par sa pure grace couvre toutes nos fautes, qu'elles nous soyent pardonnees en son nom, et qu'il supplee à nos deffauts: et que cependant il augmente tousiours de plus en plus les graces de son sainct Esprit en nous, et qu'il nous conduise par la vertu d'iceluy, iusques à ce qu'il nous ait despouillez de toutes les infirmitez et corruptions de nostre chair, et que nous soyons parvenus au but auquel nous tendons* [CO 34:570].

[73] 111 (Job 31:1-4), 525.b.23. *...et pourtant que nous prions ce bon Dieu, que quand il aura regardé en nous les fautes et les pechez que nous-mesmes ne pouvons pas voir, il lui plaise les effacer par sa misericorde: et que par ce moyen nous n'ayons autre asseurance de nostre salut, sinon d'autant qu'il nous reçoit à merci au nom de nostre Seigneur Iesus Christ, et que nous avons aussi ce lavement duquel nous sommes purgez, assavoir le sang qu'il a espandu pour nostre Redemption.* [CO 34:636]. Cf. Sermon 53, in which, following an extensive elaboration on the doctrine of original sin, Calvin ends by saying: "...we must resort to him for refuge, and that specially bycause hee hath giuen vs our Lord Iesus Christ, who hath all cleannesse in him. God seeing vs defiled and stayned, and that the way was ouerlong and high for vs to come to him: hath voutsafed to giue vs such a holiness in Iesus Christ: that if we can once wash our selues in his blood, we shall become pure and cleane from all our filthynesse." 53 (Job 14:1-4), 251.a.26. *...que nous ayons nostre refuge à lui: et sur tout d'autant qu'il nous a donné nostre Seigneur Iesus Christ, lequel a en soy toute pureté. Dieu voyant que nous estions ainsi pollus et infects, et que le chemin estoit trop long pour parvenir à lui là haut, nous a voulu donner en Iesus Christ une saincteté telle, que quand nous pourrons nous laver en son sang, nous serons purs et nets de toutes nos ordures* [CO 33:667]. Cf. the closing of Sermon 94: "As oft as men speake to vs of the meane of saluation, lette vs learne to consider where it is that we ought to repose all our trust: which is, that our God receiuing vs of his own meere goodnesse, do by his holy spirite purge and clenze vs from all our spots, and wash vs in the bloud of oure Lord Iesus Christ, the which he hath shed too clenze vs withall, thereby to make vs so pure and cleane as we may be able to stand before his face." 94 (Job

25:1-6), 444.b.6. *Apprenons toutes fois et quantes qu'on nous parle du moyen de nostre salut, de regarder où c'est que nous devons avoir toute nostre confiance, c'est assavoir, qu'estans receus de nostre Dieu par sa pure bonté, il nous purge et nettoye par son S. Esprit de toutes nos macules, et nous lave au sang de nostre Seigneur Iesus Christ, lequel il a espandu pour nostre purgation, et qu'il nous rende tellement purs et nets par ce moyen, que nous puissions consister devant sa face* [CO 34:418]. Cf. the use of 1 Corinthians 1:18 in Sermon 95, 95 (Job 26:1-7), 446.a.5 [CO 34:422].

[74] 141 (Job 36:15-19), 665.b.9. ...*que nous sommes destituez de tous moyens pour eschapper de la main de Dieu: mais qu'il faudroit que nous fussions consumez pleinement, n'estoit qu'il usast envers nous de pitié: nous cognoissions qu'il nous a donné un bon remede quand il luy a pleu d'exposer son Fils unique en sacrifice pour nous: qu'alors nous avons esté rachetez, que c'est un pris suffisant pour abolir toutes nos fautes, que le diable n'aura plus nul droit sur nous. Car quand nous serions accablez d'une multitude infinie de pechez: toutes fois si le sang de Iesus Christ respond, c'est pour satisfaire de toutes nos offenses, c'est pour appaiser l'ire de Dieu* [CO 35:289-290].

[75] Calvin's words in Sermon 3 are: "The men of old time had certayne Ceremonies, according as it was needfull that they should haue such healpes before the coming of our Lorde Iesu Christ, by reason of the rawenesse of the time. But now in these dayes we know, how we ought to haue recourse to the preciouse bloud of Gods sonne, which was shedde to wash vs withall. Therefore if we meane to be receyued for cleane before God: it behoueth vs to repayre to the bloud of our Lord Iesus Christ." 3 (Job 1:5), 10.a.36. *Les Anciens ont eu certaines ceremonies, comme il a esté besoin devant la venue de nostre Seigneur Iesus Christ, qu'il y eust de telles aides pour la rudesse du temps. Auiourd'huy nous savons qu'il nous faut avoir nostre refuge au sang precieux du Fils de Dieu, qui a esté espandu pour nostre lavement. Il nous faut donc adresser au sang de nostre Seigneur Iesus Christ, si nous voulons estre receus comme nets devant Dieu* [CO 33:45]. He adds a little later, "And this is to be done, not onely one day in a weeke, nor for some certayne time: but continually all our life long: and we must beare in minde how Sainct Paule sayeth, that our Lord Iesus Christ was sacrifyzed as the true Easterlambe, to the end that we should still be copartners of that sacrifyce, specially (as he sayeth) in all purenesse. He sayeth not that Christians ought to sanctifie themselues vnto God once a yeere: but that they ought to continew their holinesse all their lyfe through out. Wherefore? Bycause the sacrifise which Iesus Christ hath offered, and whereof we be made copartners, is euerlasting, and the verture thereof indureth for euer." 10.a.60. *Or nous n'avons point à faire cela seulement un iour la semaine, ni pour certain temps, mais il nous y faut continuer toute nostre vie: et nous doit souvenir de ce que dit S. Paul (1 Cor. 5,7,8), Que nostre Seigneur Iesus Christ a esté sacrifié comme le vray agneau Paschal, à fin que maintenant nous comuniquions à ce sacrifice, voire en toute pureté, dit-il. Il ne parle*

*point que les Chrestiens se doivent sanctifier à Dieu une fois en un an, mais qu'ils doivent continuer tout le temps de leur vie. Pourquoy? Car le sacrfice que Iesus Christ a offert, et duquel nous sommes faits participans, est perpetuel, et la vertu en demeure à iamais* [CO 33:46]. Calvin later concludes this section of the sermon with an appeal: "Behold wherin we differ from them which know not how there is not but one God whom we ought to worship, and vnto whom we must come by meanes of our Lord Iesus Christ, and that it behoueth vs to serue him according to his worde. When we know this: we may well say, that the sacrifizes which we offer vnto God are acceptable vnto him, and that he taketh them in good woorth... Nowe then let vs learne to serue God in spirit and truth, and faith wil be a good guide therevnto, when we haue our eyes fastened vpon Gods worde, which will leade vs always to our Lord Iesus Christ, who is the heaue[n]ly patterne & the mirrour wherin we must behold the will of God his father, to frame ourselues thereafter." 12.a.30,57. *Voila en quoi nous differons d'avec ceux qui ne cognoissent point qu'il y a un Dieu que nous devons adorer, et venir à lui par le moyen de nostre Seigneur Iesus Christ, et qu'il nous le faut servir selon sa parole. Quand nous aurons cognu cela, nous pourrons bien dire, que les sacrifices que nous offrirons sont agreables à Dieu, et qu'il les accepte...Ainsi donc apprenons de servir Dieu en esprit et en verité, et la foy sera une bonne guide à cela, quand nous aurons nos yeux fichez sur la parole de Dieu, laquelle nous conduira tousiours à nostre Seigneur Iesus Christ, qui est le patron celeste, et auquel il faut que nous contemplions quelle est la volonté de Dieu son pere, pour nous y ranger* [CO 33:50-51].

[76] 159 (Job 42:9-17), 747.a.4. ...*mais que Iesus Christ a cest office de nous donner accez et de nous faire ouvrir la porte...* [CO 35:503].

[77] 159 (Job 42:9-17), 748.a.13. ...*quand nostre advocat perpetuel qui est entré au Sanctuaire des cieux, assavoir Iesus Christ, iamais ne sera refusé, ni nous aussi quand nous viendrons à Dieu son Pere par ce moyen-la, tenans tousiours la voye...* [CO 35:506]. Calvin makes a similar point in Sermon 158, again dealing with the sacrifices Job offered for his sons, adding: "And therefore let vs marke: that we bee so much the lesse to be excused nowadayes; after that Christ hath suffered his death and passion, if we thinke to be quit before God by any other meane, than by the cleansing which Christ hath made...than for that he hath made satisfaction for vs, to discharge vs of the co[n]demnation of death wherin we were. Then if we seek to obtein mercy...wee must always beare in minde the death and passion of our Lord Iesus Christ, who is the sacrifice of our redemption and attonement" 158 (Job 42:6-8), 745.b.27. *Et ainsi notons que tant moins sommes nous auiourd'huy excusables, apres que Iesus Christ a souffert mort et passion, si nous cuidons estre absous devant Dieu par autre moyen, que par ceste purgation qui a esté faite, et d'autant qu'il a satisfait pour nous, afin de nous acquitter de la condamnation de mort en laquelle nous estions. Si donc nous cerchons d'obtenir misericorde...il faut que nous ayons tousiours en memoire la mort et passion de nostre Seigneur Iesus Christ,*

*qui est le sacrifice de nostre redemption et appointement* [*CO* 35:500].

[78] 159 (Job 42:9-17), 748.b.15. *...soyons certains qu'auiourd'huy Iesus Christ nous fera trouver Dieu propice et benin envers nous...*[*CO* 35:507]. Calvin precedes this section with a lengthy tirade against the "Papistes" who "wel ynough call him sonne of God, and Redeemer: but they acknowledge him not for their Aduocate: neither flee they to him for succor." 748.a.49. *Ils diront bien, Fils de Dieu et Redempteur: mais ils ne le cognoissent point pour leur Advocat, et n'y ont point leur refuge* [*CO* 35:506].

[79] 159 (Job 42:9-17), 749.b.13. *...entant que nostre Seigneur Iesus estant l'image vive de tous fideles et enfans de Dieu, ils sont conformez à lui...qu'en toutes nos miseres nous sommes configurez à nostre Seigneur Iesus Christ qui est le Fils aisné en la maison de Dieu* [*CO* 35:509-510].

[80] 159 (Job 42:9-17), 749.b.18. *Et defait si mesmes nous contemplons seulement la croix de Iesus Christ, elle est maudite par la bouche de Dieu: nous n'y verrons qu'opprobre, que frayeur: bref il semble que le gouffre d'enfer soit ouvert pour abysmer Iesus Christ. Mais quand nous conioindrons sa resurrection avec sa mort: voila pour nous resiouyr, voila pour adoucir toutes nos tristesses: afin que nous ne soyons point contristez outre mesure, quand il plaira à Dieu de nous affliger. Or cela notamment a esté accompli en nostre Seigneur Iesus, afin que nous sachions que ce n'est point seulement pour une personne que ceci est escrit: mais que nous cognoissions que le Fils de Dieu nous fera participans de sa vie, quand nous serons morts avec lui, et participans de sa gloire, quand nous porterons toutes les ignominies, et toutes les povretez qu'il plaira à Dieu nous mettre sur les espaules...* [*CO* 35:510]. Calvin then goes on to draw a parallel with David, whom he sees as a pattern, "but chiefliest in our Lord Iesus Christ, who is the true and chiefe patterne of all the faithful." 749.b.41 [*CO* 35:510].

[81] 65 (Job 17:1-5), 304.a.12. *Et au reste, n'avons–nous pas Iesus Christ pour conducteur? Allons à la mort, ne savons-nous pas que c'est une entree pour parvenir à la gloire des cieux? quand la resurrection a esté coniointe à la mort du Fils de Dieu, n'a-ce pas esté aussi bien afin que nous soyons certifiez que Dieu ne permettra point que nous demeurions en pourriture?* [*CO* 34:39]. Cf. *Institutes*. III.viii.1-11 [*CO* 2:515-523].

[82] 159 (Job 42:9-17), 750.b.16. *...voire d'autant que Iesus Christ nous est apparu, et nous a monstré que nous sommes estrangers en ce monde, pour courir à cest heritage qui nous a esté acquis par son sang* [*CO* 35:512].

[83] 159 (Job 42:9-17), 750.b.55. *Car puis que nostre Seigneur Iesus Christ est mort et ressuscité, il ne faut point que nous soyons long temps au monde pour cognoistre que Dieu nous est Pere, et que nous devons estre asseurez de nostre salut* [*CO* 35:514].

[84] 159 (Job 42:9-17), 750.b.62. *Voila donc comme nous serons tousiours rassasiez de vivre, quand en nostre Seigneur Iesus Christ Dieu nous a donné un si bon gage de son amour, qu'il ne faut point que nous demandions qu'il nous prolonge ici nostre vie pour en avoir plus ample confirmation* [*CO* 35:514].

[85] 79 (Job 21:7-12), 373.b.63. *Voila donc comme il nous faut appliquer toutes nos resiouissances à ce but, qu'il y ait une melodie qui resonne en nous, par laquelle le nom de Dieu soit benit et glorifié en nostre Seigneur Iesus Christ* [*CO* 34:228].

[86] "For not onely Iob was condemned in his sayings, but the Sonne of God also." 57 (Job 15:1-10), 266.a.6. *Car non seulement Iob a esté condamné en sa parole, mais le propre Fils de Dieu* [*CO* 33:707]. In the same sermon, Calvin takes Eliphaz to task again for suggesting that Job was too young to be wise. It is not age, but grace, that matters: "And so wee must go to God, and to our Lorde Iesus Christ, if wee will haue a sure resting stocke for our fayth to leane vnto." 57 (Job 15:1-10), 269.b.50. *Et ainsi il faut venir à Dieu, et à nostre Seigneur Iesus Christ, si nous voulons avoir un ferme appui de nostre foi* [*CO* 33:717].

[87] 15 (Job 4:7-11), 69.b.32. *Nous voyons comme il en est advenu à nostre Seigneur Iesus Christ, qui est le chef et le miroir, et le patron de tous les enfans de Dieu* [*CO* 33:196].

[88] 4 Job 1:6-8), 15.b.3. *Il est vraie que les hommes seront bien quelquefois intitulez Enfans de Dieu, à cause qu'il a imprimé son image en eux, sur tout les fideles, d'autant qu'ils sont reformez à la semblance de nostre Seigneur Iesus Christ, qui est l'image vive de Dieu son Pere, et qu'aussi ils ont receu l'Esprit d'adoption, qui leur est un gage, que Dieu leur porte un amour paternel* [*CO* 33:59]. A little later in this sermon, Calvin can say of Christ that he is God's "natural" Son: "For in asmuch as our Lord Iesus Christ, who is the onely Sonne of God his father, yea euen his naturall sonne, (for the belonging of this honour vnto him is not befalne vnto him through grace, but he is his naturall sonne, and for the same cause, his only sonne also)." 15.b.31. *Tout ainsi que le Seigneur Iesus, qui est Fils unique de Dieu son Pere, voire et naturel (car ce n'a point esté de grace qui luy soit survenue, que cest honneur luy appartient, mais il est Fils naturel, et pour ceste cause il est unique)* [*CO* 33:59]. Cf. Sermon 56: "But forasmuch as God of his owne infinite mercie hath renued vs, and adopted vs too bee his children in our Lorde Iesus Christ, and imprinted his Image againe in vs: therein wee bee his woorkemanship, and maye come with our heades vpright too call vpon him, and assure ourselues that he will not shake vs off, but that wee shall be welcome too him." 56 (Job 14:16-22), 261.a.46. *mais puis que Dieu par sa misericorde infinie nous a reformez, et nous a adoptez pour ses enfans en nostre Seigneur Iesus Christ, qu'il a imprimé son image en nous: voila comme nous sommes sa facture, afin que nous puissions venir la teste levee pour l'invoquer, que nous puissions estre asseurez qu'il ne nous reiettera point, mais que nous lui serons à gré* [*CO* 33:694]. Earlier on, Calvin stated: "True it is, that we are his woorkemanship alreadie, in that wee bee men: But there is yet more, that is to wit, he hath fashioned vs new again after his own Image, through the grace of our Lorde Iesus Christ." 261.a.25. *Or il est vrai, entant que nous sommes hommes, que desia nous sommes sa facture: mais il y a plus, c'est qu'il nous a reformez à son image par la grace de nostre*

*Seigneur Iesus Christ* [*CO* 33:693]. In Sermon 80, Calvin makes an allusion to the blotting out of the *imago Dei* as a consequence of the fall: "He hath created vs after his owne image and likenesse: & although this image be blotted out in vs by the sinne of Adam, and we bring nothing fro[m] our mothers wombe but the curse: yet had God created vs after his owne image. And this is one very great and excellent honor. And beside that, he hath vouchsafed to redeeme vs by the bloud of his onely begotten Sonne Iesus Christe, whom he woulde not spare." 80 (Job 21:13-15), 377.a.49. *Il nous a creez à son image et semblance: et encores que ceste image soit effacee en nous par le peché d'Adam, et que nous n'apportions rien que toute malediction du ventre de nos meres: si est-ce toutes fois que Dieu nous avoit creez à son image. Et voila desia un honneur trop grand et trop excellent. Et puis il nous a bien daigné racheter par le sang de Iesus Christ son Fils unique, il ne l'a point voulu espargner* [*CO* 34:236]. Cf. Sermon 148, where Calvin discusses the creation of angels, who are also called children of God. "Whyso? Bycause God created vs after his owne image and likenesse. And although this were defaced by the sin of Adam: yet was it repayred again in the chozen by the comming of our Lord Iesus Christ, who is the lyuely image of God, and we were so exalted by his spirit, as wee bee now set in our former state again, and Iesus Christ hath doone vs the honour to come of the line of Abraham, that is to say, to clothe himself with our nature, too the end to reconcyle vs to God his father." 148 (Job 38:4-11), 696.a.58. *Pourquoy? D'autant que Dieu nous a creez à son image et semblance: et combien que ceste image ait esté effacee par le peché d'Adam, si est-ce qu'elle a esté reparee aux eleus, quand nostre seigneur Iesus a esté envoyé, qui est l'image vive de Dieu, et avons esté exaltez par son Esprit, en telle sorte que nous voila restablis en nostre premier degré: et Iesus Christ nous a fait cest honneur de descendre de la race d'Abraham, c'est à dire de se vestir de nostre nature, afin de nous reconcilier à Dieu son Pere* [*CO* 35:371].

[89] 41 (Job 10:18-22), 194.a.2. *Pource qu'il falloit que Dieu luy fist sentir sa rigueur aspre et severe, et puis apres qu'il le consolast. Et c'est un passage que nous devons bien noter. Car si nous voulons bien recevoir la grace qui nous est donnee, et que Dieu nous offre tous les iours en nostre Seigneur Iesus Christ: il faut auparavant que nous ayons senti que c'est de nous et de nostre condition. Voulons nous (die-ie) bien gouster que c'est de la vie celeste? Il faut en premier lieu que nous cognoissions à quelle fin nous naissons, voire selon que nous sommes pecheurs en Adam.*[*CO* 33:516]. Cf. Sermon 105: "Seing then that when our Lorde sendeth vs his word, he will make such a triall, that all that euer lieth hid in men must come too lyght: let euery of vs walke as in the broade day, and consider that wee no more in darknesse, seing our Lord Iesus Christ reigneth among vs by his Gospell." 105 (Job 29:8-13), 494.a.39. *Puis qu'ainsi est donc que nostre Seigneur quand il nous envoye sa parole veut faire un tel examen, que tout ce qui est caché aux hommes vienne en clarté: qu'un chacun de nous chemine comme en plein midi, et que nous cognoissions que nous ne sommes plus en tenebres,*

*quand nostre Seigneur Iesus domine par son Evangile au milieu de nous* [*CO* 34:549]. Cf. Sermon 124, where Calvin makes the point (citing Psalm 62:12) that we know God's judgements only in part. This teaches us two things. One is that God makes us feel his mighty power so as to teach us to fear him. It is in order that we may learn that He is our master and that we should serve him. The second is that "we know him to be our father & Sauior, to the end to put our whole trust in him. And how shall wee know him? By grounding our selues vpon his mere mercie, knowing that there is nothing but death and damnation in vs, and acknowledging that he hath drawne vs out of death through his owne mere goodnesse, for our Lord Iesus Christes sake." 124 (Job 33:14-17), 583.b.67. ...*nous le cognoissions estre nostre pere et nostre Sauveur, afin de mettre nostre confiance pleinement en luy. Et comment le cognoistrons-nous? Nous fondans sur sa pure misericorde, cognoissans qu'il n'y a que peché en nous et perdition, cognoissans qu'il nous a retirez de la mort par sa pure bonté, au nom de nostre Seigneur Iesus Christ* [*CO* 35:68-69].

[90] 43 (Job 11:7-12), 201.a.47. *Mias tant y a qu'ils ne peuvent point voir les registres du ciel pour savoir s'ils sont là escrits: ce leur est assez que Dieu leur a donné une bonne copie de leur election, et faut qu'ils la contemplent en nostre Seigneur Iesus Christ, qu'estans ses membres, ils ne doutent pas que Dieu ne les advoüe pour ses enfans* [*CO* 33:535].

[91] 157 (Job 42:1-5), 738.a.24. *Voila, di-ie, où il nous falloit mediter la puissance de Dieu: comme il nous est monstré quand il est dit, que nul ne nous ravira de la main de Iesus Christ, lequel nous a prins en sa garde. Et pourquoy? Car le Pere qui nous a commis à luy est plus fort que tous. Pourquoy est-ce et à quel propos que Iesus Christ nous propose la puissance invincible de Dieu son Pere? C'est afin que nous soyons paisibles, ne doutans point qu'il nous sauvera...* [*CO* 35:479-480].

[92] 89 (Job 23:8-12), 416.b.65, *Iob donc en cela faut...* [*CO* 34:343]; 417.a.16, 38. *Iob donc s'abuse en disant... Et ainsi donc nous voyons comme Iob a failli en disant, Que l'homme iuste et droit pourroit plaider sa cause devant Dieu* [*CO* 34:344-345].

[93] 89 (Job 23:8-12), 417.a.31. *Il faut que nous ayons Iesus Christ pour nostre advocat: et lui, en plaidant nostre cause, n'allegue pas nos merites, il ne s'oppose pas pour dire, que Dieu nous fait tort quand il nous punira: mais il met en avant la satisfaction qu'il a faite, et que puis qu'il nous a acquitez de nos dettes, maintenant nous sommes absous devant Dieu* [*CO* 34:344-345].

[94] 89 (Job 23:8-12), 417.b.19. *Voila en quelle sorte il nous faut venir à Dieu: c'est que nous ne pretendions point d'estre iustes, ne lui pouvoir satisfaire: mais que cognoissans les pechez que nous avons commis, nous demandions qu'il nous reçoive par sa pure bonté et misericorde, et que nous n'ayons point la bouche ouverte pour plaider nostre cause: car ceste dispute-la ne nous appartient point, l'office en est donné à nostre Seigneur Iesus Christ. Que nous ayons donc la bouche close de nostre costé, et que Iesus Christ*

*A Christological Focus* 361

*soit nostre advocat, et intercede pour nous, afin que par ce moyen nos fautes soyent ensevelies, et que nous soyons absous au lieu d'estre condamnez* [*CO* 34:346].

[95] 44 (Job 11:13-20), 206.a.35. ...*nous tend la main: que son office est d'interceder pour nous: que Dieu nous a ouvert aussi la porte, et que tous les iours il ne demande sinon que nous venions à luy* [*CO* 33:547-548]. He goes on to add: "Let vs go to our God and seeke the meane to come to him: which is, that our Lord Iesus Christ make intercession for vs, & cause vs to finde fauour there. For in our owne persones God must needes hate vs, yea and of good right also holde vs accursed. But we please him and he is fauorable to vs in that we come to him in the name of our Lord Iesus." 207.b.58. *Allons donc à nostre Dieu, et cerchons le moyen d'y venir: c'est que nostre Seigneur Iesus Christ intercede pour nous, qu'il nous y face trouver grace, d'autant qu'il faut que nous soyons hays en nos personnes, et que Dieu à bon droit nous ait exercrables: mais nous luy plaisons, et aussi il nous est propice, d'autant que nous y venons au nom du Seigneur Iesus* [*CO* 33:552]. Calvin adds the insight that the Old Testament High Priest bore the names of tribes upon his shoulders and upon his breast, "but now behold, Iesus Christ hath rent asunder the veyle of the Temple, and opened the way in such wise as wee may shewe our selues before God to looke him in the face." 208.a.6. ...*mais maintenant voici Iesus Christ qui a rompu le voile du temple, il a dedié la voye, tellement que nous pouvons nous presenter à face levee devant Dieu* [*CO* 33:552].

[96] 83 (Job 22:1-8), 392.a.65. *Nostre Seigneur Iesus ne dit pas, Venez à moy vous tous qui direz, Ie suis pecheur, il y a des infirmitez en moy: nenni: mais, Vous tous qui estes chargez et qui travaillez, qui avez les espaules courbees sous la pesanteur de vos pechez. Voila ceux qui sont appellez de Iesus Christ, afin de trouver merci en lui, et en sa grace: et non pas ceux qui se mocquent ainsi de Dieu, faisans une confession à la volee sans estre touchez en leur coeur* [*CO* 34:277]. Calvin recognises that Eliphas "doth Iob great iniurie" but is keen for us to learn the general lesson that "the spirite of God intendeth heere to teach vs." 392.b.24.

[97] 84 (Job 22:9-11), 397.a.42. *Dieu nous est Pere en nostre Seigneur Iesus Christ* [*CO* 34:290].

[98] 103 (Job 28:10-24), 484.b.37. *Il ne veut point donc ici nous retirer de la foi et de ce qui en depend, c'est assavoir que nous cognoissions la bonté infinie de nostre Dieu pour estre appuyez sur icelle, que nous ne doutions point qu'il ne nous soit propice, d'autant qu'il nous pardonne nos pechez au nom de nostre Seigneur Iesus Christ: et puis qu'il nous a adoptez, qu'il nous aimera comme ses enfans pour procurer nostre salut iusques en la fin* [*CO* 34:524]. Calvin almost repeats himself entirely a little later in the same sermon, 485.a.6 [*CO* 34:524-525].

[99] 120 (Job 32:4-10), 566.b.69. *Maintenant si nous venons à la doctrine de l'Evangile, voila une sagesse qui surmonte tout sens humain, mesmes qui est admirable aux Anges: voila les secrets du ciel qui sont contenus en*

*l'Evangile: car il est question de cognoistre Dieu en la personne de son Fils: et combien que nostre Seigneur Iesus soit descendu ici bas, si est-ce qu'il nous faut comprendre sa maiesté divine, ou nous ne pouvons pas nous fonder, et reposer nostre foy en luy. Il est question, di-ie, que nous cognoissions ce qui est incomprehensible à la nature humaine* [*CO* 35:23].

[100] 4 (Job 1:6-8), 19.a.17. ...*comme chef de l'Eglise, comme figure de nostre Seigneur Iesus Christ...* [*CO* 33:68]. For Calvin's christological interpretation of Sun of righteousness in Malachi 4:2 (3:20 in Calvin's edition), see 149 (Job 38:12-17), 700.a.26 [*CO* 35:381]. Calvin engages in an interesting denial in this sermon that the sun is the cause of many diseases. Cf. his comments on Malachi 4:2 in Sermon 33, 33 (Job 9:1-6), 154.a.28 [*CO* 33:413].

[101] 112 (Job 31:5-8), 528.b.32. *Nous avons desia dit que nous sommes ainsi tentez par nos yeux de suivre des mauvais appetis au coeur, quand le mal y est desia conceu là dedans. Voila donc le peché qui precede: et ainsi il faut conclure qui si le coeur n'estoit infecté de corruption, nos yeux seroyent purs. Il est vray: mais cependant ce n'est pas à dire, que nous ne soyons tentez quelquefois sans qu'il y ait affection interieure: comme Iesus Christ mesmes a bien esté tenté, toutes fois il n'y a point eu de pollution en luy: mais il a esté tenté selon qu'une nature entiere le peut estre: il a eu des obiets, mais sa volonté l'a retenu en bien: car en tous ses sens aussi il n'y avoit rien de corrompu. C'est autre chose de nous: car tous nos sens sont corropmus à cause du peché* [*CO* 34:644]. This particular quotation is of importance given the fact that both Karl Barth and T. F. Torrance, for example, have insisted that in his incarnation Jesus assumed a fallen human nature, Torrance insisting that this was Calvin's position. For Barth, see *Church Dogmatics* I/2, 152-155, where he cites approvingly the views of Edward Irving, J. C. K. v. Hofmann of Erlangen, H. F. Kohlbrügge, Edward Bohl, and H. Bezzel. For Torrance, see *The Mediation of Christ* (Grand Rapids, MI: William B. Eerdmans, 1983), 48-50; *The Trinitarian Faith* (Edinburgh: T. & T. Clark, 1988), 157, 161, where he is alluding to Athanasius, and 165, where Torrance comments on the *non-assumptus* rubric of Cyril of Alexandria, "*what has not been taken up, has not been saved*" (ὃ γὰρ μὴ προσείληπται οὐδὲ σέσωσται); *The Christian Frame of Mind* (Edinburgh: The Handsel Press, 1985), 9-10, in which Torrance is critical of the Western church's response to the view that in the incarnation the Son of God took our depraved human nature upon himself; *Theology in Reconciliation: Essays towards Evangelical and Catholic Unity in East and West* (London: Geoffrey Chapman, 1975), 156-185; *Space, Time and Resurrection* (Edinburgh: The Handsel Press, 1976), 30-31, 46-47, 56-57, 75, 88, 91, 96-98, 116; *Scottish Theology: From John Knox to John McLeod Campbell* (Edinburgh: T. & T. Clark, 1996), 301. For a fuller refutation of this from an overall assessment of Torrance's theology, see W. D. Rankin, "Carnal Union with Christ in the Theology of T. F. Torrance" (Ph.D. diss., University of Edinburgh, 1997), 101-117. Rankin cites several other sources, including the unpublished Auburn Seminary Lectures, "The Doctrine of Jesus Christ," in which Torrance

repeats this view extensively. See also H. R. Mackintosh's *The Doctrine of the Person of Jesus Christ* (Edinburgh: T. & T. Clark, 1913), 276-288.

[102] 4 (Job 1:6-8), 15.b.51. *Quand nous voyons que le Fils de Dieu s'est ainsi approché de nous, qu'il a voulu avoir une nature commune avec les hommes, cognoissons que c'est de là que procede ceste autre grace, que les Anges s'employment pour nous, et veillent, et c'est aussi leur propre charge et vocation que de procurer nostre salut* [CO 33:60]. For a similar reference to angels and Christ, see 94 (Job 25:1-6), 441.b.64 [CO 34:411].

[103] 8 (Job 2:1-6), 36.a.18. *Car nous aurons assez de force, et nous serons asseurez de la victoire, quand mous serons appuyez en Dieu, et en la grace de nostre Seigneur Iesus Christ, de laquelle il est parlé en sainct Iean au dixieme chapitre (v.29): Le Pere (dit-il) qui vous a mis en ma main, est plus fort que tous: ne craignons point que Satan surmonte son createur. Dieu nous a rendus entre les mains de nostre Seigneur Iesus Christ, afin qu'il soit bon gardien, et fidele et de nos ames, et de nos corps* [CO 33:111]. For a similar reference, see Sermon 15, 15 (Job 4:7-11), 66.b.50 [CO 33:189]. Cf. Sermon 41: "The miseries that are in our nature, are as it were a maze: and yet for all that, if wee holde our selues by our Lorde Iesus Christ, who is the bande betweene God and vs, and looke vpon him as the partie that knitteth vs too God his father: There shall be nothing to hinder vs that we shoulde not bee alwayes merie. Lo what we haue to desire at Gods hande, when wee knowe in what plight wee bee... " 41 (Job 10:18-22), 193.b.9. *C'est comme un labyrinthe des calamitez qui sont en nostre nature: mais tant y a que si nous avons nostre Seigneur Iesus Christ, qui soit le lien entre Dieu et nous, que nous le regardions comme celuy qui nous conioint à Dieu son Pere, il n'y aura rien qui nous empesche que tousiours nous n'ayons dequoy nous resiouir. Voila la requeste que nous avons à faire à Dieu, quand nous aurons cognu que c'est de nous* [CO 33:515]. A little later, he adds: "what remedie is there? The remedie is too turne our eyes too our Lorde Iesus Christ... And howe shoulde he shewe himselfe a sheepeherde, but in the person of our Lorde Iesus Christ?... seeing we haue the Sonne of God, although oure state seeme neuer so wretched, insomuch that wee bee but as poore woormes subiect too corruption and rottenesse: yet come wee too the tasting of the benefite whiche God gaue vs..." (194.a.40). *Et le remede quel sera-il? C'est quand nous tournerons les yeux à nostre Seigneur Iesus Christ...Et comment se monstrera-il, sinon en la face de nostre Seigneur Iesus Christ?...Mais quand nous avons le Fils de Dieu, encores que nostre estat semble estre bien miserable, que nous soyons comme des povres vermines subiettes à corruption et pourriture: si est-ce que nous venons à gouster le bien que Dieu nous a fait ...* [CO 33:517].

[104] 8 (Job 2:1-6), 37.a.53. *...il faut que nous soyons sanctifiez et de corps et d'esprit, que nous soyons adonnez à Dieu, dediez à son service: ce qui ne se peut faire, que nous ne nous retirions des pollutions qui nous pourroyent corrompre.* [CO 33:114-115]. Calvin makes a similar reference to baptism into Christ in Sermon 11: "Forasmuch as we be baptized in the name of oure Lorde

Iesus Christ, and that besides oure creation, God hathe also moreouer printed his marke vpon vs for an aduantage, too the intent wee shoulde bee his deere frendes, and bee receyued into his Churche: therein wee haue cause too blesse God double." 11 (Job 3:1-10), 49.b.11. ...*d'autant que nous avons esté baptisez au nom de nostre Seigneur Iesus Christ, et que Dieu, outre la creation, nous a adiousté cest avantage-la, qu'il a imprimé sa marque en nous, afin que nous fussions comme de ses alliez, il nous a receus de son Eglise, en cela nous avons à benir Dieu doublement.* [*CO* 33:146]. In a similar way, Calvin can speak of Christ as the "generall patrone of all the faythfull" who are "graffed... into the body of his sonne." 9 (Job 2:7-10), 39.b.67. *Dieu nous a entez au corps de son Fils, ainsi qu'il est le patron general de tous fideles...* [*CO* 33:121].

[105] 16 (Job 4:12-19), 72.b.24. ...*tant par ses Prophetes, comme par nostre Seigneur Iesus Christ son Fils...* [*CO* 33:203].

[106] 16 (Job 4:12-19), 74.b.3. *Il est vray que Iesus Christ n'a point esté Redempteur des Anges: car ils n'ont point besoin d'estre rachetez de la mort, en laquelle ils ne sont iamais tombez: mais il a bien esté leur Mediateur. Et comment? afin qu'il les conioigne à Dieu en toute perfection: et puis il faut qu'il les maintiene par sa grace, et qu'ils soyent preservez afin de ne point tomber...mais les Anges qui sont maintenant plus prochains de luy, et qui contemplent sa face n'ont point encores une telle perfection qu'il n'y trouvast à redire s'il les vouloit examiner à la rigueur* [*CO* 33:208].

[107] 33 (Job 9:1-6), 152.b.13. [*CO* 33:149].

[108] 40 (Job 10:16-17), 187.b.10. *Quand nous disons que les hommes sont iustifiez par foy: c'est d'autant que Dieu leur pardonne leurs fautes, et qu'il les quitte au nom de nostre Seigneur Iesus Christ* [*CO* 33:499].

[109] 28 (Job 7:7-15), 131.b.16. ...*nous ne laissions pas de subsister en endurant...* [*CO* 33:355].

[110] 28 (Job 7:7-15), 132.b.6. *Mais apprenons de nous munir de ce qui nous est remonstré en l'Escriture saincte, que nous aurons assez ample matiere de ioye quand nous croistrons et profiterons en Iesus Christ, tant à la mort qu'en la vie. Sommes-nous donc conioints à Iesus Christ? combien que nostre vie soit plus que miserable, si est-ce qu'elle nous tournera à profit: tellement que si nous avons des afflictions en ce monde, ce nous seront autant d'aides pour nostre salut. Quand donc il semblera que nous soyons du tout perdus, ne laissons pas pourtant d'invoquer nostre Dieu, esperans que non seulement il convertira toutes nos afflictions en ioye, et ne gloire: mais qu'il continuera sa bonté sur nous iusques à ce qu'il nous la face sentir en toute perfection* [*CO* 33:358]. In the following sermon, Calvin expands on the Adam–Christ parallel, suggesting that that which was lost in Adam is restored in Christ: "And this thing is specially fulfilled in the person of our Lorde Iesus Christ. For although he be the onely sonne of God: yet notwithstanding, so it is that in respect of his manhod he was the sonne of Abraham, and was fully like vs in all poyntes, sinne onely excepted. And so when we see that God hath made much of him by giuing all things intoo his

hande, too the ende that wee shoulde recouer that thing in him, which wee lost in Adam: therein God hath shewed the great and infinite treasures of his mercie. And verely Iesus Christ is the true looking glasse of Gods grace, which afterward is spred out vpon all his members." 29 (Job 7:16-21), 133.b.14. *Et mesmes cela a esté accompli en la personne de nostre Seigneur Iesus Christ. Car combien qu'il soit Fils unique de Dieu, si est-ce toutesfois que quant à sa nature humaine il a esté fils d'Abraham, il a esté d'une telle condition que nous sommes, excepté peché. Et ainsi donc quand nous voyons que Dieu l'a magnifié, pour lui donner en main toutes choses, à fin que nous recouvrions en luy ce que nous avons perdu en Adam, en cela Dieu a monstré les grans thresors et infinis de sa misericorde. Et de fait, Iesus Christ est le vray miroir de la grace de Dieu, laquelle puis apres est espandue sur tous ses membres.*[*CO* 33:360-361]. A similar allusion to our union with Christ is made in Sermon 44, this time drawing out implications for neighbourly love: "If our neybours be members of Iesus Christe, and wee offer them wrong & violence, so as we haue no eye but to our owne profit: is it not a renting of Iesus Christes body a peeces?" 44 (Job 11:13-20), 208.a.25. *Si nos prochains sont membres de Iesus Christ, et que nous leur facions quelque extorsion et violence qu'il ne soit question que de regarder à nostre profit particulier: n'est-ce point deschirer le corps de Iesus Christ par pieces?* [*CO* 33:553]. Again, Calvin closes Sermon 54 with a similar reference: "And therefore when we see all things so confounded nowadays in the world, as we wote not what to say nor where to become: let vs runne to our good God, casting oure eyes vpon our Lorde Iesus Christ, who will deliuer vs from all miseries and from all the troubles that are at this day in this world. Well then: do we feele our selues feeble and weake? Let vs looke vpon our Lorde Iesus Christ, who is the power of God his father. Do we see our selues as good as alredy dead? The fountaine of life is come vnto vs forsomuch as God hath sent vs his only sonne. And to what ende. Euen to drawe vs out of the dungeons of death, and to assure vs that being vnited vnto him, we can neuer be set beside the saluation that is prepared for vs. Ye see then that if wee haue our eye settled vpon our Lorde Iesus Christ, wee shall not faile to thinke ourselues safe as well in the midds of death, as of the troubles of this world, bycause that by the meanes of him we be sure we shall come to the heauenly glory wherinto he is entered before vs, when we haue finished the course which we haue to runne, which now is subiect to so many miseries." 54 (Job 14:5-12), 255.b.49. *Et pourtant quand nous voyons que tout est auiourd'huy tellement confus aux choses humaines, que nous ne savons que dire ne que devenir: recourons à nostre bon Dieu, iettans les yeux sur nostre Seigneur Iesus Christ, lequel nous delivrera de toutes nos miseres et de tous les troubles qui sont auiourd'huy au monde. Et ainsi, nous sentons-nous foibles et debiles? Voila nostre Seigneur Iesus Christ qui est la vertu de Dieu son Pere. Nous voyons-nous desia comme morts? C'est la fontaine de vie qui est venue à nous, quand Dieu a envoyé son Fils unique. Et pourquoy? Afin de nous retirer des absymes de mort, afin de nous certifier, qu'estans unis à luy, nous ne pourrons iamais estre privez du salut qui nous est appresté. Voila donc comme en regardant à nostre Seigneur Iesus Christ, nous ne laisserons point de nous asseurer au milieu de la mort, et de tous les troubles de ce monde, d'autant que par ce moyen nous sommes certains de parvenir en ceste gloire celeste, en laquelle il nous a precedez, quand nous aurons achevé la course que nous aurons à faire, laquelle est subiette à tant de miseres* [CO 33:680].

[111] [CO 33:159].

[112] 12 (Job 3:11-19), 55.a.35. *Voila donc comme les fideles estans sortis de ce monde sont en ioye avec Dieu, qu'ils cognoissent qu'estans membres de Iesus Christ ils ne peuvent perir* [CO 33:160].

[113] 13 (Job 3:20-26), 59.a.59. *...et à regarder à ceste vie qui nous est preparee aux cieux, et laquelle nous sera revelee pleinement à la venue de nostre Seigneur Iesus Christ* [CO 33:170].

[114] 22 (Job 5:19-27), 101.a.44. *Pource que Iesus Christ est heritier universel de toutes creatures, que tout luy est donné en main: et si nous sommes ses membres, nous serons participans du bien que le Pere luy a commis en toute perfection* [CO 33:277].

[115] 56 (Job 14:16-22), 265.a.17. *O malheureux que ie suis (dit-il) qui est-ce qui me delivrera de ceste prison de mon corps? Mais quant et quant il rend graces à Dieu par nostre Seigneur Iesus Christ* [CO 33:704].

[116] 56 (Job 14:16-22), 265.b.14. *Mais de nostre part contentons-nous que si durant ceste vie nous sommes en langueur, que nostre chair se dueille, que nous soyons en tristesse: et bien, nous avons dequoy nous resiouir en Dieu, d'autant qu'il nous promet de nous estre tousiours Pere et Sauveur. Mourons-nous? Nous savons que la mort nous est profitable, comme dit sainct Paul, d'autant que Dieu par ce moyen-la nous retire des povretez de ce monde, pour nous faire participans de ses richesses, et de son immortalité glorieuse* [CO 33:706].

[117] "And specially let vs looke vppon our Lord Iesus Christ, too whom all power of iudgement is giuen, which serueth too maynteyne our cace, and he is our aduocate. Think wee not that he will make the bitter death auaylable which hee indured for vs? So then, if men were as well aduyzed as they ought to be: there were nothing too bee more wished, than too be iudged at Gods hand, at leastwise so they had recourse to his mercye, and yeelded them selues intoo the hands of our Lord Iesus Christ, who will not iudge vs to our condemnation, but rather acquit vs." 65 (Job 17:1-5), 305.a.67. *Et mesmes voila nostre Seigneur Iesus Christ, auquel est donnee toute puissance de iuger, qui est pour maintenir nostre cause, il est nostre advocat. Ne pensons-nous point qu'il doive faire valoir la mort qu'il a enduree tant amere pour nous? Ainsi donc, si les hommes estoyent advisez comme ils devroyent, il n'y auroit rien plus à souhaiter, que d'estre iugez de Dieu, voire moyennant qu'ils puissent avoir leur refuge à sa misericorde, et qu'ils se rendent entre les mains de nostre Seigneur Iesus Christ, qui ne veut point nous iuger à nostre condamnation, mais plustost afin de nous absoudre*

*A Christological Focus*

[*CO* 34:43]. Note that for Calvin, the future judgement is intrinsically christological: "Behold all iudgement is give[n] vnto our Lord Iesus Christ: and therfore it behoueth vs to come before him with all lowlinesse and reuerence, to heare and receyue whatsoeuer he pronounceth vpon vs without any gaynsaying." 132 (Job 34:21-26), 623.a.13. *Voila le iugement qui est donné à nostre Seigneur Iesus Christ* [*CO* 35:175]. Cf. 138 (Job 135:12-16), 651.a.45 [*CO* 35:252]. In Sermon 140, Calvin again warns us that God's temporal judgements are not all "after one rate" and that we must await the end to see the fullness of God's work. 140 (Job 36:6-14), 658.a.5 [*CO* 35:269].

[118] "Sith that me[n] shake vs of[f] (sayeth he) sith they treade vs vnder their feete, sith we be a reproche and laughingstocke to the whole world: in what cace were we if we hoped not for the resurrection that is promised vs, that our Lord Iesus Christ must come and that the[n] we shall perceiue we haue not serued God in vayne. If we had not this, there were no more God in heauen, there were no more Iustice, there were no more prouidence." 66 (Job 17:6-16), 312.a.49. *Quand (dit-il) on nous reiette, qu'on nous foule aux pieds, que nous sommes en opprobre et moquerie à tout le monde: que seroit-ce si nous n'esperions ceste resurrection qui nous est promise, que nostre Seigneur Iesus Christ doit venir, et qu'alors nous sentirons que ce n'est point en vain que nous avons servi à Dieu?* [*CO* 34:62].

[119] 81 (Job 21:16-21), 383.a.30. *Cognoissons donc les vanitez qui sont ici bas, et cognoissons-les en telle sorte qu'il ne nous face point mal quand rien ne nous sera ici certain. Et pourquoy? Car si nous voulons estre enracinez ici bas, nous renoncerons au royaume des cieux. Mais quiconques a ceste cognoissance, que nostre vie est avec Dieu, et qu'elle nous sera revelee à la venuë de nostre Seigneur Iesus Christ: il ne lui fera point mal d'estre remué en ce monde, de voir qu'il n'y a que revolutions et changemens, et qu'il n'y a rien de certain, et que pourtant il faut que nous aspirions à ceste vie celeste à laquelle Dieu nous appelle, et nous convie iournellement par sa parole. Cependant toutes fois que nous ne laissions pas parmi tous les troubles de ce monde, et les choses ainsi confuses comme on les voit, de savoir que Dieu conduit et gouverne tellement le monde par sa providence, que rien ne se fait ici bas sans sa volonté* [*CO* 34:252].

[120] 92 (Job 24:10-18), 434.b.30. *...et que nous soyons tant plus affectionnez à l'attendre comme nostre Redempteur... Et bien, Seigneur, si tout estoit ordonné comme nous desirons, nous n'aurions plus d'esperance de la venue de nostre Seigneur Iesus Christ, ne de la resurrection qui nous est promise, ne de son royaume celeste, nous serions desia comme en un paradis: mais quand nous sommes agitez comme en une mer bouillante, que nous sommes au milieu des tempestes et tourbillons, Seigneur, c'est afin que nous apprenions d'aspirer au repos qui nous est appresté au ciel, et que tu nous as promis, que nous ayons tousiours la veuë dressee à la venue de nostre Seigneur Iesus Christ ton Fils, lors qu'il viendra pour nous recueillir tous à soy, comme tu nous as commis en sa charge, et en sa protection et conduite* [*CO* 34:392].

[121] These Sermons are: 5, 7, 10, 14, 17, 18, 19, 20, 23, 31, 34, 45, 47, 48, 50, 51, 52, 55, 58, 60, 62, 63, 67, 69, 74, 76, 77, 78, 87, 91, 93, 96, 101, 102, 104, 108, 109, 117, 118, 119, 121, 129, 131, 133, 135, 136, 137, 142, 143, 145, 146, 147, 150, 151, 152, 153, 154, 155.

[122] Sermons 39, 88, and 97.

[123] For a modern, critical analysis of the concept of a mediator in the Book of Job, see D. J. A. Clines, "Belief, Desire and Wish in Job 19:23-27. Clues for the Identity of Job's 'Redeemer,'" in *"Wünschet Jerusalem Frieden": Collected Communications to the XIIth Congress of the International Organization for the Study of the Old Testament, Jerusalem 1986*, Beiträge zur Erforschung des Alten Testaments und des antiken Judentums 13, ed. M. Augustin and K.-D. Schunk (Frankfurt a.M.: Peter Lang, 1988), 363-370; J. B. Curtis, "On Job's Witness in Heaven," *JBL* 102 (1983), 549-562.

[124] Calvin takes the Hebrew לא as an interrogative "who" rather than the negative, "There is no umpire…," as in the Massoretic text.

[125] 37 (Job 9:29-35), 174.a.37. *…ie suis content si vous accomplissez ma Loy, de vous donner pour payement la vie eternelle, encores que ie puisse demander cela de vous sans aucune recompense* [*CO* 33:465].

[126] 37 (Job 9:29-35), 174.a.43. *Car il ne faut pas regarder à nostre nature telle qu'elle est vicieuse et corrompue…*[*CO* 33:465].

[127] 37 (Job 9:29-35), 174.b.7. *…au lieu d'arbitres pour plaider, cerchons Iesus Christ à ce qu'il soit moyenneur afin d'appointer. Que nous ne demandions point à Dieu d'avoir un Iuge qui mette la main sur lui, et sur nous: mais que nous lui demandions qu'il y ait un moyen pour nous reconcilier avec sa maiesté* [*CO* 33:466].

[128] 37 (Job 9:29-35), 174.b.21. *Que reste il plus? Que Iesus Christ se mette entre deux: il faut que Iesus Christ soit un arbitre, non point pour aller par dessus la maiesté de Dieu, pour renger Dieu à nous: mais que par son moyen nous soyons reconciliez à Dieu, et que comme nostre chef il nous attire tous apres soi, pour nous conioindre tellement à Dieu que nous soyons tous un en lui…* [*CO* 33:466]. Calvin ends with a prayer that God might make us "feele (his) infinite goodnesse whiche thou hast set forth in thine onely sonne our Lorde Iesus Christ, whome thou gauest too death for our sakes." *Mais puis qu'il te plaist de nous faire sentir ta bonté infinie, laquelle tu as desployee en ton Fils unique nostre Seigneur Iesus Christ, quand tu l'as exposé à la mort pour nous…* [*CO* 33:466].

[129] 64 (Job 16:18-22), 300.b.57. *Or il ne doute point d'appeller devant Dieu, sachant bien que sa cause est bonne. Vray est (comme desia nous avons dit) qu'il la deduit mal: mais en ce faisant, si est-ce qu'il avoit iuste cause de maintenir son integrité* [*CO* 34:31].

[130] 71 (Job 19:17-25), 335.b.50. *Vrai est que ceci ne se pourra pas declarer du tout pour maintenant…* [*CO* 34:125].

[131] 71 (Job 19:17-25), 336.a.11 [*CO* 34:126].

* [132] 71 (Job 19:17-25), 335.b.60. *Nous savons que les hommes travaillent tant qu'ils peuvent à s'excuser, voire d'autant qu'ils ne pensent point à*

## A Christological Focus

*Dieu: c'est assez que le monde se contente d'eux, et qu'on les estime gens de bien. Voila donc l'hypocrisie qui engendre une impudence. Car si ie ne cognoy que Dieu est mon Iuge, ô il me suffira que les hommes m'applaudissent, qu'ils me tienent en bonne reputation. Et qu'ay-ie gaigné? Rien qui soit. N'est-ce pas bien une grande impudence, quand encores que ma conscience propre me redargue, encores que ie soye convaincu d'avoir mal fait, si est-ce que ie leverai le front, et dirai, Pourquoy est-ce qu'on m'accuse? Qu'est-ce que i'ay fait? N'ay-ie pas bonne cause? Ie prendrai de belles couleurs pour couvrir mon peché, et quand i'aurai ainsi esbloui les yeux des hommes, voila ma cause gaignee* [CO 34:125-126].

[133] In line with the above interpretation of the "redeemer" of Job 19:25, Calvin further expresses doubts as to the intent of the author to convey a truth regarding the resurrection of the body in verse 26. Job is expressing faith in his recovery, rather than in his future resurrection. 72 (Job 19:26-29), 337.a.68. *Il est vrai qu'il ne parle point ici expressement et simplement de la resurrection...*[CO 34:129]. For a more christological interpretation, cf. Albert Barnes, "Job 19:25-29," in *Sitting with Job: Selected Studies on the Book of Job*, ed. Roy B. Zuck (Grand Rapids, MI: Baker Book House, 1992), 283-297.

It is beyond the scope of this dissertation to examine this issue in detail, but Calvin's comment here is all the more surprising given current interpretations of this passage. Luther's Easter Liturgy, for example, contained the hymn "Jesus Christ Our Saviour True," followed by the responsive, "V. Christ, being raised from the dead, dieth no more. R. Death hath no more dominion over him. Alleluia [Rom. 6:9]. V. I know that my Redeemer liveth. Alleluia. R. Who shall at the latter day wake me from the earth. Alleluia [Job 19:25]." See *Luther's Works*, Vol. 53, ed. Ulrich S. Leupold (Philadelphia: Fortress Press, 1965), 134.

[134] 125 (Job 33:18-25), 591.a.12. *Il est vrai que Iesus Christ nous a desliez de la servitude de peché, et de la damnation eternelle en laquelle nous estions de nature: mais si est-ce qu'il a commis ceste charge à tous Pasteurs d'Eglise* [CO 35:88].

[135] 125 (Job 33:18-25), 591.a.28. *Nous sommes donc droits, non pas en nous-mesmes, non pas de nos vertus: mais d'autant qu'il plaist à Dieu de nous pardonner* [CO 35:88].

[136] 125 (Job 33:18-25), 591.a.49. *Où est-ce donc que nostre droiture sera appuyee? C'est en la misericorde gratuite de nostre Dieu: d'autant qu'il efface nos pechez, et qu'il ne nous impute point nos offenses, apres qu'il a nettoyé nos macules par le sang de son Fils, apres qu'il nous a delivrez de damnation de mort par le payement que nostre Seigneur Iesus a fait en la croix. Voila la droiture qui nous est là annoncee par les messagers de Dieu, c'est quand nous sommes iustifiez* [CO 35:89].

[137] 126 (Job 33:29), 593.a.2. *...que l'office de ceux qui preschent l'Evangile est de pardonner les pechez* [CO 35:93].

[138] 126 (Job 33:29), 593.a.19. *...quel est le propre de l'Evangile, assavoir*

*d'estre une ambassade d'appointement de Dieu avec les hommes: c'est que Iesus Christ qui ne savoit que c'est de peché, qui estoit l'agneau sans macule, s'est assuietti à la malediction de nos pechez, afin que nous soyons trouvez iustice de Dieu en luy: c'est à dire qu'apres nous estre plongez en son sang, et venus mettre sous ce sacrifice qu'il a offert, nous sommes tenus et reputez pour iustes, à cause que ce sacrifice-la a eu ceste vertu pour abolir toutes nos fautes et offenses* [CO 35:93-94]. The rest of the sermon finds the Reformer expanding on the nature of the gospel and its ministry. He cites Matthew 16:19, that ministers have the power to "release and forgiue sinnes" by preaching the word of faith in Jesus Christ. 593.a.56. ...*de remettre et pardonner les pechez...* [CO 35:94]. He denies that Roman Catholicism has this power vested in the Pope, bulls and indulgences, which defaces "the vertue of the deathe and passion of our Lord Iesus Christ." 593.b.12. ...*la vertu de la mort et passion de nostre Seigneur Iesus Christ* [CO 35:95]. The gospel is to be received by faith and not by ceremony: "...wee say that mennes sinnes are forgiuen them by receyuing the message of the gospell, and that the same hath not to do with the ceremonies that men haue deuised, nor with the lawes which they haue inuented at their owne pleasure, but only that we must followe the order and rule which our Lord Iesus hath stablished, who hath the remission of sinnes in his hand." 593.b.32. ...*nous disons que les pechez sont pardonnez aux hommes, d'autant qu'ils reçoivent le message de l'Evangile, et qu'il n'est point question ici de ceremonies que les hommes ont controuvé, et de loix qu'on aura inventé à plaisir: mais seulement que nous suivions l'ordre et la regle que nostre Seigneur Iesus a establi, luy qui a la remission de nos pechez en main* [CO 35:95]. The gospel pricks our pride: "For so long as we bee puffed vp with pryde, Gods goodnesse hath no entrance into vs: so long as we be hardned in our sinnes, we beate back the sayd grace a greate way from vs: and so long as we be saped in our filthinesse, surely we cannot tast of the reconciliation which is made by our Lord Iesus Christ." 594.a.42. ...*car cependant que nous sommes enflez d'orgueil, la bonté de Dieu n'a point d'entree en nous: cependant que nous sommes endurcis en nos pechez, nous repoussons ceste grace-la bien loin: cependant que nous sommes confits en nos ordures, il est certain que nous ne pouvons gouster que c'est de ceste reconciliation qui a esté faite par nostre Seigneur Iesus Christ* [CO 35:97]. Still referring to ministers, Calvin adds that it is God's will that we find salvation via his ministers: "...as oft as the promises of the gospell are offered vnto vs, wherin God calleth vs to him, and sheweth himself fauorable for our Lord Iesus Christs sake, giuing vs the grace to tast of that goodnesse, and assuring vs that he is ready to receyue vs to mercye: let vs assure ourselues that then is the conuenient time which he hath appointed for our saluation: Then let vs humble ourselues, and be sure that we haue not preuented him, but that he hath sought vs." 594.b.42. *Et ainsi toutes fois et quantes que les promesses de l'Evangile nous sont offertes, où Dieu nous appelle à soy, et nous monstre qu'il nous est propice au nom de nostre Seigneur Iesus Christ, et qu'il nous fait ceste grace que*

## A Christological Focus

*nous goustons une telle bonté, et que nous sommes certains qu'il est prest de nous recevoir à merci: cognoissons que voila le temps oportun qu'il a ordonné de nostre salut. Humilions-nous donc, sachans que nous ne l'avons point prevenu, mais que c'est luy qui nous a cerché* [CO 35:98]. Thus, the assurance of the gospel: "Then if we haue this priuiledge of abilitie to call vpon our God, and can assure our selues that the gate is open to vs, and that we shall haue good accesse vnto him in the name of our Lord Iesus Christ: I say, if we ca[n] haue that boldnesse... let vs assure our selues that we must rest wholy thervpon, and though we haue neuer so many sorowes and incumbraunces." 595.a.57. *Quand donc nous avons ce privilege de pouvoir invoquer nostre Dieu, estans asseurez que la porte nous est ouverte, et que nous y aurons bon accez au nom de nostre Seigneur Iesus Christ: quand, di-ie, nous avons ceste hardiesse-la, non point de nostre temerité, mais pource qu'il a bien daigné ouvrir sa bouche sacree pour nous rendre tesmoignage de son amour...cognoissons que c'est où il nous faut arrester du tout, encores que nous ayons des tristesses, des fascheries* [CO 35:100]. We are to rejoice in our sorrows and incumbrances: "Yea and it behoueth vs to passe further, and to surmount them all, and to reioyce in our miseries and tribulations: seing that Gods loue is printed in our harts by his holy spirit: that is to wit, seing that God voutsafeth to be our father and sauiour, and hath shewed the same not only by his word, but also in very dede in the person of his only Sonne whom he hath not spared but giuen too the death for vs" 595.a.66. *Il nous faut passer outre, et surmonter tout cela, pour nous glorifier en nos miseres et tribulations, puis que cest amour de Dieu est imprimé en nos coeurs par son sainct Esprit: c'est assavoir que Dieu nous veut estre Pere et Sauveur, et qu'il nous l'a monstré non seluement de parole, mais aussi par effect en la personne de son Fils unique: lequel il n'a point espargné, mais l'a exposé à la mort pour nous* [CO 35:100]. The promises of the gospel foster trust and prayer, in the work of the Spirit sealing our adoption (enabling us to cry "Abba, Father" Romans 8:15) "by Iesus Christ wee haue beleefe in God, and this beleef ingendreth trust, to the end wee may come boldly before the throne of God to pray vnto him. Ye see then how it is shewed vs here, that when a man is so comforted by the promises of the gospell, byandby he calleth vpon God, & findeth fauour at his hand." 595.b.67. *...que par Iesus Christ nous avons la foy en Dieu, et que ceste foy engendre confiance, afin qu'en toute hardiesse nous venions devant le throne de Dieu pour le prier* [CO 35:101-102].

[139] Cf. Emil K. Kraeling's contention that Calvin "Christianized the Old Testament." See his *The Old Testament since the Reformation* (London: Lutterworth Press, 1955), 32.

[140] These include Sermons 3, 92, 125, 126 and 158.

[141] Ford Lewis Battles, *Calculus Fidei: Some Ruminations on the Structure of the Theology of John Calvin* (Grand Rapids: Calvin Theological Seminary, 1978).

[142] David Puckett, *John Calvin's Exegesis of the Old Testament* (Louisville,

Kentucky: Westminster John Knox Press, 1995).

[143] *Ibid.*, 140. See the comments at the beginning of this chapter. Puckett's qualified corroboration of Bouwsma's thesis would seem difficult to sustain in the Joban sermons.

[144] *Op. cit.*, 144-145. It might be argued that the parameters whereby a judgement is made on Calvin's so-called christological focus are too narrow. Calvin's Trinitarianism, it might be said, ensures that wherever Calvin speaks of God he has in mind complex activity of Father, Son and Holy Spirit.

# Conclusion

For it is not right for men unrestrainedly to search out things that the Lord has willed to be hid in himself, and to unfold from eternity itself the sublimest wisdom, which he would have us revere but not understand, that through this also he should fill us with wonder. He has set forth by his Word the secrets of his will that he decided to reveal to us. These he decided to reveal insofar as he foresaw that they would concern us and benefit us (*Institutes* III.xxi.1) [*CO* 2:680].

For not only does piety beget reverence toward God, but the very sweetness and delightfulness of grace so fills a man who is cast down in himself with fear, and at the same time with admiration, that he depends upon God and humbly submits himself to his power (*Institutes* III.ii.23) [*CO* 2:417].

The 159 sermons of John Calvin on the Book of Job, preached between February 1554 and March 1555, provide invaluable help, both for an understanding of the Book of Job itself and as an exemplar of effective pastoral ministry within the framework of a well-defined theological system.

It is clear that Calvin understood the argument of the Book of Job to be essentially about the nature and character of God, particularly his incomprehensibility, rather than an elaborate explanation of the problem of pain. He only rarely mentions contemporary issues, though when he does so it is with remarkable explicitness. This might indicate that for Calvin, preaching is essentially about expounding the text of Scripture. For Calvin, the text determines the preacher's emphases. In this case, the text is principally about the character of God.

In these sermons Calvin covers a wide range of theological issues. The problem of pain forces Calvin to consider the doctrine of man, particularly the *imago Dei*. His rhetoric allows him to be ambivalent, suggesting that fallen man both has lost and retains the image of God. The text of Job forces Calvin to comment upon the profitability of Scripture as God's "familiar" word. However, it is the knowledge of God that dominates the sermons: God, who makes himself known in creation and providence, also makes himself known in his word and in his Son, Jesus Christ.

For the Reformer, true discipleship is to reverence the Almighty

God. Calvin teaches that this is a response to the unfolding character of God as it is revealed in the works of providence. Providence is the belief that in every contingency, God is at work fulfilling his plan and purpose. Thus, the Joban story is an account of the perseverance of a righteous man, with a "good case." Job's friends had a bad case, which they argued well; Job himself had a good case, but argued badly. This *bonne cause* is one that Calvin struggles with, growing impatient with it as the story develops. Despite this, Job's overall steadfastness allows Calvin to urge Job upon his hearers as a model to follow. The struggle that ensues for Job's faith is a necessary one, promoting godliness in the battle against remaining sin and corruption. Job's trials were not a punishment for sin, but in the course of the trial, issues of indwelling sin do arise, suggesting to Calvin one of the purposes of trial: that trial promotes sanctification. There is much that is unclear to us in the analysis of personal pain, and only in the world to come will these issues become clear. That is why Calvin urges patience as we wait for that final revelation.

Job's *bonne cause* drives Calvin to consider the nature of the claim to "innocent" suffering. Whilst defensive of Job's innocence before the charges of Job's friends, Calvin finds himself increasingly ill at ease with Job's claim. In order to defend the character of God against the charge of injustice, Calvin resorts to the concept of a twofold justice of God: a justice that is revealed and another, secret justice before which even the pure angels of heaven are unclean. This raises the specter of universal mediatorship based on the ontological need for mediation between a Creator and the created. This, in turn, raises the charge of "tyrannical" or "absolute" power, one which Calvin consistently refutes. Calvin makes no attempt to resolve this tension, appealing instead to the doctrine of God's incomprehensibility. There is in God and his ways that which we will never be able to understand. However, Calvin's consistent suggestion that we shall be able to understand it in the world to come seems to be unproven.

Calvin's use of the doctrine of God's incomprehensibility has been shown to be not only a hermeneutical key for understanding the Book of Job, but also a key feature of Calvin's doctrine of God in general, whilst he distances himself from the arbitrariness of medieval nominalism. Our very creatureliness, notwithstanding our fallenness, renders us incapable of fully understanding God and his ways. For Calvin the very heart of godliness is submission to a God who cannot ultimately be fathomed. We are to trust his providence even when it makes no sense to us.

In preaching through the Book of Job, Calvin provides us with a comprehensive account of his understanding of the doctrine of providence. We are to learn from providence that "sometimes it is his will too trie the obedience of good men."[1] It is the way of piety to profit from such experiences, knowing that a sovereign and gracious hand is at work. When bad things happen to the righteous, the Lord is involved in the deepest possible way. Far from removing God from such crises in the interest of rescuing him from the charge of sin's authorship, Calvin regularly takes God further and further into the difficulty. He meets the ensuing theological and pastoral difficulties by resorting to God's incomprehensibility. Calvin's doctrine of providence thus reveals a focus on the incomprehensibility of God as a motif that both summarizes the message of the book of Job itself and provides a pastoral tool for responding to the tension between God's justice and power. Interestingly, if somewhat inconsistently, Calvin suggests repeatedly that this incomprehensibility is largely limited to this world. If God is ontologically incomprehensible, as Calvin seems to say, consistency would argue that he remains so even when all aspects of sin are removed in the perfect world to come.

But is providence governed by a christological agenda? If Calvin's concern in placing his discussion of predestination in Book III, rather than Book I, of the *Institutes* was to secure a firmer christological setting for the doctrine of predestination, then might not the same concerns be raised over the doctrine of providence? We have shown that in his expositions of the Book of Job, no such concern seems discernible. Indeed, at those very points where one might expect him to do so, Calvin shies away from "Christianizing" the Old Testament text, even leaving himself open to the charge of Rabbinical exegesis.

On the basis of this study of Calvin's sermons on Job, then, there can be no doubt that the doctrine of God's incomprehensibility emerges as a major theme in Calvin's analysis of the argument of the Book of Job. It would be too much to suggest that this is the "central dogma" of Calvin's theology here or elsewhere, given the fact that Calvin's work lends itself more readily to an analysis along the lines of a complex of foci. It is true, however, that Calvin seems to resort to this doctrine as a means of either defending himself against certain tensions in his theology, or as a way of avoiding any further explanation when any such attempt would be fraught with difficulty.

We would conclude, then, that the Joban sermons display a comprehensive analysis of the doctrine of providence and its implications for the believer and unbeliever. As such, they greatly supplement the doctrine as formulated in *Institutes* I:xvi-xviii. These sermons show Calvin at his most able in terms of pastoral sensitivity to the needs of his listeners and, in that sense, provide us with a model in the right use of the Book of Job today.

We have also demonstrated that Calvin is prepared to argue the doctrine of providence without resorting to christological underpinnings. Those who advocate a Christ-focus in the totality of Calvinian theology will find little support for their case in these sermons. The dilemma this raises finds a possible resolution in a consideration of Calvin's Trinitarianism. In Trinitarian terms, Christ is never absent from any of God's decrees; providence, in this sense, is thoroughly christological.[2] This would be a suitable subject for further study of these sermons.

On the negative side, Calvin can be criticised for his resort to "double justice," particularly his advocacy of ontological mediation—an issue that opens him to the charge of inconsistency in his defense of Job's *bonne cause*. If Job really does have a just case to argue, one to which God himself gives testimony in the opening prologue, it ill becomes the interpreter of the Joban drama to suggest that Job's suffering is due to his unrighteousness, even if it is an unrighteousness that only the hidden righteousness of God seems able to discern. At best, it makes Job's plea of innocence untenable from the start; at worst, it redefines the very nature of God's self-disclosure.

There is considerable scope for further study of these Joban sermons. In particular, it would be useful to compare these sermons with the work of three contemporaries who wrote commentaries on Job. Theodore Beza wrote a brief and somewhat uneven commentary on Job. There were also earlier ones by Bucer in 1528[3] and Oecolompadius in 1532.[4] Additionally, it would be of considerable interest, given the popularity of the original sermons and their translations, to study the influence these sermons may have had upon other extended sermon series on the Book of Job. One such fascinating comparison would be with that of George Hutcheson's 316 lectures on the Book of Job given in Edinburgh in the late seventeenth century.[5] These possible future studies might unearth even greater influences of the Calvin sermons.

# Conclusion

We have noted in the course of this study that Calvin engages in a discussion of several controversial issues.

1. The first of these is his use of the doctrine of the incomprehensibility of God. On some occasions, as we have seen, Calvin employs this doctrine in an ontological sense: that there exists some innate inability within us as finite creatures to understand God. On other occasions, Calvin suggests that the principal cause of our inability to comprehend God lies in our fallenness.

   Calvin's resort to the incomprehensible righteousness of God leads to suggestions that our knowledge of God is both quantitatively *and* qualitatively different from God's knowledge of himself. If this were true, it would appear to lead to the death of all theology. How can we say anything about the righteousness of God if we learn that, in reality, it differs from that form in which it has been revealed?

2. The second, and related, controversy is Calvin's resort to the concept of double justice. Given Calvin's opposition to the *potentia absoluta*, it is hard to imagine the Reformer yielding to the ghost of late medieval nominalism in these sermons; rather, as we have argued, Calvin's argument for double justice is yet another instance of his resort to incomprehensibility in the character and ways of God. We cannot expect to fully understand or justify the ways of God.

   And yet, this does not wholly satisfy. Despite the Reformer's denials, the view is dangerously nominalist in tone. On the pastoral level it introduces some uncertainty into our relationship with God precisely at the point where certainty and predictability (the predictability of covenant faithfulness) are needed. If the message of Job is that the innocent sufferer may find himself at odds with divine justice, however cogent his plea of innocence, then the Book of Job is a message of despair rather than hope.

3. The third controversial issue is Calvin's argument for ontological mediation: the necessity for a Mediator even if there had been no Fall. This finds expression in the example of sinless angels who, Calvin insists, require a Mediator in their relationship with God.

   We have noted how Calvin's interpretation of Job 4:18 finds its way into the final edition of the *Institutes*, and that, therefore, the idea of universal/ontological mediation is buried deep in Calvin's overall theological framework.[6] This is at odds with Calvin's opposition to any suggestion of the incarnation of Christ apart from the condition of sin (a view propounded by, for example, Osiander).[7] Common to both the Osiander controversy and the case of unfallen angels in Job 4:18 is the idea of the necessity of mediation *apart from* sin. The fact that Calvin gives different answers in different contexts appears contradictory.

4. The fourth controversial area is whether or not there was a specifically Christological focus in Calvin's preaching in the sermons on Job. We have noted that, despite some claims to the contrary (e.g. Miln, Puckett), Calvin's interpretation of Job is not always a "Christ-centred" one. The question may be asked, for example, as to whether Calvin is a "Christian" preacher in the Joban sermons. Miln's observation as to "the intensely Christocentric nature of the Sermons on Job"[8] is unwarranted on the evidence put forth in this book, and, for that matter, on the evidence put forth in his own thesis. It is unlikely that the sustained argument of these sermons would find a ready acceptance in those churches sympathetic to the Reformer's theology were they to be preached today, and that because many of them fail to focus on Jesus Christ. The fact, as we have suggested, that Calvin was a Trinitarian theologian, and therefore Christian by inference, fails to uphold what many would consider to be a necessary emphasis in Old Testament interpretation and homiletics.

5. And yet, despite these important and disturbing caveats, Calvin's preaching on the Book of Job is a model of sustained exposition and pastoral insight and it remains one of the finest examples of homiletical method. Calvin's unfolding of the character of God, his penetrating analysis of the human condition, his sustained argument for the essential message of the Book of Job—these continue to speak with conviction and insight.

# References

[1] "...*mais cependant si est ce que quelquefois qu'il voudra esprouver l'obessance des bons,*" 121 (Job 32:11-22), 569.b.57. [*CO* 35:30].

[2] Cf. Jacobs' point whenever he refers to "*die trinitätstheologische Verankerung*" in relation to Calvin's teaching on election. Cf. Richard Muller, *Christ and the Decree: Christology and Predestination in Reformed Theology from Calvin to Perkins* (Grand Rapids: Baker Book House, 35-38; D. N. Wiley, "Calvin's Doctrine of Predestination: His Principal Soteriological and Polemical Doctrine" (Ph.D. diss., Duke University, 1971), 255-256.

For Barth, the decree of God's election is primary, and "providence belongs to the execution of this decree." *CD* III/3,5. Scholars who agree that the twofold knowledge of God is the controlling principle in Calvin's theology, include Ford Lewis Battles, *Calculus Fidei": Some Ruminations on the Structure of the Theology of John Calvin* (Grand Rapids: Calvin Theological Seminary, 1978), 6; *Analysis of the "Institutes"* (Grand Rapids: Baker, 1980), 17; T. H. L. Parker, *Calvin's Doctrine of the Knowledge of God* (Edinburgh: Oliver & Boyd, 1969); E. Dowey, *The Knowledge of God in Calvin's Theology* (New York: Columbia University Press, 1952); J. Köstlin, "Calvins *Institutio* nach Form und Inhalt, in ihrer geschichtlichen Entwicklung," *Theologische Studien und Kritiken* 45 (1868), 6-72, 410-85. Others, such as J. H. Leith, have been more cautious, suggesting that the twofold knowledge of God is *a* way of understanding Calvin, in "Calvin's Awareness of the Holy and the Enigma of His Theology," in *In Honour of John Calvin, 1509-1564*, 217.

[3] *Commentarii in librum Jobi* (Strasbourg, 1528).

[4] *In librum Iob exegemata. Opus admodum eruditum, ac omnibus divinae Scripturae studiosis utile* (Basel, 1532).

[5] *An Exposition of the Book of Job. Being the sum of cccxvi lectures preached in the City of Edenburgh* [sic] (London, 1669).

[6] *Inst.*, III.xii.1. [*CO* 2:553-54]. C.f. III.xvii.9. [*CO* 2:597].

[7] *Ibid.* II.xii.5. [*CO* 343-344].

[8] Miln, op. cit., 125.

# BIBLIOGRAPHY

## Primary Sources

### 1. Biblia
*Biblia Hebraica Stuttgartensia.* Edited by W. Elliger and W. Rudolph. Stuttgart: Deutsche Bibelgesellschaft, 1983.
*Holy Bible.* King James Version.
*Novum Testamentum Graece.* Edited by K. Aland, M. Black, C. M. Martini, B. M. Metzger, and A. Wikgren. 26th ed. rev. Stuttgart: Deutsche Bibelstiftung, 1981.
*Septuaginta.* Edited by A. Rahlfs. Stuttgart: Deutsche Bibelgesellschaft, 1979.

### 2. Bibliographies
De Klerk, Peter. "Calvin Bibliography ____ ." *Calvin Theological Journal* 7 (1972): 221-250; 9 (1974): 38-73; 9 (1974): 210-240; 10 (1975): 175-207; 11 (1976): 19-243; 12 (1977): 164-187; 13 (1978): 166-194; 14 (1979): 187-213; 15 (1980): 244-260; 16 (1981): 206-221; 17 (1982): 231-247; 18 (1983): 206-224; 19 (1984): 192-212; 20 (1985): 268-286; 21 (1986): 194-222; 22 (1987): 275-294; 23 (1988): 195-221; 24 (1989): 278-299; 25 (1990): 225-248; 26 (1991): 389-411; 27 (1992): 326-352; 28 (1993): 393-419; 29 (1994): 451-485; 30 (1995): 419-447; 31 (1996): 420-463.

De Klerk, Peter, and Paul Fields. "Calvin Bibliography 1997." *Calvin Theological Journal* 32 (1997): 368-394.

Erichson, D. A. *Bibliographia Calviniana.* Berlin: C.A. Schwetscheke et filium, [1900], 1960.

Fields, Paul. "Calvin Bibliography 1998." *Calvin Theological Journal* 33 (1998): 377-398.

Fraenkel, Peter. "Petit supplement aux bibliographies calviniennes, 1901-1963." *Bibliothèque d'Humanisme et Renaissance* 33 (1971): 385-414.

Kempff, Dionysius. "A Bibliography of Calviniana 1959-1974." *Studies in Medieval and Reformation Thought.* 15 Leiden, 1975.

Niesel, W. *Calvin Bibliographie 1901-59.* München: Chr. Kaiser Verlag München, 1961.

Tylenda, J. N. "Calvin Bibliography, 1960-1970." *Calvin Theological Journal* 6 (1971): 156-193.

### 3. John Calvin
"Against the Fantastic and Furious Sect of the Libertines Who Are Called 'Spirituals'." In *Treatises Against the Anabaptists and Against the Libertines.* Edited by B. W. Farley. Grand Rapids, MI: Baker Book House, 1982.

*The Bondage and Liberation of the Will: A Defense of the Orthodox Doctrine of Human Choice against Pighius.* Translated by G. I. Davies. Edited by A. N. S. Lane. Grand Rapids, MI: Baker Book House, 1996.

*Calvin's Calvinism: A Defense of the Secret Providence of God.* Translated by Henry Cole. vol. 2 London: Wertheim and Macintosh, 1857.

*Calvin's Commentaries.* The Calvin Translation Society. 22 vols. Grand Rapids: Baker Book House, 1979.

*Calvin's Commentary on Seneca's De Clementia.* Translated and edited by Ford Lewis Battles & Andre Malan Hugo. Leiden: E. J. Brill, 1965.

*Calvin's Ecclesiastical Advice.* Translated by M. Beaty and B. W. Farley. Edinburgh: T. & T. Clark, 1991.

*Calvin's New Testament Commentaries.* Edited by D. W. Torrance and T. F. Torrance. 11vols. Grand Rapids: Baker Book House, 1959ff.

*Calvin's Old Testament Commentaries. Daniel 1* Chapters 1-6. Edited by D. F. Wright. Translated by T. H. L. Parker. Grand Rapids: Eerdmans/Carlisle: The Paternoster Press, 1993.

*Calvin's Old Testament Commentaries. Ezekiel 1* Chapters 1-12. Edited by D. F. Wright. Translated by D. Foxgrover and D. Martin. Grand Rapids: Eerdmans/ Carlisle: The Paternoster Press, 1993.

"Calvin's Treatise 'Against the Libertines.'" Translated by Robert Wilkie and Allen Verhey. *Calvin Theological Journal* 15, no. 2 (November 1980): 190-219.

*Calvin: Theological Treatises.* Translated by J. K. S. Reid. The Library of Christian Classics. London: SCM Press. 1954.

*Concerning the Eternal Predestination of God.* Translated by J. K. S. Reid. Cambridge: James Clarke & Co., 1961.

*The Deity of Christ and Other Sermons.* Translated by Leroy Nixon. 1950. Reprint, Audubon, NJ: Old Paths Publications, 1997.

*Institutes of the Christian Religion.* 1536 ed. Translated by F. L. Battles. London: Collins Liturgical Publications, 1975.

*Institutes of the Christian Religion.* 1559 ed. Edited by J. T. McNeill. Translated by F. L. Battles. 2 vols. Philadelphia: The Westminster Press, 1960.

*Institutes of the Christian Religion.* Edited by John T. McNeill. The Library of Christian Classics. Vols. 20-21. Philadelphia: The Westminster Press, 1960.

*Instruction in Faith.* Translated and edited by Paul T. Fuhrmann. Louisville, KY: Westminster/ John Knox Press, 1992.

*Ioannis Calvini Opera Quae Supersunt Omnia.* (*CO*) Edited by G. Baum, E. Cunitz, and E. Reuss. 59 vols. Braunschweig, 1863-1900.

*Johannis Calvini Opera Selecta.* (*OS*) Edited by Peter Barth and Wilhelm Niesel. 5 vols. Munich: Chr. Kaiser Verlag, 1926-1952.

*The Mystery of Godliness and Other Sermons.* 1830. Facsimilie reprint, Morgan, PA: Soli Deo Gloria, 1999.

*The Register of the Company of Pastors of Geneva in the Time of Calvin.* Edited and Translated by Philip Edgcumbe Hughes. Grand Rapids, MI: Eerdmans, 1966.

*Registres de la Compagnie des pasteurs de Genève au temps de Calvin*, publiés sous la direction des Archives d'Etat de Genève par R. -M. Kingdon et J.' -F. Bergier, t. I: 1546-1553, t. II. 1553-1564. Geneva, 1964 and 1962.

*Selected Works of John Calvin: Tracts and Letters* Edited by Henry Beveridge and Jules Bonnet. Translated by M. R. Gilchrist. 7 vols. Grand Rapids, MI: Baker Book House, 1948-81.

"Sermon on 1 Corinthians 11:2-3." Translated by Seth Skolnitsky. In *Men, Women, and Order in the Church.* Dallas, TX: Presbyterian Heritage Publications, 1992.

*Bibliography* 383

*Sermons of Maister Iohn Caluin, vpon the Booke of Iob.* Translated by Arthur Golding. London: 1574. Facsimile reprint: Edinburgh/Carlisle, PA: The Banner of Truth Trust, 1993.
*The Sermons of Maister Iohn Calvin Vpon the Fifth Booke of Moses Called Deuteronomie.* Translated by Arthur Golding. London: Henry Middleton, 1583. Reprint, Edinburgh: Banner of Truth Trust, 1987.
*Sermons on Deuteronomy.* Translated by Arthur Golding. 1583. Reprint, Edinburgh: The Banner of Truth, 1987.
*Sermons on Psalm 119.* Translated by Thomas Stocker. 1580. Reprint, Audubon, NJ: Old Paths Publications, 1996.
*Sermons on 2 Samuel: Chapters 1-13.* Translated by Douglas Kelly. Edinburgh: Banner of Truth Trust, 1992.
*Sermons on the Epistle to the Ephesians.* Translated by Arthur Golding. 1577. Reprint, Edinburgh: The Banner of Truth Trust, 1973.
*Sermons on the Epistle to the Galatians.* Translated by Arthur Golding. 1574. Reprint, Audubon, NJ: Old Paths Publications, 1995.
*Sermons on the Epistle to the Galatians.* Translated by Kathy Childress. Edinburgh: The Banner of Truth, 1997.
*Sermons on the Epistles to Timothy & Titus.* Translated by Laurence Tomson. 1579. Edinburgh: The Banner of Truth, 1983.
*Sermons on the Saving Work of Christ.* Translated by Leroy Nixon. 1950. Reprint, Welwyn, Herts: Evangelical Press, 1980.
*Supplementa Calviniana.* (SC) 7 vol. Sermons inédits. Neukirchen-Vluyn: Neukirchener Verlag Des Erziehungsvereins, 1936-81.

### Secondary Sources

Allen, D. *Philosophy for Understanding Theology.* Atlanta: John Knox Press, l985.
Almond, P. C. "Karl Barth and Anthropocentric Theology." *Scottish Journal of Theology* 31 (1978): 435-447.
Alden, Robert L. *Job.* The New American Commentary. 2 vols. Broadman and Holman Publishers, 1993.
Althaus, P. *The Theology of Martin Luther.* Translated by R. C. Schultz. Philadelphia, PA: Fortress Press, 1966.
Ambrose. "The Prayer of Job and David." In *Seven Exegetical Works.* Translated by M. P. McHugh. Vol. 65 of *The Fathers of the Church*, 376-385 Washington, D.C.: Catholic University of America Press, 1972.
Ames, William. *Medulla Theologiae.* English translation by John Dystra Eusden, *The Marrow of Theology.* Grand Rapids, MI: Baker Book House, 1977.
Andersen, F. I. *Job.* Tyndale Old Testament Commentary. London: Inter-Varsity Press, 1976.
Aquinas, Thomas. *Expositio super Iob ad litteram.* In *Opera omnia*, iussu Leonis XIII P.M. edita, cura et studio Fratrum Praedicatorum, vol. 26. Rome: 1965.
―――. *Summa Theologiae.* 60 vols. New York: McGraw-Hill Book Company; London: Eyre & Spottiswoode, 1963.
Armour, Michael Carl. "Calvin's Hermeneutic and the History of Christian Exegesis."

Ph.D. diss., University of California, Los Angeles, 1992.

Armstrong, B. G. *Calvinism and the Amyraut Heresy: Protestant Scholasticism and Humanism in Seventeenth-Century France*. Madison, Wisconsin: The University of Wisconsin Press, 1969.

_____. "Duplex Cognitio Dei, or, The Problem and Relation of Structure, Form and Purpose in Calvin's theology." In *Probing the Reformed Tradition,* ed. E. A. McKee and B. G. Armstrong, 135-153. Louisville, KY: Westminster/John Knox Press, 1989.

_____. "Calvin and Calvinism." In *Reformation Europe: A Guide to Research II*, ed. W. S. Maltby. St Louis: Center for Reformation Research, 1992.

Armstrong, William Park, ed. *Calvin and the Reformation: Four Studies*. New York: Fleming H. Revell, 1909.

Atkinson, David. *The Message of Job*. Leicester: Inter-Varsity Press, 1991.

Atkinson, J. *The Great Light: Luther and the Reformation*. Grand Rapids, MI: Eerdmans, 1968.

Augsburger, D. "Calvin et le second Commandment." In *Histoire de l'exegese au XVIe siecle*, ed. D. Fatio and P. Fraenkel, 83-94 Geneva: Droz, 1978.

Augustine. "Divine Providence and the Problem of Evil." Translated by Robert P. Russell. In *The Fathers of the Church*. Vol. 5, 239-334. New York: CIMA Publishing Co., Inc., 1948.

_____. "City of God." In *Patrologiae: series Latina*, ed. J. P. Migne Vol. 41, 13-804. CD-ROM (Chadwick-Healey).

_____. "John's Gospel." In *Patrologiae: series Latina*, ed. J. P. Migne, Vol. 35, 1379-1976. CD-ROM (Chadwick-Healey).

_____. "The Confessions of St. Augustine." In *A Select Library of the Nicene and Post-Nicene Fathers of the Christian Church*, ed. Philip Schaff. Vol. 1. Grand Rapids, MI: Eerdmans, 1956.

_____. "St. Augustine on the Trinity." Translated by Rev. Arthur West Haddan. In *A Select Library of the Nicene and Post-Nicene Fathers of the Christian Church*, ed. Philip Schaff. Vol. III. Grand Rapids, MI: Eerdmans, 1956.

_____. "On the Gift of Perseverance," In *Patrologiae: series Latina,* ed. J. P. Migne. Vol. 45, 993-1035. CD-ROM (Chadwick-Healey).

Bainton, R. H. *The Reformation of the Sixteenth Century*. London: Hodder & Stoughton, 1963.

_____. *Studies on the Reformation*. London: Hodder & Houghton, 1964.

Baker, D. L. *Two Testaments, One Bible*. Leicester: Inter Varsity Press, 1976.

Balke, W., and W. J. Heynen. *Calvin and the Anabaptist Radicals*. Grand Rapids, MI: Eerdmans, 1981.

Balserak, Jon. *Towards an Understanding of Calvin's View of Faith: The Twofold Presentation of the Believer's Reception of the Word.* Th.M. thesis, Reformed Theological Seminary, Jackson, 1997.

Bandstra, A. J. "Law and Gospel in Calvin and Paul." In *Exploring the Heritage of J. Calvin*, ed. D. E. Holwerda. Grand Rapids, MI: Baker Book House, 1976, 11-39.

Baron, S. W. "John Calvin and the Jews." In *H. A. Wolfson Jubilee*, ed. S. Lieberman. Jerusalem: American Academy for Jewish Research, 1965.

Barnes, Albert. "Job 19:25-29." In *Sitting with Job: Selected Studies on the Book of*

*Job*, ed. Roy B. Zuck. Grand Rapids, MI: Baker Book House, 1992.
Barth, K., and E. Brunner. *Natural Theology*. Translated by P. Fraenkel. London: The Centenary Press, 1946.
Barth, Karl. *Against the Stream*. London: SCM Press, 1954.
_____. "The Basic Forms of Theological Thought." *The Expository Times*. 49, no. 1 (1937): 5-8.
_____. *Christ and Adam: Man and Humanity in Romans 5*. In *Scottish Journal of Theology Occasional Papers* 5. Trs T. A. Smail. Edinburgh: Oliver and Boyd, 1963.
_____. *Church Dogmatics*. 13 Vols. Edited by G. W. Bromiley and T. F. Torrance. Edinburgh: T. & T. Clark, 1956-69.
_____. "Die fünf Einleitungskapitel von Calvins Institutio." *Kirchenblatt für Die Reformierte Schweiz* 40, no. 11 (1925): 41-42; 12:45-47; 13:49-50.
_____. *Epistle to the Romans*. London: Oxford University Press, 1933.
_____. "The Humanity of God." In *The Humanity of God*. Atlanta: John Knox Press, 1960.
_____. *The Knowledge of God and the Service of God According to the Teaching of the Reformation*. London: Hodder and Stoughton, 1938.
_____. *The Theology of John Calvin*. Translated by Geoffrey W. Bromiley. Grand Rapids, MI/Cambridge, U.K.: Eerdmans, 1922.
Barth, Karl and E. Brunner. *Natural Theology*. London: The Centenary Press, 1946.
Barton, J. *Reading the Old Testament: Method in Biblical Study*. Philadelphia, PA: The Westminster Press, 1984.
Bates, G. "The Typology of Adam and Christ in John Calvin." *Harvard Quarterly* 5 (1965): 42-57.
Battenhouse, R. W. "The Doctrine of Man in Calvin and in Renaissance Platonism" *Journal of the History of Ideas* 9 (1948): 447-71.
Battles, F. L. "God was Accommodating Himself to Human Capacity." *Interpretation* 31 (1977): 19-38. Also in *Readings in Calvin's Theology*, ed. D. K. McKim 21-42, Grand Rapids, MI: Baker Book House, 1984; also in *Interpreting John Calvin: Ford Lewis Battles*, ed. Robert Benedetto, Grand Rapids, Michigan: Baker Book House, 1996.
_____. *Interpreting John Calvin*. Edited by Robert Benedetto. Grand Rapids, MI: Baker Book House, 1966.
_____. "Notes on J. Calvin, Justitia and the Old Testament Law." In *Intergerini Parietis Septum*, ed. D. Y. Hadidian, 23-37. Pittsburgh Theological Monograph Series 33. Pittsburgh, PA: Pickwick Press, 1981.
_____. *The Piety of John Calvin: An Anthology Illustrative of the Spirituality of the Reformer*. Edited and translated by Ford Lewis Battles. Grand Rapids, MI: Baker Book House, 1978.
Battles, F. W., and J. Walchenbach. *Analysis of the "Institutes of the Christian Religion"*. Grand Rapids, MI: Baker Book House, 1980.
Bauke, Herman. *Dei Probleme der Theologie Calvins*. Leipzig: Hinrichs'schen, 1922.
Baumgartner, A. *Calvin hébraisant et interprete de l'Ancien Testament*. Paris: Librarie Fischbacher, 1889.
Baur, Ferdinand Christian. *Lehrbuch der Christlichen Dogmengeschichte*. Tübingen: Fues, 1858.

Bavinck, Herman. *The Doctrine of God.* Grand Rapids, MI: Baker Book House, 1977.

_____. *Our Reasonable Faith: A Survey of Christian Doctrine.* Translated by H. Zylstra. Grand Rapids, MI: Eerdmans, 1956.

Baxter, A. "John Calvin's Use and Hermeneutics of the Old Testament." Ph.D. diss., University of Sheffield, 1987.

Baxter, T. "What Did Calvin Teach about Accommodation?" *Evangel* 6 (1988): 20-22.

Beeke, J. *Assurance of Faith: Calvin, English Puritansim, and the Dutch Second Reformation.* New York: Peter Lang, 1991.

Bell, M. Charles. *Calvin and Scottish Theology: The Doctrine of Assurance.* Edinburgh: The Handel Press, 1985.

_____. "Calvin and the Extent of the Atonement." *Evangelical Quarterly* 55 (1983): 115-123.

Benoit, Jean-Daniel. *Calvin and His Letters.* Translated by R. Haig. Vol. 5 of *Courtenay Studies in Reformation Theology.* Sutton Courtenay Press, 1991.

_____. "The History and Development of the *Institutio*: How Calvin Worked." In *John Calvin*, 102-17. Vol. 1 of *Courtenay Studies in Reformation Theology.* Edited by Gervase E. Duffield. Grand Rapids, MI: Eerdmans, 1966.

Berkouwer, G. C. *Holy Scripture.* Grand Rapids, MI: Eerdmans, 1975.

_____. *The Providence of God.* Grand Rapids, MI: Eerdmans, 1952.

_____. *The Triumph of Grace in the Theology of Karl Barth.* London: The Paternoster Press, 1956.

_____. *The Work of Christ.* Grand Rapids, MI: Eerdmans, 1965.

Bettis, J. D. "Is Karl Barth a Universalist?" *Scottish Journal of Theology* 20 (1967): 423-436.

_____. "Theology in the Public Debate: Barth's Rejection of Natural Theology and the Hermeneutical Problem." *Scottish Journal of Theology* 22 (1969): 385-403.

Beza [Bèze], Theodore. *Jobus commentario et paraphrasi illustratus.* Geneva, 1583. English Translation: *Iob expounded by Theodore Beza, partly in manner of a commentary, partly in manner of a paraphrase. Faithfully translated out of Laitine into English.* Cambridge, 1589.

_____. *The Life of John Calvin.* Translated by Henry Beveridge [a translation of Beza's second *Life of Calvin* in 1844], reprinted with minor alterations in the *Banner of Truth Magazine* 227/228 [August/September], 1982.

Bierma, Lyle D. "Federal Theology in the Sixteenth Century: Two Traditions?" *Westminster Theological Journal* 45 (1983): 304-21.

_____. "The Role of Covenant Theology in Early Reformed Orthodoxy." *Sixteenth Century Journal* 21 (1990): 458-9.

Blake, R. D. Review of *John Calvin's Exegesis of the Old Testament*, by D. L. Puckett. *Perspectives* 12 (1997): 22-23.

Bloesch, Donald. *God The Almighty.* Downer's Grove, Illinois: InterVarsity Press, 1995.

Boersma, H. "Calvin and the Extent of the Atonement." *Evangelical Quarterly* 64 (1992): 333-55.

Bouwsma, W. J. "Calvin and the Renaissance Crisis of Knowing." *Calvin Theological Journal* 17, no. 2 (1982): 190-211.

———. *John Calvin: A Sixteenth Century Portrait*. New York and Oxford: Oxford University Press, 1988.

———. "John Calvin's Anxiety." In *Proceedings of the American Philosophical Society*, 128:3 (1984): 252-6.

———. "The Quest for the Historical Calvin." *Archiv für Reformationsgeschichte* 77 (1986): 47-57.

Bray, J. S. "The Value of Works in the Theology of Calvin and Beza." *Sixteenth Century Journal* 4 (1973): 77-86.

Breen, Q. *John Calvin: A Study in French Humanism*. Grand Rapids, MI: Eerdmans, 1931.

———. "John Calvin and the Rhetorical Tradition." *Church History* 26, no. 1 (1957): 3-21.

Brink, Gijsbert van den. *Almighty God: A Study of the Doctrine of Divine Omnipotence*. Th.D. diss. Kampen: Kok Pharos Publishing House, 1993.

Bromiley, G. W. *Introduction to the Theology of Karl Barth*. Edinburgh: T & T. Clark, 1979.

Bruggink, D. J. "Calvin and Federal Theology." *Reformed Review* 13 (1959): 15-22.

Brunner, E. "Allgemeine und besonder Offenbarung in Calvins Institutio." *Evangelische Theologie* 1, no. 5 (May 1934).

———. *The Christian Doctrine of God: Dogmatics*. Vol. 1. Philadelphia: The Westminster Press, 1950.

Butin, P. W. "John Calvin's Humanist Image of Popular Late-Medieval Piety and its Contribution to Reformed Worship." *Calvin Theological Journal* 29 (1994): 419-31.

———. *Revelation, Redemption and Response. Calvin's Trinitarian Understanding of the Divine-Human Relationship*. New York: Oxford University Press, 1995.

Butler, Diana. "God's Visible Glory: The beauty of nature in the thought of John Calvin and Jonathan Edwards." *The Westminster Journal* 52 (1990): 13-26.

Cairns, David. *The Image of God in Man*. London: Collins, 1973.

Campbell, Cynthia. "Response to Colin Gunton." *Theology Today* 43, no. 3 (1986): 331-333.

Carroll, Raymond E. Review of *Calvin's Perspectival Anthropology*, by Mary Potter Engel. *Theological Educator* 43 (1991): 175.

Chadwick, O. *John Cassian*. Cambridge: London: Hodder & Stoughton, 1968.

———. *The Reformation*. Grand Rapids, MI: Eerdmans, 1976.

Choisy, E. *La theocratie à Genève au temps de Calvin*. Genève: Ch. Eggimann & Cie, 1897.

Chrysostom, John. "No One Can Harm the Man Who Does Not Injure Himself." Translated by W. R. Stephens, In *Nicene and Post-Nicene Fathers*, ed. P. Schaff, et al.. Series 1, vol. 9, 269-284. Grand Rapids, MI: Eerdmans, 1954.

Cicero. *De Natura Deorum*. London: Methuen & Co., 1896.

———. *De Senectute, De Amicitia, De Divinatione*. The Loeb Classical Library. London: William Heinemann, 1923.

Clarke, F. S. "Christocentric Developments in the Reformed Doctrine of

Predestination." *The Churchman* 98, no. 3 (1984): 229-245.

Clavier, Henri. "Calvin commentateur biblique." In *Études sur le Calvinisme*, ed. H. Clavier. Paris: Fischbacher, 1936: 99-140.

Clifford, A. C. *Atonement and Justification: English Evangelical Theology 1640-1790, an Evaluation*. Oxford: Clarendon Press, 1990.

Clines, David J. "Belief, Desire and Wish in Job 19:23-27. Clues for the Identity of Job's 'Redeemer.'" In *"Wünschet Jerusalem Frieden": Collected Communications to the XIIth Congress of the International Organization for the Study of the Old Testament, Jerusalem 1986*, Beiträge zur Erforschung des Alten Testaments und des antiken Judentums 13. Edited by M. Augustin and K.-D. Schunk. Frankfurt a.M.: Peter Lang, 1988: 363-370.

_____. *Job 1-20*, Word Biblical Commentary, 17. Dallas, Texas: Word Books, 1989.

Cochrane, A. C. "A Preliminary Aspect of Calvin's Epistemology." *University of Toronto Quarterly* 14 (1944): 382-93.

Copleston, F. A. *A History of Philosophy*. 9 vols. Reprint, New York: Image Books, 1962.

Cranfield, C. E. B. "An Interpretation of the Book of Job." *Expository Times* 54 (1943): 295-298.

Crawford, Robert. "The Theological Method of Karl Barth." *Scottish Journal of Theology* 25 (1972): 320-336.

Cunningham, W. *The Reformers and the Theology of the Reformation*. Edinburgh: T. & T. Clark, 1862. Reprint, Carlisle: The Banner of Truth Trust, 1979.

Curtis, J. B. "On Job's Witness in Heaven." *Journal of Biblical Literature* 102 (1983): 549-562.

Dakin, A. *Calvinism*. London: Duckworth, 1940.

Dargan, E. C. *A History of Preaching*. Vol. 1. 1905. Reprint, Grand Rapids, MI: Baker Book House, 1954.

Davidson, R. M. *Typology in Scripture*. Grand Rapids, Michigan: Andrews University Press, 1981.

Davids, Peter. *The Epistles of James: A Commentary on the Greek Text*. Exeter: The Paternoster Press, 1982.

Davis, T. J. "Images of Intolerance: John Calvin in Nineteenth-Century History Textbooks." *Church History* 65 (1996): 234-48.

Davis, Thomas M. "The Traditions of Puritan Typology." In *Typology and Early American Literature*, ed. Sacvan Berkovich. Amherst, MA: University of Massachusetts Press, 1972.

De Gruchy, John W. Review of *Calvin and the Rhetoric of Piety*, by Serene Jones. *Modern Theology* 13 (1997): 271-272.

De Klerk, P. *Renaissance, Reformation, Resurgence: Papers and Responses Presented at the Colloquium on Calvin & Calvin Studies, Calvin Theological Seminary 1976*. Edited by P. de Klerk. Grand Rapids, MI: Calvin Theological Seminary, 1976.

De Long, I. H. "Calvin as an Interpreter of Scripture." *Reformed Review* 13 (1909): 165-82.

De Young, Jacobus. *Accommodatio Dei: A Theme in K. Schilder's Theology of Revelation*. Kampen: Dissertatie-Uitg. Mondiss., 1990.

Dekker, Harold. "Introducción" in *Sermones sobre Job*. Seleccionados y traducidos al inglés del francés por Leroy Nixon. Jenison: The Evangelical Literature League, 1988. 5-26. English text entitled "Introduction" in *Sermons from Job* by John Calvin. Selected and Translated by Leroy Nixon. Grand Rapids, MI: Eerdmans, 1952. ix-xxxvi. Earlier edition entitled "The preacher of Geneva." *The Calvin Forum* 16 (1950/51) 184-186, 205-207, 225-226.

Demarest, Bruce A. *General Revelation: Historical Views and Contemporary Issues*. Grand Rapids, MI: Zondervan Publishing House, 1982.

Dhorme, E. *A Commentary on the Book of Job*. Translated by H. Knight. London: Thomas Nelson and Sons, 1967.

Dillenberger, J. *God Hidden and Revealed: The Interpretation of Luther's deus absconditus and its Significance for Religious Thought*. Muhlenberg Press, 1953.

Doumergue, E. *Jean Calvin, les hommes et les choses de son temps*. 7 vols. Lausanne: G. Bridel & Co., 1899-1927.

Dowey, E., Jr. *The Knowledge of God in Calvin's Theology*. New York & London: Columbia University Press, 1952.

_____. "Law in Luther and Calvin." *Theology Today* 41 (1984): 146-53.

_____. "The Structure of Calvin's Theological Thought as Influenced by the Two-Fold Knowledge of God." *Calvinus Ecclesiae Genevenesis Custos*. Edited by W. Neuser. New York: Verlag Peter Lang, 1984.

Doyle, R. C. "John Calvin, his Modern Detractors and the Place of the Law in Christian Ethics." *Reformed Theological Review* 41 (1982): 74-83.

Driver, S. R., and G. B. Gray. *A Critical and Exegetical Commentary on the Book of Job*. 2 vols. New York: Charles Scribner's Sons, 1921.

Duffield, Gervase E., ed. *John Calvin: A Collection of Essays*. Vol. 1 of *Courtenay Studies in Reformation Theology*. Grand Rapids: Eerdmans, 1966.

Duthie, C. "Providence in the Theology of Karl Barth." In *Providence*, ed. M. Wiles, 62-76. London: SPCK, 1969.

Ebeling, G. "On the Doctrine of the *Triplex usus legis* in the Theology of the Reformation." In *Word and Faith*. Translated by J. W. Leith. Philadelphia, PA: Fortress Press, 1963: 62-78.

Edward, E. M. *Christianity and Philosophy*. Edinburgh: T. & T. Clark, 1932.

Edwards, Charles E. *Devotions and Prayers of John Calvin*. Grand Rapids, MI: Baker Book House, 1960.

Elert, Werner. "Uber die Herkunft des Stazes '*Finitum infiniti non capax*.'" Festschrift Carl Strange, in *Zeitschrift für Systematische Theologie*, xvi (1939).

Emerson, E. M. "Calvin and Covenant Theology." *Church History* 25 (1956): 136-144.

*The Encyclopedia of Philosophy*. Edited by P. Edwards. Vol. 8. New York: The Macmillan Co. & The Free Press, 1967.

Engel, Mary Potter. *John Calvin's Perspectival Anthropology*. American Academy of Religion Academy Series, ed. Susan Thistlethwaite, no. 52. Atlanta, GA: Scholars Press, 1988.

Engelbrecht, B. "Is Christ the Scopus of the Scripture?" in *Calvinus Reformator*, ed. B. J. van der Walt. (Potchefstroom University), Potchefstroom: Institute for Reformational Studies, 1982.

Engelland, Hans. *Gott und Mensch bei Calvin*. München: Chr. Kaiser Verlag, 1934.
Erichson, D. Alfredus, ed. *Bibliographia Calviniana*. Nieuwkoop: B. DeGraaf. 1979.
Estep, W. R. *The Anabaptist Story*, rev. ed. Grand Rapids, MI: Eerdmans, 1981.
Faber, Jelle. "Nominalisme in Calvijin's preken over Job?" In *Een sprekend begin*. Opstellen anageboden aan Heinrich Marinus Ohmann. Bij zijn afscheid als hoogleraar aan de Theoloische Unicersiteit van de Gereformeere Kerken (vrijigemaakt) te Kampen op 6 december 1993. Red. Van Rutger ter Beek, E. Brink, Cornelis van Dam [en] Gerrit Kwakkel, 68-85. Kampen: Uitgeverij van den Berg, 1993.
Fairbairn, Patrick. *The Interpretation of Prophecy*. London: Banner of Truth Trust, 1964.
_____. *The Typology of Scripture*. Grand Rapids, MI: Zondervan Publishing House, 1965.
Farley, Benjamin Wirt. "John Calvin's Sermons on the Ten Commandments." Th.D. diss., Union Theological Seminary, 1976.
_____. *The Providence of God*. Grand Rapids, MI: Baker Book House, 1988.
_____. "The providence of God in reformed perspective." In *Major themes in the Reformed Tradition*, ed. Donald Keith McKim, 87-93 Grand Rapids, MI: Eerdmans, 1992. Also entitled "The quintessential features of a reformed perspective: The triumph of God's sovereignty, goodness, and purposes" in his *The Providence of God*, 229-237. Grand Rapids, MI: Baker Book House, 1988.
_____. Review of *John Calvin's Perspectival Anthropology*, by Mary Potter Engel. *Theology Today* 45 (1991): 508.
Farmer, Craig S. Review of Susan Schreiner's *Where Shall Wisdom be Found?* by Susan Schreiner. *Pro Ecclesia* 5 (1996): 504-507.
Farrar, F. W. "Calvin as an Expositor." *The Expositor*, second series, 7 (1884): 426-44.
_____. *History of Interpretation*. Grand Rapids: MI: Baker Book House, 1961. Reprint, 1979.
Ferguson, Sinclair. *John Owen and the Christian Life*. Edinburgh: The Banner of Truth, 1987.
Floor, L. "The Hermeneutics of Calvin." In *Calvinus Reformator*, ed. B. J. van der Walt. (Potchefstroom University), Potchefstroom: Institute for Reformational Studies, 1982.
Ford, D. F. "Barth's Interpretation of the Bible." In *Karl Barth: Studies of His Theological Method*. Oxford: Clarendon Press, 1979.
Forstman, H. J. *Word and Spirit: Calvin's Doctrine of Biblical Authority*. Stanford: California: Stanford University Press, 1962.
Foxgrover, D. "Self-Examination in John Calvin and William Ames." In *Later Calvinism*, ed. W. F. Graham, 451-70. Sixteenth Century Essays and Studies, vol. 22. Kirksville, KY: Sixteenth Century Journal Publishers, 1994.
Frame, John. *The Doctrine of the Knowledge of God*. Phillipsburg, NJ: Presbyterian and Reformed Publishing Company, 1987.
Friedman, J. "Michael Servetus: The Exegesis of Divine History." *Church History* 43 (1974): 460-469.

# Bibliography 391

_____. "Sebastian Münster, the Jewish Mission, and Protestant Antisemitism." *Archiv für Reformationsgeschichte* 70 (1979): 238-59.

_____. "Servetus and the Psalms: The Exegesis of Heresy." In *Histoire de l'exégese au XVIe siecle*, ed. D. Fatio and P. Fraenkel, 164-178. Geneva: Droz, 1978.

_____. "Sixteenth Century Christian-Hebraica: Scripture and the Renaissance Myth of the Past." *Scottish Journal of Theology* 11 (1980): 67-85.

Fuhrmann, P. T. "Calvin, the Expositor of Scripture." *Interpretation* 6 (1952), 188-209.

Gagnebin, Bernard. "L'histoire des manuscrits des sermons de Calvin." In *Supplementa Calviniana* 2:xiv-xxviii.

Gamble, R. C. "*Brevitas et Facilitas*: Toward an Understanding of Calvin's Hermeneutic." *Westminster Theological Journal* 47 (1985): 1-17.

_____. "Calvin as Theologian and Exegete—Is There Anything New?" *Calvin Theological Journal* 23 (1988): 178-94.

_____. "Calvin's Theological Method: Word and Spirit, A Case Study." In *Calviniana: Ideas and Influence of Jean Calvin*. ed. R.W. Schnucker. Sixteenth Century Essays and Studies, vol. 10. Kirksville, KY: Sixteenth Century Journal Publishers, Inc., 1988.

_____. "Exposition and Method in Calvin." *Westminster Theological Journal* 47 (1985): 1-17.

Ganoczy, A. "Observations on Calvin's Trinitarian Doctrine of Grace." Translated by K. Crim. In *Probing the Reformed Tradition: Historical Studies in Honor of Edward A. Dowey, Jr.*, ed. E. A. McKee and B. G. Armstrong. Louisville, KY: Westminster/ John Knox Press, 1989.

_____. *The Young Calvin*. The Westminster Press. Philadelphia. 1987.

George, Timothy. *Theology of the Reformers*. Nashville, TN: Broadman Press, 1988.

Gerrish, B. A. "Biblical Authority and the Reformation." *Scottish Journal of Theology* 10 (1957): 337-51.

_____. *Grace and Gratitude: The Eucharistic Theology of John Calvin*. Edinburgh: T. & T. Clark, 1993.

_____. *Grace and Reason: A Study in the Theology of Luther*. Chicago: University of Chicago Press, 1979.

_____. "John Calvin and the Reformed Doctrine of the Lord's Supper." *McCormick Quarterly* 22 (1969): 85-98.

_____. *The Old Protestantism and the New: Essays on the Reformation Heritage*. Edinburgh: T. & T. Clark, 1982.

_____. *Reformers in Profile*. Philadelphia, PA: Fortress Press, 1967.

_____. *Tradition and the Modern World: Reformed Theology in the Nineteenth Century*. Chicago and London: The University of Chicago Press, 1978.

_____. "The Word of God and the Words of Scripture: Luther and Calvin on Biblical Authority." *The Old Protestantism and the New: Essays on the Reformation Heritage*. Chicago: University of Chicago Press, 1982.

Gerrish, B. A., and R. Bennedeto, ed. "Theology within the limits of piety alone: Schleiermacher and Calvin's notion of God." In *The Old Protestantism and the New*, 375-383. Essays on the Reformation Heritage. Chicago: The University of Chicago Press, 1982. Also entitled, "Theology with the limits of piety alone:

Schleiermacher and Calvin's doctrine of God." *Reformatio Perennis*. Essays on Calvin and the Reformation in honor of Ford Lewis Battles. Pittsburgh Theological Monograph Series, 32. Pittsburgh: The Pickwick Press, 1981: 67-87.

Gessert, R. A. "The Integrity of Faith: An Enquiry into the Meaning of Law in the Thought of John Calvin" *Scottish Journal of Theology* 13 (1960): 247-61.

Gibson, John C. L. *Job*. The Daily Study Bible Series. Philadelphia: The Westminster Press, 1985.

Gilkey, L. *Reaping the Whirlwind: A Christian Interpretation of History.* New York: The Seabury Press, 1981.

Gilmont, Jean-François. *Bibliotheca Calviniana: Les œuvres de Jean Calvin publiées au XVIe siècle*. 2 Vols. (Genève: Librairie Droz, 1994).

Girardin, Benoit. *Rhetorique et Théologique. Calvin: Le Commentaire de l'Epître aux Romains*. Paris: Beauchesne, 1979.

Gleason, Randall C. *John Calvin and John Owen on Mortification: A Comparative Study in Reformed Spirituality*. Studies in Church History, no. 3. New York: Peter Lang, 1995.

Gogarten, F. "Das Problem einer theologischen Anthropologie." *Zwischen den Zeiten* 7, no. 6 (1929): 493-511.

Gonzalez, J. L. *A History of Christian Thought*. Vols. 1-3. Nashville: Abingdon Press, 1975.

Gorham, G. C., ed. *Gleanings of a Few Scattered Ears*. London: Bell and Daldy, 1857.

Gotch, F. W. "Calvin as a Commentator." *Journal of Sacred Literature* 3 (1849): 222-236.

Greef, W. de. *The Writings of John Calvin: An Introductory Guide*. Trans. Lyle D. Bierma. Grand Rapids, MI: Baker Book House, 1993.

Gregory the Great. *Iob, cura et studio Marci Adriaen, Corpus Christianorum: Series Latina* 143, 143A, 143B. Turnhout: Brepols, 1979-85.

Grislis, E. "Calvin's Use of Cicero in the Institutes I. 1-5 – A Case Study in Theological Method." *Archiv fur Reformationsgeschichte* 62 (1971): 5-36.

_____. "Seneca and Cicero as Possible Sources of John Calvin's View of Double Predestination: An Inquiry in The History of Ideas." In *In Honor of John Calvin. 1509-64*. Papers from the 1986 International Calvin Symposium at McGill University, E. J. Furcha. ARC Supplement #3. Montreal: Faculty of Religious Studies, McGill University, 1987.

Guggisberg, Hans Rudolf. "Castellion, Sébastien." *The Oxford Encyclopedia of the Reformation*, ed. Hans J. Hillerbrand. Vol. 1. New York, Oxford: Oxford University Press, 1996.

Gunton, Colin. "Barth, The Trinity, and Human Freedom." *Theology Today*. 43, no. 3 (October l986): 316-330. Also Called "The Triune God and the Freedom of the Creature."

_____. *Becoming and Being: The Doctrine of God in Charles Hartshone and Karl Barth*. London: Oxford University Press. 1978.

_____. "Karl Barth and the Development of Christian Doctrine." *Scottish Journal of Theology* 25 (1972): 171-180.

_____. Karl Barth's Doctrine of Election as Part of His Doctrine of God." *Journal of Theological Studies* 25 (1974): 381-392.

_____. "The Triune God and the Freedom of the Creature." In *Karl Barth: Centenary Essays*, ed. S. W. Sykes. Cambridge: Cambridge University Press, 1989.

Habel, Norman C. *The Book of Job: A Commentary*. Philadelphia: The Westminster Press, 1985.

Haire, J. L. M. "John Calvin as an Expositor." IBS 4 (1982): 2-16.

Hall, B. "Calvin Against the Calvinists." In *John Calvin: A Collection of Distinguished Essays*, ed. Gervase Duffield, 23-27. Grand Rapids, MI: Eerdmans, 1966.

_____. "Calvin and Biblical Humanism." *The Hugenot Society of London – Proceedings 20* (1959-64): 195-209.

Hansen, Gary N. Review of *John Calvin's Exegesis of the Old Testament*, by D. L. Puckett. *Princeton Seminary Bulletin* 17, no. 3 (1996): 376-378.

Hards, Walter G. "A Critical Translation and Evaluation of the Nucleus of the 1536 Edition of Calvin's Institutes." Ph.D. diss., Princeton University, NJ 1955.

Hardy, Lee. "Our Work, God's Providence; The Calvinist Elaboration: Work and the Organic Structure of Social Life." In *The Fabric of This World*, 54-67. Grand Rapids: Eerdmans, 1990.

Harkness, G. *John Calvin – The Man and His Ethics*. New York: Abingdon Press, 1938.

Haroutunian, J. "Calvin as Biblical Commentator." In *Calvin: Commentaries*, trans and ed. J. Haroutunian, 15-50. Library of Christian Classics, no. 23. Philadelphia, PA: The Westminster Press, 1958.

Hartley, John E. *The Book of Job*. Grand Rapids, MI: Eerdmans, 1988.

Hartwell, Herbert. *The Theology of Karl Barth: An Introduction*. London: Duckworth and Co., Ltd., 1964.

Harvey, V. A. *A Handbook of Theological Terms*. New York: Macmillan Publishing Co., 1964.

Hasler, P. "The Influence of David and the Psalms upon J. Calvin's Life and Thought." *The Harvard Quarterly* 5 (1965): 7-18.

Helm, Paul. "Calvin and Bernard on Freedom and Necessity: A Reply to Brümmer." *Religious Studies* 30 (1994): 457-465.

_____. "Calvin and Natural Law." In *Articles on Calvin and Calvinism: A Fourteen-Volume Anthology of Scholarly Articles*, ed. Richard C. Gamble. Vol. 7, 177-194. London/New York: Garland Publishing, Inc., 1992.

_____. "Calvin among the Angels." Unpublished paper read at the Edinburgh Dogmatics Conference, 1992.

_____. *Calvin and the Calvinists*. Edinburgh: The Banner of Truth Trust, 1982.

_____. "Calvin and the Covenant: Unity and Continuity." *Evangelical Quarterly* 55 (1983): 71-7.

_____. "Calvin (and Zwingli) on Divine Providence." *Calvin Theological Journal* 29 (1994): 338-405.

_____. "Calvin, English Calvinism and the Logic of Doctrinal Development." *Scottish Journal of Theology* 34 (1981): 179-85.

_____. "Providence: Risky or Risk-Free? Providence and Accountability." In *The Providence of God: Contours of Christian Theology*, ed. Gerald Lewis Bray, 51-54, 178-82, 236-37. Downers Grove: InterVarsity Press, 1994.

Henderson, G. D. ed., *The Scots Confession 1560*. Edinburgh: The Saint Andrew Press, 1960.

Hendry, G. S. "The Freedom of God in the Theology of Karl Barth." *Scottish Journal of Theology* 31 (1978): 229-244.

―――――. "The Transcendental Method in the Theology of Karl Barth." *Scottish Journal of Theology* 37 (1984): 213-227.

Heppe, Heinrich. *Reformed Dogmatics Set Out and Illustrated from the Sources*. Edited by Ernst Bizer. Translated by G. T. Thompson. Grand Rapids: Baker, 1978.

Hesselink, J. *Calvin's Concept of the Law*. Princeton Theological Monographs Series, 30. Allison Park: Pickwick Publications, 1992.

―――――. *Calvin's First Catechism: A Commentary*. Louisville, KY: Westminster/John Knox Press, 1997.

―――――. "Christ the Law and the Christian: An Unexplored Aspect of the Third use of the Law in Calvin's Theology." In *Reformatio Perennis*, ed. B. A. Gerrish, 11-26. Pittsburgh Theological Monograph Series, 32. Pittsburgh: The Pickwick Press, 1981

―――――. "The Development and Purpose of Calvin's Institutes." *The Reformed Theological Review* 24, no. 3 (1965): 65-72.

―――――. "Governed and guided by the spirit—a key issue in Calvin's doctrine of the Holy Spirit." In *Calvin Studies V*. [Papers] presented at a Colloquium on Calvin Studies at Davidson College and Davidson College Presbyterian Church, Davidson, NC, January 19020, 1990, ed. John H. Leith, 29-40. Davidson: Davidson College, 1990.

―――――. *An Introduction to Calvin's Theology*. Holland, MI: Western Theological Seminary, 1993.

―――――. "Luther and Calvin on Law and Gospel in their Galatians Commentaries." *Reformed Review* 37 (1984): 69-82.

Higman, F. M. "The Reformation and the French Language." *Articles on Calvin and Calvinism: A Fourteen-Volume Anthology of Scholarly Articles*. Edited by Richard C. Gamble, vol. 14, 110-126. London/New York: Garland Publishing, Inc., 1992.

―――――. *The Style of John Calvin in his French Polemical Treatises*. Oxford: Oxford University Press, 1967.

Hodgson, Peter Crafts. "Calvin on God's Governance of History" In *God in history: Shapes of freedom*, 21-23. Nashville: Abingdon Press, 1989.

Hoekema, A. A. "The Covenant of Grace in Calvin's Teaching." *Calvin Theological Journal* 2 (1967): 133-61.

―――――. *Created in God's Image*. Grand Rapids, MI: Eerdmans, 1986.

Hoitenga, Dewey J., Jr. *John Calvin and the Will: A Critique and Corrective*. Grand Rapids, MI: Baker Book House, 1997.

Holder, R. Ward. Review of *Calvin and the Rhetoric of Piety*, by Serene Jones. *Sixteenth Century Journal* 27 (1996): 955-957.

Holmes, Rolston. "The Understanding of Sin and Responsibility in the Teaching of J. Calvin." Ph.D. diss., Edinburgh University, 1958.

Holtrop, Philip C. *The Bolsec Controversy on Predestination, from 1551 to 1555*. 2 vols. Lewiston: Edwin Mellen, 1993.

Holwerda, D. E., ed. *Exploring the Heritage of J. Calvin*. Grand Rapids, MI: Baker Book House, 1976.

Hunsinger, G. *How To Read Karl Barth*. Oxford: Oxford Univ. Press, 1991.
Hunter, A. M. *The Teaching of Calvin*. London: James Clark & Co., Ltd., 1950.
Irwin, Clarke Huston. *John Calvin: The Man and His Work*. London: The Religious Tract Society, l909.
Jacobs, P. *Prädestination und Verantwortlichkeit bei Calvin*. Neukirchen Kr. Moers, Buchhandlung des Erziehungsvereins, 1937.
Jansen, J. F. *Calvin's Doctrine of the Work of Christ*. London: J. Clark, 1956.
Jellema, Dirk William. "God's 'Baby-Talk': Calvin and the 'Errors' in the Bible." *Reformed Journal* 30 (April 1980): 25-27.
Jensen, R. *God after God. The God of the Past and the God of the Future. Seen in the Work of Karl Barth*. Indianapolis and New York : The Bobbs-Merrill Co., 1969.
Jewett, Paul K. *Election and Predestination*. Devon: Eerdmans and Paternoster Press, Ltd., 1985.
_____. "Concerning the Allegorical Interpretation of Scripture." *The Westminster Theological Journal* 17 (1954): 1-20
Johnson, G. "Calvinism and Interpretation." *Evangelical Quarterly* 4 (1932): 161-72.
Johnson, M. S. "Calvin's Handling of the Third Use of the Law and its Problems." In *Calviniana: Ideas and Influences of Jean Calvin*, ed. R. V. Schnucker, 33-50. Sixteenth Century Essays and Studies, vol. 10. Kirksville, KY: Sixteenth Century Journal Publishers, 1988.
Jones, Serene. *Columbia Series in Reformed Theology: Calvin and the Rhetoric of Piety*. Louisville, KY: Westminster/John Knox Press, 1995.
Jungel, E. *The Doctrine of the Trinity: God's Being Is in Becoming*. Edinburgh and London.: Scottish Academic Press, 1976. Original German. Pub. 1966.
Kaiser, C. B. "Calvin, Copernicus, and Castellio." *Calvin Theological Journal* 21 (1986): 5-31.
_____. "Calvin's Understanding of Aristotelian Natural Philosophy: Its Extent and Possible Origins." In *Calviniana: Ideas and Influences of Jean Calvin*, ed. R. V. Schnucker, 77-92. Sixteenth Century Essays and Studies, vol. 10. Kirksville, KY: Sixteenth Century Journal Publishers, 1988.
Kantzer, K. S. "Calvin and the Holy Scripture." *Inspiration and Interpretation*. Edited by J. F. Walvoord. Grand Rapids, MI: Eerdmans, 1957.
_____. "John Calvin's Theory of the Knowledge of God and the Word of God," Ph.D. diss., Harvard University, 1950.
Kaufman, G. *Theology for a Nuclear Age*. Philadelphia, PA: The Westminster Press, 1985.
Kelly, D. F. "The Political Ideas of John Calvin as Reflected in His Sermons on II Samuel." *Evangel* 2 (1984): 11-15.
_____. "The Transmission and Translation of the Collected Letters of John Calvin." *Scottish Journal of Theology* 30 (1977): 429-37.
Kempff, D. *A Bibliography of Calviniana 1959-1974: Studies in Medieval and Reformation Thought*. Edited by Heiko A. Oberman, Tubingen. Vol. XV. Leiden: E. J. Brill, 1975.
Kendall, R. T. *Calvin and English Calvinism to 1649*. Oxford: Oxford University Press, 1979; Carlisle: Paternoster, 1997.

Kinlaw, C. J. "Determinism and the Hiddenness of God in Calvin's Theology." *Religious Studies* 24, no. 4 (1988): 497-509.

Klauber, Martin I. Review of *John Calvin's Exegesis of the Old Testament*, by D. L. Puckett. *Calvin Theological Journal* 31 (1996): 293-294.

Kline, M. G. "Job." In *The Wycliffe Bible Commentary*. Ed. Charles F. Pfeiffer and Everett F. Harrison, 459-490. Chicago, IL: Moody Press, 1962.

———. "Trial by Ordeal." In *Through Christ's Word: A Festschrift for Dr. Philip E. Hughes*, 81-93. Phillipsburg, NJ: Presbyterian and Reformed Publishing Co., 1985.

Klooster, Fred. *Calvin's Doctrine of Predestination*. Grand Rapids, MI: Calvin Theological Seminary, 1961.

———. *The Incomprehensibility of God in the Orthodox Presbyterian Conflict*. Franeker: T. Wever, 1951.

Klooster, Fred and Cornelius van der Kooi. "Within proper limits: Basic features of John Calvin's theological epistemology." *Calvin Theological Journal* 29 (1994): 364-387.

Kraeling, E. G. *The Old Testament since the Reformation*. New York: Schocken Books, 1969.

Kraus, Hans-Joachim. "Calvin's Exegetical Principles." *Interpretation* 31 (1977): 8-18.

Kristeller, P. O. *Renaissance Thought and Its Sources*. New York: Columbia University Press, 1979.

Krusche, W. *Das wirken des Heilgen Geistes nach Calvin*. Göttingen: Vanden hoeck & Ruprect, 1957.

Lachman, David C. *The Marrow Controversy*. Edinburgh: Rutherford House, 1988.

Lane, A.N.S. "Bondage and Liberation in Calvin's Treatise against Pighius," in J.H. Leith and R.A. Johnson (edd), *Calvin Studies IX* (Davidson (NC): Davidson College and Davidson College Presbyterian Church, 1998), 16-45.

———. *Calvin and Bernard of Clairvaux*. Studies in Reformed Theology and History. Princeton, NJ: Princeton Theological Seminary, 1996.

———. "Calvin and His Times." *Evangelical Quarterly* 61 (1985): 281-85.

———. "Calvin's Doctrine of Assurance." *Vox Evangelica* 11 (1979): 42-44.

———. "Calvin's sources of St. Bernard." *Archiv für Reformationsgeschichte* 67 (1976): 253-83.

———. "Conversion: a comparison of Calvin and Spener." *Themelios* 13 (1987): 19-21.

———. "Did Calvin Believe in Freewill?" *Vox Evangelica* 12 (1981): 72-90.

———. "Early printed Patristic Anthologies to 1556: A progress report." *Studia Patristica*. Edited by E. Livingstone. 18(4): 365-370.

———. "Guide to Calvin Literature." *Vox Evangelica* 17 (1987): 35-47.

———. "John Calvin: The Witness of the Holy Spirit." *Faith and Ferment*, Papers Read at the Westminster Conference, London, 1982, 1-17.

———. *The Lion Concise Book of Christian Thought*. Oxford: Lion, 1996.

———. "The Quest for the Historical Calvin." *Evangelical Quarterly* 55 (1983): 95-113.

———. "Recent Calvin Literature: A Review Article." *Themelios* 16 (1991): 17-24.

_____. Review of *Calvin's Perspectival Anthropology*, by Mary Potter Engel. *Themelios* 16 (1991): 21-22.

Lang, August. "The Sources of Calvin's Institutes of 1536." *Evangelical Quarterly* 8 (1936): 130-41.

Lecerf, Auguste. "The Liturgy of the Holy Supper at Geneva in 1542." *Reformed Liturgics* 3 (1966), no page numbers.

Lee, Sou-Young. "Calvin's Understanding of Pietas." In *Calvinus Sincerioris Religionis Vindex*, ed. Wilhelm H. Neuser & Brian G. Armstrong, 225-240. Sixteenth Century Essays & Studies, vol. 36. Kirksville, KY: Sixteenth Century Journal Publishers, Inc., 1997.

Lehmann, P. L. "The Reformers' Use of the Bible." *Theology Today* 3 (1946): 496-502.

Leith, J. H. "Calvin's Theological Method and the Ambiguity in His Theology." In *Reformation Studies: Essays in Honor of Roland H. Bainton*, ed. F. H. Little, 106-114. Richmond, VA: John Knox Press, 1962.

_____. *An Introduction to the Reformed Tradition*. Atlanta, GA: John Knox Press, 1978.

_____. *John Calvin's Doctrine of the Christian Life*. Louisville, KY: Westminster/John Knox Press, 1989.

_____. "John Calvin – Theologian of the Bible." *Interpretation* 25 (1971): 329-44.

Leithart, Peter. "Stoic Elements in Calvin's Doctrine of the Christian Life. Part I: Original Corruption, Natural Law, and the Order of the Soul." *Westminster Theological Journal* 55 (1993): 31-54.

_____. "Stoic Elements in Calvin's Doctrine of the Christian Life. Part II: Mortification." *Westminster Theological Journal* 55 (1993): 191-208.

_____. "Stoic Elements in Calvin's Doctrine of the Christian Life. Part III: Christian Moderation." *Westminster Theological Journal* 56 (1994): 59-85.

_____. "That Eminent Pagan: Calvin's Use of Cicero in Institutes I.1.5." *Westminster Theological Journal* 52 (1990): 1-12.

Letham, R. W. A. "Saving Faith and Assurance in Reformed Theology: Zwingli to the Synod of Dordt." Ph.D. diss., Aberdeen University, 1979.

Lillback, P. A. "The Binding of God: Calvin's Role in the Development of Covenant Theology." Ph.D. diss., Westminster Theological Seminary, 1985.

_____. "Calvin's Covenantal Response to the Anabaptist View of Baptism." *Christianity and Civilization* 1 (1982): 185-232.

_____. "The Continuing Conundrum: Calvin and Conditionality of the Covenant." *Calvin Theological Journal* 29 (1994): 42-74.

_____. "Ursinus' Development of the Covenant of Creation: A Debt to Melancthon or Calvin?" *Westminster Theological Journal* 43 (1981): 247-88.

Livingston, James Craig. "A Theodicy of Submission: The Mystery of God's Sovereignty." In *Anatomy of the Sacred: An Introduction to Religion*, 275-279. New York: Macmillan Publishing Co., 1989.

Livingston, R. W., ed. *The Legacy of Greece*. Oxford: The Clarendon Press, 1921.

Long, J. H. "Calvin as an Old Testament Commentator." *Reformed Church Review* 13 (1909): 165-82.

Mackintosh, H. R. "John Calvin, Expositor and Dogmatist." *Review and Expositor* 7 (1910): 179-94.

Macleod, Donald. *The Doctrine of the Person of Jesus Christ.* Edinburgh: T. & T. Clark, 1913.

Macleod, Donald. "Living the Christian Life: Luther and Calvin on the Place of the Law." *Living the Christian Life.* The Westminster Conference Papers. 1974: 5-13.

McCarthy, David B. Review of *John Calvin's Exegesis of the Old Testament*, by D. L. Puckett. *Sixteenth Century Journal* 26, no. 4 (1995): 953-954.

McClelland [sic], J. C. "The Reformed Doctrine of Predestination." *Scottish Journal of Theology* 8 (1955): 255-271.

McCormack, Bruce L. "Recurring hermeneutical principles in Calvin's sermons, polemical treatises and correspondence," (Response) in *Calvin as Exegete.* Papers and responses presented at the Ninth Colloquium on Calvin & Calvin Studies sponsored by the Calvin Studies Society held at Princeton Theological Seminary, Princeton, NJ, on May 20, 21 and 22, 1993. Edited by Peter De Klerk, 89-93. Grand Rapids, MI: Calvin Studies Society, 1995.

McGowan, A. T. B. *The Federal Theology of Thomas Boston (1676-1732).* Carlisle, Cumbria: Paternoster Press/Edinburgh: Rutherford House, 1997.

McGrath, Alister E. *The Intellectual Origins of the European Reformation.* Oxford: Blackwell Publishers, 1987.

_____. *Iustitia Dei: A History of the Christian Doctrine of Justification.* Vol. 1, *From the Beginning to 1500.* Cambridge: Cambridge University Press, 1986.

_____. *Iustitia Dei: A History of the Christian Doctrine of Justification.* Vol. 2, *From 1500 to the Present Day.* Cambridge: Cambridge University Press, 1986.

_____. "John Calvin and Late Medieval Thought: A Study in Late Medieval Influences upon Calvin's Theological Development." *Archiv Fur Reformationsgeschichte* 77 (1986): 58-78.

_____. *A Life of John Calvin.* Oxford: Blackwell Publishers, 1990.

McKane, William. "Calvin as an Old Testament Commentator." *Nederduitse Gereformeerde Teologiese Tydskrif* 25 (1984): 250-59.

McKee, Elsie Anne. "Exegesis, Theology, and Development in Calvin's *Institutio.*" In *Probing the Reformed Tradition: Historical Studies in Honor of Edward A. Dowey, Jr.*, ed. Elsie Anne McKee and Brian G. Armstrong. Louisville, Ky.: Westminster/John Knox Press, 1989.

_____. Review of *John Calvin's Exegesis of the Old Testament*, by D. L. Puckett. *Theology Today* 52 (1996): 554-555.

McKim, Donald K. Review of *Calvin and the Rhetoric of Piety*, by Serene Jones. *Theological Studies* 58 (1997): 166-168.

_____. Review of *John Calvin's Exegesis of the Old Testament*, by D. L. Puckett. *Theological Studies* 57 (1996): 568.

_____, ed. *Encyclopedia of the Reformed Faith.* Louisville, KY: Westminster/John Knox Press, 1992.

McNeill, J. T. *The History and Character of Calvinism.* New York: Oxford University Press, 1977.

_____. "Natural Law in the Teaching of the Reformers." *Journal of Religion* 26 (1946): 168-82.

McPhee, Ian. "Conserver or Transformer of Calvin's Theology? A Study of the Origins and Development of Theodore Beza's Thought, 1550-1570." Ph.D. thesis,

Cambridge University, 1979.
Mickelsen, John K. "The Relationship between the Commentaries of J. Calvin and his Institutes of the Christian Religion ..." *The Gordon Review* 5, no. 4 (1959): 155-68.
Miln, Peter. "Hommes D'une Bonne Cause." Ph.D. diss., Nottingham University, 1989.
Milner, B. C. *Calvin's Doctrine of the Church*. Vol. 5 of *Studies in the History of Christian Thought*, ed. by H. A. Oberman. Leiden: E. J. Brill, 1970.
Mitchell, Alexander F. *Catechisms of the Second Reformation*. London: James Nisbett and Co., 1886.
Monsma, E. B. "The Preaching Style of Jean Calvin: An Analysis of the Psalm Sermons of the 'Supplementa Calviniana.'" Ph.D. diss., Rutgers University, 1986.
Monter, E. W. *Calvin's Geneva*. New York: Wiley, 1967.
Mozley, J. B. *Lectures and Other Theological Papers*. New York: E. P. Dutton, 1883.
Muller, Richard. "Biblical Interpretation in the Era of the Reformation: The View from the Middle Ages." In *Biblical Interpretation in the Era of the Reformation: Essays Presented to David C. Steinmetz in Honor of the Sixtieth Birthday*, ed. R. A. Muller and J. Thompson. Grand Rapids, MI: Eerdmans, 1996.
_____. "Calvin and the 'Calvinists': Assessing Continuities and Discontinuities between the Reformation and Orthodoxy." *Calvin Theological Journal* 30 (1995): 345-75, and 31 (1996): 125-60.
_____. "Calvin's Exegesis of Old Testament Prophecies." *In The Bible in the Sixteenth Century*, ed. David C. Steinmetz. Durham, London: Duke University Press, 1990.
_____. *Christ and the Decree: Christology and Predestination in Reformed Theology from Calvin to Perkins*. Grand Rapids, MI: Baker Book House, 1986.
_____. "Covenant and Conscience in English Reformed Theology: Three Variations on a Seventeenth Century Theme." *Westminster Theological Journal* 42 (1979-80): 308-34.
_____. *Dictionary of Latin and Greek Theological Terms*. Grand Rapids, MI: Baker Book House, 1985.
_____. "*Duplex Cognitio Dei* in the Theology of the Early Reformed Orthodoxy." *Sixteenth Century Journal* 10 (1979): 51-61.
_____. "The Era of Protestant Orthodoxy." In *Theological Education in the Evangelical Tradition*, ed. D. G. Hart and R. A. Muller. Grand Rapids, MI: Baker Book House, 1996.
_____. "*Fides* and *Cognitio* in Relation to the Problem of Intellect and Will in the Theology of John Calvin." *Calvin Theological Journal* 25 (1990): 207-224.
_____. "Giving Direction to Theology: The Scholastic Dimension." *Journal of the Evangelical Theological Society* 28 (1985): 183-193.
_____. *God, Creation and Providence in the Thought of Jacob Arminius*. Grand Rapids, MI: Baker Book House, 1991.
_____. "God, Predestination, and the Integrity of the Created Order: A Note on Patterns in Arminius' Theology." In *Later Calvinism: International Perspectives*, ed. W. F. Graham. Kirksville, KY: Sixteenth Century Journal Publishers, 1994.

_____. "The Hermeneutic of Promise and fulfillment in Calvin's Exegesis of the Old Testament Prophecies of the Kingdom." In *The Bible in the Sixteenth Century*, ed. David C. Steinmetz, 68-82, 214-221. Duke Monographs in Medieval and Renaissance Studies, 11. Durham: Duke University Press, 1990.

_____. "The Myth of 'Decretal' Theology." *Calvin Theological Journal* 30 (1995): 159-67.

_____. "Orthodoxy, Reformed." *Encyclopedia of the Reformed Faith*, ed. D. K. McKim and D. F. Wright. Louisville, KY: Westminster/ John Knox Press, 1992.

_____. "Perkins' *A Golden Chaine*: Predestinarian System or Schematized *Ordo Salutis*?" in *Sixteenth Century Journal* 9 (1978): 69-81.

_____. *Post-Reformation Reformed Dogmatics: Holy Scripture: The Cognitive Foundation of Theology*. Grand Rapids, MI: Baker Book House, 1993.

_____. *Post-Reformation Reformed Dogmatics: Prolegomena to Theology*. Grand Rapids, MI: Baker Book House, 1987.

_____. Review of *Calvin and the Rhetoric of Piety*, by Serene Jones. *Calvin Theological Journal* 31 (1996): 582-583.

_____. *The Unaccommodated Calvin*. New York and Oxford: Oxford University Press, 1999.

_____. "The Use and Abuse of a Document: Beza's *Tabula Praedestinationis*, the Bolsec Controversy, and the Origins of Reformed Orthodoxy." In *Protestant Scholasticism: Essays in Reassessment*, ed. Carl R. Trueman and R. S. Scott. Carlisle, Cumbria: Paternoster Press, 1999.

Murray, J. "Calvin as Theologian and Expositor" Lecture of the Evangelical Library, 1964. In *Collected Writings*. Vol. 1, 305-11. Edinburgh: The Banner of Truth Trust, 1976.

_____. *Calvin on Scripture and Divine Sovereignty*. Grand Rapids, MI: Baker Book House, 1960.

_____. *The Epistle to the Romans*. Grand Rapids, MI: Eerdmans, 1973.

_____. *Principles of Conduct*. London: The Tyndale Press, 1957. Reprint 1971.

Naphy, William G. *Calvin and the Consolidation of the Genevan Reformation* (Manchester/New York: Manchester University Press, 1994).

Neuser, Wilhelm H. "The Development of the *Institutes* 1536 to 1559." In *John Calvin's Institutes: His Opus Magnum*, 33-54. Potchefstroom, 1986.

_____, ed. *Calvinus Ecclesiae Doctor*. Kampen: Kok, 1980.

_____. *Calvinus Ecclesiae Genevensis Custos*. Frankfurt am Main/Bern/New York: Verlag Peter Lang, 1984.

_____. *Calvinus Sacrae Scripturae Professor*. Grand Rapids, MI: Eerdmans, 1994.

_____. *Calvinus Servus Christi*. Budapest: Presseabteilung des Ráday-Kollegiums, 1988.

_____. *Calvinus Theologus*. Neukirchen: Neukirchen-Vluyn: Neukirchener Verlag, 1976.

Neuser, Wilhelm H., and Brian G. Armstrong, ed. *Calvinus Sincerioris Religionis Vindex*. Sixteenth Century Essays & Studies, vol.36. Kirksville, KY: Sixteenth Century Journal Publishers, Inc., 1997.

Nicole, Roger. "John Calvin and Inerrancy." *Journal of the Evangelical Theological Society* 25 (December 1982): 425-44.

Niesel, Wilhelm. *Calvin - Bibliographie 1901-1959*. Kaiser Verlag Munchen, 1961.
_____. *Reformed Symbolics*. Translated by D. Lewis. Edinburgh and London: Oliver and Boyd, 1962.
_____. *The Theology of Calvin*. Translated by H. Knight. Philadelphia: The WestminsterPress, 1956.
Oberman, Heiko. *The Dawn of the Reformation*. Grand Rapids, MI: Eerdmans, 1992.
_____. *Forerunners of the Reformation*. London/New York: Holt, Rinehart and Winston, 1967.
_____. *The Harvest of Medieval Theology: Gabriel Biel and Late Medieval Nominalism*. Cambridge: MA: Harvard University Press, 1963.
_____. *Initia Calvini: The Matrix of Calvin's Reformation*. Amsterdam/New York/Oxford/Tokyo: Koninklijke Nederlandse Akademie van Weteschappen, 1991.
_____. "Some Notes on the Theology of Nominalism." *Harvard Theological Review* (1960): 47-76.
_____. "*Via Antiqua* and *Via Moderna*: Late Medieval Prolegomena to Early Reformation Thought." *Journal of the History of Ideas* 48, no. 1 (1987): 23-40.
Olson, Jeannine E. "Libertines." *The Oxford Encyclopedia of the Reformation*, ed. Hans J. Hillerbrand. New York, Oxford: Oxford University Press, 1996.
_____. Review of *John Calvin: A Sixteenth Century Portrait*, in *Theological Studies* 50.1 (1989): 188-190.
O'Malley, John W. "Sixteenth-Century Treatises on Preaching." In *Renaissance Eloquence*, ed. James J. Murphy. Berkeley: University of California Press, 1983.
Oosterbaan, J. A. "Calvin on the Covenant." *Reformed Review* 33 (1979-80): 136-49.
_____. "The Reformation of the Reformation: Fundamentals of Anabaptist Theology," *The Mennonite Quarterly Review* 51 (1977): 171-95.
Ortlund, Raymond C. Review of *Where Shall Wisdom be Found?*, by Susan Schreiner. *Journal of the Evangelical Theological Society* 39 (1996): 292.
*The Oxford English Dictionary*. 13 vols. Oxford: Clarendon Press, 1970.
Packer, J. I. "Calvin the Theologian." *The Churchman* 73 (1959): 127-136. Also in *International Reformed* Bulletin 2:4 (October 1959): 15-24. Revised in *John Calvin*, ed. Gervase E. Duffield, 149-175. Vol. 1 of Courtenay Studies in the Reformation Theology. Grand Rapids, MI: Eerdmans, 1966.
Palmer, I. B. "The Authority and Doctrine of Scripture in the Thought of J. Calvin." *Evangelical Quarterly* 49 (1977): 30-39.
Parker, T. D. "The Interpretation of Scripture: A Comparison of Calvin and Luther on Galatians." *Interpretation* 17 (1963): 61-75.
Parker, T. H. L. "The Approach to Calvin." *The Evangelical Quarterly* 16 (1944): 165-172.
_____. *Calvin: An Introduction to His Thought*. Louisville, KY: Westminster/John Knox Press, 1995.
_____. "Calvin's Doctrine of Justification." *Evangelical Quarterly* 24 (1952): 100-107.
_____. *Calvin's New Testament Commentaries*. Louisville, KY: Westminster/John Knox Press, 1993.
_____. *Calvin's New Testament Commentaries*. Grand Rapids, MI: Eerdmans, 1971.

_____. *Calvin's Old Testament Commentaries.* Edinburgh: T. & T. Clark Ltd., 1986.

_____. *The Oracles of God: An Introduction to the Preaching of John Calvin.* London: Butterworth, 1947

_____. *Calvin's Preaching.* Louisville, KY: Westminster/John Knox Press, 1992.

_____. "Calvin the Biblical Expositor." *Courtenay Studies in Reformation Theology*, No. 1. Edited by G. E. Duffield. Grand Rapids, MI: Eerdmans, 1966: 176-189.

_____. *John Calvin.* Herts, England: Lion Publishing, 1987.

_____. Review of *Dieu, la création et la providence dans la prédication de Calvin*, by Richard Stauffer. *Scottish Journal of Theology* 33, no. 1 (1980): 73-75.

_____. "The Shadow and the Sketch." In *Calvinus Reformator*, ed. B. J. Van der Walt, 142-148. Potchefstroom: Institute for Reformational Study, Potchefstroom University, 1982.

_____. *Supplementa Calviniana: An Account of the Manuscripts of Calvin's Sermons now in Course of Preparation.* London: Tyndale Press, 1962.

Partee, Charles Brooks. *Calvin and Classical Philosophy.* Studies in the History of Christian Thought, no. 14. Leiden: E. J. Brill, 1977.

_____. "Calvin and Determinism." In *An Elaboration of the Theology of Calvin*, ed. Richard Craig Gamble, 351-356. Articles on Calvin and Calvinism, 8. New York & London: Garland Publishing, 1992. Also in *Christian Scholar's Review* 5 (1975): 123-128.

_____. "Calvin, Calvinism, and Philosophy: A Prolusion." *Reformed Review* 33 (1980): 129-135.

_____. "Calvin's Central Dogma Again." *Sixteenth Century Journal* 18 (1987): 191-99.

_____. Review of *Calvin's Perspectival Anthropology*, by Mary Potter Engel. *The Journal of Religion* 69 (1989): 553-554.

Peake, A. S. *Job.* Century Bible. Edinburgh: T. & T. Clark, 1905.

Pelikan, Jaroslav. *The Christian Tradition.* Vol. 4, *Reformation of Church and Dogma (1300-1700).* Chicago: University of Chicago Press, 1984.

_____. *The Christian Tradition.* Vol. 5, *Christian Doctrine and Modern Culture (since 1700).* Chicago: University of Chicago Press, 1984.

_____. *Historical Theology: Continuity and Change in Christian Doctrine.* London, New York: Hutchinson, 1971.

Peter, Rodolphe. "Rhetorique et prédication selon Calvin." *Revue d'histoire et de philosophie religieuses* 55 (1975): 249-272.

Peterson, Robert A. *Calvin's Doctrine of the Atonement.* Phillipsburg, NJ: Presbyterian and Reformed Publishing Co., 1983.

Peyer, Etienne de. "Calvin's Doctrine of Providence" *The Evangelical Quarterly* 10 (1938): 30-44.

Phillips, Nancy Van Wyk. "Divine Providence: Meaning in the Details." *Perspectives* 6 (March 1991): 10-13.

Pitkin, Barbara. "What Pure Eyes Could See: Faith, Creation, and History in John Calvin's Theology." Ph.D. diss. University of Chicago, 1994.

Placher, William C. *A History of Christian Theology: An Introduction.* Philadelphia,

PA: The Westminster Press, 1983.

Pope, M. *Job*. Anchor Bible. Garden City, NY: Doubleday, 1965.

Postema, G. J. "Calvin's Alleged Rejection of Natural Theology." *Scottish Journal of Theology* 24 (1971): 423-34.

Potgieter, Pieter C. "The Providence of God in Calvin's Correspondence." In *Calvin: Erbe und Auftrag*, ed. von Willem van't Spijker, 85-94. Kampen: Kok Pharos Publishing House, 1991.

_____. "Perspectives on the doctrine pf providence in some of Calvin's sermons on Job." *Hervormde Teologiese Studies* 54 (1998): 36-49.

Potter, G. R. ed., Vol. I: The Renaissance: 1495-1520. In *The New Cambridge Modern History*. 14 vols. Cambridge: Cambridge University Press, 1957-61.

Preus, J. S. *From Shadow to Promise: Old Testament Interpretation from Augustine to the Young Luther*. Cambridge, MA: Belknap Press, 1969.

Prust, R. C. "Was Calvin a Biblical Literalist?" *Scottish Journal of Theology* 20 (1967): 312-28.

Puckett, David L. *John Calvin's Exegesis of the Old Testament*. Columbia Series in Reformed Theology. Louisville, KY: Westminster/John Knox Press, 1995.

Rainbow, Jonathan H. *The Will of God and the Cross: An Historical and Theological Study of John Calvin's Doctrine of Limited Atonement*. Princeton Theological Monograph Series. Allison Park: Pickwick Publications, 1990.

Raitt, Jill. "Beza, Guide for the Faithful Life. Lectures on Job, Sermons on Song of Songs, 1587." *Scottish Journal of Theology* 39 (1986): 83-87.

_____. Review of *Calvin's Perspectival Anthropology*, by Mary Potter Engel. *Sixteenth Century Journal* 21, no. 2 (1990): 324-325.

Ramm, B. *Protestant Biblical Interpretation*. Boston: Wilde, 1956.

Rankin, W. Duncan. "Carnal Union with Christ in the Theology of T. F. Torrance." Ph.D. diss., University of Edinburgh, 1997.

Reardon, P. H. "Calvin on Providence: The Development of the Insight." *Scottish Journal of* Theology 28 (1975): 517-534.

Reid, J. K. S. *The Authority of Scripture: A Study of the Reformation and Post-Reformation Understanding of the Bible*. London: Menthuen, 1957.

_____. "Reformation in France and Scotland: A Case Study in Sixteenth-Century Communication." In *Later Calvinism*, ed. W. F. Graham, 195-214. Sixteenth Century Essays and Studies, vol. 22. Kirksville, KY: Sixteenth Century Journal Publishers, 1994. 195-214.

Reid, W. B. "Calvin's Interpretation of the Reformation." *Evangelical Quarterly* 32 (1960): 4-22

Reid, W. S., ed. *John Calvin: His Influence in the Western World*. Grand Rapids, MI: Zondervan, 1982.

Reist, Benjamin A. *A Reading of Calvin's Institutes*. Louisville, KY: Westminster/John Knox Press, 1991.

Reuter, Karl. *Das Grundverständ is der Theologie Calvins*. Neukirchen: Verlag des Erziehungsvereins, 1963.

Reynolds, Blair. "Calvin's Exegesis of Jeremiah and Micah: Use or Abuse of Scripture." *Proceedings* 11 (1991): 81-91.

Richard, Lucien. "The Devotio Moderna." In *Devotio Moderna: The Spirituality of*

*John Calvin*. Atlanta: John Knox, 1974: 12-47.

Robertson, A. T. "Calvin as an Interpreter of Scripture." *Review and Expositor* 6 (1909): 577-78.

Rolston, Holmes, III. *John Calvin versus the Westminster Confession*. Richmond, VA: John Knox Press, 1972.

_____. "Responsible Man in Reformed Theology: Calvin versus the Westminster Confession." *Scottish Journal of Theology* 23 (1970): 129-55.

Rossall, Judith. Review of *Calvin and the Rhetoric of Piety*, by Serene Jones. *Expository Times* 107 (1995): 344.

Roussouw, H. W. "Calvin's Hermeneutics of Holy Scripture." In *Calvinus Reformator*, ed. B. J. Van der Walt, 149-180. Potchefstroom: Institute for Reformational Study, Potchefstroom University, 1982.

Rowley, H. H. *Job*. The Century Bible (New Series). London: Thomas Nelson and Sons Ltd., 1970.

Runia, K. "The Hermeneutics of the Reformers." *Calvin Theological Journal* 19 (1984): 121-52.

Rupp, E. G. "The Bible in the Age of Reformation." In *The Church's Use of the Bible*, ed. D. E. Nineham. London: S. P. C. K., 1963.

_____. *Patterns of Reformation*. London: Epworth Press, 1969.

_____. *The Righteousness of God*. London: Hodder & Stoughton, 1963.

Russell, S. H. "Calvin and the Messianic Interpretation of the Psalms." *Scottish Journal of Theology* 21 (1968): 37-47.

Schaff, P. "Calvin as a Commentator." *Presbyterian and Reformed Review* 3 (July 1892): 23-28.

_____. ed. *The Creeds of Christendom With a History and Critical Notes*, Vol. II "The Greek and Latin Creeds." Grand Rapids: Baker Books, 1983.

Schreiner, Susan E. "Exegesis and Double Justice in Calvin's Sermons on Job." *Church History* 58 (1989): 322-338.

_____. *The Theater of His Glory: Nature and the Natural Order in the Thought of John Calvin*. With a foreword by Richard A. Muller. Grand Rapids, MI: Baker Book House, 1991.

_____. "'Through a Mirror dimly': Calvin's Sermons on Job." In *Calvin and Hermeneutics*, ed. Richard Craig Gamble, 231-249. Articles on Calvin and Calvinism, 6. New York & London: Garland Publishing, 1992. Also in *Calvin Theological Journal* 21 (1986): 175-193.

_____. *Where Shall Wisdom Be Found? Calvin's Exegesis of Job from Medieval and Modern Perspectives*. Chicago, IL: University of Chicago Press, 1994.

Schulze, L. F. "Calvin on Preaching." *Hervormde Teoloiese Studies* 54 (1998): 50-59.

Schweizer, Alexander. *Die Glaubenslehre der evangelische-reformierten Kirche dargestellt und den Quellen belegt*. 2 vols. Zurich: Orell, Fussli, 1944-47.

_____. *Die protestantischen Centraldogmen in ihrer Entwicklung innerhalb der reformatierten Kirche*. 2 vols. Zurick: 1854-56.

Selinger, Suzanne. *Calvin Against Himself: An Inquiry in Intellectual History*. Hamden, CT: Archon Books, 1984.

Shepherd, Victor A. *The Nature and Function of Faith in the Theology of John Calvin*. NABPR Diss. Series, Number 2. Macon, GA: Mercer University Press, 1983.

Smart, J. D. *The Interpretation of Scripture*. Philadelphia: The Westminster Press, 1961.
Smeaton, George. *Christ's Doctrine of the Atonement*. Edinburgh: Banner of Truth, (1870). Reprint 1991.
Snaith, N. H. *The Book of Job*. London: SCM Press, 1968.
Spitz, Lewis, ed. *The Reformation*. Lexington: D. C. Health & Company, 1982.
Stam, David H. "England's Calvin: A Study of the Publication of John Calvin's Works in Tudor England." Ph.D. diss., Northwestern University, 1978.
Stapulensis, Jacobus Faber. "Introduction to Commentary on the Psalms." *Forerunners of the Reformation*, ed. Heiko A. Oberman. London/New York: Holt, Rinehart and Winston, 1967.
Stauffer, Richard. *Dieu, la création et la providence dans la prédication de Calvin*. Basler und Berner Studien zur historischen und systematischen Theologie, no. 33. Bern: Peter Lang, 1978.
_____. "Dieu, la Création et la Providence dans l'oeuvre homilétique de Calvin." *La Revue Réformée* 112 (1977): 196-203.
_____. "Les Sermons inedits de Calvin sur le livre de la Genese." *Regards Contemporains sur Jean Calvin*. Paris: Presses universitaires de France, 1965.
_____. "Quelques aspects insolites de la théologie du premier article dans la prédication de Calvin." In *Calvinus Ecclesiae Doctor*, ed. W. H. Neuser. Kampen: Kok Pharos Publishing House, 1978.
Steenkamp, Johan J. "A Review of the Concept of Progress in Calvin's Institutes." *Calvin: Erbe und Auftrag, Festschrift for W.H. Neuser*, ed. Willem van't Spijker, 69-76. Kampen: Kok Pharos Publishing House, 1991.
Steinmetz, David. "Calvin and Abraham: The Interpretation of Romans 4 in the Sixteenth Century." *Church History* 57 (1988): 443-88.
_____. "Calvin and the Absolute Power of God." *Journal of Medieval and Renaissance Studies* 18, no. 1 (Spring 1988): 65-79.
_____. "Calvin and the Divided Self of Romans 7." In *Augustine, the Harvest, and Theology (1300-1650)*. Essays dedicated to Heiko Augustinus Oberman in honor of his sixtieth birthday, ed. Kenneth Hagen, 300-313. Leiden: E. J. Brill, 1990.
_____. "Calvin and the Natural Knowledge of God." In *Via Augustini: Augustine in the later Middle Ages, Renaissance, and Reformation: Essays in Honor of Damasus Trapp*, ed. H. A. Oberman and F. A. James, 142-156. Leiden: E. J. Brill, 1991.
_____. "Calvin and the Patristic Exegesis of Paul." In *The Bible in the Sixteenth Century*, ed. David C. Steinmetz, 100-118, 231-235. Duke Monographs in Medieval and Renaissance Studies, 11. Durham: Duke University Press, 1990.
_____. *Calvin in Context*. New York, Oxford: Oxford University Press, 1995.
_____. "Divided by a Common Past: The Reshaping of the Christian Exegetical Tradition in the Sixteenth Century." *Journal of Medieval and Early Modern Studies*, (forthcoming).
_____. "Hermeneutic and Old Testament Interpretation in Staupitz and the young Martin Luther." *Archiv für Reformationsgeschichte* 70 (1979): 24-58.
_____. "John Calvin on Isaiah 6: A Problem in the History of Exegesis." *Interpretation* 36 (1982): 156-170.

_____. *Luther and Staupitz: An Essay in the Intellectual Origins of the Protestant Reformation*. Durham, NC: Duke University Press, 1980.

_____. *Misericordia Dei: The Theology of Jannes von Staupitz in its Late Medieval Setting*. Leiden: E. J. Brill, 1968.

_____. *Reformers in the Wings*. Philadelphia, PA: Fortress Press, 1971.

_____. "The Scholastic Calvin." In *Protestant Scholasticism: Essays in Reassessment*, ed. Carl R. Trueman and R. S. Scott. Carlisle, Cumbria: Paternoster Press, 1999.

_____. "The Theology of Calvin and Calvinism." In *Reformation Europe: A Guide to Research*, ed. S. Ozment, 211-232. St. Louis: Center for Reformation Research, 1982.

Stek, J. H. "The Modern Problem of the Old Testament in the Light of Reformation Perspective." *Calvin Theological Journal* 2 (1967): 202-25.

Stickelberger, Emmanuel. *Calvin*. Translated by David George Gelzer. Cambridge: James Clarke & Co., Ltd., 1977.

Strohl, H. "La méthode exégétique des Réformateurs." In *Le probléme biblique dans le Protestantisme*, ed. J. Boisset. Paris: Presses universitaires de France, 1955.

_____. "La Pensée de Calvin sur la Providence divine." *Revue d'Histoire et de Philosophie religieuses* 22 (1942): 154-169.

Stroup, George W. "Narrative in Calvin's Hermeneutic." In *Calvin Studies III*, ed. John H. Leith. Richmond: Union Theological Seminary in Virginia, 1986.

Tamburello, Dennis E. *Union with Christ: John Calvin and the Mysticism of St. Bernard*. Louisville, KY: Westminster/John Knox Press, 1994.

Tanner, Norman P. ed., *Decrees of the Ecumenical Councils*, Vol. 1 "Nicea 1 to Lateran V." Sheed & Ward/Georgetown University Press, 1990.

Tawney, R. H. *Religion and the Rise of Capitalism*. Harmondsworth: Penguin, 1938.

Tertullian. *Ad Nationes*. In *Ante-Nicene Fathers*, ed. A. Roberts and J. Donaldson, vol. 3, 109-147. Grand Rapids, MI: Eerdmans, 1973.

Thomas, Derek. "Calvin's Preaching on Job." In *Westminster Conference Papers*, 33-56. 1998.

_____. "Doctrine of Immediate Retribution." *Reformed Theological Journal* (November 1995): 57-74.

Thomas, G. M. *The Extent of the Atonement: A Dilemma for Reformed Theology from Calvin to the Consensus (1536-1675)*. Carlisle, Cumbria: Paternoster Publishing, 1997.

Thomas, John Newton. "The Place of Natural Theology in the Thought of John Calvin." *Articles on Calvin and Calvinism: A Fourteen-Volume Anthology of Scholarly Articles*, ed. Richard C. Gamble. Vol. 7, 147-176. London/New York: Garland Publishing, Inc., 1992.

Tillich, Paul. *A History of Christian Thought*. Edited by Carl Braaten. New York: Harper & Row, 1968.

Torrance, T. F. "Calvin and the Knowledge of God." *The Christian Century* 81 (1964): 696-699.

_____. *Calvin's Doctrine of Man*. London: Lutterworth Press, 1949.

_____. "Calvin's doctrine of the Trinity." *Calvin Theological Journal* 25 (1990): 165-193.

_____. "Calvin's Theology, Theology Proper, Eschatology." *Revue d'Histoire et de Philosophie Religieuses* 44 (1964): 402-422.

_____. *The Christian Frame of Mind*. Edinburgh: The Handsel Press, 1985.

_____. "The Doctrine of the Holy Trinity: Gregory of Nazianzen and John Calvin." *Calvin Studies V*. [Papers] presented at a Colloquium on Calvin Studies at Davidson College and Davidson College Presbyterian Church, Davidson, North Carolina, January 1920, 1990, ed. John H. Leith, 7-19. Davidson: Davidson College, 1990.

_____. *The Hermeneutics of John Calvin*. Edinburgh: Scottish Academic Press, 1988.

_____. "Intuitive and Abstractive Knowledge from Duns Scotus to John Calvin." In *De doctrina Ioannis Duns Scoti: Acta tertii Congressus Scotistici Internationalis*. Rome: 1972.

_____. *Kingdom and Church: A Study in the Theology of the Reformation*. Edinburgh: Oliver & Boyd, 1956.

_____. "La philosophie et la théologie de Jean Mair ou Major (1469-1550)." *Archives de philosophie* 32 (1969): 531-47.

_____. "Legal and Evangelical Priests: The Holy Ministry as Reflected in Calvin's Prayers." *Calvin's Books*, Festschrift (Peter de Klerk). Edited by Wilhelm H. Neuser, Herman J. Selderhuis and Wilhelm van 't Spijker, 63-74. Heerenveen: Groen, 1997.

_____. *The Mediation of Christ*. Grand Rapids, MI: Eerdmans, 1983.

_____. *Scottish Theology: From John Knox to John McLeod Campbell*. Edinburgh: T. & T. Clark, 1996.

_____. *Space, Time and Resurrection*. Edinburgh: The Handsel Press, 1976.

_____. *Theology in Reconciliation: Essays towards Evangelical and Catholic Unity in East and West*. London: Geoffrey Chapman, 1975.

_____. *The Trinitarian Faith*. Edinburgh: T. & T. Clark, 1988.

Trinkaus, C. E. "Renaissance Problems in Calvin's Theology." *Studies in Renaissance* 1 (1954): 59-80.

Troeltsch, E. "Calvin and Calvinism." *Hibbert Journal* 8 (1909): 102-121.

Turretini, Francis. *Institutio Theologiae Elenchticae*. Edinburgh: John D. Lowe, 1847. English translation by George Musgrave Giger. Edited by James T. Dennison, Jr. 3 Vols. Phillipsburg, NJ: Presbyterian and Reformed Publishing, 1992, 1994, 1997.

Tylanda [sic], Joseph. "Christ the Mediator: Calvin versus Stancaro." *Calvin Theological Journal* 8 (1973): 5-16.

Tylenda, Joseph N. "Calvin and Christ's Presence in the Supper - True or Real" *Scottish Journal of Theology* 27 (1974): 65-75.

_____. "Calvin's First Reformed Sermon? Nicholas Cop's Discourse – 1 November, 1533." *Westminster Theological Journal* 28 (1975/6): 300-18.

_____. "The Calvin-Westphal Exchange: The Genesis of Calvin's Treatises against Westphal." *Calvin Theological Journal* 9 (1974): 182-209.

_____. "The Controversy on Christ the Mediator: Calvin's Second Reply to Stancaro." *Calvin Theological Journal* 8 (1973): 131-157.

_____. "A Eucharistic Sacrifice in Calvin's Theology?" *Theological Studies* 37 (1976): 456-466.

_____. "The Warning That Went Unheeded: John Calvin on Giorgio Biandrata."

*Calvin Theological Journal* 12 (1977): 24-62.

Van Buren, Paul. *Christ in Our Place*. Edinburgh and London: Oliver and Boyd, 1957.

Van Hamersveld, Michael D. "The Concept of *Suspensio* in Calvin's Interpretation of the Gospel." Ph.D. diss. Aberdeen University, 1991.

VanderMolen, Ronald J. "Providence as Mystery, Providence as Revelation: Puritan and Anglican Modifications of John Calvin's Doctrine of Providence." *Church History* 47, no. 1 (1978): 27-47.

Van't Spijker, Willem. "The Influence of Luther on Calvin according to the *Institutes*." *John Calvin's Institutes: His Opus Magnum*, 83-105. Potchefstroom: University for Christian Higher Education, 1986.

Verhoef, P. A. "Luther's and Calvin's Exegetical Library." *Calvin Theological Journal* 3 (1968): 5-20.

Viguié, Ariste. "Les Sermons de Calvin sur le livre de Job." *Bulletin de la Societé de l'histoire du Protestantisme Francais*, Vol. 31 (1982): 548-555.

Vincent, Gilbert. "Calvin, commentateur du Psaume XXII." *Bulletin du Centre Protestant d"Etudes et de Documentation* 293 (July-August 1984): 32-52.

Vischer, Wilhelm. "Calvin exégète de 'Ancien Testament'." *La Revue Reformée* 18 (1967): 1-20.

Vos, Arvin. *Aquinas, Calvin and Contemporary Protestant Thought: A Critique of the Views of Thomas Aquinas*. Grand Rapids, MI: Eerdmans, 1982.

Vos, Clarence John. "Calvin's View of Man in the Light of Genesis 2,15 or Man: Earth's Servant or Lord." In *Calvinus Reformator: His Contribution to Theology, Church, and Society*, ed. Wilhelm H. Neuser. Institute for Reformation Studies, series F, no. 17. Potchefstroom, South Africa: Potchefstroom University for Christian Higher Education, 1982.

Walchenbach, J., and F. W. Battles. *Analysis of the Institutes of the Christian Religion*. Grand Rapids, MI: Baker Book House, 1980.

Walker, Robert. Review of *Where Shall Wisdom be Found?* by Susan Schreiner. *Biblical Interpretation* 4 (1996): 251-252.

Walker, Williston. *John Calvin: The Organizer of Reformation Protestantism, 1509-1564*. New York: Schocken Books, 1996.

Wallace, R. S. *Calvin, Geneva and the Reformation*. Edinburgh: Scottish Academic Press, 1990.

_____. *Calvin's Doctrine of the Christian Life*. Edinburgh: Oliver and Boyd, 1959.

_____. *Calvin's Doctrine of the Word and Sacrament*. Edinburgh: Oliver & Boyd, 1953.

_____. "Calvin the Expositor." *Themelios* 2 (1964): 32-37.

Warfield, B. B. *Calvin and Augustine*. Philadelphia, PA: Presbyterian and Reformed Publishing Co., 1974.

_____. *Calvin and Calvinism*. Vol. V of *The Works of Benjamin Breckinridge Warfield*. Grand Rapids, MI: Baker Book House, 1981.

_____. "On the Literary History of Calvin's 'Institutes'." *Presbyterian and Reformed Review* 10 (1899): 193-219.

_____. *Studies in Theology*. New York: Oxford University Press, 1932.

Weber, M. *The Protestant Ethic and the Spirit of Capitalism*. London:Allen & Unwin, 1930.
Wells, Paul. "John Calvin's View of Divine Providence." A translation from Calvin's French Tracts. *The Banner of Truth* 66 (1969): 36-40.
Wendel, F. *Calvin: Origins and Development of his Religious Thought*. Translated by P. Mairet. New York: Harper and Row, 1963.
Westermann, C., ed. *Essays on Old Testament Interpretation*. Richmond: John Knox Press, 1963.
Westhead, Nigel. "Calvin and Experimental Knowledge of God." *Evangel* 11, no. 3 (1993): 71-73.
Wierenga, R. "Calvin the Commentator." *Reformed Review* 32 (1978/9): 4-13.
Wiley, D. N. "Calvin's Doctrine of Predestination: His Principal Soteriological and Polemical Doctrine." Ph.D. diss., Duke University, 1971.
Wilkie, Robert G., and Allen Verhey. "Calvin's Treatise 'Against the Libertines'." *Calvin Theological Journal* 15 (1980): 190-219.
Wilkinson, J. "The medical history of John Calvin." *Proceedings of the Royal College of Physicians of Edinburgh* 22 (1992): 368-383.
Williams, G. H. *The Radical Reformation*. Philadelphia: The WestminsterPress, 1962.
Willis, E. D. *Calvin's Catholic Christology*. Vol. 2 of *Studies in Medieval and Reformation Thought*, ed. H.A. Oberman. Leiden: E.J. Brill, 1966.
Willis, R. *Servetus and Calvin*. London: H. S. King, 1877.
Wolf, Hans Heinrich. *Die Einheit des Bundes: Das Verhältnis von Altem und Neuem Testament bei Calvin*. Verlag der Buchhandlung des Erziehungsvereins Neukirchen Kreis Moers, 1958.
Wood, A. S. *The Principles of Biblical Interpretation as Enunciated by Irenaeus, Origen, Augustine, Luther and Calvin*. Grand Rapids, MI: Zondervan, 1967.
Woolsey, Andrew. "Unity and Continuity in Covenantal Thought: A Study in the Reformed Tradition to the Westminster Assembly." 2 vols. Ph.D. diss., Glasgow University, 1988.
Woudstra, M. H. "Calvin's Use of Example in his Sermons on Job." In *Bezield Verband*, ed. J. Bouma, 344-58. Kampen: Uitgeverij Van den Berg, 1964.
Wright, D. F. "Calvin's Accommodating God." In *Calvinus Sincerioris Religionis Vindex*. Sixth International Congress on Calvin Research, 1994, ed. W. H. Neuser and B. G. Armstrong. Kirksville, MO: Sixteenth Century Journal Publications, 1997.
_____. "Calvin's 'Accommodation' Revisited." In *Calvin as Exegete: Papers and Responses presented at the Ninth Coloquium on Calvin & Calvin Studies*, 171-190. Princeton Theological Seminary, Princeton, NJ, (1995). Grand Rapids, MI: Calvin Studies Society, 1995.
_____. "Accommodation and Barbarity in John Calvin's Old Testament Commentaries." In *Understanding Poets and Prophets: Essays in Honour of George Wishart Robinson*. Sheffield, England: JSOT Press, 1993, 412-427.
_____. "Calvin's Pentateuchal Criticism: Equity, Hardness of Heart and Divine Accommodation in the Mosaic Harmony Commentary." *Calvin Theological Journal* 21 (1986): 33-50.
_____. The Ethical Use of the Old Testament in Luther and Calvin: A Comparison." *Scottish Journal of Theology* 36 (1983): 463-85.

_____. Review of *Where Shall Wisdom be Found?* by Susan Schreiner. *Journal of Religion* 76 (1996): 639-640.

Zachman, Randal C. *The Assurance of Faith in the Theology of Martin Luther and John Calvin*. Philadelphia: PA: 1993.

_____. "Calvin as Analogical Theologian." *Scottish Journal of Theology* 51 (1998): 162-187.

Zucherman, Bruce. *Job the Silent: A Study in Historical Counterpoint.* New York: Oxford University Press, 1991.

# Subject Index

absolutism 54, 305
adversity 44, 48, 175, 227, 231-3, 242, 320
affections 49, 52, 96, 169, 233-5, 324
afflictions 29, 31, 51, 103, 226-30, 234-8, 240
allegory 32, 310-11
Anabaptists 308-9'
angels 15, 32, 35, 49, 93-4, 105-10, 112-13, 159-60, 162-4, 166, 174, 176, 324-5, 329, 374, 377-8
anthropology 34, 36
apostasy 47
Apostles' Creed 158
assurance 48, 308, 317, 331
atonement 15, 330, 332

Christology 54, 305-7, 320, 329, 333-4, 375-6, 378
condemnation 111-12, 160
conscience 40, 107, 331
corruption 159-60, 324, 374
covenant 162, 308-9, 311-12, 334
   of grace 233, 309
creation 34, 36, 38-9, 46, 112, 156-7, 159, 165, 167, 174, 240, 373
cross (of Christ) 50, 158, 311, 319, 332

damnation 111, 160, 332
death 50, 53, 113, 240-1, 313, 315-17, 320, 325-6, 332
   of Christ 50, 314, 319-20, 326, 331
depravity 38
despair 236-7, 377
determinism 306
discipleship 43-4, 373
discipline, ecclesiastical 30
doctrine 10, 36, 41-2, 54, 153, 170, 173, 226, 306, 309, 313, 324

double justice 7, 15-16, 54, 94, 105-6, 118, 159, 174, 322, 376-7
dualism 44

election 15, 47, 110, 160, 168, 172, 238, 306, 317, 321-2
eschatology 34, 240-1
evil 38-9, 44, 46, 99, 108, 160, 312, 324

faith 10-11, 31, 36, 42, 47-51, 102, 118, 163 166-7, 174, 232, 236, 239, 317, 323-4, 326, 331, 374
Fall 17, 36, 39, 53, 113, 118, 153, 377
fear 241, 373
   (Godly) 98, 102, 105, 157, 159, 164, 177, 231, 238, 312, 323
forgiveness 312, 318-19
free will 15, 38

glory (of God) 36, 39, 45, 106, 109, 112, 118, 154, 156, 158, 161, 163, 167, 173-4, 239, 308, 316, 320, 327-8
God, attributes of 10-11, 34, 106, 170, 227
   character of 44, 117, 158, 167, 305, 373-4, 377-8
   doctrine of 44, 50, 94, 305, 374
   essence of 156-7, 160, 166-7
godliness 9, 52-3, 95, 98-9, 153, 227, 323, 325, 374
goodness (of God) 40, 42, 45, 109, 111, 115, 166, 172, 176, 227, 231-4, 241-2, 308, 322-4, 326
grace 37-9, 96-8, 107-9, 111, 113, 152, 164, 229, 233-4, 236, 309, 312-15, 318, 321, 323, 325-6, 373
   *See also* covenant of grace
guilt 97, 313, 322

heaven 36, 53, 104, 108, 159, 161, 168, 174, 176, 240, 307, 314, 317, 319-20, 322, 324, 327-30, 374
hell 103, 116, 158, 319
hiddenness of God 151, 154, 159
holiness 36, 97, 107, 111
Holy Spirit (role of) 9, 38, 40, 48, 97-8, 111, 160, 162, 171, 173, 176, 226, 229, 232-3, 308-9, 313, 315, 318
hope 43, 46, 101, 104, 114, 236, 319, 326, 328, 377
humanism 11, 171-2
humility 11, 14, 31, 43, 111, 117, 164, 238, 314

idol 156, 173
idolatry 43, 168, 171, 242
ignorance 161, 165-6, 173, 177, 239
image of God / *imago Dei* 36-7, 39-40, 112, 319, 321, 373
images *See* idol
imitation of Christ 36
immortality 48, 53, 109, 160, 315, 327
immutability (of God) 11
impassibility (of God) 11, 162
impatience 232
incarnation 118, 378
incomprehensibility (of God) 11-17, 54, 106, 110, 113, 115, 117-18, 152-62, 164, 167, 169-76, 226, 232, 238-42, 305, 373-5, 377
infinity (of God) 11, 114, 156
injustice 31-2, 95, 101, 374
innocence (of Job) 38, 47, 54, 94, 97, 99, 227, 234, 374, 376-7
integrity 94-6, 172, 331

joy 52, 231-2, 235, 320, 326
judgment (future / final) 13, 96-7, 99, 106, 109-10, 167, 232, 327-8
    secret 47, 100, 117, 153, 162, 170, 174, 228

judgments (of God) 46, 100-4, 157-8, 160, 162-4, 169-70, 174, 226, 230-1, 238, 242, 328, 330
justice (of God) 13, 16, 35, 45, 54, 94-5, 99-101, 103-6, 116-17, 166, 226-7, 242, 305, 322, 374-5, 377
    *See also* double justice
justification 14, 173, 239, 326

knowability (of God) 12, 152, 154
knowledge 12, 117, 161, 324
    (of God) 15-16, 39, 42, 47, 151, 156-7, 161, 167-8, 170, 174, 176, 237, 242, 373, 377

law (of God) 15, 94, 105-7, 110-12, 159, 165, 167-8, 174, 235, 309-10, 322, 329-30
    natural 34
Libertines 30-1, 307
Lord's Prayer 159
Lord's Supper 31, 161
love (God's) 49, 158, 242, 313, 320-1

majesty (of God) 12, 14-15, 41, 44, 105-6, 108, 115-16, 151, 156-7, 159, 163-7, 169-71, 173-7, 231, 234, 238-9, 242, 324, 330
man, doctrine of 10, 36-7, 373
Manichaeism 37
mediation, ontological 15, 112-13, 118, 322, 374, 376-8
mediator 113, 118, 158-9, 167, 309, 325, 329, 377
mediatorship (of Christ) 112-13
    universal *See* mediation, ontological
meekness 230
mercy (of God) 45, 96-7, 102-3, 106, 109, 111, 160, 234, 316, 318, 322-3, 332
mind (human) 37, 42, 151-2, 155-7, 162-6, 231, 238, 325
    (divine) 152
ministry, pastoral 13-14, 373
mortification 50-1, 236

*Index* 413

mysticism 152

nominalism 12-13, 16, 35, 115, 117-18, 161, 305, 374, 377

obedience 40-3, 46, 53, 106-7, 109-11, 227, 230, 242, 313, 316, 375
omnipotence (of God) 94, 115
omniscience (of God) 171, 231
ontological mediation *See* mediation, ontological

pain 16, 53-4, 94, 115, 231, 240, 321, 326, 373-4
patience 46-7, 49, 52, 102, 174, 231-3, 238, 374
perfectionism 98
perseverance 36, 43-4, 46-7, 175, 233, 235, 314, 374
piety 16-17, 52, 153, 229, 236, 373, 375
plan (of God) 159-60 *See also* purposes (of God)
power (of God) 13-14, 16, 33, 35-7, 44-5, 49, 54, 94-5, 109, 113-17, 160, 162-7, 170, 227, 231, 305, 308, 310, 315, 322, 373-5, 377
prayer 46, 53, 108, 159, 227, 233, 235, 315, 318-19, 323, 328
preaching 10, 12, 14, 34-6, 41-3, 53, 110, 151, 167, 307, 328, 332, 334, 373, 378
predestination 9, 14, 48, 160, 168, 306-7, 375
pride 32, 49, 98, 171, 177, 240, 310
promises (of God) 48-9, 103-4, 118, 165, 232-3, 309-10, 315
prosperity, material 50, 232
providence (divine) 7, 9, 10, 13, 15, 17, 32, 34, 36, 43-6, 51, 54, 94-5, 99-101, 103-4, 110, 117, 153, 157, 159, 163-4, 167, 171-4, 176, 225-41, 305-7, 327-8, 334, 373-6
    secret 11

punishment 50, 99-100, 102-4, 164, 170, 374
purposes (of God) 11, 41, 164, 176, 309, 374 *See also* plan (of God)

rationalism 152
reason 10, 37, 40, 45, 105, 110, 116, 162-3, 167, 171
redemption 9, 173, 308, 312, 318
    metaphysical 7, 16
regeneration 40
repentance 51, 95, 102, 162, 227, 233, 323
reprobation 110, 160, 168, 307
resurrection 164, 167, 307, 315, 319-20, 326-8, 330
retribution 97, 99, 102-3, 109, 234
revelation (of God) 42, 94, 152-3, 233, 237, 241, 305-6, 313, 317, 321, 323, 374
    doctrine of 36, 40, 42
reverence 41, 43, 51, 153, 157, 159, 164, 170, 172-4, 176-7, 230-1, 239, 373
rhetoric 29, 35, 39, 171, 373
righteousness (of God) 15, 36, 40, 43, 45, 51, 93-6, 100, 105-8, 110, 112-18, 159, 166, 168, 174, 176, 239, 242, 316-17, 326, 329, 331-2, 376-7
    (of men) 47, 94-6, 98, 105-6, 110-11, 331-2

sacraments 159-60
sacrifice 163, 225, 311-12, 318, 332
salvation 47-8, 54, 159, 317-18, 320, 323, 326
Satan 38, 44, 51, 95, 160, 163, 227, 236-7, 305, 310, 313-14, 324-5
Scripture, authority of 40, 305, 311
    nature of 40-1, 373
Scots Confession (1560) 155
self-control 52
self-denial 50, 233
simplicity (of God) 11
sin 13, 36, 38-9, 42, 47, 51, 53, 95-6, 99, 102-3, 107, 117-18, 153, 159, 163, 167, 170, 173, 226-7, 229-30, 234, 236, 239,

sin, cont., 312-13, 316, 318, 322-4, 326, 332, 374-5, 378
  original 38, 95
soteriology 306
sovereignty (of God) 14, 17, 33, 43-5, 151, 160, 170, 232-3
spirituality 16
subjection (to God) 11, 238
submission (to God) 17, 49, 51, 153, 161, 175, 230, 237, 242, 374
suffering 13, 16-17, 33, 36, 38-9, 44, 50, 53, 94-7, 99, 103, 105, 117, 153, 158, 226-8, 234, 236, 305, 318-21, 326-8, 376
  innocent 7, 95-6, 98-9, 106, 118, 374, 377

temptation 45-6, 49-51, 110, 163, 228, 235, 237, 312, 317, 324
theism, Christian 152
theodicy 16, 44, 93
theology 10, 15, 29, 34-5, 42, 54, 155, 225, 305-7, 334, 375-8
  natural 10, 154
  pastoral 7, 13, 43, 151
transcendence 152, 174, 226-7

trials 17, 31, 48-9, 51, 53, 95, 171, 175-6, 225-33, 235, 237-8, 240-2, 314, 320-1, 326, 328, 374
Trinity 43, 158, 307
Trinitarianism 376, 378
truth 37, 43, 164, 166, 225, 310
typology 32, 311

understanding 37, 41, 107, 162, 165, 169, 171-4, 226, 231, 234, 239, 242, 324
union with Christ 160, 236, 318, 326
  with God 108

vengeance 102-3

Westminster Confession (1647) 155
will (of God) 42, 45-6, 53, 94, 100, 114-15, 151, 159-60, 164, 225-8, 233, 235, 305, 323, 328, 373
  (human) 38, 235 *See also* free will
wisdom (of God) 11, 36, 45, 157, 160-1, 164, 166, 168, 173, 175-6, 225, 238-9, 310, 313, 323-4, 373
  (human) 168, 226, 237-9, 317
worldliness 42
wrath (of God) 97, 102, 229, 234, 318

# Author Index

Ambrose 32
Aquinas, Thomas 11, 13, 32, 34, 39, 108, 136-7, 154-5
Armstrong, Brian 16, 22, 26
Augustine (of Hippo) 32, 155, 158

Baillie, John 155
Barth, Karl 9, 151-2, 155, 180, 335, 379
Battles, Ford Lewis 307, 333
Bavinck, Herman 177
Berkouwer, G C. 26, 93
Beza, Theodore 57, 376
Bohatec, Josef 10
Bouwsma, William J. 10-14, 22, 25, 34, 68, 134, 208, 211, 218, 333
Bucer, Martin 376
Bullinger, Heinrich 30, 35
Büser, Fritz 19

Calvin, John 7, 9-10 *et passim*
Castellio, Sebastian 158

Dekker, Harold 43, 151
Doumergue, Emil 14

Engel, Mary Potter 34, 36, 180, 241, 295, 300

Forstman, Jackson 343
Friedman, Jerome 337

Gerrish, Brian 152
Golding, Arthur 33
Gregory the Great 32, 34

Habel, Norman C. 122
Hall, B. 306
Helm, Paul 109
Hesselink, I. John 12
Hilary (of Poitiers) 32
Hunnius, Aegidius 307, 332
Hutcheson, George 376

Jacobs, P. 306
Jerome 32
Joachim-Kraus, Hans 308

Kafka, Franz 13

Lane, A.N.S. 88
Lee, Sou-Young 283
Leith, John H. 306
Leithart, Peter 52
Luther, Martin 14, 154-5

McGrath, Alister E. 120-2, 139
MacLeish, Archibald 13
McLelland, Joseph 23
McNeill, John T. 66
McPhee, Ian 306

Maimonides 12
Miln, Peter 13-15, 24, 169, 204, 378
Milner, B.C. Jr. 305
Mülhaupt, Erwin 10
Muller, Richard A. 119, 336, 339
Murray, John 9, 262

Naphy, William 32
Niesel, Wilhelm 72, 306

Oecolompadius, Johannes 376
Origen 310
Osiander 118, 159, 378

Parker, T.H.L. 10, 12, 14, 22, 41, 61, 64, 205
Partee, Charles 67, 306
Plotinus 154
Perkins, William 14
Puckett, David 307-8, 310, 333, 343, 378

Raguenier, Denis 33
Rowley, H.H. 122

415

Schreiner, Susan 10, 12-13, 17, 26, 29, 32, 34-5, 64, 94, 105, 117, 119, 121, 134, 226, 246, 300
Schweizer, A. 306
Selinger, Suzanne 134
Servetus, Michael 157, 308
Stancaro, Francesco 112
Stauffer, Richard 10-11, 13, 19, 34, 133

Tawney, R.H. 50
Torrance, Thomas F. 10, 13, 34, 36, 91, 204

Wallace, Ronald 50
Warfield, B.B. 59-60
Weisel, Elie 13
Wendel, F. 306, 336
Wiley, D.N. 307
William of Ockham 11
Willis, David 142, 200
Willis-Watkins, David 283
Wolf, Hans Heinrich 342
Wright, David F. 139
Wycliffe, John 35

Zachman, Randall C. 191, 343
Zwingli, Ulrich 35